Rock 'n' Roll through 1969

*To my parents, John and Doris, without whose love and
support this book would not have been completed.*

*To my best friends, Kelpie, Foley, Boo Boo Frank and Tibet,
for their unquestioning love.*

*In memory of Cactus Cholla Edwards,
my bright little star in the sky.*

Rock 'n' Roll Through 1969

Discographies of All Performers Who Hit the Charts, Beginning in 1955

by

John W. Edwards

McFarland & Company, Inc., Publishers
Jefferson, North Carolina, and London

British Library Cataloguing-in-Publication data are available

Library of Congress Cataloguing-in-Publication Data

Edwards, John W., 1958–
    Rock 'n' roll through 1969 : discographies of all performers who hit the charts, beginning in 1955 / by John W. Edwards.
      p. cm.
    Includes bibliographical references.
    ISBN 0-89950-655-0 (lib. bdg. : 50# alk. paper) ∞
    1. Rock music—To 1961—Discography. 2. Rock music—1961–1970—
Discography. I. Title.
ML156.4.R6E33 1992
016.7842166'026'6—dc20   91-50945
                                             CIP
                                            MN

Manufactured in the United States of America

McFarland & Company, Inc., Publishers
Box 611, Jefferson, North Carolina 28640

Table of Contents

Acknowledgments

Thanks to those individuals who have helped to make my interest in writing a reality:
Dr. Walter J. Arnell
Dr. & Mrs. John R. Edwards, Jr.
Terry Hounsome

Sincerest appreciation to those individuals who have enhanced my interest in music:
Billboard Magazine
James A. Brenden
Carl Damhesel
John Hankinson
Loco, Zip's & Tower Records
Dr. James O'Brien

Thanks to the following professionals who have encouraged this project to succeed:
Tina Isaac at Kodansha International
Dr. Kevin Leman, Psychologist
Margaret L. Maxwell, Attorney at Law
Laura Shepherd at Putnam
Lissa W. Walls, Newspaper Executive

Deepest gratitude to those individuals that have contributed information to this project:
Suzy Fisher
Peter Frame and his Family Trees
John Jones Management
David Koppel
Kimberley E. Long at Cornerstone
  Management
Lora at Dept. Z
The Michael Ochs Archives
The Staff of Rhino Records
Raquel M. Tucker
Dan Wiley at Chuck Morris Enter-
  tainment
Rebekah Williamson at EMI
  Records
Maxine Young

Thanks to those individuals who have been friends throughout:
Chris & Debbie at Bingo Cash 'n'
  Carry
Victor Cordero
David Goehring
Gene & Wendy Holdt
Wade & Cheryl Holt
David & Lori Hsu
Joyce, Roy & Misty Ledsham
Jim & Denise Kalemba
Jerry & Sharon McDonald
Peter & Paula Partch
Tom & Kathleen Stevenson
Tom Struck and the gang (Drew,
  Charlie & Roger) at Fantasy
  Comics
Joe Warnock

Introduction

What is Rock and Roll? How does one define it? What are the parameters that separate it from other musical forms? These questions have puzzled many in the late twentieth century, particularly parents of teenagers.

Rock and Roll is a unique music format which has captured the interest and imagination of the younger generation for nearly 40 years. The early days of rock are very distinctive as they combined many musical influences (country, rhythm & blues and jazz) to create a new format to appeal to a varied audience. The mid-fifties through the early sixties brought us the talents of Chuck Berry, Bill Haley & the Comets, Little Richard, Jerry Lee Lewis and Elvis Presley to name a few. A change began in 1962 as a different form of Rock and Roll began to be heard. In America it was Jan & Dean, the Four Seasons and the Beach Boys; throughout Europe it was the sounds of Cliff Richard and the Beatles. Highlighted by moonshots, Presidential assassinations, Vietnam, flower power, riots and music, this book details the performers of Rock and Roll's most dynamic period, 1955–1969.

Exactly who qualifies for inclusion? What designates a performer as a Rock and Roll act? The Billboard trade charts, for the most part, have been the indicative force behind popular music. What's hot and what is not? This book includes the majority of performers who have achieved a charting single on the Billboard Hot 100 or an album on the Top 200 Albums, that fall into the classification of popular or rock music. Included are performers whose careers began in the fifties and crossed over into the sixties, performers whose career existed solely in the sixties and those performers whose first sounds were heard in the late sixties and continued into the seventies and beyond.

From the Amboy Dukes to the Zombies, the Association to Yes, Genesis, the Beatles, Jethro Tull, Fleetwood Mac, Chicago, the Moody Blues, Status Quo, the Guess Who, the Rolling Stones, Pink Floyd, the Beach Boys and more, they're all here. The emphasis is not only on the supergroups, the chartbusters, but also the one-hit wonders, the album-oriented performers and the cult bands. Music categories include hard rock, acid rock, country rock, dance rock, pop rock, art rock, jazz rock, blues rock, cajun rock, southern rock and more. Performers come from the United States, England, Ireland, Sweden, Germany, France, Canada, Mexico, Japan, Denmark, Norway, Scotland, Australia, New Zealand, the Netherlands and elsewhere. Featured are as many popular music performers of the last thirty years as possible. Whether you are a trivia buff, music aficionado, casual listener or music student there is something to both inform and entertain in this book. Keep listening to the music and happy reading.

—John W. Edwards
June 1992

Glossary

Albums — long playing recordings, listed by year of release.

Category — describes the type or genre of music performed by the artist, as well as the region of origin of the artist. The categories are:

Acid Rock
Art Rock
Art/Progressive Rock
Avant Garde Rock
Blue-Eyed Soul
Blues/Boogie Rock
Blues/Jazz
Blues Rock
Blues/Rock
Blues/Soul
Boogie Rock
Bubblegum Pop
Cajun Rock
Comedy/Folk
Country Rock
Dance Pop
Dance Rock
Dixieland Pop
Elvis Rock
Folk
Folk/Blues/Rock
Folk/Country
Folk/Inspirational
Folk Rock
Folk/Rock
Folk Vocal
Glam Rock
Hard Rock
Heavy Metal
Heavy Metal/Blues
Instrumental Rock
Jazz/Blues Rock
Jazz/Pop
Jazz Rock
Jazz/Rock
Latin/Jazz Rock
Mod Rock
Musical Comedy
Novelty/Pop
Pop
Pop/Folk Vocal
Pop Rock
Pop/Rock
Pop/Soft Rock
Pop/Soul
Pop Vocal
Progressive/Art Rock
Progressive Rock
Psychedelic Pop
Psychedelic Rock
Pub Rock
Punk Pop
Rhythm & Blues
Rhythm & Blues/Rock
R & B/Funk
R & B/Soul
R & B Vocal
Rockabilly

Glossary

Rockabilly/Country
Skiffle
Soft Rock
Soul
Soul/Boogie Rock
Soul/Funk
Soul/Pop Vocal
Soul Vocal
Soul/Rock Vocal
Space Rock
Surf Rock

Swamp Rock
Tex/Mex Rock

Personnel — a listing of group members, the instruments they played and in some cases replacements of members, by date.

Singles — 45 rpm records of individual songs, listed by date of release, with the peak Billboard chart position high-lighted.

Photograph Credits

A & M Records: pages 268, 330
Abcko Records: page 152
Apple Records: page 17
Arista Records: pages 114, 127, 142, 186, 230, 332, 371
Asylum Records: pages 229, 290 (Bonnie Lippel)
Atco Records: page 40
Atlantic Records: pages 78, 134, 386
Buddah Records: page 222
Capitol Records: pages 45, 135, 181, 183, 226, 257, 260
Caribou Records: page 15
Casablanca Records: page 56 (Harry Langdon)
Chrysalis Records: page 175
Colpix Records: page 109
Columbia/CBS Records: pages 13, 40, 44, 57, 89, 179, 280, 299, 302, 314, 319, 341, 385, 390
Decca Records: pages 49, 194, 237
Dolton Records: page 118
E. G. Records: page 184
Elektra Records: pages 69 (Francesco Scavullo), 97, 304
EMI Records: pages 30, 281
Epic Records: pages 62, 154, 173, 207, 241, 367
Fantasy Records: page 76
Folklore Productions: page 278 (Andrew de la Rue)
Geffen Records: pages 196, 387
Island Records: page 111
John Jones: page 110
Laurie Records: page 92
Liberty Records: pages 170, 198, 363
London Records: page 353
MCA Records: pages 26, 140, 213, 287, 330, 348, 351, 376
Mercury Records: pages 129, 139, 324
MGM Records: pages 5, 92, 126
Chuck Morris Entertainment: page 242 (Dan Wiley)

The Performers

The Accents

Personnel: Robert Draper, Jr. (vocals)

Single: Wiggle, Wiggle, 1958 **(55)**

R & B—American

Johnny Ace

Album: Memorial Album for Johnny Ace, 1955

Single: Pledging My Love, 1955 **(17)**

R & B—Memphis; died from a self-inflicted gunshot wound in 1954; real name was John Marshall Alexander, Jr.

Barbara Acklin

Albums: Love Makes a Woman, 1968; Seven Days of Night, 1969; Someone Else's Arms, 1970; I Did It, 1971; A Place in the Sun, 1975

Singles: Love Makes a Woman, 1968 **(15)**; From the Teacher to the Preacher, 1968 **(57)** (with Gene Chandler); Just Ain't No Love, 1968 **(67)**; Am I the Same Girl, 1969 **(79)**; I Did It, 1970 **(121)**

R & B Vocal—Chicago

Action

Personnel: Alan "Bam" King (guitars); Reg King (vocals); Pete Watson (guitars); Mike Evans (bass); Roger Powell (drums)

Album: The Ultimate Action, 1980

Singles: Land of a Thousand Dances, 1965; I'll Keep on Holding On, 1966; Baby You've Got It, 1966; Never Ever, 1967; Shadows and Reflections, 1967; I'll Keep Holding On, 1981; Since I Lost My Baby, 1981; Hey Sha Lo Ney, 1984

Pub Rock—British

The Ad Libs

Personnel: Mary Ann Thomas (vocals); Hugh Harris (vocals); Danny Austin (vocals); Norman Donegan (vocals); Dave Watt (vocals)

Album: The Ad Libs, 1965

Singles: The Boy from New York City, 1965 **(8)**; He Ain't No Angel, 1965 **(100)**

Pop Vocal—New Jersey

Johnny Adams

Albums: Heart & Soul, 1968; Reconsider Me, 1969; Stand By Me, 1970; After All the Good Is Gone, 1971

Singles: Release Me, 1968 **(82)**; Reconsider Me, 1969 **(28)**; I Can't

Be All Bad, 1969 **(89)**; Proud
Woman, 1970 **(121)**
   Soul Vocal — New Orleans

Jewel Akens

Singles: The Birds and the Bees,
1965 **(3)**; Georgie Porgie, 1965 **(68)**;
It's the Only Way to Fly, 1965 **(120)**
   R & B Vocal — Houston

Steve Alaimo

Albums: Twist with Steve Alaimo,
1961; Mashed Potatoes, 1962; Every
Day I Have to Cry, 1963; Steve
Alaimo, 1963; Starring Steve
Alaimo, 1965; Where the Action Is,
1965; Sings and Swings, 1966
   Singles: Mashed Potatoes, 1962
(81); Every Day I Have to Cry,
1963 **(46)**; Don't Let the Sun Catch
You Crying, 1963 **(125)**; Michael —
Pt. 1, 1963 **(100)**; Gotta Lotta Love,
1963 **(74)**; I Don't Know, 1964 **(103)**;
Real Live Girl, 1965 **(77)**; Cast Your
Fate to the Wind, 1965 **(89)**; So
Much Love, 1966 **(92)**; New Orleans,
1967 **(126)**; Denver, 1968 **(118)**; One
Woman, 1969 **(101)**; When My Lit-
tle Girl Is Smiling, 1971 **(72)**;
Amerikan Music, 1972 **(79)**
   Pop Vocal — American; star of
TV's "Where the Action Is"

Arthur Alexander

Albums: You Better Move On,
1962; Alexander the Great, 1964;
Arthur Alexander, 1965; Arthur
Alexander, 1975
   Singles: You Better Move On,
1962 **(24)**; Where Have You Been
(All My Life), 1962 **(58)**; Anna (Go
to Him), 1962 **(68)**; Go Home Girl,
1963 **(102)**; Pretty Girls Everywhere,
1963 **(118)**; Every Day I Have to
Cry Some, 1975 **(45)**
   Soul Vocal — Alabama

Davie Allan & The Arrows

Albums: The Wild Angels, 1966;
The Wild Angels, Vol. II, 1967;
Devil's Angels, 1967
   Singles: Apache '65, 1965 **(64)**;
Theme from the Wild Angels, 1966
(99); Blue's Theme, 1967 **(37)**;
Devil's Angels, 1967 **(97)**
   Instrumental Pop — L.A.

The Alley Cats

Personnel: Billy Storm (vocals);
Chester Pipkin (vocals); Ed Willis
(vocals); Bryce Caufield (vocals)
   Singles: Puddin' n' Tain (Ask Me
Again, I'll Tell You the Same), 1963
(43)
   Pop Vocal — Los Angeles

Gene Allison

Album: Gene Allison, 1959
   Singles: You Can Make It If You
Try, 1957 **(36)**; Have Faith, 1958 **(73)**
   R & B Vocal — Nashville

The Amboy Dukes

Personnel: Ted Nugent (guitars,
vocals); Steve Farmer (guitars); Bill
White (bass) replaced (1969) by Greg
Arama (bass); John Drake (vocals)
replaced (1969) by John Angelos (vocals); Rick Lober (keyboards) replaced
(1969) by Andy Solomon (keyboards);
Dave Palmer (drums) replaced (1969)
by K. J. Knight (drums)
   Albums: The Amboy Dukes,
1968; Journey to the Center of the
Mind, 1969; Migration, 1969; Mar-
riage on the Rocks, 1970
   Singles: Baby Please Don't Go,
1968 **(106)**; Journey to the Center of
the Mind, 1968 **(16)**; You Talk Sunshine, I Breathe Fire, 1968 **(114)**;

The Amboy Dukes: *(left to right)* **Nugent, Farmer, Lober, Drake, White, Palmer**

The Inexhaustible Quest for the Cosmic Cabbage, 1969
  Acid Rock—Detroit

Amen Corner

Personnel: Andy Fairweather-Low (guitars, vocals); Neil Jones (guitars); Blue Weaver (organ); Clive Tayler (bass); Dennis Byron (drums); Allen Jones (baritone saxophone); Mike Smith (saxophones)

Albums: Round Amen, 1968; National Welsh Coast Live, 1969; Farewell Magnificent Seven, 1969; Amen Corner and Small Faces, 1975; Return of the Magnificent Seven, 1976; Greatest Hits, 1978

Singles: Gin House, 1967; Bend Me, Shape Me, 1968; High in the Sky, 1968; (If Paradise Is) Half as Nice, 1969; Hello Suzie, 1969; Natural Sinner, 1969
  Mod Rock—British; early glam-rock band in England

American Breed

Personnel: Al Ciner (guitars); Gary Lorzio (guitars, vocals); Chuck Colbert (bass); Lee Graziano (drums); added (1968): Kevin Murphy (keyboards)

Albums: American Breed, 1967; Bend Me, Shape Me, 1968; Pumpkin, Powder, Scarlet & Green, 1968; Lonely Side of the City, 1969

Singles: Step Out of Your Mind, 1967 **(24)**; Don't Forget About Me, 1967 **(107)**; Bend Me, Shape Me, 1967 **(5)**; Green Light, 1968 **(39)**; Ready, Willing and Able, 1968 **(84)**; Anyway That You Want Me, 1968 **(88)**; Hunky Funky, 1969 **(107)**
  Pop/Rock—Midwest

Ed Ames

Albums: More I Cannot Wish You, 1966; My Cup Runeth Over, 1967; Time, Time, 1967; When the Snow Is on the Roses, 1967; Who Will Answer & Other Songs of Our Time, 1968; Apologize, 1968; The Hits of Broadway and Hollywood, 1968; A Time for Living, a Time for Hope, 1969; The Windmills of Your Mind, 1969; The Best of Ed Ames, 1969; Love of the Common People, 1970; Sing Away the World, 1970; The Songs of Bacharach and David, 1971

Singles: Try to Remember, 1965 **(73)**; My Cup Runneth Over, 1967 **(8)**; Time, Time, 1967 **(61)**; When

The American Breed: *(left to right)* **Lorzio, Ciner, Colbert, Graziano**

the Snow Is on the Roses, 1967 **(98)**; Who Will Answer?, 1967 **(19)**; Apologize, 1968 **(79)**; All My Love's Laughter, 1968 **(122)**; Changing, Changing, 1969 **(130)**; Son of a Travelin' Man, 1969 **(92)**

Pop Vocal—Massachusetts; starred on TV's "Daniel Boone"

The Ames Brothers

Personnel: Ed Ames (vocals); Gene Ames (vocals); Joe Ames (vocals); Vic Ames (vocals; deceased 1978)

Album: There'll Always Be a Christmas, 1957

Singles: The Naughty Lady of Shady Lane, 1954 **(3)**; My Bonnie Lassie, 1955 **(11)**; Forever Darling, 1956 **(35)**; I'm Gonna Love You, 1956 **(84)**; It Only Hurts for a Little While, 1956 **(11)**; If You Wanna See Mamie Tonight, 1956 **(89)**; 49 Shades of Green, 1956 **(49)**; Summer Sweetheart, 1956 **(67)**; I Saw Esau, 1956 **(51)**; Tammy, 1957 **(5)**; Rockin' Shoes, 1957 **(64)**; Melodie d'Amour, 1957 **(5)**; Little Gypsy, 1958 **(67)**; A Very Precious Love, 1958 **(23)**; Stay, 1958 **(90)**; Little Serenade, 1958 **(98)**; Pussy Cat, 1958 **(17)**; No One but You (In My Heart), 1958 **(45)**; Red River Rose, 1958 **(37)**; Someone to Come Home To, 1959 **(78)**; China Doll, 1960 **(38)**; Washington Square, 1963 **(129)**

Pop Vocal—Massachusetts

Eric Andersen

Albums: Today Is the Highway, 1965; 'Bout Changes 'n' Things, 1966; 'Bout Changes 'n' Things, Take 2, 1968; More Hits from Tin Can Alley, 1968; A Country Dream, 1968; Avalanche, 1969; Eric Andersen, 1970; The Best of Eric Andersen, 1971; Blue River, 1973; Stages, 1974; Be True to You, 1975; Sweet Surprise!, 1976; The Best Songs, 1977

Folk Rock—American

Lee Andrews & The Hearts

Personnel: Lee Andrews (vocals); Thomas Curry (vocals); Ted Weems (vocals); Roy Calhoun (vocals); Wendell Calhoun (vocals)

Album: Lee Andrews & the Hearts, 1957

Singles: Long Lonely Nights, 1957 **(45)**; Tear Drops, 1958 **(20)**; Try the Impossible, 1958 **(33)**

Soul Vocal—Philadelphia; Andrews' real name is Arthur Thompson

Andromeda

Personnel: Mick Hawksworth (bass, vocals); John Cann (guitars, vocals); Ian McClane (drums, vocals)

Album: Andromeda, 1969

Hard Rock—British

The Angels

Personnel: Barbara Allbut (vocals) replaced (1972) by Lana Shan (vocals); Phyllis Allbut Meister (vocals); Linda Jansen (vocals) replaced (1962) by Peggy Santiglia McGannon (vocals)

Albums: My Boyfriend's Back, 1963; A Halo to You, 1963

Singles: 'Til, 1961 **(14)**; Cry Baby Cry, 1962 **(38)**; My Boyfriend's Back, 1963 **(1)**; I Adore Him, 1963 **(25)**; Thank You and Goodnight, 1963 **(84)**; Wow Wow Wee (He's the Boy for Me), 1964 **(41)**

Pop Vocal—New Jersey

The Animals

Personnel: Eric Burdon (vocals); Alan Price (keyboards, vocals) replaced (1966) by Dave Rowberry (keyboards) replaced (1966) by Danny McCullough (guitars); Hilton Valentine (guitars) replaced (1966) by Andy Summers (guitars) replaced (1966) by Vic Briggs (guitars); Bryan "Chas" Chandler (bass) replaced (1966) by John Weider (bass); John Steel (drums) replaced (1966) by Barry Jenkins (drums)

The Animals: Steel, Rowberry, Burdon, Chandler, Valentine

Albums: The Animals, 1964; Get Yourself a College Girl, 1965; Animals on Tour, 1965; Animal Tracks, 1965; British Go Go, 1965; Best of the Animals, 1966; Animalization, 1966; Animalisms, 1966; Most of the Animals, 1966, Wind of Change, 1967; Best of the Animals Volume 2, 1967; Eric Is Here, 1967; Everyone of Us, 1968; Twain Shall Meet, 1968; Love Is, 1968; Greatest Hits, 1969; Live in Newcastle, 1976; Newcastle '63, 1977; Before We Were So Rudely Interrupted, 1977; Ark, 1983; Rip It to Shreds/Greatest Hits Live, 1984

Singles: House of the Rising Sun, 1964 **(1)**; Gonna Send You Back to Walker, 1964 **(57)**; I'm Crying, 1964 **(19)**; Baby Let Me Take You Home, 1964 **(102)**; Boom Boom, 1964 **(43)**; Don't Let Me Be Misunderstood, 1965 **(15)**; Bring It on Home, 1965 **(32)**; We Gotta Get Out of This Place, 1965 **(13)**; It's My Life, 1965 **(23)**; Inside Looking Out, 1966 **(34)**; Don't Bring Me Down, 1966 **(12)**; See See Rider, 1966 **(10)**; Help Me Girl, 1966 **(29)**; When I Was Young, 1967 **(15)**; San Franciscan Nights, 1967 **(9)**; Monterrey, 1967 **(15)**; Anything, 1968 **(80)**; Sky Pilot, 1968 **(14)**; White Houses, 1968 **(67)**; The Night, 1983 **(48)**

Blues/Rock—British

Paul Anka

Albums: Paul Anka, 1958; It's Christmas Everywhere, 1960; His Big 15, 1960; At the Copa, 1960; Swings for Young Lovers, 1960; His Big 15, Volume 2, 1961; Strictly Instrument, 1961; Diana, 1962; His Big 15, Volume 3, 1962; Young, Alive and in Love, 1962; Let's Sit This One Out, 1962; Our Man Around the World, 1963; Songs I Wish I'd Written, 1963; 21 Golden Hits, 1963; Excitement on Park Avenue, 1964; Strictly Nashville, 1966; Paul Anka Live, 1967; Goodnight My Love, 1969; Life Goes On, 1969; Sincerely, 1969; Paul Anka 70's, 1970; Paul Anka, 1971; Jubilation, 1972; Anka, 1974; My Way, 1974, Paul Anka Gold, 1974; This Is Anka, 1974; Feelings, 1975; Remember Diana, 1975; She's a Lady, 1975; Times of Your Life, 1975; The Essential Paul Anka, 1976; The Painter, 1976; Sings His Favorites, 1976; The Music Man, 1977; Listen to Your Heart, 1978; Paul Anka at His Best, 1978; Vintage Years 1957/61, 1978; Golden Hour, 1978; Headlines, 1979; 21 Greatest Hits, 1980; Both Sides of Love, 1981; 21 Golden Hits, 1981; Songs, 1983; Original Hits, 1983; Walk a Fine Line, 1983

Singles: Diana, 1957 **(1)**; I Love You, Baby, 1957 **(97)**; You Are My Destiny, 1958 **(7)**; Crazy Love, 1958 **(15)**; Let the Bells Keep Ringing, 1958 **(16)**; Midnight, 1958 **(69)**; Just Young, 1958 **(80)**; The Teen Commandments, 1958 **(29)** (with Geo. Hamilton IV, Johnny Nash); (All of a Sudden) My Heart Sings, 1958 **(15)**; I Miss You So, 1959 **(33)**; Lonely Boy, 1959 **(1)**; Put Your Head on My Shoulder, 1959 **(2)**; It's Time to Cry, 1959 **(4)**; Puppy Love, 1960 **(2)**; Adam and Eve, 1960 **(90)**; My Home Town, 1960 **(8)**; Something Happened, 1960 **(41)**; Hello Young Lovers, 1960 **(23)**; I Love You in the Same Old Way, 1960 **(40)**; Summer's Gone, 1960 **(11)**; Rudolph, The Red-Nose Reindeer, 1960 **(104)**; Don't Say Your Sorry, 1961 **(108)**; The Story of My Love,

1961 **(16)**; Tonight My Love, Tonight, 1961 **(13)**; Dance on Little Girl, 1961 **(10)**; Kissin' on the Phone, 1961 **(35)**; Cinderella, 1961 **(70)**; The Bells at My Wedding, 1961 **(104)**; Loveland, 1961 **(110)**; The Fools Hall of Fame, 1962 **(103)**; Love Me Warm and Tender, 1962 **(12)**; I'd Never Find Another You, 1962 **(106)**; A Steel Guitar and a Glass of Wine, 1962 **(13)**; Every Night (Without You), 1962 **(46)**; I'm Coming Home, 1962 **(94)**; Eso Beso (That Kiss!), 1962 **(19)**; Love (Makes the World Go 'Round), 1963 **(26)**; Remember Diana, 1963 **(39)**; Hello Jim, 1963 **(97)**; Did You Have a Happy Birthday?, 1963 **(89)**; My Baby's Comin' Home, 1964 **(113)**; Goodnight My Love, 1969 **(27)**; In the Still of the Night, 1969 **(64)**; Sincerely, 1969 **(80)**; Happy, 1969 **(86)**; Do I Love You, 1971 **(53)**; Jubilation, 1972 **(65)**; Let Me Get to Know You, 1974 **(80)**; (You're) Having My Baby, 1974 **(1)** (with Odia Coates); One Man Woman/One Woman Man, 1974 **(7)** (with Odia Coates); I Don't Like to Sleep Alone, 1975 **(8)** (with Odia Coates); (I Believe) There's Nothing Stronger Than Our Love, 1975 **(15)** (with Odia Coates); Times of Your Life, 1975 **(7)**; Anytime (I'll Be There), 1976 **(33)**; Happier, 1976 **(60)**; My Best Friend's Wife, 1977 **(80)**; Everybody Ought to Be in Love, 1977 **(75)**; This Is Love, 1978 **(35)**; I've Been Waiting for You All of My Life, 1981 **(48)**; Hold Me 'Til the Mornin' Comes, 1982 **(40)**

Pop Vocal — Canadian

Annette

Albums: Annette Sings Anka, 1960; Hawaiiannette, 1960; Annette's Beach Party, 1963

Singles: Tall Paul, 1959 **(7)**; Jo-Jo the Dog-Faced Boy, 1959 **(73)**; Lonely Guitar, 1959 **(50)**; First Name Initial, 1959 **(20)**; My Heart Became of Age, 1959 **(74)**; O Dio Mio, 1960 **(10)**; Train of Love, 1960 **(36)**; Pineapple Princess, 1960 **(11)**; Talk to Me Baby, 1960 **(92)**; Dream Boy, 1961 **(87)**; Blue Muu Muu, 1961 **(107)**; Dreamin' About You, 1961 **(106)**; Promise Me Anything, 1963 **(123)**

Pop Vocal — New York; "Beach" film star and original Disney Mouseketeer; last name Funicello

Ann-Margret

Singles: I Just Don't Understand, 1961 **(17)**; It Do Me So Good, 1961 **(97)**; What Am I Supposed to Do, 1962 **(82)**; Sleep in the Grass, 1969 **(113)** (with Lee Hazlewood)

Pop Vocal — Illinois; movie actress; full name is Ann-Margret Olsson

Appaloosa

Personnel: John Crompton (vocals); David Reiser (bass); Robin Batteau (violin); Al Kooper (keyboards)

Album: Appaloosa, 1969

Folk Rock — American

The Applejacks

Personnel: Dave Appell (guitars)

Singles: Mexican Hat Rock, 1958 **(16)**; Rocka-Conga, 1958 **(38)**; Bunny Hop, 1959 **(70)**

Instrumental — Philadelphia

The Applejacks

Personnel: Al Jackson (vocals); Phil Cash (guitars); Martin Baggott (guitars); Megan Davies (bass); Don Gould (keyboards); Gerry Freeman (drums)

Album: The Applejacks, 1964
Single: Tell Me When, 1964 **(135)**
Pop Rock—British

The Aquatones

Personnel: Lynn Nixon (vocals); Larry Vannata (vocals); David Goddard (vocals); Eugene McCarthy (vocals)

Singles: You, 1958, **(21)**; Crazy for You, 1961 **(119)**
Pop Vocal—New York

The Arbors

Personnel: Edward Farran (vocals); Fred Farran (vocals); Scott Herrick (vocals); Tom Herrick (vocals)

Album: A Symphony for Susan, 1967
Singles: A Symphony for Susan, 1966 **(51)**; Just Let It Happen, 1967 **(113)**; Graduation Day, 1967 **(59)**; The Letter, 1969 **(20)**; I Can't Quit Her, 1969 **(67)**
Pop Rock—Michigan; from University of Michigan

The Archies

Personnel: Ron Dante (vocals); Jeff Barry (vocals); Andy Kim (vocals); Ellie Greenwich (vocals); Ray Stevens (guitars, vocals); Toni Wine (vocals); Tony Passalacqua (vocals)

Albums: The Archies, 1968; Everything's Archie, 1969; Jingle Jangle, 1969; Sunshine, 1970; The Archies' Greatest Hits, 1970

Singles: Bang Shang a Lang, 1968 **(22)**; Feeling So Good, 1968 **(53)**; Sugar Sugar, 1969 **(1)**; Jingle Jangle, 1969 **(10)**; Who's Your Baby, 1970 **(40)**; Sunshine, 1970 **(57)**; Together We Two, 1971 **(122)**

Bubblegum Pop—American; group had Saturday morning cartoon based on Archie comic book characters

Area Code 615

Personnel: Weldon Myrick (steel guitars); Buddy Spicher (fiddle); Mac Gayden (guitars); Charlie McCoy (harmonica); Ken Lauber (piano) replaced (1969) by David Briggs (piano); Wayne Moss (guitars, bass); Norbert Putnam (bass); Bobby Thompson (keyboards, banjo); Kenny Buttrey (drums)

Albums: Area Code 615, 1969; A Trip in the Country, 1970
Folk/Country Rock—California

Art

Personnel: Luther Grosvenor (guitars); Mike Harrison (keyboards, vocals); Greg Ridley (bass); Mike Kellie (drums)

Album: Supernatural Fairytales, 1969
Art Rock—British; group evolved into Spooky Tooth

Artwoods

Personnel: Art Wood (vocals); Jon Lord (keyboards); Derek Griffiths (guitars); Malcolm Pool (bass); Keef Hartley (drums)

Albums: Gallery, 1964; Jazz in Jeans, 1966; Artwoods, 1973; Art Gallery, 1974
Jazz/Rock—British

Arzachel

Personnel: Steve Hillage (guitars), Mont Campbell (bass); Dave Stewart (keyboards); Clive Brooks (drums)
Album: Arzachel, 1969
Jazz Rock—British

Jan Ashton

Single: Cold Dreary Morning, 1967
Folk/Rock—American; Ashton was a member of the Mojo Men and the Vejtables

The Association

Personnel: Russ Giguere (guitars, vocals) replaced (1970) by Richard Thompson (guitars, vocals) replaced (1974) by Larry Ulsky (guitars); Gary Alexander (guitars, vocals) replaced (1967) by Larry Ramos (guitars, vocals) replaced (1969) by Gary Alexander (guitars, vocals); Jim Yester (guitars, keyboards, vocals); Terry Kirkman (woodwinds, keyboards, vocals); Ted Bluechel (drums, vocals); Brian Cole (bass, deceased 1972)
Albums: And Then ... Along Came the Association, 1966; Renaissance, 1967; Insight Out, 1967; Birthday, 1968; Greatest Hits, 1969; Goodbye Columbus, 1969; Association, 1969; Live, 1970; Stop Your Motor, 1971; Waterbeds in Trinidad, 1972
Singles: Along Comes Mary, 1966 **(7)**; Cherish, 1966 **(1)**; Pandora's Golden Heebie Jeebies, 1966 **(35)**; Looking Glass, 1967 **(113)**; No Fair at All, 1967 **(51)**; Windy, 1967 **(1)**; Never My Love, 1967 **(2)**; Requiem for the Masses, 1967 **(100)**; Everything That Touches You, 1968 **(10)**; Time for Livin', 1968 **(39)**; Six Man Band, 1968 **(47)**; Goodbye Columbus, 1969 **(80)**; Under Branches, 1969 **(117)**; Yes, I Will, 1969 **(120)**; Just About the Same, 1970 **(106)**; Darling Be Home Soon, 1972 **(104)**; Names, Tags, Numbers & Labels, 1973 **(91)**; Dreamer, 1981 **(66)**; Small Town Lovers, 1981
Soft Rock—Los Angeles; reformed in 1980 with surviving original members

The Astors

Personnel: Curtis Johnson (vocals); Eddie Stanback (vocals); Richard Harris (vocals); Sam Byrnes (vocals)
Single: Candy, 1965 **(63)**
R & B Vocal—Memphis

The Astronauts

Personnel: Bob Demmon (guitars); Dennis Lindsey (guitars); Rich Fifield (guitars, vocals); Storm Patterson (bass, vocals); Jim Gallagher (drums)
Albums: Surfin' with the Astronauts, 1963; Everything Is A OK, 1964; Rockin' with the Astronauts, 1964; Astronauts Orbit Kampus, 1964; Competition Coupe, 1964; Down the Line, 1965; Favourites for You, 1965; Go Go Go, 1965; Travelin' Men, 1967
Singles: Baja, 1963 **(94)**; Competition Coupe, 1964 **(124)**
Surf Rock—Colorado

Brian Auger

Personnel: Brian Auger (keyboards, vocals); Richard Brown (bass) replaced (1967) by Dave Ambrose (bass) replaced (1970) by

Roger Sutton (bass) replaced (1977) by Clive Chaman (bass) replaced (1978) by David McDaniels (bass); Julie Driscoll (vocals) replaced (1970) by Alex Ligertwood (vocals); Gary Boyle (guitars) replaced (1970) by Jim Mullen (guitars) replaced (1973) by Jack Mills (guitars); Micky Waller (drums) replaced (1967) by Clive Thacker (drums) replaced (1970) by Rob McIntosh (drums) replaced (1973) by Lennox Laington (drums) replaced (1974) by Steve Ferrone (drums) replaced (1978) by Dave Crigger (drums); added (1971) Barry Dean (guitars) replaced (1978) by George Doering (guitars)

Albums: Open, 1967; Definitely What, 1968; Streetnoise, 1968; Befour, 1970; Best of Brian Auger & Trinity, 1970; Brian Auger & Trinity, 1971; Oblivion Express, 1971; A Better Land, 1971; Second Wind, 1972; Straight Ahead, 1973; Live Oblivion Volume 1, 1974; Live Oblivion Volume 2, 1974; Jam Session, 1975; Genesis, 1975; Reinforcements, 1975; Best of Brian Auger, 1976; London '64/'67, 1977; Happiness Heartaches, 1977; Encore, 1978; Search Party, 1981; Planet Earth Calling, 1989

Singles: This Wheel's on Fire, 1968 **(106)**; Listen Here, 1970 **(100)**

Jazz/Rock/Fusion — British; Brian's groups were known as Trinity and Oblivion Express

Frankie Avalon

Albums: Venus, 1959; Swingin' on a Rainbow, 1959; Where Are You, 1960; A Whole Lotta Frankie, 1961

Singles: Dede Dinah, 1958 **(7)**; You Excite Me, 1958 **(49)**; Ginger Bread, 1958 **(9)**; I'll Wait for You, 1958 **(15)**; What Little Girl, 1958 **(79)**; Venus, 1959 **(1)**; Bobby Sox to Stockings, 1959 **(8)**; A Boy Without a Girl, 1959 **(10)**; Just Ask Your Heart, 1959 **(7)**; Two Fools, 1959 **(54)**; Why, 1959 **(1)**; Swingin' on a Rainbow, 1959 **(39)**; Don't Throw Away All Those Teardrops, 1960 **(22)**; Where Are You, 1960 **(32)**; Tuxedo Junction, 1960 **(82)**; Togetherness, 1960 **(26)**; Don't Let Love Pass Me By, 1960 **(85)**; A Perfect Love, 1960 **(47)**; The Puppet Song, 1960 **(56)**; Call Me Anything, 1961 **(102)**; All of Everything, 1961 **(70)**; Who Else But You, 1961 **(82)**; Voyage to the Bottom of the Sea, 1961 **(101)**; True, True Love, 1961 **(90)**; Married, 1961 **(112)**; After You've Gone, 1962 **(117)**; You Are Mine, 1962 **(26)**; A Miracle, 1962 **(75)**; Don't Let Me Stand in Your Way, 1962 **(111)**; Welcome Home, 1962 **(129)**; Venus, 1976 **(46)**

Pop Vocal — Philadelphia; "Beach" film star; real name is Francis Avallone

The Avant-Garde

Singles: Naturally Stoned, 1968 **(40)**; Fly with Me, 1968 **(130)**

Pop — American

The Bachelors

Personnel: Declan Cluskey (vocals); Con Cluskey (vocals); John Stokes (vocals)

Albums: Presenting: The Bachelors, 1964; Back Again, 1964; No Arms Can Ever Hold You, 1965; Marie, 1965

Singles: Diane, 1964 **(10)**; I Believe, 1964 **(33)**; I Wouldn't Trade You for the World, 1964 **(69)**; No Arms Can Ever Hold You, 1964

(27); Marie, 1965 (15); Chapel in the Moonlight, 1965 (32); Love Me with All of Your Heart, 1966 (38); Can I Trust You?, 1966 (49); Walk with Faith in Your Heart, 1967 (83)

Folk Vocal—Irish; trio from Dublin, Ireland

Joan Baez

Albums: Joan Baez, 1960; Joan Baez, Volume 2, 1961; Joan Baez in Concert, 1962; The Best of Joan Baez, 1963; Joan Baez in Concert, Part 2, 1963; Joan Baez/5, 1964; Farewell, Angelina, 1965; Joan, 1967; Baptism, 1968; Any Day Now, 1969; David's Album, 1969; One Day at a Time, 1970; The First 10 Years, 1970; Blessed Are, 1971, Carry It On, 1972; Come from the Shadows, 1972; The Joan Baez Ballad Book, 1972; Where Are You Now, My Son?, 1973; Hits/Greatest and Others, 1973; Diamonds and Rust, 1975; From Every Stage, 1976; Gulf Winds, 1976; Blowin' Away, 1977; The Best of Joan C. Baez, 1977; Honest Lullaby, 1979; Live in Concert, 1980; Classics, 1985; Recently, 1986; Diamonds and Rust in the Bullring, 1988

Singles: We Shall Overcome, 1963 (90); There But for Fortune, 1965 (50); Love Is Just a Four-Letter Word, 1969 (86); The Night They Drove Old Dixie Down, 1971 (3); Let It Be, 1971 (49); In the Quiet Morning (for Janis Joplin), 1972 (69); Blue Sky, 1975 (57); Diamonds and Rust, 1975 (35)

Folk/Rock—California

LaVern Baker

Albums: LaVern, 1956; LaVern Baker, 1957; Blues Ballads, 1959; Precious Memories, 1959; Saved, 1961; See See Rider, 1963; The Best of LaVern Baker, 1963

Singles: Tweedle Dee, 1955 (14); I Can't Love You Enough, 1956 (22); Tra La La, 1956 (94); Jim Dandy, 1956 (17); Still, 1956 (97); Jim Dandy Got Married, 1957 (76); Humpty Dumpty Heart, 1957 (71); I Cried a Tear, 1958 (6); I Waited Too Long, 1959 (33); So High So Low, 1959 (52); If You Love Me, 1959 (79); Tiny Tim, 1959 (63); Wheel of Fortune, 1960 (83); Shadows of Love, 1960 (83); Bumble Bee, 1960 (46); I'll Never Be Free, 1961 (103) (with Jimmy Ricks); You're the Boss, 1961 (81) (with Jimmy Ricks); Saved, 1961 (37); See See Rider, 1962 (34); You'd Better Find Yourself Another Fool, 1964 (128); Fly Me to the Moon, 1965 (84); Think Twice, 1966 (93) (with Jackie Wilson); Please Don't Hurt Me, 1966 (128) (with Jackie Wilson); Batman to the Rescue, 1966 (135)

Blues Vocal—Chicago

Bakerloo

Personnel: Dave Clempson (guitars, keyboards); Terry Poole (bass); Keith Baker (drums)

Album: Bakerloo, 1969

Blues/Rock—British

Long John Baldry

Albums: Long John Blues, 1964; Looking at Long John, 1966; Let the Heartache Begin, 1968; Let There Be Long John, 1968; Wait for Me, 1969; It Ain't Easy, 1971; Everything Stops for Tea, 1972; Heartaches (Golden Hour), 1974; Good to Be Alive, 1976; Welcome to the Club, 1977; Baldry's Out, 1979; Long John Baldry, 1980; Rock with the Best, 1981

Singles: Let the Heartaches Begin, 1968 **(88)**; Mexico, 1968; Don't Try to Lay No Boogie-Woogie on the King of Rock and Roll, 1971 **(73)**; You've Lost That Lovin' Feelin', 1979**(89)** (with Kathi MacDonald)

Blues/Rock — British; "Long" John stands 6'7" and is now a Canadian citizen

Kenny Ball & His Jazzmen

Album: Midnight in Moscow, 1962

Singles: Midnight in Moscow, 1962 **(2)**; March of the Siamese Children, 1962 **(88)**; The Green Leaves of Summer, 1962 **(87)**; Heartaches, 1963 **(119)**

Jazz/Rock — British

Hank Ballard and The Midnighters

Personnel: Henry Booth (vocals) replaced (1965) by Walter Miller (vocals); Charles Sutton (vocals) replaced (1965) by Frank Stadford (vocals); Lawson Smith (vocals) replaced (1953) by Hank Ballard (vocals); Sonny Woods (vocals) replaced (1965) by Wesley Hargrove (vocals)

Albums: Their Greatest Hits, 1954; Their Greatest Hits 2, 1956; The Midniters, 1957; Greatest Juke Box Hits, 1958; Singin' and Swingin', 1959; One & Only, 1960; Mr. Rhythm & Blues, 1960; Sing Along, 1961; Spotlight on Hank Ballard, 1961; Let's Go Again, 1961; Jumpin' Hank Ballard, 1962; Twistin' Fools, 1962; The 1963

Sound, 1963; Hank Ballard's Biggest Hits, 1963; Star in Your Eyes, 1964; Those Lazy Days, 1965; 24 Hits, 1966; Glad Songs, Sad Songs, 1966; 24 Greatest Hits, 1968; You Can't Keep a Good Man Down, 1969; 20 Hits, 1977

Singles: Teardrops on Your Letter, 1959 **(87)**; Kansas City, 1959 **(72)**; Cute Little Ways, 1959 **(106)**; Finger Poppin' Time, 1960 **(7)**; The Twist, 1960 **(28)**; Let's Go, Let's Go, Let's Go, 1960 **(6)**; The Hoochi Coochi Coo, 1960 **(23)**; Let's Go Again (Where We Went Last Night), 1961 **(39)**; The Continental Walk, 1961 **(33)**; The Switch-a-Roo, 1961 **(26)**; The Float, 1961 **(92)**; Nothing But Good, 1961 **(49)**; Keep on Dancing, 1961 **(66)**; Do You Know How to Twist, 1962 **(87)** (Hank Ballard solo)

Soul/R & B Vocal — Detroit

Balloon Farm

Personnel: Mike Appel (vocals, guitars)

Album: Balloon Farm, 1968

Single: A Question of Temperature, 1968 **(37)**

Psychedelic Pop — American

The Band

Personnel: Robbie Robertson (guitars, vocals) replaced (1988) by Jim Weider (guitars); Rick Danko (bass, vocals); Garth Hudson (keyboards); Richard Manuel (piano, vocals; deceased 1986); Levon Helm (drums, vocals)

Albums: Music from the Big Pink, 1968; The Band, 1969; Stage Fright, 1970; Cahoots, 1971; Rock of Ages, 1972; Moondog Matinee, 1973; Northern Lights Southern

The Band: Danko, Helm, Manuel, Hudson, Robertson

Cross, 1975; The Best of the Band, 1976; Islands, 1977; The Last Waltz, 1978; Anthology, 1978; Anthology Volume 2, 1984; To Kingdom Come — The Definitive Collection, 1990

Singles: The Weight, 1968 **(63)**; Up on Cripple Creek, 1969 **(25)**; Rag Mama Rag, 1970 **(57)**; Time to Kill, 1970 **(77)**; The Shape I'm In, 1971 **(121)**; Life Is a Carnival, 1971 **(72)**; Don't Do It, 1972 **(34)**; (I Don't Want To) Hang Up My Rock and Roll Shoes, 1972 **(113)**; Ain't Got No Home, 1973 **(73)**; Most Likely You Go Your Way (I'll Go Mine), 1974 **(66)**; Ophelia, 1976 **(62)**

Video: The Last Waltz, 1978
Folk/Rock — Canadian

Bangor Flying Circus

Personnel: Alan De Carlo (guitars, vocals); David "Hawk" Wolinski (bass, keyboards, vocals); Michael Tegza (drums, percussion)

Album: Bangor Flying Circus, 1969
Pop/Rock — American

Darrell Banks

Albums: Darrell Banks Is Here, 1968; Here to Stay, 1969
Singles: Open the Door to Your Heart, 1966 **(27)**; Somebody (Somewhere) Needs You, 1966 **(55)**; Here Come the Tears, 1967 **(124)**

Soul Vocal — Buffalo; shot to death in 1970; real last name was Eubanks

The Barbarians

Personnel: Bruce Benson (guitars); Jeff Morris (guitars); Jerry Causi (bass); Victor Moulton (drums, vocals)
Album: The Barbarians, 1965
Singles: Are You a Boy or Are You a Girl?, 1965 **(55)**; What the New Breed Say, 1965 **(102)**; Moulty, 1966, **(90)**

The Barbarians: *(left to right)* **Moulton, Morris, Causi, Benson**

Psychedelic Pop—Massachusetts; drummer "Moulty" had a hook for a left hand

Keith Barbour

Album: Echo Park, 1969
Single: Echo Park, 1969 **(40)**
Pop Vocal—American

The Bar-Keys

Personnel: Jimmy King (guitars; deceased 1967) replaced (1968) by Frank Thompson (guitars) replaced (1971) by Lloyd Smith (guitars); Ronnie Caldwell (organ; deceased 1967) replaced (1968) by Winston Stewart (organ) replaced (1971) by Michael Beard (organ); James Alexander (bass); Phalon Jones (saxophones; deceased 1967) replaced (1968) by Harvey Henderson (saxophones); Ben Cauley (trumpet); Carl Cunningham (drums; deceased 1967) replaced (1968) by Willie Hall (drums) replaced (1971) by Charles Allen (drums); added (1968) Vernon Burch (vocals)

Albums: Soul Finger, 1967; Gotta Groove, 1969; Black Rock, 1971; Do You See What I See, 1972; Cold Blooded, 1974; Too Hot to Stop, 1976; Flying High on Your Love, 1977; Money Talks, 1978; Light of Life, 1978; Injoy, 1979; As One, 1980, Nightcruisin', 1981; Propositions, 1982; Dangerous, 1984
Singles: Soul Finger, 1967 **(17)**; Knucklehead, 1967 **(76)**; Give Everybody Some, 1967 **(91)**; Son of Shaft, 1971 **(53)**; Shake Your Rump to the Funk, 1976 **(23)**; Too Hot to Stop, 1977 **(74)**; Let's Have Some Fun, 1978 **(102)**; Shine, 1979 **(102)**; Move Your Boogie Body, 1979 **(57)**; Today Is the Day, 1980 **(60)**; Hit and Run, 1981 **(101)**; Freakshow on the Dance Floor, 1984 **(73)**
R & B—American

Joe Barry

Singles: I'm a Fool to Care, 1961 **(24)**; Teardrops in My Heart, 1961 **(63)**
Pop Vocal—Louisiana; real name is Joe Barrios

Len Barry

Album: 1-2-3, 1965
Singles: Lip Sync (to the Tongue Twisters), 1965 **(84)**; 1-2-3, 1965 **(2)**; Like a Baby, 1966 **(27)**; Somewhere, 1966 **(26)**; It's That Time of the Year, 1966 **(91)**; I Struck It Rich, 1966 **(98)**; Moving Finger Writes, 1967 **(124)**
Pop Vocal—Philadelphia; former lead singer of the Dovells; real name is Leonard Borisoff

Barry and The Tamerlanes

Personnel: Barry DeVorzon (keyboards, vocals); Terry Smith (vocals); Bodie Chandler (vocals); Perry Botkin, Jr. (keyboards)
Singles: I Wonder What She's Doing Tonight, 1963 **(21)**; Roberta, 1964 **(127)**
Pop—California

Chris Bartley

Album: The Sweetest Thing This Side of Heaven, 1967
Singles: The Sweetest Thing This Side of Heaven, 1967 **(32)**; Baby It's Wonderful, 1967 **(125)**
Soul/R & B—New York

Fontella Bass

Albums: The New Look, 1966; Free, 1972
Singles: Don't Mess Up a Good Thing, 1965 **(33)** (with Bobby McClure); You'll Miss Me (When I'm Gone), 1965 **(91)** (with Bobby McClure); Rescue Me, 1965 **(4)**; Recovery, 1965 **(37)**; I Surrender, 1966 **(78)**; Safe and Sound, 1966 **(100)**
Soul Vocal—St. Louis

B. Bumble & The Stingers

Personnel: Plas Johnson (saxophones); Rene Hall (bass); Earl Palmer (drums); Al Hassan (guitars); Ernie Freeman (piano) replaced (1962) by Lincoln Mayorga (piano) replaced (1963) by R. C. Gamble (piano)
Singles: Bumble Boogie, 1961 **(21)**; Boogie Woogie, 1961 **(89)**; Nut Rocker, 1962 **(23)**
Instrumental—Los Angeles

The Beach Boys

back row: **B. Wilson, A. Jardine, D. Wilson,** *front row:* **M. Love, C. Wilson**

Personnel: Brian Wilson (vocals, keyboards); Carl Wilson (guitars, vocals); Dennis Wilson (drums, vocals; deceased 1984); Al Jardine (guitars, bass, vocals); Mike Love (vocals, percussion); added: Daryl Dragon (keyboards, guitars) replaced (1965) by Bruce Johnston (keyboards, guitars)
Albums: Surfin' Safari, 1962; Surfin U.S.A., 1963; Surfer Girl, 1963; Little Deuce Coupe, 1963; Shut Down Volume 2, 1964; All Summer Long, 1964; Christmas Album, 1964; Beach Boys Concert, 1964; Beach Boys Today, 1965; Summer Days Summer Nights, 1965; Beach Boys Party, 1965; Pet Sounds, 1966; Best of the Beach Boys, 1966; Smiley Smile, 1967; Best of the Beach Boys, Volume 2, 1967; Wild Honey, 1967; Friends, 1968; Best of the Beach Boys, Volume 3,

1968; 20/20, 1969; Close Up, 1969; Beach Boys '69, 1969; Sunflower, 1970; Greatest Hits, 1970; Surf's Up, 1971; Live in London, 1972; So Tough, 1972; Holland, 1973; In Concert, 1973; Endless Summer, 1974; Good Vibrations, 1975; Spirit of America, 1975; 15 Big Ones, 1976; Stack O' Tracks, 1976; 20 Golden Greats, 1977; The Beach Boys Love You, 1977; M I U, 1978; The Light Album, 1979; Keepin' the Summer Alive, 1980; Ten Years of Harmony, 1981; Sunshine Dream, 1982; The Beach Boys, 1985; Made in the U.S.A., 1986; California Girls, 1987; Best of the Beach Boys, 1987; Still Cruisin', 1989

Singles: Surfin', 1962 **(75)**; Surfin' Safari, 1962 **(14)**; 409, 1962 **(76)**; Ten Little Indians, 1962 **(49)**; Surfin' U.S.A., 1963 **(3)**; Shut Down, 1963 **(23)**; Little Deuce Coupe, 1963 **(15)**; Surfer Girl, 1963 **(7)**; Be True to Your School, 1963 **(6)**; In My Room, 1963 **(23)**; Fun, Fun, Fun, 1964 **(5)**; Why Do Fools Fall in Love, 1964 **(120)**; I Get Around, 1964 **(1)**; Don't Worry Baby, 1964 **(24)**; When I Grow Up to Be a Man, 1964 **(9)**; She Knows Me Too Well, 1964 **(101)**; Little Honda, 1964 **(65)**; Wendy, 1964 **(44)**; Dance, Dance, Dance, 1964 **(8)**; Little Saint Nick, 1964; Do You Wanna Dance, 1965 **(12)**; Please Let Me Wonder, 1965 **(52)**; Help Me Rhonda, 1965 **(1)**; California Girls, 1965 **(3)**; The Little Girl I Once Knew, 1965 **(20)**; Barbara Ann, 1966 **(2)**; Sloop John B, 1966 **(3)**; Wouldn't It Be Nice, 1966 **(8)**; God Only Knows, 1966 **(39)**; Good Vibrations, 1966 **(1)**; Heroes and Villains, 1967 **(12)**; Wild Honey, 1967 **(31)**; Darlin', 1967 **(19)**; Friends, 1968 **(47)**; Do It Again, 1968 **(20)**; Bluebirds Over the Mountain, 1968 **(61)**; I Can Hear Music, 1969 **(24)**; Breakaway, 1969 **(63)**; Add Some Music to Your Day, 1970 **(64)**; Cottonfields, 1970 **(103)**; Long Promised Road, 1971 **(89)**; Marcella, 1972 **(110)**; Sail on Sailor, 1973 **(79)**; California Saga, 1973 **(89)**; Surfin U.S.A., 1974 **(36)**; Sail on Sailor, 1975 **(49)**; Barbara Ann, 1975 **(101)**; Wouldn't It Be Nice, 1975 **(103)**; Rock and Roll Music, 1976 **(5)**; It's O.K., 1976 **(29)**; Susie Cincinnati, 1976; Peggy Sue, 1978 **(59)**; Here Comes the Night, 1979 **(44)**; Good Timin', 1979 **(40)**; Lady Lynda, 1979; Goin' On, 1980 **(83)**; Livin' with a Heartache, 1980; Beach Boys Medley, 1981 **(12)**; Come Go with Me, 1981 **(18)**; Getcha Back, 1985 **(26)**; It's Gettin' Late, 1985 **(82)**; She Believes in Love, 1985; Rock 'n' Roll to the Rescue, 1985 **(68)**; California Dreamin', 1986 **(57)**; Wipe Out, 1989 **(12)** (with the Fat Boys); Kokomo, 1988 **(1)**; Still Crusin', 1989 **(93)**

Surf/Soft Rock — California; Brian's daughters Wendy and Carnie are ⅔ of the group Wilson Phillips

Beacon Street Union

Personnel: Paul Tartachny (guitars, vocals); John Wright (vocals, percussion); Wayne Ulaky (bass, vocals); Robert Rhodes (keyboards, woodwinds); Richard Weisburg (drums)

Albums: The Eyes of the Beacon Street Union, 1968; The Clown Died in Marvin Gardens, 1968

Psychedelic Rock — Boston

Beast

Personnel: David Raines (vocals); Robert Yeazel (guitars, vocals);

Kenny Passarelli (bass, harmonica) replaced (1969) by Robert Bryant (bass); Mike Kearns (woodwinds); Larry Ferris (drums)

Albums: Prelude for Today, 1969; Beast, 1970

Hard Rock—Denver

The Beatles

McCartney, Harrison, Lennon, Starr

Personnel: John Lennon (guitars, vocals, keyboards; deceased 1980); Paul McCartney (bass, vocals, guitars, keyboards); George Harrison (guitars, vocals, sitar); Stu Sutcliffe (bass; deceased 1962); Peter Best (drums) replaced (1962) by Richard "Ringo Starr" Starkey (drums, vocals)

Albums: Please Please Me, 1963; With the Beatles, 1963; Meet the Beatles, 1964; Beatles Second, 1964; Something New, 1964; Beatles' Story, 1964; Hard Day's Night, 1964; Beatles for Sale, 1964; Beatles '65, 1965; The Early Beatles, 1965; Beatles VI, 1965; Help, 1965; Rubber Soul, 1966; Yesterday & Today, 1966; Revolver, 1966; Sergeant Pepper's Lonely Hearts Club Band, 1967; Magical Mystery Tour, 1968; The Beatles (White Album), 1968; Yellow Submarine, 1969; Abbey Road, 1969; Let It Be, 1970; Hey Jude, 1970; 1962–1966, 1973; 1967–1970, 1973; Rock 'n' Roll Music, 1976; Live at the Hollywood Bowl, 1976; Love Songs, 1977; Live at the Star Club: Hamburg, 1977; Rarities, 1980; Beatles Ballads, 1980; Reel Music, 1982; 20 Greatest Hits, 1982

Singles: From Me to You, 1963 **(116)**; She Love You, 1964 **(1)**; I Want to Hold Your Hand, 1964 **(1)**; I Saw Her Standing There, 1964 **(14)**; Please Please Me, 1964 **(3)**; From Me to You, 1964 **(41)**; Do You Want to Know a Secret, 1964 **(2)**; Can't Buy Me Love, 1964 **(1)**; All My Loving, 1964 **(45)**; Twist and Shout, 1964 **(2)**; Love Me Do, 1964 **(1)**; There'a a Place, 1964 **(74)**; Roll Over Beethoven, 1964 **(68)**; You Can't Do That, 1964 **(48)**; Thank You Girl, 1964 **(35)**; P.S. I Love You, 1964 **(10)**; Why, 1964 **(88)** (with Tony Sheridan); Sie Lieb Dich, 1964 **(97)**; Ain't She Sweet, 1964 **(19)**; Hard Day's Night, 1964 **(1)**; I Should Have Known Better, 1964 **(53)**; And I Love Her, 1964 **(12)**; If I Fell, 1964 **(53)**; I'll Cry Instead, 1964 **(25)**; I'm Happy Just to Dance with You, 1964 **(95)**; Matchbox, 1964 **(17)**; Slow Down, 1964 **(25)**; She's a Woman, 1964 **(4)**; I Feel Fine, 1964 **(1)**; Eight Days a Week, 1965 **(1)**; I Don't Want to Spoil the Party, 1965 **(39)**; Ticket to Ride, 1965 **(1)**; Yes It Is, 1965 **(46)**; I'm Down, 1965 **(101)**; Help!, 1965 **(1)**; Yesterday, 1965 **(1)**; Boys, 1965 **(102)**; Act Naturally, 1965 **(47)**; Day Tripper, 1965 **(5)**; We Can Work It Out, 1965 **(1)**; Nowhere Man, 1966 **(3)**; Michelle, 1966 **(3)**; What Goes On, 1966 **(81)**; Rain, 1966 **(23)**;

Paperback Writer, 1966 **(1)**; Yellow Submarine, 1966 **(2)**; Eleanor Rigby, 1966 **(11)**; Penny Lane, 1967 **(1)**; Strawberry Fields Forever, 1967 **(8)**; All You Need Is Love, 1967 **(1)**; Here Comes the Sun, 1967 **(1)**; Baby You're a Rich Man, 1967 **(34)**; Lucy in the Sky with Diamonds, 1967; Hello Goodbye, 1967 **(1)**; I Am the Walrus, 1967 **(56)**; Lady Madonna, 1968 **(4)**; The Inner Light, 1968 **(96)**; Magical Mystery Tour, 1968 **(1)**; Hey Jude, 1968 **(1)**; Revolution, 1968 **(12)**; Get Back, 1969 **(1)**; Don't Let Me Down, 1969 **(35)**; The Ballad of John & Yoko, 1969 **(8)**; Something, 1969 **(3)**; Come Together, 1969 **(1)**; Let It Be, 1970 **(1)**; The Long and Winding Road, 1970 **(1)**; For You Blue, 1970 **(71)**; Got to Get You into My Life, 1976 **(7)**; Ob-La-Di, Ob-La-Da, 1976 **(49)**; Sergeant Pepper's Lonely Hearts Club Band/with a Little Help from My Friends, 1978 **(71)**; Beatles' Movie Medley, 1982 **(12)**; Love Me Do, 1982; Twist and Shout, 1986

Pop/Rock—British; biggest selling group of the 1960s, with 20 #1 singles and 15 #1 albums

The Beau Brummels

Personnel: Ron Elliott (guitars, vocals); Sal Valentino (vocals); Declan Mulligan (bass) left group (1965); Ron Meagher (bass, guitars, vocals) replaced (1968) by Norbert Putnam (bass); John Peterson (drums) replaced (1968) by Ken Buttrey (drums)

Albums: Introducing, 1965; Beau Brummels, 1966; The Beau Brummels, 1966; Beau Brummels '66, 1966; Triangle, 1967; Best of the Beau Brummels, 1967; Volume 44, 1968; Bradley's Barn, 1968; The Beau Brummels, 1975; Greatest Hits, 1976; Best of 1964/1968, 1981

Singles: Laugh Laugh, 1965 **(15)**; Just a Little, 1965 **(8)**; You Tell Me Why, 1965 **(38)**; Don't Talk to Strangers, 1965 **(52)**; Good Time Music, 1965 **(97)**; One Too Many Mornings, 1966 **(95)**

Pop/Rock—San Francisco

The Beau-Marks

Personnel: Joey Frechette (vocals)
Single: Clap Your Hands, 1960 **(45)**

Pop Vocal—Canadian

Beau Brummels: Elliot, Meagher, Valentino, Peterson

Jeff Beck Group

Personnel: Jeff Beck (guitars, vocals); Rod Stewart (vocals) replaced (1969) by Alexander Ligertwood (vocals) replaced (1971) by Bob Tench (vocals; left group 1972); Jet Harris (bass) replaced (1967) by Ron Wood (bass, guitars) replaced (1971) by Clive Chaman (bass) replaced (1973) by Tim Bogert (bass) replaced (1975) by Phil Chen (bass) replaced (1976) by Wilbur Bascomb (bass) replaced (1977) by Stanley Clarke (bass) replaced (1980) by Mo Foster (bass); Viv Prince (drums) replaced (1967) by Aynsley Dunbar (drums) replaced (1967) by Rod Coombes (drums) replaced (1967) by Ray Cook (drums) replaced (1967) by Micky Waller (drums) replaced (1968) by Tony Newman (drums) replaced (1971) by Cozy Powell (drums) replaced (1973) by Carmine Appice (drums) replaced (1975) by Bernard Purdie (drums) replaced (1980) by Simon Phillips (drums) replaced (1988) by Terry Bozzio (drums); added (1968): Nicky Hopkins (keyboards) replaced (1971) by Max Middleton (keyboards) replaced (1980) by Tony Hymas (keyboards)

Albums: Truth, 1968; Beck-Ola, 1969; Rough and Ready, 1971; The Jeff Beck Group, 1972; Beck, Bogert & Appice, 1973; Blow by Blow, 1975; Wired, 1976; Live . . . with the Jan Hammer Group, 1977; There and Back, 1980; Flash, 1985; Guitar Shop, 1989

Singles: Hi-Ho Silver Lining, 1968 **(123)**; People Get Ready, 1985 **(48)** (with Rod Stewart); Ambitious, 1985

Jazz/Rock—British; Beck attended Wimbledon Art College in London and is considered a guitar master and innovator by his peers

Bob Beckham

Singles: Just as Much as Ever, 1959 **(32)**; Crazy Arms, 1960 **(36)**; Mais Oui, 1960 **(105)**
  Country Vocal—Oklahoma

Bee Gees

Personnel: Barry Gibb (guitars, vocals); Robin Gibb (vocals); Maurice Gibb (bass, vocals); Vince Melouney (guitars) left group (1969) replaced (1974) by Alan Kendall (guitars); Colin Petersen (drums) left group (1969) replaced (1974) by Dennis Bryon (drums); added (1974) Blue Weaver (keyboards)

Albums: Bee Gees First, 1967; Horizontal, 1968; Rare, Precious and Beautiful, 1968; Idea, 1968; Odessa, 1969; The Best of the Bee Gees, 1969; Cucumber Castle, 1970; The Sound of Love, 1970; Marley Purt Drive, 1970; Two Years On, 1971; Trafalgar, 1971; To Whom It May Concern, 1972; Life in a Tin Can, 1973; The Best of the Bee Gees Volume 2, 1973; Mr. Natural, 1974; Main Course, 1975; Children of the World, 1976; Bee Gees Gold, 1977; Here at Last . . . Bee Gees . . . Live, 1977; Saturday Night Fever (Soundtrack), 1978; Spirits Having Flown, 1979; Living Eyes, 1981; Stayin' Alive (Soundtrack), 1983; ESP, 1987; One, 1989; Tales from the Brothers Gibb, 1990; High Civilisation, 1991

Singles: New York Mining Disaster 1941, 1967 **(14)**; I Can't See Nobody, 1967 **(128)**; To Love Somebody, 1967 **(17)**; Holiday, 1968 **(16)**; Massachusetts, 1968 **(11)**;

The Bee Gees: *left to right,* **Maurice, Robin, Barry Gibb**

Words, 1968 **(15)**; The Singer Sang His Songs, 1968 **(116)**; Jumbo, 1968 **(57)**; I've Gotta Get a Message to You, 1968 **(8)**; I Started a Joke, 1968 **(6)**; First of May, 1969 **(37)**; Tomorrow Tomorrow, 1969 **(54)**; Don't Forget to Remember, 1969 **(73)**; If I Had My Mind on Something Else, 1970 **(91)**; I.U.I.U., 1970 **(94)**; Lonely Days, 1970 **(3)**; How Can You Mend a Broken Heart, 1971 **(1)**; Don't Wanna Live Inside Myself, 1971 **(53)**; My World, 1971 **(16)**; Run to Me, 1972 **(16)**; Alive, 1972 **(34)**; Saw a New Morning, 1973 **(94)**; Wouldn't I Be Someone, 1973 **(115)**; Mr. Natural, 1974 **(93)**; Charade, 1974 **(103)**; Jive Talkin', 1975 **(1)**; Nights on Broadway, 1975 **(7)**; Fanny (Be Tender with My Love), 1975 **(12)**; You Should Be Dancing, 1976 **(1)**; Love So Right, 1976 **(3)**; Boogie Child, 1976 **(12)**; Edge of the Universe, 1977 **(26)**; How Deep Is Your Love, 1977 **(1)**; Stayin' Alive, 1977 **(1)**; Night Fever, 1978 **(1)**; Too Much Heaven, 1978

(1); Tragedy, 1979 **(1)**; Love You Inside Out, 1979 **(1)**; He's a Liar, 1981 **(30)**; Living Eyes, 1981 **(45)**; The Woman in You, 1983 **(24)**; Someone Belongs to Someone, 1983 **(49)**; You Win Again, 1987 **(75)**; Ordinary Lives, 1989; One, 1989 **(7)**; Bodyguard, 1990; Secret Love, 1991

Soft Rock — British; Robin and Maurice are twins

Archie Bell & The Drells

Personnel: Archie Bell (vocals); Billy Butler (vocals) replaced (1975) by Lee Bell (vocals); Joe Cross (vocals) replaced (1976) by Willie Parnell (vocals); James Wise (vocals)

Albums: Tighten Up, 1968; There's Gonna Be a Showdown, 1969; Dance Your Troubles Away, 1976; Hard Not to Like It, 1977; I Never Had It So Good, 1981

Singles: Tighten Up, 1968 **(1)**; I

Can't Stop Dancing, 1968 **(9)**; Do
the Choo Choo, 1968 **(44)**; There's
Gonna be a Showdown, 1968 **(21)**; I
Love My Baby, 1969 **(94)**; Girl
You're Too Young, 1969 **(59)**; Just
a Little Closer, 1969 **(128)**; My Bal-
loon's Going Up, 1969 **(87)**; A
World Without Music, 1969 **(90)**;
Here I Go Again, 1970 **(112)**; Don't
Let the Music Slip Away, 1970
(100); Wrap It Up, 1970 **(93)**;
Dancing to Your Music, 1973 **(61)**
   R & B—Houston

Madeline Bell

Albums: Bell's a Poppin', 1967;
Doin' Things, 1969; Madeline Bell,
1971; Comin' Atcha, 1974; This Is
One Girl, 1976
Single: I'm Gonna Make You
Love Me, 1967 **(26)**
   Blues/Rock—British; Madeline
became lead vocalist for British
group Blue Mink

William Bell

Albums: Phases of Reality, 1967;
Bound to Happen, 1968; It's Time
You Took Another Listen, 1968;
Relating, 1969; Wow William Bell,
1970; Comin' Back for More, 1977;
Do Right Man, 1984
Singles: You Don't Miss Your
Water, 1962 **(95)**; Any Other Way,
1962 **(131)**; Everybody Loves a Win-
ner, 1967 **(95)**; Every Man Oughta
Have a Woman, 1968 **(115)**; A
Tribute to a King, 1968 **(86)**;
Private Number, 1968 **(75)** (with
Judy Clay); I Forgot to Be Your
Lover, 1969 **(45)**; Happy, 1969
(129); Lovin' on Borrowed Time,
1973 **(101)**; Tryin' to Love Two,
1977 **(10)**

R & B/Soul Vocal—Memphis;
real last name is Yarborough

The Bell Notes

Personnel: Ray Ceroni (guitars);
Lenny Giambalvo (bass); Peter
Kane (piano); Carl Bonura (saxo-
phones); John Casey (drums)
Singles: I've Had It, 1959 **(6)**; Old
Spanish Town, 1959 **(76)**; Shortnin'
Bread, 1960 **(96)**
   Pop—New York

The Belmonts

Personnel: Angelo D'Aleo (vocals); Fred Milano (vocals); Carlo
Mastrangelo (vocals) replaced (1962)
by Frank Lyndon (vocals)
Album: The Belmonts' Carnival of
Hits, 1962
Singles: We Belong Together, 1961
(108); Tell Me Why, 1961 **(18)**;
Don't Get Around Much Anymore,
1961 **(57)**; I Need Some One, 1961
(75); Come on Little Angel, 1962
(28); Diddle-Dee-Dum (What Happens When Your Love Has Gone),
1962 **(53)**; Ann-Marie, 1963 **(86)**;
Let's Put the Fun Back in Rock 'n'
Roll, 1981 **(81)** (with Freddy Cannon)
   Pop Vocal—New York; formerly
recorded with Dion

Jesse Belvin

Singles: Funny, 1958 **(81)**; Guess
Who, 1959 **(31)**
   R & B Vocal—Texas; killed with
his wife in an auto accident in 1960

Boyd Bennett & His Rockets

Singles: Seventeen, 1955 **(5)**; My
Boy—Flat Top, 1955 **(39)**; Blue

Suede Shoes, 1956 **(63)**; Boogie Bear, 1959 **(73)**
  Rockabilly — Alabama

Joe Bennett & The Sparkletones

Personnel: Joe Bennett (vocals, guitars); Howard Childress (guitars); Wayne Arthur (bass); Irving Denton (drums)
Singles: Black Slacks, 1957 **(17)**; Penny Loafers and Bobby Socks, 1957 **(42)**; Boys Do Cry, 1959 **(105)**
  Pop/Rock — South Carolina

George Benson

Albums: Benson & McDuff, 1964; It's Uptown, 1965; George Benson Cookbook, 1966; Giblet Gravy, 1967; George Benson Goodies, 1968; Shape of Things to Come, 1968; Tell It Like It Is, 1969; The Other Side of Abbey Road, 1969; Beyond the Blue Horizon, 1971; White Rabbit, 1972; Benson Burner, 1972; Willow Weep for Me, 1973; Body Talk, 1974; Bad Benson, 1975; Good King Bad, 1976; Benson & Farrell, 1976; Blue Benson, 1976; In Concert, 1976; Breezin', 1976; In Flight, 1977; Summertime, 1977; Weekend in L.A., 1978; Stormy Weather, 1978; Living Inside Your Love, 1979; Give Me the Night, 1980; The George Benson Collection, 1981; The Best of George Benson, 1982; In Your Eyes, 1983; 20/20, 1984; Silver Collection, 1985; Electrifying, 1985; While the City Sleeps, 1986; Collaboration, 1987 (with Earl Klugh); Twice the Love, 1988; Tenderly, 1989; Compact Jazz, 1990
Singles: My Woman's Good to Me, 1969 **(113)**; Supership, 1975 **(105)**; This Masquerade, 1976 **(10)**;

Breezin', 1976 **(63)**; Everything Must Change, 1977 **(106)**; Gonna Love You More, 1977 **(71)**; The Greatest Love of All, 1977 **(24)**; On Broadway, 1978 **(7)**; Unchained Melody, 1978; Love Ballad, 1979 **(18)**; Give Me the Night, 1980 **(4)**; Love × Love, 1980 **(61)**; Love All the Hurt Away, 1981 **(46)**; Turn Out the Lamplight, 1980 **(109)**; Turn Your Love Around, 1981 **(5)**; Never Give Up on a Good Thing, 1982 **(52)**; Inside Love (So Personal), 1983 **(43)**; Lady Love Me, 1983 **(30)**; Feel Like Making Love, 1983; In Your Eyes, 1983; 20/20, 1984 **(48)**; I Just Wanna Hang Around You, 1985 **(102)**; New Day, 1985
  Jazz/Pop — Pittsburgh

Brook Benton

Albums: The Two of Us, 1960 (with Dinah Washington); Brook Benton's Golden Hits, 1961; The Boll Weevil Song and 11 Other Great Hits, 1961; If You Believe, 1962; Singing the Blues — Lie to Me, 1962; Golden Hits, Volume 2, 1963; Laura (What's He Got That I Ain't Got), 1967; Do Your Own Thing, 1969; Brook Benton Today, 1970; Home Style, 1970; The Gospel Truth, 1971; Something for Everyone, 1973; Brook Benton Sings a Love Story, 1975; This Is Brook Benton, 1976; Making Love Is Good for You, 1977
Singles: A Million Miles from Nowhere, 1958 **(82)**; It's Just a Matter of Time, 1959 **(3)**; Hurtin' Inside, 1959 **(78)**; Endlessly, 1959 **(12)**; So Close, 1959 **(38)**; Thank You Pretty Baby, 1959 **(16)**; With All of My Heart, 1959 **(82)**; So Many Ways, 1959 **(6)**; This Time of the

Year, 1959 (**66**); The Ties That
Bind, 1960 (**37**); Hither and Thither
and Yon, 1960 (**58**); Kiddio, 1960
(**7**); The Same One, 1960 (**16**); Fools
Rush In, 1960 (**24**); Someday You'll
Want Me to Want You, 1960 (**93**);
Think Twice, 1961 (**11**); For My
Baby, 1961 (**28**); The Boll Weevil
Song, 1961 (**2**); Frankie and Johnny,
1961 (**20**); It's Just a House Without
You, 1961 (**45**); Revenge, 1961 (**15**);
Shadrack, 1962 (**19**); The Lost
Penny, 1962 (**77**); Walk on the Wild
Side, 1962 (**43**); Hit Record, 1962
(**45**); Thanks to the Fool, 1962
(**106**); With the Touch of Your
Hand, 1962 (**120**); Lie to Me, 1962
(**13**); Hotel Happiness, 1962 (**3**);
Still Waters Run Deep, 1962 (**89**); I
Got What I Wanted, 1963 (**28**);
Dearer Than Life, 1963 (**59**); My
True Confession, 1963 (**22**); Two
Tickets to Paradise, 1963 (**32**); Go-
ing Going Gone, 1964 (**35**); Too
Late to Turn Back Now, 1964 (**43**);
Another Cup of Coffee, 1964 (**47**);
A House Is Not a Home, 1964 (**75**);
Lumberjack, 1964 (**53**); Please,
Please Make It Easy, 1964 (**119**); Do
It Right, 1964 (**67**); The Special
Years, 1965 (**129**); Love Me Now,
1965 (**100**); Mother Nature, Father
Time, 1965 (**53**); Only a Girl Like
You, 1966 (**122**); Too Much Good
Lovin' (No Good for Me), 1966
(**126**); Laura (Tell Me What He's
Got That I Ain't Got), 1967 (**78**);
Do Your Own Thing, 1968 (**99**);
Nothing Can Take the Place of You,
1969 (**74**); Rainy Night in Georgia,
1970 (**4**); My Way, 1970 (**72**); Don't
It Make You Want to Go Home,
1970 (**45**); Shoes, 1970 (**67**); If
You've Got the Time, 1972 (**104**)

Soul/R & B — South Carolina;
Brook's real name was Benjamin
Franklin Peay; died in 1988

Chuck Berry

Albums: Rock Rock, 1957; Louis-
iana, 1957; After School Session,
1958; One Dozen Berry's, 1958;
Chuck Berry Is on Top, 1958;
Rockin' at the Hops, 1959; New
Juke Box Hits, 1959; Chuck Berry,
1960; More Chuck Berry, 1960;
Twist, 1960; Latest and Greatest,
1962; Chuck Berry on Stage, 1963;
You Never Can Tell, 1964; Chuck
Berry's Greatest Hits, 1964; St.
Louis to Liverpool, 1964; Chuck
Berry in London, 1965; Fresh Ber-
rys, 1965; Chuck Berry's Golden
Decade, 1967; At the Fillmore, 1967;
Medley, 1967; In Memphis, 1968;
Concerto in B Goode, 1969; Home
Again, 1971; The London Chuck
Berry Sessions, 1972; St. Louis to
Frisco to Memphis, 1972; San Fran-
cisco Dues, 1972; Chuck Berry's
Golden Decade, Vol. 2, 1973;
Chuck Berry/Bio, 1973; All Time
Greatest Rock 'n' Roll Party Hits,
1974; Golden Decade, Vol. 3, 1974;
I'm a Rocker, 1975; Chuck Berry
'75, 1975; Motorvatin', 1976; Rockit,
1979; Spotlight, 1980; Chess Mas-
ters, 1983

Singles: Maybelline, 1955 (**5**);
Roll Over Beethoven, 1956 (**29**);
School Day, 1957 (**3**); Oh Baby
Doll, 1957 (**57**); Rock & Roll Music,
1957 (**8**); Sweet Little Sixteen, 1958
(**2**); Johnny B. Goode, 1958 (**8**);
Beautiful Delilah, 1958 (**81**); Carol,
1958 (**18**); Sweet Little Rock and
Roll, 1958 (**47**); Joe Joe Gun, 1958
(**83**); Run Rudolph Run, 1958 (**69**);
Merry Christmas Baby, 1958 (**71**);
Anthony Boy, 1959 (**60**); Almost
Grown, 1959 (**32**); Little Queenie,
1959 (**80**); Back in the U.S.A., 1959
(**37**); Too Pooped to Pop ("Casey"),
1960 (**42**); Let It Rock, 1960 (**64**);

Nadine (Is It You?), 1964 **(23)**; No Particular Place to Go, 1964 **(10)**; You Never Can Tell, 1964 **(14)**; Little Marie, 1964 **(54)**; Promised Land, 1964 **(41)**; Dear Dad, 1965 **(95)**; My Ding-a-Ling, 1972 **(1)**; Reelin' & Rockin', 1972 **(27)**

Blues/Rock—St. Louis

The Big Bopper

Album: Chantilly Lace, 1958
Singles: Chantilly Lace, 1958 **(6)**; Big Bopper's Wedding, 1958 **(38)**; Little Red Riding Hood, 1958 **(72)**

Rockabilly—Texas; real name was J. P. Richardson; died in 1959 plane crash that also killed Buddy Holly and Richie Valens

Big Brother & The Holding Company

Personnel: Janis Joplin (vocals; deceased 1970) replaced (1969) by Nick Gravenites (vocals) and Kathy McDonald (vocals); Pete Albin (bass, guitars); James Gurley (guitars, bass) replaced (1984) by Michael Pendergrass (guitars); Sam Andrews (guitars, bass, vocals); David Getz (drums); added (1969) Mike Finnigan (keyboards); added (1969) David Shallock (guitars, vocals)
Albums: Big Brother & the Holding Company, 1967; Cheap Thrills, 1968; Be a Brother, 1971; How Hard It Is, 1971; Cheaper Thrills, 1984
Singles: Blindman, 1967 **(110)**; Bye Bye Baby, 1967 **(118)**; Piece of My Heart, 1968 **(12)**; Down on Me, 1968 **(43)**; Coo Coo, 1968 **(84)**

Blues/Rock—American; band hailed from California and Texas, launched Joplin's career

Big Three

Personnel: Brian Griffiths (guitars); John Gustafson (bass); John Hutchinson (drums) replaced by Nigel Olsson (drums)
Albums: Live at the Cavern, 1963; Resurrection, 1973; Cavern Stomp, 1982

Pop Rock—British

Billy & Lillie

Personnel: Billy Ford (vocals); Lillie Bryant (vocals)
Singles: La Dee Dah, 1958 **(9)**; Happiness, 1958 **(56)**; Lucky Ladybug, 1958 **(14)**; Bells, Bells, Bells (The Bell Song), 1959 **(88)** (with The Thunderbirds)

Pop Vocal—New Jersey

Cilla Black

Albums: Cilla, 1965; Cilla Sings for a Rainbow, 1966; Sher-oo!, 1968; Best of Cilla, 1968; Surround Yourself with Cilla, 1969; Sweet Inspiration, 1970; You're My World, 1970; Images, 1971; Day by Day, 1973; In My Life, 1974; Yesterday, 1975; It Makes Me Feel So Good, 1978; Modern Priscilla, 1978; Especially for You, 1980; Very Best of Cilla Black, 1983; Unlaced, 1984
Singles: You're My World, 1964 **(26)**; It's for You, 1964 **(79)**; Is It Love?, 1965 **(133)**; Alfie, 1966 **(95)**

Pop Vocal—British; Cilla hails from Liverpool; real name is Priscilla Maria Veronica White

Jeanne Black

Singles: He'll Have to Stay, 1960 **(4)**; Lisa, 1960 **(43)**; Oh, How I Miss You Tonight, 1960 **(63)**

Pop Vocal—California

Black Pearl

Personnel: Jeff Morris (guitars, vocals); Lefty Benson (guitars); Whitey White (guitars); Jerry Causi (bass); Bernie "B.B." Fieldings (vocals, keyboards); Victor Moulton (drums)

Albums: Black Pearl, 1969; Live, 1970

Psychedelic Rock — American

Blades of Grass

Single: Happy, 1967 **(87)**

Pop/Rock — New Jersey

Billy Bland

Singles: Let the Little Girl Dance, 1960 **(7)**; You Were Born to Be Loved, 1960 **(94)**; Pardon Me, 1960 **(102)**; Harmony, 1960 **(91)**; My Heart's on Fire, 1960 **(90)**

R & B Vocal — North Carolina

Marcie Blane

Singles: Bobby's Girl, 1962 **(3)**; What Does a Girl Do?, 1963 **(82)**

Pop Vocal — New York

The Blenders

Personnel: Hilliard "Johnny" Jones (vocals); Albert Hunter (vocals); Goldie Coates (vocals); Delores Johnson (vocals); Gail Mapp (vocals)

Single: Daughter, 1963 **(61)**

Soul/R & B Vocal — Chicago

Blind Faith

Personnel: Steve Winwood (keyboards, guitars, vocals); Eric Clapton (guitars, vocals); Ric Grech (bass); Peter "Ginger" Baker (drums)

Album: Blind Faith, 1969

Single: Can't Find My Way Home, 1969

Blues/Jazz Rock — British

Blodwyn Pig

Personnel: Mick Abrahams (guitars, vocals) replaced (1970) by Barry Reynolds (guitars, vocals); Jack Lancaster (saxophones); Andy Pyle (bass, vocals); Ron Berg (drums); added (1970) Graham Waller (keyboards); added (1970) Peter Banks (guitars)

Albums: Ahead Rings Out, 1969; Getting to This, 1970

Jazz/Blues Rock — British

Blood, Sweat & Tears

Personnel: Al Kooper (vocals, keyboards) replaced (1969) by David Clayton-Thomas (vocals) replaced (1972) by Jerry Fischer (vocals) replaced (1975) by David Clayton-Thomas (vocals); Steven Katz (guitars, vocals) replaced (1972) by George Wadenius (guitars) replaced (1976) by Mike Stern (guitars) replaced (1980) by Richard Martinez (guitars); Jim Fielder (bass) replaced (1974) by Ron McClure (bass) replaced (1976) by Danny Trifan (bass) replaced (1980) by Wayne Pedziwiatr (bass); Bobby Colomby (drums) replaced (1978) by Roy McCurdy (drums) replaced (1980) by Bobby Economou (drums); Jerry Weiss (trumpet) replaced (1969) by Lewis Soloff (trumpet) replaced (1974) by Tony Klatka (trumpet) replaced (1980) by Robert Piltch (trumpet); Alan Rubin (trumpet) replaced (1969) by Charles Winfield (trumpet) replaced (1973) by Tom Malone (trumpet) replaced (1974) by

Blood, Sweat & Tears: R. Piltch, Cassidy, D. Piltch, Economou, Martinez, Dorge, Seymour, Clayton-Thomas

Jerry LaCroix (saxophones, vocals) replaced (1976) by Joe Giorgianni (trumpet) replaced (1976) by Forrest Butchell (trumpet); Richard Halligan (trombone, keyboards, flute) replaced (1980) by Earl Seymour (trombone); Jerry Hyman (trombone, recorder) replaced (1971) by Dave Bargeron (trombone) replaced (1980) by Vernon Dorge (guitars); Fred Lipsius (piano, saxophones) replaced (1972) by Lou Marini (saxes) replaced (1974) by Bill Tillman (saxes) replaced (1980) by David Piltch (saxes); added (1972) Larry Willis (keyboards) replaced (1980) by Bruce Cassidy (keyboards); added (1976) Don Alias (percussion) left group (1979)

Albums: Child Is Father to the Man, 1968; Blood, Sweat & Tears, 1969; Three, 1970; Four, 1971; New Blood, 1972; Greatest Hits, 1972; No Sweat, 1973; Mirror Image, 1974; New City, 1975; More Than Ever, 1976; In Concert, 1977; Brand New Day, 1978; Classic Blood, Sweat & Tears, 1980; Nuclear Blues, 1980; The Challenge, 1984

Singles: You've Made Me So Very Happy, 1969 **(2)**; Spinning Wheel, 1969 **(2)**; And When I Die, 1969 **(2)**; Hi-De-Ho, 1970 **(14)**; Lucretia Mac Evil, 1970 **(29)**; Go Down Gamblin', 1971 **(32)**; Lisa Listen to Me, 1971 **(73)**; Sing a Song, 1972 **(112)**; So Long Dixie, 1972 **(44)**; I Can't Move No Mountains, 1972 **(103)**; Tell Me That I'm Wrong, 1974 **(83)**; Got to Get You Into My Life, 1975 **(62)**; Yesterday's Music, 1975; You're the One, 1976 **(106)**; Nuclear Blues, 1980

Blues/Jazz Rock — American; lead

singer Clayton-Thomas hails from
Canada

Michael Bloomfield

Albums: Super Session, 1968; It's
Not Killing Me, 1969; Live at Bill
Graham's Fillmore West, 1969; Live
Adventures, 1969; Try It Before
You Buy It, 1973; Triumvirate,
1973; Mill Valley Session, 1976; If
You Love These Blues, Play 'Em as
You Please, 1977; Analine, 1977;
Count Talent & the Originals, 1978;
Michael Bloomfield, 1978; Between
the Hard Place, 1978; Living in the
Fast Lane, 1980; Live in Italy, 1980,
Bloomfield & Harris, 1980; Cruisin'
for a Bruisin', 1981; Gospel Duets,
1981; Red Hot & Blues, 1981; A
Retrospective, 1984; Bloomfield,
1984

　　Blues/Rock—American; member
of Electric Flag and KGB; died of
an overdose in early 1981; "Super
Session" LP featured Al Kooper and
Stephen Stills

Blossom Toes

Personnel: Jim Cregan (guitars,
vocals); Brian Godding (guitars,
vocals, keyboards); Brian Belshaw
(bass, vocals); Kevin Westlake
(drums) replaced (1968) by Barry
Reeves (drums)
　　Albums: We Are Ever So Clean,
1967; If Only for a Moment, 1969
　　Hard/Blues Rock—British

Blue Cheer

Personnel: Leigh Stephens (guitars) replaced (1969) by Bruce
Stephens (vocals, guitars); Dick
Peterson (bass, vocals); Paul Whaley
(drums) replaced (1969) by Norman
Mayell (drums) replaced (1984) by
Paul Whaley (drums); added (1968)
Ralph Burns Kellogg (keyboards);
added (1969) Gene Estes (percussion); added (1969) Randy Holden
(guitars)
　　Albums: Vincebus Eruptum,
1968; Outside Inside, 1968; New Improved, 1969; Blue Cheer, 1969;
Original Human Beings, 1970; Best

Blue Cheer: L. Stephens, Peterson, Whaley

of Blue Cheer, 1982; Good Times Are So Hard to Find, 1988; Highlights and Lowlives, 1990
   Singles: Summertime Blues, 1968 **(14)**; Just a Little, 1968 **(92)**
   Acid Rock—San Francisco

Blues Image

Personnel: Mike Pinera (guitars, vocals) replaced (1970) by Kent Henry (guitars); Skip Konte (keyboards); Malcolm Jones (bass); Joe Lala (drums); Manuel Bertenatti (percussion); added (1970) Dennis Correll (vocals)
   Albums: Blues Image, 1969; Open, 1970; Red, White & Blues Image, 1970
   Singles: Ride Captain Ride, 1970 **(4)**; Gas Lamps and Clay, 1970 **(81)**
   Hard Rock—Florida

The Blue Jays

Personnel: Leon Peels (vocals)
Single: Lover's Island, 1961 **(31)**
R & B Vocal—Los Angeles

Blues Magoos

Personnel: Mike Esposito (guitars) replaced by John Liello (percussion); Ralph Scala (keyboards, vocals) replaced by Eric Kaz (keyboards, vocals); Emil "Peppy" Thielheim (guitars, vocals); Ron Gilbert (bass, vocals) replaced by Roger Eaton (bass) replaced by John Cooker LoPresti (bass); Geoff Daking (drums) replaced by Herb Lovell (drums) replaced by Jim Payne (drums); added (1969) Richie Dickon (percussion)
   Albums: Blues Magoos, 1966; Psychedelic Lollipop, 1966; Electric Comic Book, 1967; Basic Blues

Blues Magoos: Scala, Gilbert, Thielheim, Esposito, Daking

Magoos, 1968; Never Going Back to Georgia, 1969; Gulf Coast Bound, 1970
   Singles: (We Ain't Got) Nothin' Yet, 1966 **(5)**; Pipe Dream, 1967 **(60)**; There's a Chance We Can Make It, 1967 **(81)**; One by One, 1967 **(71)**
   Blues/Rock—New York; Peppy Thielheim changed his last name to Castro in the 1970s

The Blues Project

Personnel: Steve Katz (guitars) replaced (1968) by John Gregory (guitars) replaced (1972) by Bill Lussenden (guitars); Al Kooper (keyboards) replaced (1971) by David Cohen (guitars, keyboards); Danny Kalb (guitars); Andy Kulberg (bass) replaced (1971) by Don Kretmar (bass, saxophones); Roy Blumenfeld (drums); Tommy Flanders (vocals)

The Blues Project: Kalb, Katz, Blumenfeld, Kooper, Kulberg

left group (1966); rejoined (1972)

Albums: Live at the Cafe au Go Go, 1966; Projections, 1967; Live at the Town Hall, 1967; Planned Obsolescence, 1968; Best of the Blues Project, 1969; Lazarus, 1971; Blues Project, 1972; Reunion in Central Park, 1973

Single: No Time Like the Right Time, 1967 **(96)**

Blues/Rock—New York; the original group reformed for 1973 reunion album

The Bobbettes

Personnel: Emma Pought (vocals); Janice Pought (vocals); Laura Webb (vocals); Helen Gathers (vocals); Reather Dixon (vocals)

Singles: Mr. Lee, 1957 **(6)**; I Shot Mr. Lee, 1960 **(52)**; Have Mercy Baby, 1960 **(66)**; Dance with Me Georgie, 1960 **(95)**; Mr. Johnny Q,
1961 **(120)**; I Don't Like It Like That, 1961 **(72)**

Pop Vocal—New York

Bob B. Soxx & The Blue Jeans

Personnel: Bobby Sheen (vocals); Darlene Love (vocals) replaced (1964) by Carolyn Willis (vocals); Fanita James (vocals) replaced (1964) by Gloria Jones (vocals)

Album: Zip-a-Dee-Doo-Dah, 1963

Singles: Zip-a-Dee-Doo-Dah, 1962 **(8)**; Why Do Lovers Break Each Other's Heart?, 1963 **(38)**; Not Too Young to Get Married, 1963 **(63)**

Pop/Soul Vocal—Philadelphia

Bodast

Personnel: Steve Howe (guitars); Clive Skinner (guitars, vocals); Clive Muldoon (guitars, vocals); Dave Curtis (bass, vocals); Bobby Clarke (drums)

Album: The Bodast Tapes, 1981

Progressive Rock—British; this was Steve Howe's band pre–Yes in the mid–1960s

Graham Bond

Albums: The Sound of '65, 1965; There's a Bond Between Us, 1966; Mighty Graham Bond, 1968; Love Is the Law, 1968; Solid Bond, 1970; Holy Magick, 1971; We Put Our Magick on You, 1971; Bond in America, 1971; This Is Graham Bond, 1972; Two Heads Are Better Than One, 1972; Beginning of Jazz Rock, 1977

Jazz/Rock—British; Graham died May 8, 1974

Gary U. S. Bonds

Albums: Dance 'Til Quarter to Three, 1961; Twist the Calypso, 1962; Greatest Hits, 1963; Dedication, 1981; On the Line, 1982; Standing in the Line of Fire, 1984; Best of Gary U.S. Bonds, 1990

Singles: New Orleans, 1960 **(6)**; Not Me, 1961 **(116)**; Quarter to Three, 1961 **(1)**; School Is Out, 1961 **(5)**; School Is In, 1961 **(28)**; Dear Lady Twist, 1962 **(9)**; Twist, Twist Senora, 1962 **(9)**; Seven Day Weekend, 1962 **(27)**; Copy Cat, 1962 **(92)**; I Dig This Station, 1962 **(101)**; Take Me Back to New Orleans, 1966 **(121)**; This Little Girl, 1981 **(12)**; Jole Blon, 1981 **(65)**; Your Love, 1981; Out of Work, 1982 **(21)**; Turn the Music Down, 1982; Standing in the Line of Fire, 1984

R & B/Rock — Florida; real name is Gary Anderson

Bonzo Dog Band

Personnel: Roger Ruskin Spear (kazoo, Jew's harp) replaced (1972) by Bubs White (guitars); Rodney Desborough Slater (saxophones) replaced (1972) by Dick Parry (flutes); Vivian Stanshall (vocals, trumpet, ukelele); Neil Innes (vocals, keyboards); Vernon Dudley Bohay-Nowell (guitars) replaced (1972) by Andy Roberts (fiddle, guitars, mandolin); Martin "Sam Spoons" Stafford (percussion) left group (1972); Larry "Legs" Smith (drums) replaced 1972) by Hughie Flint (drums); added (1968) Dennis Cowan (bass); added (1972) Dave Richards (bass)

Albums: Gorilla, 1967; The Doughnut in Granny's Greenhouse, 1968; Tadpoles, 1969; Keynsham, 1969; Let's Make Up and Be Friendly, 1972

Single: I'm the Urban Spaceman, 1968

Comedy/Rock — British; Neil Innes joined Monty Python's Eric Idle to form the satirical Rutles

Booker T. & The MGs

Personnel: Booker T. Jones (organ); Steve Cropper (guitars); Lewis Steinberg (bass) replaced (1964) by Donald "Duck" Dunn (bass); Al Jackson (drums; deceased 1975) replaced (1975) by Willie Hall (drums)

Albums: Green Onions, 1962; And Now, Booker T. and the MGs, 1966; Hip Hug-Her, 1967; Back to Back, 1967; Doin' Our Thing, 1968; Soul Limbo, 1968; Best of Booker T. and the MGs, 1968; Uptight, 1969; The Booker T. Set, 1969; McLemore Street, 1970; Booker T. & the MGs Greatest Hits, 1970; Melting Pot, 1971; Star Collection, 1973; Memphis Sound, 1975; Union Extended, 1976; Time Is Tight, 1976; Universal Language, 1977; Try and Love Again, 1978

Singles: Green Onions, 1962 **(3)**; Jellybread, 1962 **(82)**; Chinese Checkers, 1963 **(78)**; Tic-Tac-Toe, 1964 **(109)**; Mo-Onions, 1964 **(97)**; Soul Dressing, 1964 **(95)**; Boot-Leg, 1965 **(58)**; My Sweet Potato, 1966 **(85)**; Hip Hug-Her, 1967 **(37)**; Groovin', 1967 **(21)**; Slim Jenkin's Place, 1967 **(70)**; Soul Limbo, 1968 **(17)**; Hang 'Em High, 1968 **(9)**; Time Is Tight, 1969 **(6)**; Mrs. Robinson, 1969 **(37)**; Slum Baby, 1969 **(88)**; Something, 1970 **(76)**; Melting Pot, 1971 **(45)**

R & B/Soul; Jones was married to Rita Coolidge's sister Priscilla

Pat Boone

Albums: Howdy!, 1956; A Closer Walk with Thee, 1957; Pat, 1957; Four by Pat (EP), 1957; Pat Boone, 1957; Pat's Greatest Hits, 1957; April Love, 1957; Hymns We Love, 1957; Star Dust, 1958; Yes Indeed!, 1958; Tenderly, 1959; Moonglow, 1960; Moody River, 1961; White Christmas, 1962; Pat Boone's Golden Hits, 1962

Singles: Two Hearts, 1955 **(16)**; Ain't That a Shame, 1955 **(1)**; At My Front Door (Crazy Little Mama), 1955 **(7)**; No Other Arms (No Arms Can Ever Hold You), 1955 **(26)**; Gee Whittakers!, 1955 **(19)**; I'll Be Home, 1956 **(4)**; Tutti' Fruitti, 1956 **(12)**; Long Tall Sally, 1956 **(8)**; Just As Long As I'm with You, 1956 **(76)**; I Almost Lost My Mind, 1956 **(1)**; I'm in Love with You, 1956 **(57)**; Friendly Persuasion (Thee I Love), 1956 **(5)**; Chains of Love, 1956 **(10)**; Don't Forbid Me, 1956 **(1)**; Anastasia, 1956 **(37)**; Why Baby Why, 1957 **(5)**; I'm Waiting for You, 1957 **(27)**; Love Letters in the Sand, 1957 **(1)**; Bernardine, 1957 **(14)**; Remember You're Mine, 1957 **(6)**; There's a Gold Mine in the Sky, 1957 **(14)**; April Love, 1957 **(1)**; When the Swallows Come Back to Capistrano, 1957 **(80)**; A Wonderful Time Up There, 1958 **(4)**; It's Too Soon to Know, 1958 **(4)**; Sugar Moon, 1958 **(5)**; Cherie, I Love You, 1958 **(63)**; If Dreams Came True, 1958 **(7)**; That's How Much I Love You, 1958 **(39)**; For My Good Fortune, 1958 **(23)**; Gee, But It's Lonely, 1958 **(21)**; I'll Remember Tonight, 1958 **(34)**; With the Wind and the Rain in Your Hair, 1959 **(21)**; Good Rockin' Tonight, 1959 **(49)**; For a Penny, 1959 **(23)**; The Wang Dang Taffy-Apple Tango, 1959 **(62)**; Twixt Twelve and Twenty, 1959 **(17)**; Fools Hall of Fame, 1959 **(29)**; Beyond the Sunset, 1959 **(71)**; Welcome New Lovers, 1960 **(18)**; Words, 1960 **(94)**; Walking the Floor Over You, 1960 **(44)**; Spring Rain, 1960 **(50)**; Delia Gone, 1960 **(66)**; Candy Sweet, 1960 **(72)**; Dear John, 1960 **(44)**; Alabam, 1960 **(47)**; The Exodus Song (This Land Is Mine), 1961 **(64)**; Moody River, 1961 **(1)**; Big Cold Wind, 1961 **(19)**; (If I'm Dreaming) Just Let Me Dream, 1961 **(114)**; Johnny Will, 1961 **(35)**; I'll See You in My Dreams, 1962 **(32)**; Pictures in the Fire, 1962 **(77)**; Willing and Eager, 1962 **(113)**; Quando, Quando, Quando (Tell Me When), 1962 **(95)**; Speedy Gonzales, 1962 **(6)**; Ten Lonely Guys, 1962 **(45)**; Meditation (Meditacao), 1963 **(91)**; Days of Wine and Roses, 1963 **(117)**; Rosemarie, 1964 **(129)**; Beach Girl, 1964 **(72)**; Five Miles from Home (Soon I'll See Mary), 1966 **(127)**; Wish You Were Here Buddy, 1966 **(49)**; July You're a Woman, 1969 **(100)**

Pop Vocal—Tennessee; real first name is Charles

David Bowie

Personnel: David Bowie (vocals, guitars, saxophones); Mick Ronson (guitars) replaced (1975) by Carlos Alomar (guitars); Tony Visconti (bass) replaced (1971) by Trevor Bolder (bass) replaced (1976) by George Murray (bass) replaced (1980) by Chuck Hammer (bass, guitars); Mick Woodmansey (drums) replaced (1973) by Aynsley Dunbar (drums) replaced (1974) by Tony Newman (drums) replaced (1975) by Dennis Davies (drums); added (1974) Earl Slick (guitars, vocals) replaced (1977) by Ricky Gardiner (guitars) replaced (1978) by Adrian Belew (guitars) replaced (1988) by Peter Frampton (guitars); added (1973) Mike Garson (keyboards) replaced (1978) by Roger Powell (keyboards)

Albums: David Bowie, 1967; The World of David Bowie, 1967; Man of Words, 1969; The Man Who Sold the World, 1970; Hunky Dory, 1971; The Rise and Fall of Ziggy Stardust and the Spiders from Mars, 1972; Aladdin Sane, 1973; Pin Ups, 1973; Images '66 '67, 1973; Diamond Dogs, 1974; Live, 1974; Young Americans, 1975; Station to Station, 1976; ChangesOneBowie, 1976; Low, 1977; Heroes, 1977; Peter & the Wolf, 1978; Stage, 1978; Lodger, 1979; Scary Monsters, 1980; ChangesTwoBowie, 1981; Christiane F (Soundtrack), 1982; Cat People (Soundtrack), 1982; Baal, 1982; Let's Dance, 1983; Golden Years, 1983; Ziggy Stardust the Motion Picture, 1983; Fame & Fashion, 1984; Tonight, 1984; Never Let Me Down, 1985; Sound and Vision, 1989; ChangesBowie, 1990

Singles: Space Oddity, 1969 **(124)**; Changes, 1972 **(66)**; Starman, 1972 **(65)**; Jean Genie, 1973 **(71)**; Space Oddity, 1973 **(15)**; Rebel Rebel, 1974 **(64)**; Changes, 1974 **(41)**; Let's Spend the Night Together, 1973 **(109)**; Diamond Dogs, 1974; Young Americans, 1975 **(28)**; Fame, 1975 **(1)**; Golden Years, 1976 **(10)**; TVC15, 1976 **(64)**; John I'm Only Dancing, 1976; Sound and Vision, 1977 **(69)**; Be My Wife, 1977; Boys Keep Swinging, 1977; Heroes, 1977; Beauty & the Beast, 1978; DJ, 1979 **(106)**; Ashes to Ashes, 1980 **(101)**; Fashion, 1980 **(70)**; Scary Monsters, 1980; Up the Hill Backwards, 1982; Wild as the Wind, 1982; Under Pressure, 1981 **(29)** (with Queen); Cat People (Putting Out Fire), 1982 **(67)**; Baal's Hymn, 1982; Let's Dance, 1983 **(1)**; China Girl, 1983 **(10)**; Modern Love, 1983 **(14)**; White Light/White Heat, 1983; Without You, 1984 **(73)**; 1984, 1984; Blue Jean, 1984 **(8)**; Tonight, 1984 **(53)**; This Is Not America, 1985 **(32)** (with Pat Metheney Group); Lovin' the Alien, 1985; Dancing in the Streets, 1985 **(7)** (with Mick Jagger); Absolute Beginners, 1986 **(53)**; Underground, 1986; Day In, Day Out, 1987 **(21)**; Never Let Me Down, 1987 **(27)**; Fame '90, 1990

Glam Rock/Pop—British; real name is David Robert Jones

Alan Bown Set

Personnel: Alan Bown (trumpet); Jeff Bannister (keyboards, vocals); Stan Haldane (bass, vocals) replaced (1971) by Andy Bown (bass, vocals); John A. Helliwell (saxophones); Jess Roden (vocals) replaced (1970) by Gordon Neville (vocals); Tony Catchpole (guitars); Vic Sweeney (drums)

Albums: London Swings, 1966; Outward Bown, 1967; The Alan Bown Set, 1968; Second Album?, 1968; Listen, 1970; Stretchin' Out, 1971

Jazz/Rock—British

The Box Tops

Talley, Chilton, Allen, Cunningham, Boggs

Personnel: Alex Chilton (vocals); Gary Talley (guitars, bass); Bill Cunningham (keyboards, bass); Rick Allen (organ, bass); Tom Boggs (drums)

Albums: The Letter/Neon Rainbow, 1967; Cry Like a Baby, 1968; The Box Tops Super Hits, 1968; Dimensions, 1969; Greatest Hits, 1982

Singles: The Letter, 1967 **(1)**; Neon Rainbow, 1967 **(24)**; Cry Like a Baby, 1968 **(2)**; Choo Choo Train, 1968 **(26)**; I Met Her in Church, 1968 **(37)**; Sweet Cream Ladies, Forward March, 1968 **(28)**; I Shall Be Released, 1969 **(67)**; Soul Deep, 1969 **(18)**; Turn on a Dream, 1969 **(58)**; You Keep Tightening Up on Me, 1970 **(92)**

Blue-Eyed Soul—Memphis

Tommy Boyce & Bobby Hart

Tommy Boyce, Bobby Hart

Albums: Test Patterns, 1967; I Wonder What She's Doing Tonite, 1968; Which One's Boyce and Which One's Hart, 1968; It's All Happening on the Inside, 1969

Singles: Along Came Linda, 1962 **(118)** (Boyce); I'll Remember Carol, 1962 **(80)** (Boyce); Sunday, the Day Before Monday, 1966 **(132)** (Boyce); Out & About, 1967 **(39)**; Sometimes She's a Little Girl, 1967 **(110)**; I Wonder What She's Doing Tonite,

1967 **(8)**; Goodbye Baby (I Don't Want to See You Cry), 1968 **(53)**; Alice Long (You're Still My Favorite Girlfriend), 1968 **(27)**; We're All Going to the Same Place, 1968 **(123)**; L.U.V. (Let Us Vote), 1969 **(111)**

Bubblegum Pop—American; hit songwriting team for the Monkees; toured with Davy Jones and Mickey Dolenz in the 70s

Jan Bradley

Singles: Mama Didn't Lie, 1963 **(14)**; I'm Over You, 1965 **(93)**

Soul Vocal—Mississippi; real first name is Addie

Brenda & The Tabulations

Personnel: Brenda Payton (vocals); Jerry Jones (vocals) replaced (1970) by Pat Mercer (vocals); Eddie Jackson (vocals) replaced (1970) by Deborah Martin (vocals); Maurice Coates (vocals) left group (1970); added (1969) Bernard Murphy (vocals) left group (1970)

Albums: Dry Your Eyes, 1967; Brenda & The Tabulations, 1970

Singles: Dry Your Eyes, 1967 **(20)**; Stay Together Young Lovers, 1967 **(66)**; Who's Lovin' You, 1967 **(66)**; Just Once in a Lifetime, 1967 **(97)**; When You're Gone, 1967 **(58)**; Baby You're So Right for Me, 1968 **(86)**; The Touch of You, 1970 **(50)**; And My Heart Sang (Tra La La), 1970 **(64)**; Don't Make Me Over, 1970 **(77)**; A Child No One Wanted, 1971 **(120)**; Right on the Tip of My Tongue, 1971 **(23)**; A

Part of You, 1971 **(94)**; Why Didn't I Think of That, 1972 **(107)**

Soul Vocal—Philadelphia

Teresa Brewer

Singles: Let Me Go, Lover!, 1954 **(6)** (with The Lancers); I Gotta Go Get My Baby, 1955 **(59)**; Pledging My Love/How Important Can It Be?, 1955 **(17)**; Silver Dollar, 1955 **(20)**; The Banjo's Back in Town, 1955 **(15)**; Shoot It Again, 1955 **(66)**; A Tear Fell, 1956 **(5)**; Bo Weevil, 1956 **(17)**; A Sweet Old Fashioned Girl, 1956 **(7)**; I Love Mickey, 1956 **(87)** (with Mickey Mantle); Mutual Admiration Society, 1956 **(21)**; Crazy with Love, 1956 **(73)**; Empty Arms, 1957 **(13)**; Teardrops in My Heart, 1957 **(64)**; You Send Me, 1957 **(8)**; Pickle Up a Doodle, 1958 **(99)**; The Hula Hoop Song, 1958 **(38)**; The One Rose (That's Left in My Heart), 1959 **(75)**; Heavenly Lover, 1959 **(40)**; Bye Bye Baby Goodbye, 1959 **(115)**; Peace of Mind, 1960 **(66)**; Anymore, 1960 **(31)**; Have You Ever Been Lonely (Have You Ever Been Blue), 1960 **(84)**; Milord, 1961 **(74)**; She'll Never Love You (Like I Do), 1963 **(122)**; He Understands Me, 1963 **(130)**; Music, Music, Music, 1973 **(109)**

Pop Vocal—Ohio; real name is Theresa Breuer

Brewer & Shipley

Personnel: Mike Brewer (guitars, vocals); Tom Shipley (guitars, vocals)

Albums: Brewer and Shipley Down in L.A., 1968; Weeds, 1969; Tarkio, 1970; Shake Off the Demon, 1971; Rural Space, 1972; Brewer and Shipley, 1974; Welcome to Riddle

Bridge, 1975; Best of Brewer and Shipley, 1976; Not Far from Free, 1978

Singles: One Toke Over the Line, 1971 **(10)**; Tarkio Road, 1971 **(55)**; Shake Off the Demon, 1972 **(98)**

Folk/Rock—Los Angeles

British Road Runners

Album: British Road Runners, 1968

Single: Do Something to Me, 1968

Bubblegum Pop—British; Kasenetz-Katz (Ohio Express) produced British studio group

The Brogues

Personnel: Gary Duncan (guitars, vocals, bass); Greg Elmore (drums)

Album: The Brogues, 1966

Single: I Ain't No Miracle Worker, 1966

Psychedelic Pop—California

The Brooklyn Bridge

Personnel: Johnny "Maestro" Mastrangelo (vocals); Fred Ferrara (vocals); Mike Gregorio (vocals); Les Cauchi (vocals); Tom Sullivan (musical director); Carolyn Woods (organ); Jim Macioce (guitars); Jim Rosica (bass); Shelly Davis (trumpet, keyboards); Joe Ruvio (saxophones); Artie Cantanzarita (drums)

Albums: Brooklyn Bridge, 1969; The Second Brooklyn Bridge, 1969; Bridge in Blue, 1970

Singles: Worse That Could Happen, 1968 **(3)**; Blessed Is the Rain, 1969 **(45)**; Welcome Me Love, 1969 **(48)**; Your Husband—My Wife, 1969 **(46)**; You'll Never Walk Alone, 1969 **(51)**; Free as the Wind, 1970 **(109)**; Down by the River, 1970

(91); Day Is Gone, 1970 **(98)**

Pop/Soft Rock—New York; the four vocalists known as the Del-Satins joined with The Rhythm Method to form Brooklyn Bridge

Donnie Brooks

Singles: Mission Bell, 1960 **(7)**; Doll House, 1960 **(31)**; Memphis, 1961 **(90)**; Round Robin, 1960 **(115)**

Pop Vocal—Dallas; real name is John Faircloth

The Brothers Four

Personnel: Dick Foley (vocals); Bob Flick (vocals); John Paine (vocals); Mike Kirkland (vocals)

Albums: The Brothers Four, 1960; B.M.O.C. (Best Music On/Off Campus), 1961; The Brothers Four Songbook, 1961; The Brothers Four: In Person, 1962; Cross-Country Concert, 1963; The Big Folk Hits, 1963; More Big Folk Hits, 1964; The Honey Wind Blows, 1965; Try to Remember, 1965; A Beatles' Songbook, 1966

Singles: Greenfields, 1960 **(2)**; My Tani, 1960 **(50)**; The Green Leaves of Summer, 1960 **(65)**; Frogg, 1961 **(32)**; Blue Water Line, 1962 **(68)**; Hootenanny Saturday Night, 1963 **(89)**; Four Strong Winds, 1963 **(114)**; Somewhere, 1965 **(131)**; Try to Remember, 1965 **(91)**

Folk/Pop—Washington; quartet formed at the University of Washington

Crazy World of Arthur Brown

Personnel: Arthur Brown (vocals); Vincent Crane (keyboards) replaced

(1972) by Michael Harris (keyboards) replaced (1973) by Victor Peraino (keyboards) replaced (1974) by Errol Nelson (keyboards); Andy Dalby (guitars); Sean Nicholas (bass) replaced (1972) by Phil Curtis (bass) replaced (1974) by Lee Robinson (bass); Carl Palmer (drums) replaced (1968) by Drachen Theaker (drums) replaced (1972) by Martin Steer (drums) replaced (1974) by Drachen Theaker (drums)

Albums: The Crazy World of Arthur Brown, 1968; Galactic Zoo Dossier, 1972; Kingdom Come, 1973; The Journey, 1973; Dance, 1974; Lost Ears, 1976; Chisolm in My Bosom, 1978; Faster Than the Speed of Sound, 1980; Requiem, 1982; Speaknotech, 1983

Singles: Fire, 1968 **(2)**; Nightmare, 1968 **(107)**; I Put a Spell on You, 1968

Psychedelic Rock — British

James Brown

Albums: Live at the Apollo, 1963; Prisoner of Love, 1963; Amazing James Brown, 1963; Pure Dynamite! Live at the Royal, 1964; Showtime, 1964; Grits & Soul, 1965; Please Please, 1965; Unbeatable Hits, 1965; Papa's Got a Brand New Bag, 1965; James Brown Plays James Brown — Today & Yesterday, 1965; I Got You (I Feel Good), 1966; James Brown Plays New Breed, 1966; It's a Man's Man's Man's World, 1966; Handful of Soul, 1966; Raw Soul, 1967; Live at the Garden, 1967; James Brown Plays the Real Thing, 1967; Cold Sweat, 1967; I Can't Stand Myself (When You Touch Me), 1968; I Got the Feelin', 1968; James Brown Plays Nothing but Soul, 1968; Thinking About Little Willie, 1968; Live at the Apollo, Volume II, 1969; Say It Loud — I'm Black and Proud, 1969; Gettin' Down to It, 1969; James Brown Plays & Directs the Popcorn, 1969; It's a Mother, 1969; Ain't It Funky, 1970; Soul on Top, 1970; It's a New Day So Let a Man Come In, 1970; Sex Machine, 1970; Super Bad, 1971; Sho Is Funky Down Here, 1971; Hot Pants, 1971; Revolution of the Mind — Live at the Apollo Volume III, 1971; James Brown Soul Classics, 1972; There It Is, 1972; Get on the Good Foot, 1972; Black Caesar, 1973; Slaughter's Big Rip-Off, 1973; The Payback, 1974; Hell, 1974; Reality, 1975; Sex Machine Today, 1975; Everybody's Doin' the Hustle & Dead on the Double Bump, 1975; Soul Classics Volume 2, 1975; Soul Classics Volume 3, 1975; Get Up Offa That Thing, 1976; Bodyheat, 1977; Mutha's Nature, 1977; Jam/1980's, 1978; Take a Look at Those Cakes, 1979; The Original Disco Man, 1979; Soul Syndrome, 1980; People, 1980; James Brown ... Live/Hot on the One, 1980; CD of JB — Sex Machine

& Other Soul Classics, 1985; CD of JB II—Cold Sweat & Other Soul Classics, 1987; In the Jungle Groove, 1987; Gravity, 1988; I'm Real, 1988; Motherlode, 1988; Roots of the Revolution, 1989; Soul Session, 1989; Star Time, 1991; Love Over-Due, 1991

Singles: Try Me, 1958 **(48)**; Think, 1960 **(33)**; You've Got the Power, 1960 **(86)**; This Old Heart, 1960 **(79)**; Please, Please, Please, 1960 **(105)**; The Bells, 1960 **(68)**; Hold It, 1961 **(109)**; Bewildered, 1961 **(40)**; I Don't Mind, 1961 **(47)**; Baby, You're Right, 1961 **(49)**; Lost Someone, 1961 **(48)**; Night Train, 1962 **(35)**; Shout and Shimmy, 1962 **(61)**; Mashed Potatoes U.S.A., 1962 **(82)**; Three Hearts in a Tangle, 1962 **(93)**; Every Beat of My Heart, 1963 **(99)**; Prisoner of Love, 1963 **(18)**; These Foolish Things, 1963 **(55)**; Signed, Sealed, Delivered, 1963 **(77)**; Oh Baby Don't You Weep (Part 1), 1964 **(23)**; Please, Please, Please, 1964 **(95)**; In the Wee Hours (of the Nite), 1964 **(125)**; Again, 1964 **(107)**; Caledonia, 1964 **(95)**; How Long Darling, 1964 **(134)**; So Long, 1964 **(132)**; The Things That I Used to Do, 1964 **(99)**; Out of Sight, 1964 **(24)**; Maybe the Last Time, 1964 **(107)**; Have Mercy Baby, 1964 **(92)**; Devil's Hideaway, 1965 **(114)**; Papa's Got a Brand New Bag, 1965 **(8)**; I Got You (I Feel Good), 1965 **(3)**; Try Me, 1965 **(63)**; I'll Go Crazy, 1966 **(73)**; Lost Someone, 1966 **(94)**; Ain't That a Groove (Part 1), 1966 **(42)**; It's a Man's Man's Man's World, 1966 **(8)**; New Breed (The Boo-Ga-Loo), 1966 **(102)**; Money Won't Change You (Part 1), 1966 **(53)**; Don't Be a Drop-Out, 1966 **(50)**; Bring It Up, 1967 **(29)**; Kansas City, 1967 **(55)**; Think, 1976 **(100)** (with Vicki Anderson); Let Yourself Go, 1967 **(46)**; Cold Sweat (Part 1), 1967 **(7)**; Get It Together, 1967 **(40)**; I Can't Stand Myself (When You Touch Me), 1967 **(28)**; There Was a Time, 1968 **(36)**; I Got the Feelin', 1968 **(6)**; Licking Stick— Licking Stick, 1968 **(14)**; America Is My Home (Part 1), 1968 **(52)**; Shhhhhhhh (for a Little While), 1968 **(104)**; I Guess I'll Have to Cry, Cry, Cry, 1968 **(55)**; Say It Loud— I'm Black and I'm Proud, 1968 **(10)**; Goodbye My Love, 1968 **(31)**; Tit for Tat (Ain't No Taking Back), 1968 **(86)**; Give It Up or Turnit a Loose, 1969 **(15)**; Soul Pride (Part 1), 1969 **(117)**; I Don't Want Nobody to Give Me Nothing (Open Up the Door, I'll Get It Myself), 1969 **(20)**; The Popcorn, 1969 **(30)**; Mother Popcorn (You Got to Have a Mother for Me) (Part 1), 1969 **(11)**; Lowdown Popcorn, 1969 **(41)**; World (Part 1), 1969 **(37)**; Let a Man Come In and Do the Popcorn (Part One), 1969 **(21)**; Ain't It Funky Now (Part 1), 1969 **(24)**; Let a Man Come In and Do the Popcorn (Part Two), 1969 **(40)**; It's a New Day (Part 1 & 2), 1970 **(32)**; Funky Drummer (Part 1), 1970 **(51)**; Brother Rapp (Part 1 & Part 2), 1970 **(32)**; Get Up I Feel Like Being a Sex Machine (Part 1), 1970 **(15)**; Super Bad (Part 1 & 2), 1970 **(13)**; Hey America, 1970 **(105)**; Get Up, Get Into It, Get Involved, 1971 **(34)**; Soul Power (Part 1), 1971 **(29)**; Spinning Wheel (Part 1), 1971 **(90)**; I Cried, 1971 **(50)**; Escape-ism (Part 1), 1971 **(35)**; Hot Pants (She Got to Use What She Got, to Get What She Wants) (Part 1), 1971 **(15)**; Make It Funky (Part 1), 1971 **(22)**; My Part/Make It Funky (Part 3), 1971

(68); I'm a Greedy Man, 1971 (35); Talking Loud and Saying Nothing, 1972 (27); King Heroin, 1972 (40); There It Is (Part 1), 1972 (43); Honky Tonk (Part 1), 1972 (44); Get on the Good Foot (Part 1), 1972 (18); I Got a Bag of My Own, 1972 (44); What My Baby Needs Now Is a Little More Lovin', 1972 (56) (with Lyn Collins); I Got Ants in My Pants (and I Want to Dance) (Part 1), 1973 (27); Down and Out in New York City, 1973 (50); Think, 1973 (77) (version 1); Think, 1973 (80) (version 2); Sexy, Sexy, Sexy, 1973 (50); Stoned to the Bone (Part 1), 1973 (58); The Payback (Part 1), 1974 (26); My Thang, 1974 (29); Papa Don't Take No Mess (Part 1), 1974 (31); Funky President (People It's Bad)/Coldblooded, 1974 (44); Reality, 1975 (80); Sex Machine (Part 1), 1975 (61) (version 2); Get Up Offa That Thing, 1976 (45); Bodyheat (Part 1), 1977 (88); Living in America, 1986 (4); Gravity, 1986 (93)

Soul—Georgia; James, the "Godfather" of soul, is the "hardest working man in show business today"

Maxine Brown

Album: We'll Cry Together, 1969
Singles: All in My Mind, 1960 (19); Funny, 1961 (25); After All We've Been Through, 1961 (102); I Got a Funny Kind of Feeling, 1962 (104); My Time for Cryin', 1962 (98); Ask Me, 1963 (75); Coming Back to You, 1964 (99); Oh No Not My Baby, 1964 (24); It's Gonna Be Alright, 1965 (56); Something You Got, 1965 (55) (with Chuck Jackson); One Step at a Time, 1965 (55); Can't Let You Out of My Sight, 1965 (91) (with Chuck Jackson); I Need You So, 1965 (98) (with Chuck Jackson); It You Gotta Make a Fool of Somebody, 1965 (63); I'm Satisfied, 1966 (112) (with Chuck Jackson); I Don't Need Anything, 1966 (129); Hold On I'm Coming, 1967 (91) (with Chuck Jackson); Daddy's Home, 1967 (91) (with Chuck Jackson); We'll Cry Together, 1969 (73)

Soul Vocal—South Carolina

Ruth Brown

Singles: Lucky Lips, 1957 (25); This Little Girl's Gone Rockin', 1958 (24); Jack O'Diamonds, 1959 (96); I Don't Know, 1959 (64); Don't Deceive Me, 1960 (62); Shake a Hand, 1962 (97); Mama (He Treats Your Daughter Mean), 1962 (99)

Pop Vocal—Virginia

The Browns

Personnel: Jim Ed Brown (vocals); Maxine Brown (vocals); Bonnie Brown (vocals)
Singles: The Three Bells, 1959 (1); Scarlet Ribbons (for Her Hair), 1959 (13); The Old Lamplighter, 1960 (5); Teen-Ex, 1960 (47); Lonely Little Robin, 1960 (105); Whiffenpoof Song, 1960 (112); Send Me the Pillow You Dream On, 1960 (56); Blue Christmas, 1960 (97); Ground Hog, 1961 (97); Buttons and Bows, 1962 (104); The Old Master Painter, 1962 (118); Everybody's Darlin, Plus Mine, 1964 (135); You Can't Grow Peaches on a Cherry Tree, 1965 (120); Morning, 1970 (47) (Jim Ed solo)

Country Vocal—Arkansas

Bruce & Terry

Personnel: Bruce Johnston (guitars, vocals); Terry Melcher (guitars, vocals)

Singles: Custom Machine, 1964
(85); Summer Means Fun, 1964
(72); Carmen, 1965 **(107)**
Surf Rock—California

Anita Bryant

Albums: In a Velvet Mood, 1962;
Mine Eyes Have Seen the Glory,
1967

Singles: Till There Was You, 1959
(30); Six Boys and Seven Girls,
1959 **(62)**; Promise Me a Rose (A
Slight Detail), 1959 **(78)**; Do-Re-Mi,
1959 **(94)**; Paper Roses, 1960 **(5)**; In
My Little Corner of the World, 1960
(10); One of the Lucky Ones, 1960
(62); Wonderful by Night, 1960
(18); A Texan and a Girl from
Mexico, 1961 **(85)**; I Can't Do It by
Myself, 1961 **(87)**; Lonesome for
You, Mama, 1961 **(108)**; Step by
Step, Little by Little, 1962 **(106)**;
The World of Lonely People, 1964
(59); Welcome, Welcome Home,
1964 **(130)**

Pop Vocal—Oklahoma; former 2nd
runner-up to Miss America in 1958

Bubble Puppy

Personnel: Rod Prince (guitars,
vocals); Todd Potter (guitars,
vocals); Roy Cox (bass); M Taylor
(drums)
Album: A Gathering of Promises,
1969
Singles: Hot Smoke and Sassafras,
1969 **(14)**; If I Had a Reason, 1969
(128)
Psychedelic Rock—Texas

Buchanan & Goodman

Personnel: Bill Buchanan (vocals);
Dickie Goodman (vocals)

Singles: The Flying Saucer (Parts
1 & 2), 1956 **(3)**; Buchanan and
Goodman on Trial, 1956 **(80)**; Fly-
ing Saucer the 2nd, 1957 **(18)**; The
Creature, 1957 **(85)** (Buchanan &
Bob Ancell); Santa and the Satellite
(Parts I & II), 1957 **(32)**; The Inva-
sion, 1964 **(120)** (Buchanan &
Howard Greenfield)
Novelty Pop—American

The Buckinghams

Personnel: Dennis Tufano (vocals,
guitars); Carl Giamarese (guitars);
Nicholas Fortune (bass); Martin
Grebb (keyboards) replaced (1968)
by Dennis Miccoli (keyboards); Joe
Poulos (drums; deceased 1980)
Albums: Kind of a Drag, 1966;
Time and Changes, 1967; Portraits,
1968; In One Ear and Gone Tomor-
row, 1968; Greatest Hits, 1969;
Made in Chicago, 1975
Singles: I'll Go Crazy, 1966 **(112)**;
Kind of a Drag, 1967 **(1)**; Laudy
Miss Claudy, 1967 **(41)**; Don't You
Care, 1967 **(6)**; Mercy, Mercy,
Mercy, 1967 **(5)**; Hey Baby (They're
Playing Our Song), 1967 **(12)**;
Susan, 1967 **(11)**; Back in Love
Again, 1968 **(57)**; Where Did You
Come From, 1968 **(117)**; It's a
Beautiful Day (for Loving), 1969
(126); Music Everywhere, 1973 **(68)**;
Veronica, 1985

Pop/Rock—Midwest; band ar-
rested on drug charges in 1968,
group soon disbanded

Tim Buckley

Albums: Tim Buckley, 1967;
Goodbye and Hello, 1967; Happy
Sad, 1969; Blue Afternoon, 1970;
Lorca, 1970; Starsailor, 1971; Greet-
ings from L.A., 1972; Look at the

The Buckinghams: *back row,* **Tufano, Grebb, Fortune;** *front row:* **Giamarese, Poulos**

Fool, 1974; Dream Letter: Live in London 1968, 1991

Jazz/Rock—American; died in the summer of 1975 from a drug overdose

Buffalo Springfield

Personnel: Neil Young (guitars, vocals); Stephen Stills (guitars, vocals); Bruce Palmer (bass) replaced (1967) by Ken Koblun (bass) replaced (1967) by Jim Fielder (bass) replaced (1967) by Ken Forssi (bass) replaced (1967) by Jim Messina (bass, vocals); Richie Furay (guitars, vocals); Dewey Martin (drums); added (1967) Doug Hastings (guitars) left group (1967)

Albums: Buffalo Springfield, 1967; Buffalo Springfield Again, 1967; Last Time Around, 1968; Expecting

Buffalo Springfield: Furay, Martin, Young, Stills, Palmer

to Fly, 1970; Retrospective, 1972; Buffalo Springfield, 1973

Singles: Nowadays Clancy Can't Even Sing, 1966 **(110)**; For What It's Worth, 1967 **(7)**; Bluebird, 1967 **(58)**; Rock 'n' Roll Woman, 1967 **(44)**; Expecting to Fly, 1968 **(98)**; Uno Mundo, 1968 **(105)**; Special Care, 1968 **(107)**; On the Way Home, 1968 **(82)**

Psychedelic/Folk Rock—Int.; Young, Martin and Palmer are Canadians

Solomon Burke

Albums: Greatest, 1963; Rock 'n' Soul, 1964; The Best of Solomon Burke, 1965; I Wish I Knew, 1965; King of Rock 'n' Soul, 1966; Proud Mary, 1969; Electronic Magnetism, 1969; We're Almost Home, 1971; Get Up and Do Something, 1972; I Have a Dream, 1974; Music to Make Love To, 1975

Singles: Just Out of Reach (Of My Two Open Arms), 1961 **(24)**; Cry to Me, 1962 **(44)**; Down in the Valley, 1962 **(71)**; I'm Hanging Up My Heart for You, 1962 **(85)**; I Really Don't Want to Know, 1962 **(93)**; Words, 1963 **(121)**; If You Need Me, 1963 **(37)**; Can't Nobody Love You, 1963 **(66)**; You're Good for Me, 1963 **(49)**; He'll Have to Go, 1964 **(51)**; Goodbye Baby (Baby Goodbye), 1964 **(33)**; Everybody Needs Somebody to Love, 1964 **(58)**; Yes I Do, 1964 **(92)**; The Price, 1964 **(57)**; Got to Get You Off My Mind, 1965 **(22)**; Tonight's the Night, 1965 **(28)**; Someone Is Watching, 1965 **(89)**; Only Love (Can Save Me Now), 1965 **(94)**; Baby Come on Home, 1966 **(96)**; I Feel a Sin Coming On, 1966 **(97)**; Keep Looking, 1966 **(109)**; Keep a Light in the Window Till I Come Home, 1967 **(64)**; Take Me (Just As

I Am), 1967 **(49)**; Detroit City, 1967 **(104)**; Party People, 1968 **(112)**; I Wish I Knew (How It Would Feel to be Free), 1968 **(68)**; Up Tight Good Woman, 1969 **(116)**; Proud Mary, 1969 **(45)**; That Lucky Old Sun, 1969 **(129)**; The Electronic Magnetism (That's Heavy, Baby), 1971 **(96)**; Love's Street and Fool's Road, 1972 **(89)**; You and Your Baby Blues, 1975 **(96)**

Soul/R & B—Philadelphia

Dorsey Burnette

Albums: Talk Oak Tree, 1960; Dorsey Burnett, 1963; Greatest Hits, 1964; Here and Now, 1972; Dorsey Burnette, 1973; Comin' Back, 1974; Dorsey Burnette, 1974; Bertha Lou Devil's Queen, 1975; Things I Treasure, 1977; Golden Hits, 1979

Singles: (There Was a) Tall Oak Tree, 1960 **(23)**; Hey Little One, 1960 **(48)**; Big Rock Candy Mountain, 1960 **(102)**; The Ghost of Billy Malloo, 1960 **(103)**; Feminine Touch, 1961 **(117)**; The Greatest Love, 1969 **(67)**

Rockabilly—Memphis; father of Fleetwood Mac's Billy Burnette and brother of Johnny; Dorsey died in 1979

Johnny Burnette

Albums: Rock 'n' Roll Trio, 1956; Dreamin', 1960; Roses Are Red, 1961; Johnny Burnette, 1962; Johnny Burnette Sings, 1963; Very Best of Johnny Burnette, 1964; Tear It Up, 1969; Hits and Other Favourites, 1970; 10th Anniversary Album, 1974; Together Again, 1978; Johnny & Dorsey, 1982

Singles: Dreamin', 1960 **(11)**; You're Sixteen, 1960 **(8)**; Little Boy

Sad, 1961 **(17)**; Big Big World, 1961 **(58)**; I've Got a Lot of Things to Do, 1961 **(109)**; God, Country and My Baby, 1961 **(18)**; Clown Shoes, 1962 **(113)**; I Wanna Thank You Folks, 1962 **(117)**

Rockabilly—Memphis; father of Rocky Burnette and brother of Dorsey; Johnny drowned in 1964

The Busters

Personnel: Jack Baker (saxophones); Fran Parda (drums)
Single: Bust Out, 1963 **(25)**
Instrumental—Massachusetts

Jerry Butler

Albums: He Will Break Your Heart, 1963; Folk Songs, 1963; Delicious Together, 1964 (with Betty Everett); For Your Precious Love, 1967; Love Me, 1968; Mr. Dream Merchant, 1968; Jerry Butler's Golden Hits Live, 1968; The Soul Goes On, 1968; The Ice Man Cometh, 1969; Ice on Ice, 1969; The Best of Jerry Butler, 1970; You & Me, 1970; Sings Assorted Sounds, 1971; Gene & Jerry—One & One, 1971 (with Gene Chandler); The Sagittarius Movement, 1971; The Spice of Life, 1972; The Love We Have, 1972; Stuff Dreams Are Made Of, 1973; Power of Jerry Butler, 1973; Sweet 16, 1974; Love's on the Menu, 1976; The Vintage Years, 1977; Suite for the Single Girl, 1977; Thelma & Jerry, 1977 (with Thelma Houston); It All Comes Out, 1978; Two to One, 1978; Nothing Says I Love You Like I Love You, 1979; Best Love, 1981; Street Carols, 1991
Singles: For Your Precious Love, 1958 **(11)**; He Will Break Your Heart, 1960 **(7)**; Find Another Girl, 1961 **(27)**; I'm a Telling You, 1961 **(25)**; Moon River, 1961 **(11)**; Aware of Love, 1961 **(105)**; Make It Easy on Yourself, 1962 **(20)**; You Can Run (But You Can't Hide), 1962 **(63)**; Theme from Taras Bulba (The Wishing Star), 1962 **(100)**; Whatever You Want, 1963 **(68)**; Need to Belong, 1963 **(31)**; Giving Up on Love, 1964 **(56)**; I Don't Want to Hear Anymore, 1964 **(95)**; I Stand Accused, 1964 **(61)**; Let It Be Me, 1964 **(5)** (with Betty Everett); Ain't That Lovin' You Baby, 1964 **(108)** (with Betty Everett); Smile, 1964 **(42)** (with Betty Everett); Good Times, 1965 **(64)**; I Can't Stand to See You Cry, 1965 **(122)**; For Your Precious Love, 1966 **(99)**; Love (Oh, How Sweet It Is), 1966 **(103)**; I Dig You Baby, 1967 **(60)**; Mr. Dream Merchant, 1967 **(38)**; Lost, 1967 **(62)**; Never Give You Up, 1968 **(20)**; Hey, Western Union Man, 1968 **(16)**; Are You Happy, 1968 **(39)**; Only the Strong Survive, 1969 **(4)**; Moody Woman, 1969 **(24)**; What's the Use of Breaking Up, 1969 **(20)**; A Brand New Me, 1969 **(109)**; Don't Let Love Hang You Up, 1969 **(44)**; Got to See If I Can't Get Mommy (To Come Back Home), 1970 **(62)**; I Could Write a Book, 1970 **(46)**; Where Are You Going, 1970 **(95)**; Special Memory, 1970 **(109)**; You Just Can't Win (by Making the Same Mistake), 1971 **(94)** (with Gene Chandler); If It's Real What I Feel, 1971 **(69)**; How Did We Lose It Baby, 1971 **(85)**; Ten and Two (Take This Woman Off the Corner), 1971 **(126)** (with Gene Chandler); Walk Easy My Son, 1971 **(93)**; Ain't Understanding Mellow, 1971 **(21)** (with Brenda Lee Eager); I Only Have Eyes for You, 1972 **(85)**; They Long to Be) Close

to You, 1972 **(91)** (with Brenda Lee Eager); One Night Affair, 1972 **(52)**; I Wanna Do It to You, 1977 **(51)**

Soul Vocal — Mississippi; former Impressions vocalist

Paul Butterfield Blues Band

Personnel: Paul Butterfield (vocals, harmonica); Otis "Smokey" Smothers (guitars) replaced (1965) by Elvin Bishop (guitars, vocals); Jerome Arnold (bass) replaced (1967) by Bugsy Maugh (bass) replaced (1969) by Rod Hicks (bass, vocals) replaced (1973) by Billy Rich (bass); Sam Lay (drums) replaced (1966) by Bill Davenport (drums) replaced (1967) by Phil Wilson (drums) replaced (1970) by George Davidson (drums) replaced (1971) by Denny Whitted (drums) replaced (1972) by Chris Parker (drums); added (1965) Mike Bloomfield (guitars) replaced (1967) by Gene Dinwiddie (saxophones); added (1965) Mark Naftalin (keyboards) replaced (1969) by Ted Harris (keyboards) replaced (1973) by Ronnie Barron (keyboards) replaced (1975) by Richard Bell (keyboards)

Albums: The Paul Butterfield Blues Band, 1965; East-West, 1966; The Resurrection of Pigboy Crabshaw, 1967; In My Own Dream, 1968; Keep on Moving, 1969; Live, 1970; Sometimes I Just Feel Like Smilin', 1971; Golden Butter — The Best of the Paul Butterfield Blues Band, 1972; Offer You Can't Refuse, 1972; Better Days, 1973; It All Comes Back, 1974; Put It in Your Ear, 1975; North-South, 1981

Blues/Rock — American; Butterfield died in 1987

The Byrds

Personnel: Roger McGuinn (guitars, vocals); Gene Clark (guitars, vocals; deceased 1991) replaced (1966) by Carlos Bernal (guitars, vocals) replaced (1968) by Clarence White (guitars, vocals) replaced (1973) by Gene Clark (vocals); Chris Hillman (bass, guitars, vocals) replaced (1968) by John York (bass, vocals) replaced (1969) by Skip Battin (bass, vocals) replaced (1973) by Chris Hillman (bass, vocals); David Crosby (guitars, vocals) replaced (1968) by Gram Parsons (guitars, vocals) replaced (1968) by "Sneaky" Pete Kleinow (pedal steel guitar) left group (1968) replaced (1973) by David Crosby (vocals); Michael Clarke (drums) replaced (1967) by Kevin Kelley (drums) replaced (1969) by Gene Parsons (drums) replaced (1972) by John Guerin (drums) replaced (1973) by Dennis Dragon (drums) replaced (1973) by Jim Moon (drums) replaced (1973) by Joe Lala (drums); added (1968) Doug Dillard (banjo) left group (1968)

Albums: Early Flight, 1964; Preflyte, 1964; Mr. Tambourine Man, 1965; Turn! Turn! Turn!, 1966; Fifth Dimension, 1966; Younger Than Yesterday, 1967; Greatest Hits, 1967; The Notorious Byrd Brothers, 1968; Sweetheart of the Rodeo, 1968; Dr. Byrds & Mr. Hyde, 1969; The Ballad of Easy Rider, 1970; Untitled, 1970; Byrdmaniax, 1971; Farther Along, 1972; Greatest Hits Volume 2, 1972; The Byrds, 1973; History of the Byrds, 1973; L.A. Full Circle, 1974; Greatest Hits Volume 3, 1975; Mr. Tambourine Man (Best of), 1976; The Byrds Play Dylan, 1980; Original

The Byrds: Hillman, Crosby, McGuinn, Clarke, Clark

Singles 1965 –1967, 1980; Original Singles 1967 –1969, 1981; Never Before, 1988; The Byrds (Box Set), 1990

Singles: Mr. Tambourine Man, 1965 **(1)**; All I Really Want to Do, 1965 **(40)**; I'll Feel a Whole Lot Better, 1965 **(103)**; Turn! Turn! Turn!, 1965 **(1)**; It Won't Be Wrong, 1966 **(63)**; Set You Free This Time, 1966 **(79)**; Eight Miles High, 1966 **(14)**; 5-D, 1966 **(44)**; Mr. Spaceman, 1966 **(36)**; So You Want to Be a Rock & Roll Star, 1967 **(29)**; My Back Pages, 1967 **(30)**; Have You Seen Her Face, 1967 **(74)**; Lady Friend, 1967 **(82)**; Going Back, 1967 **(89)**; You Ain't Going Nowhere, 1968 **(74)**; Lay Lady Lay, 1969 **(132)**; The Ballad of Easy Rider, 1969 **(65)**; Jesus Is Just Alright, 1970 **(97)**; Chestnut Mare, 1970 **(121)**; Glory, Glory, 1971 **(110)**; Full Circle, 1973 **(109)**

Folk/Country Rock — L.A.; Roger McGuinn was originally known as Jim McGuinn; the 1973 album "The Byrds" was a reunion album; Gene Clark left the band due to his fear of flying

Edward Byrnes

Singles: Kookie Kookie (Lend Me Your Comb), 1959 **(4)** (with Connie Stevens); Like I Love You, 1959 **(42)** (with Friend)

Novelty Pop — New York; starred in TV's "77 Sunset Strip"

The Cadets

Personnel: Aaron Collins (vocals); Ted Taylor (vocals); William "Dub" Jones (vocals); Willie Davis (vocals); Lloyd McCraw (vocals)

Albums: Rockin' 'n' Reelin', 1956; The Cadets, 1957

Single: Stranded in the Jungle, 1956 **(15)**

R & B Vocal — Los Angeles

The Cadillacs

Personnel: Earl "Speedy" Carroll (vocals)

Albums: The Fabulous Cadillacs, 1956; Crazy Cadillacs, 1957; Twisting with the Cadillacs, 1958

Singles: Speedoo, 1955 **(17)**; Peek-a-Boo, 1958 **(28)**; Romeo, 1959 **(105)**

R & B Vocal — New York

Glen Campbell

Albums: Gentle on My Mind, 1967; By the Time I Get to Phoenix, 1967; Hey Little One, 1968; A New Place in the Sun, 1968; Bobbie Gentry and Glen Campbell, 1968; Wichita Lineman, 1968; Galveston, 1969; Glen Campbell Live, 1969; Try a Little Kindness, 1970; Oh Happy Day, 1970; Norwood, 1970; The Glen Campbell Goodtime Album, 1970; Greatest Hits, 1971; The Last Time I Saw Her, 1971; Anne Murray/Glen Campbell, 1971; Glen Travis Campbell, 1972; I Knew Jesus (Before He Was a Star), 1973; Reunion (The Songs of Jimmy Webb), 1974; Rhinestone Cowboy, 1975; Bloodline, 1976; The Best of Glen Campbell, 1976; Southern Nights, 1977; Live at the Royal Festival Hall, 1978; Basic, 1978; Highwayman, 1979; Somethin' 'Bout You Baby I Like, 1980; It's the World Gone Crazy, 1981; Letting Go, 1983; Still Within the Sound of My Voice, 1987; Light Years, 1988; Classics Collection, 1990; Walkin' in the Sun, 1990

Singles: Turn Around, Look at Me, 1961 **(62)**; Too Late to Worry, Too Blue to Cry, 1962 **(76)**; Kentucky Means Paradise, 1962 **(114)**; Prima Donna, 1963 **(103)**; Tomorrow Never Comes, 1965 **(118)**; The Universal Soldier, 1965 **(45)**; Private John Q, 1965 **(114)**; Gentle on My Mind, 1967 **(62)**; By the Time I Get to Phoenix, 1967 **(26)**; Hey Little One, 1968 **(54)**; I Wanna Live, 1968 **(36)**; Dreams of the Everyday Housewife, 1968 **(32)**; Gentle on My Mind, 1968 **(39)**; Mornin' Glory, 1968 **(74)**; Wichita Lineman, 1968 **(3)**; Let It Be Me, 1969 **(36)**; Galveston, 1969 **(4)**; Where's the Playground Susie, 1969 **(26)**; True Grit, 1969 **(35)**; Try a Little Kindness, 1969 **(23)**; Honey Come Back, 1970 **(19)**; All I Have to Do Is Dream, 1970 **(27)**; Oh Happy Day, 1970 **(40)**; Everything a Man Could Ever Need, 1970 **(52)**; It's Only Make Believe, 1970 **(10)**; Dream Baby (How Long Must I Dream), 1971 **(31)**; The Last Time I Saw Her, 1971 **(61)**; I Say a Little Prayer, 1971 **(81)**; Oklahoma Sunday Morning, 1972 **(104)**; Manhattan Kansas, 1972 **(114)**; I Will Never Pass This Way Again, 1972 **(61)**; One Last Time, 1972 **(78)**; I Knew Jesus (Before He Was a Star), 1973 **(45)**; Wherefore and Why, 1973 **(111)**; Houston (I'm Comin' to See You), 1974 **(68)**; Rhinestone Cowboy, 1975 **(1)**; Country Boy (You Got Your Feet in L.A.), 1975 **(11)**; My Prayer, 1976; See You on Sunday, 1976; Don't Pull Your Love Out/Then You Can Tell Me Goodbye, 1976 **(27)**; Southern Nights, 1977 **(1)**; Sunflower, 1977 **(39)**; Hound Dog Man, 1977; God Must Have Blessed America, 1978; Can You Fool, 1978 **(38)**; Somethin' 'Bout You Baby I Like, 1980 **(42)** (with Rita Coolidge); California, 1979; Another Fine Mess, 1979; I'm Gonna Love You, 1979; Any Which Way You Can, 1980; I Don't Want to Know Your Name, 1981 **(65)**; I Love My Truck, 1981 **(94)**; Old Home Town, 1982; I Know You Love Me, 1983; On the Wings of My Victory, 1983; Letting Go, 1983; Faithless Love, 1984; A Lady Like You, 1984; (Love Always) Letter to Home, 1985; It's Just a Matter of Time, 1985; Cowpoke, 1986; Still Within the Sound of My Voice, 1987; On a Good Night, 1990; She's Gone, Gone, Gone, 1990

Country/Pop—Arkansas

Jo Ann Campbell

Singles: A Kookie Little Paradise, 1960 **(61)**; (I'm the Girl on) Wolverton Mountain, 1962 **(38)**; Mother, Please!, 1963 **(88)**

Country/Pop Vocal—Florida; married to Troy Seals

Can

Personnel: Holger Czukay (bass) replaced (1977) by Roscoe Gee (bass); Michael Karoli (guitars, violin); Malcolm Mooney (vocals) re-

placed (1971) by Kenji Suzuki (vocals) replaced (1976) by Peter Gilmore (vocals); Irmin Schmidt (keyboards, vocals); Dave Johnson (flutes, electronics) left group (1970); Jaki Liebezeit (drums) replaced (1977) by Rebop Kwaku Baah (drums)

Albums: Delay 1968, 1968; Monster Movie, 1969; Deep End (Soundtrack), 1970; Tago Mago, 1971; Ege Bamyasi, 1972; Future Days, 1973; Soon Over Babaluma, 1974; Limited Edition, 1974; Landed, 1975; Unlimited Edition, 1976; Opener, 1976; Flow Motion, 1976; Saw Delight, 1977; Out of Reach, 1978; Cannibalisms, 1978; Can, 1979; Inner Space, 1980

Jazz/Rock—European

The Candymen

Personnel: Rodney Justo (vocals); John Rainey Adkins (guitars); Billy Gilmore (bass); Dean Daughtry (keyboards); Robert Nix (drums)

Albums: The Candymen, 1967; Bring You Candypower, 1968

Single: Georgia Pines, 1967 **(81)**

Southern Rock—Georgia

Canned Heat

Personnel: Bob Hite (vocals; deceased 1980) replaced (1981) by Ricky Kellogg (vocals); Henry Vestine (guitars) replaced (1981) by Mike Halby (guitars, vocals); Alan Wilson (guitars; deceased 1970) replaced (1970) by Harvey Mandel (guitars) replaced (1973) by Edward Beyer (keyboards) replaced (1981) by Walter Trout (guitars, vocals); Larry Taylor (bass) replaced (1971) by Antonio Barrada (bass) replaced (1973) by Richard Hite (bass) replaced (1981) by Ernie Rodriguez (bass); Frank Cook (drums) replaced (1968) by Adolfo de la Parra (drums); added (1972) Joel Scott Hill (vocals, guitars) replaced (1973) by James Shane (guitars) replaced (1980) by Chris Morgan (guitars)

Albums: Canned Heat, 1967; Boogie with Canned Heat, 1968; Living the Blues, 1969; Hallelujah, 1969; Vintage Heat, 1970; Live in Europe, 1970; Future Blues, 1970; Cookbook, 1970; Hooker & Heat, 1971; Memphis Heat, 1971; Live at the Topanga Corral, 1971; Historical Figures, 1972; Portrait, Volume 1 and 2, 1972; New Age, 1973; Rollin' and Tumblin', 1973; One More River to Cross, 1974; Collage, 1975; Very Best of Canned Heat, 1976; Human Condition, 1978; Dog House Blues, 1982

Singles: Rollin' and Tumblin', 1967 **(115)**; On the Road Again, 1968 **(16)**; Going Up the Country, 1968 **(11)**; Time Was, 1969 **(67)**; Poor Moon, 1969 **(119)**; Let's Work Together, 1970 **(26)**; Wooly Bully, 1971 **(105)**; Rocking with the King, 1972 **(88)**

Blues/Rock — Los Angeles; Bob "The Bear" Hite weighed over 300 pounds

Cannibal and The Headhunters

Personnel: Frankie "Cannibal" Garcia (vocals)

Album: Land of 1000 Dances, 1965

Singles: Land of 1000 Dances, 1965 **(30)**; Nau Ninny Nau, 1965 **(133)**; Land of 1000 Dances, 1966 **(106)**

Mex/Rock — Los Angeles

Ace Cannon

Albums: Tuff, 1962; Looking Back, 1962; Moaning Sax, 1964; Aces High, 1964; Great Show Tunes, 1964; Christmas Cheer, 1964; Live, 1965; Nashville Hits, 1965; Sweet & Tuff, 1966; Misty Sax, 1967; Memphis Golden Sax, 1968; In the Spotlight, 1969; Ace of Sax, 1970; Happy & Mellow, 1970; Cool & Saxy, 1971; Blowing Wind, 1972; Country Cannon, 1972; Baby Don't Get Hooked on Me, 1973; Country Comfort, 1973; That Music City Feeling, 1974; Super Sax, 1975; Very Best of Ace Cannon, 1975; Sax Man, 1978

Singles: Tuff, 1961 **(17)**; Blues (Stay Away from Me), 1962 **(36)**; Sugar Blues, 1962 **(92)**; Volare (Nel Blu Dipinto Di Blu), 1962 **(107)**; Since I Met You Baby, 1963 **(130)**; Cottonfields, 1963 **(67)**; Swanee River, 1963 **(103)**; Searchin', 1964 **(84)**; Empty Arms, 1964 **(120)**; Sea Cruise, 1965 **(135)**; Funny (How Time Slips Away), 1966 **(102)**; By the Time I Get to Phoenix, 1968 **(110)**

Instrumental — Mississippi; sax man for Bill Black's Combo

Freddy Cannon

Albums: The Explosive Freddy Cannon, 1960; Freddy Cannon Favourites, 1961; Happy Shades of Blue, 1962; Freddy Cannon at Palisades Park, 1962; Bang On, 1963; Steps Out, 1964; Freddy Cannon, 1965; Greatest Hits, 1966

Singles: Tallahassee Lassie, 1959 **(6)**; Okefenokee, 1959 **(43)**; Way Down Yonder in New Orleans, 1959 **(3)**; Chattanooga Shoe Shine Boy, 1960 **(34)**; Jump Over, 1960 **(28)**; The Urge, 1960 **(60)**; Happy Shades of Blue, 1960 **(83)**; Humdinger, 1960 **(59)**; Muskrat Ramble, 1961 **(54)**; Opportunity, 1961 **(114)**; Buzz Buzz A-Diddle-It, 1961 **(51)**; Transistor Sister, 1961 **(35)**; For Me and My Gal, 1961 **(71)**; Teen Queen of the Week, 1962 **(92)**; Palisades Park, 1962 **(3)**; What's Gonna Happen When Summer's Done, 1962 **(45)**; If You Were a Rock and Roll Record, 1962 **(67)**; Four Letter Man, 1963 **(121)**; Patty Baby, 1963 **(65)**; Everybody Monkey, 1963 **(52)**; Abigail Beecher, 1964 **(16)**; In the Night, 1965 **(132)**; Action, 1965 **(13)**; Let Me Show You Where It's At, 1965 **(127)**; The Dedication Song, 1966 **(41)**; The Laughing Song, 1966 **(111)**; Rock Around the Clock, 1968 **(121)**; Let's Put the Fun Back in Rock 'n' Roll, 1981 **(81)** (with The Belmonts)

Pop/Rock—Massachusetts; real name is Frederick Picariello

The Capitols

Personnel: Sam George (vocals; deceased 1982); Donald Norman (vocals); Richard Mitchell (vocals)

Albums: Dance the Cool Jerk, 1966; We Got a Thing, 1967

Singles: Cool Jerk, 1966 **(7)**; I Got to Handle It, 1966 **(74)**; We Got a Thing That's in the Groove, 1966 **(65)**; Patty Cake, 1967 **(125)**

R & B Vocal—Detroit

The Capris

Personnel: Nick "Santo" Santamaria (vocals) left group (1961) rejoined (1981); Mike Miniceli (vocals); Frank Reina (vocals); John Cassese (vocals) replaced (1980) by Tony Danno (vocals); Vinny Nar-

cardo (vocals) replaced (1980) by Tom Ferrara (vocals)

Albums: There's a Moon Out Tonight, 1961; There's a Moon Out Tonight Again, 1981

Singles: There's a Moon Out Tonight, 1960 **(3)**; Where I Fell in Love, 1961 **(74)**; Girl in My Dreams, 1961 **(92)**; Limbo, 1962 **(99)**

Pop Vocal—New York

Captain Beefheart & The Magic Band

St. Claire, French, Van Vliet, Handley, Cotton

Personnel: Don "Captain Beefheart" Van Vliet (vocals, saxophones, bass, harmonica); Ry Cooder (guitars) replaced (1967) by Jeff Cotton (guitars) replaced (1969) by Art Tripp (percussion) replaced (1972) by Mark Marcellino (keyboards) replaced (1974) by Jim Caravan (keyboards) replaced (1975) by Bruce Fowler (trombone); Alex "Snuffy" St. Claire (guitars) replaced (1968) by Bill Harkleroad (guitars) replaced (1972) by Eliot Ingber (guitars) replaced (1972) by Alex St. Claire (guitars) replaced (1974) by Dean Smith (guitars) replaced (1975) by Rich Redus (guitars) replaced (1978)

by Gary Lucas (guitars); Jerry
Handley (bass) replaced (1968) by
Mark Boston (bass) replaced (1974)
by Ira Ingber (bass) replaced (1975)
by Eric Drew Feldman (bass, keyboards); John "Toxey" French
(drums) replaced (1970) by Roy Estrada (drums) replaced (1972) by
John French (drums) replaced (1974)
by Gene Pello (drums) replaced
(1975) by Rob Williams (drums) replaced (1978) by John French
(drums) replaced (1980) by Cliff
Martinez (drums); added (1974)
Mike Smotherman (keyboards) replaced (1974) by Jeff Tepper (guitars); added (1974) Ty Grimes (percussion) left group (1975)

Albums: Safe As Milk, 1967;
Drop Out Boogie, 1967; Mirror
Man, 1968; Strictly Personal, 1968;
Trout Mask Replica, 1969; Lick My
Decals Off, Baby, 1970; Clear Spot,
1972; The Spotlight Kid, 1972; Un-
conditionally Guaranteed, 1974;
Bluejeans and Moonbeams, 1975;
Bongo Fury, 1975; Shiny Beast (Bat
Chain Puller), 1978; Doc at the
Radar Station, 1980; Ice Cream for
Crow, 1982; Music in Sea Minor,
1983; Top Secret, 1984

Psychedelic Pop—American

Caravan

Personnel: Pye Hastings (vocals,
guitars); Richard Sinclair (bass, vocals) replaced (1972) by Stuart Evans
(bass) replaced (1972) by John G.
Perry (bass) replaced (1974) by Mike
Wedgwood (bass) replaced (1977) by
Dek Messecar (bass, vocals) replaced by Richard Sinclair (bass,
vocals); Dave Sinclair (keyboards)
replaced by Steve Miller (keyboards)
replaced by Derek Austin (keyboards) replaced by Dave Sinclair

Caravan: Wedgwood, D. Sinclair, Richardson, Hastings,
Coughlan

(keyboards) replaced by Jan Schel-
haas (keyboards) replaced by Dave
Sinclair (keyboards); Richard
Coughlan (drums, percussion); added
Geoff Richardson (guitars, viola)

Albums: Caravan, 1968; If I
Could Do It All Over Again, I'd Do
It All Over You, 1970; In the Land
of Grey and Pink, 1971; Waterloo
Lily, 1972; For Girls Who Grow
Plump in the Night, 1972; Caravan
and the New Symphonia, 1973;
Cunning Stunts, 1975; Blind Dog at
St. Dunstans, 1976; Canterbury
Tales/The Best of Caravan, 1976;
Better by Far, 1977; The Album,
1980; The Best of Caravan Live,
1980; The Show of Our Lives, 1981;
Back and Forth, 1982; Back to
Front, 1982

Singles: If I Could Do It All Over
Again, I'd Do It All Over You,
1970; Golf Girl, 1971; Aristocracy,
1972; Hoedown, 1973; Virgin on the

Ridiculous, 1973; Stuck in a Hole, 1975 **(110)**
Art Rock — British

The Caravelles

Personnel: Andrea Simpson (vocals); Lois Wilkinson (vocals)
Album: You Don't Have to Be a Baby to Cry, 1964
Singles: You Don't Have to Be a Baby to Cry, 1963 **(3)**; Have You Ever Been Lonely (Have You Ever Been Blue), 1964 **(94)**
Pop Vocal — British

The Carefrees

Single: We Love You Beatles, 1964 **(39)**
Pop/Rock — British

Cathy Carr

Singles: Ivory Tower, 1956 **(2)**; Heart Hideaway, 1956 **(67)**; First Anniversary, 1959 **(42)**; I'm Gonna Change Him, 1959 **(63)**; Little Sister, 1960 **(106)**; Sailor Boy, 1962 **(103)**
Pop Vocal — New York; died in November, 1988

James Carr

Singles: You've Got My Mind Messed Up, 1966 **(63)**; Love Attack, 1966 **(99)**; Pouring Water on a Drowning Man, 1966 **(85)**; The Dark End of the Street, 1967 **(77)**; Let It Happen, 1967 **(106)**; I'm a Fool for You, 1967 **(97)**; A Man Needs a Woman, 1968 **(63)**; Life Turned Her That Way, 1968 **(112)**
Soul Vocal — Memphis

Valerie Carr

Single: When the Boys Talk About Girls, 1958 **(19)**
Soul/Pop Vocal — New York

Vikki Carr

Albums: Discovery!, 1964; It Must Be Him, 1967; Vikki!, 1968; For Once in My Life, 1969; Nashville by Carr, 1970; Vikki Carr's Love Story, 1971; Superstar, 1972; The First Time Ever (I Saw Your Face), 1972; En Espanol, 1972; Ms. America, 1973; Live at the Greek Theatre, 1973; One Hell of a Woman, 1974
Singles: He's a Rebel, 1962 **(115)**; It Must Be Him, 1967 **(3)**; The Lesson, 1967 **(34)**; She'll Be There, 1968 **(99)**; Your Heart Is Free Just Like the Wind, 1968 **(91)**; Don't Break My Pretty Balloon, 1968 **(114)**; With Pen in Hand, 1969 **(35)**; Eternity, 1969 **(79)**; I'll Be Home, 1971 **(96)**; Big Hurt, 1972 **(108)**
Pop Vocal — Texas; real name is Florence Cardona

Andrea Carroll

Single: It Hurts to Be Sixteen, 1963 **(45)**
Pop Vocal — Cleveland; real last name is DeCapite

Bernadette Carroll

Single: Party Girl, 1964 **(47)**
Pop Vocal — American

Clarence Carter

Albums: This Is Clarence Carter, 1968; The Dynamic Clarence Carter, 1969; Testifyin', 1969; Patches, 1970; The Best of Clarence

Carter, 1971; Let's Burn, 1973; Real, 1974; Loneliness and Temptation, 1975; Heart Full of Song, 1976; In Person, 1981

Singles: Thread the Needle, 1967 **(98)**; Looking for a Fox, 1968 **(62)**; Funky Fever, 1968 **(88)**; Slip Away, 1968 **(6)**; Too Weak to Fight, 1968 **(13)**; Snatching It Back, 1969 **(31)**; The Feeling Is Right, 1969 **(65)**; Doin' Our Thing, 1969 **(46)**; Take It Off Him and Put It on Me, 1970 **(94)**; I Can't Leave Your Love Alone, 1970 **(42)**; Patches, 1970 **(4)**; It's All in Your Mind, 1970 **(51)**; The Court Room, 1971 **(61)**; Slipped, Tripped and Fell in Love, 1971 **(84)**; Scratch My Back (and Mumble in My Ear), 1971 **(101)**; Put on Your Shoes and Walk, 1973 **(112)**; Mother-in-Law, 1973 **(80)**; Sixty Minute Man, 1973 **(65)**; I'm the Midnight Special, 1973 **(101)**

R & B/Soul — Alabama

Mel Carter

Albums: Hold Me, Thrill Me, Kiss Me, 1965; Easy Listening, 1966

Singles: When a Boy Falls in Love, 1963 **(44)**; The Richest Man Alive, 1965 **(104)**; Hold Me, Thrill Me, Kiss Me, 1965 **(8)**; (All of a Sudden) My Heart Sings, 1965 **(38)**; Love Is All We Need, 1966 **(50)**; Band of Gold, 1966 **(32)**; You You You, 1966 **(49)**; Take Good Care of Her, 1966 **(78)**; As Time Goes By, 1967 **(111)**; Be My Love, 1967 **(132)**; I Only Have Eyes for You, 1974 **(104)**

Soul Vocal — Cincinnati; starred on TV's "Sanford & Son"

Martin Carthy

Albums: The Word Is, 1964; Martin Carthy, 1965; Second

Album, 1966; Landfall, 1971; Selections, 1971; This Is Martin Carthy, 1972; Sweet Wivelfield, 1974; Shearwater, 1975; Crown of Horn, 1976; Because It's There, 1979; Out of the Cut, 1982

Folk/Rock — British; became a member of Steeleye Span and Fairport Convention

Martin Carthy & Dave Swarbrick

Albums: Byker Hill, 1967; But Two Came By, 1968; Prince Heathen, 1969; Life and Limb, 1990

Folk/Rock — British

The Cascades

Personnel: John Gummoe (vocals); Eddie Snyder (vocals); David Stevens (vocals); David Wilson (vocals); David Zabo (vocals)

Album: The Rhythm of the Rain, 1963

Singles: Rhythm of the Rain, 1963 **(3)**; The Last Leaf, 1963 **(60)**; Shy Girl, 1963 **(91)**; A Little Like Lovin', 1963 **(116)**; For Your Sweet Love, 1963 **(86)**; Cheryl's Goin' Home, 1966 **(131)**; Maybe the Rain Will Fall, 1969 **(61)**

Pop Vocal — San Diego

The Casinos

Personnel: Gene Hughes (vocals)

Album: Then You Can Tell Me Goodbye, 1967

Singles: Then You Can Tell Me Goodbye, 1967 **(6)**; It's All Over Now, 1967 **(65)**; How Long Has It Been, 1967 **(121)**

Pop/Soft Rock — Cincinnati

The Castaways

Personnel: Richard Robey (vocals, bass); Robert Folschow (guitars); Roy Hensley (guitars); James Donna (keyboards); Dennis Craswell (drums)
Album: The Castaways, 1965
Singles: Liar Liar, 1965 **(12)**; Goodbye Babe, 1965 **(101)**
Pop/Rock — Minnesota

The Castells

Personnel: Bob Ussery (vocals); Tom Hicks (vocals); Joe Kelly (vocals); Chuck Girard (vocals)
Singles: Little Sad Eyes, 1961 **(101)**; Sacred, 1961 **(20)**; Make Believe Wedding, 1961 **(98)**; So This Is Love, 1962 **(21)**; Oh! What It Seemed to Be, 1962 **(91)**
Pop Vocal — California

Cat Mother & The All Night News Boys

Personnel: Roy Michaels (guitars, bass, vocals); Bob Smith (keyboards, drums, vocals); Larry Packer (guitars, vocals) replaced (1973) by Steve Davidson (guitars); Charlie Chin (banjo, guitars, vocals) replaced (1970) by Jay Ungar (guitars, vocals) replaced (1974) by Charlie Harcourt (guitars); Michael Equine (drums, guitars, vocals)
Albums: The Street Giveth . . . The Street Taketh Away, 1969; Albion Doowah, 1970; Last Chance Dance, 1973; Cat Mother, 1974
Singles: Good Old Rock & Roll, 1969 **(21)**; Can You Dance to It, 1969 **(115)**
Hard Rock — New York

Cathy Jean & The Roommates

Personnel: Cathy Jean (vocals); Steve Susskind (vocals); Jack Sailson (vocals); Felix Alvarez (vocals); Bob Minsky (vocals)
Singles: Please Love Me Forever, 1961 **(12)**; Band of Gold, 1961 **(119)**
Pop Vocal — New York

Chad & Jeremy

Personnel: Chad Stuart (vocals, guitars, piano); Jeremy Clyde (vocals, guitars)
Albums: Before & After, 1964; I Don't Wanna Lose You Baby, 1965; More, 1966; Distant Shores, 1966; Best Of, 1967; Of Cabbages and Kings, 1967; The Ark, 1968
Singles: Yesterday's Gone, 1964 **(21)**; A Summer Song, 1964 **(7)**; Willow Weep for Me, 1964 **(15)**; If I Loved You, 1965 **(23)**; What Do You Want with Me, 1965 **(51)**; Before and After, 1965 **(17)**; From a Window, 1965 **(97)**; I Don't Wanna Lose You Baby, 1965 **(35)**; Should I, 1965 **(128)**; I Have Dreamed, 1965 **(91)**; Teenage Failure, 1966 **(131)**; Distant Shores, 1966 **(30)**; You Are She, 1966 **(87)**; Bite the Bullet, 1984
Pop Vocal — British

Chambers Brothers

Personnel: Joe Chambers (guitars, vocals); George Chambers (bass); Willie Chambers (guitars, vocals); Lester Chambers (vocals, harmonica); added (1965): Brian Keenan (drums)
Albums: People Get Ready, 1965; Now, 1966; Shout, 1968; The Time Has Come Today, 1968; A New

Chambers Brothers

Time, a New Day, 1968; Greatest
Hits, 1969; Live at Fillmore East,
1970; Feeling the Blues, 1970; A
New Generation, 1971; Oh My God,
1972; Unbonded, 1973; Love, Peace
and Happiness, 1974; Right Move,
1975; Live in Concert on Mars,
1977; Best Of, 1977

Singles: Uptown, 1967 **(126)**;
Time Has Come Today, 1968 **(11)**; I
Can't Turn You Loose, 1968 **(37)**;
Shout! (Part 1), 1968 **(83)**; Are You
Ready, 1969 **(113)**; Wake Up, 1969
(92); Love, Peace and Happiness,
1970 **(96)**; Let's Do It Together,
1970 **(103)**; Funky, 1970 **(106)**; Let's
Go, Let's Go, Let's Go, 1974 **(106)**

Soul/Rock — Mississippi

The Champs

Personnel: Dave Burgess (guitars);
Buddy Bruce (guitars) replaced
(1958) by Dale Norris (guitars)
replaced (1960) by Glen Campbell
(guitars); Danny Flores (saxophones)
replaced (1958) by James Seals
(saxophones); Cliff Hills (bass)

replaced (1958) by Joe Burnas
(bass); Gene Alden (drums) replaced
(1958) by Dash Crofts (drums)

Albums: Go Champs Go, 1958;
Everybody's Rockin', 1960; Great
Dance Hits, 1962; Play All Ameri-
can, 1962; Play Joshua Logan, 1963;
Best of the Champs, 1977

Singles: Tequila, 1958 **(1)**; El
Rancho Rock, 1958 **(30)**; Mid-
nighter, 1958 **(94)**; Chariot Rock,
1958 **(59)**; Too Much Tequila, 1960
(30); Tequila Twist, 1962 **(99)**;
Limbo Rock, 1962 **(40)**; Limbo
Dance, 1962 **(97)**; Mr. Cool, 1963
(111)

Instrumental — Los Angeles

Gene Chandler

Albums: The Duke of Earl, 1962;
Gene Chandler — Live on Stage in
'65, 1966; Gene Chandler, 1967; The
Girl Don't Care, 1967; There Was a

Time, 1968; Two Sides of Gene Chandler, 1969; The Gene Chandler Situation, 1970; Gene Chandler & Jerry Butler—One & One, 1971; Album, 1974; Get Down, 1978; When You're #1, 1979; Gene Chandler '80, 1980

Singles: Duke of Earl, 1962 **(1)**; Walk on with the Duke, 1962 **(91)**; Tear for Tear, 1962 **(114)**; You Threw a Lucky Punch, 1962 **(49)**; Rainbow, 1963 **(47)**; Check Yourself, 1963 **(119)**; Man's Temptation, 1963 **(71)**; Think Nothing About It, 1964 **(107)**; Soul Hootenanny (Part 1), 1964 **(92)**; Just Be True, 1964 **(19)**; Bless Our Love, 1964 **(39)**; What Now, 1964 **(40)**; You Can't Hurt Me No More, 1965 **(92)**; Nothing Can Stop Me, 1965 **(18)**; Good Times, 1965 **(92)**; Here Come the Tears, 1965 **(102)**; Rainbow '65 (Part 1), 1965 **(69)**; (I'm Just a) Fool for You, 1966 **(88)**; I Fooled You This Time, 1966 **(45)**; Girl Don't Care, 1967 **(66)**; To Be a Lover, 1967 **(94)**; There Goes the Lover, 1967 **(98)**; There Was a Time, 1968 **(82)**; From the Teacher to the Preacher, 1968 **(57)** (with Barbara Acklin); Groovy Situation, 1970 **(12)**; Simply Call It Love, 1970 **(75)**; You Just Can't Win (by Making the Same Mistake), 1971 **(94)** (with Jerry Butler); You're a Lady, 1971 **(116)**; Ten and Two (Take This Woman Off the Corner, 1971 **(126)** (with Jerry Butler); Get Down, 1979 **(53)**; When You're #1, 1979 **(99)**; Does She Have a Friend?, 1980 **(101)**

Soul/Rock—Chicago; real last name is Dixon

Bruce Channel

Albums: Hey! Baby (and 11 Other Songs About Your Baby),

1962; Goin' Back to Louisiana, 1964

Singles: Hey! Baby, 1962 **(1)**; Number One Man, 1962 **(52)**; Come on Baby, 1962 **(98)**; Somewhere in This Town, 1962 **(117)**; Going Back to Louisiana, 1964 **(89)**; Mr. Bus Driver, 1967 **(90)**

Pop Vocal—Texas

The Chantays

Personnel: Brian Carman (guitars); Bob Welsh (drums); Bob Marshall (keyboards); Warren Waters (bass); Bob Spickard (guitars)

Album: Pipeline, 1963

Singles: Pipeline, 1963 **(4)**; Pipeline, 1966 **(106)**

Surf Rock—California

The Chantels

Personnel: Arlene Smith (vocals); Sonia Goring (vocals); Rene Minus (vocals); Jackie Landry (vocals); Lois Harris (vocals)

Albums: We Are the Chantels, 1958; Here's Our Song Again, 1959

Singles: He's Gone, 1957 **(71)**; Maybe, 1958 **(15)**; Every Night (I Pray), 1958 **(39)**; I Love You So, 1958 **(42)**; Summer's Love, 1959 **(93)** (with Richard Barrett); Look in My Eyes, 1961 **(14)**; Well, I Told You, 1961 **(29)**; Here It Comes Again, 1962 **(118)**; Eternally, 1963 **(77)**; Maybe, 1969 **(116)**

Pop Vocal—New York

The Chanters

Personnel: Larry Pendergrass (vocals); Fred Paige (vocals); Bud Johnson (vocals); Elliott Green (vocals); Bobby Thompson (vocals)

Single: No, No, No, 1961 **(41)**

Pop Vocal—New York

The Charlatans

Olsen, Hicks, Wilhelm, Devore, Wilson

Personnel: George Hunter (vocals) left group (1968); Mike Wilhelm (guitars, vocals); Richard Olsen (bass); Michael Ferguson (keyboards) replaced (1967) by Patrick Bogerty (keyboards) replaced (1968) by Darryl Devore (keyboards); Dan Hicks (guitars, vocals, drums) left group (1968); Sam Linde (drums) replaced (1967) by Terry Wilson (drums)
 Album: The Charlatans, 1969
 Single: Codine, 1969
 Psychedelic Pop — American

The Charms

Personnel: Otis Williams (vocals); Richard Parker (vocals); Donald Peak (vocals); Joe Penn (vocals); Rolland Bradley (vocals)
Singles: Hearts of Stone, 1954 **(15)**; Ling, Ting, Tong, 1955 **(26)**; That's Your Mistake, 1956 **(48)**; Ivory Tower, 1956 **(11)**; Little Turtle Dove, 1961 **(95)**; Panic, 1961 **(99)**
 R & B Vocal — Cincinnati

The Chartbusters

Personnel: Vernon Sandusky (vocals)

Album: The Chartbusters, 1964
Singles: She's the One, 1964 **(33)**; Why (Doncha Be My Girl), 1964 **(92)**; New Orleans, 1965 **(134)**
 Pop/Rock — Washington, D.C.

Chubby Checker

Albums: Twist with Chubby Checker, 1960; It's Pony Time, 1961; Let's Twist Again, 1961; For Twisters Only, 1961; Your Twist Party, 1961; Bobby Rydell/Chubby Checker, 1961; For Teen Twisters Only, 1962; Twistin' 'Round the World, 1962; Don't Knock the Twist, 1962; All the Hits (Your Dancin' Party), 1962; Down to Earth, 1962 (with Dee Dee Sharp); Limbo Party, 1962; Chubby Checker's Biggest Hits, 1962; Let's Limbo Some More, 1963; Beach Party, 1963; Chubby Checker in Person, 1963; Chubby Checker's Greatest Hits, 1972; The Change Has Come, 1982
 Singles: The Class, 1959 **(38)**; The Twist, 1960 **(1)**; The Hucklebuck, 1960 **(14)**; Whole Lotta Shakin' Goin' On, 1960 **(42)**; Pony Time, 1961 **(1)**; Dance the Mess Around, 1961 **(24)**; Good Good Lovin', 1961 **(43)**; Let's Twist Again, 1961 **(8)**; The Fly, 1961 **(7)**; The Twist, 1961 **(1)**; Twistin' U.S.A., 1961 **(68)**; Jingle Bell Rock, 1961 **(21)** (with Bobby Rydell); Slow Twistin', 1962 **(3)** (with Dee Dee Sharp); La Paloma Twist, 1962 **(72)**; Teach Me to Twist, 1962 **(109)** (with Bobby Rydell); Dancin' Party, 1962 **(12)**; Limbo Rock, 1962 **(2)**; Popeye the Hitchhiker, 1962 **(10)**; Jingle Bell Rock, 1962 **(92)** (with Bobby Rydell); Twenty Miles, 1963 **(15)**; Let's Limbo Some More, 1963 **(20)**; Birdland, 1963 **(12)**; Black Cloud,

1963 (**98**); Twist It Up, 1963 (**25**); Surf Party, 1963 (**55**); Loddy Lo, 1963 (**12**); Hooka Tooka, 1963 (**17**); Hey, Bobba Needle, 1964 (**23**); Lazy Elsie Molly, 1964 (**40**); Rosie, 1964 (**116**); She Wants t' Swim, 1964 (**50**); Lovely, Lovely (Loverly, Loverly), 1965 (**70**); Let's Do the Freddie, 1965 (**40**); Hey You! Little Boo-Ga-Loo, 1966 (**76**); Back in the U.S.S.R., 1969 (**82**); Running, 1982 (**91**); The Twist (Yo, Twist!), 1988 (**16**) (with The Fat Boys)

Dance Rock — Philadelphia; real name is Ernest Evans

The Checkmates, Ltd.

Personnel: Sonny Charles (vocals); Bobby Stevens (vocals); Harvey Trees (vocals); Bill Van Buskirk (vocals); Marvin Smith (vocals)

Album: Love Is All We Have to Give, 1969

Singles: Love Is All I Have to Give, 1969 (**65**); Black Pearl, 1969 (**13**); Proud Mary, 1969 (**69**)

Soul Vocal — Indiana

Cher

Albums: All I Really Want to Do, 1965; Sonny Side of Cher, 1966; Cher, 1967; With Love, 1968; Backstage, 1968; Golden Greats, 1968; 3614 Jackson Highway, 1969; Cher, 1971; Cher, 1972; Foxy Lady, 1972; Hits of Cher, 1972; Bittersweet White Light, 1973; Half Breed, 1974; Dark Lady, 1974; Stars, 1975; Greatest Hits, 1975; I'd Rather Believe in You, 1977; Cherished, 1977; Take Me Home, 1979; Prisoner, 1979; Cher, 1981; I Paralyze, 1982; Best Of, 1985; Cher, 1987; Heart of

Cher

Stone, 1989; Love Hurts, 1991

Singles: All I Really Want to Do, 1965 (**15**); Where Do You Go, 1965 (**25**); Bang Bang (My Baby Shot Me Down), 1966 (**2**); Alfie, 1966 (**32**); Behind the Door, 1966 (**97**); Hey Joe, 1967 (**94**); You Better Sit Down Kids, 1967 (**9**); Gypsys, Tramps & Thieves, 1971 (**1**); The Way of Love, 1972 (**7**); Living in a House Divided, 1972 (**22**); Don't Hide Your Love, 1972 (**46**); Half Breed, 1973 (**1**); Dark Lady, 1974 (**1**); Train of Thought, 1974 (**27**); I Saw a Man and He Danced with His Wife, 1974 (**42**); Pirate, 1977 (**93**); Take Me Home, 1979 (**8**); Wasn't It Good, 1979 (**49**); Hell on Wheels, 1979 (**59**); I Found Someone, 1987 (**10**); We All Sleep Alone, 1988 (**14**); Skin Deep, 1988 (**79**); After All, 1989 (**6**) (with Peter Cetera); If I Could Turn Back Time, 1989 (**3**); Just Like Jesse James, 1989 (**8**); Heart of Stone, 1990 (**20**); It's in His Kiss (The Shoop Shoop Song), 1990; Love

Hurts, 1991; Save Up All Your Tears, 1991
　Rock Vocal—California

Don Cherry

Album: Swingin' for Two, 1956
Singles: Band of Gold, 1955 **(4)**; Wild Cherry, 1956 **(29)**; I'm Still a King to You, 1956 **(72)**; Ghost Town, 1956 **(22)**; I'll Be Around, 1956 **(78)**; Namely You, 1956 **(65)**; I Love You Drops, 1966 **(112)**; There Goes My Everything, 1967 **(113)**
　Pop Vocal—Texas

The Cherry People

Personnel: Dougy Grimes (vocals); Chris Grimes (guitars); Punky Meadows (guitars); Jan Zukowski (bass); Rocky Isaac (drums)
Album: The Cherry Tree, 1968

Singles: And Suddenly, 1968 **(45)**; Feelings, 1969 **(134)**
　Hard Rock—American

Chicago

Personnel: Peter Cetera (bass, vocals) replaced (1987) by Jason Scheff (bass, vocals); Robert Lamm (keyboards, vocals); Terry Kath (guitars, vocals; deceased 1977) replaced (1977) by Donnie Dacus (guitars, vocals) replaced (1979) by Chris Pinnick (guitars) replaced (1986) by DaWayne Bailey (guitars, vocals); James Pankow (trombone, vocals); Lee Loughnane (trumpet, vocals); Walter Parazaider (woodwinds); Daniel Seraphine (drums) replaced (1990) by John Keane (drums); added (1972) Laudir de Oliveira (percussion) replaced (1982)

Chicago: *left to right,* **de Oliveira, Loughnane, Cetera, Parazaider, Lamm, Seraphine, Pankow, Kath**

by Bill Champlin (guitars, keyboards, vocals)

Albums: Chicago Transit Authority, 1969; Chicago II, 1970; Chicago III, 1970; Chicago IV/Live at Carnegie Hall, 1971; Chicago V, 1972; Chicago VI, 1973; Chicago VII, 1974; Chicago VIII, 1975; Chicago IX/Greatest Hits, 1976; Chicago X, 1976; Chicago XI, 1977; Hot Streets, 1978; Chicago 13, 1979; Chicago XIV, 1980; Chicago XV/Greatest Hits Volume 2, 1981; Chicago 16, 1982; If You Leave Me Now, 1983; Chicago 17, 1984; Take Me Back to Chicago, 1985; Chicago 18, 1986; Chicago 19, 1988; Greatest Hits 1982–1989, 1989; Twenty 1, 1991; Group Portrait (box), 1991

Singles: Questions 67 & 68, 1969 **(71)**; Make Me Smile, 1970 **(9)**; 25 or 6 to 4, 1970 **(4)**; Does Anybody Really Know What Time It Is?, 1970 **(7)**; Free/Flight 602, 1971 **(20)**; Lowdown, 1971 **(35)**; Beginnings, 1971 **(7)**; Colour My World, 1971 **(7)**; I'm a Man, 1971 **(49)**; Questions 67 & 68, 1971 **(24)**; Saturday in the Park, 1972 **(3)**; Dialogue, 1972 **(24)**; Alma Mater, 1972; Feelin' Stronger Every Day, 1973 **(10)**; Just You 'n' Me, 1973 **(4)**; (I've Been) Searchin' So Long, 1974 **(9)**; Call on Me, 1974 **(6)**; Happy Man, 1974; Wishing You Were Here, 1974 **(11)**; Harry Truman, 1975 **(13)**; Old Days, 1975 **(5)**; Brand New Love Affair, 1975 **(61)**; Another Rainy Day in New York City, 1976 **(32)**; If You Leave Me Now, 1976 **(1)**; You Are on My Mind, 1977 **(49)**; Baby, What a Big Surprise, 1977 **(4)**; Little One, 1978 **(44)**; Take Me Back to Chicago, 1978 **(63)**; Alive Again, 1978 **(14)**; No Tell Lover, 1979 **(14)**; Gone Long Gone, 1979 **(73)**; Must Have Been Crazy, 1979 **(83)**; Street Player, 1979; Run Away, 1980; Thunder and Lightning, 1980 **(56)**; Song for You, 1980; Hard to Say I'm Sorry, 1982 **(1)**; Love Me Tomorrow, 1982 **(22)**; What You're Missing, 1982 **(81)**; Prima Donna, 1984; Stay the Night, 1984 **(16)**; Hard Habit to Break, 1984 **(3)**; You're the Inspiration, 1984 **(3)**; Along Comes a Woman, 1985 **(14)**; 25 or 6 to 4 (1987 version), 1987 **(48)**; Will You Still Love Me?, 1986 **(3)**; If She Would Have Been Faithful, 1987 **(17)**; Niagara Falls, 1987 **(91)**; I Don't Want to Live Without Your Love, 1988 **(3)**; Look Away, 1988 **(1)**; You're Not Alone, 1989 **(10)**; We Can Last Forever, 1989 **(55)**; What Kind of Man Would I Be, 1989 **(5)**; Hearts in Trouble, 1990 **(75)**; Chasin' the Wind, 1991; You Come to My Senses, 1991

Jazz/Pop Rock—Chicago; guitarist Kath killed himself accidentally while playing Russian Roulette with a friend

Chicken Shack

Personnel: Stan Webb (guitars, vocals); Andy Sylvester (bass) replaced (1971) by John Glascock (bass) replaced (1973) by Bob Daisley (bass) replaced (1974) by Rob Hull (bass) replaced (1978) by Steve York (bass) replaced (1978) by Paul Martinez (bass) replaced (1979) by Alan Scott (bass) replaced (1981) by Andy Pyle (bass); Christine Perfect (keyboards, vocals) replaced (1969) by Paul Raymond (keyboards) replaced (1974) by Dave Wilkinson (keyboards) replaced (1978) by Robbie Blunt (guitars) replaced (1978) by Tony Ashton (keyboards) replaced (1979) by Paul

Butler (guitars, vocals); Dave Bidwell (drums) replaced (1970) by Hughie Flint (drums) replaced (1971) by Paul Hancox (drums) replaced (1974) by Alan Powell (drums) replaced (1978) by Ed Spevock (drums) replaced (1979) by Ric Lee (drums)

Albums: Forty Blue Fingers Freshly Packed and Ready to Serve, 1968; O.K. Ken, 1968; 100 Ton Chicken, 1969; Accept! Chicken Shack, 1970; Imagination Lady, 1972; Unlucky Boy, 1973; Goodbye, 1974; The Best of Chicken Shack, 1976; The Creeper, 1978; Chicken Shack, 1979; In the Can, 1980; Roadies Concerto, 1981

Blues Rock—British

The Chiffons

Personnel: Barbara Lee (vocals); Patricia Bennett (vocals); Sylvia Peterson (vocals); Judy Craig (vocals)

Albums: The Chiffons, 1963; He's So Fine, 1963; One Fine Day, 1963; Everything You Always Wanted to Hear, 1964; Sweet Talkin' Guy, 1966

Singles: Tonight's the Night, 1960 **(76)**; He's So Fine, 1963 **(1)**; One Fine Day, 1963 **(5)**; A Love So Fine, 1963 **(40)**; I Have a Boyfriend, 1963 **(36)**; Easy to Love, 1964 **(105)**; Sailor Boy, 1964 **(81)**; Nobody Knows What's Goin' On (in My Mind but Me), 1965 **(49)**; Sweet Talkin' Guy, 1966 **(10)**; Out of This World, 1966 **(67)**; Stop, Look and Listen, 1966 **(85)**; My Boyfriend's Back, 1966 **(117)**

Pop Vocal—New York

The Chi-Lites

Personnel: Eugene Record (vocals); Robert Lester (vocals); Marshall Thompson (vocals); Cradel "Red" Jones (vocals)

Albums: Give It Away, 1969; I Like Your Lovin', 1970; (For God's Sake) Give More Power to the People, 1971; A Lonely Man, 1972; The Chi-Lites Greatest Hits, 1972; A Letter to Myself, 1973; Chi-Lites, 1973; Toby, 1974; Half a Love, 1975; Happy Being Lonely, 1976; Greatest Hits Volume 2, 1976; The Fantastic Chi-Lites, 1977; Heavenly Body, 1980; Me and You, 1982; Bottom's Up, 1983

Singles: Give It Away, 1969 **(88)**; Let Me Be the Man My Daddy Was, 1969 **(94)**; The Twelfth of Never, 1969 **(122)**; 24 Hours of Sadness, 1970 **(119)**; I Like Your Lovin' (Do You Like Mine), 1970 **(72)**; Are You My Woman? (Tell Me So), 1970 **(72)**; (For God's Sake) Give More Power to the People, 1971 **(26)**; We Are Neighbors, 1971 **(70)**; Have You Seen Her, 1971 **(3)**; I Want to Pay You Back (For Loving Me), 1971 **(95)**; Oh Girl, 1972 **(1)**; The Coldest Days of My Life (Part 1), 1972 **(47)**; A Lonely Man/The Man & the Woman (The Boy & the Girl), 1972 **(57)**; We Need Order, 1972 **(61)**; A Letter to Myself, 1973 **(33)**; My Heart Just Keeps on Breakin', 1973 **(92)**; Stoned Out of My Mind, 1973 **(30)**; I Found Sunshine, 1973 **(47)**; Homely Girl, 1974 **(54)**; There Will Never Be Any Peace (Until God Is Seated at the Conference Table), 1974 **(63)**; You Got to Be the One, 1974 **(83)**; Toby/That's How Long, 1975 **(78)**; It's Time for Love, 1975 **(94)**

Soul/R & B Vocal—Chicago

The Chimes

Personnel: Leonard Cocco (vocals)

Singles: Once in Awhile, 1960 **(11)**; I'm in the Mood for Love, 1961 **(38)**

Pop Vocal — New York

The Chipmunks

Albums: Let's All Sing with the Chipmunks, 1959; Sing Again with the Chipmunks, 1960; Christmas with the Chipmunks, 1962; The Chipmunks Sing the Beatle Hits, 1964; Chipmunks A-Go-Go, 1965; Chipmunk Punk, 1980; Urban Chipmunk, 1981; A Chipmunk Christmas, 1981; Chipmunk Rock, 1982

Singles: The Chipmunk Song, 1958 **(1)**; Alvin's Harmonica, 1959 **(3)**; Ragtime Cowboy Joe, 1959 **(16)**; The Chipmunk Song, 1959 **(41)**; Alvin's Orchestra, 1960 **(33)**; Alvin for President, 1960 **(95)**; The Chipmunk Song, 1960 **(45)**; Rudolph the Red Nosed Reindeer, 1960 **(21)**; The Chipmunk Song, 1961 **(39)**; Alvin's Harmonica, 1961 **(73)**; Rudolph the Red Nosed Reindeer, 1961 **(47)**; The Alvin Twist, 1962 **(40)**; The Chipmunk Song, 1962 **(40)**; Alvin's Harmonica, 1962 **(87)**; Rudolph the Red Nosed Reindeer, 1962 **(77)**; All My Loving, 1964 **(134)**; You May Be Right, 1980 **(101)**

Novelty Pop — American; created by Ross Bagdasarian (a.k.a. David Seville); Alvin, Simon and Theodore became cartoon characters in the 1960s; following his death in 1972, Bagdasarian's son Ross, Jr. became "David Seville"

Chocolate Watchband

Personnel: Gary Osborne (vocals, guitars); Paul Vigrass (vocals, guitars); Billy Lawrie (vocals, bass); Colin Allen (drums)

Albums: No Way Out, 1967; The Inner Mystique, 1967; One Step Beyond, 1968; Let's Talk About Girls, 1969

Singles: Sweet Young Thing, 1967; Are You Going to Be There (at the Love-In)?, 1967

Acid Rock — British

Chocolate Watchband: Lawrie, Osborne, Allen, Vigrass

The Choir

Personnel: Wally Bryson (guitars, vocals); David Smalley (bass); James Bonfanti (drums)
Album: The Choir, 1967
Single: It's Cold Outside, 1967 **(68)**
Pop/Rock—Cleveland

The Chordettes

Personnel: Janet Ertel Buschman (vocals; deceased 1988); Carol Buschman (vocals); Dorothy Schwartz (vocals) replaced (1953) by Lynn Evans (vocals); Jinny Lockard (vocals) replaced (1953) by Margie Needham (vocals)
Albums: The Chordettes, 1956; Lollipop, 1958
Singles: The Wedding, 1956 **(91)**; Eddie My Love, 1956 **(14)**; Born to Be with You, 1956 **(5)**; Lay Down Your Arms, 1956 **(16)**; Teen Age Goodnight, 1956 **(45)**; Just Between You and Me, 1957 **(8)**; Soft Sands, 1957 **(73)**; Lollipop, 1958 **(2)**; Zorro, 1958 **(17)**; No Other Arms, No Other Lips, 1959 **(27)**; A Girl's Work Is Never Done, 1959 **(89)**; A Broken Vow, 1960 **(102)**; Never on Sunday, 1961 **(13)**; Faraway Star, 1961 **(90)**
Pop Vocal—Wisconsin

Lou Christie

Albums: Lou Christie, 1963; Lightnin' Strikes, 1966; Painter of Hits, 1966; Strikes Back, 1967; Strikes Again, 1968; Lou Christie, 1974
Singles: The Gypsy Cried, 1963 **(24)**; Two Faces Have I, 1963 **(6)**; How Many Teardrops, 1963 **(46)**; Shy Boy, 1963 **(119)**; Guitars and Bongos, 1964 **(123)**; Lightnin' Strikes, 1965 **(1)**; Outside the Gates of Heaven, 1966 **(45)**; Big Time, 1966 **(95)**; Rhapsody in the Rain, 1966 **(16)**; Painter, 1966 **(81)**; If My Car Could Only Talk, 1966 **(118)**; Since I Don't Have You, 1966 **(102)**; Shake Hands and Walk Away Cryin', 1967 **(95)**; I'm Gonna Make You Mine, 1969 **(10)**; Are You Getting Any Sunshine, 1969 **(73)**; Indian Lady, 1970 **(106)**; Beyond the Blue Horizon, 1974 **(80)**
Pop Vocal—Pennsylvania; real name is Lugee Geno Sacco

Susan Christie

Single: I Love Onions, 1966 **(63)**
Pop Vocal—Pennsylvania; sister of Lou Christie

Eugene Church

Singles: Pretty Girls Everywhere, 1958 **(36)**; Miami, 1959 **(67)**; Good News, 1960 **(106)**
R & B Vocal—Los Angeles

Circus

Personnel: Chris Burrows (vocals, guitars); Ian Jelts (guitars); Phillip Goodhand-Tait (keyboards); Kirk Riddle (bass); Mel Collins (saxophones); Alan Bunn (drums)
Albums: Circus, 1969; Listen to the Band, 1970
Jazz/Rock—British

Jimmy Clanton

Albums: Just a Dream, 1958; Go, Jimmy, Go, 1960
Singles: Just a Dream, 1958 **(4)**; A Letter to an Angel, 1958 **(25)**; A Part of Me, 1958 **(38)**; My Own True Love, 1959 **(33)**; Go, Jimmy, Go, 1959 **(5)**; Another Sleepless

Night, 1960 **(22)**; Come Back, 1960 **(63)**; Wait, 1960 **(91)**; What Am I Gonna Do, 1961 **(50)**; Venus in Blue Jeans, 1962 **(7)**; Darkest Street in Town, 1963 **(77)**; Red Don't Go with Blue, 1963 **(115)**; Curly, 1969 **(97)**

Soul Vocal—Louisiana

Claudine Clark

Album: Claudine Clark's Party Lights, 1962
Single: Party Lights, 1962 **(5)**
Pop Vocal—Georgia

Dave Clark Five

Huxley, Payton, Smith, Davidson, Clark

Personnel: Dave Clark (drums, vocals); Lenny Davidson (guitars, bass); Rick Huxley (guitars, bass); Dennis Payton (saxophones, keyboards); Michael Smith (keyboards, vocals)
Albums: A Session with the Dave Clark 5, 1963; Glad All Over, 1964; American Tour, 1964; Return, 1964; Coast to Coast, 1965; Catch Us If You Can, 1965; Wild Weekend, 1965; I Like It Like That, 1966; Greatest Hits, 1966; Try Too Hard,

1966; Satisfied with You, 1966; More Greatest Hits, 1966; 5 By 5, 1967; You Got What It Takes, 1967; Everybody Knows, 1968; 14 Titles by Dave Clark, 1968; Weekend in London, 1968; Glad All Over, 1975
Singles: Glad All Over, 1964 **(6)**; Bits and Pieces, 1964 **(4)**; Do You Love Me, 1964 **(11)**; I Knew It All the Time, 1964 **(53)**; Can't You See That She's Mine, 1964 **(4)**; Because, 1964 **(3)**; Everybody Knows, 1964 **(15)**; Any Way You Want It, 1964 **(14)**; Come Home, 1965 **(14)**; I'm Thinking, 1965 **(128)**; Reelin' and Rockin', 1965 **(23)**; I Like It Like That, 1965 **(7)**; Catch Us If You Can, 1965 **(4)**; Over and Over, 1965 **(1)**; At the Scene, 1966 **(18)**; Try Too Hard, 1966 **(12)**; Look Before You Leap, 1966 **(101)**; Please Tell Me Why, 1966 **(28)**; Satisfied with You, 1966 **(50)**; Nineteen Days, 1966 **(48)**; I've Got to Have a Reason, 1967 **(44)**; Everybody Knows, 1967 **(43)**; You Got What It Takes, 1967 **(7)**; You Must Have Been a Beautiful Baby, 1967 **(35)**; A Little Bit Now, 1967 **(67)**; Red and Blue, 1967 **(89)**; Please Stay, 1968 **(115)**

Pop Rock—British

Dee Clark

Albums: Keep It Up, 1959; How About That, 1960; Your Friends, 1961
Singles: Nobody but You, 1958 **(21)**; Just Keep It Up, 1959 **(18)**; Hey Little Girl, 1959 **(20)**; Blues, Get Off My Shoulder, 1959 **(109)**; How About That, 1959 **(33)**; At My Front Door, 1960 **(56)**; You're Looking Good, 1960 **(46)**; Because I Love You, 1961 **(105)**; Your Friends, 1961 **(34)**; Raindrops, 1961 **(2)**; Don't

Walk Away from Me, 1961 **(104)**; I'm Going Back to School, 1962 **(52)**; Shook Up Over You, 1963 **(125)**; Crossfire Time, 1963 **(92)**; Heartbreak, 1964 **(119)**; T.C.B., 1965 **(132)**

Soul/Rock — Chicago

Gene Clark

Albums: Gene Clark & the Gosdin Brothers, 1967; Fantastic Expedition, 1969 (with Doug Dillard); Through the Morning, 1969; White Light, 1972; Road Master, 1973; No Other, 1974; Early L.A. Sessions, 1975; Kansas City Southern, 1975; Two Sides to Every Story, 1977; Firebyrd, 1987; So Rebellious a Rebel, 1988 (with Carla Olson)

Country/Rock — American; former member of The Byrds and McGuinn, Clark & Hillman; died in 1991

Petula Clark

Albums: Downtown, 1965; I Know a Place, 1965; The World's Greatest International Hits, 1965;

My Love, 1966; I Couldn't Live Without Your Love, 1966; Color My World/Who Am I, 1967; These Are My Songs, 1967; The Other Man's Grass Is Always Greener, 1968; Petula, 1968; Petula Clark's Greatest Hits, Volume 1, 1968; Portrait of Petula, 1969; Just Pet, 1969; Memphis, 1970; Warm and Tender, 1971

Singles: Downtown, 1964 **(1)**; I Know a Place, 1965 **(3)**; You'd Better Come Home, 1965 **(22)**; Round Every Corner, 1965 **(21)**; My Love, 1965 **(1)**; A Sign of the Times, 1966 **(11)**; I Couldn't Live Without Your Love, 1966 **(9)**; Who Am I, 1966 **(21)**; Color My World, 1966 **(16)**; This Is My Song, 1967 **(3)**; Don't Sleep in the Subway, 1967 **(5)**; The Cat in the Window (the Bird in the Sky), 1967 **(26)**; The Other Man's Grass Is Always Greener, 1967 **(31)**; Kiss Me Goodbye, 1968 **(15)**; Don't Give Up, 1968 **(37)**; American Boys, 1968 **(59)**; Happy Heart, 1969 **(62)**; Look at Mine, 1969 **(89)**; No One Better Than You, 1969 **(93)**; My Guy, 1972 **(70)**; Wedding Song (There Is Love), 1972 **(61)**; Natural Love, 1982 **(66)**

Pop Vocal — British; Petula began hitting the U.K. charts in 1954 at the age of 21, with hits including "The Little Shoemaker," "Sailor," "Romeo" and "Majorca"

Sanford Clark

Albums: The Fool, 1956; They Call Me Country, 1957; Modern Romance, 1975

Singles: The Fool, 1956 **(7)**; A Cheat, 1956 **(74)**

Country/Pop — Oklahoma

Tony Clarke

Singles: (The Story of) Woman, Love and a Man, 1964 **(88)**; The Entertainer, 1965 **(31)**
Soul Vocal—Detroit; died in 1970

The Classics

Personnel: Emil Stucchio (vocals); Johnny Gambale (vocals); Tony Victor (vocals); Jamie Troy (vocals)
Singles: Cinderella, 1960 **(109)**; Life Is But a Dream Sweetheart, 1961 **(109)**; Till Then, 1963 **(20)**; P.S. I Love You, 1963 **(120)**
Pop Vocal—New York

Classics IV

Personnel: Dennis Yost (vocals); J. R. Cobb (guitars); Wally Eaton (guitars) replaced (1971) by Dean Daughtry (guitars, keyboards); Joe Wilson (bass) replaced (1971) by Billy Gilmore (bass); Kim Venable (drums) replaced (1971) by Michael Huey (drums)
Albums: Spooky (1968); Mamas and Papas Soul Train, 1968; Traces, 1969; Golden Greats, 1970; Dennis Yost & Classics IV, 1972; Very Best of Classics IV, 1975
Singles: Pollyanna, 1966 **(106)**; Spooky, 1968 **(3)**; Soul Train, 1968 **(90)**; Stormy, 1968 **(5)**; Traces, 1969 **(2)**; Everyday with You Girl, 1969 **(19)**; Change of Heart, 1969 **(49)**; Midnight, 1969 **(58)**; The Funniest Thing, 1970 **(59)**; God Knows I Loved Her, 1970 **(128)**; Where Did All the Good Times Go, 1970 **(69)**; What Am I Crying For, 1972 **(39)**; Rosanna, 1973 **(95)**; My First Day Without Her, 1975 **(94)**
Soft Rock—Florida

Judy Clay

Singles: Storybook Children, 1967 **(54)** (with Billy Vera); Country Girl—City Man, 1968 **(36)** (with Billy Vera); Where Do We Go, 1968 **(107)** (with Billy Vera); Private Number, 1968 **(75)** (with William Bell); My Baby Specializes, 1968 **(104)** (with William Bell); Greatest Love, 1970 **(122)**
Soul Vocal—New York; real last name is Guion

Clear Light

Personnel: Cliff De Young (vocals); Danny Kortchmar (guitars); Bob Seal (guitars); Doug Lubahn (bass); Ralph Shuckett (keyboards); Michael Ney (drums); Dallas Taylor (drums)
Album: Clear Light, 1967
Country Rock—American; De Young starred in the movie *Sunshine*

The Cleftones

Personnel: Herbie Cox (vocals); Charlie James (vocals); Berman Patterson (vocals); William McClain (vocals); Warren Corbin (vocals)
Singles: You Baby You, 1956 **(78)**; Little Girl of Mine, 1956 **(57)**; Heart and Soul, 1961 **(18)**; For Sentimental Reasons, 1961 **(60)**; Lover Come Back to Me, 1962 **(95)**
Soul Vocal—New York; originally called the Silvertones

Buzz Clifford

Albums: Baby Sittin' with Buzz, 1961; See Your Way Clear, 1969
Single: Baby Sittin' Boogie, 1961 **(6)**
Novelty Pop—Illinois

Mike Clifford

Singles: Close to Cathy, 1962 **(12)**; What to Do with Laurie, 1962 **(68)**; One Boy Too Late, 1963 **(96)**
Pop Vocal—Los Angeles

Climax Blues Band

Personnel: Peter Haycock (guitars, vocals); Colin Cooper (vocals, saxophones, guitars); Derek Holt (bass, vocals); Richard Jones (keyboards, vocals) replaced (1969) by Arthur Wood (keyboards) replaced (1972) by Peter Filleul (keyboards, vocals) replaced (1974) by Richard Jones (keyboards, vocals) replaced (1983) by George Glover (keyboards); George Newsome (drums) replaced (1972) by John Cuffley (drums)
Albums: Climax Chicago Blues Band, 1969; Climax Chicago Blues Band Plays On, 1969; A Lot of Bottle, 1970; Tightly Knit, 1971; Rich Man, 1972; FM Live, 1974; Sense of Direction, 1974; Stamp Album, 1975; 1969/1972, 1975; Gold Plated, 1977; Shine On, 1978; Real to Reel, 1979; Flying the Flag, 1980; Lucky for Some, 1981; Sample and Hold, 1983; Best Of, 1983; Loosen Up 74/76, 1984
Singles: Using the Power, 1975 **(110)**; Couldn't Get It Right, 1977 **(3)**; Makin' Love, 1978 **(91)**; Gotta Have More Love, 1980 **(47)**; I Love You, 1981 **(12)**; Dance the Night Away, 1981; Darlin', 1981; Breakdown, 1982
Blues/Jazz Rock—British

The Clique

Personnel: Dave; Oscar; Sid; Randy Shaw
Album: The Clique, 1969

Singles: Splash 1, 1967 **(113)**; Sugar on Sunday, 1969 **(22)**; I'll Hold Out My Hand, 1969 **(45)**; Sparkle and Shine, 1970 **(100)**
Pop/Rock—Texas

The Cliques

Personnel: Jesse Belvin (vocals); Eugene Church (vocals)
Single: The Girl in My Dreams, 1956 **(45)**
R & B Vocal—American

The Clovers

Personnel: John "Buddy" Bailey (vocals); Matthew McQuater (vocals); Harold Lucas (vocals); Harold Winely (vocals); Bill Harris (vocals); added (1952) Billy Mitchell (vocals)
Albums: The Clovers, 1956; Dance Party, 1957; In Clover, 1958; Love Potion No. 9, 1959; Their Greatest Recordings, 1960; Good Lovin', 1960; One Mint Julep, 1961
Singles: Love, Love, Love, 1956 **(30)**; Love Potion No. 9, 1959 **(23)**; The Honeydripper, 1961 **(110)**; Stop Pretending, 1963 **(134)**
R & B—Washington, D.C.

Clouds

Personnel: Ian Ellis (guitars, bass, vocals); Billy Ritchie (keyboards, bass, guitars, vocals); Harry Hughes (drums)
Albums: Scrapbook, 1969; Up Above Our Heads, 1969; Watercolour Days, 1970
Art Rock—British

The Coasters

Personnel: Carl Gardner (vocals); Leon Hughes (vocals); Billy Guy (vocals); Adolph Jacobs (guitars); Bobby Nunn (bass; deceased 1986) replaced (1958) by Will Jones (vocals); added (1957) Cornelius Gunter (vocals; deceased 1990) replaced (1961) by Earl Carroll (vocals)

Albums: The Coasters, 1957; Rock 'n' Roll with the Coasters, 1957; Keep Rockin' with the Coasters, 1958; Greatest Hits, 1958; The Coasters, 1959; Top Hits, 1960; One by One, 1961; Coastin' Along, 1962; All Time Greatest Hits, 1967; On Broadway, 1971; 20 Great Originals, 1978

Singles: One Kiss Led to Another, 1956 (**73**); Searchin', 1957 (**3**); Young Blood, 1957 (**8**); Idol with the Golden Head, 1957 (**64**); Yakety Yak, 1958 (**1**); Charlie Brown, 1959 (**2**); Along Came Jones, 1959 (**9**); Poison Ivy, 1959 (**7**); I'm a Hog for You, 1959 (**38**); What About Us, 1959 (**47**); Run Red Run, 1959 (**36**); Besame Mucho (Part 1), 1960 (**70**); Wake Me, Shake Me, 1960 (**51**); Shoppin' for Clothes, 1960 (**83**); Wait a Minute, 1961 (**37**); Little Egypt (Ying-Yang), 1961 (**23**); Girls Girls Girls (Part 2), 1961 (**96**); T'ain't Nothin' to Me, 1964 (**64**); Love Potion Number Nine, 1971 (**76**)

R & B Vocal—Los Angeles

Eddie Cochran

Albums: Eddie Cochran, 1960; Cherished Memories, 1962; Memorial Album, 1963; Singing to My Baby, 1963; Never to Be Forgotten, 1963; My Way, 1964; Summertime Blues, 1969; C'mon Everybody, 1970; Legendary, 1971; Legendary Masters, 1972; Very Best of Eddie Cochran, 1975; Singles

Album, 1979; 20th Anniversary Album, 1980

Singles: Sittin' in the Balcony, 1957 (**18**); Drive In Show, 1957 (**82**); Jeannie Jeannie Jeannie, 1958 (**94**); Summertime Blues, 1958 (**8**); C'mon Everybody, 1958 (**35**); Teenage Heaven, 1959 (**99**); Something Else, 1959 (**58**); Three Steps to Heaven, 1960 (**108**)

Pop/Rock—Oklahoma; killed in an auto accident in England on 4/17/60

Wayne Cochran

Albums: High & Ridin', 1966; Alive & Well, 1967; Old King Gold, 1968; Wayne Cochran, 1968; Cochran, 1973

Single: Harlem Shuffle, 1965 (**127**)

Pop/Rock—American

Joe Cocker

Albums: With a Little Help from My Friends, 1969; Joe Cocker, 1969; Mad Dogs & Englishmen, 1971; Cocker Happy, 1971; Something to Say, 1973; I Can Stand a Little Rain, 1974; Jamaica Say You Will, 1975; Stingray, 1976; Live in L.A., 1976; Greatest Hits, 1977; Luxury You Can Afford, 1978; Space Captain, 1982; Sheffield Steel, 1982; Joe Cocker Collection, 1982; One More Time, 1983; Off the Record, 1984; Civilized Man, 1984; Cocker, 1986; Unchain My Heart, 1987; Classics, 1988; One Night of Sin, 1989

Singles: With a Little Help from My Friends, 1968 (**68**); Feeling Alright, 1969 (**69**); Delta Lady, 1969 (**69**); She Came in Through the Bathroom Window, 1969 (**30**); The Letter, 1970 (**7**); Cry Me a River, 1970 (**11**); High Time We Went,

1971 **(22)**; Black-Eyed Blues, 1971 **(95)**; Feeling Alright, 1972 **(33)**; Midnight Rider, 1972 **(27)**; Woman to Woman, 1972 **(56)**; Pardon Me Sir, 1973 **(51)**; Put Out the Light, 1974 **(46)**; It's a Sin When You Love Somebody, 1974 **(95)**; You Are So Beautiful, 1975 **(5)**; Fun Time, 1978 **(43)**; Up Where We Belong, 1982 **(1)** (with Jennifer Warnes); Threw It Away, 1983 **(104)**; Civilized Man, 1984; Crazy in Love, 1984; Edge of a Dream, 1984 **(69)**; Shelter Me, 1986 **(91)**; You Can Leave Your Hat On, 1986; Don't You Love Me Anymore, 1986; Love Lives On, 1987; Unchain My Heart, 1987; A Woman Loves a Man, 1988; When the Night Comes, 1989 **(11)**; What Are You Doing with a Fool Like Me, 1990 **(96)**

Blues/Rock — British; Joe starred in the film *Mad Dogs and Englishmen* and appeared at the Woodstock festival

The C.O.D.'s

Personnel: Larry Brownlee (vocals; deceased 1978); Robert Lewis (vocals); Carl Washington (vocals)

Singles: Michael, 1965 **(41)**; I'm a Good Guy, 1966 **(128)**

R & B Vocal — Chicago

Leonard Cohen

Albums: Songs of Leonard Cohen, 1968; Songs from a Room, 1969; Songs of Love and Hate, 1971; Live Songs, 1973; New Skin for Old Ceremony, 1974; Best of Leonard Cohen, 1975; Death of a Ladies Man, 1977; Recent Songs, 1979;

Various Positions, 1985; I'm Your Man, 1988

Folk/Poetic Vocal — Canadian

Cold Blood

Personnel: Lydia Pense (vocals); Raul Matute (keyboards); Larry Field (guitars) replaced (1973) by Michael Sasaki (guitars); Rod Ellicott (bass) replaced (1976) by Domingo Balinton (bass); Larry Jonutz (trumpet) replaced (1973) by Max Haskett (trumpet, vocals); Danny Hull (saxophones, vocals) replaced (1973) by Mel Martin (saxophones) replaced (1974) by David Luell (saxophones) replaced (1976) by Danny Hull (saxophones, vocals); Frank J. Davis (drums) replaced (1971) by Sandy McKee (drums) replaced (1973) by Gaylord Birch (drums) replaced (1976) by Harvey Hughes (drums); Mic Gillette (horns) left group (1971)

Albums: Cold Blood First Blood, 1969; Sisyphus, 1971; First Taste of Sin, 1972; Thriller, 1973; Lydia, 1974; Lydia Pense & Cold Blood, 1976

Singles: You Got Me Hummin', 1970 **(52)**; I'm a Good Woman, 1970 **(125)**; Too Many People, 1970 **(107)**

Psychedelic Rock — San Francisco; Pense had a reputation for using the occult in her stage persona

Nat King Cole

Albums: Ballads of the Day, 1956; After Midnight, 1957; Love Is the Thing, 1957; This Is Nat "King" Cole, 1957; Just One of Those Things, 1957; St. Louis Blues, 1958; Cole Espanol, 1958; The Very Thought of You, 1958; To Whom It May Concern, 1959; Tell Me All

About Yourself, 1960; Wild Is Love, 1960; The Touch of Your Lips, 1961; Nat King Cole Sings, 1962; Ramblin' Rose, 1962; Dear Lonely Hearts, 1962; Where Did Everyone Go?, 1963; Those Lazy-Hazy-Crazy Days of Summer, 1963; I Don't Want to Be Hurt Anymore, 1964; My Fair Lady, 1964; L-O-V-E, 1965; Unforgettable, 1965; Songs from "Cat Ballou" and Other Motion Pictures, 1965; Looking Back, 1965; Nat King Cole at the Sands, 1966; The Great Songs!, 1966; The Best of Nat King Cole, 1968; Close-Up, 1969

Singles: Darling Je Vous Aime Beaucoup, 1955 **(7)**; The Sand and the Sea, 1955 **(23)**; A Blossom Fell, 1955 **(2)**; If I May, 1955 **(8)**; My One Sin, 1955 **(24)**; Someone You Love, 1955 **(13)**; Forgive My Heart, 1955 **(13)**; Take Me Back to Toyland, 1955 **(47)**; I'm Gonna Laugh You Right Out of My Life, 1956 **(57)**; Ask Me, 1956 **(18)**; Nothing Ever Changes My Love for You, 1956 **(72)**; Too Young to Go Steady, 1956 **(21)**; Never Let Me Go, 1956 **(79)**; That's All There Is to That, 1956 **(16)**; My Dream Sonata, 1956 **(59)**; Night Lights, 1956 **(11)**; To the Ends of the Earth, 1956 **(25)**; Ballerina, 1957 **(18)**; You Are My First Love, 1957 **(65)**; When Rock and Roll Come to Trinidad, 1957 **(48)**; Stardust, 1957 **(79)**; Send for Me, 1957 **(6)** (with The Four Knights); My Personal Possession, 1957 **(21)**; With You on My Mind/The Song of Raintree County, 1957 **(30)**; Angel Smile, 1958 **(33)**; Looking Back, 1958 **(5)**; Do I Like It, 1958 **(67)**; Come Closer to Me, 1958 **(38)**; Nothing in the World, 1958 **(99)**; Non Dimenticar (Don't Forget), 1958 **(45)**; Give Me Your Love, 1959 **(82)**; Madrid, 1959 **(85)**; You Made Me Love You, 1959 **(45)**; I Must Be Dreaming, 1959 **(69)**; Midnight Flyer, 1959 **(51)**; Sweet Bird of Youth, 1959 **(96)**; Time and the River, 1960 **(30)**; Whatcha' Gonna Do, 1960 **(92)**; That's You, 1960 **(101)**; My Love, 1960 **(47)** (with Stan Kenton); The Christmas Song, 1960 **(80)**; If I Knew, 1960 **(86)**; Illusion, 1961 **(108)**; Take a Fool's Advice, 1961 **(71)**; Let True Love Begin, 1961 **(73)**; Cappucina, 1961 **(115)**; Step Right Up (and Say You Love Me), 1962 **(106)**; The Right Thing to Say, 1962 **(110)**; Ramblin' Rose, 1962 **(2)**; Dear Lonely Hearts, 1962 **(13)**; The Christmas Song, 1962 **(65)**; All Over the World, 1963 **(42)**; Nothing Goes Up (Without Coming Down), 1963 **(87)**; Those Lazy-Hazy-Crazy Days of Summer, 1963 **(6)**; That Sunday, That Summer, 1963 **(12)**; Mr. Wishing Well, 1963 **(92)**; My True Carrie, Love, 1964 **(49)**; I Don't Want to Be Hurt Anymore, 1964 **(22)**; People, 1964 **(100)**; More and More of Your Amor, 1964 **(102)**; I Don't Want to See Tomorrow, 1964 **(34)**; L-O-V-E, 1964 **(81)**; Looking Back, 1965 **(123)**; Let Me Tell You, Babe, 1966 **(90)**

Soul/Pop Vocal — Chicago; father of Natalie Cole; died of lung cancer in 1965; real last name was Coles

The Collectors

Personnel: Bill Henderson (vocals, guitars, keyboards); Glenn Miller (bass, vocals); Howie Vickers (vocals); Claire Lawrence (woodwinds, keyboards, vocals); Ross Turney (drums)

Albums: The Collectors, 1968; Grass and Wild Strawberries, 1968 Hard Rock—Canadian

Judy Collins

Albums: Maid of Constant Sorrow, 1962; Golden Apple of the Sun, 1963; 3rd Album, 1963; Concert, 1964; Fifth Album, 1965; Wild Flowers, 1967; In My Life, 1968; Who Knows Where the Time Goes, 1968; Recollections, 1969; Both Sides Now, 1971; Whales and Nightingales, 1971; Living, 1972; True Stories and Other Dreams, 1973; Judith, 1975; Bread and Roses, 1976; So Early in Spring, 1977; Save the Children, 1978; Hard Time for Lovers, 1979; Running for My Life, 1980; Times of Our Lives, 1982; Shooting Star, 1984; Home Again, 1984; Colors of the Day, 1986; Trust Your Heart, 1987; Sanity and Grace, 1988; Fires of Eden, 1991

Singles: Hard Loving Loser, 1967 **(97)**; Both Sides Now, 1968 **(8)**; Someday Soon, 1969 **(55)**; Chelsea Morning, 1969 **(78)**; Turn! Turn! Turn!, 1969 **(69)**; Amazing Grace, 1970 **(15)**; Open the Door (Song for Judith), 1971 **(90)**; Cook with Honey, 1973 **(32)**; Secret Gardens, 1975 **(122)**; Send in the Clowns, 1975 **(36)**; Send in the Clowns, 1977 **(19)**; Hard Time for Lovers, 1979 **(66)**; It's Gonna Be One of Those Nights, 1982; Memory, 1982; Home Again, 1984; Only You, 1985; Fires of Eden, 1991

Folk/Rock—Denver; Judy was the inspiration for CSN song "Suite: Judy Blue Eyes"

Colosseum

Personnel: Jon Hiseman (drums); Dick Heckstall-Smith (saxophones); David Greenslade (keyboards); Jim Roche (guitars) replaced (1969) by James Litherland (guitars, vocals) replaced (1970) by Dave Clempson (guitars); Tony Reeves (bass) replaced (1970) by Mark Clarke (bass); added (1970) Chris Farlowe (vocals)

Albums: Those Who Are About to Die Salute You, 1969; Valentyne Suite, 1969; Daughter of Time, 1970; Grass Is Greener/Best Of, 1970; Colosseum Live, 1971; The Collector's Colosseum, 1971

Jazz/Rock—British

Perry Como

Albums: So Smooth, 1955; We Get Letters, 1957; Merry Christmas Music, 1957; Dream Along with Me, 1957; Saturday Night with Mr. C., 1958; Como's Golden Records, 1958; When You Come to the End of the Day, 1959; Como Swings, 1959; Season's Greetings, 1960; Sing to Me, Mr. C., 1961; By Request, 1962; The Best of Irving Berlin's Songs from "Mr. President," 1962;

The Songs I Love, 1963; The Scene Changes, 1965; Lightly Latin, 1966; Perry Como in Italy, 1966; Seattle, 1969; It's Impossible, 1971; I Think of You, 1971; And I Love You So, 1973; Perry, 1974; Just Out of Reach, 1975

Singles: Ko Ko Mo (I Love You So), 1955 **(2)**; Chee Chee-Oo-Chee (Sang the Little Bird), 1955 **(12)** (with Jaye P. Morgan); Two Lost Souls, 1955 **(18)** (with Jaye P. Morgan); Tina Marie, 1955 **(5)**; Fooled, 1955 **(20)**; All at Once You Love Her, 1955 **(11)**; The Rose Tattoo, 1955 **(79)**; Hot Diggity (Dog Ziggity Boom), 1956 **(1)**; Juke Box Baby, 1956 **(10)**; More, 1956 **(4)**; Glendora, 1956 **(8)**; Somebody Up There Likes Me, 1956 **(18)**; Dream Along with Me (I'm on My Way to a Star), 1956 **(85)**; Moonlight Love, 1956 **(42)**; Chincherinchee, 1956 **(59)**; Round and Round, 1957 **(1)**; Mi Casa, Su Casa (My House Is Your House), 1957 **(50)**; The Girl with the Golden Braids, 1957 **(13)**; My Little Baby, 1957 **(48)**; Dancin', 1957 **(76)**; Just Born (to Be Your Baby), 1957 **(12)**; Ivy Rose, 1957 **(18)**; Jingle Bells, 1957 **(74)**; Catch a Falling Star, 1958 **(1)**; Magic Moments, 1958 **(4)**; Kewpie Doll, 1958 **(6)**; Dance Only with Me, 1958 **(19)**; Moon Talk, 1958 **(28)**; Love Makes the World Go 'Round, 1958 **(33)**; Mandolins in the Moonlight, 1958 **(47)**; Tomboy, 1959 **(29)**; I Know, 1959 **(47)**; Delaware, 1960 **(22)**; I Know What God Is, 1960 **(81)**; Make Someone Happy, 1960 **(80)**; You're Following Me, 1961 **(92)**; Caterina, 1962 **(23)**; (I Love You) Don't You Forget It, 1963 **(39)**; Dream On Little Dreamer, 1965 **(25)**; Oowee, Oowee, 1965 **(88)**; Coo Coo Roo Coo Coo

Paloma, 1966 **(128)**; Here Comes My Baby, 1967 **(124)**; Stop! And Think It Over, 1967 **(92)**; The Father of Girls, 1968 **(92)**; Happy Man, 1968 **(134)**; Seattle, 1969 **(38)**; It's Impossible, 1970 **(10)**; I Think of You, 1971 **(53)**; And I Love You So, 1973 **(29)**; Love Don't Care (Where It Grows), 1973 **(106)**; Christmas Dream, 1974 **(92)**

Pop Vocal — Pennsylvania; appeared in the films *Doll Face, Something for the Boys, If I'm Lucky* and *Words and Music*

Arthur Conley

Albums: Sweet Soul Music, 1967; Shake, Rattle & Roll, 1967; Soul Directions, 1968; More Sweet Soul, 1968

Singles: Sweet Soul Music, 1967 **(2)**; Shake, Rattle & Roll, 1967 **(31)**; Whole Lotta Woman, 1967 **(73)**; Funky Street, 1968 **(14)**; People Sure Act Funny, 1968 **(58)**; Aunt Dora's Love Soul Shack, 1968 **(85)**; Ob-La-Di, Ob-La-Da, 1969 **(51)**; Run On, 1969 **(115)**; God Bless, 1970 **(107)**

Soul/Rock — Atlanta

The Contours

Personnel: Joe Billingslea (vocals); Billy Gordon (vocals); Hubert Johnson (vocals; deceased 1981); Huey Davis (vocals); Billy Hoggs (vocals); Sylvester Potts (vocals)

Albums: Do You Love Me, 1962; Baby Hit & Run, 1974

Singles: Do You Love Me, 1962 **(3)**; Shake Sherry, 1962 **(43)**; Don't Let Her Be Your Baby, 1963 **(64)**; Can You Do It, 1964 **(41)**; Can You Jerk Like Me, 1964 **(47)**; First I Look at the Purse, 1965 **(57)**; Just a Little Misunderstanding, 1966 **(85)**;

It's So Hard Being a Loser, 1967
(79); Do You Love Me, 1988 **(11)**
R & B Vocal — Detroit

Sam Cooke

Albums: Sam Cooke, 1958; Only
Sixteen, 1959; Cooke's Tour, 1960;
Hits of the 50's, 1960; My Kind of
Blues, 1961; Twistin' the Night
Away, 1962; The Best of Sam
Cooke, 1962; Mr. Soul, 1963; Night
Beat, 1963; Soul Stirrers, 1964; Ain't
That Good News, 1964; Sam Cooke
at the Copa, 1964; Two Sides of
Sam Cooke, 1964; Shake, 1965; The
Best of Sam Cooke, Volume 2,
1965; Try a Little Love, 1965; Un-
forgettable Sam Cooke, 1966; Man
Who Invented Soul, 1968; Forever,
1976; Feel It! — Sam Cooke Live at
the Harlem Square Club 1963, 1985;
A Man and His Music, 1986
Singles: You Send Me, 1957 **(1)**;
Summertime, 1957 **(81)**; I'll Come
Running Back to You, 1957 **(18)**;
Forever, 1957 **(60)**; (I Love You) for
Sentimental Reasons, 1957 **(17)**;
Desire Me, 1957 **(47)**; Lonely
Island, 1958 **(26)**; You Were Made
for Me, 1958 **(39)**; Win Your Love
for Me, 1958 **(22)**; Love You Most
of All, 1958 **(26)**; Everybody Likes
to Cha Cha Cha, 1959 **(31)**; Only
Sixteen, 1959 **(28)**; Summertime
(Part 2), 1959 **(106)**; There, I've
Said It Again, 1959 **(81)**; No One
(Can Ever Take Your Place), 1960
(103); Teenage Sonata, 1960 **(50)**;
Wonderful World, 1960 **(12)**; Chain
Gang, 1960 **(2)**; Sad Mood, 1960
(29); That's It — I Quit — I'm Movin'
On, 1961 **(31)**; Cupid, 1961 **(17)**; Feel
It, 1961 **(56)**; It's All Right, 1961
(93); Twistin' the Night Away, 1962
(9); Having a Party, 1962 **(17)**;
Bring It on Home to Me, 1962 **(13)**;

Nothing Can Change This Love,
1962 **(12)**; Somebody Have Mercy,
1962 **(70)**; Send Me Some Lovin',
1963 **(13)**; Baby, Baby, Baby, 1963
(66); Love Will Find a Way, 1963
(105); Another Saturday Night, 1963
(10); Frankie and Johnny, 1963 **(14)**;
Little Red Rooster, 1963 **(11)**; Good
News, 1964 **(11)**; Good Times, 1964
(11); Tennessee Waltz, 1964 **(35)**;
Cousin of Mine, 1964 **(31)**; That's
Where It's At, 1964 **(93)**; Shake,
1965 **(7)**; A Change Is Gonna
Come, 1965 **(31)**; It's Got the Whole
World Shakin', 1965 **(41)**; (Somebody) Ease My Troublin' Mind,
1965 **(115)**; When a Boy Falls in
Love, 1965 **(52)**; Sugar Dumpling,
1965 **(32)**; Feel It, 1966 **(95)**; Let's
Go Steady Again, 1966 **(97)**
Soul/Pop Vocal — Chicago; Sam
was shot to death on 12/11/64 at the
age of 29

The Cookies

Personnel: Earl-Jean McCrea
(vocals)
Album: The Cookies, 1963
Singles: Chains, 1962 **(17)**; Don't
Say Nothin' Bad (About My Baby),
1963 **(7)**; Will Power, 1963 **(72)**;
Girls Grow Up Faster Than Boys,
1963 **(33)**
Pop Vocal — American

Alice Cooper

Albums: Pretties for You, 1969;
Easy Action, 1969; Love It to
Death, 1971; Killer, 1971; School's
Out, 1972; Billion Dollar Babies,
1973; Muscle of Love, 1974;
Greatest Hits, 1974; Welcome to My
Nightmare, 1975; Alice Cooper Goes
to Hell, 1976; Lace & Whiskey,
1977; The Alice Cooper Show, 1977;

Alice Cooper

From the Inside, 1978; Flush the Fashion, 1980; Special Forces, 1981; Zipper Catches Skin, 1982; Da Da, 1983; Ladies Man, 1984; Constrictor, 1986; Raise Your Fist and Yell, 1987; Prince of Darkness, 1988; Trash, 1989; Hey Stoopid, 1991

Singles: I'm Eighteen, 1971 **(21)**; Caught in a Dream, 1971 **(94)**; Under My Wheels, 1971 **(59)**; Be My Lover, 1972 **(49)**; School's Out, 1972 **(7)**; Elected, 1972 **(26)**; Hello Hooray, 1973 **(35)**; No More Mr. Nice Guy, 1973 **(25)**; Billion Dollar Babies, 1973 **(57)**; Teenage Lament '74, 1973 **(48)**; Muscle of Love, 1974; Only Women Bleed, 1975 **(12)**; Department of Youth, 1975 **(67)**; Welcome to My Nightmare, 1975 **(45)**; I Never Cry, 1976 **(12)**; You and Me, 1977 **(9)**; Lace & Whiskey, 1977; Love at Your Convenience, 1978; How You Gonna See Me Now, 1978 **(12)**; Clones (We're All), 1980 **(40)**; Talk Talk, 1980; You Want It, You Got It, 1981; Seven and Seven Is, 1981; I Like Girls, 1982; I Am the Future, 1982; Freedom, 1987; Poison, 1989 **(7)**; House on Fire, 1990 **(56)**; Only My Heart Talkin', 1990 **(89)**; Hey Stoopid, 1991

Hard Rock—Arizona; real name is Vincent Furnier

The Corsairs

Personnel: Jay Uzzell (vocals); James Uzzell (vocals); Moses Uzell (vocals); George Wooten (vocals)

Singles: Smoky Places, 1961 **(12)**; I'll Take You Home, 1962 **(68)**

R & B Vocal—North Carolina

Dave "Baby" Cortez

Albums: Happy Organ, 1959; Fabulous Organ, 1960; Music 'Round the Clock, 1961; Rinky Dink, 1962; Organ Shindig, 1963; In Orbit with Dave "Baby" Cortez, 1964; Dave "Baby" Cortez, 1965; "Baby" & Jerry's House Rockers, 1966

Singles: The Happy Organ, 1959 **(1)**; The Whistling Organ, 1959 **(61)**; Piano Shuffle, 1959 **(103)**; Rinky Dink, 1962 **(10)**; Happy Weekend, 1962 **(67)**; Fiesta, 1962 **(96)**; Hot Cakes! 1st Serving, 1963 **(91)**; Organ Shout, 1963 **(76)**; Count Down, 1963 **(91)**; Popping Popcorn, 1965 **(132)**; Tweetie Pie, 1965 **(135)**

Instrumental—Detroit

Count Five

Personnel: Kenn Ellner (vocals); John Michalski (guitars); Sean Byrne (guitars); Roy Chaney (bass); Craig Atkinson (drums)

Album: Psychotic Reaction, 1966

Singles: Psychotic Reaction, 1966 **(5)**; Peace of Mind, 1966 **(125)**

Psychedelic Rock—California; band wore vampire costumes during some stage performances; Byrne is British

Count Five: *left to right,* Byrne, Chaney, Atkinson, Ellner, Michalski

Country Joe & The Fish

Hirsch, Cohen, Barthol, Melton, McDonald

Personnel: "Country" Joseph McDonald (vocals, guitars); Barry "The Fish" Melton (guitars, vocals); Bruce Barthol (bass); David Cohen (keyboards, guitars); Chicken Hirsch (drums)

Albums: Electric Music for the Mind, 1967; I Feel Like I'm Fixin' to Die, 1967; Together, 1968; Here We Go Again, 1969; Thinking of Woody Guthrie, 1969; Greatest Hits, 1969; Tonight I'm Singing for You, 1970; C. J. Fish, 1970; Quiet Day in Clichy, 1971; From Ashbury to Woodstock, 1971; Hold On It's Coming, 1971; War War War, 1971; Incredible Live, 1972; Paris Sessions, 1973; The Best of Country Joe & The Fish, 1973; Country Joe, 1975; Paradise with an Ocean View, 1975; The Essential, 1976; Love Is a Fire, 1976; Goodbye Blues, 1977; Reunion, 1977; Rock 'n' Roll from the Planet Earth, 1978; Leisure Suite, 1979; Child's Play, 1983

Singles: Not So Sweet Martha Lorraine, 1967 **(95)**; Who Am I, 1968 **(114)**; Here I Go Again, 1969 **(106)**; Breakfast for Two, 1975 **(92)**

Psychedelic Pop—California; popularized the "FISH" cheer at Woodstock, coined the phrase "political rock"

The Cowsills

Personnel: Barbara Cowsill (deceased 1985); Barry Cowsill; John Cowsill; Mary Cowsill; Paul Cowsill; Susan Cowsill

Albums: The Cowsills, 1967; We Can Fly, 1968; Captain Sad and His Ship of Fools, 1968; The Best of the Cowsills, 1969; The Cowsills in Concert, 1969; On My Side, 1971

Singles: Most of All, 1966 **(118)**; The Rain, The Park and Other Things, 1967 **(2)**; We Can Fly, 1968 **(21)**; In Need of a Friend, 1968 **(54)**; Indian Lake, 1968 **(10)**; Poor Baby, 1968 **(44)**; The Path of Love, 1968 **(132)** (John); The Candy Kid, 1968 **(118)**; Hair, 1969 **(2)**; The Prophecy of Daniel and John the Divine (Six-Six-Six), 1969 **(75)**; Silver Threads and Golden Needles, 1969 **(74)**; On My Side, 1971 **(108)**

Pop/Soft Rock—Rhode Island

Johnny Crawford

Albums: A Young Man's Fancy, 1962; His Greatest Hits, 1963

Singles: Daydreams, 1961 **(70)**; Patti Ann, 1962 **(43)**; Cindy's Birthday, 1962 **(8)**; Your Nose Is Gonna Grow, 1962 **(14)**; Rumors, 1962 **(12)**; Proud, 1963 **(29)**; Cry on My Shoulder, 1963 **(126)**; Cindy's Gonna Cry, 1963 **(72)**; Sandy, 1964

(108); Judy Loves Me, 1964 **(95)**

Pop Vocal—Los Angeles; starred with Chuck Connors in TV's "The Rifleman"

Crazy Elephant

Personnel: Robert Spencer (vocals); Hal Hing (vocals, guitars); Ronnie Bretone (bass); Larry Alufer (keyboards, vocals); Kenny Cohen (keyboards, saxophones, vocals); Bob Avery (drums)

Album: Crazy Elephant, 1969

Singles: Gimme Gimme Good Lovin', 1969 **(12)**; Sunshine, Red Wine, 1969 **(104)**; Gimme Some More, 1969 **(116)**

Psychedelic Pop—American

Cream

Personnel: Eric Clapton (guitars, vocals); Jack Bruce (bass, keyboards, vocals); Ginger Baker (drums, vocals)

Albums: Fresh Cream, 1966; Full Cream, 1966; Disraeli Gears, 1967; Wheels of Fire, 1968; Goodbye, 1969; The Best of Cream, 1969; Live Cream, 1970; Live Cream Volume 2, 1972; Off the Top, 1972; Heavy Cream, 1973; The Best of Cream Volume 2, 1975; The Best of Cream Live, 1977; Strange Brew—The Very Best of Cream, 1983

Singles: I Feel Free, 1967 **(116)**; Sunshine of Your Love, 1968 **(5)**; Anyone for Tennis, 1968 **(64)**; White Room, 1968 **(6)**; Crossroads, 1969 **(28)**; Badge, 1969 **(60)**; Strange Brew, 1969; Spoonful, 1969

Blues/Rock—British; made the film *Goodbye Cream* documenting final performance

Cream: Clapton, Baker, Bruce

Creedence Clearwater Revival

Personnel: John Fogerty (guitars, vocals); Tom Fogerty (guitars, vocals; deceased 1990); Stu Cook (bass); Doug Clifford (drums)

Albums: Creedence Clearwater Revival, 1968; Bayou Country, 1969; Green River, 1969; Willy and the Poorboys, 1969; Cosmo's Factory, 1970; Pendulum, 1971; Mardi Gras, 1972; Creedence Gold, 1973; More Creedence Gold, 1973; Live in Europe, 1974; Chronicle, 1976; CCR 1968/1969, 1978; CCR 1969, 1978; CCR 1970, 1978; The Royal Albert Hall Concert, 1980; Creedence Country, 1981; Chooglin', 1982; Chronicle Volume 2, 1984

Singles: Suzie Q, 1968 **(11)**; I Put a Spell on You, 1968 **(58)**; Proud Mary, 1969 **(2)**; Lodi/Bad Moon Rising, 1969 **(52)/(2)**; Green River/Commotion, 1969 **(2)/(30)**; Down on the Corner/Fortunate Son, 1969 **(3)/(14)**; Travelin' Band/Who'll Stop the Rain, 1970 **(2)**; Up Around the Bend/Run Through the Jungle, 1970 **(4)**; Lookin' Out My Back Door/Long As I Can See the Light, 1970 **(2)**; Hey Tonight/Have You Ever Seen the Rain, 1971 **(8)**; Sweet Hitch-Hiker, 1971 **(6)**; Someday Never Comes, 1972 **(25)**; I Heard It Through the Grapevine, 1976 **(43)**; Tombstone Shadow, 1981; Cotton Fields, 1981

Psychedelic Rock—California; group formed in Berkeley, California under the name The Golliwogs

The Crescendos

Personnel: George Lanuis (vocals); James Lanuis (vocals); Ken

Creedence Clearwater Revival: T. Fogerty, J. Fogerty, Cook, Clifford

Brigham (vocals); Tom Fortner (vocals); Jim Hall (vocals)
Single: Oh Julie, 1958 **(5)**
Pop Vocal—Nashville

The Crests

Personnel: Johnny Mastrangelo (vocals) replaced (1960) by James Ancrum (vocals); Harold Torres (vocals); Talmadge Gough (vocals); J. T. Carter (vocals); Patricia Van Dross (vocals)
Albums: The Crests Sing, 1958; Sing All the Biggies, 1959; Best of the Crests, 1960
Singles: Sweetest One, 1957 **(86)**; 16 Candles, 1958 **(2)**; Six Nights a Week, 1959 **(28)**; Flower of Love, 1959 **(79)**; The Angels Listened In, 1959 **(22)**; A Year Ago Tonight, 1959 **(42)**; Step by Step, 1960 **(14)**; Trouble in Paradise, 1960 **(20)**; Journey of Love, 1960 **(81)**; Isn't It Amazing, 1960 **(100)**; I Remember (in the Still of the Night), 1960 **(102)**; Guilty, 1963 **(123)**
R & B Vocal—New York

The Crew-Cuts

Personnel: John Perkins (vocals); Ray Perkins (vocals); Pat Barrett (vocals); Rudi Maugeri (vocals)
Albums: The Crew Cuts on the Campus, 1954; Gum Drop, 1955
Singles: Earth Angel, 1955 **(3)**; Ko Ko Mo (I Love You So), 1955 **(6)**; Don't Be Angry/Chop Chop Boom, 1955 **(14)**; A Story Untold, 1955 **(16)**; Gum Drop, 1955 **(10)**; Angels in the Sky, 1955 **(11)**; Mostly

Martha, 1955 **(31)**; Seven Days, 1956 **(18)**; Tell Me Why, 1956 **(45)**; Young Love, 1957 **(17)**

Pop Vocal—Canadian

The Crickets

Personnel: Buddy Holly (guitars, vocals; deceased 1959) left group (1958); Niki Sullivan (guitars); Joe B. Mauldin (bass); Jerry Allison (drums)

Albums: Chirpin' Crickets, 1958; In Style with the Crickets, 1960; Bobby Vee Meets the Crickets, 1961; Something Old, Something New, 1962; We Gotta Get Together, 1963

Singles: That'll Be the Day, 1957 **(1)**; Oh, Boy!, 1957 **(10)**; Maybe Baby, 1958 **(17)**; Think It Over, 1958 **(27)**; Fool's Paradise, 1958 **(58)**

Pop/Rock—American

The Critters

Gorka, Ryan, Ciccone, Decker, Daraway

Personnel: Don Ciccone (guitars, vocals); James Ryan (guitars); Kenneth Gorka (bass); Christopher Daraway (organ); Jack Decker (drums)

Albums: The Critters, 1966;

Younger Girl, 1966; Touch 'n' Go with the Critters, 1967

Singles: Younger Girl, 1966 **(42)**; Mr. Diengly Sad, 1966 **(17)**; Bad Misunderstanding, 1966 **(55)**; Marryin' Kind of Love, 1967 **(111)**; Don't Let the Rain Fall Down on Me, 1967 **(39)**; Little Girl, 1967 **(113)**

Pop/Rock—New Jersey

Crosby, Stills & Nash

Personnel: David Crosby (vocals, guitars); Stephen Stills (vocals, guitars, bass, keyboards); Graham Nash (vocals, guitars); Dallas Taylor (drums) replaced (1975) by Russ Kunkel (drums) replaced (1979) by Joe Vitale (drums, keyboards); added (1977) George Perry (bass); added (1977) Craig Doerge (keyboards)

Albums: Crosby, Stills & Nash, 1969; C S N, 1977; Replay, 1980; Daylight Again, 1982; Allies, 1983; Live It Up, 1990

Singles: Marrakesh Express, 1969 **(28)**; Suite: Judy Blue Eyes, 1969 **(21)**; Just a Song Before I Go, 1977 **(7)**; Fair Game, 1977 **(43)**; I Give, You Give Blind, 1978; Carry On, 1980; Wasted on the Way, 1982 **(9)**; Southern Cross, 1982 **(18)**; Too Much Love to Hide, 1982 **(69)**; War Games, 1983 **(45)**; Raise a Voice, 1983; Live It Up, 1990

Pop/Rock—American/British; made their second live appearance with Neil Young at Woodstock; played at the No Nukes and US festival concerts

Crow

Personnel: Dave Wagner (vocals); Dick Wiegand (guitars); Larry Wiegand (bass); Kirk Middlemist (key-

CSN: Crosby, Stills, Nash

boards); Denny Caswell (drums, vocals)

Albums: Crow Music, 1969; Crow by Crow, 1970; Mosaic, 1971; Best of Crow, 1972; Dave Wagner, Crow, 1972

Singles: Time to Make a Turn, 1969 **(123)**; Evil Woman Don't Play Your Games with Me, 1969 **(19)**; Slow Down, 1970 **(103)**; Cottage Cheese, 1970 **(56)**; Don't Try to Lay No Boogie Woogie on the King of Rock & Roll, 1970 **(52)**

Hard Rock—Minnesota

Cryan Shames

Personnel: Jim Fairs (guitars, bass, flutes); Tom Doody (vocals); Lenny Kerley (guitars, bass, vocals) replaced (1967) by Jerry Stone (guitars); Isaac Guillory (guitars, bass, keyboards) replaced (1967) by Dave Purple (bass, keyboards); J. C.

Cryan Shames: *back row,* **Fairs, Kerley, Guillory, Conroy;** *front,* **Doody, Hooke**

Hooke (vocals, percussion) replaced (1967) by Jim Pilster (percussion); Dennis Conroy (drums)

Albums: Sugar & Spice, 1966; A Scratch in the Sky, 1967; Synthesis, 1968

Singles: Sugar and Spice, 1966 **(49)**; I Wanna Meet You, 1966 **(85)**; It Could Be We're in Love, 1967 **(85)**; Mr. Unreliable, 1967 **(127)**; Up on the Roof, 1968 **(85)**; Young Birds Fly, 1968 **(99)**; Greenburg, Glickstein, Charles, David Smith & Jones, 1968 **(115)**

Pop/Rock—Chicago

The Crystals

Personnel: Dee Dee Kennibrew (vocals); Dolores "La La" Brooks (vocals); Mary Thomas (vocals) replaced (1963) by Darlene Love (vocals); Barbara Alston (vocals); Pat Wright (vocals) replaced (1963) by Frances Collins (vocals)

Albums: Twist Uptown, 1962; He's a Rebel, 1963; Greatest Hits, 1964

Singles: There's No Other (Like My Baby), 1961 **(20)**; Uptown, 1962 **(13)**; He's a Rebel, 1963 **(1)**; He's Sure the Boy I Love, 1962 **(11)**; Da Doo Ron Ron (When He Walked Me Home), 1963 **(3)**; Then He Kissed Me, 1963 **(6)**; Little Boy, 1964 **(92)**; All Grown Up, 1964 **(98)**

Pop Vocal—Brooklyn

The Cues

Personnel: Jimmy Breedlove (vocals); Ollie Jones (vocals); Abel DeCosta (vocals); Robie Kirk (vocals); Eddie Barnes (vocals)

Singles: Burn That Candle, 1955 **(86)**; Why, 1957 **(77)**

R & B Vocal—American

The Cuff Links

Personnel: Ron Dante (vocals)
Album: Tracy, 1969
Singles: Tracy, 1969 **(9)**; When Julie Comes Around, 1969 **(41)**; Run Sally Run, 1970 **(76)**

Bubblegum Pop—American

The Cyrkle

Back row, **Freed, Dawes;** *front row,* **Losekamp, Danneman**

Personnel: Michael Losekamp (guitars, vocals, keyboards); Donald Danneman (guitars, vocals); Earl Pickens (bass, vocals) replaced (1966) by Tom Dawes (bass, guitars); Martin Freed (drums, guitars); added (1967) John Simon (keyboards)

Albums: Red Rubber Ball, 1966; Neon, 1967

Singles: Red Rubber Ball, 1966 **(2)**; Turn-Down Day, 1966 **(16)**; Please Don't Ever Leave Me, 1966 **(59)**; I Wish You Could Be Here, 1967 **(70)**; We Had a Good Thing Goin', 1967 **(72)**; Penny Arcade, 1967 **(95)**; Turn of the Century, 1967 **(112)**

Pop/Rock—Pennsylvania; band was signed by Beatles' manager Brian Epstein

The Daily Flash

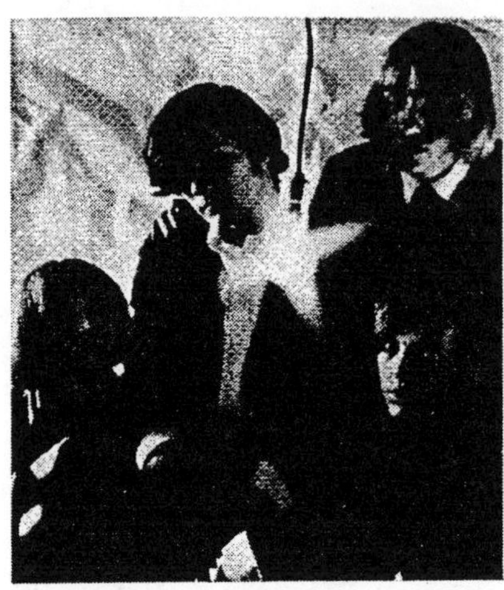

Personnel: Lalor; Keliehor; Hastings; MacAllister
Album: The Daily Flash, 1966
Singles: Jack of Diamonds, 1965; Violets of Dawn, 1966
Folk/Rock—California; appeared on the "Girl from U.N.C.L.E." TV show in 1966

Dale & Grace

Personnel: Dale Houston (vocals); Grace Broussard (vocals)
Album: I'm Leaving It Up to You, 1964
Singles: I'm Leaving It Up to You, 1963 **(1)**; Stop and Think It Over, 1964 **(8)**; The Loneliest Night, 1964 **(65)**; Darling It's Wonderful, 1964 **(114)**
Pop Vocal—Louisiana

Dick Dale & His Del-Tones

Albums: Surfer's Choice, 1963; Checkered Flag, 1963; Greatest Hits, 1966
Singles: Let's Go Trippin', 1961 **(60)**; King of the Surf Guitar, 1963 **(124)**; The Scavenger, 1963 **(98)**
Surf Rock—California

Vic Dana

Albums: More, 1963; Shangri-La, 1964; Red Roses for a Blue Lady, 1965
Singles: Little Altar Boy, 1961 **(45)**; I Will, 1962 **(47)**; Danger, 1963 **(96)**; More, 1963 **(42)**; Shangri-La, 1964 **(27)**; Love Is All We Need, 1964 **(53)**; Garden in the Rain, 1964 **(97)**; Red Roses for a Blue Lady, 1965 **(10)**; Bring a Little Sunshine (to My Heart), 1965 **(66)**; Moonlight and Roses (Bring Mem'ries of You, 1965 **(51)**; Crystal Chandelier, 1965 **(51)**; I Love You Drops, 1966 **(30)**; A Million and One, 1966 **(71)**; Distant Drums, 1966 **(114)**; If I Never Knew Your Name, 1970 **(47)**; Red Red Wine, 1970 **(72)**
Pop Vocal—California

The Danleers

Personnel: Jimmy Weston (vocals)
Single: One Summer Night, 1958 **(7)**
R & B Vocal—New York

Danny & The Juniors

Personnel: Danny Rapp (vocals; deceased 1983); Bill Carlucci (vocals); Frank Maffei (vocals); Joe Terranova (vocals); Dave White (vocals)
Albums: Rock & Roll Is Here to Stay, 1958; Twistin' All Night Long, 1958; Twistin' U.S.A., 1960; Pony Express, 1961
Singles: At the Hop, 1957 **(1)**; Rock and Roll Is Here to Stay, 1958

(19); Dottie, 1958 (39); Twistin'
U.S.A., 1960 (27); Pony Express,
1961 (60); Back to the Hop, 1960
(80); Twistin' All Night Long, 1962
(68) (with Freddy Cannon); Doin'
the Continental Walk, 1962 (93);
Oo-La-La-Limbo, 1963 (99)
Pop Vocal — Philadelphia

Dante & The Evergreens

Personnel: Donald Drowty (vo-
cals); Bill Young (vocals); Tony
Moon (vocals); Frank D. Rosenthal
(vocals)
Singles: Alley-Oop, 1960 (15);
Time Machine, 1960 (73); What
Are You Doing New Year's Eve,
1960 (107); Yeah Baby, 1961 (104)
Pop Vocal — Los Angeles

Bobby Darin

Albums: Bobby Darin, 1958;
That's All, 1959; This Is Darin,
1960; Darin at the Copa, 1960; For
Teenagers Only, 1960; Two of a
Kind, 1961; The Bobby Darin Story,
1961; Love Swings, 1961; Twist with
Bobby Darin, 1962; Bobby Darin
Sings Ray Charles, 1962; Things &
Other Things, 1962; Oh! Look at
Me Now, 1962; You're the Reason
I'm Living, 1963; 18 Yellow Roses,
1963; Golden Folk Hits, 1964; From
Hello Dolly to Goodbye Charlie,
1964; Venice Blue, 1965; Best of
Bobby Darin, 1966; I Wanna Be
Around, 1966; Shadow of Your
Smile, 1966; Dr. Doolittle, 1967; If I
Were a Carpenter, 1967; Winners,
1968; In a Broadway Bag, 1969;
Bobby Darin, 1936/73, 1975
Singles: Splish Splash, 1958 (3);
Queen of the Hop, 1958 (9); Plain
Jane, 1959 (38); Dream Lover, 1959

(2); Mack the Knife, 1959 (1);
Beyond the Sea, 1960 (6); Clemen-
tine, 1960 (21); Won't You Come
Home Bill Bailey, 1960 (19); I'll Be
There, 1960 (79); Beachcomber,
1960 (100); Artificial Flowers, 1960
(20); Somebody to Love, 1960 (45);
Christmas Auld Lang Syne, 1960
(51); Child of God, 1960 (95); Lazy
River, 1961 (14); Nature Boy, 1961
(40); Theme from "Come
September," 1961 (113); You Must
Have Been a Beautiful Baby, 1961
(5); Irresistible You, 1961 (15);
Multiplication, 1961 (30); What I'd
Say (Part 1), 1962 (24); Things, 1962
(3); If a Man Answers, 1962 (32);
Baby Face, 1962 (42); A True, True
Love (Love Theme from If a Man
Answers), 1962 (105); I Found a
New Baby, 1962 (90); You're the
Reason I'm Living, 1963 (3); 18
Yellow Roses, 1963 (10); Treat My
Baby Good, 1963 (43); Be Mad Lit-
tle Girl, 1963 (64); I Wonder Who's
Kissing Her Now, 1964 (93);
Milord, 1964 (45); The Things in
This House, 1964 (86); Hello,
Dolly!, 1965 (79); Venice Blue, 1965
(133); We Didn't Ask to Be Brought
Here, 1965 (117); Mame, 1966 (53);
If I Were a Carpenter, 1966 (8);
The Girl That Stood Beside Me,
1966 (66); Lovin' You, 1967 (32);
The Lady Came from Baltimore,
1967 (62); Darling Be Home Soon,
1967 (93); She Knows, 1967 (106);
Long Line Rider, 1969 (79); Me
and Mr. Hohner, 1969 (123); Jive,
1969 (111); Happy, 1973 (67)
Pop Vocal — New York; Bobby
died during heart surgery in 1973
and was married to movie star Sandra Dee; real name was Walden
Robert Cassotto

James Darren

Albums: Gidget Goes Hawaiian (James Darren Sings the Movies), 1961; Teenage Triangle, 1961 (with Shelley Fabares and Paul Petersen); James Darren/All, 1967

Singles: Gidget, 1959 (**41**); Angel Face, 1959 (**47**); Goodbye Cruel World, 1961 (**3**); Her Royal Majesty, 1962 (**6**); Conscience, 1962 (**11**); Mary's Little Lamb, 1962 (**39**); Hail to the Conquering Hero, 1962 (**97**); Pin a Medal on Joey, 1963 (**54**); All, 1967 (**35**); Since I Don't Have You, 1967 (**123**); Mammy Blue, 1971 (**107**); You Take My Heart Away, 1977 (**52**)

Pop Vocal—Philadelphia; James starred in the "T. J. Hooker" and "Time Tunnel" TV series and many films; real name is Ercolani

The Dartells

Personnel: Doug Phillips (vocals, bass); Dick Burns (guitars); Corky Wilkie (guitars); Rich Peil (saxophones); Randy Ray (keyboards); Gary Peeler (drums)

Album: Hot Pastrami!, 1963

Singles: Hot Pastrami, 1963 (**11**); Dance, Everybody, Dance, 1963 (**99**)

Pop/Rock—California

Dave Dee, Dozy, Beaky, Mick & Tich

Personnel: Dave "Dee" Harman (vocals); Trevor "Dozy" Davies (bass); John "Beaky" Diamond (guitars, drums) replaced (1970) by Peter Lucas (guitars); Michael "Mick" Wilson (drums); Ian "Tich" Amey (guitars)

Albums: Dave Dee, Dozy, Beaky, Mick & Tich, 1966; If Music Be the Food of Love, 1966; Golden Hits, 1967; What's in a Name, 1967; If No One Sang, 1968; Greatest Hits, 1968; Together, 1969; The Legend of Dave Dee, Dozy, Beaky, Mick & Tich, 1969; Fresh Air, 1970; Attention, 1970; Greatest Hits 2, 1971; Time to Take Off, 1972; Bend It, 1982

Singles: Bend It, 1966 (**110**); Zabadak, 1967 (**52**); The Legend of Zanadu, 1968 (**123**); Staying with It, 1983

Psychedelic Rock—British

David & Jonathan

Personnel: Roger Greenaway (vocals); Roger Cook (vocals)

Single: Michelle, 1966 (**18**)

Pop Vocal—British

Skeeter Davis

Albums: The End of the World, 1963; Let Me Get Close to You, 1964

Singles: (I Can't Help You) I'm Falling Too, 1960 (**39**); My Last Date (With You), 1960 (**26**); The End of the World, 1963 (**2**); I'm Saving My Love, 1963 (**41**); I Can't Stay Mad at You, 1963 (**7**); He Says the Same Things to Me, 1964 (**47**); How Much Can a Lonely Heart Stand, 1964 (**92**); Gonna Get Along Without You Now, 1964 (**48**); Let Me Get Close to You, 1964 (**106**); What Am I Gonna Do Without You, 1964 (**123**); A Dear John Letter, 1965 (**114**) (with Bobby Bare); I Can't Help It (If I'm Still in Love with You), 1965 (**126**); Sun Glasses, 1965 (**120**); What Does It Take (to Keep a Man Like You Satisfied),

1967 **(121)**; I Can't Believe That It's All Over, 1973 **(101)**

Country Vocal—Kentucky; real name is Mary Frances Penick; former husband is Ralph Emery; also married to NRBQ's Joey Spampinato

Spencer Davis Group

Personnel: Spencer Davis (vocals, guitars); Steve Winwood (vocals, guitars, keyboards) replaced (1970) by Eddie Hardin (keyboards); Muff Winwood (bass, vocals) replaced (1970) by Dee Murray (bass) replaced (1973) by Charlie McCracken (bass); Peter York (drums) replaced (1969) by Nigel Olsson (drums) replaced (1971) by Peter York (drums); added (1967) Phil Sawyer (guitars) replaced (1968) by Ray Fenwick (guitars)

Albums: Every Little Bit Hurts, 1965; Their First Album, 1965; You Put the Hurt on Me, 1965; Second Album, 1966; Sittin' and Thinkin', 1966; Autumn '66, 1966; Gimme Some Lovin', 1967; I'm a Man, 1967; Very Best of Spencer Davis Group, 1968; Here We Go Round the Mulberry Bush, 1968; Greatest Hits, 1968; With Their New Face On, 1968; Heavies, 1969; The Best of Spencer Davis, 1977; Keep on Running, 1978

Singles: Keep on Running, 1966 **(76)**; Gimme Some Lovin', 1966 **(7)**; I'm a Man, 1967 **(10)**; Somebody Help Me, 1967 **(47)**; Time Seller, 1967 **(100)**; Looking Back, 1968 **(113)**

Blues/Rock—British; Spencer was a lecturer in German at the University of Birmingham; Muff Winwood became a recording executive

Tyrone Davis

Albums: Can I Change My Mind, 1969; Turn Back the Hands of Time, 1970; I Had It All the Time, 1972; Without You in My Life, 1973; Love and Touch, 1976; In the Mood with Tyrone Davis, 1979; Tyrone Davis, 1983

Singles: Can I Change My Mind, 1968 **(5)**; Is It Something You've Got, 1969 **(34)**; All the Waiting Is Not in Vain, 1969 **(125)**; Turn Back the Hands of Time, 1970 **(3)**; I'll Be Right Here, 1970 **(53)**; Let Me Back In, 1970 **(58)**; Could I Forget You, 1970 **(60)**; One-Way Ticket, 1971 **(75)**; You Keep Me Holding On, 1971 **(94)**; I Had It All the Time, 1972 **(61)**; Come and Get This Ring, 1972 **(119)**; If You Had a Change in Mind, 1972 **(107)**; Without You in My Life, 1973 **(64)**; There It Is, 1973 **(32)**; I Wish It Was Me, 1974 **(57)**; What Goes Up (Must Come Down), 1974 **(89)**; Give It Up (Turn It Loose), 1976 **(38)**; This I Swear, 1977 **(102)**; Get on Up (Disco), 1978 **(102)**; Are You Serious, 1982 **(57)**

Soul Vocal—Michigan

Bobby Day

Album: Rockin' Robin, 1958

Singles: Little Bitty Pretty One, 1957 **(57)**; Rock-In Robin, 1958 **(2)**; Over and Over, 1958 **(41)**; The Bluebird, the Buzzard & the Oriole, 1958 **(54)**; That's All I Want, 1959 **(98)**; Gotta New Girl, 1959 **(82)**; Gee Whiz, 1960 **(103)**

R & B Vocal—Texas; died in 1990 of cancer

Bill Deal & The Rhondels

Album: The Best of Bill Deal & The Rhondels, 1970

Singles: May I, 1969 **(39)**; I've Been Hurt, 1969 **(35)**; What Kind of Fool Do You Think I Am, 1969 **(23)**; Swingin' Tight, 1969 **(85)**; Nothing Succeeds Like Success, 1970 **(62)**; It's Too Late, 1972 **(108)**

Pop/Rock — New York

Jimmy Dean

Albums: Big Bad John and Other Fabulous Songs and Tales, 1961; Portrait of Jimmy Dean, 1962

Singles: Deep Blue Sea, 1957 **(67)**; Little Sandy Sleighfoot, 1957 **(32)**; Sing Along, 1959 **(106)**; Big Bad John, 1961 **(1)**; Dear Ivan, 1962 **(24)**; To a Sleeping Beauty, 1962 **(26)**; The Cajun Queen, 1962 **(22)**; P.T. 109, 1962 **(8)**; Steel Men, 1962 **(41)**; Little Black Book, 1962 **(29)**; Gonna Raise a Rukus Tonight, 1962 **(73)**; This Ole House, 1963 **(128)**; The First Thing Ev'ry Morning (And the Last Thing Ev'ry Night), 1965 **(91)**; I.O.U., 1976 **(35)**

Country/Pop Vocal — Texas; starred in his own TV series 1957–58 and 1963–66

Dean and Jean

Personnel: Welton Young (vocals); Brenda Lee Jones (vocals)

Album: Hey Jean, Hey Dean, 1964

Singles: Tra La La La Suzy, 1963 **(35)**; Hey Jean, Hey Dean, 1964 **(32)**; I Wanna Be Loved, 1964 **(91)**; Thread Your Needle, 1964 **(123)**

Pop Vocal — Ohio

Dean and Marc

Personnel: Dean Mathis (vocals); Marc Mathis (vocals)

Single: Tell Him No, 1959 **(42)**

Pop Vocal — Georgia

The De Castro Sisters

Personnel: Peggy De Castro (vocals); Babette De Castro (vocals); Cherie De Castro (vocals)

Singles: Boom Boom Boomerang, 1955 **(17)**; Too Late Now, 1955 **(66)**; Snowbound for Christmas, 1955 **(84)**; It's Yours, 1956 **(74)**; Who Are They to Say, 1958 **(99)**; Teach Me Tonight Cha Cha, 1959 **(76)**

Pop Vocal — Cuban

Jimmy Dee & The Offbeats

Single: Henrietta, 1958 **(47)**

Rockabilly — Texas

Joey Dee & The Starlighters

Personnel: Joey Dee (vocals); David Brigati (vocals, saxophones); Larry Vernieri (vocals) replaced (1963) by Eddie Brigati (vocals); Carlton Latimore (organ) replaced (1963) by Felix Cavalierre (keyboards); Willie Davis (drums, vocals) replaced (1963) by Gene Cornish (guitars) replaced (1966) by Jimi Hendrix (guitars)

Albums: Doin' the Twist at the Peppermint Lounge, 1961; Hey, Let's Twist!, 1962; Back at the Peppermint Lounge — Twistin', 1963

Singles: Peppermint Twist (Part 1), 1961 **(1)**; Hey, Let's Twist, 1962 **(20)**; Roly Poly, 1962 **(74)**; Shout — Part 1, 1962 **(6)**; Everytime (I Think

About You)—Part 1, 1962 **(105)**;
What Kind of Love Is This, 1962
(18); I Lost My Baby, 1962 **(61)**;
Baby, You're Driving Me Crazy,
1963 **(100)**; Hot Pastrami with
Mashed Potatoes—Part 1, 1963
(36); Dance, Dance, Dance, 1963
(89)

Dance Pop—New Jersey; Joey's
real name is Joseph Dinicola

Dee Jay & The Runaways

Personnel: Gary Lind (vocals,
guitars); John "Jay" Senn (bass);
Denny "Dee" Storey (drums)
Single: Peter Rabbit, 1966
(45)

Pop/Rock—Iowa

Deep Purple

Personnel: Rod Evans (vocals)
replaced (1970) by Ian Gillan (vocals) replaced (1974) by David
Coverdale (vocals) replaced (1984)

**Deep Purple: Lord, Hughes,
Coverdale, Paice, Blackmore**

by Ian Gillan (vocals) replaced
(1990) by Joe Lynn Turner (vocals);
Ritchie Blackmore (guitars) replaced
(1975) by Tommy Bolin (guitars;
deceased 1976) replaced (1984) by
Ritchie Blackmore (guitars); Nic
Simper (bass) replaced (1970) by
Roger Glover (bass, vocals) replaced
(1974) by Glenn Hughes (bass, vocals) replaced (1984) by Roger
Glover (bass, vocals); Jon Lord
(keyboards); Ian Paice (drums)

Albums: Shades of Deep Purple,
1968; Book of Taliesyn, 1969; Deep
Purple, 1969; Concerto for Group
and Orchestra, 1970; Deep Purple in
Rock, 1970; Fireball, 1971; Machine
Head, 1972; Made in Japan, 1972;
Who Do We Think We Are, 1973;
Burn, 1974; Stormbringer, 1974; Mk
1 & 2, 1974; Come Taste the Band,
1975; 24 Carat Purple, 1975; Purple
Passages, 1975; Made in Europe,
1976; Powerhouse, 1977; The Last
Concert in Japan, 1977; When We
Rock, We Rock and When We
Roll, We Roll, 1978; The Singles
A's & B's, 1978; New, Live & Rare,
1978; Deep Purple Mk 2 Singles,
1979; Deepest Purple, 1980; In Con-
cert, 1982; Live in London, 1982;
Perfect Strangers, 1984; House of
Blue Light, 1987; Nobody's Perfect,
1988; Slaves and Masters, 1990; Anthology, 1991; Knebworth '85, 1991

Singles: Hush, 1968 **(4)**; Kentucky
Woman, 1968 **(38)**; River Deep—
Mountain High, 1969 **(53)**; Em-
maretta, 1969 **(128)**; Hallelujah (I
Am the Preacher), 1969 **(108)**; Black
Night, 1970 **(66)**; Fireball, 1971;
Speed King, 1971; Space Truckin',
1972; Smoke on the Water, 1973 **(4)**;
Woman from Tokyo, 1973 **(60)**;
Highway Star, 1973; Just Might
Take Your Life, 1974 **(91)**; Burn,
1974 **(105)**; Stormbringer, 1974;

Child in Time, 1975; Strange Kind of Woman, 1975; Knocking at Your Back Door, 1984 **(61)**; Nobody's Home, 1985; Perfect Strangers, 1985; Bad Attitude, 1987; Call of the Wild, 1987; King of Dreams, 1990; Fire in the Basement, 1990; Love Conquers All, 1991

Hard Rock — British

Deep Six

Album: Deep Six, 1966
Single: Rising Sun, 1965 **(122)**
Pop/Rock — American

Delaney & Bonnie & Friends

Personnel: Delaney Bramlett (guitars, vocals); Bonnie Bramlett (vocals); Bobby Whitlock (keyboards, vocals); Steve Cropper (guitars) replaced (1969) by Jerry McGee (guitars) replaced (1970) by Dave Mason (guitars) replaced (1971) by Charlie Freeman (guitars); Donald "Duck" Dunn (bass) replaced (1969) by Carl Radle (bass) replaced (1970) by Kenny Gradney (bass); Al Jackson (drums) replaced (1969) by Jim Keltner (drums) replaced (1970) by Jim Gordon (drums) replaced (1971) by Sam Creason (drums)

Albums: Home, 1969; Accept No Substitute, 1969; On Tour, 1970; To Bonnie from Delaney, 1970; Motel Shot, 1971; Country Life, 1971; Genesis, 1971; Mobius Strip, 1971 (Delaney); Together, 1972; Something's Coming, 1972 (Delaney); Best Of, 1973; Sweet Bonnie Bramlett, 1973 (Bonnie); Giving Birth to a Song, 1974 (Delaney); It's Time, 1975 (Bonnie); Lady's Choice, 1976 (Bonnie); Class Reunion, 1977 (Delaney); Memories, 1978, (Bonnie)

Singles: Free the People, 1970 **(75)**; Comin' Home, 1970 **(84)**; Soul Shake, 1970 **(43)**; They Call It Rock and Roll Music, 1970 **(119)**; Never Ending Song of Love, 1971 **(13)**; Only You and I Know, 1971 **(20)**; Move 'em Out, 1972 **(59)**; Where There's a Will There's a Way, 1972 **(99)**

Folk Rock — American; Delaney and Bonnie divorced in 1972

The Delfonics

Personnel: William Hart (vocals); Wilbert Hart (vocals); Randy Cain (vocals) replaced (1971) by Major Harris (vocals) replaced (1973) by Bruce Peterson (vocals); Ritchie Daniels (vocals)

Albums: La La Means I Love You, 1968; The Sound of Sexy Soul, 1969; The Delfonics Super Hits, 1969; The Delfonics, 1970; Tell Me This Is a Dream, 1972; Alive and Kicking, 1974; Let It Be Me, 1975

Singles: La La Means I Love You, 1968 **(4)**; I'm Sorry, 1968 **(42)**; He Don't Really Love You, 1968 **(92)**; Break Your Promise, 1968 **(35)**; Ready or Not Here I Come (Can't Hide from Love), 1968 **(35)**; Somebody Loves You, 1969 **(72)**; Funny Feeling, 1969 **(94)**; You Got Yours and I'll Get Mine, 1969 **(40)**; Didn't I (Blow Your Mind This Time), 1970 **(10)**; Trying to Make a

Fool of Me, 1970 **(40)**; When You Get Right Down to It, 1970 **(53)**; Hey! Love/Over and Over, 1971 **(52)**; Walk Right Up to the Sun, 1971 **(81)**; Tell Me This Is a Dream, 1972 **(86)**; Think It Over, 1973 **(101)**; I Don't Want to Make You Wait, 1973 **(91)**; I Told You So, 1974 **(101)**

Soul Vocal—Philadelphia

The Dells

Personnel: Marvin Junior (vocals); Mickey McGill (vocals) left group (1958); Johnny Funches (vocals) replaced (1958) by Johnny Carter (vocals); Chuck Barksdale (vocals); Vern Allison (vocals)

Albums: There Is, 1968; The Dells Musical Menu/Always Together, 1969; The Dells Greatest Hits, 1969; Love Is Blue, 1969; Like It Is, Like It Was, 1970; Freedom Means, 1971; The Dells Sing Dionne Warwicke's Greatest Hits, 1972; Give Your Baby a Standing Ovation, 1973; Sweet As Funk Can Be, 1973; The Dells vs. The Dramatics, 1974; The Mighty Mighty Dells, 1974; We Got Together, 1975; No Way Back, 1976; They Said It Couldn't Be Done, but We Did, 1977; Love Connection, 1978; New Beginnings, 1978; I Touched a Dream, 1980; Whatever Turns You On, 1981

Singles: The (Bossa Nova) Bird, 1962 **(97)**; Stay in My Corner, 1965 **(122)**; O-O, I Love You, 1967 **(61)**; There Is, 1968 **(20)**; Wear It on Our Face, 1968 **(44)**; Stay in My Corner, 1968 **(10)**; Always Together, 1968 **(18)**; Does Anybody Know I'm Here, 1968 **(38)**; Hallways of My Mind, 1969 **(92)**; I Can't Do Enough, 1969 **(98)**; Oh, What a Night, 1969 **(10)**; On the Dock of the Bay, 1969 **(42)**; When I'm in Your Arms, 1969 **(108)**; Oh What a Day, 1970 **(43)**; Open Up My Heart/Nadine, 1970 **(51)**; Long Lonely Nights, 1970 **(74)**; The Glory of Love, 1971 **(92)**; The Love We Had (Stays on My Mind), 1971 **(30)**; It's All Up to You, 1972 **(94)**; Give Your Baby a Standing Ovation, 1973 **(34)**; My Pretending Days Are Over, 1973 **(51)**; I Miss You, 1974 **(60)**; I Wish It Was Me You Loved, 1974 **(94)**; Bring Back the Love of Yesterday, 1974 **(87)**; We Got to Get Our Thing Together, 1975 **(104)**; The Power of Love, 1976 **(106)**; Slow Motion, 1976 **(102)**; Super Woman, 1978 **(108)**

Soul Vocal—Illinois

The Del-Vetts

Album: The Del-Vetts, 1966
Single: Last Time Around, 1966
Punk Pop—Chicago; group drove matching white Corvettes

The Dell-Vikings

Personnel: Norman Wright (vocals); Cornithian Johnson (vocals; deceased 1990); Donald "Gus" Backus (vocals); David Lerchey (vocals); Clarence Quick (vocals)

Albums: Newies & Oldies, 1956; Come Go with Me, 1957; The Dell-Vikings and the Sonnets, 1957; Swinging Singing Record Session, 1957; They Sing They Swing, 1958; Del-Vikings, 1959

Singles: Come Go with Me, 1957 **(4)**; Whispering Bells, 1957 **(9)**; Cool Shake, 1957 **(12)**; Bring Back Your Heart, 1961 **(101)**; Come Go with Me, 1973 **(112)**

R & B Vocal—Pittsburgh; shortened name to Del-Vikings in 1957

The Demensions

Personnel: Phil Del Giudice (vocals); Lenny Dell (vocals); Howard Margolin (vocals); Marisa Martelli (vocals)

Singles: Over the Rainbow, 1960 **(16)**; My Foolish Heart, 1963 **(95)**

Pop Vocal—New York

Derek

Singles: Cinnamon, 1968 **(11)**; Back Door Man, 1969 **(59)**

Pop Vocal—American; also recorded as Johnny Cymbal

Jackie DeShannon

Albums: Jackie DeShannon, 1963; This Is Jackie DeShannon, 1964; You Won't Forget Me, 1964; In the Wind, 1964; Breaking Up, 1965; Are You Ready for This, 1965; New Image, 1965; For You, 1965; Me About You, 1965; What the World Needs Now, 1965; Laurel Canyon, 1966; C'mon Live a Little, 1967; Lonely Girl, 1968; Jackie DeShannon, 1968; Here's Jackie, 1969; Put a Little Love in Your Heart, 1969; To Be Free, 1970; Songs, 1971; Jackie, 1972; Your Baby Is a Lady, 1973; New Arrangement, 1975; You're the Only Dancer, 1977; The Very Best of Jackie DeShannon, 1978

Singles: The Prince, 1962 **(108)**; Faded Love, 1963 **(97)**; Needles and Pins, 1963 **(84)**; Little Yellow Roses, 1963 **(110)**; When You Walk in the Room, 1964 **(99)**; Oh Boy, 1964 **(112)**; What the World Needs Now Is Love, 1965 **(7)**; A Lifetime of Loneliness, 1965 **(66)**; Come and Get Me, 1966 **(83)**; I Can Make It with You, 1966 **(68)**; Windows and Doors, 1966 **(108)**; Come on Down, 1967 **(121)**; It's All in the Game, 1967 **(110)**; Me About You, 1968 **(119)**; The Weight, 1968 **(55)**; Put a Little Love in Your Heart, 1969 **(4)**; Love Will Find a Way, 1969 **(40)**; Brighton Hill, 1970 **(82)**; You Keep Me Hangin' On/Hurts So Bad, 1970 **(96)**; It's So Nice, 1970 **(84)**; Vanilla Olay, 1972 **(76)**; Paradise, 1972 **(110)**; Don't Let the Flame Burn Out, 1977 **(68)**; I Don't Need You Anymore, 1980 **(86)**

Pop Vocal—Kentucky; Jackie wrote hits for Evie Sands, the Searchers, Brenda Lee, the Fashionettes and the Byrds; real name is Sharon Myers

The Detergents

Personnel: Ron Dante (vocals); Tommy Wynn (vocals); Danny Jordan (vocals)

Album: The Man Faces of the Detergents, 1964

Singles: Leader of the Laundromat, 1964 **(19)**; Double-O-Seven, 1965 **(89)**

Bubblegum Pop—New York

Detroit Emeralds

Personnel: Abrim Tilmon (vocals; deceased 1982); Ivory Tilmon (vocals) replaced (1977) by Paul Riser (vocals); Cleophus Tilmon (vocals) left group (1970) replaced (1977) by Maurice King (vocals); Raymond Tilmon (vocals) replaced (1970) by James Mitchell (vocals) replaced (1977) by Johnny Allen (vocals)

Albums: Show Time, 1968; Do Me Right, 1971; You Want It, You Got It, 1972; I'm in Love with You, 1973; Abe, James & Ivory, 1973;

Feel the Need, 1977; Let's Get Together, 1978

Singles: Show Time, 1968 **(89)**; Do Me Right, 1971 **(43)**; Wear This Ring (With Love), 1971 **(91)**; You Want It, You Got It, 1972 **(36)**; Baby Let Me Take You (In My Arms), 1972 **(24)**; Feel the Need in Me, 1972 **(110)**; You're Gettin' a Little Too Smart, 1973 **(101)**; Feel the Need, 1977 **(90)**

R & B Vocal—Arkansas

The Devotions

Personnel: Ray Sanchez (vocals); Bob Weisbrod (vocals); Bob Hovorka (vocals); Frank Pardo (vocals); Joe Pardo (vocals)

Single: Rip Van Winkle, 1964 **(36)**

Pop Vocal—New York

Tracey Dey

Singles: Teenage Cleopatra, 1963 **(75)**; Here Comes the Boy, 1963 **(93)**; Gonna' Get Along Without You Now, 1964 **(51)**; Hangin' on to My Baby, 1964 **(107)**

Pop Vocal—American

Neil Diamond

Albums: The Feel of Neil Diamond, 1966; Just for You, 1967; Velvet Gloves & Spit, 1968; Shilo, 1968; Brother Love's Travelling Salvation Show, 1969; Touching Me Touching You, 1969; Gold, 1969; Tap Root Manuscript, 1970; Stones, 1971; Hot August Night, 1972; Rainbow, 1973; Jonathan Livingston Seagull, 1973; Greatest Hits, 1974; Serenade, 1974; Diamonds, 1975; Beautiful Noise, 1976; And the Singer Sings His Songs, 1976; Love

Neil Diamond

at the Greek, 1977; I'm Glad You're Here with Me Tonight, 1977; You Don't Bring Me Flowers, 1978; September Morn, 1979; The Jazz Singer (Soundtrack), 1980; Love Songs, 1980; On the Way to the Sky, 1981; Greatest Hits Volume 2, 1982; Live Diamond, 1982; Heartlight, 1982; Moods, 1983; Classic Hits, 1983; Primitive, 1984; Headed for the Future, 1986; Hot August Night II, 1987; Best Years of Our Lives, 1988; Lovescape, 1991

Singles: Solitary Man, 1966 **(55)**; Cherry Cherry, 1966 **(6)**; I Got the Feelin', 1966 **(16)**; You Got to Me, 1967 **(18)**; Girl, You'll Be a Woman Soon, 1967 **(10)**; Thank the Lord for the Night Time, 1967 **(13)**; Kentucky Woman, 1967 **(22)**; New Orleans, 1968 **(51)**; Red Red Wine, 1968 **(62)**; Brooklyn Roads, 1968 **(58)**; Two Bit Manchild, 1968 **(66)**; Sunday Sun, 1968 **(68)**; Brother Love's Travelling Salvation Show, 1969 **(22)**; Sweet Caroline, 1969 **(4)**; Holly Holy, 1969 **(6)**; Shilo, 1970 **(24)**; Until It's Time for You to Go,

1970 (**53**); Soolaimon, 1970 (**30**); Solitary Man, 1970 (**21**); Cracklin' Rosie, 1970 (**1**); Do It, 1970 (**36**); He Ain't Heavy, He's My Brother, 1970 (**20**); I Am I Said, 1971 (**4**); Done Too Soon, 1971 (**65**); I'm a Believer, 1971 (**51**); Stones, 1971 (**14**); Song Sung Blue, 1972 (**1**); Play Me, 1972 (**11**); Walk on Water, 1972 (**17**); Cherry Cherry, 1973 (**31**); The Last Thing on My Mind, 1973 (**56**); The Long Way Home, 1973 (**91**); Be, 1973 (**34**); Skybird, 1974 (**75**); Longfellow Serenade, 1974 (**5**); I've Been This Way Before, 1975 (**34**); If You Know What I Mean, 1976 (**11**); Don't Think . . . Feel, 1976 (**43**); Beautiful Noise, 1976; Desiree, 1977 (**16**); You Don't Bring Me Flowers, 1978 (**1**) (with Barbra Streisand); Forever in Blue Jeans, 1979 (**20**); Say Maybe, 1979 (**56**); September Morn, 1979 (**17**); The Good Lord Loves You, 1980 (**67**); Love on the Rocks, 1980 (**2**); Hello Again, 1981 (**6**); America, 1981 (**8**); Yesterday's Songs, 1981 (**11**); On the Way to the Sky, 1982 (**27**); Be Mine Tonight, 1982 (**35**); Heartlight, 1982 (**5**); I'm Alive, 1983 (**35**); Front Page Story, 1983 (**65**); Turn Around, 1984 (**62**); Sleep with Me Tonight, 1984; You Make It Feel Like Christmas, 1984; Headed for the Future, 1986 (**53**); The Best Years of Our Lives, 1987; I Dreamed a Dream, 1987; This Time, 1988

Pop Vocal — New York; Neil starred in the film *The Jazz Singer* and wrote "I'm a Believer" for the Monkees; his songs have been covered by Deep Purple, Lulu, The Hollies, Cliff Richard and UB40

The Diamonds

Personnel: Dave Somerville (vo-cals) replaced (1978) by Bob Duncan (vocals); Ted Kowalski (vocals) replaced (1959) by John Felten (vocals; deceased 1982); Phil Leavitt (vocals) replaced (1958) by Michael Douglas (vocals); Bill Reed (vocals) replaced (1959) by Evan Fisher (vocals)

Albums: America's No. 1 Singing Stylists, 1956; Meet Pete Rugolo, 1957; Old West, 1957; The Stroll, 1957; Diamonds, 1958

Singles: Why Do Fools Fall in Love, 1956 (**12**); The Church Bells May Ring, 1956 (**14**); Love, Love, Love, 1956 (**30**); Ka-Ding-Dong, 1956 (**35**); Soft Summer Breeze, 1956 (**34**); Little Darlin', 1957 (**2**); Words of Love, 1957 (**13**); Zip Zip, 1957 (**16**); Silhouettes, 1957 (**10**); The Stroll, 1957 (**4**); High Sign, 1958 (**37**); Kathy-O, 1958 (**16**); Happy Years, 1958 (**73**); Walking Along, 1958 (**29**); She Say (Oom Dooby Doom), 1959 (**18**); One Summer Night, 1961 (**22**)

Pop Vocal — Canadian

Dick & DeeDee

Personnel: Dick St. John (vocals); DeeDee Sperling (vocals)

Albums: Tell Me, 1962; Young and in Love, 1963; Turn Around, 1963; Thou Shalt Not Steal, 1964; Songs We've Sung, 1964

Singles: The Mountain's High, 1961 (**2**); Tell Me, 1962 (**22**); Young and in Love, 1963 (**17**); Love Is a Once in a Lifetime Thing, 1963 (**103**); Where Did the Good Times Go, 1963 (**93**); Turn Around, 1963 (**27**); All My Trials, 1964 (**89**); Thou Shalt Not Steal, 1964 (**13**); Be My Baby, 1965 (**87**)

Pop Vocal — California

"Little" Jimmy Dickens

Singles: May the Bird of Paradise Fly Up Your Nose, 1965 **(15)**; When the Ship Hit the Sand, 1966 **(103)**

Novelty Songs—West Virginia

Dicky Doo & The Don'ts

Personnel: Gerry Granahan (vocals); Harvey Davis (bass); Ray Gangi (guitars); Al Ways (saxophones); Dave Alldred (drums)

Albums: The Madison, 1958; Teen Scene, 1960

Singles: Click-Clack, 1958 **(28)**; Nee Nee Na Na Na Na Nu Nu, 1958 **(40)**; Flip Top Box, 1958 **(61)**; Leave Me Alone (Let Me Cry), 1958 **(44)**; Teardrops Will Fall, 1959 **(61)**

Pop/Rock—New York

Bo Diddley

Albums: Go Bo Diddley, 1959; Boss Man, 1960; Have Guitar Will Travel, 1960; Bo Diddley, 1962; In the Spotlight, 1963; Bo Diddley Is a Gunslinger, 1963; Bo Diddley Is a Lover, 1963; Bo Diddley Is a Twister, 1963; Bo Diddley Rides Again, 1963; Beach Party, 1963; Bo Diddley & Company, 1964; Surfin' with Bo Diddley, 1964; Road Runner, 1964; Two Great Guitars, 1964; Hey Good Looking, 1964; 16 All Time Hits, 1965; Let Me Pass, 1965; Hey Bo Diddley, 1967; 500% More Man, 1967; Originator, 1967; Super Blues Band, 1968; Black Gladiator, 1968; Big Bad Bo, 1970; London Sessions, 1972; Got Another Bag of Tricks, 1973; Another

Dimension, 1975; 20th Anniversary, 1976; Where It All Began, 1977

Singles: Crackin Up, 1959 **(62)**; Say Man, 1959 **(20)**; Say Man, Back Again, 1959 **(106)**; Road Runner, 1960 **(75)**; Crawdad, 1960 **(111)**; You Can't Judge a Book by the Cover, 1962 **(48)**; Ooh Baby, 1967 **(88)**

Blues/Rock—Mississippi; real name is Otha Elias Bates McDaniel

Doug Dillard & Gene Clark

Albums: Fantastic Expedition, 1968; Through the Morning, 1969; Dillard Clark, 1975; Kansas City Southern, 1975

Single: Through the Morning, 1969

Folk/Country Rock—Missouri

The Dillards

Personnel: Rodney Dillard (guitars); Doug Dillard (banjo, guitars) replaced (1968) by Herb Pedersen (banjo) replaced (1972) by Billy Ray Latham (banjo, guitars) replaced (1978) by Herb Pedersen (banjo); Dean Webb (mandolin); Mitch Jayne (bass, vocals) replaced (1977) by Doug Haywood (bass, vocals) replaced (1977) by Jeff Gilkenson (bass, vocals); Toxey French (drums) replaced (1970) by Paul York (drums); added (1979) Doug Bounsall (guitars, vocals)

Albums: Back Porch Blue Grass, 1963; Live Almost, 1964; Pickin' and Fiddlin', 1965; Wheatsheaf Straw, 1968; Copperfields, 1970; Roots and Branches, 1972; Tribute to the American Duck, 1973; Best of the Dillards, 1976; The Dillards vs. The Incredible L.A. Time Machine,

1977; Decade Waltz, 1979; Mountain Rock, 1980; Homecoming and Family Reunion, 1980; Out on a Limb, 1991
Singles: It's About Time, 1971 **(92)**; One A.M., 1972 **(111)**; Out on a Limb, 1991
Country/Rock—Missouri

Mark Dinning

Albums: Teen Angel, 1960; Mark Dinning, 1961
Singles: Teen Angel, 1959 **(1)**; A Star Is Born (a Love Has Died), 1960 **(68)**; The Lovin' Touch, 1960 **(84)**; Top Forty, News, Weather and Sports, 1961 **(81)**
Pop Vocal—Oklahoma; brother of the Dinning Sisters Trio; died 03/22/86 from a heart attack

Kenny Dino

Single: Your Ma Said You Cried in Your Sleep Last Night, 1961 **(24)**
Pop Vocal—New York

Paul Dino

Single: Ginnie Bell, 1961 **(38)**
Pop Vocal—Philadelphia

Dino, Desi & Billy

Personnel: Billy Hinsche (guitars, vocals); Dino Martin, Jr. (bass, vocals); Desi Arnaz, Jr. (drums, vocals)
Albums: I'm a Fool, 1965; Our Time's Coming, 1966
Singles: I'm a Fool, 1965 **(17)**; Not the Lovin' Kind, 1965 **(25)**; Please Don't Fight It, 1965 **(60)**; Superman, 1966 **(94)**; If You're Thinkin' What I'm Thinkin', 1967 **(128)**; Two in the Afternoon, 1967 **(99)**; Kitty Doyle, 1967 **(108)**; Tell Someone You Love Them, 1968 **(92)**
Pop/Rock—California; the sons of Dean Martin, Desi Arnaz and Lucille Ball formed group with their realtor's son

Dion & The Belmonts

Milano, DiMucci, Mastrangelo

Personnel: Dion DiMucci (vocals); Angelo D'Aleo (vocals) replaced (1960) by Frank Lyndon (vocals); Freddie Milano (vocals); Carlo Mastrangelo (vocals)
Albums: Presenting Dion & The Belmonts, 1958; Teenager in Love,

1959; Wish Upon a Star, 1960; Together with The Belmonts, 1960

Singles: I Wonder Why, 1958 **(22)**; No One Knows, 1958 **(19)**; Don't Pity Me, 1958 **(40)**; A Teenager in Love, 1959 **(5)**; Every Little Thing I Do, 1959 **(48)**; A Lover's Prayer, 1959 **(73)**; Where or When, 1959 **(3)**; When You Wish Upon a Star, 1960 **(30)**; In the Still of the Night, 1960 **(38)**

Pop Vocal — New York

Dion

Albums: Runaround Sue, 1961; Lovers Who Wander, 1962; Dion Sings His Greatest Hits, 1962; Ruby Baby, 1963; Dion Sings to Sandy (And All His Other Girls), 1963; Dion, 1968; Sit Down Old Friend, 1969; You're Not Alone, 1971; Sanctuary, 1972; Suite for Late Summer, 1972; Reunion — Live at MSG 1972, 1973; Dion's Greatest Hits, 1973; Streetheart, 1976

Singles: Lonely Teenager, 1960 **(12)**; Little Miss Blue, 1960 **(96)**; Havin' Fun, 1961 **(42)**; Kissin' Game, 1961 **(82)**; Somebody Nobody Wants, 1961 **(103)**; Runaround Sue, 1961 **(1)**; The Wanderer, 1961 **(2)**; The Majestic, 1961 **(36)**; Lovers Who Wander, 1962 **(3)**; (I Was) Born to Cry, 1962 **(42)**; Little Diane, 1962 **(8)**; Love Came to Me, 1962 **(10)**; Ruby Baby, 1963 **(2)**; Sandy, 1963 **(21)**; This Little Girl, 1963 **(21)**; Come Go with Me, 1963 **(48)**; Be Careful of Stones That You Throw, 1963 **(31)**; Lonely World, 1963 **(101)**; Donna the Prima Donna, 1963 **(6)**; Drip Drop, 1963 **(6)**; I'm Your Hoochie Coochie Man, 1964 **(113)**; Shout, 1964 **(108)**; Johnny B. Goode, 1964 **(71)**; Abraham, Martin and John, 1968

(4); Purple Haze, 1969 **(63)**; From Both Sides Now, 1969 **(91)**; Your Own Back Yard, 1970 **(75)**; Sanctuary, 1971 **(103)**; Born to Be with You, 1976 **(108)**; And the Night Stood Still, 1989 **(75)**

Pop Vocal — New York

The Dixie Belles

Personnel: Shirley Thomas (vocals); Mary Hunt (vocals); Mildred Pratcher (vocals)

Singles: (Down at) Papa Joe's, 1963 **(9)**; Southtown, U.S.A., 1964 **(15)**; New York Town, 1964 **(119)**

Soul Vocal — Memphis; recorded with pianist Jerry Smith

The Dixie Cups

Personnel: Barbara Ann Hawkins (vocals); Rosa Lee Hawkins (vocals); Joan Marie Johnson (vocals)

Albums: Chapel of Love, 1964; Iko Iko, 1964; Riding High, 1965

Singles: Chapel of Love, 1964 **(1)**; People Say, 1964 **(12)**; You Should Have Seen the Way He Looked at Me, 1964 **(39)**; Little Bell, 1964 **(51)**; Iko Iko, 1965 **(20)**; Gee the Moon Is Shining Bright, 1965 **(102)**

Pop Vocal — New Orleans

Carl Dobkins, Jr.

Singles: My Heart Is an Open Book, 1959 **(3)**; If You Don't Want My Lovin', 1959 **(67)**; Lucky Devil, 1959 **(25)**; Exclusively Yours, 1960 **(62)**

Pop Vocal — Cincinnati

Dr. John

Albums: Dr. John & His New Orleans Cong, 1966; Gris Gris,

1968; Babylon, 1969; Remedies, 1970; Dr. John, The Night Tripper (Sun, Moon and Herbs), 1971; Gumbo, 1972; The Right Place, 1973; Triumvirate, 1974 (with Michael Bloomfield & John Hammond); Desitively Bonaroo, 1974; Cut Me While I'm Hot, 1975; Hollywood Know Thy Name, 1975; Mardi Gras, 1976; City Lights, 1978; Tango Palace, 1979; Dr. John Plays Mac Rebennack, 1980; Loser for My Baby, 1982; Take Me Back to New Orleans, 1982; Brightest Smile in Town, 1983; I Been Hoodood, 1984; Such a Night! Live in London, 1984; Ultimate Dr. John, 1988; In a Sentimental Mood, 1989

Singles: Wash Mama Wash, 1970 **(108)**; Iko Iko, 1972 **(71)**; Right Place, Wrong Time, 1973 **(9)**; Such a Night, 1973 **(42)**; (Everybody Wanna Get Rich) Rite Away, 1974 **(92)**; Mac's Boogie, 1982; Jet Set, 1984; Makin' Whoopee, 1989 (with Rickie Lee Jones)

Swamp Rock — New Orleans; real name is Mac Rebennack

Dr. West's Medicine Show & Junk Band

Personnel: Norman Greenbaum (vocals); Jack Carrington (guitars, vocals); Bonnie Wallach (guitars, vocals); Evan Engber (percussion, vocals)

Album: The Eggplant That Ate Chicago, 1966

Single: The Eggplant That Ate Chicago, 1966 **(52)**

Novelty Pop — American

Bill Doggett

Albums: Honky Tonk, 1956; Prelude to the Blues, 1956; Finger-tips, 1956; Moondust, 1956; Hot Doggett, 1956; As You Desire, 1957; Everybody Dance the Honky Tonk, 1957; Dame Dreaming, 1957; A Salute to Ellington, 1957; Doggett Best for Dancing Feet, 1957; Ram Bunk Shush, 1957; Soft, 1957; Candle Glow, 1958; Swingin' Easy, 1958; Dance Awhile, 1958; Christmas, 1958; Hold It, 1958; High and Wide, 1959; Big City Dance Party, 1959; On Tour, 1959; For Reminiscent Lovers, 1959; Back Again with More, 1959; Many Moods, 1959; Plays American Songs, 1960; Impressions, 1960; Honky Tonk a la Mode, 1960; 3046 People Danced Till 4 A.M., 1960; The Band with the Beat, 1961; The Best of Bill Doggett, 1961; Bonanza of 24 Hit Songs, 1961; Honky Tonk Popcorn, 1962; The Nearness of You, 1962; Swings, 1962; Sentimental Journey, 1963; Wow, 1965

Singles: Honky Tonk (Parts 1 & 2), 1956 **(2)**; Slow Walk, 1956 **(26)**; Ram-Bunk-Shush, 1957 **(67)**; Soft, 1957 **(35)**; Blip Blop, 1958 **(82)**; Hold It, 1958 **(92)**; Smokie — Part 2, 1960 **(95)**; (Let's Do) the Hully Gully Twist, 1960 **(66)**; Honky Tonk (Part 2), 1961 **(57)**

R & B/Jazz — Philadelphia

Mickey Dolenz

Single: Don't Do It, 1967 **(75)**

Pop Vocal — California; member of the Monkees

Fats Domino

Albums: Rock and Rollin' with Fats Domino, 1955; Carry on Rockin', 1955; Fats Domino — Rock and Rollin', 1956; This Is Fats Domino, 1957; Here Stands Fats

Domino, 1957; This Is Fats, 1958; Fabulous Mr. D., 1958; Fats Domino Swings, 1959; Let's Play Fats Domino, 1959; Fats Domino Sings, 1960; A Lot of Domino's, 1960; I Miss You So, 1961; Let the Four Winds Blow, 1961; What a Party, 1961; Twistin' the Stomp, 1962; Million Sellers by Fats, 1962; Just Domino, 1963; Let's Dance, 1963; Here He Comes Again, 1963; Walking to New Orleans, 1963; Here Comes . . . Fats Domino, 1963; Fats on Fire, 1963; '65, 1965; Southwind U.S.A., 1965; Getaway with Fats, 1966; Fantastic Fats, 1966; Cooking with Fats, 1966; Fats Is Back, 1968; Very Best of Fats Domino, 1969; Fats, 1970; Million Sellers Volume 2, 1970; Million Sellers Volume 3, 1971; Legendary Masters, 1972; Live in Las Vegas, 1973; Live at Montreux, 1974; Live in New York, 1976; Story, Volumes 1–6, 1977; Live in Europe, 1978; Sleeping on the Job, 1979; When in Walking, 1979

Singles: Ain't That a Shame, 1955 (**10**); Bo Weevil, 1956 (**35**); I'm in Love Again, 1956 (**3**); My Blue Heaven, 1956 (**21**); When My Dreamboat Comes Home, 1956 (**14**); So-Long, 1956 (**44**); Blueberry Hill, 1956 (**2**); Blue Monday, 1957 (**5**); What's the Reason I'm Not Pleasing, 1957 (**50**); I'm Walkin', 1957 (**4**); Valley of Tears, 1957 (**8**); It's You I Love, 1957 (**6**); When I See You, 1957 (**29**); What Will I Tell My Heart, 1957 (**64**); Wait and See, 1957 (**23**); I Still Love You, 1957 (**79**); The Big Beat, 1957 (**26**); I Want You to Know, 1957 (**32**); Yes, My Darling, 1958 (**55**); Sick and Tired, 1958 (**22**); No, No, 1958 (**55**); Little Mary, 1958 (**48**); Young School Girl, 1958 (**92**); Whole Lotta

Loving, 1958 (**6**); Coquette, 1958 (**92**); Telling Lies, 1959 (**50**); When the Saints Go Marching In, 1959 (**50**); I'm Ready, 1959 (**16**); Margie, 1959 (**51**); I Want to Walk You Home, 1959 (**8**); I'm Gonna Be a Wheel Some Day, 1959 (**17**); Be My Guest, 1959 (**8**); I've Been Around, 1959 (**33**); Country Boy, 1960 (**25**); If You Need Me, 1960 (**98**); Tell Me That You Love Me, 1960 (**51**); Before I Grow Too Old, 1960 (**84**); Walking to New Orleans, 1960 (**6**); Don't Come Knockin', 1960 (**21**); Three Nights a Week, 1960 (**15**); Put Your Arms Around Me Honey, 1960 (**58**); My Girl Josephine, 1960 (**14**); Natural Born Lover, 1960 (**38**); What a Price, 1961 (**22**); Ain't That Just Like a Woman, 1961 (**33**); Shu Rah, 1961 (**32**); Fell in Love on Monday, 1961 (**32**); It Keeps Rainin', 1961 (**23**); Let the Four Winds Blow, 1961 (**15**); What a Party, 1961 (**22**); Rockin' Bicycle, 1961 (**83**); Jambalaya (on the Bayou), 1961 (**30**); I Hear You Knocking, 1961 (**67**); You Win Again, 1962 (**22**); Ida Jane, 1962 (**90**); My Real Name, 1962 (**59**); Nothing New (Same Old Thing), 1962 (**77**); Dance with Mr. Domino, 1962 (**98**); Did You Ever See a Dream Walking, 1962 (**79**); Stop the Clock, 1962 (**103**); Hum Diddy Doo, 1963 (**124**); You Always Hurt the One You Love, 1963 (**102**); Can't Go on Without You, 1963 (**123**); When I'm Walking (Let Me Walk), 1963 (**114**); I've Got a Right to Cry, 1963 (**128**); There Goes (My Heart Again), 1963 (**59**); Red Sails in the Sunset, 1963 (**35**); I Can't Give You Anything but Love, 1963 (**114**); Just a Lonely Man, 1963 (**108**); Who Cares, 1964 (**63**); Lazy Lady, 1964 (**86**); Your Cheatin' Heart, 1964

(112); I Don't Want to Set the World on Fire, 1964 (122); Mary, Oh Mary, 1964 (127); Sally Was a Good Old Girl, 1964 (99); Heartbreak Hill, 1964 (99); Lady Madonna, 1968 (100)

Blues/Rock—New Orleans; real first name is Antoine

Don & Juan

Personnel: Roland Trone (vocals); Claude Johnson (vocals)
Singles: What's Your Name, 1962 (7); Magic Wand, 1962 (91)
R & B Vocal—New York

Don & The Goodtimes

Personnel: Don Gallucci (vocals)
Album: So Good, 1967
Singles: I Could Be So Good to You, 1967 (56); Happy and Me, 1967 (98)
Pop Vocal—Seattle

Lonnie Donegan

Albums: Showcase, 1956; Tops with Lonnie, 1957; Lonnie, 1958; Lonnie Donegan Rides Again, 1959; More Tops with Lonnie, 1961; Sings Hallelujah, 1962; Golden Age of Donegan, 1962; Golden Age of Donegan 2, 1963; Folk Album, 1965; Lonnie Pops, 1970; My Old Man's a Dustman, 1971; Lonnie Donegan, 1972; Puttin' on the Style, 1977; Sundown, 1978; Jubilee Concert, 1981
Singles: Rock Island Line, 1956 (8); Lost John, 1956 (58); Does Your Chewing Gum Lose Its Flavor (on the Bedpost Over Night), 1961 (5)
Skiffle—Scottish

Ral Donner

Albums: Takin' Care of Business, 1961; Takin' Care of Business, Volume 2, 1962; Elvis Scrapbook, 1977; You Don't Know What You've Got, 1978; Ral Donner, Ray Smith & Bobby Dale, 1978
Singles: Girl of My Best Friend, 1961 (19); You Don't Know What You've Got (Until You Lose It), 1961 (4); Please Don't Go, 1961 (39); She's Everything (I Wanted You to Be), 1961 (18); (What a Sad Way) to Love Someone, 1962 (74); Loveless Life, 1962 (117); I Got Burned, 1963 (124)
Elvis Rock—Chicago

Donnie & The Dreamers

Personnel: Louis Burgio (vocals)
Singles: Count Every Star, 1961 (35); My Memories of You, 1961 (79)
Pop Vocal—New York

Donovan

Albums: What's Bin Did, 1965; Catch the Wind, 1965; Fairytale, 1965; Sunshine Superman, 1966; The Real Donovan, 1966; Mellow Yellow, 1967; For Little Ones, 1967; Wear Your Love Like Heaven, 1967; Universal Soldier, 1967; In Concert, 1968; Hurdy Gurdy Man, 1968; Barabajagal, 1968; A Gift from a Flower to a Garden, 1968; Like It Is, 1968; Greatest Hits, 1969; Best of Donovan, 1969; World of Donovan, 1969; Open Road, 1970; Golden Hour, 1970; Cosmic Wheels, 1973; Essence to Essence, 1973; Live in Japan, 1973; 7 Tease, 1974; Donovan, 1974; Slow Down World,

1976; Donovan, 1977; Donovan File, 1977; Spotlight, 1981; Love I Only Feeling, 1982; Minstrel Boy, 1983; Neutronic, 1983; Lady of the Stars, 1984; Classics Live, 1991

Singles: Catch the Wind, 1965 **(23)**; Colours, 1965 **(61)**; Universal Soldier, 1965 **(53)**; Sunshine Superman, 1966 **(1)**; Mellow Yellow, 1966 **(2)**; Epistle to Dippy, 1967 **(19)**; Summer Day Reflection Song, 1967 **(135)**; There Is a Mountain, 1967 **(11)**; Wear Your Love Like Heaven, 1967 **(23)**; Jennifer Juniper, 1968 **(26)**; Hurdy Gurdy Man, 1968 **(5)**; Lalena, 1968 **(33)**; To Susan on the West Coast Waiting, 1969 **(35)**; Atlantis, 1969 **(7)**; Goo Goo Barabajagal (Love Is Hot), 1969 **(36)**; Riki Tikki Tavi, 1970 **(55)**; Celia of the Seals, 1971 **(84)**; I Like You, 1973 **(66)**; Lady of the Stars, 1983

Pop Vocal—British; full name is Donovan Leitch

The Doors

Personnel: Jim Morrison (vocals; deceased 1971); Robby Krieger (guitars); Ray Manzarek (keyboards, vocals); John Densmore (drums); Doug Lubahn (bass) replaced (1970) by Lonnie Mack (bass) replaced (1971) by Jerry Scheff (bass) replaced (1972) by Jack Conrad (bass) replaced (1978) by Jerry Scheff (bass)

Albums: The Doors, 1967; Strange Days, 1968; Waiting for the Sun, 1968; The Soft Parade, 1969; Morrison Hotel, 1970; Absolutely Live, 1970; 13, 1970; L.A. Woman, 1971; Other Voices, 1971; Weird Scenes Inside the Goldmine, 1972; Full Circle, 1972; The Best of the Doors, 1973; An American Prayer, 1978; The Doors Greatest Hits, 1980; Alive, She Cried, 1983;

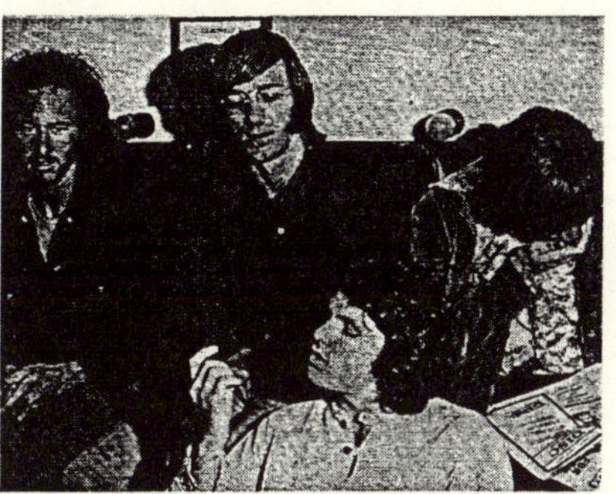

Doors: Krieger, Manzarek, Morrison, Densmore

Classics, 1985; Live at the Hollywood Bowl, 1986

Singles: Break on Through, 1967 **(126)**; Light My Fire, 1967 **(1)**; People Are Strange, 1967 **(12)**; Love Me Two Times, 1967 **(25)**; The Unknown Soldier, 1968 **(39)**; Hello, I Love You, 1968 **(1)**; Light My Fire, 1968 **(87)**; Touch Me, 1968 **(3)**; Wishful Sinful, 1969 **(44)**; Tell All the People, 1969 **(57)**; Running Blue, 1969 **(64)**; Roadhouse Blues, 1970 **(76)**; You Make Me Real, 1970 **(50)**; Love Her Madly, 1971 **(11)**; Riders on the Storm, 1971 **(14)**; Tightrope Ride, 1971 **(71)**; L.A. Woman, 1972; Break on Through, 1972; The Mosquito, 1972 **(85)**; Gloria, 1983 **(71)**

Psychedelic Rock—L.A.

Lee Dorsey

Albums: Lee Dorsey, 1966; The New Lee Dorsey, 1966; Yes We Can, 1970; Greatest Hits, 1974; Night People, 1978; Gonna Be Funky, 1980; Always Funky, 1982

Singles: Ya Ya, 1961 **(7)**; Do-Re-Mi, 1961 **(27)**; Ride Your Pony, 1965 **(28)**; Work, Work, Work, 1965 **(121)**; Get Out of My Life, Woman

1966 (**44**); Working in the Coal Mine, 1966 (**8**); Holy Cow, 1966 (**23**); Rain Rain Go Away, 1967 (**105**); My Old Car, 1967 (**97**); Go-Go Girl, 1967 (**62**); Love Lots of Lovin', 1967 (**110**) (with Betty Harris); Everything I Do Gohn Be Funky (From Now On), 1969 (**95**)

Soul/Rock — New Orleans; died from emphysema in 1986

Ronnie Dove

Albums: One Kiss for Old Times' Sake, 1965; The Best of Ronnie Dove, 1966; Ronnie Dove Sings the Hits for You, 1966; Cry, 1967

Singles: Say You, 1964 (**40**); Right or Wrong, 1964 (**14**); Hello Pretty Girl, 1965 (**54**); One Kiss for Old Times' Sake, 1965 (**14**); A Little Bit of Heaven, 1965 (**16**); I'll Make All Your Dreams Come True, 1965 (**21**); Kiss Away, 1965 (**25**); When Liking Turns to Loving, 1966 (**18**); Let's Start All Over Again, 1966 (**20**); Happy Summer Days, 1966 (**27**); I Really Don't Want to Know, 1966 (**22**); Cry, 1966 (**18**); One More Mountain to Climb, 1967 (**45**); My Babe, 1967 (**50**); I Want to Love You for What You Are, 1967 (**54**); Dancin' Out of My Heart, 1967 (**87**); In Some Time, 1968 (**99**); Mountain of Love, 1968 (**67**); Tomboy, 1968 (**96**); What's Wrong with My World, 1969 (**131**); I Need You Now, 1969 (**93**)

Pop Vocal — Virginia

The Dovells

Personnel: Len Barry (vocals); Arnie Satin (vocals); Jerry Summers (vocals); Mike Dennis (vocals); Danny Brooks (vocals)

Albums: Bristol Stomp, 1961; All the Hits for Your Hully Gully Party, 1962; You Can't Sit Down, 1963; Biggest Hits, 1963

Singles: Bristol Stomp, 1961 (**2**); Do the New Continental, 1962 (**37**); Bristol Twistin' Annie, 1962 (**27**); Hully Gully Baby, 1962 (**25**); The Jitterbug, 1962 (**82**); You Can't Sit Down, 1963 (**3**); Betty in Bermudas, 1963 (**50**); Stop Monkeyin' Around, 1963 (**94**); Dancing in the Street, 1974 (**105**)

Pop Vocal — Philadelphia

Joe Dowell

Album: Wooden Heart, 1961

Singles: Wooden Heart, 1961 (**1**); The Bridge of Love, 1961 (**50**); A Kiss for Christmas (O Tannenbaum), 1961 (**110**); Little Red Rented Rowboat, 1962 (**23**)

Pop Vocal — Indiana

Charlie Drake

Single: My Boomerang Won't Come Back, 1962 (**21**)

Pop Vocal — British

Pete Drake

Albums: Forever, 1964; Pete Drake & His Talking Steel Guitar, 1965; Fabulous Steel Guitar, 1966; Amazing, 1967; The Hits I Played On, 1969; Plays All Time Country Favorites, 1971; Steel Away, 1973; Pete Drake Show, 1974

Singles: Forever, 1964 (**25**); I'm Sorry, 1964 (**122**)

Country/Pop — Atlanta; died in 1988; was Nashville session steel guitarist

The Dreamlovers

Singles: When We Get Married, 1961 **(10)**; Let Them Love (and Be Loved), 1961 **(102)**; I Miss You, 1962 **(115)**; If I Should Lose You, 1962 **(62)**; You Gave Me Somebody to Love, 1965 **(121)**

Pop Vocal—Philadelphia

The Dream Weavers

Personnel: Wade Buff (vocals)

Singles: It's Almost Tomorrow, 1955 **(7)**; Into the Night, 1956 **(82)**; You're Mine, 1956 **(100)**; A Little Love Can Go a Long, Long Way, 1956 **(33)**; Is There Somebody Else, 1956 **(87)**

Pop Vocal—Miami

Patti Drew

Albums: Tell Him, 1967; Workin' on a Groovy Thing, 1968

Singles: Tell Him, 1964 **(90)** (with The Drew-Vels); Tell Him, 1967 **(85)**; Workin' on a Groovy Thing, 1968 **(62)**; Hard to Handle, 1968 **(93)**; The Love That a Woman Should Give to a Man, 1969 **(119)**

Soul/Pop Vocal—South Carolina

The Drifters

Personnel: Clyde McPhatter (vocals; deceased 1972) replaced (1955) by Dave Baughn (vocals) replaced (1956) by Johnny Moore (vocals) replaced (1957) by Bobby Hendricks (vocals) replaced (1959) by Ben E. King (vocals) replaced (1960) by Rudy Lewis (vocals; deceased 1964) replaced (1964) by Johnny Moore (vocals); Billy Pinkney (vocals); Andrew Thrasher (vocals) replaced (1959) by Charlie Thomas (vocals); Gerhart Thrasher (vocals) replaced (1959) by Elsbeary Hobbs (vocals)

Albums: Clyde McPhatter & The Drifters, 1958; Rockin' and Driftin', 1958; Drifters' Greatest Hits, 1960; Save the Last Dance for Me, 1962; Up on the Roof—The Best of the Drifters, 1963; Under the Boardwalk, 1964; The Good Life with the Drifters, 1965; I'll Take You Where the Music's Playing, 1965; Our Biggest Hits, 1966; The Drifters' Golden Hits, 1966; The Drifters, 1972; Love Games, 1973; There Goes My First Love, 1975; 24 Original Hits, 1975; The Drifters' Story, 1975; Every Night Is Saturday Night, 1976

Singles: White Christmas, 1955 **(80)**; Fools Fall in Love, 1957 **(69)**; Hypnotized, 1957 **(79)**; Moonlight Bay, 1958 **(72)**; Drip Drop, 1958 **(58)**; There Goes My Baby, 1959 **(2)**; Dance with Me, 1959 **(15)**; (If You Cry) True Love, True Love, 1959 **(33)**; This Magic Moment, 1960 **(16)**; Lonely Winds, 1960 **(54)**; Save the Last Dance for Me, 1960 **(1)**; I Count the Tears, 1960 **(17)**; White Christmas, 1960 **(96)**; Some Kind of Wonderful, 1961 **(32)**; Please Stay, 1961 **(14)**; Sweets for My Sweet, 1961 **(16)**; Room Full of Tears, 1961 **(72)**; When My Little Girl Is Smiling, 1962 **(28)**; Stranger on the Shore, 1962 **(73)**; Up on the Roof, 1962 **(5)**; White Christmas, 1962 **(88)**; On Broadway, 1963 **(9)**; Rat Race, 1963 **(71)**; If You Don't Come Back, 1963 **(101)**; I'll Take You Home, 1963 **(25)**; Vaya Con Dios, 1964 **(43)**; One Way Love, 1964 **(56)**; Under the Boardwalk, 1964 **(4)**; I've Got Sand in My Shoes, 1964 **(33)**; He's Just a Playboy, 1964 **(115)**; Saturday Night at the Movies, 1964 **(18)**; At the Club,

1965 **(43)**; Come on Over to My Place, 1965 **(60)**; Chains of Love, 1965 **(90)**; Follow Me, 1965 **(91)**; I'll Take You Where the Music's Playing, 1965 **(51)**; Memories Are Made of This, 1966 **(48)**; You Can't Love Them All, 1966 **(127)**; Baby What I Mean, 1966 **(62)**; Still Burning in My Heart, 1968 **(111)**

Soul/Pop Vocal—American; McPhatter died of complications of heart, liver and kidney disease

The Dubs

Personnel: Richard Blandon (vocals)

Singles: Don't Ask Me (to Be Lonely), 1957 **(72)**; Could This Be Magic, 1957 **(23)**; Chapel of Dreams, 1959 **(74)**

R & B Vocal—American

The Dukays

Personnel: Gene Chandler (vocals)

Singles: The Girl's a Devil, 1961 **(64)**; Nite Owl, 1962 **(73)**

Soul/Pop Vocal—Chicago

Patty Duke

Album: Don't Just Stand There, 1965

Singles: Don't Just Stand There, 1965 **(8)**; Say Something Funny, 1965 **(22)**; Funny Little Butterflies, 1965 **(77)**; Whenever She Holds You, 1966 **(64)**

Pop Vocal—New York; star of the "Patty Duke Show" and other productions

Aynsley Dunbar

Albums: Aynsley Dunbar Retaliation, 1968; Doctor Dunbar's Pre-

scription, 1969; Retaliation, 1969; Remains to Be Heard, 1970; Blue Whale, 1970; Joy to the World, 1971

Hard Rock—British; hard rock drummer for Journey, Jefferson Starship and others

The Duprees

Personnel: Joseph "Joey Vann" Canzano (vocals; deceased 1984); Mike Arnone (vocals); Tom Bialablow (vocals); John Salvato (vocals); Joe Santollo (vocals)

Album: You Belong to Me, 1962

Singles: You Belong to Me, 1962 **(7)**; My Own True Love, 1962 **(13)**; I'd Rather Be Here in Your Arms, 1963 **(91)**; Gone with the Wind, 1963 **(89)**; Why Don't You Believe Me, 1963 **(37)**; Have You Heard, 1963 **(18)**; (It's No) Sin, 1964 **(74)**; Where Are You, 1964 **(114)**; Around the Corner, 1965 **(91)**; Goodnight My Love, 1968 **(113)**

Pop Vocal—New Jersey

Dyke & The Blazers

Personnel: Arlester Christian (vocals; deceased 1971)

Albums: The Funky Broadway, 1967; So Sharp, 1968

Singles: Funky Broadway—Part 1, 1967 **(65)**; So Sharp, 1967 **(130)**; Funky Walk—Part 1, 1968 **(67)**; Funky Bull, 1968 **(102)**; We Got More Soul, 1969 **(35)**; Let a Woman Be a Woman—Let a Man Be a Man, 1969 **(36)**; You Are My Sunshine, 1970 **(101)**; Uhh, 1970 **(118)**; Runaway People, 1970 **(119)**

Soul/Pop—New York

Bob Dylan

Albums: Bob Dylan, 1962; Freewheelin' Bob Dylan, 1963; The

Times They Are a Changin', 1964; Another Side of Bob Dylan, 1964; Bringing It All Back Home, 1965; Highway 61 Revisited, 1965; 11 Years in the Life of Bob Dylan, 1966; Blonde on Blonde, 1966; Greatest Hits, 1967; John Wesley Harding, 1968; Nashville Skyline, 1969; Self Portrait, 1970; New Morning, 1970; Greatest Hits Volume 2, 1971; Greatest Hits Volume 3, 1971; Nobody Sings Like Bob Dylan, 1972; More Greatest Hits, 1972; Pat Garrett and Billy the Kid, 1973; Dylan, 1973; Planet Waves, 1974; Before the Flood, 1974 (with The Band); Blood on the Tracks, 1974; The Basement Tapes, 1975 (with The Band); Desire, 1975; Hard Rain, 1976; Street Legal, 1978; At Budokan, 1978; Slow Train Coming, 1979; Saved, 1980; Shot of Love, 1981; Infidels, 1983; Real Live, 1984; Empire Burlesque, 1985; Biograph, 1985; Knocked Out Loaded, 1986; Dylan & The Dead, 1987 (with The Grateful Dead); Down in the Groove, 1987; Oh Mercy, 1989; The Bootleg Series (Rare & Unreleased) 1961–1991, 1991; Under the Red Sky, 1991

Singles: Subterranean Homesick Blues, 1965 **(39)**; Like a Rolling Stone, 1965 **(2)**; Positively 4th Street, 1965 **(7)**; Can You Please Crawl Out Your Window?, 1965 **(58)**; One of Us Must Know, 1966 **(119)**; Rainy Day Woman #12 & 35, 1966 **(2)**; I Want You, 1966 **(20)**; Just Like a Woman, 1966 **(33)**; Leopard-Skin Pill-Box Hat, 1967 **(81)**; I Threw It All Away, 1969 **(85)**; Lay Lady Lay, 1969 **(7)**; Tonight I'll Be Staying Here with You, 1969 **(50)**; Wigwam, 1970 **(41)**; Watching the River Flow, 1971 **(41)**; George Jackson, 1971 **(33)**; Knockin' on Heaven's Door, 1973 **(12)**; A Fool Such As I, 1973 **(55)**; On a Night Like This, 1974 **(44)**; Something There Is About You, 1974 **(107)**; Most Likely You Go Your Way (and I'll Go Mine), 1974 **(66)**; Tangled Up in Blue, 1975 **(31)**; Million Dollar Bash, 1975 (with The Band); Hurricane, 1975 **(33)**; Mozambique, 1976 **(54)**; Rita May/ Stuck Inside of Mobile with the Memphis Blues Again, 1977 **(110)**; Gotta Serve Somebody, 1979 **(24)**; Slow Train, 1980; Solid Rock, 1980; Saved, 1980; Heart of Mine, 1981; Sweetheart Like You, 1983 **(55)**; Jokerman, 1984; Tight Connection to My Heart, 1985 **(103)**; Emotionally Yours, 1985; Band of the Hand, 1986; The Usual, 1987 (with Eric Clapton); Silvio, 1988

Folk/Rock—Minnesota; real last name is Zimmerman

The Dynamics

Personnel: Samuel Stevenson (vocals); Isaac "Zeke" Harris (vocals); George White (vocals); Fred "Sonny" Baker (vocals)
Singles: Misery, 1963 **(44)**; Ice Cream Song, 1969 **(59)**

R & B Vocal—Detroit

The E-Types

Personnel: Bob Wence (vocals); Randy Barlow (vocals, guitars); Craig Williams (vocals, bass); Larry Hosford (vocals, drums)
Album: The E-Types, 1967
Single: Put the Clock Back on the Wall, 1967

Psychedelic Rock—California

Earl-Jean

Single: I'm Into Somethin' Good, 1964 **(38)**

Soul/Pop Vocal — New York; last name is McCrea; leader of The Cookies

The Earls

Personnel: Larry Figueiredo (vocals); Bob Del Din (vocals); Eddie Harder (vocals); Jack Wray (vocals)

Singles: Life Is But a Dream, 1961 **(107)**; Remember Then, 1962 **(24)**; Never, 1963 **(119)**; Eyes, 1963 **(123)**

Pop Vocal — New York

Earth Opera

Personnel: Peter Rowan (vocals, guitars, saxophones); John Nagy (bass); David Grisman (keyboards, saxophones); Bill Stevenson (keyboards) replaced (1969) by David Horowitz (keyboards); Billy Mundi (percussion) replaced (1969) by Bob Zachary (percussion); Paul Dillon (drums, guitars, vocals)

Albums: Earth Opera, 1968; The Great American Eagle Tragedy, 1969

Single: Home to You, 1969 **(97)**

Country/Rock — California

The Easybeats

Personnel: Stevie Wright (vocals); Harry Vanda (guitars, vocals); George Young (guitars, vocals); Richard Diamonde (bass); Gordon Fleet (drums)

Albums: Friday on My Mind, 1967; Good Friday, 1967; Falling Off the Edge of the World, 1968; Vigil, 1968; Friends, 1970; Absolute Anthology, 1972; Nostalgia, 1974; The Shame Just Drained, 1978

Singles: Friday on My Mind, 1967 **(16)**; St. Louis, 1969 **(100)**

Pop/Rock — Australian

The Echoes

Personnel: Tommy Duffy (vocals); Harry Doyle (vocals); Tom Morrissey (vocals)

Singles: Baby Blue, 1961 **(12)**; Sad Eyes (Don't You Cry), 1961 **(88)**; Gee Oh Gee, 1961 **(112)**; Bluebirds Over the Mountain, 1962 **(112)**

Pop Vocal — New York

Eclection

Personnel: Kerilee Male (vocals) replaced (1969) by Dorris Henderson (vocals); Michael Rosen (guitars, vocals, trumpet) replaced (1969) by Gary Boyle (guitars); Trevor Lucas (guitars, vocals); George Hultgren (guitars, bass, vocals) replaced (1969) by Eric Johns (guitars, bass); Gerry Conway (drums) replaced (1969) by Mick Woods (drums); added (1969) Kevin Westlake (guitars, percussion); added (1969) John "Poli" Palmer (vocals, vibes)

Album: Eclection, 1968

Folk/Rock — British

Duane Eddy

Albums: Have Twangy' Guitar Will Travel, 1959; Especially for You, 1959; The "Twangs" the "Thang," 1960; Songs for Our Heritage, 1960; $1,000,000.00 Worth of Twang, 1960; Girls! Girls! Girls!, 1961; Twistin' 'n' Twangin', 1962; Twangy Guitar — Silky Strings, 1962; Dance with the Guitar Man, 1963; "Twangs" a Country Song, 1963; "Twangin'" Up a Storm, 1963; Lonely Guitar, 1964; Twistin', 1964;

Surfin', 1964; In Person, 1965; Greatest Hits, 1964; Duane a Go-Go, 1965; Duane Does Dylan, 1965; "Twangin'" Golden Hits, 1965; Twangsville, 1965; Best of Duane Eddy, 1965; Biggest Twang of All, 1966; Roarin' Twangies, 1967; Movin' & Groovin', 1970; Vintage Years, 1975; Duane Eddy, 1979; 20 Terrific Twangies, 1980

Singles: Moovin' 'n' Groovin', 1958 **(72)**; Rebel-'Rouser, 1958 **(6)**; Ramrod, 1958 **(27)**; Cannonball, 1958 **(15)**; The Lonely One, 1959 **(23)**; "Yep!", 1959 **(30)**; Forty Miles of Bad Road, 1959 **(9)**; The Quiet Three, 1959 **(46)**; Some Kind-a Earthquake, 1959 **(37)**; First Love, First Tears, 1959 **(59)**; Bonnie Came Back, 1959 **(26)**; Shazam!, 1960 **(45)**; Because They're Young, 1960 **(4)**; Kommotion, 1960 **(78)**; Peter Gunn, 1960 **(27)**; "Pepe," 1960 **(18)**; Theme from Dixie, 1961 **(39)**; Gidget Goes Hawaiian, 1961 **(101)**; Ring of Fire, 1961 **(84)**; Drivin' Home, 1961 **(87)**; My Blue Heaven, 1961 **(50)**; The Avenger, 1962 **(101)**; The Battle, 1962 **(114)**; Deep in the Heart of Texas, 1962 **(78)**; The Ballad of Paladin, 1962 **(33)** (from "Have Gun Will Travel"); (Dance with the) Guitar Man, 1962 **(12)**; Boss Guitar, 1963 **(28)**; Lonely Boy, Lonely Guitar, 1963 **(82)**; Your Baby's Gone Surfin', 1963 **(93)**; The Son of Rebel Rouser, 1964 **(97)**; Freight Train, 1970 **(110)**; Peter Gunn, 1986 **(50)** (with Art of Noise)

Guitar Rock — New York

Eden's Children

Personnel: Richard Schamach (guitars, vocals); Larry Kiley (bass); Jimmy Sturman (drums)

Albums: Eden's Children, 1968; Sure Looks Real, 1969

Pop Rock — Boston

The Edsels

Personnel: George Jones, Jr. (vocals); Marshall Sewell (vocals)

Single: Rama Lama Ding Dong, 1961 **(21)**

Pop Vocal — Ohio

Tommy Edwards

Singles: It's All in the Game, 1958 **(1)**; Please Love Me Forever, 1958 **(61)**; Love Is All We Need, 1958 **(15)**; Please Mr. Sun, 1959 **(11)**; The Morning Side of the Mountain, 1959 **(27)**; My Melancholy Baby, 1959 **(26)**; It's Only the Good Times, 1959 **(86)**; I've Been There, 1959 **(53)**; I Looked at Heaven, 1959 **(100)**; Honestly and Truly, 1959 **(65)**; (New in) The Ways of Love, 1959 **(47)**; Don't Fence Me In, 1960 **(45)**; I Really Don't Want to Know, 1960 **(18)**; It's Not the End of Everything, 1960 **(78)**

R & B Vocal — Virginia; died in 1969

The El Dorados

Personnel: Pirkle Lee Moses, Jr. (vocals)

Single: At My Front Door, 1955 **(17)**

R & B Vocal — Chicago

The Elastik Band

Personnel: Sean Jenkins; Andy Scott; Dave Scott; Ted Yeadon

Album: Expansions on Life, 1969

Single: Spazz, 1969

Psychedelic Pop — Midwest

Electric Banana

Personnel: Phil May (guitars, bass, vocals); Dick Taylor (guitars, bass, vocals) replaced (1973) by Pete Tolson (bass, guitars); Wally Allen Walter (guitars, bass, vocals) replaced (1973) by Gordon Edwards (bass, guitars, vocals); John Povey (keyboards, drums); Skip Allen (drums, vocals) left group (1967)

Albums: Electric Banana, 1967; More Electric Banana, 1968; Even More Electric Banana, 1972; Hot Licks, 1973; The Return of Electric Banana, 1979; Electric Banana the 70's, 1979; Electric Banana the 60's, 1980

Hard Rock—British

Electric Flag

Personnel: Nick Gravenites (vocals, guitars); Michael Bloomfield (guitars) replaced (1969) by Hoshal Wright (guitars) replaced (1971) by Michael Bloomfield (guitars; deceased 1981); Barry Goldberg (keyboards) replaced (1969) by John Simon (keyboards) replaced (1971) by Barry Goldberg (keyboards); Harvey Brooks (bass, guitars, vocals) replaced (1970) by Roger Troy (bass); Buddy Miles (drums, vocals); Herbie Rich (saxophones, keyboards, guitars) replaced (1969) by George Terry (guitars) replaced (1971) by Herbie Rich (guitars, keyboards, saxophones); Marcus Doubleday (trumpet) left group (1971); Peter Strazza (saxophones) left group (1971)

Albums: A Long Time Comin', 1968; Electric Flag, 1969; The Best of Electric Flag, 1971; The Band Kept Playing, 1974; Groovin' Is Easy, 1983

Blues/Rock—American

The Electric Prunes

Kincaid, Wade, Whetstone, Herren

Personnel: James Lowe (vocals, guitars, autoharp) replaced (1968) by Mark Kincaid (guitars) replaced (1970) by Kenny Loggins (guitars); Kenneth Williams (guitars) replaced (1968) by Ron Morgan (guitars); Weasel Spagnola (guitars, vocals) replaced (1968) by John Herren (keyboards); Mark Tulin (bass, keyboards) replaced (1968) by Brett Wade (bass); Preston Ritter (drums, percussion) replaced (1967) by Quint (drums) replaced (1968) by Richard Whetstone (drums, vocals)

Albums: Electric Prunes, 1967; Underground, 1967; Mass in F Minor, 1968; Release of an Oath, 1968; Just Good Old Rock 'n' Roll, 1969; I Had Too Much to Dream Last Night, 1984

Singles: I Had Too Much to Dream Last Night, 1967 **(11)**; Get Me to the World on Time, 1967 **(27)**; Dr. Do Good, 1967 **(128)**

Psychedelic Rock—Seattle; entire band was replaced following their second album

The Elegants

Personnel: Vito Picone (vocals); Arthur Venosa (vocals); Frank Tardogna (vocals); Carmen Romano (vocals); James Moschella (vocals)
Single: Little Star, 1958 **(1)**
Pop Vocal—New York

Elephant's Memory

Personnel: Stan Bronstein (saxophones, vocals); Gary Van Scyoc (bass, vocals); Rick Frank (drums, vocals)
Albums: Elephant's Memory, 1969; Midnight Cowboy (Soundtrack), 1969; Take It to the Streets, 1971; Elephant's Memory, 1972; Angels Forever, 1974
Singles: Crossroads of the Stepping Stones, 1969 **(120)**; Mongoose, 1970 **(50)**
Psychedelic Rock—New York

The Elgins

Personnel: Saundra Mallett Edwards (vocals); Johnny Dawson (vocals); Cleotha Miller (vocals); Robert Fleming (vocals); Norbert McClean (vocals)
Singles: Put Yourself in My Place, 1966 **(92)**; Darling Baby, 1966 **(72)**; Heaven Must Have Sent You, 1966 **(50)**; It's Been a Long Long Time, 1967 **(92)**
Pop Vocal—Detroit

Cass Elliott

Albums: Cass Elliott, 1968; Dream a Little Dream, 1968; Bubble Gum, Lemonade & Something, 1969; Make Your Own Kind of Music, 1970; Mama's Big Ones, 1971; Dave Mason & Cass Elliott, 1971; The Road Is No Place for a Lady, 1974; Don't Call Me Mama Anymore, 1974
Singles: Dream a Little Dream of Me, 1968 **(12)**; California Earthquake, 1968 **(67)**; Move in a Little Closer, Baby, 1969 **(58)**; It's Getting Better, 1969 **(30)**; Make Your Own Kind of Music, 1969 **(36)**; New World Coming, 1970 **(42)**; A Song That Never Comes, 1970 **(99)**; Good Times Are Coming, 1970 **(104)**; Don't Let the Good Life Pass You By, 1970 **(110)**
Pop Vocal—Baltimore; Cass died in 1974

Shirley Ellis

Singles: The Nitty Gritty, 1963 **(8)**; (That's) What the Nitty Gritty Is, 1964 **(72)**; Shy One, 1964 **(130)**; The Name Game, 1964 **(3)**; The Clapping Song (Clap Pat Clap Slap), 1965 **(8)**; The Puzzle Song (a Puzzle in Song), 1965 **(78)**; Ever See a Diver Kiss His Wife (While the Bubbles Bounce About Above the Water), 1966 **(135)**; Soul Time, 1967 **(67)**
Soul Vocal—New York

Elmer Gantry's Velvet Opera

Personnel: Elmer Gantry (vocals, guitars); Colin Forster (guitars) replaced (1968) by Paul Brett (guitars); John Ford (bass); Richard Hudson (drums)
Album: Elmer Gantry's Velvet Opera, 1968
Art Rock—British

The Enchanters

Personnel: Zola Pearnell (vocals); Samuel Bell (vocals); Charles Boyer (vocals)

Single: I Wanna Thank You, 1964 **(91)**

    R & B Vocal—Philadelphia; Garnet Mimms' backing group

Scott English

Singles: High on a Hill, 1964 **(77)** (with The Accents); Brandy, 1972 **(91)**

    Pop Vocal—American

The Equals

Personnel: Eddy Grant (guitars, vocals) replaced (1968) by Jimmy Haynes (guitars) replaced (1968) by Dave Martin (guitars); Lincoln Gordon (guitars); Dervin Gordon (vocals); Pat Lloyd (bass, guitars); John Hall (drums) replaced (1968) by Neil McBain (drums)

Albums: Unequalled, 1967; Equal Sensation, 1968; Sensational Equals, 1968; Equals Supreme, 1968; Baby Come Back, 1968; Equals Strike Back, 1969; Best of the Equals, 1969; At the Top, 1970; Equals Rock Around the Clock, 1974; Doin' the 45's, 1975; Born Ya, 1976; Mystic Syster, 1978; 20 Greatest Hits, 1984

Single: Baby, Come Back, 1968 **(32)**

    Reggae/Rock—British/Jamaican

The Esquires

Personnel: Gilbert Alvis (vocals); Betty Moorer (vocals) replaced (1965) by Shawn Taylor (vocals); Sam Pace (vocals); added (1967) Millard Edwards (vocals)

Album: The Esquires, 1967

Singles: Get on Up, 1967 **(11)**; And Get Away, 1967 **(22)**; You Say, 1968 **(126)**; You've Got the Power,
1968 **(91)**; Girls of the City, 1971 **(120)**

    Soul/Pop Vocal—Milwaukee

The Essex

Personnel: Anita Humes (vocals); Walter Vickers (vocals); Rodney Taylor (vocals); Rudy Johnson (vocals); Billie Hill (vocals)

Album: Easier Said Than Done, 1963

Singles: Easier Said Than Done, 1963 **(1)**; A Walkin' Miracle, 1963 **(12)**; She's Got Everything, 1963 **(56)**

    Soul Vocal—North Carolina; members were former Marines

The Eternals

Personnel: Charles Girona (vocals); Ernest Sierra (vocals); Fred Hodge (vocals); Arnie Torres (vocals); Alex Miranda (vocals)

Single: Rockin' in the Jungle, 1959 **(78)**

    Pop Vocal—New York

Eternity's Children

Personnel: Bruce Blackman (keyboards, vocals)

Album: Eternity's Children, 1968

Singles: Mrs. Bluebird, 1968 **(69)**; Sunshine Among Us, 1968 **(117)**

    Folk/Rock—American

Paul Evans

Singles: Seven Little Girls Sitting in the Back Seat, 1959 **(9)**; Midnite Special, 1960 **(16)**; Happy-Go-Lucky-Me, 1960 **(10)**; The Brigade of Broken Hearts, 1960 **(81)**

    Pop Vocal—New York

Betty Everett

Albums: You're No Good, 1963; It's in His Kiss, 1964; They're Delicious Together, 1965; The Very Best of Betty Everett, 1967; Betty Everett & Ketty Lester, 1967; Betty Everett, 1968; There'll Come a Time, 1969; Starring Betty Everett, 1970; Together, 1971; Love Rhymes, 1973; Happy Endings, 1975; Hot to Hold, 1980

Singles: You're No Good, 1963 **(51)**; The Shoop Shoop Song (It's in His Kiss), 1964 **(6)**; I Can't Hear You, 1964 **(66)**; Happy I Long to Be, 1964 **(126)**; It Hurts to Be in Love, 1964 **(109)**; Let It Be Me, 1964 **(5)** (with Jerry Butler); Getting Mighty Crowded, 1964 **(65)**; Smile, 1964 **(42)** (with Jerry Butler); Gonna Be Ready, 1965 **(117)**; There'll Come a Time, 1969 **(26)**; I Can't Say No to You, 1969 **(78)**; Maybe, 1969 **(116)**; It's Been a Long Time, 1969 **(96)**; I Got to Tell Somebody, 1970 **(96)**; Ain't Nothing Gonna Change Me, 1971 **(113)**

Soul Vocal—Mississippi

The Everly Brothers

Personnel: Don Everly (guitars, vocals); Phil Everly (guitars, vocals)

Albums: The Everly Brothers, 1958; Songs Our Daddy Taught Us, 1958; Folk Songs by the Everly Brothers, 1959; Their Best, 1959; It's Everly Time!, 1960; The Fabulous Style of the Everly Brothers, 1960; A Date with the Everly Brothers, 1960; Both Sides of an Evening, 1961; Instant Party, 1962; The Golden Hits of the Everly Brothers, 1962; Christmas with the Everly Brothers, 1962; Sing Country Hits, 1963; Very Best of the Everly Brothers, 1965; Rock 'n' Soul, 1965; Gone, Gone, Gone, 1965; Beat & Soul, 1965; In Our Image, 1965; Two Yanks in England, 1965; Hit Sound of the Everly Brothers, 1967; The Everly Brothers Sing, 1967; Roots, 1968; Wake Up Little Susie, 1969; Chained to a Memory, 1970; The Everly Brothers' Show, 1970; The Everly Brothers' Original Greatest Hits, 1970; End of an Era, 1970; Stories We Could Tell, 1972; The History of the Everly Brothers, 1972; Pass the Chicken, 1973; Most Beautiful Songs of the Everly Brothers, 1973; Everly's, 1975; Walk Right Back, 1975; New Album, 1977; Greatest Hits 1, 1978; Greatest Hits 2, 1978; Greatest Hits 3, 1978; Rock 'n' Roll Forever, 1981; The Everly Brothers, 1981; The Everly Brothers Reunion Concert, 1984; EB 84, 1984

Singles: Bye Bye Love/I Wonder If I Care as Much, 1957 **(2)**; Wake Up Little Susie, 1957 **(1)**; This Little Girl of Mine/Should We Tell Him, 1958 **(26)**; All I Have to Do Is Dream, 1958 **(1)**; Claudette, 1958 **(30)**; Bird Dog, 1958 **(1)**; Devoted

The Everly Brothers

to You, 1958 **(10)**; Problems, 1958 **(2)**; Love of My Life, 1958 **(40)**; Take a Message to Mary, 1959 **(16)**; Poor Jenny, 1959 **(22)**; ('Til) I Kissed You, 1959 **(4)**; Let It Be Me, 1960 **(7)**; Cathy's Clown, 1960 **(1)**; Always It's You, 1960 **(56)**; When Will I Be Loved, 1960 **(8)**; Be Bop-a-Lula, 1960 **(74)**; So Sad (to Watch Good Love Go Bad), 1960 **(7)**; Lucille, 1960 **(21)**; Like Strangers, 1960 **(22)**; Brand New Heartache, 1960 **(109)**; Ebony Eyes, 1961 **(8)**; Walk Right Back, 1961 **(7)**; Temptation, 1961 **(27)**; Stick with Me Baby, 1961 **(41)**; All I Have to Do Is Dream, 1961 **(96)**; Don't Blame Me, 1961 **(20)**; Muskrat, 1961 **(82)**; Crying in the Rain, 1962 **(6)**; That's Old Fashioned (That's the Way Love Should Be), 1962 **(9)**; How Can I Meet Her?, 1962 **(75)**; I'm Here to Get My Baby Out of Jail, 1962 **(76)**; Don't Ask Me to Be Friends, 1962 **(48)**; No One Can Make My Sunshine Smile, 1963 **(117)**; Nancy's Minuet, 1963 **(107)**; (So It Was . . . So It Is) So It Always Will Be, 1963 **(116)**; It's Been Nice (Goodnight), 1963 **(101)**; Love Her, 1963 **(117)**; Ain't That Lovin' You, Baby, 1964 **(133)**; The Ferris Wheel, 1964 **(72)**; Gone, Gone, Gone, 1964 **(31)**; You're My Girl, 1965 **(110)**; That'll Be the Day, 1965 **(111)**; The Price of Love, 1965 **(104)**; Love Is Strange, 1965 **(128)**; Bowling Green, 1967 **(40)**; Love of the Common People, 1967 **(114)**; It's My Time, 1968 **(112)**; On the Wings of a Nightingale, 1984 **(50)**

Folk/Pop Vocal — American

Every Father's Teenage Son

Single: A Letter to Dad, 1967 **(93)**

Spoken Word; a reply to "An Open Letter to My Teenage Son" by Victor Lundberg

Every Mother's Son

Personnel: Larry Larden (guitars, vocals); Dennis Larden (guitars, banjo, vocals); Schuyler Larden (bass); Bruce Milner (keyboards); Christopher Augustine (drums)

Albums: Every Mother's Son, 1967; Back, 1968

Singles: Come on Down to My Boat, 1967 **(6)**; Put Your Mind at Ease, 1967 **(46)**; Pony with the Golden Mane, 1967 **(93)**; No One Knows, 1968 **(96)**

Pop/Rock — New York

Everything Is Everything

Personnel: Danny Weiss (vocals, guitars); Chris Hill (vocals, guitars)

Single: Witchi Tai To, 1969 **(69)**

Pop/Rock — American

The Excellents

Single: Coney Island Baby, 1962 **(51)**

Pop Vocal — New York

The Exciters

Personnel: Carol Johnson (vocals); Brenda Reid (vocals); Lilian Walker (vocals); Herbert Rooney (vocals)

Albums: Tell Him, 1963; Exciters, 1965; Caviar & Chitling, 1966; Black Beauty, 1967

Singles: Tell Him, 1962 **(4)**; He's Got the Power, 1963 **(57)**; Get Him, 1963 **(76)**; Do-Wah-Diddy, 1964 **(78)**; I Want You to Be My Boy,

1965 **(98)**; A Little Bit of Soap, 1966 **(58)**
Soul/Pop Vocal—New York

Eyes of Blues

Personnel: Gary Pickford Hopkins (vocals); Ritchie Francis (guitars, vocals); Ray Williams (bass) replaced (1969) by Ray Bennett (bass); Phil Ryan (keyboards); Wyndham Rees (drums) replaced (1969) by John Weathers (drums)
Albums: Crossroads of Time, 1968; In Fields of Ardath, 1969
Blues/Rock—British

Shelley Fabares

Albums: Shelley!, 1962; The Things We Did Last Summer, 1962
Singles: Johnny Angel, 1962 **(1)**; Johnny Loves Me, 1962 **(21)**; The Things We Did Last Summer, 1962 **(46)**; Telephone (Won't You Ring), 1963 **(109)**; Ronnie, Call Me When You Get a Chance, 1963 **(72)**
Pop Vocal—California; played "Mary Stone" on the Donna Reed TV show

Fabian

Albums: Hold That Tiger, 1959; Fabulous Fabian, 1959; Good Old Summertime, 1960; Rockin' Hot, 1960; 16 Greatest Hits, 1962; Facade, 1963; Very Best of Fabian, 1974
Singles: I'm a Man, 1959 **(31)**; Turn Me Loose, 1959 **(9)**; Tiger, 1959 **(3)**; Come On and Get Me, 1959 **(29)**; Got the Feeling, 1959 **(54)**; Hound Dog Man, 1959 **(9)**; This Friendly World, 1959 **(12)**; String Along, 1960 **(39)**; About This Thing Called Love, 1960 **(31)**; Kissin' and Twistin', 1960 **(91)**
Pop Vocal—Philadelphia; last name is Forte

Tommy Facenda

Single: High School U.S.A., 1959 **(28)**
Novelty Pop—Virginia

Faces (The Small Faces)

Personnel: Steve Marriott (guitars, vocals; deceased 1991) replaced (1970) by Rod Stewart (vocals) replaced (1978) by Steve Marriott (guitars, vocals); Ronnie Lane (bass, vocals) replaced (1974) by Testu Yamauchi (bass) replaced (1978) by Rick Wills (bass); Ian McLagan (keyboards); Jimmy Winston (organ) left group (1965); Kenney Jones (drums); added Ron Wood (guitars, vocals) replaced (1978) by Jimmy McCulloch (guitars, vocals; deceased 1979)
Albums: Small Faces, 1966; From the Beginning, 1967; Ogden's Nut Gone Flake, 1968; Autumn Stone, 1969; In Memoriam, 1970; First

Step, 1970; Long Player, 1971; A Nod's as Good as a Wink to a Blind Horse, 1971; Ooh La La, 1973; Coast to Coast: Overture and Beginners, 1974; There Are But Four Small Faces, 1975; Greatest Hits, 1976; Snakes and Ladders: The Best of the Faces, 1977; Playmates, 1977; Stay with Me, 1977; 78 in the Shade, 1978; Big Music, 1984

Singles: Itchykoo Park, 1967 **(16)**; Tin Soldier, 1968 **(73)**; Lazy Sunday, 1968 **(114)**; (I Know) I'm Losing You, 1971 **(24)**; Stay with Me, 1972 **(17)**; Cindy Incidentally, 1973 **(48)**

Blues/Rock — British

Fairport Convention

Personnel: Richard Thompson (guitars, vocals, mandolin) replaced (1971) by Roger Hill (guitars, vocals) replaced (1972) by David Rea (guitars) replaced (1972) by Trevor Lucas (guitars, vocals) replaced (1976) by Dan Arbras (guitars) replaced (1976) by Richard Thompson (guitars, vocals) replaced (1985) by Martin Allcock (guitars, bass); Ashley Hutchings (bass, vocals) replaced (1969) by Dave Pegg (bass, vocals, mandolin); Simon Nicol (guitars, vocals) replaced (1972) by Jerry Donohue (guitars) replaced (1976) by Simon Nicol (guitars, vocals); Ian Matthews (vocals, percussion) replaced (1969) by Dave Swarbrick (vocals, violin, mandolin) replaced (1976) by Roger Burridge (violin) replaced (1976) by Dave Swarbrick (vocals, violin, mandolin) replaced (1985) by Ric Sanders (violin); Judy Dyble (vocals,

Fairport Convention: *bottom row:* **Mattacks, Allcock;** *top row:* **Nicol, Pegg, Sanders**

autoharp) replaced (1968) by Sandy Denny (vocals, guitars; deceased 1978); Martin Lamble (drums; deceased 1969) replaced (1969) by Dave Mattacks (drums) replaced (1972) by Tom Farnell (drums) replaced (1972) by David Mattacks (drums, keyboards) replaced (1975) by Paul Warren (drums) replaced (1975) by Bruce Rowland (drums) replaced (1979) by David Mattacks (drums, keyboards); added (1974) Sandy Denny (vocals) replaced (1976) by Bob Brady (piano) left group (1979)

Albums: Fairport Convention, 1968; What We Did on Our Holidays, 1969; Unhalfbricking, 1969; Liege and Lief, 1970; Full House, 1970; Angel Delight, 1971; Babbacombe Lee, 1971; Fairport Chronicles, 1972; Rosie, 1973; Nine, 1973; Fairport Live/A Moveable Feast, 1974; Rising for the Moon, 1975; Gottle o' Gear, 1976; Live at the L.A. Troubador, 1976; The Bonny Bunch of Roses, 1977; Tipplers Tales, 1978; Farewell Farewell, 1979; Moat on the Ledge, 1982; A T 2, 1984; Gladys' Leap, 1985; Expletive Delighted, 1986; In Real Time, 1987; Heyday, 1988; Five Seasons, 1991; The Woodworm Years, 1991

Folk/Rock—British; band holds a reunion concert every August with past members

Adam Faith

Albums: Adam, 1964; Beat Girl, 1964; Adam Faith, 1965; From Adam with Love, 1965; For You, 1966; On the Move, 1967; Faith Alive, 1968; Best of Adam Faith, 1974; I Survive, 1976

Singles: It's Alright, 1965 **(31)**; Talk About Love, 1965 **(97)**

Pop/Rock—British; real name is Terence Nelhams

Marianne Faithfull

Albums: Come My Way, 1965; Marianne Faithfull, 1965; Go Away from My World, 1965; North Country Maid, 1966; Faithfull Forever, 1966; Love in a Mist, 1967; Greatest Hits, 1968; The World of Marianne Faithfull, 1969; Dreamin' My Dreams, 1976; Faithless, 1978; Broken English, 1980; As Tears Go By, 1981; Dangerous Acquaintances, 1981; A Child's Adventure, 1983; Strange Weather, 1987; Blazing Away, 1990

Singles: As Tears Go By, 1964 **(22)**; Come and Stay with Me, 1965 **(26)**; This Little Bird, 1965 **(32)**; Summer Nights, 1965 **(24)**; Go Away from My World, 1965 **(89)**; Is This What I Get for Loving You?, 1967 **(125)**; The Ballad of Lucy Jordan, 1980; Broken English, 1980; Sweetheart, 1981; Blue Millionaire, 1983; Running for Our Lives, 1983; As Tears Go By, 1987

Pop/Rock Vocal—British; starred

in the French film "The Girl on the Motorcycle"

The Falcons

Personnel: Eddie Floyd (vocals) replaced (1961) by Wilson Pickett (vocals); Bonny "Mack" Rice (vocals); Joe Stubbs (vocals); Willie Schofield (vocals); Lance Finnie (vocals)

Singles: You're So Fine, 1959 **(17)**; You're Mine, 1959 **(107)**; I Found a Love, 1962 **(75)**; Standing on Guard, 1966 **(107)**

R & B Vocal — Detroit

Georgie Fame & The Blue Flames

Personnel: Georgie Fame (keyboards, vocals); Colin Green (guitars); Cliff Barton (bass) replaced (1966) by Phil Bates (bass); John Mitchell (drums) replaced (1966) by Bill Eyden (drums)

Albums: R & B at the Flamingo, 1964; Fame at Last, 1964; Yeh Yeh, 1965; Sweet Thing, 1966; Sound Venture, 1966; Get Away, 1966; Hall of Fame, 1967; Two Faces of Fame, 1967; Third Face of Fame, 1968; The Ballad of Bonnie and Clyde, 1968; Seventh Son, 1969; Does His Own Thing with Strings, 1970; Going Home, 1971; Fame & Price, 1971; All Me Own Work, 1972; Georgie Fame, 1974; Georgie Fame Right Now!, 1979; That's What Friends Are For, 1979; Closing the Gap, 1980; In Hogland, 1981; 20 Beat Classics, 1983; Together, 1985; Cool Cat Blues, 1991

Singles: Yeh Yeh, 1965 **(21)**; In the Meantime, 1965 **(97)**; Get Away, 1966 **(70)**; The Ballad of Bonnie and Clyde, 1968 **(7)**

Glam Rock — British; real name is Clive Powell

Family

Personnel: Roger Chapman (vocals); Charlie Whitney (guitars); Jim King (saxophones, flutes) replaced (1970) by John Palmer (keyboards) replaced (1973) by Tony Ashton (keyboards, vocals); Ric Grech (bass, violin, vocals) replaced (1970) by John Weider (bass, violin, vocals) replaced (1971) by John Wetton (bass, vocals) replaced (1973) by Jim Cregan (bass, guitars); Rob Townsend (drums)

Albums: Music in a Doll's House, 1968; Family Entertainment, 1969; A Song for Me, 1970; Anyway, 1970; Fearless, 1971; Old Songs, New Songs, 1971; Bandstand, 1972; It's Only a Movie, 1973; Best of Family, 1974

Blues/Rock — British

Fantastic Four

Personnel: James Epps (vocals); Robert Pruitt (vocals) replaced (1972) by Cleveland Horne (vocals); Joseph Pruitt (vocals); Toby Childs (vocals) replaced (1972) by Ernest Newsome (vocals)

Albums: The Whole World Is a Stage, 1967; Alvin Stone (the Birth and Death of a Gangster), 1975

Singles: The Whole World Is a Stage, 1967 **(63)**; You Gave Me Something (and Everything's Alright), 1967 **(55)**; To Share Your Love, 1967 **(68)**; I Love You Madly, 1968 **(56)**; I Feel Like I'm Falling in Love Again, 1969 **(111)**; Alvin Stone (the Birth and Death of a Gangster), 1975 **(74)**

R & B Vocal — Detroit

Fantastic Johnny C

Singles: Boogaloo Down Broadway, 1967 **(7)**; Got What You Need, 1968 **(56)**; Hitch It to the Horse, 1968 **(34)**; (She's) Some Kind of Wonderful, 1968 **(87)**; Is There Anything Better Than Making Love, 1969 **(130)**

Soul Vocal—South Carolina; last name is Corley

Don Fardon

Albums: The Lament of the Cherokee, 1968; I've Paid My Dues, 1970; Released, 1970

Singles: (The Lament of the Cherokee) Indian Reservation, 1968 **(20)**; Delta Queen, 1973 **(86)**

Pop Vocal—British; real last name is Maughn

Chris Farlowe

Albums: Chris Farlowe & the Thunderbirds, 1966; Stormy Monday, 1966; Out of Time, 1966; Paint It Black, 1966; 14 Things to Think About, 1966; The Art of Chris Farlowe, 1966; The Best of Chris Farlowe, 1968; The Last Goodbye, 1969; From Here to Mama Rosa, 1970; Chris Farlowe Band Live, 1975; Greatest Hits, 1977; Out of the Blue, 1980

Singles: Out of Time, 1966 **(122)**; Out of Time, 1975

Pop/Rock—British; real name is John Henry Deighton; member of Atomic Rooster and Colosseum

Fat Mattress

Personnel: Neil Landon (vocals); Noel Redding (guitars, bass, vocals) replaced by Steven Hammond (guitars); James Leverton (bass, keyboards, vocals); Eric Dillon (drums)

Albums: Fat Mattress, 1969; Fat Mattress 2, 1970

Blues/Rock—British

Jose Feliciano

Albums: Feliciano, 1968; Souled, 1968; Feliciano/10 to 23, 1969; Alive Alive-O!, 1969; Fireworks, 1970; Encore! Jose Feliciano's Finest Performances, 1971; That the Spirit Needs, 1971; Compartments, 1973; And the Feeling's Good, 1974; Just Wanna Rock 'n' Roll, 1975

Singles: Light My Fire, 1968 **(3)**; Hi-Heel Sneakers, 1968 **(25)**; Hitchcock Railway, 1968 **(77)**; The Star Spangled Banner, 1968 **(50)**; Hey! Baby, 1969 **(71)**; My World Is Empty Without You, 1969 **(87)**; Marley Purt Drive, 1969 **(70)**; She's a Woman, 1969 **(103)**; Rain, 1969 **(76)**; Destiny, 1970 **(83)**; Susie-Q, 1970 **(84)**; I Only Want to Say (Gethsemane), 1971 **(122)**; Chico and the Man, 1975 **(96)**

Latin/Pop—Puerto Rico; born blind; also became TV actor

The Fendermen

Personnel: Phil Humphrey (vocals); Jim Sundquist (vocals)

Singles: Mule Skinner Blues, 1960 **(5)**; Don't You Just Know It, 1960 **(110)**

Folk Vocal—Wisconsin

Johnny Ferguson

Single: Angela Jones, 1960 **(27)**

Pop Vocal—Nashville

Ferris Wheel

Personnel: Linda Lewis (vocals); Keith Anthony (guitars) replaced (1969) by Terry Edmunds (guitars); Micky Liston (guitars) replaced (1969) by Bernie Holland (guitars, vocals); Michael Snow (keyboards, guitars, vocals); George Sweetnam-Ford (bass, vocals); David Sweetnam-Ford (saxophones); Dennis Elliott (drums)

Albums: Can't Break the Habit, 1967; Ferris Wheel, 1970

Art Rock — British

Fever Tree

Personnel: Dennis Keller (vocals); Michael (guitars); E. E. Wolfe (bass); Rob Landes (woodwinds, keyboards); John Tuttle (drums, percussion)

Albums: Fever Tree, 1968; Another Time, Another Place, 1968; Creation, 1969; For Sale, 1970

Single: San Francisco Girls (Return of the Native), 1968 **(91)**

Psychedelic Pop — Houston

The Fiestas

Personnel: Tommy Bullock (vocals); Eddie Morris (vocals); Sam Ingalls (vocals); Preston Lane (vocals)

Singles: So Fine, 1959 **(11)**; Broken Heart, 1962 **(81)**; I Feel Good All Over, 1962 **(123)**

R & B Vocal — New Jersey

Fifth Dimension

Personnel: Marilyn McCoo (vocals); Billy Davis, Jr. (vocals); Lamonte McLemore (vocals); Florence LaRue Gordon (vocals); Ron Townson (vocals)

Fifth Dimension: McLemore, Gordon, Davis, McCoo, Townson

Albums: Up, Up and Away, 1967; The Magic Garden, 1968; Stoned Soul Picnic, 1968; The Age of Aquarius, 1969; Portrait, 1970; The 5th Dimension/Greatest Hits, 1970; The July 5th Album, 1970; Love's Lines, Angles and Rhymes, 1971; The 5th Dimension/Live!!, 1971; Reflections, 1971; Individually & Collectively, 1972; Greatest Hits on Earth, 1972; Living Together, Growing Together, 1973; Earthbound, 1975; Star Dancing, 1978

Singles: Go Where You Wanna Go, 1967 **(16)**; Another Day, Another Heartache, 1967 **(45)**; Up, Up and Away, 1967 **(7)**; Paper Cup, 1967 **(34)**; Carpet Man, 1968 **(29)**; Stoned Soul Picnic, 1968 **(3)**; Sweet Blindness, 1968 **(13)**; California Soul, 1968 **(25)**; Aquarius/Let the Sunshine In, 1969 **(1)**; Workin' on a Groovy Thing, 1969 **(20)**; Wedding Bell Blues, 1969 **(1)**; Blowing Away, 1970 **(21)**; A Change Is Gonna Come & People Gotta Be Free (medley)/The Declaration, 1970 **(60)**; The Girls' Song, 1970 **(43)**;

Puppet Man, 1970 **(24)**; Save the Country, 1970 **(27)**; On the Beach (in the Summertime), 1970 **(54)**; One Less Bell to Answer, 1970 **(2)**; Love's Lines, Angles and Rhymes, 1971 **(19)**; Light Sings, 1971 **(44)**; Never My Love, 1971 **(12)**; Together Let's Find Love, 1972 **(37)**; (Last Night) I Didn't Get to Sleep at All, 1972 **(8)**; If I Could Reach You, 1972 **(10)**; Living Together, Growing Together, 1973 **(32)**; Everything's Been Changed, 1973 **(70)**; Ashes to Ashes, 1973 **(52)**; Flashback, 1973 **(82)**; No Love in the Room, 1975 **(105)**; Love Hangover, 1976 **(80)**

Pop Vocal—Los Angeles; McCoo hosted the "Solid Gold" TV show in the 1980s; Davis and McLemore are cousins

The Fifth Estate

Singles: Ding Dong! The Witch Is Dead, 1967 **(11)**; Do Drop Inn, 1968 **(122)**

Pop Vocal—American

Larry Finnegan

Singles: Dear One, 1962 **(11)**; The Other Ringo (A Tribute to Ringo Starr), 1964 **(130)**

Pop Vocal—New York; died of a brain tumor in 1973; real name was John Finneran

The Fireballs

Personnel: Chuck Tharp (vocals) replaced (1960) by Jimmy Gilmer (vocals, keyboards); George Tomsco (guitars); Dan Trammell (guitars) left group (1959); Stan Lark (bass); Eric Budd (drums) replaced (1962) by Doug Roberts (drums; deceased 1982)

Albums: Torquay, 1960; Vaquero, 1961; Here We Go, 1961; Sugar Shack, 1963; Firewater, 1963; Campusology, 1964; Bottle of Wine, 1968; Come On, React, 1969

Singles: Torquay, 1959 **(39)**; Bulldog, 1960 **(24)**; Vaquero (Cowboy), 1960 **(99)**; Quite a Party, 1961 **(27)**; Sugar Shack, 1963 **(1)**; Daisy Petal Pickin', 1963 **(15)**; Ain't Gonna Tell Anybody, 1964 **(53)**; Look at Me, 1964 **(133)**; What Kinda Love, 1964 **(133)**; Bottle of Wine, 1967 **(9)**; Goin' Away, 1968 **(79)**; Come On, React!, 1968 **(63)**; Long Green, 1969 **(73)**

Rockabilly—New Mexico

Fireflies

Personnel: Ritchie Adams (vocals); Lee Reynolds (vocals); Paul Giacolone (vocals); Johnny Viscelli (vocals)

Album: You Were Mine, 1959
Singles: You Were Mine, 1959 **(21)**; I Can't Say Goodbye, 1960 **(90)**

Pop Vocal—New York

Five Americans

Albums: I See the Light, 1966; Western Union, 1967; Progressions, 1967; Now and Then, 1968
Singles: I See the Light, 1966 **(26)**; Evol-Not Love, 1966 **(52)**; Western Union, 1967 **(5)**; Sound of Love, 1967 **(36)**; Zip Code, 1967 **(36)**; Stop Light, 1967 **(132)**; 7:30 Guided Tour, 1968 **(96)**; Virginia Girl, 1969 **(133)**
Blue-Eyed Soul—Dallas

Five by Five

Personnel: Ronnie Plants (vocals)
Album: Next Exit, 1968
Singles: Fire, 1968 **(52)**; Apple Cider, 1969 **(133)**
Hard Rock—American

The Five Keys

Personnel: Rudy West (vocals); Bernie West (vocals); Ripley Ingram (vocals); Raphael Ingram (vocals) replaced (1952) by Dickie Smith (vocals) replaced (1953) by Ramon Loper (vocals); Maryland Pierce (vocals)
Singles: Ling, Ting, Tong, 1954 **(28)**; Out of Sight, Out of Mind, 1956 **(23)**; Wisdom of a Fool, 1956 **(35)**; Let There Be You, 1957 **(69)**
R & B Vocal—Virginia

The 5 Royales

Personnel: Lowman Pauling (vocals); Clarence Pauling (vocals); Windsor King (vocals); Eugene Tanner (vocals); John Tanner (vocals)
Albums: Dedicated to You, 1960; Five Royales, 1961; All Time Hits, 1961; Rockin', 1962
Singles: Think, 1957 **(66)**; I Know It's Hard, But It's Fair, 1959 **(103)**;

I'm with You, 1960 **(107)**; Please Please Please, 1960 **(114)**; Dedicated to the One I Love, 1961 **(81)**
R & B Vocal—North Carolina

The Five Satins

Personnel: Fred Parris (vocals) replaced (1956) by Bill Baker (vocals) replaced (1958) by Fred Parris (vocals); Al Denby (vocals); Jim Freeman (vocals); Eddie Martin (vocals); Jessie Murphy (vocals, piano)
Album: In the Still of the Nite, 1960
Singles: In the Still of the Night, 1956 **(24)**; To the Aisle, 1957 **(25)**; When Your Love Comes Along, 1959 **(112)**; Shadows, 1959 **(87)**; In the Still of the Nite, 1960 **(81)**; I'll Be Seeing You, 1960 **(79)**; Your Memory, 1960 **(107)**; In the Still of the Nite, 1961 **(99)**; The Masquerade Is Over, 1962 **(102)**; Memories of Days Gone By, 1982 **(71)**
R & B Vocal—Connecticut

The Five Stairsteps

Personnel: Clarence Burke, Jr. (vocals); James Burke (vocals); Kenneth Burke (vocals); Aloha Burke (vocals); Dennis Burke (vocals); added (1967) Cubie Burke (vocals)
Albums: The Five Stairsteps, 1967; Our Family Portrait, 1968; Love's Happening, 1969; Stairsteps, 1970; Step by Step by Step, 1970
Singles: You Waited Too Long, 1966 **(94)**; World of Fantasy, 1966 **(49)**; Come Back, 1966 **(61)**; Danger! She's a Stranger, 1967 **(89)**; Ain't Gonna Rest (Till I Get You), 1967 **(87)**; Oooh, Baby Baby, 1967 **(63)**; Something's Missing, 1967 **(88)**; A Million to One, 1968 **(68)**;

The Shadow of Your Love, 1968 **(94)**; Don't Change Your Love, 1968 **(59)**; Stay Close to Me, 1968 **(91)**; Baby Make Me Feel So Good, 1969 **(101)**; We Must Be in Love, 1969 **(88)**; Dear Prudence, 1970 **(66)**; O-oh Child, 1970 **(8)**; America/Standing (medley)/Because I Love You, 1970 **(83)**; Didn't It Look So Easy, 1971 **(81)**; I Love You—Stop, 1972 **(115)**; From Us to You, 1976 **(102)**; Tell Me Why, 1976 **(106)**

Soul Vocal—Chicago

The Flamingos

Personnel: Zeke Carey (vocals) replaced (1956) by Tommy Hunt (vocals) replaced (1958) by Zeke Carey (vocals); Jake Carey (vocals); Paul Wilson (vocals); Johnny Carter (vocals) replaced (1956) by Terry Johnson (vocals); Sollie McElroy (vocals) replaced (1954) by Nate Nelson (vocals; deceased 1984)

Singles: Lovers Never Say Goodbye, 1959 **(52)**; I Only Have Eyes for You, 1959 **(11)**; Love Walked In, 1959 **(88)**; I Was Such a Fool (to Fall in Love with You), 1960 **(71)**; Nobody Loves Me Like You, 1960 **(30)**; Mio Amore, 1960 **(74)**; Your Other Love, 1960 **(54)**; Kokomo, 1961 **(92)**; Time Was, 1961 **(45)**; Golden Teardrops, 1961 **(108)**; Lovers Never Say Goodbye, 1961 **(117)**; I Know Better, 1963 **(107)**; The Boogaloo Party, 1966 **(93)**; Buffalo Soldier, 1970 **(86)**

R & B Vocal—Chicago

The Flares

Personnel: Aaron Collins (vocals)
Singles: Foot Stomping—Part 1,

1961 **(25)**; The Monkey Walk, 1963 **(133)**

R & B Vocal—Los Angeles

Fleetwood Mac

Personnel: Mick Fleetwood (drums, percussion); John McVie (bass); Jeremy Spencer (guitars, vocals) replaced (1971) by Bob Welch (guitars, vocals) replaced (1975) by Lindsey Buckingham (guitars, vocals) replaced (1988) by Billy Burnette (guitars, vocals); Peter Green (guitars, vocals) replaced (1969) by Danny Kirwan (guitars, vocals) replaced (1973) by Bob Weston (guitars) replaced (1975) by Stevie Nicks (vocals) left group (1991); added (1968) Christine McVie (keyboards, vocals) left group (1991); added (1969) Walter Horton (harmonica) replaced (1973) by Dave Walker (vocals) left group (1973); added (1988) Rick Vito (guitars, vocals) left group (1991)

Albums: Fleetwood Mac, 1968; Mr. Wonderful, 1968; English Rose, 1969; Blues Jam at Chess, 1969; Fleetwood Mac in Chicago, 1969; Then Play On, 1969; Pious Bird of Good Omen, 1969; Kiln House, 1970; Black Magic Woman, 1970; Original Fleetwood Mac, 1971; Future Games, 1971; Greatest Hits, 1971; Bare Trees, 1972; Penguin, 1973; Mystery to Me, 1974; Heroes Are Hard to Find, 1974; Vintage Years, 1975; Fleetwood Mac, 1975; Albatross, 1977; Rumours, 1977; The Best of Fleetwood Mac, 1978; Man of the World, 1978; Tusk, 1979; Live, 1980; Mirage, 1982; Jumping at Shadows 1969, 1985; Tango in the Night, 1987; Greatest Hits, 1988; Behind the Mask, 1990

Singles: Albatross, 1969 **(104)**; Oh

Fleetwood Mac: J. McVie, Fleetwood, Nicks, C. McVie, Buckingham

Well, 1970 **(55)**; Black Magic Woman, 1970; Hypnotized, 1974; Over My Head, 1975 **(20)**; Rhiannon (Will You Ever Win), 1976 **(11)**; Say You Love Me, 1976 **(11)**; Go Your Own Way, 1976 **(10)**; Dreams, 1977 **(1)**; Don't Stop, 1977 **(3)**; You Make Loving Fun, 1977 **(9)**; Silver Springs, 1978; Tusk, 1979 **(8)**; Sara/Angel, 1979 **(7)**; Think About Me, 1980 **(20)**; Sisters of the Moon, 1980 **(86)**; Fireflies, 1980 **(60)**; The Farmer's Daughter, 1981; Hold Me, 1982 **(4)**; Gypsy, 1982 **(12)**; Love in Store, 1982 **(22)**; Oh Diane, 1983; Big Love, 1987 **(5)**; Seven Wonders, 1987 **(19)**; Little Lies, 1987 **(4)**; Everywhere, 1987 **(14)**; Family Man, 1988 **(90)**; As Long as You Follow, 1988 **(43)**; Save Me, 1990 **(33)**; Love Is Dangerous, 1990; Skies the Limit, 1990

Pop/Rock — British/American; John and Christine McVie were formerly married

The Fleetwoods

Ellis, Troxel, Christopher

Personnel: Gary Troxel (vocals); Barbara Ellis (vocals); Gretchen Christopher (vocals)

Album: The Fleetwoods' Greatest Hits, 1962

Singles: Come Softly to Me, 1959 **(1)**; Graduation's Here, 1959 **(39)**; Mr. Blue, 1959 **(1)**; You Mean Everything to Me, 1959 **(84)**; Outside My Window, 1960 **(28)**; Magic Star, 1960 **(113)**; Runaround, 1960 **(23)**; The Last One to Know, 1960 **(96)**; Tragedy, 1961 **(10)**; (He's) the Great Inposter, 1961 **(30)**; Lovers by Night, Strangers by Day, 1962 **(36)**; You Should Have Been There, 1963 **(114)**; Goodnight My Love, 1963 **(32)**; Ruby Red, Baby Blue, 1964 **(134)**; Mr. Sandman, 1964 **(113)**

Pop Vocal—Washington

Shelby Flint

Singles: Angel on My Shoulder, 1960 **(22)**; Little Dancing Doll, 1963 **(103)**; Cast Your Fate to the Wind, 1966 **(61)**

Pop Vocal—California

The Flirtations

Personnel: Shirley Pearce (vocals); Ernestine Pearce (vocals); Viola Billups (vocals)

Singles: Nothing but a Heartache, 1969 **(34)**; South Carolina, 1969 **(111)**

Pop Vocal—Southeast

Floating Bridge

Personnel: Rick Dangel (guitars); Joe Johansen (guitars); Joe Johnson (bass); Kent Morrill (keyboards); Mike Marinelli (drums)

Albums: Floating Bridge, 1969; Brought Up Wrong, 1970

Single: Don't Mean a Thing, 1969

Psychedelic Pop—Northwest

The Flock

Personnel: Fred Glickstein (guitars, vocals); Jerry Goodman (violin) replaced (1971) by Mike Zydowsky (violin); Rick Canoff (saxophones) replaced (1971) by James L. Hirsen (keyboards, vocals); Tom Webb (saxophones) left group (1971); Frank Posa (trumpet) left group (1971); Jerry Smith (bass, vocals); Ron Karpman (drums, vocals)

Albums: The Flock, 1969; Dinosaur Swamps, 1971; Inside Out, 1975

Progressive Rock—Midwest

Eddie Floyd

Albums: Knock on Wood, 1967; Never Found a Girl, 1968; Rare Stamps, 1969; You've Got to Have Eddie, 1969; California Girl, 1970; Down to Earth, 1971; Think About It, 1972; Soul Street, 1974; Baby Lay Your Head, 1975; Experience, 1977; Chronicle, 1978

Singles: Knock on Wood, 1966 **(28)**; Raise Your Hand, 1967 **(79)**; Don't Rock the Boat, 1967 **(98)**; Love Is a Doggone Good Thing, 1967 **(97)**; On a Saturday Night, 1967 **(92)**; Big Bird, 1968 **(132)**; I've Never Found a Girl (to Love Me Like You Do), 1968 **(40)**; Bring It Home to Me, 1968 **(17)**; I've Got to Have Your Love, 1969 **(102)**; Don't Tell Your Mama (Where You've Been), 1969 **(73)**; Why Is the Wine Sweeter (on the Other Side), 1969 **(98)**; California Girl, 1970 **(45)**; My Girl, 1970 **(116)**; The Best Years of

My Life, 1971 **(118)**; Yum Yum Yum (I Want Some), 1972 **(122)**
Soul Vocal—Alabama

Flying Burrito Brothers

Personnel: Gram Parsons (guitars, vocals; deceased 1973) replaced (1970) by Rick Roberts (guitars, vocals) replaced (1974) by Floyd "Gib" Guilbeau (guitars, vocals); Chris Hillman (guitars, bass, vocals) replaced (1972) by Roger Bush (bass) replaced (1975) by Joel Scott Hill (bass); "Sneaky" Pete Kleinow (pedal steel guitar) replaced (1971) by Al Perkins (pedal steel guitar) replaced (1972) by Don Beck (pedal steel guitar) replaced (1974) by Pete Kleinow (pedal steel guitar); Chris Etheridge (bass, vocals, keyboards) replaced (1969) by Bernie Leadon (guitars, vocals, banjo) replaced (1971) by Kenny Wertz (guitars, vocals) replaced (1974) by Chris Etheridge (bass, vocals, keyboards) replaced (1975) by Skip Battin (guitars, vocals) replaced (1980) by John Beland (guitars, vocals); Jon Corneal (drums) replaced (1969) by Michael Clarke (drums) replaced (1972) by Erik Dalton (drums) replaced (1974) by Gene Parsons (drums) replaced (1976) by Ed Ponder (drums) replaced (1980) by Mick McGee (drums); added (1971) Byron Berline (violin) replaced (1972) by Alan Munde (banjo, guitars) left group (1972)
Albums: Gilded Palace of Sin, 1969; Burrito Deluxe, 1970; Flying Burrito Brothers, 1971; Last of the Red Hot Burritos, 1971; Close Up the Honky Tonks, 1974; Flying Again, 1975; Hot Burrito, 1975; Live in Amsterdam, 1975; Airborne, 1976; Sleepless Nights, 1976; Bluegrass Special, 1977; Live from Tokyo, 1978; Close Encounters to the West Coast, 1978; Farther Along/Best Of, 1980; Hearts on the Line, 1981; Sunset Sundown, 1982; Cabin Fever, 1984; Live from Europe, 1985
Singles: Waitin' for Love to Begin, 1976; She's a Friend of a Friend, 1981; Does She Wish She Was Single Again, 1981; She Belongs to Everyone but Me, 1981; If Something Should Come Between Us (Let It Be Love), 1981; Closer to You, 1982; Almost Saturday Night, 1984; My Kind of Lady, 1984
Country/Rock—American

Flying Machine

Personnel: Steve Jones (guitars, vocals); Tony Newman (guitars); Stuart Coleman (bass, vocals); Paul Wilkinson (drums, vocals)
Album: Down to Earth, 1969
Singles: Smile a Little Smile for Me, 1969 **(5)**; Baby Make It Soon, 1970 **(87)**
Pop/Rock—British

Wayne Fontana & The Mindbenders

Personnel: Wayne Fontana (vocals) replaced (1966) by James O'Neil (guitars); Eric Stewart (guitars, vocals); Bob Land (bass); Rick Rothwell (drums)
Albums: Wayne Fontana & the Mindbenders, 1965; Eric Rick Wayne Bob, 1966; Wayne One, 1966; The Mindbenders, 1966; With Woman in Mind, 1967; A Groovy Kind of Love, 1967; To Sir with Love (Soundtrack), 1967

Singles: Game of Love, 1965 **(1)**; It's a Little Bit Too Late, 1965 **(45)**; A Groovy Kind of Love, 1966 **(2)**; Ashes to Ashes, 1966 **(55)**; Come on Home, 1966 **(117)** (Wayne Fontana solo)

Pop/Rock — British; group became the Mindbenders after Fontana went solo in 1966

Frankie Ford

Singles: Sea Cruise, 1959 **(14)**; Alimony, 1959 **(97)**; Time After Time, 1960 **(75)**; You Talk Too Much, 1960 **(87)**; Seventeen, 1961 **(72)**

Pop Vocal — Louisiana; real name is Frank Guzzo

Forest

Personnel: Hadrian Welham (vocals, guitars, keyboards); Martin Welham (vocals, guitars, keyboards, percussion); Derek Allenby (keyboards, vocals, harmonica)

Albums: Forest, 1969; Full Circle, 1970

Progressive Rock — British

The Fortunes

Personnel: Barry Pritchard (guitars, vocals); Glen Dale (guitars, vocals); Rod Allen (bass); John Davey (keyboards, vocals) replaced (1971) by David Carr (keyboards); John Trickett (drums) replaced (1971) by Andy Brown (drums)

Albums: Fortunes, 1965; Here Comes That Rainy Day Feeling Again, 1971; Fortunes, 1972; Storm in a Teacup, 1972; Remembering the Fortunes, 1976; You've Got Your Troubles, 1980; Hit Collection, 1984

Singles: You've Got Your Troubles, 1965 **(7)**; Here It Comes Again, 1965 **(27)**; This Golden Ring, 1966 **(82)**; That Same Old Feeling, 1970 **(62)**; Here Comes That Rainy Day Feeling Again, 1971 **(15)**; Freedom Comes, Freedom Goes, 1971 **(72)**

Pop/Rock — British

The Forum

Personnel: Phil Campos (vocals); Rene Nole (vocals); Riselle Bain (vocals)

Single: The River Is Wide, 1977 **(63)**

Pop Vocal — California

The Foundations

Personnel: Alan Warner (guitars); Peter Macbeth (bass); Clem Curtis (vocals); Colin Young (vocals); Tony Gomez (keyboards); Eric Allan Dale (trombone); Pat Burke (saxophones, flutes); Mike Elliot (saxophones); Tim Harris (drums)

Albums: From the Foundations, 1967; Baby Now That I've Found You, 1967; Build Me Up Buttercup, 1968; The Foundations, 1968; It's All Right, 1968; Digging the Foundations, 1969; Golden Hour, 1973

Singles: Baby, Now That I've Found You, 1967 **(11)**; Back on My Feet Again, 1968 **(59)**; Build Me Up Buttercup, 1969 **(3)**; In the Bad, Bad Old Days (Before You Loved Me), 1969 **(51)**; My Little Chickadee, 1969 **(99)**; Stoney Ground, 1972 **(113)**

Pop Rock — British; members hailed from England, Trinidad, the West Indies, Ceylon, Jamaica and Barbados

The Four Aces

Personnel: Al Alberts (vocals);
Dave Mahoney (vocals); Sol Vac-
caro (vocals); Lou Silvestri (vocals)
Singles: Melody of Love, 1955
(3); Heart, 1955 **(13)**; Love Is a
Many-Splendored Thing, 1955 **(1)**;
A Woman in Love, 1955 **(14)**; Of
This I'm Sure, 1955 **(56)**; If You
Can Dream, 1956 **(62)**; The Gal
with the Yaller Shoes, 1956 **(91)**; To
Love Again, 1956 **(43)**; I Only
Know I Love You, 1956 **(22)**;
Dreamer, 1956 **(86)**; Friendly Per-
suasion (Thee I Love), 1956 **(45)**;
You Can't Run Away from It, 1956
(20); Someone to Love, 1956 **(47)**;
Written on the Wind, 1956 **(61)**;
Bahama Mama, 1957 **(53)**; You're
Mine, 1957 **(76)**; Rock and Roll
Rhapsody, 1958 **(66)**; The World
Outside, 1958 **(63)**; No Other Arms,
No Other Lips, 1959 **(74)**
   Pop Vocal—Pennsylvania; sang
on many film scores

The Four Coins

Personnel: George Mantalis (vo-
cals); George Gregorakis (vocals);
Michael Mahramas (vocals); George
Mahramas (vocals)
Singles: I Love You Madly, 1955
(28); Memories of You, 1955 **(22)**;
Shangri-La, 1957 **(11)**; My One Sin,
1957 **(28)**; Wendy, Wendy, 1958
(72); The World Outside, 1958 **(21)**;
My First Love, 1959 **(106)**; One
Love, One Heart, 1959 **(82)**
   Pop Vocal—Pennsylvania

The Four Esquires

Personnel: Bill Courtney (vocals);
Frank Mahoney (vocals); Bob
Golden (vocals); Wally Gold (vocals)
Singles: Look Homeward Angel,

1956 **(55)**; Love Me Forever, 1957
(25); Hideaway, 1958 **(21)**
   Pop Vocal—Boston

The Four Freshmen

Personnel: Ross Barbour (vocals);
Don Barbour (vocals); Bob Flanigan
(vocals); Ken Errair (vocals)
Albums: Four Freshmen and 5
Trombones, 1956; Freshmen Favor-
ites, 1956; 4 Freshmen and 5
Trumpets, 1957; Four Freshmen
and Five Saxes, 1957; The Four
Freshmen in Person, 1958; Voices in
Love, 1958; The Four Freshmen and
Five Guitars, 1960
Singles: Day by Day, 1955 **(42)**;
Charmaine, 1955 **(69)**; Graduation
Day, 1956 **(17)**
   Pop Vocal—Indianapolis

Four Jacks and a Jill

Personnel: Glenys "Jill" Lynne
(vocals)
Album: Master Jack, 1968
Singles: Master Jack, 1968 **(18)**;
Mister Nico, 1968 **(96)**; Hey Mister,
1968 **(130)**
   Pop Vocal—South Africa

The Four Knights

Personnel: Gene Alford (vocals);
Clarence Dixon (vocals); Oscar
Broadway (vocals); John Wallace
(vocals)
Single: O' Falling Star, 1959 **(83)**
   R & B Vocal—North Carolina

The Four Lads

Personnel: Bernie Toorish (vocals); Jimmie Arnold (vocals); Frank
Busseri (vocals); Connie Codarini
(vocals)

Album: On the Sunny Side, 1956
Singles: Moments to Remember,
1955 **(2)**; No, Not Much, 1956 **(2)**;
I'll Never Know, 1956 **(52)**; Standing on the Corner, 1956 **(3)**; My
Little Angel, 1956 **(22)**; The Mocking Bird, 1956 **(67)**; The Bus Stop
Song (a Paper of Pins), 1956 **(17)**; A
House with Love in It, 1956 **(16)**;
Who Needs You/It's So Easy to Forget, 1957 **(9)**; I Just Don't Know,
1957 **(17)**; Put a Light in the Window, 1957 **(8)**; There's Only One of
You, 1958 **(10)**; Enchanted Island,
1958 **(12)**; The Mocking Bird, 1958
(32); The Girl on Page 44, 1959
(52); The Fountain of Youth, 1959
(90); Happy Anniversary, 1959 **(77)**
Pop Vocal—Canadian

The Four Preps

Personnel: Bruce Belland (vocals);
Glen Larson (vocals); Ed Cobb (vo-
cals); Marvin Ingraham (vocals)
Albums: The Four Preps on Cam-
pus, 1961; Campus Encore, 1962
Singles: Dreamy Eyes, 1956 **(56)**;
26 Miles (Santa Catalina), 1958 **(2)**;
Big Man, 1958 **(3)**; Lazy Summer
Night/Summertime Lies, 1958 **(21)**;
Cinderella, 1958 **(69)**; Big Surprise,
1959 **(111)**; I Ain't Never, 1959 **(79)**;
Down by the Station, 1959 **(13)**; Got
a Girl, 1960 **(24)**; Calcutta, 1961
(96); More Money for You and Me,
1961 **(17)**; The Big Draft, 1962 **(61)**;
Charmaine, 1963 **(116)**; A Letter to
the Beatles, 1964 **(85)**
Pop Vocal—California

The Four Seasons

Personnel: Frankie Valli (vocals);
Tommy DeVito (guitars) replaced
(1966) by John Paiva (guitars) replaced (1981) by Larry Lingle (gui-

**The Four Seasons: DeVito,
Valli, Gaudio, Massi**

tars); Nick DeVito (guitars) replaced
(1963) by Bob Gaudio (guitars, keyboards); Hank Majewski (bass) replaced (1963) by Nick Massi (bass)
replaced (1965) by Charles Callelo
(bass) replaced (1969) by Joey Long
(bass) replaced (1975) by Don Ciccone (bass); added (1975) Gerry
Polci (drums, vocals); added (1975)
Lee Shapiro (keyboards) replaced
(1981) by Jerry Corbetta (keyboards)
Albums: Sherry, 1963; Greetings,
1963; Big Girls Don't Cry, 1963;
Ain't That a Shame, 1963; Golden
Hits, 1963; Born to Wander, 1964;
Dawn, 1964; Stay, 1964; Rag Doll,
1964; More Golden Hits, 1964; We
Love Girls, 1965; Live on Stage,
1965; The Four Seasons Sing Big
Hits, 1965; The Four Seasons Enter-
tain You, 1965; The Four Seasons
Vault of Big Hits, 1965; Big Hits by
Bacharach, David & Dylan, 1965;
Working My Way Back to You,
1966; 2nd Vault of Hits, 1966;
Lookin' Back, 1966; Christmas
Album, 1966; New Gold Hits, 1967;
Edizione d'Oro, 1968; The Genuine

Imitation Life Gazette, 1969; Half and Half, 1970; Chameleon, 1972; Gold, 1975; Who Loves You, 1975; The Four Seasons Story, 1975; Helicon, 1977; Reunited, 1981; Streetfighter, 1985; 25th Anniversary Collection, 1988

Singles: You're the Apple of My Eye, 1956 **(62)**; Sherry, 1962 **(1)**; Big Girls Don't Cry, 1962 **(1)**; Walk Like a Man, 1963 **(1)**; Peanuts, 1963 **(108)**; Ain't That a Shame, 1963 **(22)**; Since I Don't Have You, 1963 **(123)**; Candy Girl/Marlena, 1963 **(3)**; New Mexican Rose, 1963 **(36)**; Dawn, 1964 **(3)**; Stay, 1964 **(16)**; Ronnie, 1964 **(6)**; Rag Doll, 1964 **(1)**; Long Lonely Nights, 1964 **(102)**; Alone, 1964 **(28)**; Save It for Me/Sincerely, 1964 **(10)**; Big Man in Town/Apple of My Eye, 1964 **(106)**; Bye Bye Baby, 1965 **(12)**; Toy Soldier, 1965 **(64)**; Since I Don't Have You, 1965 **(105)**; Girl Come Running, 1965 **(30)**; Let's Hang On, 1965 **(3)**; Don't Think Twice, 1965 **(12)**; Little Boy (in Grown Up Clothes), 1965 **(60)**; Working My Way Back to You, 1966 **(9)**; Opus 17 (Don't You Worry 'Bout Me), 1966 **(13)**; On the Good Ship Lollipop, 1966 **(87)**; You're Nobody Till Somebody Loves You, 1966 **(96)**; I've Got You Under My Skin, 1966 **(9)**; Tell It to Rain, 1966 **(10)**; Beggin', 1967 **(16)**; C'mon Marianne, 1967 **(9)**; Lonesome Road, 1967 **(89)**; Watch the Flowers Grow, 1967 **(30)**; Will You Love Me Tomorrow, 1968 **(24)**; Saturday's Father, 1968 **(103)**; Electric Stories, 1968 **(61)**; Something's on Her Mind/Idaho, 1969 **(95)**; And That Reminds Me, 1969 **(45)**; Patch of Blue, 1970 **(94)**; Who Loves You, 1975 **(3)**; December, 1963 (Oh, What a Night), 1975 **(1)**; Silver Star, 1976 **(38)**; Down the Hall, 1977 **(65)**; I Believe in You, 1977; Rhapsody, 1977; Spend the Night in Love, 1980 **(91)**; Heaven Must Have Sent You (Here in the Night), 1981; East Meets West, 1984 (with the Beach Boys); Streetfighter, 1985

Pop/Rock — New Jersey; Valli's real name is Francis Castelluccio

The Four Sonics

Personnel: Willie Frazier (vocals); Steve Gaston (vocals); Eddy Daniels (vocals); James "Jay" Johnson (vocals)

Single: You Don't Have to Say You Love Me, 1968 **(89)**

R & B Vocal — American

The Four Tops

Personnel: Levi Stubbs (vocals); Abdul "Duke" Fakir (vocals); Renaldo "Obie" Benson (vocals); Lawrence Payton (vocals)

Albums: Four Tops, 1965; Four Tops Second Album, 1965; 4 Tops on Top, 1966; Four Tops Live!, 1966; 4 Tops on Broadway, 1967; Four Tops Reach Out, 1967; The Four Tops Greatest Hits, 1967; Yesterday's Dreams, 1968; Four Tops Now!, 1969; Soul Spin, 1969; Still Waters Run Deep, 1970; Changing Times, 1970; The Magnificent Seven, 1970 (with the Supremes); The Return of the Magnificent Seven, 1971 (with the Supremes); Four Tops Greatest Hits, Volume 2, 1971; Dynamite, 1972 (with the Supremes); Nature Planned It, 1972; Keeper of the Castle, 1972; The Best of the 4 Tops, 1973; Main Street People, 1973; Meeting of the Minds, 1974; Live and in Concert, 1974; Night Lights

Harmony, 1975; Super Hits, 1976; Catfish, 1976; Anthology, 1976; The Show Must Go On, 1977; At the Top, 1978; Reach Out and 20 Golden Greats, 1981; Tonight!, 1981

Singles: Baby I Need Your Loving, 1964 (**11**); Without the One You Love (Life's Not Worth While), 1964 (**43**); Ask the Lonely, 1964 (**24**); I Can't Help Myself, 1965 (**1**); It's the Same Old Song, 1965 (**5**); Ain't That Love, 1965 (**93**); Something About You, 1965 (**19**); Shake Me, Wake Me (When It's Over), 1966 (**18**); Loving You Is Sweeter Than Ever, 1966 (**45**); Reach Out I'll Be There, 1966 (**1**); Standing in the Shadows of Love, 1966 (**6**); Bernadette, 1967 (**4**); 7 Rooms of Gloom, 1967 (**14**); I'll Turn to Stone, 1967 (**76**); You Keep Running Away, 1967 (**19**); Walk Away Renee, 1968 (**14**); If I Were a Carpenter, 1968 (**20**); Yesterday's Dreams, 1968 (**49**); I'm in a Different World, 1968 (**51**); What Is a Man, 1969 (**53**); Don't Let Him Take Your Love from Me, 1969 (**45**); It's All in the Game, 1970 (**24**); Still Water (Love), 1970 (**11**); River Deep—Mountain High, 1970 (**14**) (with the Supremes); Just Seven Numbers (Can Straighten Out My Life), 1971 (**40**); You Gotta Have Love in Your Heart, 1971 (**55**) (with the Supremes); In These Changing Times, 1971 (**70**); MacArthur Park (Part II), 1971 (**38**); A Simple Game, 1972 (**90**); I Can't Quit Your Love, 1972 (**102**); (It's the Way) Nature Planned It, 1972 (**53**); Keeper of the Castle, 1972 (**10**); Ain't No Woman (Like the One I've Got), 1973 (**4**); Are You Man Enough, 1973 (**15**); Sweet Understanding Love, 1973 (**33**); I Just Can't Get You Out of My Mind, 1974 (**62**); One Chain Don't

Make No Prison, 1974 (**41**); Midnight Flower, 1974 (**55**); Seven Lonely Nights, 1975 (**71**); We All Gotta Stick Together, 1975 (**97**); Mama You're All Right with Me, 1976 (**107**); Catfish, 1976 (**71**); When She Was My Girl, 1981 (**11**); Sad Hearts, 1982 (**84**); Back to School Again, 1982 (**71**); I Just Can't Walk Away, 1983 (**71**); Indestructible, 1988 (**35**)

Soul/Pop Vocal—Detroit

The Four Voices

Personnel: Allan Chase (vocals); Frank Fosta (vocals); Sal Mayo (vocals); Bill McBride (vocals)

Singles: Lovely One, 1956 (**20**); Dancing with My Shadow, 1958 (**50**)

Pop Vocal—American

Inez & Charles Foxx

Albums: Mockingbird, 1964; Come by Here, 1968; Hits, 1968; Inez & Charles Foxx, 1969; At Memphis, 1973

Singles: Mockingbird, 1963 (**7**); Here's the One You Love, 1963 (**113**); Hi Diddle Diddle, 1963 (**98**); Ask Me, 1964 (**91**); Hurt by Love, 1964 (**54**); La De Da I Love You, 1964 (**124**); I Stand Accused, 1967 (**127**); (1-2-3-4-5-6-7) Count the Days, 1968 (**76**)

Pop Vocal—North Carolina

Connie Francis

Albums: Italian Favorites, 1960; Connie's Greatest Hits, 1960; More Italian Favorites, 1960; Connie Francis at the Copa, 1961; Jewish Favorites, 1961; More Greatest Hits, 1961; Never on Sunday (and Other

Connie Francis

Title Songs from Motion Pictures),
1961; Do the Twist, 1962; Connie
Francis Sings, 1962; Country Music
Connie Style, 1962; Modern Italian
Hits, 1963; Follow the Boys, 1963;
Award Winning Motion Picture
Hits, 1963; Greatest American
Waltzes, 1963; Mala Femmena &
Connie's Big Hits from Italy, 1963;
The Very Best of Connie Francis,
1963; In the Summer of His Years,
1964; Looking for Love, 1964; A
New Kind of Connie, 1964; Connie
Francis Sings for Mama, 1965;
When the Boys Meet the Girls, 1966
    Singles: The Majesty of Love,
1957 **(93)** (with Marvin Rainwater);
Who's Sorry Now, 1958 **(4)**; I'm
Sorry I Made You Cry, 1958 **(36)**;
Stupid Cupid, 1958 **(14)**; Fallin',
1958 **(30)**; My Happiness, 1958 **(2)**;
If I Didn't Care, 1959 **(22)**; Lipstick
on Your Collar, 1959 **(5)**; Frankie,
1959 **(9)**; You're Gonna Miss Me,
1959 **(34)**; Plenty Good Lovin', 1959
(69); Among My Souvenirs, 1959
(7); God Bless America, 1959 **(36)**;
Mama, 1960 **(8)**; Teddy, 1960 **(17)**;
Everybody's Somebody's Fool, 1960
(1); Jealous of You, 1960 **(19)**; My
Heart Has a Mind of Its Own, 1960
(1); Malaguena, 1960 **(42)**; Many
Tears Ago, 1960 **(7)**; Senza Mamma
(with No One), 1960 **(87)**; Where
the Boys Are, 1961 **(4)**; No One,
1961 **(34)**; Breakin' in a Brand New
Broken Heart, 1961 **(7)**; Together,
1961 **(6)**; Too Many Rules, 1961
(72); (He's My) Dreamboat, 1961
(14); Hollywood, 1961 **(42)**; When
the Boy in Your Arms (Is the Boy
in Your Heart), 1961 **(10)**; Baby's
First Christmas, 1961 **(26)**; Don't
Break the Heart That Loves You,
1962 **(1)**; Second Hand Love, 1962
(7); Vacation, 1962 **(9)**; The Biggest
Sin of All, 1962 **(116)**; I Was Such a
Fool (to Fall in Love with You),
1962 **(24)**; He Thinks I Still Care,
1962 **(57)**; I'm Gonna Be Warm
This Winter, 1962 **(18)**; Baby's First
Christmas, 1962 **(113)**; Al Di La,
1963 **(90)**; Follow the Boys, 1963
(17); Waiting for Billy, 1963 **(127)**;
If My Pillow Could Talk, 1963 **(23)**;
Drownin' My Sorrows, 1963 **(36)**;
Mala Femmena, 1963 **(114)**; Your
Other Love, 1963 **(28)**; In the Sum-
mer of His Years, 1963 **(46)**; Blue
Winter, 1964 **(24)**; Be Anything
(But Mine), 1964 **(25)**; Looking for
Love, 1964 **(45)**; Don't Ever Leave
Me, 1964 **(42)**; We Have Something
More (Than a Summer Love), 1964
(128); Whose Heart Are You Breaking Tonight, 1965 **(43)**; For Mama,
1965 **(48)**; Wishing It Was You,
1965 **(57)**; Forget Domani, 1965
(79); Roundabout, 1965 **(80)**;
Jealous Heart, 1965 **(47)**; Love Is
Me, Love Is You, 1966 **(66)**; It's a
Different World, 1966 **(134)**; A Letter from a Soldier (Dear Mama),
1966 **(105)**; Spanish Nights and
You, 1966 **(99)**; Another Page, 1967
(121); My Heart Cries for You, 1967
(118); Why Say Goodbye?, 1968
(132); Time Alone Will Tell, 1967

(94); The Wedding Cake, 1969 **(91)**; The Answer (Should I Tie a Yellow Ribbon 'Round the Ole Oak Tree?), 1973 **(104)**

Pop Vocal — New Jersey; real name is Concetta Rosa Maria Franconero

Aretha Franklin

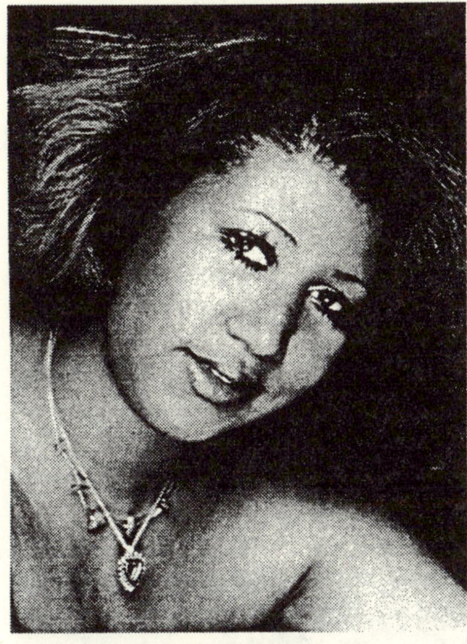

Albums: Aretha, 1961; Electrifying, 1962; The Tender, the Moving & the Swinging Aretha Franklin, 1962; Laughing on the Outside, 1963; Unforgettable, 1964; Songs of Faith, 1964; Running Out of Fools, 1964; Yeah!!!, 1965; Soul Sister, 1966; I've Never Loved a Man the Way I Love You, 1967; Queen of Soul, 1967; Take It Like You Give It, 1967; Greatest Hits, 1967; Aretha Arrives, 1967; Take a Look, 1967; Greatest Hits Volume 2, 1968; Aretha: Lady Soul, 1968; Aretha Now, 1968; Aretha in Paris, 1968; Aretha Franklin: Soul '69, 1969; Aretha's Gold, 1969; This Girl's in Love with You, 1970; Spirit in the Dark, 1970; Aretha Live at Fillmore West, 1971; Aretha's Greatest Hits, 1971; Young, Gifted and Black, 1972; Amazing Grace, 1972; In the Beginning/The World of Aretha Franklin 1960–1967, 1972; Hey Now Hey (the Other Side of the Sky), 1973; Let Me in Your Life, 1974; With Everything I Feel in Me, 1974; You, 1975; Sparkle, 1976; Ten Years of Gold, 1976; Sweet Passion, 1977; Almighty Fire, 1978; La Diva, 1979; Aretha, 1980; Love All the Hurt Away, 1981; Jump to It, 1982; Sweet Bitter Love, 1982; Get It Right, 1983; Who's Zoomin' Who, 1985; Sings the Blues, 1985; After Hours, 1987; First 12 Sides, 1988; Aretha's Jazz, 1989; Through the Storm, 1989; What You See Is What You Sweat, 1991

Singles: Won't Be Long, 1961 **(76)**; Rock-a-Bye Your Baby with a Dixie Melody, 1961 **(37)**; I Surrender, Dear, 1962 **(87)**; Rough Lover, 1962 **(94)**; Don't Cry, Baby, 1962 **(92)**; Try a Little Tenderness, 1962 **(100)**; Just for a Thrill, 1962 **(111)**; Trouble in Mind, 1962 **(86)**; Here's Where I Came In, 1963 **(125)**; Say It Isn't So, 1963 **(113)**; Soulville, 1964 **(121)**; Runnin' Out of Fools, 1964 **(57)**; Can't You Just See Me, 1965 **(96)**; One Step Ahead, 1965 **(119)**; I'm Losing You, 1965 **(114)**; You Made Me Love You, 1965 **(109)**; Cry Like a Baby, 1966 **(113)**; I Never Loved a Man (the Way I Love You), 1967 **(9)**; Respect, 1967 **(1)**; Baby I Love You, 1967 **(4)**; Take a Look, 1967 **(56)**; A Natural Woman (You Make Me Feel Like), 1967 **(8)**; Chain of Fools, 1967 **(2)**; Mockingbird, 1967 **(94)**; Soulville, 1968 **(83)**; (Sweet Sweet

Baby) Since You've Been Gone, 1968 **(5)**; Ain't No Way, 1968 **(16)**; Think, 1968 **(7)**; You Send Me, 1968 **(56)**; The House That Jack Built, 1968 **(6)**; I Say a Little Prayer, 1968 **(10)**; See Saw, 1968 **(14)**; My Song, 1968 **(31)**; The Weight, 1969 **(19)**; Tracks of My Tears, 1969 **(71)**; I Can't See Myself Leaving You, 1969 **(28)**; Gentle on My Mind, 1969 **(76)**; Share Your Love with Me, 1969 **(13)**; Today I Sing the Blues, 1969 **(101)**; Eleanor Rigby, 1969 **(17)**; Call Me, 1970 **(13)**; Spirit in the Dark, 1970 **(23)**; Don't Play That Song, 1970 **(11)**; Border Song (Holy Moses)/You and Me, 1970 **(37)**; You're All I Need to Get By, 1971 **(19)**; Bridge Over Troubled Water/Brand New Me, 1971 **(6)**; Spanish Harlem, 1971 **(2)**; Rock Steady, 1971 **(9)**; Oh Me Oh My (I'm a Fool for You Baby), 1972 **(73)**; Day Dreaming, 1972 **(5)**; All the King's Horses, 1972 **(26)**; Wholly Holy, 1972 **(81)**; Master of Eyes (The Deepness of Your Eyes), 1973 **(33)**; Angel, 1973 **(20)**; Until You Come Back to Me (That's What I'm Gonna Do), 1973 **(3)**; I'm in Love, 1974 **(19)**; Ain't Nothing Like the Real Thing, 1974 **(47)**; Without Love, 1974 **(45)**; Mr. D. J. (5 for the D. J.), 1975 **(53)**; Something He Can Feel, 1976 **(28)**; Jump, 1976 **(72)**; Look Into Your Heart, 1977 **(82)**; Break It to Me Gently, 1977 **(85)**; Almighty Fire (Woman of the Future), 1978 **(103)**; United Together, 1980 **(56)**; Come to Me, 1981 **(84)**; Love All the Hurt Away, 1981 **(46)** (with George Benson); Jump to It, 1982 **(24)**; Get It Right, 1983 **(61)**; Freeway of Love, 1985 **(3)**; Who's Zoomin' Who, 1985 **(7)**; Another Night, 1986 **(22)**; Jumpin' Jack Flash, 1986 **(21)**; Jimmy Lee, 1986 **(28)**; I Knew You Were Waiting (For Me), 1987 **(1)** (with George Michael); Rock-a-Lott, 1987 **(82)**; Through the Storm, 1989 **(16)** (with Elton John); It Isn't, It Wasn't, It Ain't Never Gonna Be, 1989 **(41)** (with Whitney Houston)

Soul Vocal — Memphis

Stan Freberg

Album: Stan Freberg Presents the United States of America, 1961

Singles: The Yellow Rose of Texas, 1955 **(16)**; Nuttin' for Christmas, 1955 **(53)**; Heartbreak Hotel, 1956 **(79)**; Banana Boat (Day-O), 1957 **(25)**; Wun'erful, Wun'erful! (Sides uh-one & uh-two), 1957 **(32)**; Green Chritma, 1958 **(44)**; The Old Payola Roll Blues, 1960 **(99)**

Novelty Pop — California

John Fred & His Playboy Band

back row: **Goodson, Bernard, Spinosa, Cowart;** *front row:* **Micely, Fred, O'Rourke, DeGeneres**

Personnel: John Fred Gourrier (vocals); Jimmy O'Rourke (guitars); Harold Cowart (bass); Tommy

DeGeneres (keyboards); Andrew Bernard (saxophones); Charlie Spinosa (trumpet); Ronnie Goodson (trumpet); Joe Micely (drums)

Albums: John Fred & His Playboys, 1965; 34:40 of John Fred & His Playboys, 1966; Agnes English, 1967; Permanently Stated, 1969; Love in My Soul, 1970

Singles: Shirley, 1959 **(82)** (with Tommy Bryan); Judy in Disguise (with Glasses), 1967 **(1)**; Agnes English, 1967 **(125)**; Hey Hey Bunny, 1968 **(57)**; We Played Games, 1968 **(130)**

Pop/Rock — Louisiana; John's father played baseball for the Detroit Tigers

Freddie & The Dreamers

Personnel: Freddie Garrity (vocals); Roy Crewsdon (guitars); Derek Quinn (guitars); Peter Birrell (bass); Bennie Dwyer (drums)

Albums: Freddie & the Dreamers, 1963; You Were Made for Me, 1964; Sing Along, 1965; In Disneyland, 1966; Freddie & the Dreamers, 1966; Do the Freddie, 1966; Seaside Swingers, 1966; Fanatic Freddie, 1967; Fun Lovin', 1967; King Freddie & Dreaming Knights, 1967; Oliver in Overworld, 1970; Freddie Garrity, 1974; I'm Telling You Now, 1977; Best of Freddie & the Dreamers, 1977

Singles: I'm Telling You Now, 1965 **(1)**; I Understand (Just How You Feel), 1965 **(36)**; Do the Freddie, 1965 **(18)**; You Were Made for Me, 1965 **(21)**; A Little You, 1965 **(48)**

Pop/Rock — British

Free

Personnel: Paul Rodgers (vocals) left group (1971) returned (1972); Paul Kossoff (guitars, vocals; deceased 1976); Andy Fraser (bass) replaced (1971) by Tetsu Yamauchi (bass); Simon Kirke (drums); added (1971) John Bundrick (keyboards); added (1976) Wendell Richardson (guitars)

Albums: Tons of Sobs, 1968; Free, 1969; Fire and Water, 1970; Highway, 1970; Live, 1971; Kossoff,

Freddie & The Dreamers: Birrell, Quinn, Garrity, Crewsdon

Kirke, Tetsu & Rabbit, 1971; Free at Last, 1972; Heartbreaker, 1973; The Free Story, 1973; Best of Free, 1975; Free & Easy, Rough & Ready, 1976; All Right Now, 1978

Singles: All Right Now, 1970 **(4)**; Stealer, 1970 **(49)**; A Little Bit of Love, 1972 **(119)**; Wishing Well, 1973 **(112)**

Hard/Blues Rock—British; Rodgers quit the band for one album and returned to record "Free at Last" in 1972

Bobby Freeman

Albums: Do You Wanna Dance, 1958; Get in the Swim, 1959; Lovable Side of Bobby Freeman, 1960; Twist with Bobby Freeman, 1962; C'mon and Swim, 1964

Singles: Do You Want to Dance, 1958 **(5)**; Betty Lou Got a New Pair of Shoes, 1958 **(37)**; Need Your Love, 1958 **(54)**; Mary Ann Thomas, 1959 **(90)**; Ebb Tide, 1959 **(93)**; (I Do the) Shimmy Shimmy, 1960 **(37)**; The Mess Around, 1961 **(89)**; C'mon and Swim, 1964 **(5)**; S-W-I-M, 1964 **(56)**; I'll Never Fall in Love Again, 1965 **(131)**; Everybody's Got a Hang Up, 1966 **(122)**

R & B Vocal—San Francisco

Friend and Lover

Personnel: James Post (vocals); Cathy Post (vocals)

Singles: Reach Out of the Darkness, 1968 **(10)**; If Love Is in Your Heart, 1968 **(86)**

Pop Vocal—American; husband and wife team

Friends of Distinction

Personnel: Harry Elston (vocals); Floyd Butler (vocals); Jessica Cleaves (vocals); Barbara Love (vocals)

Albums: Grazin', 1969; Friends of Distinction, 1970

Singles: Grazing in the Grass, 1969 **(3)**; Let Yourself Go, 1969 **(63)**; Going in Circles, 1969 **(15)**; Love or Let Me Be Lonely, 1970 **(6)**; Time Waits for No One, 1970 **(60)**; I Need You, 1971 **(79)**

Soul/Pop Vocal—Los Angeles

The Frogmen

Single: Underwater, 1961 **(44)**

Pop/Rock—American

Max Frost & The Troopers

Personnel: Christopher Jones (vocals)

Album: Wild in the Streets (Soundtrack), 1968

Singles: Shape of Things to Come, 1968 **(22)**; Fifty-Two Percent, 1968 **(123)**

Psychedelic Pop—California; Jones starred in the film "Wild in the Streets" with Diana Varsi

Frost

Personnel: Dick Wagner (guitars, vocals); Don Hartman (guitars, vocals); Gerdy Garris (bass, keyboards, vocals); Bob Riggs (drums)

Albums: Frost Music, 1969; Rock 'n' Roll Music, 1969; Through the Eyes of Love, 1970

Single: Rock and Roll Music, 1970 **(105)**

Hard Rock—Midwest

The Fugs

Personnel: Tuli Kupferberg (vocals, bass); Steve Weber (guitars)

replaced (1966) by Ed Sanders (guitars, vocals); John Anderson (bass, vocals) replaced (1966) by Charles Larkey (bass) replaced (1970) by Bill Wolf (bass) replaced (1975) by Mark Kramer (keyboards); Vinny Leary (guitars) replaced (1966) by Kenny Pine (guitars, vocals) replaced (1975) by Vinny Leary (guitars); Peter Stampfel (violin, banjo, vocals) replaced (1966) by Danny Kortchmar (guitars, vocals) replaced (1968) by Carl Lynch (guitars) replaced (1969) by Dan Hamburg (guitars) replaced (1975) by Steve Taylor (guitars); Ken Weaver (drums, vocals) replaced (1969) by Bob Mason (drums) replaced (1975) by Cody Batty (drums)

Albums: First Album, 1965; The Fugs (Kill for Peace), 1966; Virgin Fugs, 1966; Tenderness Junction, 1966; It Crawled Into My Hand, Honest, 1967; Golden Filth, 1968; Belle of Avenue A, 1969; Fugs 4 Rounders Score, 1975; Proto-punk, 1983

Psychedelic Rock — New York

Bobby Fuller Four

Personnel: Bobby Fuller (guitars, vocals; deceased 1966); Randy Fuller (bass, vocals); Wayne Quirico (drums); Jim Reese (guitars)

Albums: I Fought the Law, 1965; K R L A King of Wheels, 1966; Civil Defense, 1966; Memorial Album, 1967; The Best of the Bobby Fuller Four, 1981

Singles: Let Her Dance, 1965 (**133**); I Fought the Law, 1966 (**9**); Love's Made a Fool of You, 1966 (**26**); The Magic Touch, 1966 (**117**)

Pop/Rock — Texas; Bobby died of asphyxiation under mysterious circumstances

Billy Fury

Albums: The Sound of Fury, 1960; Billy Fury, 1960; Halfway to Paradise, 1961; Billy, 1963; We Want Billy, 1963; I Gotta Horse, 1964; Best of Billy Fury, 1967; World of Billy Fury, 1972; The Billy Fury Story, 1977; World of Billy Fury, Volume 2, 1980; Hit Parade, 1982

Singles: Maybe Tomorrow, 1959; Colette, 1960; That's Love, 1960; Halfway to Paradise, 1963; Jealousy, 1963; I'd Never Find Another You, 1964

Pop/Rock — British; real name was Ron Wycherly; died in 1983; was in film *That'll Be the Day*

Fuse

Personnel: Joe Sundberg (vocals); Craig Meyers (guitars); Rick Nielsen (guitars, vocals); Tom Petersson (bass, vocals); Chip Greenman (drums)

Album: Fuse, 1968

Hard Rock — Midwest

Gabriel & The Angels

Single: That's Life (That's Tough), 1962 (**51**)

Pop Vocal — American

The Gadabouts

Single: Stranded in the Jungle, 1956 (**39**)

Pop Vocal — American

The Galens

Personnel: Galen (vocals); Bob Hubener (vocals); Charlene Knight (vocals); George Ross (vocals)

Single: Baby I Do Love You, 1963 **(70)**
Pop Vocal—American

The Gallahads

Singles: The Fool, 1956 **(62)**;
Lonely Guy, 1960 **(111)**
Pop Vocal—Northeast

The Gants

Single: Road Runner, 1965 **(46)**
R & B Vocal—Mississippi

Don Gardner & Dee Dee Ford

Singles: I Need Your Loving,
1962 **(20)**; Glory of Love, 1962 **(75)**;
Don't You Worry, 1962 **(66)**; My
Baby Likes to Boogaloo, 1966 **(126)**
R & B Vocal—Philadelphia

Frank Gari

Album: Utopia, 1960
Singles: Utopia, 1960 **(27)**;
Lullaby of Love, 1961 **(23)**; Princess,
1961 **(30)**
Pop Vocal—New York

Gale Garnett

Album: My Kind of Folk Songs,
1964
Singles: We'll Sing in the Sunshine, 1964 **(4)**; Lovin' Place, 1964
(54); I'll Cry Alone, 1965 **(108)**
Pop Vocal—New Zealand

Marvin Gaye

Albums: Soulful Mood, 1961;
That Stubborn Kinda Fellow, 1962;
Live on Stage, 1963; When I'm
Alone I Cry, 1964; Together (1964)
(with Mary Wells); Marvin Gaye/
Greatest Hits, 1964; Hello Broad-
way, 1964; How Sweet It Is to Be
Loved by You, 1965; Tribute to Nat
King Cole, 1965; Moods of Marvin
Gaye, 1966; Take Two, 1966; Mar-
vin Gaye/Greatest Hits, Vol. 2,
1967; United, 1967 (with Tammi
Terrell); You're All I Need, 1968
(with Tammi Terrell); In the
Groove, 1968; M.P.G., 1969; Mar-
vin Gaye and His Girls, 1969 (with
Tammi Terrell, Mary Wells and
Kim Weston); Easy, 1969 (with
Tammi Terrell); That's the Way
Love Is, 1969; Marvin Gaye &
Tammi Terrell Greatest Hits, 1970;
Marvin Gaye Super Hits, 1970;
What's Going On, 1971; Trouble
Man (Soundtrack), 1972; Let's Get
It On, 1973; Diana & Marvin, 1973
(with Diana Ross); Marvin Gaye
Anthology, 1974; Marvin Gaye
Live!, 1974; I Want You, 1976;
Marvin Gaye's Greatest Hits, 1976;
Marvin Gaye Live at the London
Palladium, 1977; Here, My Dear,
1979; Love Man, 1979; In Our Life-
time, 1981; Midnight Love, 1982;
Every Great Motown Hit of Marvin
Gaye, 1983; 15 Greatest Hits, 1984;
Compact Command Performances,
1984; Compact Command Perfor-
mances, Volume 2, 1985
Singles: Stubborn Kinda Fellow,
1962 **(46)** (with the Vandellas);
Hitch Hike, 1963 **(30)**; Pride and
Joy, 1963 **(10)**; Can I Get a Witness,
1963 **(22)**; I'm Crazy 'Bout My
Baby, 1963 **(77)**; You're a Wonder-
ful One, 1964 **(15)**; Once Upon a
Time, 1964 **(19)** (with Mary Wells);
What's the Matter with You Baby,
1964 **(17)** (with Mary Wells); Try It
Baby, 1964 **(15)**; Baby Don't You
Do It, 1964 **(27)**; What Good Am I
Without You, 1964 **(61)** (with Kim
Weston); How Sweet It Is to Be

Loved by You, 1964 **(6)**; I'll Be Doggone, 1965 **(8)**; Pretty Little Baby, 1965 **(25)**; Ain't That Peculiar, 1965 **(8)**; One More Heartache, 1966 **(29)**; Take This Heart of Mine, 1966 **(44)**; Liι .e Darling, I Need You, 1966 **(47)**; It Takes Two, 1967 **(14)** (with Kim Weston); Ain't No Mountain High Enough, 1967 **(19)** (with Tammi Terrell); Your Unchanging Love, 1967 **(33)**; Your Precious Love, 1967 **(5)** (with Tammi Terrell); If I Could Build My Whole World Around You, 1967 **(10)** (with Tammi Terrell); You, 1968 **(34)**; If This World Were Mine, 1968 **(68)** (with Tammi Terrell); Ain't Nothing Like the Real Thing, 1968 **(8)** (with Tammi Terrell); You're All I Need to Get By, 1968 **(7)** (with Tammi Terrell); Chained, 1968 **(32)**; Keep on Lovin' Me Honey, 1968 **(24)** (with Tammi Terrell); I Heard It Through the Grapevine, 1968 **(1)**; Good Lovin' Ain't Easy to Come By, 1969 **(30)** (with Tammi Terrell); Too Busy Thinking About My Baby, 1969 **(4)**; That's the Way Love Is, 1969 **(7)**; What You Gave Me, 1969 **(49)** (with Tammi Terrell); How Can I Forget, 1970 **(41)**; Gonna Give Her All the Love I've Got, 1970 **(67)**; The Onion Song/ California Soul, 1970 **(50)** (with Tammi Terrell); The End of Our Road, 1970 **(40)**; What's Going On, 1971 **(2)**; Mercy Mercy Me (The Ecology), 1971 **(4)**; Inner City Blues (Make Me Wanna Holler), 1971 **(9)**; You're the Man, 1972 **(50)**; Trouble Man, 1972 **(7)**; Let's Get It On, 1973 **(1)**; You're a Special Part of Me, 1973 **(12)** (with Diana Ross); Come Get to This, 1973 **(21)**; You Sure Love to Ball, 1974 **(50)**; My Mistake (Was to Love You), 1974 **(19)** (with Diana Ross); Don't Knock My Love, 1974 **(46)** (with Diana Ross); Distant Lover, 1974 **(28)**; I Want You, 1976 **(15)**; After the Dance, 1976 **(74)**; Got to Give It Up—Part 1, 1977 **(1)**; A Funky Space Reincarnation—Part 1, 1979 **(106)**; Praise, 1981 **(101)**; Sexual Healing, 1982 **(3)**

Soul Vocal—Washington, D.C.; Marvin was shot to death on April 1, 1984 by his father; his singing partner Tammi Terrell died in 1970 at the age of 23 from a brain tumor

The G-Clefs

Personnel: Teddy Scott (vocals); Timmy Scott (vocals); Arnold Scott (vocals); Chris Scott (vocals); Ray Gibson (vocals)

Singles: Ka-Ding Dong, 1956 **(24)**; I Understand (Just How You Feel), 1961 **(9)**; A Girl Has to Know, 1962 **(81)**

Pop Vocal—Massachusetts

Gene & Debbe

Personnel: Gene Thomas (vocals); Debbe Nevills (vocals)

Album: Go with Me, 1967

Singles: Go with Me, 1967 **(78)**; Playboy, 1968 **(17)**; Lovin' Season, 1968 **(81)**; Make a Noise Like Love, 1968 **(127)**; Memories Are Made of This, 1969 **(114)**

Pop Vocal—Texas

Genesis

Personnel: Michael Rutherford (bass, guitars, vocals); Tony Banks (keyboards, guitars, vocals); Peter Gabriel (vocals, flute) left group (1975); Anthony Phillips (guitars, vocals) replaced (1971) by Steve

Genesis: Banks, Thompson, Rutherford, Collins, Hackett

Hackett (guitars, vocals) replaced (1978) by Daryl Steurmer (guitars); Chris Stewart (drums) replaced (1968) by John Silver (drums) replaced (1969) by John Mayhew (drums) replaced (1971) by Phil Collins (drums, vocals); added (1977) Bill Bruford (drums) replaced (1978) by Chester Thompson (drums)

Albums: From Genesis to Revelation, 1969; Trespass, 1970; Nursery Cryme, 1971; Foxtrot, 1972; Genesis Live, 1973; Selling England by the Pound, 1973; The Lamb Lies Down on Broadway, 1974; A Trick of the Tail, 1976; Wind and Wuthering, 1977; Seconds Out, 1977; Spot the Pigeon (EP), 1977; . . .And Then There Were Three, 1978; The Story of Genesis, 1979; Duke, 1980; Abacab, 1981; Three Sides Live, 1982; 3 × 3 (EP), 1982; Genesis, 1983; Invisible Touch, 1986; We Can't Dance, 1991

Singles: The Lamb Lies Down on Broadway, 1974; Robbery, Assault and Battery, 1976; Ripples, 1976; Your Own Special Way, 1977 **(62)**; Eleventh Earl of Mar, 1977; Robbery, Assault and Battery, 1978; Follow You, Follow Me, 1978 **(23)**; Many Too Many, 1978; Spot the Pigeon/Inside & Out, 1978; Misunderstanding, 1980 **(14)**; Turn It on Again, 1980 **(58)**; Behind the Lines, 1980; No Reply at All, 1981 **(29)**; Abacab, 1981 **(26)**; Keep It Dark, 1982; Man on the Corner, 1982 **(40)**; Paperlate, 1982 **(32)**; Mama, 1983 **(73)**; That's All, 1983 **(6)**; Illegal Alien, 1984 **(44)**; Taking It All Too Hard, 1984 **(50)**; Invisible Touch, 1986 **(1)**; Throwing It All Away, 1986 **(4)**; Land of Confusion, 1986 **(4)**; In Too Deep, 1987 **(3)**; Tonight, Tonight, Tonight, 1987 **(3)**; No Son of Mine, 1991

Videos: Seconds Out, 1977; Three Sides Live, 1982; Genesis: The Mama Tour, 1983; Invisible Touch,

1987; Genesis: The Videos, Volume 1, 1988; Genesis: The Videos, Volume 2, 1988

Art Rock—British; band was formed in 1966 by schoolmates Banks, Gabriel, Rutherford and Phillips

Bobbie Gentry

Albums: Ode to Billy Joe, 1967; The Delta Sweete, 1968; Bobbie Gentry & Glen Campbell, 1968; Touch 'em with Love, 1969; Bobbie Gentry's Greatest, 1969; Fancy, 1970

Singles: Ode to Billy Joe, 1967 **(1)**; Okolona River Bottom Band, 1967 **(54)**; Louisiana Man, 1968 **(100)**; Mornin' Glory, 1968 **(74)** (with Glen Campbell); Let It Be Me, 1969 **(36)** (with Glen Campbell); Fancy, 1969 **(31)**; Touch 'em with Love, 1969 **(113)**; All I Have to Do Is Dream, 1970 **(27)** (with Glen Campbell); He Made a Woman Out of Me, 1970 **(71)**; Apartment 21, 1970 **(81)**; Ode to Billie Joe, 1976 **(54)**; Ode to Billy Joe, 1976 **(65)** (new film version)

Country/Pop—Mississippi; real name is Bobbie Lee Street

The Gentrys

Personnel: Larry Raspberry (guitars, vocals); Jimmy Hart (vocals); Bruce Bowles (vocals); Pat Neal (bass); Jimmy Johnson (trumpet, organ); Bobby Fisher (saxophones, piano); Larry Wall (drums)

Albums: Keep on Dancing, 1965; Time, 1966; The Gentrys, 1970

Singles: Keep on Dancing, 1965 **(4)**; Spread It on Thick, 1966 **(50)**; Brown Paper Sack, 1966 **(101)**; Everyday I Have to Cry, 1966 **(77)**; A Woman of the World, 1966 **(112)**; You Make Me Feel So Good, 1967 **(130)**; I Can't Go Back to Denver, 1968 **(132)**; Why Should I Cry, 1970 **(61)**; Cinnamon Girl, 1970 **(52)**; He'll Never Love You, 1970 **(116)**; Goddess of Love, 1970 **(119)**; Wild World, 1971 **(97)**

Pop/Rock—Memphis

Barbara George

Album: I Know, 1961

Singles: I Know (You Don't Love Me No More), 1961 **(3)**; You Talk About Love, 1962 **(46)**; If You Think, 1962 **(114)**; Send for Me (If You Need Some Lovin'), 1962 **(96)**

Pop Vocal—Memphis

Gerry & The Pacemakers

Personnel: Gerrard Marsden (vocals, guitars); Les McGuire (bass, vocals, keyboards); Les Chadwick (keyboards, bass); Fred Marsden (drums)

Albums: How Do You Do It, 1963; Ferry Across the Mersey,

1964; Don't Let the Sun Catch You Crying, 1964; Second Album, 1964; I'll Be There, 1965; Greatest Hits, 1965; Girl on a Swing, 1966

Singles: Don't Let the Sun Catch You Crying, 1964 **(4)**; I'm the One, 1964 **(82)**; How Do You Do It, 1964 **(9)**; I Like It, 1964 **(17)**; I'll Be There, 1964 **(14)**; Ferry Across the Mersey, 1965 **(6)**; It's Gonna Be Alright, 1965 **(23)**; You'll Never Walk Alone, 1965 **(48)**; You're the Reason, 1965 **(117)**; Give All Your Love to Me, 1965 **(68)**; Walk Hand in Hand, 1965 **(103)**; La La La, 1966 **(90)**; Girl on a Swing, 1966 **(28)**; Don't Let the Sun Catch You Crying, 1970 **(112)**

Pop/Rock — British

The Gestures

Personnel: Dale Menton (vocals); Gus Dewey (vocals); Bruce Waterson (vocals); Tom Klugertz (vocals)
Single: Run, Run, Run, 1964 **(44)**

Pop Vocal — Minnesota

Georgia Gibbs

Singles: Tweedle Dee, 1955 **(2)**; Dance with Me Henry (Wallflower), 1955 **(1)**; Sweet and Gentle, 1955 **(12)**; I Want You to Be My Baby, 1955 **(14)**; Goodbye to Rome (Arrivederci Roma), 1955 **(51)**; 24 Hours a Day (365 a Year), 1955 **(74)**; Rock Right, 1956 **(36)**; Kiss Me Another, 1956 **(30)**; Happiness Street, 1956 **(20)**; Tra La La, 1956 **(24)**; Silent Lips, 1957 **(68)**; I'm Walkin' the Floor Over You, 1957 **(92)**; The Hula Hoop Song, 1958 **(32)**; Let Me Cry on Your Shoulder, 1965 **(132)**

Pop Vocal — Massachusetts; real name is Fredda Gibbons

Steve Gibson and The Red Caps

Single: Silhouettes, 1957 **(63)**
Pop Vocal — Virginia

Giles, Giles & Fripp

Personnel: Mike Giles (drums); Peter Giles (bass); Robert Fripp (guitars); Judy Dyble (vocals)
Album: The Cheerful Insanity of Giles, Giles & Fripp, 1968

Art/Progressive Rock — British

Terry Gilkyson and The Easy Riders

Personnel: Terry Gilkyson (vocals); Rick Dehr (vocals); Frank Miller (vocals)
Singles: Marianne, 1957 **(4)**; Tina, 1957 **(96)**

Folk/Pop Vocal — American; Gilkyson's son Tony is the bassist for X

James Gilreath

Single: Little Band of Gold, 1963 **(21)**
Pop Vocal — Mississippi

Gino & Gina

Personnel: Aristedes Glosasi (vocals); Irene Glosasi (vocals)
Single: (It's Been a Long Time) Pretty Baby, 1958 **(20)**
Pop Vocal — New York

The Girlfriends

Personnel: Gloria Goodson (vocals); Nannette Jackson (vocals); Carolyn Willis (vocals)

Single: My One and Only, Jimmy Boy, 1963 **(49)**
R & B Vocal—Los Angeles

The Gladiolas

Personnel: Maurice Williams (vocals); Earl Gainey (vocals); William Massey (vocals); Willie Jones (vocals); Norman Wade (vocals)
Single: Little Darlin', 1957 **(41)**
R & B Vocal—South Carolina

The Glass House

Personnel: Larry Mitchell (vocals); Ty Hunter (vocals; deceased 1981); Sherrie Payne (vocals); Pearl Jones (vocals); Eric Dunham (vocals)
Albums: The Glass House, 1969; I Can't Be You, 1970
Singles: Crumbs Off the Table, 1969 **(59)**; I Can't Be You (You Can't Be Me), 1970 **(90)**; Stealing Moments from Another Woman's Life, 1970 **(121)**; Look What We've Done to Love, 1971 **(101)**
Soul/Pop Vocal—Detroit

Tom Glazer

Album: On Top of Spaghetti, 1963
Single: On Top of Spaghetti, 1963 **(14)**
Folk Vocal—Philadelphia

The Glencoves

Personnel: Don Connors (guitars, vocals); Bill Byrne (guitars, vocals); Brian Bolger (vocals)
Single: Hootenanny, 1963 **(38)**
Folk/Pop—New York

The Gods

Personnel: Ken Hensley (keyboards, guitars, vocals); Mick Taylor (guitars, vocals) replaced (1966) by Joe Jonas (guitars, vocals); Brian Glascock (drums) replaced (1968) by Lee Kerslake (drums); John Glascock (bass, vocals) replaced (1966) by Paul Newton (bass) replaced (1967) by Greg Lake (bass, vocals) replaced (1968) by John Glascock (bass)
Albums: Genesis, 1968; To Samuel a Son, 1970; Gods, 1976
Hard Rock—British; group evolved into Uriah Heep

Golden Earring

Hay, Zuiderwijk, Kooymans, Gerritsen

Personnel: George Kooymans (guitars, vocals); Marinus Gerritsen (bass, vocals); Franz Krassenburg (vocals) replaced (1966) by Barry Hay (vocals); Jaap Eggermont (drums) replaced (1966) by Pim Koopman (drums) replaced (1967) by Sieb Warner (drums) replaced (1968) by Cesar Zuiderwijk (drums); added (1975) Robert Jan Stips (keyboards) replaced (1977) by Kevin Nance (keyboards) replaced (1977) by Robert Jan Stips (keyboards) left group (1980); added (1971) Eelco Gelling (guitars) left group (1979)

Albums: Just Earring, 1964; Winter Harvest, 1966; Miracle Mirror, 1967; On the Double, 1968; Eight Miles High, 1969; Golden Earring, 1970; Seven Tears, 1971; Together, 1972; Best of Golden Earring, 1973; Hearing Earring, 1973; Moontan, 1974; Switch, 1975; To the Hilt, 1976; Mad Love, 1977; Live, 1977; Contraband, 1977; Story, 1977; Grab It for a Second, 1978; No Promises, No Debts, 1979; Prisoner of the Night, 1980; Long Blond Animal, 1980; 2nd Live, 1981; Cut, 1982; N.E.W.S., 1984; Something Heavy Going Down, 1984; The Continuing Story of Radar Love, 1989

Singles: Radar Love, 1974 **(13)**; Candy's Going Bad, 1974 **(91)**; Sleep Walkin', 1976 **(109)**; Weekend Love, 1979; Twilight Zone, 1982 **(10)**; The Devil Made Me Do It, 1983 **(79)**; When the Lady Smiles, 1984 **(76)**; Something Heavy Going Down, 1984; Quiet Eyes, 1986

Hard Rock — The Netherlands

Bobby Goldsboro

Albums: Solid Goldsboro — Bobby Goldsboro's Greatest Hits, 1967; Honey, 1967; Word Pictures Featuring Autumn of My Life, 1968; Today, 1969; Muddy Mississippi Line, 1970; Bobby Goldsboro's Greatest Hits, 1970; We Gotta Start Lovin', 1971; Come Back Home, 1971; Summer (The First Time), 1973; Bobby Goldsboro's 10th Anniversary Album, 1974; A Butterfly for Bucky, 1976; Brand New Kind of Love, 1978

Singles: Molly, 1962 **(70)**; See the Funny Little Clown, 1964 **(9)**; Whenever He Holds You, 1964 **(39)**; Me Japanese Boy I Love You, 1964 **(74)**; I Don't Know You Anymore, 1964 **(105)**; Little Things, 1965 **(13)**; Voodoo Woman, 1965 **(27)**; If You Wait for Love, 1965 **(75)**; If You've Got a Heart, 1965 **(60)**; Broomstick Cowboy, 1965 **(53)**; It's Too Late, 1966 **(23)**; I Know You Better Than That, 1966 **(56)**; Take Your Love, 1966 **(114)**; It Hurts Me, 1966 **(70)**; Blue Autumn, 1966 **(35)**; Goodbye to All You Women, 1967 **(102)**; Jo-Jo's Place, 1967 **(111)**; Pledge of Love, 1967 **(118)**; Honey, 1968 **(1)**; Autumn of My Life, 1968 **(19)**; The Straight Life, 1968 **(36)**; Glad She's a Woman, 1969 **(61)**; I'm a Drifter, 1969 **(46)**; Muddy Mississippi Line, 1969 **(53)**; Mornin' Mornin', 1970 **(78)**; Can You Feel It, 1970 **(75)**; It's Gonna Change, 1970 **(108)**; Watching Scotty Grow, 1970 **(11)**; And I Love You So, 1971 **(83)**; Come Back Home, 1971 **(69)**; Danny Is a Mirror to Me, 1971 **(107)**; California Wine, 1972 **(108)**; With Pen in Hand, 1972 **(94)**; Brand New Kind of Love, 1973 **(116)**; Summer (The First Time), 1973 **(21)**; A Butterfly for Bucky, 1976 **(101)**; Me and the Elephants, 1977 **(104)**

Pop Vocal — Florida; Bobby was a member of Roy Orbison's band in the 1960s

The Goodees

Single: Condition Red, 1968 **(46)**

Pop/Rock — American

Dickie Goodman

Album: Mr. Jaws and Other Fables, 1975

Singles: The Touchables, 1961 **(60)**; The Touchables in Brooklyn, 1961 **(42)**; Berlin Top Ten, 1961 **(116)**; Santa & the Touchables, 1961 **(99)**; Ben Crazy, 1962 **(44)**; Senate Hearing, 1963 **(116)**; Batman & His Grandmother, 1966 **(70)**; On Campus, 1969 **(45)**; Luna Trip, 1969 **(95)**; Watergate, 1973 **(42)**; Purple People Eater, 1973 **(119)**; Energy Crisis '74, 1974 **(33)**; Mr. President, 1974 **(73)**; Mr. Jaws, 1975 **(4)**; Kong, 1977 **(48)**

Novelty/Pop — New York

Barry Gordon

Singles: Nuttin' for Christmas, 1955 **(6)**; Rock Around Mother Goose, 1955 **(52)**

Novelty/Pop — Massachusetts

Lesley Gore

Albums: I'll Cry If I Want To, 1963; Lesley Gore Sings of Mixed-Up Hearts, 1964; Boys, Boys, Boys, 1964; Girl Talk, 1964; The Golden Hits of Lesley Gore, 1965; My Town, My Guy & Me, 1965; California Nights, 1967; The Golden Hits of Lesley Gore, Volume 2, 1968; Someplace Else Now, 1972; Love Me by Name, 1978

Singles: It's My Party, 1963 **(1)**; Judy's Turn to Cry, 1963 **(5)**; She's a Fool, 1963 **(5)**; You Don't Own Me, 1963 **(2)**; That's the Way Boys Are, 1964 **(12)**; I Don't Wanna Be a Loser, 1964 **(37)**; Maybe I Know, 1964 **(14)**; Hey Now, 1964 **(76)**; Sometimes I Wish I Were a Boy, 1964 **(86)**; Look of Love, 1964 **(27)**; All of My Life, 1965 **(71)**; Sunshine, Lollipops and Rainbows, 1965 **(13)**; My Town, My Guy and Me, 1965 **(32)**; I Won't Love You Anymore (Sorry), 1965 **(80)**; We Know We're in Love, 1966 **(76)**; Young Love, 1966 **(50)**; Off and Running, 1966 **(108)**; Treat Me Like a Lady, 1966 **(115)**; California Nights, 1967 **(16)**; Summer and Sandy, 1967 **(65)**; Brink of Disaster, 1967 **(82)**; Small Talk, 1968 **(124)**; He Gives Me Love (La La La), 1968 **(119)**

Pop Vocal — New Jersey; worked with brother Michael on the soundtrack to *Fame;* first hit was at the age of 16

Charlie Gracie

Singles: Butterfly, 1957 **(1)**; Fabulous, 1957 **(16)**; I Love You So Much It Hurts, 1957 **(71)**

Pop — Philadelphia

The Graduates

Personnel: John Cappello (vocals); Bruce Hammond (vocals); Fred

Mancuso (vocals); Jack Scorsone (vocals)

Singles: Ballad of a Girl and a Boy, 1959 **(74)**; What Good Is Graduation, 1959 **(110)**

Pop Vocal—New York

Gerry Granahan

Singles: No Chemise, Please, 1958 **(23)**; Unchained Melody, 1961 **(109)**

Pop Vocal—Pennsylvania

Grand Funk Railroad

Personnel: Mark Farner (guitars, vocals, organ); Mel Schacher (bass, vocals) replaced (1977) by Dennis Bellinger (bass, vocals); Don Brewer (drums, percussion, vocals); added (1972) Craig Frost (keyboards, vocals) left group (1977)

Albums: On Time, 1969; Grand Funk, 1970; Close to Home, 1970; Live Album, 1971; Survival, 1971; E Pluribus Funk, 1972; Mark, Don & Mel 1969–1971, 1972; Phoenix, 1973; We're an American Band, 1973; Shinin' On, 1974; All the Girls in the World, 1975; Caught in the Act, 1975; Born to Die, 1976; Good Singin', Good Playin', 1976; Grand Funk Hits, 1977; Grand Funk Lives, 1981; What's Funk, 1983; More of the Best, 1991

Singles: Time Machine, 1969 **(48)**; Mr. Limousine Driver, 1969 **(97)**; Heartbreaker, 1970 **(72)**; Closer to Home, 1970 **(22)**; Mean Mistreater, 1970 **(47)**; Feeling Alright, 1971 **(54)**; Gimme Shelter, 1971 **(61)**; Footstomping Music, 1972 **(29)**; Upsetter, 1972 **(73)**; Rock & Roll Soul, 1972 **(29)**; We're an American Band, 1973 **(1)**; Walk Like a Man (You Can Call Me Your Man), 1973 **(19)**; The Loco-Motion, 1974 **(1)**; Shinin' On, 1974 **(11)**; Some Kind of Wonderful, 1974 **(3)**; Bad Time, 1975 **(4)**; Take Me, 1976 **(53)**; Sally, 1976 **(69)**; Can You Do It, 1976 **(45)**; Just Couldn't Wait

Grand Funk Railroad: Farner, Brewer, Schacher, Frost

1976; Queen Bee, 1981; Y.O.U., 1981; Stuck in the Middle, 1981 **(108)**
Hard Rock — Michigan

Earl Grant

Albums: Ebb Tide, 1961; Beyond the Reef, 1962; Earl Grant at Basin Street East, 1962; Fly Me to the Moon, 1964; Just for a Thrill, 1964; Trade Winds, 1965; Gently Swingin', 1968
Singles: The End, 1958 **(7)**; Evening Rain, 1959 **(63)**; House of Bamboo, 1960 **(88)**; Swingin' Gently, 1962 **(44)**; Sweet Sixteen Bars, 1962 **(55)**; Stand by Me, 1965 **(75)**
Pop Vocal — Oklahoma; appeared in the films *Tokyo Night, Imitation of Life* and *Tender Is the Night;* died in a car accident in 1970

Gogi Grant

Singles: Suddenly There's a Valley, 1955 **(9)**; Who Are We, 1956 **(62)**; The Wayward Wind, 1956 **(1)**; You're in Love, 1956 **(69)**; When the Tide Is High, 1956 **(75)**; Strange Are the Ways of Love, 1958 **(80)**; The Wayward Wind, 1961 **(50)**
Pop Vocal — Philadelphia; real name is Audrey Brown

Janie Grant

Singles: Triangle, 1961 **(29)**; Romeo, 1961 **(75)**; That Greasy Kid Stuff, 1962 **(74)**
Pop Vocal — New Jersey; real name is Rose Marie Cosili

Grapefruit

Personnel: John Perry (guitars, vocals); George Alexander (bass); Geoff Swettenham (drums)

Albums: Deep Water, 1968; Around Grapefruit, 1969
Singles: Dear Delilah, 1968 **(98)**; Elevator, 1968 **(113)**
Progressive Rock — British

The Grass Roots

Personnel: Creed Bratton (guitars, vocals) replaced (1969) by Terry Furlong (guitars) replaced (1972) by Reed Kailing (guitars) replaced (1982) by Terry Oubry (guitars, vocals); Dennis Provisor (keyboards, vocals) replaced (1972) by Virgil Weber (keyboards) replaced (1982) by Charles Judge (keyboards); Warren Entner (guitars) left group (1976); Robert Grill (bass, vocals); Rick Coonce (drums) replaced (1972) by Joel Larson (drums) replaced (1982) by Ralph Gilmore (drums, vocals)
Albums: The Grass Roots, 1966; Let's Live for Today, 1967; Feelings, 1968; Golden Grass, 1969; Lovin' Thing, 1969; Leaving It All Behind, 1969; More Golden Grass, 1970; Walking Through the Country, 1970; 16 Greatest Hits, 1971; Sooner or Later, 1971; Move Along, 1972; A Lot of Mileage, 1974; Powers of the Night, 1982
Singles: Mr. Jones (Ballad of a Thin Man), 1965 **(121)**; Where Were You When I Needed You, 1966 **(28)**; Only When You're Lonely, 1966 **(96)**; Let's Live for Today, 1967 **(8)**; The Things I Should Have Said, 1967 **(23)**; Wake Up, Wake Up, 1967 **(68)**; A Melody for You, 1968 **(123)**; Midnight Confession, 1968 **(5)**; Bella Linda, 1968 **(28)**; Loving Things, 1969 **(49)**; The River Is Wide, 1969 **(31)**; I'd Wait a Million Years, 1969 **(15)**; Heaven Knows, 1969 **(24)**; Walking

Through the Country, 1970 **(44)**; Baby Hold On, 1970 **(35)**; Come on and Say It, 1970 **(61)**; Temptation Eyes, 1970 **(15)**; Sooner or Later, 1971 **(9)**; Two Divided by Love, 1971 **(16)**; Glory Bound, 1972 **(34)**; The Runaway, 1972 **(39)**; Anyway the Wind Blows, 1972 **(107)**; Love Is What You Make It, 1973 **(55)**; Mamacita, 1975 **(71)**; Here Comes the Feeling Again, 1982

Pop/Rock—California

The Grateful Dead

Hart, Lesh, Garcia, Mydland, Kreutzmann, Weir

Personnel: Bob Weir (guitars, vocals); Jerry Garcia (guitars, vocals); Phil Lesh (bass); Rod McKernan (keyboards, vocals; deceased 1973) replaced (1971) by Keith Godchaux (keyboards; deceased 1980); replaced (1980) by Brent Mydland (keyboards; deceased 1990) replaced (1991) by Vince Welnick (keyboards); Bill Kreutzmann (drums); added (1967) Mickey Hart (drums, percussion); added (1971) Donna Godchaux (vocals) left group (1978)

Albums: The Grateful Dead, 1967; Anthem of the Sun, 1968; Aoxomoxoa, 1969; Live Dead, 1969; Workingman's Dead, 1970; American Beauty, 1970; The Grateful Dead Live, 1971; Europe '72, 1972; Vintage Dead, 1972; History of the Grateful Dead, Volume 1, 1973; Historic Dead, 1973; Wake of the Flood, 1973; Grateful Dead from the Mars Hotel, 1974; Best Of/Skeletons in the Closet, 1974; Blues for Allah, 1975; Steal Your Face, 1976; Terrapin Station, 1977; What a Long Strange Trip It's Been/Greatest Hits, 1978; Shakedown Street, 1978; Go to Heaven, 1980; Reckoning, 1981; Dead Set, 1981; For the Faithful, 1981; Dead Zone, 1987; In the Dark, 1987; Built to Last, 1989; Without a Net, 1990; One from the Vault, 1991

Singles: Uncle John's Band, 1970 **(69)**; Truckin', 1971 **(64)**; Sugar Magnolia, 1973 **(91)**; The Music Never Stopped, 1975 **(81)**; Alabama Getaway, 1980 **(68)**; Don't Ease Me In, 1980; Touch of Grey, 1987 **(9)**; Hell in a Bucket, 1987; Foolish Heart, 1989

Psychedelic Rock—California; thousands of fans, "Deadheads," follow the group on tour worldwide

Dobie Gray

Albums: Drift Away, 1973; Loving Arms, 1973; Hey Dixie, 1974; New Ray of Sunshine, 1975; Midnight Diamond, 1979; Dobie Gray, 1979; Best of Dobie Gray, 1982

Singles: Look at Me, 1963 **(91)**; The "In" Crowd, 1965 **(13)**; See You at the "Go-Go," 1965 **(69)**; Rose Garden, 1969 **(119)**; Drift Away, 1973 **(5)**; Loving Arms, 1973 **(61)**; Good Old Song, 1973 **(103)**; Watch Out for Lucy, 1974 **(107)**; If Love Must Go, 1976 **(78)**; Find 'em, Fool 'em & Forget 'em, 1976 **(94)**; You Can Do It, 1978 **(37)**

Soul/Pop Vocal—Texas; real name is Leonard Ainsworth

Great Society

Personnel: Grace Slick (vocals); Darby Slick (guitars); David Minor (guitars); Peter Van Der Geld (bass); Jerry Slick (drums)

Albums: Great Society, 1966; Conspicuous Only in Its Absence, 1968; How It Was, 1968; Somebody to Love, 1969

Single: Somebody to Love, 1966

Psychedelic Rock—San Francisco

R. B. Greaves

Album: R. B. Greaves, 1970

Singles: Take a Letter Maria, 1969 **(2)**; Always Something There to Remind Me, 1970 **(27)**; Fire & Rain, 1970 **(82)**; Georgia Took Her Back, 1970 **(88)**; Whiter Shade of Pale, 1970 **(82)**; Who's Watching the Baby (Margie), 1972 **(115)**

Pop Vocal—American; real name is Ronald Bertram Aloysius Greaves III; Sam Cooke's nephew

Garland Green

Singles: Jealous Kind of Fella, 1969 **(20)**; Don't Think That I'm a Violent Guy, 1969 **(113)**; Plain & Simple Girl, 1971 **(109)**

Soul Vocal—Mississippi

Norman Greenbaum

Albums: Spirit in the Sky, 1969; Back Home Again, 1972; Petaluma, 1973

Singles: Spirit in the Sky, 1970

(3); Canned Ham, 1970 **(46)**; California Earthquake, 1970 **(93)**

Pop/Rock—Boston

Ellie Greenwich

Album: Let It Be Written, Let It Be Sung, 1973

Singles: I Want You to Be My Baby, 1967 **(83)**; Maybe I Know, 1973 **(122)**

Pop Vocal—New York; wrote many 60s hits with ex-husband Jeff Barry

The Groundhogs

Personnel: Tony McPhee (guitars, vocals); David Wellbeloved (guitars); Peter Cruickshank (bass) replaced (1973) by Martin Kentin (bass); Ken Pustelnik (drums) replaced (1972) by Clive Brooks (drums) replaced (1976) by Mick Cook (drums)

Albums: Scratching the Surface, 1968; Blues Obituary, 1969; Thank Christ for the Bomb, 1970; Split, 1971; Who Will Save the World?, 1972; Hogwash, 1973; The Groundhogs with John Lee Hooker and John Mayall, 1973; Solid, 1974; Best of the Groundhogs, 1969–1972, 1974; Black Diamond, 1976; Crosscut Saw, 1976; Hoggin' the Stage, 1984

Heavy Metal/Blues—British

The Guess Who

Personnel: Burton Cummings (vocals, keyboards) replaced (1978) by Bruce Fuhr (vocals) replaced (1979) by Allan McDougall (vocals); Randy Bachman (guitars, vocals) replaced (1970) by Kurt Winter (guitars) replaced (1975) by Domenic Troiano (guitars, vocals) replaced

The Guess Who: *back row:* **Cummings, Troiano;** *front row:* **Peterson, Wallace**

(1979 by David Inglis (guitars); Chad Allan (bass, vocals) replaced (1969) by Jim Kale (bass) replaced (1971) by Bill Wallace (bass) replaced (1979) by Jim Kale (bass); Garry Peterson (drums) replaced (1979) by Vance Masters (drums, vocals); added (1970) Gregory Leskiw (guitars) replaced (1972) by Don McDougall (guitars)

Albums: Shakin' All Over, 1968; Guess Who, 1969; Wheatfield Soul, 1969; Canned Wheat, 1970; American Woman, 1970; Share the Land, 1971; Best of the Guess Who, 1971; So Long Bannatyne, 1972; Rockin', 1973; Live at the Paramount, 1973; Artificial Paradise, 1974; Ten, 1974; Best of the Guess Who, Volume 2, 1974; Road Food, 1974; Flavours, 1975; Power in the Music, 1975; Greatest, 1976; Born in Canada, 1976; Best of Live, 1976; All This for a Song, 1979

Singles: Shakin' All Over, 1965 **(22)**; Hey Ho What You Do to Me, 1965 **(125)**; These Eyes, 1969 **(6)**; Laughing, 1969 **(10)**; Undun, 1969 **(22)**; No Time, 1969 **(5)**; American Woman, 1970 **(1)**; No Sugar To-night, 1970 **(39)**; Hand Me Down World, 1970 **(17)**; Share the Land, 1970 **(10)**; Hang on to Your Life, 1971 **(43)**; Albert Flasher, 1971 **(29)**; Broken, 1971 **(55)**; Rain Dance, 1971 **(19)**; Sour Suite, 1971 **(50)**; Heart-broken Bopper, 1972 **(47)**; Guns Guns Guns, 1972 **(70)**; Running Back to Saskatoon, 1972 **(96)**; Follow Your Daughter Home, 1973 **(61)**; Star Baby, 1974 **(39)**; Clap for the Wolfman, 1974 **(6)**; Dancin' Fool, 1974 **(28)**; Glamour Boy, 1975; Roseanne, 1975 **(105)**; When the Band Was Singin' "Shakin' All Over," 1975 **(102)**

Hard Rock — Canadian

Gun

Personnel: Adrian Gurvitz (guitars, vocals); Paul Gurvitz (bass, vocals); Louis Farrell (drums) replaced (1969) by Peter Dunton (drums)

Albums: Gun, 1968; Gunsight, 1969

Progressive Rock — British

Arlo Guthrie

Albums: Alice's Restaurant, 1967; Arlo, 1968; Running Down the Road, 1969; Washington County, 1970; Alice's Restaurant (Soundtrack), 1970; Hoboes Lullabye, 1972; Last of the Brooklyn Cowboys, 1973; Arlo Guthrie, 1974; Together, 1975; Amigo, 1975; The Best of Arlo Guthrie, 1977; One Night, 1978; Outlasting the Blues, 1979; Power of Love, 1981

Singles: Alice's Rock & Roll

Restaurant, 1969 **(97)**; Valley to Play, 1970 **(102)**; City of New Orleans, 1972 **(18)**; Gypsy Davy, 1973 **(105)**; If I Could Only Touch Your Life, 1981

Folk/Rock—New York; Arlo is the son of legendary folk performer Woody Guthrie

Hackamore Brick

Personnel: Robbie Biege (guitars, vocals); Tommy Moonlig (guitars, vocals); Chick Newman (bass); Bob Roman (drums)
Albums: Hackamore Brick, 1969; One Kiss Leads to Another, 1970
Single: Got a Gal Named Wilma, 1970

Psychedelic Pop—American

Bill Haley & His Comets

Personnel: Bill Haley (vocals, guitars; deceased 1981); Danny Cedrone (guitars) replaced (1956) by Frannie Beecher (guitars); Joey D'Ambrose (saxophones) replaced (1956) by Rudy Rompilli (saxophones; deceased 1976); Billy Williamson (steel guitar); Johnny Grande (piano); Marshall Lytle (bass) replaced (1956) by Al Rex (bass); Dick Richards (drums) replaced (1956) by Ralph Jones (drums)
Albums: Live It Up, 1955; Shake, Rattle & Roll, 1955; Rock Around the Clock, 1956; Rock 'n' Roll Stage Show, 1956; Rockin' the Oldies, 1957; Rockin' Around the World, 1957; Rockin' the Joint, 1957; Chicks, 1959; Bill Haley & the Comets, 1959; He Digs Rock 'n' Roll, 1960; Strictly Instrumental, 1960; Haley's Juke Box, 1960; Twisting Knights, 1962; Greatest Hits, 1968; On Stage, 1970; Rock Around the Country, 1971; King of Rock, 1973; Traveling Band, 1973; Razzle Dazzle, 1974; Live in London '74, 1974; Golden Hits, 1974; Rare Items, 1975; Collections, 1976; Armchair Rock 'n' Roll, 1978; Rock 'n' Roll Revival, 1981; Rock 'n' Roll Forever, 1981; Rockin' Rollin' Bill Haley, 1984
Singles: Dim, Dim the Lights (I Want Some Atmosphere), 1954 **(11)**; Mambo Rock, 1955 **(18)**; Birth of the Boogie, 1955 **(17)**; (We're Gonna) Rock Around the Clock, 1955 **(1)**; Razzle-Dazzle/Two Hound Dogs, 1955 **(15)**; Burn That Candle, 1955 **(9)**; Rock-a-Beatin' Boogie, 1955 **(41)**; See You Later Alligator, 1956 **(6)**; R-O-C-K, 1956 **(16)**; The Saints Rock 'n' Roll, 1956 **(18)**; Hot Dog Buddy Buddy, 1956 **(60)**; Rockin' Through the Rye, 1956 **(78)**; Rip It Up, 1956 **(25)**; Teenager's Mother (Are You Right?), 1956 **(68)**; Rudy's Rock, 1956 **(34)**; Don't Knock the Rock/Choo Choo Ch' Boogie, 1956 **(45)**; Forty Cups of Coffee/Hook, Line and Sinker, 1957 **(70)**; (You Hit the Wrong Note) Billy Goat, 1957 **(60)**; Skinny Minnie, 1958 **(22)**; Lean Jean, 1958 **(67)**; Joey's Song, 1959 **(46)**; Skokiaan (South African Song), 1960 **(70)**; Tamiami, 1960 **(101)**; Rock Around the Clock, 1968 **(118)**; (We're Gonna) Rock Around the Clock, 1974 **(39)**

Rock/Pop—Michigan

Larry Hall

Single: Sandy, 1959 **(15)**
Pop Vocal—Cincinnati

The Halos

Single: "Nag," 1961 **(25)**
R & B Vocal — New York

George Hamilton IV

Album: Abilene, 1963
Singles: A Rose and a Baby Ruth, 1956 **(6)**; Only One Love, 1957 **(33)**; High School Romance, 1957 **(80)**; Why Don't They Understand, 1957 **(10)**; Now and For Always, 1958 **(25)**; I Know Where I'm Goin', 1958 **(43)**; When Will I Know, 1958 **(65)**; Your Cheatin' Heart, 1958 **(72)**; The Teen Commandments, 1958 **(29)** (with Paul Anka & Johnny Nash); Gee, 1959 **(73)**; Abilene, 1963 **(15)**; There's More Pretty Girls Than One, 1963 **(116)**
Country/Pop Vocal — North Carolina

Roy Hamilton

Singles: Unchained Melody, 1955 **(6)**; Forgive This Fool, 1955 **(45)**; Without a Song, 1955 **(77)**; Everybody's Got a Home, 1955 **(42)**; Don't Let Go, 1958 **(13)**; Pledging My Love, 1958 **(45)**; I Need Your Lovin', 1959 **(62)**; Time Marches On, 1959 **(84)**; Ebb Tide, 1959 **(105)**; You Can Have Her, 1961 **(12)**; You're Gonna Need Magic, 1961 **(80)**; I'll Come Running Back to You, 1962 **(110)**; Let Go, 1963 **(129)**
R & B Vocal — Georgia; died of a stroke in 1969

Russ Hamilton

Single: Rainbow, 1957 **(4)**
Pop Vocal — British; real name is Ronald Hulme

The Happenings

Personnel: Bob Miranda (vocals); Tom Giuliano (vocals); Ralph DiVito (vocals) replaced (1968) by Bernie LaPorta (vocals); Dave Libert (vocals)
Albums: The Happenings, 1966; Back to Back, 1967 (with the Tokens); The Happenings Golden Hits, 1968; Piece of Mind, 1969
Singles: See You in September, 1966 **(3)**; Go Away Little Girl, 1966 **(12)**; Goodnight My Love, 1966 **(51)**; I Got Rhythm, 1967 **(3)**; My Mammy, 1967 **(13)**; Why Do Fools Fall in Love, 1967 **(41)**; Music Music Music, 1968 **(96)**; Randy, 1968 **(118)**; Breaking Up Is Hard to Do, 1968 **(67)**; Crazy Rhythm, 1968 **(114)**; Where Do I Go/Be-In/Hare Krishna, 1969 **(66)**; Answer Me My Love, 1970 **(115)**
Pop Vocal — New Jersey

The Harbinger Complex

Album: The Harbinger Complex, 1969
Single: I Think I'm Down, 1969
Psychedelic Pop — American

The Harden Trio

Personnel: Bobby Harden (vocals); Arlene Harden (vocals); Robbie Harden (vocals)
Album: Tippy Toeing, 1966
Single: Tippy Toeing, 1966 **(44)**
Country/Folk — Arkansas

Tim Hardin

Albums: Tim Hardin I, 1966; Tim Hardin II, 1967; This Is Tim Hardin, 1967; Tim Hardin III Live in Concert, 1968; Tim Hardin IV,

1969; Suite for Susan Moore and Damion-We Are-One, All in One, 1969; The Best of Tim Hardin, 1970; Bird on a Wire, 1971; Painted Head, 1973; Archetypes, 1973; Nine, 1973; State of Grace, 1981; Memorial Album, 1982

Single: Simple Song of Freedom, 1969 **(50)**

Folk/Blues—Oregon; Tim died in 1980 from a heroin overdose at the age of 39

The Hardtimes

Personnel: Rudy Romero (vocals); Bill Richardson (guitars); Bob Morris (guitars); Lee Kiefer (bass); Paul Wheatbread (drums)

Single: Fortune Teller, 1966 **(97)**

Pop/Rock—San Diego

Janice Harper

Singles: Bon Voyage, 1957 **(46)**; That's Why I Was Born, 1957 **(84)**; Devotion, 1958 **(82)**; Cry Me a River, 1960 **(91)**

Pop Vocal—New York

Roy Harper

Albums: Sophisticated Beggar, 1967; Come Out Fighting Ghengis Smith, 1967; Folkjokeopus, 1969; Flat, Baroque and Beserk, 1970; Stormcock, 1971; Life Mask, 1973; Valentine, 1974; Flashes from the Archives, 1974; When an Old Cricketer, 1975; H.Q., 1975; Bullinamingvase, 1977; Commercial Break, 1977; The Early Years, 1977; One of Those Days in England, 1977; Roy Harper 70/75, 1978; Unknown Soldier, 1980; Once, 1991

Folk Rock—British

Harper's Bizarre

Personnel: Ted Templeman (guitars, vocals); Dick Scoppettone (guitars); Eddie James (guitars); Dick Yount (bass); John Petersen (drums)

Albums: Feelin' Groovy, 1967; Anything Goes, 1967; Secret Life of Harper's Bizarre, 1968; Harper's Bizarre 4, 1969; Best of Harper's Bizarre, 1974; As Time Goes By, 1976

Singles: The 59th Street Bridge Song (Feelin' Groovy), 1966 **(13)**; Come to the Sunshine, 1967 **(37)**; Anything Goes, 1967 **(43)**; Chattanooga Choo Choo, 1967 **(45)**; Both Sides Now, 1968 **(123)**; Battle of New Orleans, 1968 **(95)**

Pop/Rock—San Francisco; formerly known as the Tikis; Templeman produced LPs for the Doobie Brothers and Van Halen

Betty Harris

Singles: Cry to Me, 1963 **(23)**; His Kiss, 1964 **(89)**; Nearer to You, 1967 **(85)**

Soul Vocal—Florida

Richard Harris

Albums: A Tramp Shining, 1968; The Yard Went on Forever..., 1968; My Boy, 1971; Slides, 1972; Jonathan Livingston Seagull, 1973; The Prophet by Kahlil Gibran, 1974

Singles: MacArthur Park, 1968 **(2)**; The Yard Went on Forever, 1968 **(64)**; Didn't We, 1968 **(63)**; My Boy, 1971 **(41)**; There Are Too Many Saviors on My Cross, 1972 **(107)**; I Don't Want to Tell You, 1973 **(106)**

Pop Vocal—Irish; Richard is best known as an actor

Rolf Harris

Album: Tie Me Kangaroo Down, Sport & Sun Arise, 1963

Singles: Sun Arise, 1963 **(61)**; Tie Me Kangaroo Down, Sport, 1963 **(3)**; Nick Teen and Al K. Hall, 1963 **(95)**; The Court of King Caractacus, 1964 **(116)**; Two Little Boys, 1970 **(119)**

Pop Vocal—Australian

Thurston Harris

Singles: Little Bitty Pretty One, 1957 **(6)**; Do What You Did, 1958 **(57)**; Over and Over, 1958 **(96)**

R & B Vocal—Indiana; died of a heart attack in 1990

Noel Harrison

Album: Collage, 1967

Singles: A Young Girl, 1965 **(51)**; Suzanne, 1967 **(56)**

Pop Vocal—British; son of actor Rex Harrison

Wilbert Harrison

Albums: Kansas City, 1959; Battle of the Giants, 1962; Shoot You Full of Love, 1967; Let's Work Together, 1969; Wilbert Harrison, 1972; Soul Food Man, 1973; Anything You Want, 1974

Singles: Kansas City, 1959 **(1)**; Let's Work Together (Part 1), 1969 **(32)**; My Heart Is Yours, 1971 **(98)**

R & B Vocal—North Carolina

Tim Hart & Maddy Prior

Albums: Folk Songs of Olde England 1, 1968; Folk Songs of Olde England 2, 1968; Summer Solstice, 1972

Folk/Rock—British

John Hartford

Albums: Looks at Life, 1967; Earthwords & Music, 1967; The Love Album, 1968; Housing Project, 1968; Gentle on My Mind, 1969; John Hartford, 1969; Iron Mountain Depot, 1970; Aero Plain, 1971; Morning Bugle, 1972; Mark Twang, 1976; Nobody Knows What You Do, 1976; All in the Name of Love, 1977; Heading Down Into the Mystery Below, 1978; Slumberin' on the Cumberland, 1979; You and Me at Home, 1981; Me Oh My, How Does the Time Fly, 1983; Annual Waltz, 1987

Folk/Country—New York; appeared on the Glen Campbell and Smothers Brothers TV shows

Sensational Alex Harvey Band

Personnel: Alex Harvey (guitars, vocals; deceased 1982); Zal Cleminson (guitars) replaced (1979) by Matthew Lang (guitars); Chris Glen (bass) replaced (1979) by Gordon Sellars (bass); Ted McKenna (drums) replaced (1979) by Simon Chatterton (drums); Hugh McKenna (keyboards) replaced (1978) by Tommy Eyre (keyboards); Bud Beadle (saxophones) left group (1972) replaced (1979) by Don Weller (saxophones)

Albums: Alex Harvey Soul Band, 1964; The Blues, 1964; Attention, 1968; Roman Wall Blues, 1969; This Is Alex Harvey, 1970; Joker Is Wild, 1972; Framed, 1972; Next, 1974; Impossible Dream, 1974;

Tomorrow Belongs to Me, 1975; Live, 1975; Penthouse Tapes, 1975; SAHB Stories, 1976; Big Hits and Close Shaves, 1977; Fourplay, 1977; Presents the Loch Ness Monster, 1977; Rock Drill, 1978; Vambo Rools, 1978; The Mafia Stole My Guitar, 1979; Collectors Items, 1980; Soldier on the Wall, 1983; The Best of the Sensational Alex Harvey Band, 1984

Hard Rock—British

The Hassles

Personnel: John Edward Dizek (vocals, percussion); Billy Joel (vocals, keyboards); Richard McKenner (guitars); Howard Arthur Blauvelt (bass); Jonathan Small (drums)

Albums: The Hassles, 1967; Hour of the Wolf, 1968

Single: You've Got Me Hummin', 1967 **(112)**

Pop/Rock—New York

Richie Havens

Albums: Richie Havens Record, 1965; Electric Havens, 1966; Mixed Bag, 1967; Something Else Again, 1968; Richard D. Havens 1983, 1969; Stonehenge, 1970; Alarm Clock, 1971; The Great Blind Degree, 1971; Richie Havens on Stage, 1972; Portfolio, 1973; Mixed Bag II, 1974; The End of the Beginning, 1976; Mirage, 1977; Richie Havens, 1978; Connections, 1980; Simple Things, 1985; Sings Beatles & Dylan, 1988

Singles: Handsome Johnny, 1970 **(115)**; Here Comes the Sun, 1971 **(16)**; Eyesight to the Blind, 1973 **(111)**; I'm Not in Love, 1976 **(102)**

Black Folk/Rock—New York

Dale Hawkins

Albums: Susie Q, 1958; Dale Hawkins, 1959; Let's Twist at the Peppermint Lounge, 1961; L.A., Memphis & Tyler, Texas, 1970

Singles: Susie-Q, 1957 **(27)**; La-Do-Dada, 1958 **(32)**; A House, a Car and a Wedding Ring, 1958 **(88)**; Class Cutter (Yeah Yeah), 1959 **(52)**

Rockabilly—Louisiana; real first name is Delmar

Ronnie Hawkins

Albums: Ronnie Hawkins, 1969; Mr. Dynamo, 1960; Folk Ballads, 1960; Sings Hank Williams, 1961; Arkansas Rockpile, 1962; The Best of Ronnie Hawkins, 1963; Mojo Man, 1964; Rrrracket Time, 1965; Ronnie Hawkins, 1968; Ronnie Hawkins, 1970; The Hawk, 1971; Rock & Roll Resurrection, 1972; Giant of Rock 'n' Roll, 1974; Rockin', 1977; The Hawk, 1979

Singles: Forty Days, 1959 **(45)**; Mary Lou, 1959 **(26)**; Bo Diddley, 1963 **(117)**; Down in the Alley, 1970 **(75)**; Bitter Green, 1970 **(118)**

Blues/Rock—Arkansas

Bill Hayes

Singles: The Ballad of Davy Crockett, 1955 **(1)**; Wringle, Wrangle, 1957 **(33)**

Pop Vocal—Illinois; soap star of "Days of Our Lives"

Isaac Hayes

Albums: Presenting Isaac Hayes, 1967; Hot Buttered Soul, 1969; The Isaac Hayes Movement, 1970; To Be Continued, 1970; Shaft, 1971; Black Moses, 1971; Live at the

Sahara Tahoe, 1973; Joy, 1973; Tough Guys, 1974; Truck Turner, 1974; Chocolate Chip, 1975; The Best of Isaac Hayes, 1975; Disco Connection, 1976; Groove-a-Thon, 1976; Juicy Fruit (Disco Freak), 1976; A Man and a Woman, 1977 (with Dionne Warwick); New Horizon, 1977; For the Sake of Love, 1978; Hotbed, 1978; Don't Let Go, 1979; Royal's Rappin', 1979 (with Millie Jackson); And Once Again, 1980

Singles: Walk On By, 1969 **(30)**; By the Time I Get to Phoenix, 1969 **(37)**; I Stand Accused, 1970 **(42)**; The Look of Love, 1971 **(79)**; Never Can Say Goodbye, 1971 **(22)**; Theme from Shaft, 1971 **(1)**; Do Your Thing, 1972 **(30)**; Let's Stay Together, 1972 **(48)**; Ain't That Loving You (for More Reasons Than One), 1972 **(86)** (with David Porter); Theme from the Men, 1972 **(38)**; Rolling Down a Mountainside, 1973 **(104)**; Joy—Pt. I, 1973 **(30)**; Wonderful, 1974 **(71)**; Chocolate Chip, 1975 **(92)**; Disco Freak, 1976 **(102)**; Out of the Ghetto, 1978 **(107)**; Don't Let Go, 1979 **(18)**; It's All in the Game, 1980 **(107)**

Soul/R & B—Tennessee

Leon Haywood

Albums: It's Got to Be Mellow, 1967; Keep It in the Family, 1974; Come and Get Yourself Some, 1975; Just Your Fool, 1976; Naturally, 1980

Singles: She's with Her Other Love, 1965 **(92)**; It's Got to Be Mellow, 1967 **(63)**; Mellow Moonlight, 1967 **(92)**; Keep It in the Family, 1974 **(50)**; Sugar Lump, 1974 **(108)**; Believe Half of What You See (and None of What You Hear), 1975 **(94)**; Come An' Get Yourself Some, 1975 **(83)**; I Want'a Do Something Freaky to You, 1975 **(15)**; Just Your Fool, 1976 **(102)**; Strokin' (Pt. 1), 1976 **(101)**; The Streets Will Love You to Death— Pt. 1, 1976 **(107)**; Don't Push It Don't Force It, 1980 **(49)**

Soul/R & B—Houston

Roy Head

Albums: Treat Me Right, 1965; Get Back, 1966; Puff of Smoke, 1970

Singles: Treat Her Right, 1965 **(2)**; Just a Little Bit, 1965 **(39)**; Apple of My Eye, 1965 **(32)**; Get Back, 1966 **(88)**; My Babe, 1966 **(99)**; Wigglin' and Gigglin', 1966 **(110)**; To Make a Big Man Cry, 1966 **(95)**; Puff of Smoke, 1971 **(96)**

Pop/Country Vocal—Texas

Hearts and Flowers

Personnel: Dave Dawson (vocals, autoharp); Rick Cunha (guitars, vocals); Larry Murray (guitars, vocals); added (1968) Bernie Leadon (guitars, vocals)

Albums: Now Is the Time, 1967; Of Old Horses, Kings and Forgotten Heroes, 1968
Single: Rock 'n' Roll Gypsies, 1967
Folk/Rock — California

The Heartbeats

Personnel: James "Shep" Sheppard (vocals; deceased 1970); Wally Roker (vocals); Walter Crump (vocals); Robbie Adams (vocals); Vernon Walker (vocals)
Singles: A Thousand Miles Away, 1957 **(53)**; Everybody's Somebody's Fool, 1957 **(78)**; A Thousand Miles Away, 1960 **(96)**
R & B Vocal — New York

Bobby Hebb

Album: Sunny, 1966
Singles: Sunny, 1966 **(2)**; A Satisfied Man, 1966 **(39)**; Love Me, 1966 **(84)**
Pop Vocal — Nashville

Hedgehoppers Anonymous

Singles: It's a Good News Week, 1965 **(48)**; Don't Push Me, 1966 **(110)**
Pop/Rock — British

Bobby Helms

Singles: Fraulein, 1957 **(36)**; My Special Angel, 1957 **(7)**; Jingle Bell Rock, 1957 **(6)**; Jacqueline, 1958 **(63)**; Borrowed Dreams, 1958 **(60)**; The Fool and the Angel, 1958 **(75)**; Jingle Bell Rock, 1958 **(35)**; Jingle Bell Rock, 1960 **(36)**; Jingle Bell Rock, 1961 **(41)**; Jingle Bell Rock, 1962 **(56)**
Country/Pop — Indiana

Dorris Henderson

Albums: There You Go, 1965; Watch the Stars, 1967; Rotterdam Blues, 1969
Pop Vocal — British

Joe Henderson

Album: Snap Your Fingers, 1962
Singles: Snap Your Fingers, 1962 **(8)**; Big Love, 1962 **(74)**; The Searching Is Over, 1962 **(94)**
R & B Vocal — Indiana; died in 1966

Bobby Hendricks

Singles: Itchy Twitchy Feeling, 1958 **(25)**; Psycho, 1960 **(73)**
R & B Vocal — Ohio

Jimi Hendrix Experience

Personnel: Jimi Hendrix (guitars, vocals; deceased 1970); Noel Redding (bass) replaced (1970) by Billy Cox (bass); Mitch Mitchell (drums) replaced (1970) by Buddy Miles (drums)
Albums: Are You Experienced, 1967; Axis Bold As Love, 1967; Smash Hits, 1968; Electric Ladyland, 1968; Electric Hendrix, 1968; Monterrey, 1970; Band of Gypsys, 1970; Cry of Love, 1971; Rainbow Bridge, 1971; Isle of Wight, 1971; In the West, 1972; War Heroes, 1973; Jimi Hendrix, 1973; Loose Ends, 1973; Crash Landing, 1975; Jimi Hendrix (Special), 1975; Jimi Hendrix 2, 1975; Legacy, 1976;

Midnight Lightning, 1976; Jimi
Hendrix Story, 1977; The Essential,
1978; The Essential 2, 1979; Box
Set, 1980; 9 to the Universe, 1980;
Legendary, 1980; Stone Free, 1981;
The Jimi Hendrix Concerts, 1982;
Kiss the Sky, 1984; Live at Winter-
land, 1987; Radio One, 1988

Singles: Purple Haze, 1967 **(65)**;
Foxey Lady, 1968 **(67)**; Up from the
Skies, 1968 **(82)**; All Along the
Watchtower, 1968 **(20)**; Crosstown
Traffic, 1968 **(52)**; Stone Free, 1969
(130); Freedom, 1971 **(59)**; Dolly
Dagger, 1971 **(74)**

Psychedelic Rock — Texas; Jimi's
rendition of "The Star Spangled
Banner" brought down the house at
Woodstock

Clarence Henry

Singles: Ain't Got No Home, 1956
(20); But I Do, 1961 **(4)**; You
Always Hurt the One You Love,
1961 **(12)**; Lonely Street, 1961 **(57)**;
On Bended Knees, 1961 **(64)**; Standing in the Need of Love, 1961 **(109)**;
A Little Too Much, 1962 **(77)**;
Dream Myself a Sweetheart, 1962
(112); Have You Ever Been Lonely,
1964 **(135)**

R & B Vocal — Louisiana

Herd

Personnel: Peter Frampton (guitars, vocals); Andy Bown (keyboards, vocals); Gary Taylor (bass);
Andrew Steele (drums)

Albums: Paradise Lost, 1968;
Lookin' Thru You, 1968; Nostalgia,
1972

Single: From the Underworld,
1968

Progressive Rock — British

Herman's Hermits

**Hopwood, Greene, Noone,
Leckenby, Whitham**

Personnel: Peter Noone (vocals);
Karl Greene (bass, harmonica);
Keith Hopwood (guitars); Derek
Leckenby (guitars); Barry Whitham
(drums); added (1968) Frank Ren-
shaw (keyboards)

Albums: Herman's Hermits, 1965;
Introducing Herman's Hermits,
1965; On Tour, 1965; The Best of
Herman's Hermits, 1965; When the
Boys Meet the Girls, 1965; Both
Sides of Herman's Hermits, 1966;
Herman's Hermits Again, 1966;
Lucky 13, 1966; Hold On, 1966;
Best of Herman's Hermits Vol. 2,
1966; There's a Kind of Hush, 1967;
Blaze, 1967; Mrs. Brown You've
Got a Lovely Daughter, 1968; Best
of Herman's Hermits Volume 3,
1968; Their 20 Greatest Hits, 1973

Singles: I'm Into Something
Good, 1964 **(13)**; Can't You Hear
My Heartbeat, 1965 **(2)**; Silhouettes,
1965 **(5)**; Mrs. Brown You've Got a
Lovely Daughter, 1965 **(1)**;

Wonderful World, 1965 (4); I'm Henry VIII, I Am, 1965 (1); Just a Little Bit Better, 1965 (7); A Must to Avoid, 1965 (8); Listen People, 1966 (3); Leaning on the Lamp Post, 1966 (9); This Door Swings Both Ways, 1966 (12); Dandy, 1966 (5); East West, 1966 (27); There's a Kind of Hush (All Over the World), 1967 (4); No Milk Today, 1967 (35); Don't Go Out in the Rain, 1967 (18); Museum, 1967 (39); I Can't Take Or Leave Your Loving, 1968 (22); Sleepy Joe, 1968 (61); Sunshine Girl, 1968 (101); The Most Beautiful Thing in My Life, 1968 (131); Something's Happening, 1969 (130)

Pop/Rock—British

The Hesitations

Personnel: George "King" Scott (vocals; deceased 1968); Fred Deal (vocals)

Album: The New Born Free, 1968
Singles: Born Free, 1968 (38); The Impossible Dreams, 1968 (42); Climb Every Mountain, 1968 (90); Who Will Answer, 1968 (112); A Whiter Shade of People, 1968 (100)

Soul Vocal—Cleveland

The High Keyes

Personnel: Troy Keyes (vocals); Jimmy Williams (vocals); Bobby Haggard (vocals); Cliff Rice (vocals)
Single: Que Sera, Sera (Whatever Will Be, Will Be), 1963 (47)

R & B Vocal—American

High Tide

Personnel: Tony Hill (guitars); Peter Pavli (bass); Simon House (violin); Roger Hadden (drums)

Albums: Sea Shanties, 1969; High Tide, 1970

Space Rock—British

The Highlights

Personnel: Frank Pizani (vocals); Frank Calzaretta (vocals); Tony Calzaretta (vocals); Bill Melshimer (vocals); Jerry Oleski (vocals)
Singles: City of Angels, 1956 (19); To Be with You, 1956 (84)

Pop Vocal—Chicago

The Highwaymen

Personnel: Dave Fisher (banjo, vocals); Bob Burnett (percussion, vocals); Steve Trott (guitars, vocals) replaced (1962) by Gil Robbins (vocals); Steve Butts (bass, vocals); Chan Daniels (charango, vocals)

Albums: The Highwaymen, 1961; Standing Room Only!, 1962; Hootenanny with the Highwaymen, 1963
Singles: Michael, 1961 (1); The Gypsy Rover, 1961 (42); Cotton Fields, 1961 (13); I'm on My Way, 1962 (90); The Bird Man, 1962 (64) (with Burt Lancaster)

Pop/Folk Vocal—Connecticut; group formed at Wesleyan University in Connecticut

Jessie Hill

Album: Naturally, 1960
Singles: Ooh Poo Pah Doo—Part II, 1960 (28); Whip It on Me, 1960 (91)

R & B Vocal—New Orleans

The Hilltoppers

Personnel: Jimmy Sacca (vocals); Don McGuire (vocals); Seymour Spiegelman (vocals); Billy Vaughn (vocals) left group (1955)

Singles: The Kentuckian Song, 1955 **(20)**; Only You (and You Alone), 1955 **(8)**; Searching, 1955 **(81)**; My Treasure, 1955 **(31)**; Ka-Ding-Dong, 1956 **(38)**; Marianne, 1957 **(3)**; I'm Serious, 1957 **(74)**; I Love My Girl, 1957 **(75)**; A Fallen Star, 1957 **(58)**; The Joker (That's What They Call Me), 1957 **(22)**
Folk/Pop Vocal — Kentucky

Eddie Hodges

Album: I'm Gonna Knock on Your Door, 1961
Singles: I'm Gonna Knock on Your Door, 1961 **(12)**; Bandit of My Dreams, 1962 **(65)**; (Girls, Girls, Girls) Made to Love, 1962 **(14)**; Halfway, 1963 **(118)**; New Orleans, 1965 **(44)**; Love Minus Zero, 1965 **(134)**
Pop Vocal — Mississippi

Ron Holden

Singles: Love You So, 1960 **(7)**; Gee, But I'm Lonesome, 1960 **(106)**
R & B Vocal — Seattle

Jimmy Holiday

Singles: How Can I Forget, 1963 **(57)**; Poor Boy, 1963 **(124)**; The New Breed, 1965 **(115)**; Baby I Love You, 1966 **(98)**; Everybody Needs Help, 1967 **(116)**; I Wanna Hurry My Brothers Home, 1967 **(132)**
Soul Vocal — Mississippi; died in 1987

The Holidays

Personnel: Edwin Starr (vocals); Steve Mancha (vocals); J. J. Barnes (vocals)

Single: I'll Love You Forever, 1966 **(63)**
R & B Vocal — Detroit

Eddie Holland

Singles: Jamie, 1962 **(30)**; Leaving Here, 1964 **(76)**; Just Ain't Enough Love, 1964 **(54)**; Candy to Me, 1964 **(58)**
R & B Vocal — Detroit; part of the Holland-Dozier-Holland songwriting team

The Hollies

Elliott, Calvert, Nash, Clarke, Hicks

Personnel: Allan Clarke (vocals) replaced (1971) by Mikael Rickfors (vocals) replaced (1973) by Allan Clarke (vocals); Tony Hicks (guitars); Graham Nash (guitars, vocals) replaced (1969) by Terry Sylvester (guitars, vocals) replaced (1983) by Graham Nash (vocals); Eric Haydock (bass, vocals) replaced (1965) by Bernard Calvert (bass) replaced (1981) by Eric Haydock (bass) replaced (1983) by Steve Stroud (bass); Donald Rathbone (drums) replaced (1964) by Robert Elliott (drums);

added (1983) Paul Bliss (keyboards); added (1983) Frank Christopher (guitars)

Albums: Stay with the Hollies, 1964; In the Hollies Style, 1965; Here I Go, 1965; Hear Here, 1965; The Hollies, 1965; Bus Stop, 1966; Stop, Stop, Stop, 1966; Would You Believe, 1966; For Certain Because, 1966; Evolution, 1967; Butterfly, 1967; Hollies' Greatest, 1968; King Midas, 1968; Sing Dylan, 1969; Sing Hollies, 1969; Moving Finger, 1969; Confessions of the Mind, 1970; Distant Light, 1971; Romany, 1972; Greatest Hits, Volume 2, 1972; The Hollies, 1974; Another Night, 1975; Write On, 1976; Russian Roulette, 1976; Live Hits, 1977; Best of the Hollies, 1978; The Other Side of the Hollies, 1978; A Crazy Steal, 1978; Double Seven O Four, 1979; Buddy Holly, 1980; What Goes Around, 1983

Singles: Just One Look, 1964 **(98)**; Here I Go Again, 1964 **(107)**; I'm Alive, 1965 **(104)**; Look Through Any Window, 1965 **(32)**; I Can't Let Go, 1966 **(42)**; Bus Stop, 1966 **(5)**; Stop, Stop, Stop, 1966 **(7)**; On a Carousel, 1967 **(11)**; Pay You Back with Interest, 1967 **(28)**; Carrie Ann, 1967 **(9)**; Just One Look, 1967 **(44)**; King Midas in Reverse, 1967 **(51)**; Dear Eloise, 1967 **(50)**; Jennifer Eccles, 1968 **(40)**; Do the Best You Can, 1968 **(93)**; Sorry, Suzanne, 1969 **(56)**; He Ain't Heavy, He's My Brother, 1969 **(7)**; I Can't Tell the Bottom from the Top, 1970 **(82)**; Hey Willy, 1971 **(110)**; Long Cool Woman, 1972 **(2)**; Long Dark Road, 1972 **(26)**; Magic Woman Touch, 1973 **(60)**; The Air That I Breathe, 1974 **(6)**; Sandy, 1975 **(85)**; Another Night, 1975 **(71)**; I'm Down, 1975 **(104)**; Stop in the

Name of Love, 1983 **(29)**; If the Lights Go Out, 1983; Someone Else's Eyes, 1983; Casualty, 1983
  Pop/Rock — British

Brenda Holloway

Albums: Every Little Bit Hurts, 1964; Artistry of Brenda Holloway, 1965

Singles: Every Little Bit Hurts, 1964 **(13)**; I'll Always Love You, 1964 **(60)**; When I'm Gone, 1965 **(25)**; Operator, 1965 **(78)**; You Can Cry on My Shoulder, 1965 **(116)**; Together Till the End of Time, 1966 **(125)**; Just Look What You've Done, 1967 **(69)**; You've Made Me So Very Happy, 1967 **(39)**
  Soul Vocal — California

Buddy Holly

Albums: Buddy Holly, 1958; The Buddy Holly Story, 1959; The Buddy Holly Story 2, 1960; That'll Be the Day, 1961; Reminiscing, 1963; Showcase, 1964; Holly in the Hills, 1965; Best of Buddy Holly, 1966; The Great Buddy Holly, 1967; Rave On, 1968; True Love Ways, 1968; Giant, 1969; Greatest Hits, 1969; Greatest Hits 2, 1970; Remember, 1971; Rock 'n' Roll Collection, 1972; Legend, 1974; Buddy Holly/The Crickets 20 Golden Greats, 1978; Buddy Holly, 1979

Singles: That'll Be the Day, 1957 **(1)**; Peggy Sue, 1957 **(3)**; Oh, Boy!, 1957 **(10)**; Maybe Baby, 1957 **(17)**; Rave On, 1958 **(37)**; Think It Over, 1958 **(27)**; Fool's Paradise, 1958 **(58)**; Early in the Morning, 1958 **(32)**; Real Wild Child, 1958 **(68)**; Heartbeat, 1958 **(82)**; It Doesn't Matter Anymore, 1959 **(13)**; Raining in My Heart, 1959 **(88)**

Rock/Pop—Texas; killed in a 1959 plane crash

The Hollywood Argyles

Personnel: Gary Paxton (vocals); Ted Marsh (vocals); Bobby Rey (vocals); Deany Weaver (guitars); Ted Winters (bass); Gary Webb (drums)

Album: The Hollywood Argyles, 1960

Single: Alley-Oop, 1960 **(1)**

Pop—American

Eddie Holman

Album: I Love You, 1970

Singles: This Can't Be True, 1966 **(57)**; Don't Stop Now, 1966 **(104)**; Am I a Loser, 1966 **(101)**; Hey There Lonely Girl, 1969 **(2)**; Don't Stop Now/Since I Don't Have You, 1970 **(48)**; I'll Be There, 1970 **(115)**; This Will Be a Night to Remember, 1977 **(90)**

Soul Vocal—Virginia

Holy Modal Rounders

Personnel: Peter Stampfel (banjo, fiddle, vocals); Steve Weber (guitars, vocals); John Wesley Annis (bass); Ken Crabtree (keyboards); Sam Shepard (drums)

Albums: Indian War Hoop, 1967; Moray Eels Eat the Holy Modal Rounders, 1968; Holy Modal Rounders, Volume 1, 1968; Holy Modal Rounders, Volume 2, 1968; Good Taste Is Timeless, 1969; Stampfel & Weber, 1972; Alleged in Their Own Time, 1975; Last Round, 1979; Goin' Nowhere Fast, 1981

Singles: If You Wanna Be a Bird, 1969; Boobs a Lot, 1970

Folk/Bluegrass—American

The Hombres

Personnel: Gary W. McEwan (guitars, vocals); Jerry Masters (bass, vocals); B. B. Cunningham (keyboards, vocals); John W. Hunter (drums)

Album: Let It Out (Let It All Hang Out), 1967

Singles: Let It Out (Let It All Hang Out), 1967 **(12)**; It's a Gas, 1968 **(113)**

Psychedelic Rock—Memphis

The Hondells

Personnel: Ritchie Burns (guitars, vocals)

Album: Go Little Honda, 1964

Singles: Little Honda, 1964 **(9)**; My Buddy Seat, 1964 **(87)**; Sea Cruise, 1965 **(131)**; Younger Girl, 1966 **(52)**; Kissin' My Life Away, 1966 **(118)**

Surf Rock—California

The Honeycombs

Personnel: Martin Murray (guitars); Alan Ward (guitars, keyboards); Dennis Dalziel (guitars, keyboards, vocals); John Lantree (bass); Ann "Honey" Lantree (drums)

Albums: Here Are the Honeycombs, 1965; All Systems Go, 1965; Meek & Honey, 1983

Singles: Have I the Right?, 1964 **(5)**; I Can't Stop, 1964 **(48)**

Pop/Rock — British

The Honey Cone

Personnel: Carolyn Willis (vocals); Edna Wright (vocals); Shellie Clark (vocals)

Albums: Sweet Replies, 1971; Soulful Tapestry, 1971; Love, Peace & Soul, 1973

Singles: While You're Out Looking for Sugar, 1969 **(62)**; Girls It Ain't Easy, 1969 **(68)**; Take Me with You, 1970 **(108)**; When Will It End, 1970 **(117)**; Want Ads, 1971 **(1)**; Stick-Up, 1971 **(11)**; One Monkey Don't Stop No Show — Part 1, 1971 **(15)**; The Day I Found Myself, 1972 **(23)**; Sittin' on a Time Bomb (Waitin' for the Hurt to Come), 1972 **(96)**; Innocent Til Proven Guilty, 1972 **(101)**

Soul/Pop Vocal — Los Angeles

Mary Hopkin

Albums: Postcard, 1969; Earth Song, 1971; Those Were the Days, 1972; Welsh World of Mary Hopkin, 1979; Kidnapped, 1979

Singles: Those Were the Days, 1968 **(2)**; Goodbye, 1969 **(13)**; Temma Harbour, 1970 **(39)**; Que Sera Sera (Whatever Will Be, Will Be), 1970 **(77)**; Think About Your Children, 1970 **(87)**; Water, Paper & Clay, 1972 **(113)**; Knock Knock Who's There, 1972 **(92)**

Pop Vocal — Welsh; formerly married to record producer Tony Visconti; "Goodbye" was produced and written by Paul McCartney

Johnny Horton

Albums: The Spectacular Johnny Horton, 1959; Johnny Horton Makes History, 1960; Johnny Horton's Greatest Hits, 1961; Honky-Tonk Man, 1962; The World of Johnny Horton, 1971

Singles: The Battle of New Orleans, 1959 **(1)**; Sal's Got a Sugar Lip, 1959 **(81)**; Johnny Reb, 1959 **(54)**; Sink the Bismarck, 1960 **(3)**; Johnny Freedom, 1960 **(69)**; North to Alaska, 1960 **(4)**; Sleep-Eyed John, 1961 **(54)**; Ole Slew-Foot, 1961 **(110)**; Honky-Tonk Man, 1962 **(96)**

Pop Vocal — Texas; killed in an auto crash in 1960

Hourglass

Personnel: Duane Allman (guitars); Gregg Allman (keyboards, vocals); Jesse Willard Carr (guitars); Pete Carr (bass); Paul Hornsby (keyboards); Johnny Sandlin (guitars, bass); Mabron McKinney (drums)

Albums: Hourglass, 1968; Power of Love, 1969

Southern Rock — Georgia

Fred Hughes

Singles: Oo Wee Baby, I Love You, 1965 **(23)**; You Can't Take It Away, 1965 **(96)**

Soul Vocal — Arkansas

Jimmy Hughes

Singles: Steal Away, 1964 **(17)**; Try Me, 1964 **(65)**; Neighbor, Neighbor, 1966 **(65)**; Why Not Tonight, 1967 **(90)**; Don't Lose Your Good Thing, 1967 **(121)**
Soul Vocal—Alabama

The Hullaballoos

Album: The Hullaballoos, 1964
Singles: I'm Gonna Love You Too, 1964 **(56)**; Did You Ever, 1964 **(74)**; Learning the Game, 1965 **(121)**
Pop Rock—British

Human Beinz

Album: Nobody But Me, 1968
Singles: Nobody But Me, 1967 **(8)**; Turn on Your Love Light, 1968 **(80)**
Hard Rock—Cleveland

Humble Pie

Personnel: Steve Marriott (vocals, guitars, keyboards, harmonica; deceased 1991); Peter Frampton (guitars, vocals) replaced (1972) by Dave Clempson (guitars) replaced (1980) by Bobby Tench (guitars, vocals); Greg Ridley (bass, vocals) replaced (1980) by Anthony Jones (bass, vocals); Jerry Shirley (drums)
Albums: As Safe As Yesterday Is, 1969; Town and Country, 1969; Humble Pie, 1970; Rock On, 1971; Rockin' the Fillmore, 1972; Smokin', 1972; Eat It, 1973; Thunderbox, 1974; Street Rats, 1975; Lost & Found, 1976; Back Home Again, 1976; Greatest Hits, 1977; On to Victory, 1980; Go for the Throat, 1981
Singles: I Don't Need No Doctor, 1971 **(73)**; Hot & Nasty, 1972 **(52)**; Black Coffee, 1973 **(113)**; Rock &

Roll Music, 1975 **(105)**; Fool for a Pretty Face, 1980 **(52)**
Hard/Blues Rock—British

Humblebums

Personnel: Billy Connolly (guitars, vocals); Tim Harvey (guitars, vocals, mandolin) replaced (1969) by Gerry Rafferty (guitars, vocals); Ronnie Rae (bass) replaced (1969) by Jimmy Tagford (bass); Terry Cox (drums); added (1970) Reg Guest (keyboards)
Albums: First Collection, 1969; Humblebums, 1969; Open Up the Door, 1970
Pop/Rock—British

Engelbert Humperdinck

Albums: Release Me, 1967; The Last Waltz, 1967; A Man Without Love, 1968; Engelbert, 1969; Engelbert Humperdinck, 1970; We Made It Happen, 1970; Sweetheart, 1971; Another Time, Another Place, 1971; Live at the Riviera, Las Vegas, 1972; In Time, 1972; King of Hearts, 1973; His Greatest Hits, 1974; After the Lovin', 1976; Miracles by Englebert Humperdinck, 1977; Christmas Tyme, 1977; This Moment in Time, 1979
Singles: Release Me (and Let Me Love Again), 1967 **(4)**; There Goes My Everything, 1967 **(20)**; The Last Waltz, 1967 **(25)**; Am I That Easy to Forget, 1967 **(18)**; A Man Without Love, 1968 **(19)**; Les Bicyclettes de Belsize, 1968 **(31)**; The Way It Used to Be, 1969 **(42)**; I'm a Better Man, 1969 **(38)**; Winter World of Love, 1969 **(16)**; My Marie, 1970 **(43)**; Sweetheart, 1970 **(47)**; When There's No You, 1971 **(45)**; Another

Time, Another Place, 1971 **(43)**; Too Beautiful to Last, 1972 **(86)**; In Time, 1972 **(69)**; I Never Said Goodbye, 1972 **(61)**; I'm Leavin' You, 1973 **(99)**; Love Is All, 1973 **(91)**; This Is What You Mean to Me, 1975 **(102)**; After the Lovin', 1976 **(8)**; Goodbye My Friend, 1977 **(97)**; This Moment in Time, 1978 **(58)**; Love's Only Love, 1980 **(83)**; Til You and Your Lover Are Lovers Again, 1983 **(77)**

Pop Vocal—British; real name is Arnold Dorsey; born in India

Tommy Hunt

Singles: Human, 1961 **(48)**; The Door Is Open, 1962 **(92)**; I Am a Witness, 1963 **(71)**; I Just Don't Know What to Do with Myself, 1964 **(119)**; Biggest Man, 1967 **(124)**

R & B Vocal—Pittsburgh; real first name is Charles

Ivory Joe Hunter

Singles: Since I Met You Baby, 1956 **(12)**; Empty Arms, 1957 **(43)**; Yes I Want You, 1958 **(94)**; City Lights, 1959 **(92)**

R & B Vocal—Texas; died of lung cancer in 1974

Tab Hunter

Singles: Young Love, 1957 **(1)**; Red Sails in the Sunset, 1957 **(57)**; Ninety-Nine Ways, 1957 **(11)**; Don't Get Around Much Anymore, 1957 **(74)**; Jealous Heart, 1958 **(62)**; (I'll Be with You in) Apple Blossom Time, 1959 **(31)**; There's No Fool Like a Young Fool, 1959 **(68)**

Pop Vocal—New York; real name is Arthur Kelm; appeared in films *Damn Yankees, Ride the Wild Surf,*

Lust in the Dust and *Island of Desire*

Pop Vocal—New York

Danny Hutton

Album: Danny Hutton, 1966
Singles: Roses and Rainbows, 1965 **(73)**; Big Bright Eyes, 1966 **(102)**; Funny How Love Can Be, 1966 **(120)**

Pop Vocal—American; became a member of Three Dog Night

Brian Hyland

Albums: Itsy Bitsy Teenie Weenie Yellow Polka Dot Bikini, 1960; Sealed with a Kiss, 1962; The Joker Went Wild, 1966; Tragedy/A Million to One, 1969; Brian Hyland, 1971
Singles: Itsy Bitsy Teenie Weenie Yellow Polka Dot Bikini, 1960 **(1)**; (The Clickity Clack Song) Four Little Heels, 1960 **(73)**; That's How Much, 1960 **(74)**; I Gotta Go ('Cause I Love You), 1960 **(101)**; Lop-Sided Over-Loaded (and It Wiggled When We Rode It), 1960 **(105)**; Let Me Belong to You, 1961 **(20)**; I'll Never Stop Wanting You,

1961 **(83)**; Ginny Come Lately, 1962 **(21)**; Sealed with a Kiss, 1962 **(3)**; Warmed Over Kisses (Left Over Love), 1962 **(25)**; I May Not Live to See Tomorrow, 1962 **(69)**; If Mary's There, 1963 **(88)**; I'm Afraid to Go Home, 1963 **(63)**; Let Us Make Our Own Mistakes, 1963 **(123)**; Here's to Our Love, 1964 **(129)**; 3000 Miles, 1966 **(99)**; The Joker Went Wild, 1966 **(20)**; Run, Run, Look and See, 1966 **(25)**; Hung Up in Your Eyes, 1967 **(58)**; Holiday for Clowns, 1967 **(94)**; Get the Message, 1967 **(91)**; Tragedy, 1969 **(56)**; A Million to One, 1969 **(90)**; Stay and Love Me All Summer, 1969 **(82)**; Gypsy Woman, 1970 **(3)**; Lonely Teardrops, 1971 **(54)**; So Long, Marianne, 1971 **(120)**

Pop Vocal—New York

Janis Ian

Albums: Janis Ian, 1967; For All the Seasons, 1968; Secret Life of Eddie Fink, 1968; Who Really Cares, 1969; Present Company, 1971; Stars, 1974; Between the Lines, 1975; Aftertones, 1975; Miracle Row, 1977; Janis Ian, 1978; Night Rains, 1979; Best of Janis Ian, 1980; My Favourites, 1980; Restless Eyes, 1981

Singles: Society's Child (Baby I've Been Thinking), 1967 **(14)**; Insanity Comes Quietly to the Structured Mind, 1967 **(109)**; The Man You Are in Me, 1974 **(104)**; At Seventeen, 1975 **(3)**; Under the Covers, 1981 **(71)**

Folk/Pop Vocal—New York; real name is Janis Fink

Ian & Sylvia

Personnel: Ian Tyson (guitars, vocals); Sylvia Fricker Tyson (autoharp, vocals)

Albums: Ian & Sylvia, 1962; Four Strong Winds, 1964; Northern Journey, 1964; Early Morning Rain, 1965; Play One More, 1966; So Much Dreaming, 1967; Lovin' Sound, 1967; Ian & Sylvia, 1967; Nashville, 1968; Full Circle, 1968; Best of Ian & Sylvia, 1968; Greatest Hits, Volume 1, 1970; Greatest Hits, Volume 2, 1971; You Were on My Mind, 1972; Best of Ian & Sylvia 2, 1973; Ol'Eon, 1975 (Ian); Woman's World (1975) (Sylvia); One Jump Ahead of the Devil, 1979 (Ian)

Singles: Four Strong Winds, 1964; You Were on My Mind, 1964; Lovin' Sound, 1967 **(101)**

Folk/Rock—Canadian; Ian and Sylvia married in 1964

Ides of March

Personnel: Jim Peterik (guitars, vocals); Larry Millas (guitars, bass, vocals); Ray Herr (guitars, bass, vocals) left group (1970); Bob Bergland (bass, vocals); Chuck Soumar (percussion, harmonica, vocals); Mike Borch (drums, vibes)

Albums: Ides of March, 1966; Vehicle, 1970; Common Bond, 1971; World Woven, 1972; Midnight Oil, 1973

Singles: You Wouldn't Listen, 1966 **(42)**; Roller Coaster, 1966 **(92)**; Vehicle, 1970 **(2)**; Superman, 1970 **(64)**; Melody, 1970 **(122)**; L.A. Goodbye, 1971 **(73)**; Tie-Dye Princess, 1971 **(113)**

Pop/Rock—Chicago

Idle Race

Personnel: Jeff Lynne (guitars, vocals) replaced (1971) by Mike Hopkins (guitars); Greg Masters (bass); Dave Pritchard (guitars);

Roger Spencer (drums) replaced (1972) by Bob Lamb (drums); added (1972) Bob Wilson (keyboards); added (1972) Ritchie Walker (guitars); added (1971) Dave Walker (vocals)

Albums: Birthday Party, 1968; Idle Race, 1969; Time Is, 1971; Impostors of Life Magazine, 1972; On with the Show, 1973

Progressive Rock — British

Frank Ifield

Album: Jolly What! The Beatles & Frank Ifield, 1964

Singles: I Remember You, 1962 **(5)**; Lovesick Blues, 1962 **(44)**; The Wayward Wind, 1963 **(104)**; I'm Confessin' (That I Love You), 1963 **(58)**; Please, 1963 **(71)**; Don't Blame Me, 1964 **(128)**; Out of Nowhere, 1967 **(132)**

Pop Vocal — British

Igginbottom's Wrench

Personnel: Steve Robinson (guitars, vocals); Allan Holdsworth (guitars, vocals); Mick Skelly (bass); Dave Freeman (drums)

Album: Igginbottom's Wrench, 1969

Progressive Rock — British

The Ikettes

Personnel: Delores Johnson (vocals); Eloise Hester (vocals); Jo Armstead (vocals)

Singles: I'm Blue (The Gong-Gong Song), 1962 **(19)**; Prisoner in Love, 1963 **(126)**; Camel Walk, 1965 **(107)**; Peaches 'n' Cream, 1965 **(36)**; (He's Gonna Be) Fine, Fine, Fine, 1965 **(125)**; I'm So Thankful, 1965 **(74)**; Lonely for You, 1966 **(126)**

Soul Vocal — American; formed by Ike & Tina Turner

Illinois Speed Press

Personnel: Paul Cotton (guitars, vocals); Kal David (guitars, vocals); Rob Lewine (bass); Mike Anthony (keyboards); Fred Page (drums)

Albums: Illinois Speed Press, 1969; Dou, 1970

Singles: Sadly Out of Place, 1969; Bad Weather, 1969

Pop/Rock — Illinois

The Illusion

Personnel: John Vinci (vocals); Richie Cerniglia (guitars); Mike Maniscalco (guitars, keyboards); Chuck Adler (bass); Michael Ricciardella (drums)

Albums: Illusion, 1969; Together, 1969; If It's So, 1970

Singles: Did You See Her Eyes, 1969 **(32)**; How Does It Feel, 1969 **(110)**; Together, 1969 **(80)**; Let's Make Each Other Happy, 1970 **(98)**

Pop/Rock — New York

The Impalas

Personnel: Joe Frazier (vocals); Richard Wagner (vocals); Lenny Renda (vocals); Tony Carlucci (vocals)

Singles: Sorry (I Ran All the Way Home), 1959 **(2)**; Oh, What a Fool, 1959 **(86)**

Pop Vocal — New York

The Impressions

Personnel: Curtis Mayfield (vocals) replaced (1970) by Leroy

Hutson (vocals) replaced (1973) by Ralph Johnson (vocals); Jerry Butler (vocals) replaced (1959) by Fred Cash (vocals); Arthur Brooks (vocals) left group (1961) replaced (1973) by Reggie Torian (vocals); Richard Brooks (vocals) left group (1961); Sam Gooden (vocals)

Albums: The Impressions, 1963; The Never Ending Impressions, 1964; Keep on Pushing, 1964; People Get Ready, 1965; The Impressions Greatest Hits, 1965; One by One, 1965; Ridin' High, 1966; The Fabulous Impressions, 1967; We're a Winner, 1968; The Best of the Impressions, 1968; This Is My Country, 1968; The Young Mods' Forgotten Story, 1969; The Versatile Impressions, 1970; 16 Greatest Hits, 1971; Check Out Your Mind, 1972; Times Have Changed, 1972; Curtis Mayfield/His Early Years with the Impressions, 1973; Preacher Man, 1973; Finally Got Myself Together, 1974; First Impressions, 1975; Sooner or Later, 1975; For Your Precious Love, 1976; Loving Power, 1976; It's About Time, 1976; The Originals, 1976; Three the Hard Way, 1977; The Vintage Years, 1977

Singles: For Your Precious Love, 1958 **(11)**; Gypsy Woman, 1961 **(20)**; Grow Closer Together, 1962 **(99)**; Little Young Lover, 1962 **(96)**; Minstrel and Queen, 1962 **(113)**; I'm the One Who Loves You, 1963 **(73)**; Sad, Sad Girl and Boy, 1963 **(84)**; It's All Right, 1964 **(4)**; Talking About My Baby, 1964 **(12)**; I'm So Proud, 1964 **(14)**; Keep On Pushing, 1964 **(10)**; You Must Believe Me, 1964 **(15)**; Amen, 1964 **(7)**; I've Been Trying, 1965 **(133)**; People Get Ready, 1965 **(14)**; Woman's Got Soul, 1965 **(29)**; Meeting Over Yonder, 1965 **(48)**; I Need You, 1965 **(64)**; Just One Kiss from You, 1965 **(76)**; You've Been Cheatin', 1965 **(33)**; Since I Lost the One I Love, 1966 **(90)**; Too Slow, 1966 **(91)**; Can't Satisfy, 1966 **(65)**; You Always Hurt Me, 1967 **(96)**; I Can't Stay Away from You, 1967 **(80)**; We're a Winner, 1967 **(14)**; We're Rolling On (Part 1), 1968 **(59)**; I Loved and Lost, 1968 **(61)**; Fool for You, 1968 **(22)**; Don't Cry My Love, 1968 **(71)**; This Is My Country, 1968 **(25)**; My Deceiving Heart, 1969 **(104)**; Seven Years, 1969 **(84)**; Choice of Colors, 1969 **(21)**; Say You Love Me, 1969 **(58)**; Amen (1970), 1969 **(110)**; Wherever She Leadeth Me, 1970 **(128)**; Check Out Your Mind, 1970 **(28)**; (Baby) Turn on to Me, 1970 **(56)**; Ain't Got Time, 1971 **(53)**; Love Me, 1971 **(94)**; Finally Got Myself Together (I'm a Changed Man), 1974 **(17)**; Sooner or Later, 1975 **(68)**; Same Thing It Took, 1975 **(75)**; Loving Power, 1976 **(103)**

Soul/Pop Vocal—Chicago

Incredible String Band

Personnel: Mike Heron (keyboards, guitars, vocals, bass, flute); Robin Williamson (guitars, vocals, keyboards, violin); Clive Palmer (vocals, guitars, banjo) replaced (1967) by Licorice McKechnie (violin, keyboards) replaced (1972) by Gerald Dott (keyboards, clarinet); Mike Tomich (bass) replaced (1967) by Danny Thompson (bass) replaced (1968) by Rose Simpson (bass, percussion) replaced (1971) by Stan Lee (bass, vocals) replaced (1974) by Graham Forbes (bass, guitars); John Gilston (drums) replaced (1970) by

Dave Mattacks (drums) replaced (1970) by David Barker (drums) replaced (1970) by Gerry Conway (drums) replaced (1973) by Jack Ingram (drums, vocals) replaced (1974) by John Gilston (drums); added (1971) Malcolm LeMaistre (vocals, bass, keyboards)

Albums: The Incredible String Band, 1966; The 5000 Spirits, 1967; The Hangman's Beautiful Daughter, 1968; The Big Huge, 1968; Wee Tam, 1968; Changing Horses, 1969; I Looked Up, 1970; "U," 1970; Relics of the Incredible String Band, 1970; Be Glad for the Song, 1970; Liquid Acrobat, 1971; Earth Span, 1972; No Ruinous Feud, 1973; Hard Rope and Silken Twine, 1974; Seasons They Change, 1976

Folk/Rock — Scotland

Initial Shock

Mojo Collins in middle

Personnel: Mojo Collins (organ)
Album: The Initial Shock, 1967
Single: Mind Disaster, 1967
Psychedelic Pop — Montana

The Innocence

Personnel: Peter Anders (guitars, vocals); Vinnie Poncia (guitars, vocals)

Albums: Innocence, 1966; Anders & Poncia, 1969
Singles: There's Got to Be a Word, 1966 **(34)**; Mairzy Doats, 1967 **(75)**
Pop/Soft Rock — American

The Innocents

Personnel: James West (vocals); Al Candelaria (bass, vocals); Darron Stankey (guitars, vocals)
Album: The Innocents, 1960
Singles: Honest I Do, 1960 **(28)**; Gee Whiz, 1960 **(28)**
Pop — California

The Intrigues

Album: The Intrigues, 1969
Singles: In a Moment, 1969 **(31)**; I'm Gonna Love You, 1969 **(86)**; The Language of Love, 1970 **(100)**
Soul Vocal — Philadelphia

The Intruders

Personnel: Samuel "Little Sonny" Brown (vocals); Phil Terry (vocals); Robert Edwards (vocals); Eugene Daughtry (vocals)
Albums: United, 1966; Together, 1967; Cowboys to Girls, 1968; The Intruders Greatest Hits, 1969; I'm Girl Scoutin', 1971; Save the Children, 1973
Singles: (We'll Be) United, 1966 **(78)**; Together, 1967 **(48)**; Baby I'm Lonely, 1967 **(70)**; A Love That's Real, 1967 **(82)**; Cowboys to Girls, 1968 **(6)**; (Love Is Like a) Baseball Game, 1968 **(26)**; Slow Drag, 1968 **(54)**; Give Her a Transplant, 1969

(104); Lollipop (I Like You), 1969
(101); Sad Girl, 1969 (47); Tender
(Is the Love We Knew), 1970 (119);
When We Get Married, 1970 (45);
This Is My Love Song, 1970 (85);
I'm Girl Scoutin', 1971 (88); Pray for
Me, 1971 (105); I Bet He Don't
Love You (Like I Love You), 1971
(92); I'll Always Love My Mama,
1973 (36); I Wanna Know Your
Name, 1973 (60)

Soul/Pop Vocal—Philadelphia

The Irish Rovers

Personnel: Will Millar (vocals);
George Millar (vocals); Joe Millar
(vocals); Jimmy Ferguson (vocals);
Wilcil McDowell (vocals)

Albums: The Unicorn, 1968; All
Hung Up, 1968; Tales to Warm
Your Mind, 1969; Wasn't That a
Party, 1981; The Rovers, 1982

Singles: The Unicorn, 1968 (7);
(The Puppet Song) Whiskey on a
Sunday, 1968 (75); The Biplane,
Ever More, 1968 (91); Lily the Pink,
1969 (113); Wasn't That a Party,
1981 (37); Mexican Girl, 1981; Pain

in My Past, 1982; People Who Read
People Magazine, 1982

Folk Vocal—Irish/Canadian

Iron Butterfly

Personnel: Danny Weiss (guitars)
replaced (1970) by Larry Reinhardt
(guitars); Jerry Penrod (guitars) replaced (1968) by Erik Braunn (guitars, vocals) replaced (1970) by Mike
Pinera (guitars, vocals) replaced
(1975) by Erik Braunn (guitars,
vocals); Darryl de Loach (bass) replaced (1968) by Lee Dorman (bass,
keyboards) replaced (1975) by Phil
Kramer (bass); Doug Ingle (keyboards) replaced (1974) by Bill de
Martines (keyboards) replaced
(1975) by Howie Reitzes (keyboards); Ron Bushy (drums)

Albums: Heavy, 1967; In-a-
Gadda-Da-Vida, 1968; Ball, 1969;
Live, 1970; Metamorphosis, 1970;
Evolution/Best of Iron Butterfly,
1971; Sun & Steel, 1975; Scorching
Beauty, 1975

Singles: In-a-Gadda-Da-Vida,
1968 (30); Soul Experience, 1969

Iron Butterfly: Bushy, Ingle, Dorman, Braunn

(75); In the Time of Our Lives, 1969 (96); I Can't Help but Deceive You Little Girl, 1969 (118); Easy Rider (Let the Wind Pay the Way), 1970 (66); Beyond the Milky Way, 1975 (108)

Acid Rock—San Diego

Big Dee Irwin

Singles: Swinging on a Star, 1963 (38) (with Little Eva); By the Time I Get to Phoenix/I Say a Little Prayer, 1968 (114) (with Mamie Galore)

R & B Vocal—American; real name is Defosca Ervin

The Isley Brothers

Personnel: Rudolph Isley (vocals); Ronald Isley (vocals); O'Kelly Isley (vocals; deceased 1986); added (1969) Ernie Isley (bass, guitars); added (1969) Marvin Isley (bass); added (1969) Chris Jasper (keyboards); added (1969) Everett Collins (drums)

Albums: Shout, 1969; Twist and Shout, 1962; Twisting and Shouting, 1963; Take Some Time Out, 1966; This Old Heart of Mine, 1966; Soul on the Rocks, 1966; Tamla Motown Presents the Isley Brothers, 1967; Doin' Their Thing, 1969; It's Our Thing, 1969; Live at Yankee Stadium, 1969 (side A only); The Brothers: Isley, 1969; Get Into Something, 1970; In the Beginning, 1970; Givin' It Back, 1971; Brother, Brother, Brother, 1972; The Isleys Live, 1973; 3 + 3, 1973; Isleys' Greatest Hits, 1973; Live It Up, 1974; The Heat Is On, 1975; Harvest for the World, 1976; Go for Your Guns, 1977; Forever Gold, 1977; Showdown, 1978; Timeless,

1978; Winner Takes All, 1979; Go All the Way, 1980; Grand Slam, 1981; Inside You, 1981; The Real Deal, 1982; Between the Sheets, 1983; Greatest Hits Volume 1, 1984; Smooth Sailin', 1988; Spend the Night, 1989

Singles: Shout—Part 1, 1959 (47); Shout—Part 2, 1962 (94); Twist and Shout, 1962 (17); Twistin' with Linda, 1962 (54); Nobody but Me, 1963 (106); Simon Says, 1965 (131); This Old Heart of Mine (Is Weak for You), 1966 (12); Take Some Time Out for Love, 1966 (66); I Guess I'll Always Love You, 1966 (61); Love Is a Wonderful Thing, 1966 (110); Got to Have You Back, 1967 (93); That's the Way Love Is, 1967 (125); Take Me in Your Arms (Rock Me a Little While), 1968 (121); It's Your Thing, 1969 (2); I Turned You On, 1969 (23); Black Berries—Part 1, 1969 (79); Was It Good to You, 1969 (83); Bless Your Heart, 1969 (105); Keep on Doin', 1970 (75); If He Can, You Can, 1970 (113); Girls Will Be Girls, Boys Will Be Boys, 1970 (75); Get Into Something, 1970 (89); Freedom, 1971 (72); Warpath, 1971 (111); Love the One You're With, 1971 (18); Spill the Wine, 1971 (49); Lay Lady Lay, 1971 (71); Lay-Away, 1972 (54); Pop That Thang, 1972 (24); Work to Do, 1972 (51); That Lady, 1973 (6); What It Comes Down To, 1973 (55); Summer Breeze (Part 1), 1974 (60); Live It Up—Part 1, 1974 (52); Midnight Sky (Part 1), 1975 (73); Fight the Power, 1975 (4); For the Love of You (Part 1 & 2), 1975 (22); Who Loves You Better—Part 1, 1976 (47); Harvest for the World, 1976 (63); The Pride (Part 1), 1977 (63); Livin' in the Life, 1977 (40); It's a Disco Night, 1979 (90); Don't

Say Goodnight (It's Time for Love) (Parts 1 & 2), 1980 **(39)**; Hurry Up and Wait, 1981 **(58)**
R & B/Soul—Ohio

It's a Beautiful Day

Personnel: David LaFlamme (vocals, violin, flutes); Hal Wagenet (guitars, vocals) replaced (1971) by Bill Gregory (guitars); Mitchell Holman (bass, vocals) replaced (1971) by Tom Fowler (bass) replaced (1973) by Bud Cockrell (bass, vocals); Linda LaFlamme (keyboards) replaced (1970) by Fred Webb (keyboards, vocals); Pattie Santos (vocals, percussion); Val Fuentes (drums, vocals)
Albums: It's a Beautiful Day, 1968; Marrying Maiden, 1970; Choice Quality Stuff, 1971; Live at Carnegie Hall, 1972; Today, 1973; 1001 Nights, 1974; It's a Beautiful Day (Compilation), 1979
Single: White Bird, 1969 **(118)**
Folk/Rock—San Francisco

The Iveys

Personnel: Peter Ham (guitars, vocals; deceased 1975); Tom Evans (bass, vocals; deceased 1983); Ron Wood (guitars); Mickey Gibbons (drums)
Album: Maybe Tomorrow, 1969
Single: Maybe Tomorrow, 1969 **(67)**
Pop/Rock—British; became Badfinger in 1970 and was the first group signed to The Beatles "Apple" label

The Ivy League

Personnel: John Carter (vocals); Ken Lewis (vocals)

Single: Tossing & Turning, 1965 **(83)**
Pop Vocal—British

The Ivy Three

Personnel: Charles Koppelman (vocals); Art Berkowitz (vocals); Don Rubin (vocals)
Single: Yogi, 1960 **(8)**
Pop Vocal—New York; Koppelman and Rubin founded SBK Records

The Jacks

Personnel: Aaron Collins (vocals); Willie Davis (vocals); William Jones (vocals); Lloyd McCraw (vocals); Ted Taylor (vocals)
Single: Why Don't You Write Me?, 1955 **(82)**
R & B Vocal—Los Angeles; group became the Cadets

Chuck Jackson

Singles: I Don't Want to Cry, 1961 **(36)**; (It Never Happens) in Real Life, 1961 **(46)**; Mr. Pride, 1961 **(91)**; I Wake Up Crying, 1961 **(59)**; Any Day Now (My Wild Beautiful Bird), 1962 **(23)**; Who's Gonna Pick Up the Pieces, 1962 **(119)**; I Keep Forgettin', 1962 **(55)**; Getting Ready for the Heartbreak, 1962 **(88)**; Tell Him I'm Not Home, 1963 **(42)**; Tears of Joy, 1963 **(85)**; I Will Never Turn My Back on You, 1963 **(110)**; Any Other Way, 1963 **(81)**; Hand It Over, 1964 **(92)**; Beg Me, 1964 **(45)**; Somebody New, 1964 **(93)**; Since I Don't Have You, 1964 **(47)**; Something You Got, 1965 **(55)** (with Maxine Brown); I Need You, 1965 **(75)**; If I Didn't Love You, 1965 **(46)**; Can't Let You Out of My

Sight, 1965 **(91)** (with Maxine Brown); I Need You So, 1965 **(98)** (with Maxine Brown); Hold On I'm Coming, 1967 **(91)** (with Maxine Brown); Good Things Come to Those Who Wait, 1965 **(105)**; I'm Satisfied, 1966 **(112)**; Daddy's Home, 1967 **(91)** (with Maxine Brown); Shame On Me, 1967 **(76)**; (You Can't Let the Boy Overpower) The Man in You, 1968 **(94)**; Are You Lonely for Me Baby, 1969 **(107)**; I Only Get This Feeling, 1973 **(117)**

R & B Vocal — South Carolina

Deon Jackson

Singles: Love Makes the World Go Round, 1966 **(11)**; Love Takes a Long Time Growing, 1966 **(77)**; Ooh Baby, 1967 **(65)**; I Can't Do Without You, 1966 **(111)**

Soul Vocal — Michigan

J. J. Jackson

Albums: With the Greatest Little Soul Band, 1967; The Greatest Little Soul Band, 1969; J. J. Jackson's Dilemma, 1971

Singles: But It's Alright, 1966 **(22)**; I Dig Girls, 1966 **(83)**; Four Walls (Three Windows and Two Doors), 1967 **(123)**; But It's Alright, 1969 **(45)**

Soul Vocal — New York; real name is Jerome Louis Jackson

Stonewall Jackson

Singles: Waterloo, 1959 **(4)**; Igmoo (The Pride of South Central High), 1959 **(95)**; Mary Don't You Weep, 1959 **(41)**; Why I'm Walkin', 1960 **(83)**

Country/Pop — North Carolina

Walter Jackson

Albums: Speak Her Name, 1967; Feeling Good, 1976; I Want to Come Back as a Song, 1977

Singles: It's All Over, 1964 **(67)**; Suddenly I'm All Alone, 1965 **(96)**; Welcome Home, 1965 **(95)**; I'll Keep On Trying, 1965 **(120)**; Funny (Not Much), 1966 **(103)**; It's an Uphill Climb to the Bottom, 1966 **(88)**; After You, There Can Be Nothing, 1966 **(130)**; A Corner in the Sun, 1966 **(83)**; Speak Her Name, 1967 **(89)**; Deep in the Heart of Harlem, 1967 **(110)**; My Ship Is Comin' In, 1967 **(124)**; Any Way That You Want Me, 1969 **(111)**; Feelings, 1976 **(93)**

Soul Vocal — Florida; died in 1983

Wanda Jackson

Albums: Rockin' with Wanda, 1960; Right or Wrong, 1961; Wonderful Wanda, 1962; There's a Party Going On, 1962; Wanda Jackson, 1963; Love Me Forever, 1963; I Got to Sing, 1964; Two Sides of Wanda, 1965; Blues in My Heart, 1965; Sings Country Songs, 1966; Country Music Hall of Fame, 1967; You'll Have My Love, 1968; Cream of the Crop, 1969; Best of Wanda Jackson, 1969; A Portrait of Wanda Jackson, 1970; A Woman Lives to Love, 1970; Country, 1970; Praise the Lord, 1972; Country Keepsakes, 1973; I Wouldn't Want You Any Other Way, 1973; Country Classics, 1973; When It's Time to Fall in Love Again, 1974; Country Gospel, 1974; Now I Have Everything, 1975; Make Me a Child Again, 1976; Closer to Jesus, 1978; Rock 'n' Roll History, 1979; Greatest Hits, 1979; My Testament, 1982

Singles: Let's Have a Party, 1960

(37); Right Or Wrong, 1961 (29); In the Middle of a Heartache, 1961 (27); A Little Bitty Tear, 1962 (84); If I Cried Every Time You Hurt Me, 1962 (58); I Misunderstood, 1962 (117); The Greatest Actor, 1962 (117)

Rockabilly—Oklahoma

Etta James

Albums: At Last!, 1961; Second Time Around, 1961; Etta James, 1962; Sings for Lovers, 1963; Etta James Top Ten, 1963; Etta James Rocks the House, 1964; Queen of Soul, 1965; Call My Name, 1966; Tell Mama, 1968; Funk, 1969; Miss Etta James, 1969; Best of Etta James, 1970; Twist with Etta James, 1971; Golden Decade, 1972; Etta James, 1973; Peaches, 1973; Come a Little Closer, 1974; Loser's Weepers, 1974; Etta Is Betta Than Evah, 1975; Sings, 1976; Best of Etta James, 1977; Deep in the Night, 1978; Chess Masters, 1981; Good Rockin' Mama, 1981; Tuff Lover, 1983

Singles: All I Could Do Was Cry, 1960 (33); If I Can't Have You, 1960 (52) (with Harvey Fuqua); My Dearest Darling, 1960 (34); Spoonful, 1960 (78) (with Harvey Fuqua); At Last, 1961 (47); Trust in Me, 1961 (30); Fool That I Am, 1961 (50); Dream, 1961 (55); Don't Cry, Baby, 1961 (39); It's Too Soon to Know, 1961 (54); Seven Day Fool, 1961 (95); Something's Got a Hold On Me, 1962 (37); Stop the Wedding, 1962 (34); Next Door to the Blues, 1962 (71); Fools Rush In, 1962 (87); How Do You Talk to an Angel, 1963 (109); Would It Make Any Difference to You, 1963 (64); Pushover, 1963 (25); Pay Back, 1963 (78); Two Sides (to Every Story), 1963 (63); I Worry 'Bout You, 1963 (118); Baby What You Want Me to Do, 1964 (82); Loving You More Every Day, 1964 (65); Do I Make Myself Clear, 1965 (96) (with Sugar Pie DeSanto); In the Basement—Part 1, 1966 (97) (with Sugar Pie DeSanto); Tell Mama, 1967 (23); Security, 1968 (35); I Got You Babe, 1968 (69); You Got It, 1968 (113); Almost Persuaded, 1969 (79); Losers Weepers—Part 1, 1970 (94); I've Found a Love, 1972 (108); All the Way Down, 1973 (101)

Soul Vocal—Los Angeles; real name is Jamesetta Hawkins

Jimmy James & The Vagabonds

Personnel: Jimmy James (vocals); Count Prince Miller (vocals); Wallace Wilson (guitars); Phil Chen (bass); Carl Noel (keyboards) replaced (1974) by Arthur Regis (keyboards); Nat Frederick (saxophones); Milton James (saxophones) replaced (1974) by Pat Gravesend (saxophones); Rupert Balgobin (drums)

Albums: New Religion, 1966; Come Softly to Me, 1967; Open Up Your Soul, 1968; This Is Jimmy James, 1968; London Swings (1 Side), 1969; You Don't Stand a Chance, 1975; Now, 1976; Life, 1977; Dancin' Till Dawn, 1979; Golden Hour, 1979

Singles: Come to Me Softly, 1968 (76); Red Red Wine, 1969 (127); I Am Somebody, 1976 (94)

R & B/Soul—British

Joni James

Singles: How Important Can It Be?, 1955 (2); You Are My Love,

1955 **(6)**; My Believing Heart, 1955 **(49)**; Don't Tell Me Not to Love You, 1956 **(83)**; I Woke Up Crying, 1956 **(72)**; Give Us This Day, 1956 **(30)**; How Lucky You Are, 1956 **(70)**; Summer Love, 1957 **(97)**; There Goes My Heart, 1958 **(19)**; There Must Be a Way, 1959 **(33)**; I Still Get a Thrill (Thinking of You), 1959 **(51)**; I Still Get Jealous, 1959 **(63)**; Are You Sorry, 1959 **(102)**; I Laughed at Love, 1959 **(108)**; Little Things Mean a Lot, 1959 **(35)**; I Need You Now, 1960 **(98)**; You Belong to Me, 1960 **(101)**; My Last Date (with You), 1960 **(38)**

Pop Vocal—Chicago; real name is Joan Babbo

Sonny James

Albums: True Love's a Blessing, 1965; The Best of Sonny James, 1966; I'll Never Find Another You, 1967; Only the Lonely, 1969; The Astrodome Presents in Person ... Sonny James, 1969; It's Just a Matter of Time, 1970; My Love/Don't Keep Me Hanging On, 1970; #1, 1970; Empty Arms, 1971; The Sensational Sonny James, 1971; When the Snow Is on the Roses, 1972

Singles: Young Love, 1956 **(1)**; First Date, First Kiss, First Love, 1957 **(25)**; Uh-Huh-mm, 1957 **(92)**; You Got That Touch, 1958 **(94)**; Talk of the School, 1959 **(85)**; Pure Love, 1959 **(107)**; I Forgot More Than You'll Ever Know, 1960 **(80)**; Jenny Lou, 1960 **(67)**; Apache, 1961 **(87)**; The Minute You're Gone, 1963 **(95)**; Baltimore, 1964 **(134)**; You're the Only World I Know, 1964 **(91)**; I'll Keep Holding On (Just to Your Love), 1965 **(116)**; Behind the Tear, 1965 **(113)**; I'll Never Find Another You, 1967 **(97)**;

A World of Our Own, 1968 **(118)**; Born to Be with You, 1968 **(81)**; Only the Lonely, 1969 **(92)**; Running Bear, 1969 **(94)**; Since I Met You, Baby, 1969 **(65)**; It's Just a Matter of Time, 1970 **(87)**; My Love, 1970 **(125)**; Endlessly, 1970 **(108)**; Empty Arms, 1971 **(93)**; Bright Lights, Big City, 1971 **(91)**; When the Snow Is on the Roses, 1972 **(103)**

Country/Pop—Alabama; real name is James Loden

Tommy James & The Shondells

Lucia, Vale, James, Gray, Rosman

Personnel: Tommy James (vocals); Joe Kessler (guitars) replaced (1966) by Eddie Gray (guitars); Mike Vale (bass); Ron Rosman (keyboards); George Magura (saxophone, organ, bass) left group (1967); Vince Pietropaoli (drums) replaced (1966) by Pete Lucia (drums)

Albums: Hanky Panky, 1966; It's Only Love, 1966; I Think We're Alone Now, 1967; Something

Special, 1967; Getting Together, 1967; Mony Mony, 1968; Crimson & Clover, 1968; Cellophane Symphony, 1969; Best of Tommy James, 1970; Travelin', 1970

Singles: Hanky Panky, 1966 **(1)**; Say I Am, 1966 **(21)**; It's Only Love, 1966 **(31)**; I Think We're Alone Now, 1967 **(4)**; Mirage, 1967 **(10)**; I Like the Way, 1967 **(25)**; Gettin' Together, 1967 **(18)**; Out of the Blue, 1967 **(43)**; Get Out Now, 1968 **(48)**; Mony, Mony, 1968 **(3)**; Somebody Cares, 1968 **(53)**; Do Something to Me, 1968 **(38)**; Crimson & Clover, 1968 **(1)**; Sweet Cherry Wine, 1969 **(7)**; Crystal Blue Persuasion, 1969 **(2)**; Balls of Fire, 1969 **(19)**; She, 1969 **(23)**; Gotta Get Back to You, 1970 **(45)**; Come to Me, 1970 **(47)**

Pop/Rock—Michigan; Tommy's real name is Thomas Gregory Jackson

The James Gang

Personnel: Jim Fox (drums, vocals); Tom Kriss (bass, vocals) replaced (1970) by Dale Peters (bass, vocals); Glenn Schwartz (guitars) replaced (1968) by Joe Walsh (guitars, vocals, keyboards) replaced (1972) by Domenic Troiano (guitars, vocals) replaced (1973) by Tommy Bolin (guitars; deceased 1976) replaced (1975) by Richard Shack (guitars) replaced (1976) by Bob Webb (guitars); added (1972) Roy Kenner (vocals) replaced (1975) by Bubba Keith (vocals, guitars) replaced (1976) by Phil Giallombardo (keyboards)

Albums: James Gang, 1969; Yer Album, 1969; The James Gang Rides Again, 1970; Thirds, 1971; Live in Concert, 1971; Straight

Shooter, 1972; Passin' Through, 1972; Best of the James Gang, 1972; Bang, 1973; Gold Record, 1973; 16 Greatest Hits, 1973; Miami, 1974; Newborn, 1975; Jesse Come Home, 1976; The Last Ride, 1976

Singles: Funk #48, 1969 **(126)**; Funk #49, 1970 **(59)**; The Bomber, 1970; Walk Away, 1971 **(51)**; Midnight Man, 1971 **(80)**; Looking for My Lady, 1972 **(108)**; Had Enough, 1972 **(111)**; Must Be Love, 1974 **(54)**

Hard Rock—Cleveland

The Jamies

Personnel: Tom Jamison (vocals); Serena Jamison (vocals)

Singles: Summertime, Summertime, 1958 **(26)**; Summertime, Summertime, 1962 **(38)**

Pop Vocal—Massachusetts

Jan & Dean

Jan Berry, Dean Torrence

Personnel: Jan Berry (vocals, guitars); Dean Torrence (vocals, guitars)

Albums: Golden Hits, 1962; Take Linda Surfin', 1963; Surf City, 1963; Drag City, 1963; Dead Man's Curve/New Girl in School, 1964; Ride the Wild Surf, 1964; Little Old

Lady from Pasadena, 1964; Command Performance, 1965; Golden Hits Volume 2, 1965; Folk & Roll, 1965; Filet of Soul, 1966; Meet Batman, 1966; Popsicle, 1966; Golden Hits Volume 3, 1966; Save for a Rainy Day, 1967; Jan & Dean, 1968; Legendary Masters, 1971; Remember (EP), 1973; Gotta Take That One Last Ride, 1974; 20 Rock 'n' Roll Hits, 1979; Jan & Dean Story, 1980; Deadman's Curve/Greatest Hits, 1980; One Summer Night/Live, 1982; Surf City/Best of Jan & Dean, 1986

Singles: Jenny Lee, 1958 (**8**) (Jan & Arnie); Gas Money, 1958 (**81**) (Jan & Arnie); Baby Talk, 1959 (**10**); There's a Girl, 1959 (**97**); Clementine, 1960 (**65**); We Go Together, 1960 (**53**); Gee, 1960 (**81**); Heart and Soul, 1961 (**25**); Wanted: One Girl, 1961 (**104**); A Sunday Kind of Love, 1962 (**95**); Tennessee, 1962 (**69**); Linda, 1963 (**28**); Surf City, 1963 (**1**); Honolulu Lulu, 1963 (**11**); Drag City, 1963 (**10**); Deadman's Curve, 1964 (**8**); The New Girl in School, 1964 (**37**); Little Old Lady from Pasadena, 1964 (**3**); Ride the Wild Surf, 1964 (**16**); The Anaheim, Azusa & Cucamonga Sewing Circle, Book Review and Timing Association, 1964 (**77**); Sidewalk Surfin', 1964 (**25**); From All Over the World, 1965 (**56**); You Really Know How to Hurt a Guy, 1965 (**27**); I Found a Girl, 1965 (**30**); A Beginning from an End, 1965 (**109**); Batman, 1966 (**66**); Popsicle, 1966 (**21**); Fiddle Around, 1966 (**93**); Yellow Balloon, 1967 (**111**); Sidewalk Surfin', 1976 (**107**)

Surf Rock — California; Jan was seriously injured in a car accident in April, 1966 and suffered partial paralysis

Bert Jansch

Albums: Bert Jansch, 1965; It Don't Bother Me, 1965; Bert Jansch & John Renbourn, 1966; Jack Orion, 1966; Lucky Thirteen, 1966; Nicola, 1967; Birthday Blues, 1968; Stepping Stones, 1969; Sampler, 1969; Rosemary Lane, 1971; Box of Love, 1972; Moonshine, 1973; L.A. Turnaround, 1974; Santa Barbara Honeymoon, 1975; A Rare Conundrum, 1977; Anthology, 1978; Avocet, 1979; 13 Down, 1980; Best of Bert Jansch, 1980; Heartbreak, 1982; The Ornament Tree, 1991

Folk/Rock — British; member of the Pentangle

The Jarmels

Personnel: Nathaniel Ruff (vocals); Ray Smith (vocals); Paul Burnett (vocals); Earl Christian (vocals); Tom Eldridge (vocals)

Single: A Little Bit of Soap, 1961 (**12**)

R & B Vocal — Virginia

Carol Jarvis

Single: Rebel, 1957 (**48**)

Pop Vocal — American

Jasper

Personnel: Nicky Payne (vocals, flutes, harmonica); Steve Radford (guitars); Jon Taylor (bass); Alan Feldman (keyboards); Chico Greenwood (drums)

Album: Liberation, 1969

Pub Rock — British

Jay & The Americans

Personnel: John "Jay" Traynor (vocals) replaced (1962) by David Jay Black (vocals); Howie Kane (vocals) left group (1969); Sandy "Deane" Yaguda (vocals); Marty Sanders (guitars, vocals); Kenny Vance (vocals)

Albums: She Cried, 1962; At the Cafe Wha, 1963; Come a Little Bit Closer, 1965; Blockbusters, 1965; Greatest Hits Volume 1, 1965; Sunday and Me, 1966; Living Above Your Head, 1966; Greatest Hits Volume 2, 1967; Try Some of This, 1967; Sand of Time, 1969; Wax Museum Volume 1, 1970; Wax Museum Volume 2, 1971; Very Best of Jay & the Americans, 1975; Greatest Hits, 1980

Singles: Tonight, 1961 **(120)**; This Is It, 1962 **(109)**; She Cried, 1962 **(5)**; Only in America, 1963 **(25)**; Come Dance with Me, 1963 **(76)**; Come a Little Bit Closer, 1964 **(3)**; Let's Lock the Door (and Throw Away the Key), 1964 **(11)**; Think of the Good Times, 1965 **(57)**; Cara, Mia, 1965 **(4)**; Some Enchanted Evening, 1965 **(13)**; When It's All Over, 1965 **(129)**; Sunday and Me, 1965 **(18)**; Why Can't You Bring Me Home, 1966 **(63)**; Crying, 1966 **(25)**; Livin' Above Your Head, 1966 **(76)**; (He's) Raining in My Sunshine, 1966 **(90)**; (We'll Meet in the) Yellow Forest, 1967 **(131)**; No Other Love, 1968 **(114)**; This Magic Moment, 1968 **(6)**; When You Dance, 1969 **(70)**; Hushabye, 1969 **(62)**; Walkin' in the Rain, 1969 **(19)**; Capture the Moment, 1970 **(57)**

Pop Vocal — New York

Jay & The Techniques

Personnel: Jay Proctor (vocals); Karl Landis (vocals); Ronnie Goosly (vocals); Dante Dancho (vocals); Chuck Crowl (vocals); John Walsh (vocals); George Lloyd (vocals)

Albums: Apples, Peaches, Pumpkin Pie, 1967; Strawberry Shortcake, 1968

Singles: Apples, Peaches, Pumpkin Pie, 1967 **(6)**; Keep the Ball Rollin', 1967 **(14)**; Strawberry Shortcake, 1968 **(39)**; Baby Make Your Own Sweet Music, 1968 **(64)**; Singles Game, 1968 **(116)**; Change Your Mind, 1969 **(107)**

R & B/Pop — Pennsylvania

Jerry Jaye

Singles: My Girl Josephine, 1967 **(29)**; Let the Four Winds Blow, 1967 **(107)**

Country/Pop — Arkansas; real name is Jerald Jaye Hatley

The Jayhawks

Personnel: Dave Govan (vocals); Carlton Fisher (vocals); Carver Bunkum (vocals); James Johnson (vocals)

Single: Stranded in the Jungle, 1956 **(18)**

R & B Vocal — Los Angeles

The Jaynetts

Personnel: Zelma Sanders (vocals); Johnnie Louise Richardson (vocals)

Singles: Sally, Go 'Round the Roses, 1963 **(2)**; Keep an Eye on Her, 1963 **(120)**

R & B Vocal — New York

Jefferson

Album: Jefferson, 1969

Singles: The Colour of My Love, 1969 **(68)**; Baby Take Me in Your Arms, 1969 **(23)**

Pop/Rock — British

Jefferson Airplane

Personnel: Paul Kantner (vocals, guitars); Signe Anderson (vocals) replaced (1966) by Grace Slick (vocals); Bob Harvey (bass) replaced (1966) by Jack Casady (bass, vocals) replaced (1971) by Peter Kaukonen (bass) replaced (1973) by David Freiberg (bass, vocals) replaced (1990) by Jack Casady (bass, vocals); Jorma Kaukonen (guitars, vocals) left group (1973) rejoined (1990); Marty Balin (vocals) replaced (1971) by Papa John Creach (violin, vocals) replaced (1990) by Marty Balin (vocals); Skip Spence (drums) replaced (1967) by Spencer Dryden (drums) replaced (1969) by Joey Covington (drums) replaced (1972) by John Barbata (drums) replaced (1990) by Kenny Aronoff (drums)

Albums: Jefferson Airplane Takes Off, 1966; Surrealistic Pillow, 1967; After Bathing at Baxter's, 1967; Crown of Creation, 1968; Bless Its Pointed Little Head, 1969; Volunteers, 1969; The Worst of Jefferson Airplane, 1970; Bark, 1971; Long John Silver, 1972; 30 Seconds Over Winterland, 1973; Early Flight, 1974; 2400 Fulton Street, 1988; Jefferson Airplane, 1989

Singles: My Best Friend, 1967 **(103)**; Somebody to Love, 1967 **(5)**; White Rabbit, 1967 **(8)**; The Ballad of You & Me & Pooneil, 1967 **(42)**; Two Heads, 1967 **(124)**; Watch Her Ride, 1967 **(61)**; Greasy Heart, 1968 **(98)**; Crown of Creation, 1968 **(64)**; Plastic Fantastic Lover, 1969 **(133)**; Volunteers, 1969 **(65)**; Mexico/Have You Seen the Saucers, 1970 **(102)**; Pretty as You Feel, 1971 **(60)**; Long John Silver, 1972 **(104)**; Planes, 1990; True Love, 1990

Psychedelic Rock — San Francisco

Jefferson Airplane: Kaukonen, Casady, Balin, Kantner, Slick

Joe Jeffrey Group

Singles: My Pledge of Love, 1969 **(14)**; Dreamin' Till Then, 1969 **(108)**; Hey Hey Woman, 1969 **(109)**; My Baby Loves Lovin', 1970 **(115)**

R & B Vocal—American

The Jelly Beans

Personnel: Elyse Herbert (vocals); Maxine Herbert (vocals); Alma Brewer (vocals); Diane Taylor (vocals); Charles Thomas (vocals)

Album: Jelly Beans, 1964

Singles: I Wanna Love Him So Bad, 1964 **(9)**; Baby Be Mine, 1964 **(51)**

Pop Vocal—New Jersey

Jellybread

Personnel: Pete Wingfield (keyboards, vocals) replaced (1972) by Rick Hayward (guitars); Paul Butler (guitars, vocals); John Best (bass); Chris Waters (drums) replaced (1972) by Kenny Lamb (drums)

Albums: First Slice, 1969; 65 Parkway, 1970; Back to Begin Again, 1972

Pop/Rock—British

Kris Jensen

Singles: Torture, 1962 **(20)**; Don't Take Her from Me, 1963 **(112)**

Country/Pop—Connecticut; real first name is Peter

The Jesters

Personnel: Adam Jackson (vocals); Noel Grant (vocals); Leo Vincent (vocals); Lennie McKay (vocals)

Singles: So Strange, 1957 **(100)**; The Plea, 1958 **(74)**; The Wind, 1960 **(110)**

R & B Vocal—New York

Jethro Tull

Personnel: Ian Anderson (vocals, flute, keyboards, guitars); Mick Abrahams (guitars, vocals) replaced (1968) by Martin Barre (guitars, vocals); Glenn Cornick (bass) replaced (1971) by Jeffrey Hammond-Hammond (bass) replaced (1975) by John Glascock (bass; deceased 1979) replaced (1979) by Tony Williams (bass) replaced (1979) by Dave Pegg (bass, vocals); Clive Bunker (drums) replaced (1971) by Barriemore Barlow (drums) replaced (1980) by Mark Craney (drums) replaced (1981) by Gerry Conway (drums); added (1981) Paul Burgess (drums) replaced (1983) by Doane Perry (drums); added (1970) John Evan (keyboards) replaced (1979) by David Palmer (keyboards) replaced (1980) by Eddie Jobson (keyboards, violin) replaced (1981) by Peter-John Vettesse (keyboards, vocals) replaced (1987) by Don Airey (keyboards) replaced (1988) by Martin Allcock (keyboards)

Albums: This Was Jethro Tull, 1968; Stand Up, 1969; Benefit, 1970; Aqualung, 1971; Life Is a Long Song, 1971; Living in the Past, 1972; Thick as a Brick, 1972; A Passion Play, 1973; War Child, 1974; Minstrel in the Gallery, 1975; MU—The Best of Jethro Tull, 1976; Too Old to Rock 'n' Roll, Too Young to Die, 1976; Winter Solstice (EP), 1976; Songs from the Wood, 1977; Repeat—The Best of Jethro Tull Volume 2, 1977; Heavy Horses, 1978; Live Bursting Out, 1978; Stormwatch, 1979; A, 1980; The Broadsword and the Beast, 1982; Under Wraps, 1984; Original Masters, 1985; Crest of a Knave, 1987; 20 Years of Jethro Tull, 1988; Rock

Jethro Tull: Perry, Anderson, Pegg, Allcock, Barre

Island, 1989; Live at Hammersmith, 1991; Catfish Rising, 1991

Singles: Aqualung, 1971; Hymn 43, 1971 **(91)**; Thick as a Brick, 1972; Living in the Past, 1972 **(11)**; A Passion Play, 1973 **(80)**; A Passion Play #10, 1973 **(105)**; Wond'ring Aloud, 1973; Bungle in the Jungle, 1974 **(12)**; Minstrel in the Gallery, 1975 **(79)**; Locomotive Breath, 1976 **(62)**; Ring Out Solstice, 1976; The Whistler, 1977 **(59)**; Crossfire, 1980; Working John, Working Joe, 1981; Fallen on Hard Times, 1982 **(108)**; Lap of Luxury, 1984; Under Wraps, 1984; Steel Monkey, 1987; Farm on the Freeway, 1987; Part of the Machine, 1988; Kissing Willie, 1990; This Is Not Love, 1991

Progressive Rock—British; band named for the 18th century agronomist/inventor

The Jive Bombers

Personnel: Clarence Palmer (vocals); Earl Johnson (vocals); Al Tinney (vocals); William Tinney (vocals)

Single: Bad Boy, 1957 **(36)**
R & B Vocal — New York

The Jive Five

Personnel: Eugene Pitt (vocals); Billy Prophet (vocals) replaced (1971) by Casey Spencer (vocals) replaced (1982) by Billy Prophet (vocals); Richard Harris (vocals) replaced (1971) by Webster Harris (vocals) replaced (1982) by Frank Pitt (vocals); Norman Johnson (vocals; deceased 1970) replaced (1982) by Beatrice Best (vocals); Jerome Hanna (vocals) replaced (1971) by Johnny Watson (vocals) left group (1973)

Albums: My True Story, 1961; Here We Are!, 1982; Our True Story, 1983

Singles: My True Story, 1961 **(3)**; Never, Never, 1961 **(74)**; Hully Gully Callin' Time, 1962 **(105)**; What Time Is It?, 1962 **(67)**; Rain, 1963 **(128)**; I'm a Happy Man, 1965 **(36)**; A Bench in the Park, 1965 **(106)**; Crying Like a Baby, 1967 **(127)**; Sugar, 1968 **(119)**

R & B Vocal — New York

Damita Jo

Albums: This Is Damita Jo, 1965; If You Go Away, 1967

Singles: I'll Save the Last Dance for You, 1960 **(22)**; Keep Your Hands Off of Him, 1961 **(75)**; I'll Be There, 1961 **(12)**; Dance with a Dolly (with a Hole in Her Stocking), 1961 **(105)**; Stop Foolin', 1963 **(108)** (with Brook Benton); Baby, You've Got It Made, 1963 **(111)** (with Brook Benton); Tomorrow Night, 1965 **(124)**; Gotta Travel On, 1965 **(119)**; If You Go Away, 1966 **(68)**

R & B Vocal — Texas; full name is Damita Jo DuBlanc

Jo Ann & Troy

Personnel: Jo Ann Campbell (vocals); Troy Seals (vocals)

Single: I Found a Love, Oh What a Love, 1964 **(67)**

Pop Vocal — American; husband and wife team

Jody Grind

Personnel: Tim Hinkley (keyboards, vocals); Ivan Zagni (guitars) replaced (1970) by Bernie Holland (guitars); Louis Cennamo (bass); Barry Wilson (drums) replaced (1970) by Pete Gavin (drums)

Albums: One Step On, 1969; Far Canal, 1970

Progressive Rock — British

Little Willie John

Singles: Fever, 1956 **(24)**; Talk to Me, Talk to Me, 1958 **(20)**; You're a Sweetheart, 1958 **(66)**; Let Nobody Love You, 1959 **(108)**; Leave My Kitten Alone, 1959 **(60)**; Let Them Talk, 1960 **(100)**; A Cottage for Sale, 1960 **(63)**; Heartbreak (It's Hurtin' Me), 1960 **(38)**; Sleep, 1960 **(13)**; Walk Slow, 1960 **(48)**; Leave My Kitten Alone, 1961 **(60)**; The Very Thought of You, 1961 **(61)**; (I've Got) Spring Fever, 1961 **(71)**; Now You Know, 1961 **(93)**; Take My Love (I Want to Give It All to You), 1961 **(87)**; I Wish I Could Cry, 1962 **(116)**

R & B Vocal — Arkansas

Johnny & Joe

Personnel: Johnnie Louise Richardson (vocals; deceased 1988); Joe Rivers (vocals)

Singles: Over the Mountain;
Across the Sea, 1957 **(8)**; Over the
Mountain; Across the Sea, 1960 **(89)**
R & B Vocal—New York

Johnny & The Hurricanes

Personnel: John Pocisk (saxo-
phones); Paul Tesluk (organ); Dave
Yorko (guitars); Lionel Mattice
(bass); Tony Kaye (drums) replaced
(1959) by Bill "Bo" Savich (drums)
Albums: Red River Rock, 1959;
Johnny & the Hurricanes, 1960;
Stormsville, 1960; Big Sound, 1960;
Beatnik Fly, 1961; Live at the Star
Club Hamburg, 1962; Best Of, 1964
Singles: Crossfire, 1959 **(23)**; Red
River Rock, 1959 **(5)**; Reveille
Rock, 1959 **(25)**; Beatnik Fly, 1960
(15); Down Yonder, 1960 **(48)**;
Rocking Goose, 1960 **(60)**; Revival,
1960 **(97)**; You Are My Sunshine,
1960 **(91)**; Ja-Da, 1961 **(86)**; Old
Smokie, 1961 **(116)**
Pop/Rock—Ohio

Betty Johnson

Singles: I'll Wait, 1956 **(94)**; Clay
Idol, 1956 **(72)**; I Dreamed, 1956
(9); Little White Lies, 1957 **(25)**;
1492, 1957 **(70)**; The Little Blue
Man, 1958 **(17)**; Dream, 1958 **(19)**;
Hoopa Hoola, 1958 **(56)**; You Can't
Get to Heaven on Roller Skates,
1959 **(99)**; There's a Star Spangled
Banner Waving Somewhere No. 2
(1960) (The Ballad of Francis Gary
Powers), 1960 **(111)**; Slipping
Around, 1960 **(109)**
Pop Vocal—North Carolina

Lou Johnson

Singles: Reach Out for Me, 1963
(74); It Ain't No Use, 1964 **(117)**;
(There's) Always Something There
to Remind Me, 1964 **(49)**; Kentucky
Bluebird, 1964 **(104)**; A Time to
Love—A Time to Cry (Petite
Fleur), 1965 **(59)**
Soul Vocal—American

Marv Johnson

Album: Early Classics, 1980
Singles: Come to Me, 1959 **(30)**;
I'm Coming Home, 1959 **(82)**; You
Got What It Takes, 1959 **(10)**; I
Love the Way You Love, 1960 **(9)**;
Ain't Gonna Be That Way, 1960
(74); All the Love I've Got, 1960
(63); (You've Got to) Move Two
Mountains, 1960 **(20)**; Happy Days,
1960 **(58)**; Merry-Go-Round, 1961
(61)
R & B Vocal—Detroit

Syl Johnson

Albums: Different Strokes, 1967;
We Did It, 1973
Singles: Come on Sock It to Me,
1967 **(97)**; Different Strokes, 1967
(95); Is It Because I'm Black, 1969
(68); One Way Ticket to Nowhere,
1970 **(125)**; We Did It, 1973 **(95)**;
Back for a Taste of Your Love, 1973
(72); Take Me to the River, 1975
(48)
R & B/Soul—Chicago; real name
is Syl Thompson

Bruce Johnston

Albums: Surfin' Pajama Party,
1967; Surfin' Around the World,
1969; Going Public, 1977
Single: Pipeline, 1977 **(109)**
Surf Rock—California; member
of the Beach Boys

Jon & Robin

Personnel: Jon Abnor (vocals);
Robin Wright (vocals)
Singles: Do It Again a Little Bit
Slower, 1967 **(18)**; Drums, 1967
(100); I Want Some More, 1967
(109); Dr. Jon (the Medicine Man),
1968 **(87)**; Hangin' from Your
Lovin' Tree, 1968 **(131)**; You Got
Style, 1968 **(110)**
   Pop Vocal—Texas

Davey Jones

Album: David Jones, 1967
Singles: What Are You Going to
Do?, 1965 **(93)**; Rainy Jane, 1971
(52); I Really Love You, 1971 **(107)**
   Pop Vocal—British; member of
the Monkees

Jack Jones

Albums: Call Me Irresponsible,
1963; Wives and Lovers, 1963; Be-
witched, 1964; Where Love Has
Gone, 1964; Dear Heart, 1965; My
Kind of Town, 1965; There's Love
& There's Love & There's Love,
1965; For the "In" Crowd, 1966; The
Impossible Dream, 1966; Jack Jones
Sings, 1966; Lady, 1967; Our Song,
1967; Without Her, 1967; What the
World Needs Now Is Love!, 1968; If
You Ever Leave Me, 1968; Where
Is Love?, 1968; A Time for Us, 1969
Singles: Lollipops and Roses, 1962
(66); Call Me Irresponsible, 1963
(75); Toys in the Attic, 1963 **(92)**;
Wives and Lovers, 1963 **(14)**; Love
with the Proper Stranger, 1964 **(62)**;
The First Night of the Full Moon,
1964 **(59)**; Where Love Has Gone,
1964 **(62)**; Dear Heart, 1964 **(30)**;
The Race Is On, 1965 **(15)**; Seein'
the Right Love Go Wrong, 1965
(46); Travellin' On, 1965 **(132)**; Just

Yesterday, 1965 **(73)**; The True Picture, 1965 **(134)**; Love Bug, 1965
(71); The Weekend, 1966 **(123)**; The
Impossible Dream (The Quest),
1966 **(35)**; A Day in the Life of a
Fool, 1966 **(62)**; Lady, 1967 **(39)**;
I'm Indestructible, 1967 **(81)**; Now I
Know, 1967 **(73)**; Our Song, 1967
(92); Live for Life, 1967 **(99)**; Open
for Business as Usual, 1968 **(130)**; If
You Ever Leave Me, 1968 **(92)**;
Follow Me, 1968 **(117)**; L.A. Breakdown, 1968 **(106)**
   Pop Vocal—Los Angeles; son of
actor Allan Jones

Jimmy Jones

Singles: Handy Man, 1959 **(2)**;
Good Timin', 1960 **(3)**; That's When
I Cried, 1960 **(83)**; Ee-I Ee-I Oh!
(Sue MacDonald), 1960 **(102)**;
Itchin', 1960 **(106)**; I Told You So,
1961 **(85)**
   R & B Vocal—Alabama

Joe Jones

Singles: You Talk Too Much,
1960 **(3)**; California Sun, 1961 **(89)**
   Blues/Soul—New Orleans

Linda Jones

Album: Your Precious Love, 1972
Singles: Hypnotized, 1967 **(21)**;
What've I Done (to Make You
Mad), 1967 **(61)**; Give My Love a
Try, 1968 **(93)**; I Who Have
Nothing, 1968 **(116)**; Your Precious
Love, 1972 **(74)**
   R & B Vocal—New Jersey; died
of diabetes in 1972

Tom Jones

Albums: It's Not Unusual, 1965;
What's New Pussycat?, 1965; Green,

Green Grass of Home, 1967; Thirteen Smash Hits, 1967; The Tom Jones Fever Zone, 1968; Help Yourself, 1969; Tom Jones Live!, 1969; This Is Tom Jones, 1969; Tom Jones Live in Las Vegas, 1969; Tom, 1970; I (Who Have Nothing), 1970; She's a Lady, 1971; Tom Jones Live at Caesar's Palace, 1971; Close Up, 1972; The Body and Soul of Tom Jones, 1973; Tom Jones' Greatest Hits, 1974; Say You'll Stay Until Tomorrow, 1976; What a Night, 1977; Tom Jones Greatest Hits, 1977; Darlin', 1981; Carrying a Torch, 1991

Singles: It's Not Unusual, 1965 **(10)**; Little Lonely One, 1965 **(42)**; What's New Pussycat?, 1965 **(3)**; With These Hands, 1965 **(27)**; Thunderball, 1965 **(25)**; Chills and Fever, 1965 **(125)**; Promise Her Anything, 1966 **(74)**; Not Responsible, 1966 **(58)**; What a Party, 1966 **(120)**; Green, Green Grass of Home, 1966 **(11)**; Detroit City, 1967 **(27)**; Funny Familiar Forgotten Feelings, 1967 **(49)**; Sixteen Tons, 1967 **(68)**; I'll Never Fall in Love Again, 1967 **(49)**; I'm Coming Home, 1967 **(57)**; Delilah, 1968 **(15)**; Help Yourself, 1968 **(35)**; A Minute of Your Time, 1968 **(48)**; Love Me Tonight, 1969 **(13)**; I'll Never Fall in Love Again, 1969 **(6)**; Without Love (There Is Nothing), 1969 **(5)**; Daughter of Darkness, 1970 **(13)**; I (Who Have Nothing), 1970 **(14)**; Can't Stop Loving You, 1970 **(25)**; She's a Lady, 1971 **(2)**; Puppet Man, 1971 **(26)**; Resurrection Shuffle, 1971 **(38)**; Till, 1971 **(41)**; The Young New Mexican Puppeteer, 1972 **(80)**; Letter to Lucille, 1973 **(60)**; Say You'll Stay Until Tomorrow, 1977 **(15)**; Take Me Tonight, 1977 **(101)**; Darlin', 1981 **(103)**; What in the World's Come Over You, 1981 **(109)**; Kiss, 1988 **(31)** (with Art of Noise)

Pop Vocal—Welsh; real name is Thomas Jones Woodward; hosted TV variety show in 1969 and 1970

Janis Joplin

Albums: I Got Dem' Ol Kozmic Blues Again, 1969; Pearl, 1971; In Concert, 1972; Greatest Hits, 1973; Janis, 1974; Anthology, 1980; Farewell Song, 1982

Singles: Kozmic Blues, 1969 **(41)**; Try (Just a Little Bit Harder), 1970 **(103)**; Maybe, 1970 **(110)**; Me and Bobby McGee, 1971 **(1)**; Cry Baby, 1971 **(42)**; Get It While You Can, 1971 **(78)**; Down On Me, 1972 **(91)**

Blues/Rock—Texas; Janis died of a drug overdose on October 4, 1970; had been a member of Big Brother & the Holding Company

July

Personnel: Tom Newman (vocals); Jon Field (flutes, percussion); Tony Duhig (guitars); Alan James (bass); Chris Jackson (keyboards)

Album: July, 1968

Art Rock—British

Just Us

Personnel: Chip Taylor (vocals); Al Gorgoni (vocals)
Singles: I Can't Grow Peaches on a Cherry Tree, 1966 (34); Used to Be, 1971 (103)
Pop Vocal—New York

Kaleidoscope

Personnel: David Lindley (guitars, vocals, violin) replaced (1976) by DeParis Letante (guitars); Soloman Feldthouse (guitars, vocals); Fenrus Epp (violin, keyboards); Chris Darrow (guitars, bass, violin) replaced (1969) by Stuart Brotman (bass, vocals); John Vidican (drums, percussion) replaced (1969) by Paul Lagos (drums, vocals)
Albums: Side Trips, 1967; Beacon from Mars, 1968; Incredible Kaleidoscope, 1969; Bernice, 1970; When Scopes Collide, 1976; Bacon from Mars, 1983; Rampe Pampe, 1984; Greetings from Kartooniskin, 1991
Folk/Rock—American; Lindley became famous for his work with Jackson Browne

The Kalin Twins

Personnel: Herbert Kalin (vocals); Harold Kalin (vocals)
Album: When, 1958
Singles: When, 1958 (5); Forget Me Not, 1958 (12); It's Only the Beginning, 1959 (42); Sweet Sugar Lips, 1959 (97); Zing! Went the Strings of My Heart, 1960 (112)
Pop Vocal—New York

Kasenetz—Katz Singing Orchestral Circus

Personnel: Jerry Kasenetz (vocals); Jeff Katz (vocals)
Album: Kasenetz-Katz Singing Orchestral Circus, 1968
Singles: Down in Tennessee, 1968 (124); Quick Joey Small (Run Joey Run), 1968 (25); I'm in Love with You, 1969 (105)
Bubblegum Pop—American

Ernie K-Doe

Singles: Mother-in-Law, 1961 (1); Te-Ta-Te-Ta-Ta, 1961 (53); I Cried My Last Tear, 1961 (69); A Certain Girl, 1961 (71); Popeye Joe, 1962 (99); Later for Tomorrow, 1967 (122)
R & B Vocal—New Orleans; real last name is Kador

Keith

Album: 98.6/Ain't Gonna Lie, 1967
Singles: Ain't Gonna Lie, 1966 (39); 98.6, 1966 (7); Tell Me to My Face, 1967 (37); Daylight Savin'

Time, 1967 **(79)**; I'm So Proud, 1967 **(135)**

Pop Vocal—Philadelphia; real name is James Barry Keefer

Jerry Keller

Singles: Here Comes Summer, 1959 **(14)**; Be Careful How You Drive, Young Joey, 1961 **(112)**

Pop Vocal—Oklahoma

Chris Kenner

Album: Land of a Thousand Dances, 1963

Singles: I Like It Like That, 1961 **(2)**; A Very True Story, 1961 **(103)**; Land of 1000 Dances, 1963 **(77)**

Pop Vocal—New Orleans; Chris died in 1976

Kenny & The Kasuals

back row: **Smith, Roach, Lightfoot, Blackley;** *front row:* **Daniels**

Personnel: Kenny Daniels (guitars, vocals, bass); Jerry Smith (guitars) replaced (1967) by Jack Morgan (guitars); Lee Lightfoot (bass) replaced (1967) by Gregg Daniels (bass); Paul Roach (keyboards) replaced (1967) by Wally Wilson (keyboards); David Blackley (drums) replaced (1967) by Ron Mason (drums)

Albums: Impact, 1965; Kenny & the Kasuals, 1966; Live at the Studio Club, 1966; Things Gettin' Better, 1967

Single: Journey to Tyme, 1966

Pop Rock—Texas

Troy Keyes

Single: Love Explosion, 1968 **(92)**

R & B Vocal—American; lead singer of the High Keyes

Andy Kim

Albums: Rainbow Ride, 1968; Baby I Love You, 1969; It's Your Life, 1970; I Wish I Were, 1971; Andy Kim, 1974; Andy Kim's Greatest Hits, 1974

Singles: How'd We Ever Get This

Way, 1968 **(21)**; Shoot 'em Up Baby, 1968 **(31)**; Rainbow Ride, 1968 **(49)**; Tricia Tell Your Daddy, 1969 **(110)**; Baby, I Love You, 1969 **(9)**; So Good Together, 1969 **(36)**; A Friend in the City, 1970 **(90)**; It's Your Life, 1970 **(85)**; Be My Baby, 1970 **(17)**; I Wish I Were Here, 1971 **(62)**; I Been Moved, 1971 **(97)**; Who Has the Answers?, 1972 **(111)**; Rock Me Gently, 1974 **(1)**; Fire, Baby I'm On Fire, 1974 **(28)**; Amour, 1982

Pop Vocal—Canadian; also recorded as Baron Longfellow

Albert King

Albums: The Big Blues, 1962; Travelling to California, 1967; Born Under a Bad Sign, 1967; Live Wire/ Blues Power, 1968; Does the King Thing, 1968; King of the Blues Guitar, 1969; Years Gone By, 1969; Jammed Together, 1969 (with Steve Cropper & Pop Staples); Lovejoy, 1971; I'll Play the Blues for You, 1972; I Wanna Get Funky, 1974; Montreux Festival, 1974; Truckload of Lovin', 1976; Albert Live, 1977; Albert, 1977; King Albert, 1977; The Pinch, 1978; Chronicle, 1979; Albert Live, 1979; New Orleans Heat, 1980; San Francisco '83, 1983; Laundromat Blues, 1984

Country/Blues—Mississippi; real name is Albert Nelson

Ben E. King

Albums: Spanish Harlem, 1961; Sings for Soulful Lovers, 1962; Don't Play That Song, 1962; Ben E. King's Greatest Hits, 1964; Seven Letters, 1965; Beginning of It All, 1971; Rough Edges, 1972; Supernatural, 1975; Ben E. King Story, 1975; I Had a Love, 1976; Benny

and Us, 1977 (with Average White Band); Let Me Live in Your Life, 1978; Music Trance, 1980; Street Tough, 1981; Ultimate Collection, 1984; Stand by Me—Best of Ben E. King, 1987

Singles: Spanish Harlem, 1960 **(10)**; First Taste of Love, 1960 **(53)**; Stand by Me, 1961 **(4)**; Amor, 1961 **(18)**; Here Comes the Night, 1961 **(81)**; Young Boy Blues, 1961 **(66)**; Ecstasy, 1962 **(56)**; Don't Play That Song (You Lied), 1962 **(11)**; Too Bad, 1962 **(88)**; I'm Standing By, 1962 **(111)**; Tell Daddy, 1963 **(122)**; How Can I Forget, 1963 **(85)**; I (Who Have Nothing), 1963 **(29)**; I Could Have Danced All Night, 1963 **(72)**; What Now My Love, 1964 **(102)**; Around the Corner, 1964 **(125)**; That's When It Hurts, 1964 **(63)**; What Can a Man Do, 1964 **(113)**; It's All Over, 1964 **(72)**; Seven Letters, 1964 **(45)**; The Record (Baby I Love You), 1965 **(84)**; She's Gone Again, 1965 **(128)**; Goodnight My Love, 1966 **(91)**; So Much Love, 1966 **(96)**; Tears, Tears, Tears, 1967 **(93)**; We Got a Thing Going On, 1968 **(127)** (with Dee Dee Sharp); Don't Take Your Love from Me, 1968 **(117)**; Till I Can't Take It Anymore, 1968 **(134)**; Supernatural Thing—Part 1, 1975 **(5)**; Do It in the Name of Love, 1975 **(60)**; Stand by Me, 1986 **(9)**

Soul Vocal—North Carolina; real name is Benjamin Earl Soloman; former lead singer for the Drifters

Carole King

Albums: Now That Everything's Been Said, 1969; Writer, 1970; Tapestry, 1971; Music, 1972; Rhymes & Reasons, 1972; Fantasy, 1973; Wrap Around Joy, 1974; Really Rosie,

Carole King

1975; Thoroughbred, 1976; Simple Things, 1977; Welcome Home, 1978; Her Greatest Hits, 1978; Touch the Sky, 1979; Pearls, 1980; One to One, 1982; Speeding Time, 1983; City Streets, 1989

Singles: It Might As Well Rain Until September, 1962 **(22)**; School Bells Are Ringing, 1962 **(123)**; He's a Bad Boy, 1963 **(94)**; It's Too Late, 1971 **(1)**; I Feel the Earth Move, 1971 **(80)**; So Far Away, 1971 **(14)**; Smackwater Jack, 1971 **(90)**; Sweet Seasons, 1972 **(9)**; Been to Canaan, 1972 **(24)**; You Light Up My Life, 1973 **(67)**; Believe in Humanity, 1973 **(28)**; Corazon, 1973 **(37)**; Jazzman, 1974 **(2)**; Nightingale, 1974 **(9)**; Move Lightly, 1975; High Out of Time, 1976 **(76)**; Only Love Is Real, 1976 **(28)**; Hard Rock Cafe, 1977 **(30)**; Morning Sun, 1977; One Fine Day, 1980 **(12)**; Oh No, Not My Baby, 1980; Chains, 1980; One to One, 1982 **(45)**; Read Between the Lines, 1982; Crying in the Rain, 1983; Speeding Time, 1984; City Streets, 1989

Pop Vocal—New York; real name is Carole Klein

Claude King

Album: Meet Claude King, 1962

Singles: Big River, Big Man, 1961 **(82)**; The Comancheros, 1961 **(71)**; Wolverton Mountain, 1962 **(6)**; The Burning of Atlanta, 1962 **(53)**; I've Got the World by the Tail, 1962 **(111)**; Tiger Woman, 1965 **(110)**

Country Vocal—Louisiana

Freddie King

Albums: Freddie King Sings, 1960; Let's Hideaway and Danceaway, 1961; Girl Boy Girl, 1962; Bossa Nova Blues, 1963; Freddie King Goes Surfin', 1964; Bonanza of Instrumentals, 1964; Vocals & Instrumentals, 1965; Hideaway, 1966; Freddie King Is a Blues Master, 1969; My Feeling for the Blues, 1970; Getting Ready, 1971; Texas Cannonball, 1972; Woman Across the River, 1973; Burglar, 1974; Best of Freddie King, 1974; Larger Than Life, 1975; Rest of Freddie King, 1976; Original Hits, 1977; 1934 to 1976, 1977; Rockin' Blues Live, 1983

Singles: You've Got to Love Her with a Feeling, 1961 **(93)**; Hide Away, 1961 **(29)**; Lonesome Whistle Blues, 1961 **(88)**; San-Ho-Zay, 1961 **(47)**; The Bossa Nova Watusi Twist, 1963 **(103)**; Play It Cool, 1969 **(127)**

Blues/Soul Vocal—Texas; died from heart attack in 1976; real name was Freddie Christian

Jonathan King

Singles: Everyone's Gone to the Moon, 1965 **(17)**; Where the Sun Has Never Shone, 1966 **(97)**; Round, Round, 1967 **(122)**

Pop Vocal—British; real first name is Kenneth

P. Giles, Tippett, Fripp, Lake, M. Giles

King Crimson

Personnel: Robert Fripp (guitars, mellotron); Greg Lake (bass, vocals) replaced (1970) by Pete Giles (bass) replaced (1970) by Gordon Haskell (bass, vocals) replaced (1971) by Boz Burrell (bass, vocals) replaced (1973) by John Wetton (bass, vocals) replaced (1981) by Tony Levin (bass); Ian McDonald (keyboards, saxophones, vocals) replaced (1970) by Keith Tippett (piano) replaced (1972) by Mel Collins (saxophones) replaced (1973) by David Cross (violin, flute, keyboards) replaced (1981) by Adrian Belew (guitars, vocals); Michael Giles (drums, vocals) replaced (1970) by Andy McCulloch (drums) replaced (1971) by Ian Wallace (drums) replaced (1973) by Bill Bruford (drums); added (1973) Jamie Muir (percussion) replaced (1975) by Eddie Jobson (violin, keyboards) left group (1977); Peter Sinfield (lyrics) replaced (1973) by Richard Palmer-James (lyrics)

Albums: In the Court of the Crimson King, 1969; In the Wake of Poseidon, 1970; Lizard, 1970; Islands, 1971; Earthbound, 1972; Lark's Tongue in Aspic, 1973; Starless and Bible Black, 1974; Red, 1974; USA, 1975; The Young Person's Guide to King Crimson, 1975; Greatest, 1977; Discipline, 1981; Beat, 1982; Three of a Perfect Pair, 1984; Compact King Crimson, 1988; Essential King Crimson/Frame by Frame, 1991

Singles: In the Court of the Crimson King, 1969 **(80)**; 21st Century Schizoid Man, 1969; Groon/Cat Food, 1970; Starless and Bible Black, 1974; Heartbeat, 1982; Sleepless, 1984

Progressive Rock — British; Fripp invented several guitar and recording techniques including Frippertronics and has produced LPs for Daryl Hall & the Roches

The Kingsmen

Sundholm, Gallucci, Easton, Mitchell, Abbot

Personnel: Lynn Easton (vocals, saxophones, drums); Mike Mitchell (guitars); Jack Ely (guitars, vocals); Bob Nordby (bass) replaced (1966) by Norman Sundholm (bass, guitars); Don Gallucci (organ); added (1966) Gary Abbot (drums)

Albums: In Person, 1963; Volume II, 1964; Volume III, 1965; On

Campus, 1965; 15 Great Hits, 1966; Best of the Kingsmen, 1972

Singles: Louie Louie, 1963 (2); Money, 1964 (16); Little Latin Lupe Lu, 1964 (46); Death of an Angel, 1964 (42); The Jolly Green Giant, 1965 (4); The Climb, 1965 (65); Annie Fanny, 1965 (47); (You Got) The Gamma Goochee, 1965 (122); Killer Joe, 1966 (77); Louie Louie, 1966 (97); I Guess I Was Dreaming, 1966; Bo Diddley Back, 1967 (128)

Bar Rock—Portland

The Kingston Trio

Personnel: Bob Shane (vocals); Nick Reynolds (vocals) replaced (1973) by Roger Gamble (vocals); Dave Guard (vocals; deceased 1991) replaced (1961) by John Stewart (vocals) replaced (1973) by George Grove (vocals)

Albums: The Kingston Trio, 1958; From the Hungry i, 1959; The Kingston Trio at Large, 1959; Here We Go Again!, 1959; Sold Out, 1960; String Along, 1960; Stereo Concert, 1960; The Last Month of the Year, 1960; Make Way!, 1961; Goin' Places, 1961; Close Up, 1961; College Concert, 1962; The Best of the Kingston Trio, 1962; Something Special, 1962; New Frontier, 1962; The Kingston Trio #16, 1963; Sunny Side!, 1963; Sing Along with the Kingston Trio, 1964; Time to Think, 1964; Back in Town, 1964; The Kingston Trio (Nick-Bob-John), 1965; Stay Awhile, 1965; The Best of the Kingston Trio, Volume 2, 1965; Once Upon a Time, 1969

Singles: Tom Dooley, 1958 (1); Raspberries, Strawberries, 1959 (70); The Tijuana Jail, 1959 (12); M.T.A., 1959 (15); A Worried Man, 1959 (20); CooCoo-U, 1959 (98); Home from the Hill, 1960 (102); El Matador, 1960 (32); Bad Man Blunder, 1960 (37); Everglades, 1960 (60); Where Have All the Flowers Gone, 1962 (21); Scotch and Soda, 1962 (81); Jane, Jane, Jane, 1962 (93); Old Joe Clark, 1962 (113); One More Town, 1962 (97); Greenback Dollar, 1963 (21); Reverend Mr. Black, 1963 (8); Desert Pete, 1963 (33); Ally Ally Oxen Free, 1963 (61); Last Night I Had the Strangest Dream, 1964 (124); If You Don't Look Around, 1964 (123); I'm Going Home, 1965 (104); Scotch and Soda, 1969 (124)

Folk/Pop—San Francisco

The Kinks

Personnel: Ray Davies (guitars, vocals); Dave Davies (guitars, vocals); Mick Avory (drums) replaced (1987) by Robert Henrit (drums); Peter Quaife (bass) replaced (1969) by John Dalton (bass) replaced (1977) by Andy Pyle (bass) replaced (1979) by Jim Rodford (bass, vocals); added (1970) John Gosling (keyboards) replaced (1979) by Gordon Edwards (keyboards) replaced (1980) by Ian Gibbons (keyboards) replaced (1987) by Mark Haley (keyboards)

Albums: The Kinks, 1964; You Really Got Me, 1965; Kinks—Size, 1965; Kinda Kinks, 1965; Kinks Kinkdom, 1966; The Kink Kontroversy, 1966; Face to Face, 1966; Live at the Kelvin Hall, 1967; Something Else by the Kinks, 1967; The Kinks Are the Village Green Preservation Society, 1968; Arthur (or the Decline and Fall of the British Empire), 1969; Lola Versus Powerman and the Moneygoround, 1970; Percy, 1971; Muswell Hillbillies,

The Kinks: D. Davies, Rodford, R. Davies, Avory

1971; Golden Hour, 1971; Everybody's in Showbiz—Everybody's a Star, 1972; The Kink Kronikles, 1972; The Great Lost Kinks Album, 1972; Preservation, Act I, 1973; All the Good Times, 1973; Golden Hour Volume 2, 1973; Preservation, Act II, 1974; Soap Opera, 1975; Celluloid Heroes, 1976; Schoolboys in Disgrace, 1976; Sleepwalker, 1977; Misfits, 1978; Low Budget, 1979; One More for the Road, 1980; Second Time Around—Greatest Hits, 1980; You Really Got Me, 1980; Give the People What They Want, 1981; State of Confusion, 1983; Word of Mouth, 1984; Come Dancing with the Kinks/Best of the Kinks, 1986; Think Visual, 1987; Live/The Road, 1988; UK Jive, 1989; Fab Forty, 1991

Singles: You Really Got Me, 1964 **(7)**; All Day and All of the Night, 1964 **(7)**; Long Tall Sally, 1965 **(129)**; Tired of Waiting for You, 1965 **(6)**; Set Me Free, 1965 **(23)**; Who'll Be the Next in Line, 1965 **(34)**; See My Friends, 1965 **(111)**; A Well Respected Man, 1965 **(13)**; Till the End of the Day, 1966 **(50)**; Dedicated Follower of Fashion, 1966 **(36)**; Sunny Afternoon, 1966 **(14)**; Deadend Street, 1967 **(73)**; Mr. Pleasant, 1967 **(80)**; Victoria, 1970 **(62)**; Lola, 1970 **(9)**; Apeman, 1971 **(45)**; 20th Century Man, 1972 **(106)**; Supersonic Rocketship, 1972 **(111)**; One of the Survivors, 1973 **(108)**; Sleepwalker, 1977 **(48)**; Rock & Roll Fantasy, 1978 **(30)**; (I Wish I Could Fly Like) Superman, 1979 **(41)**; Gallon of Gas, 1979; Celluloid Heroes, 1980; Lola, 1980 **(81)**; Destroyer, 1981 **(85)**; Better Things, 1981 **(92)**; Come Dancing, 1983 **(6)**; Don't Forget to Dance, 1983 **(29)**; State of Confusion, 1983; Do It Again, 1984 **(41)**; Living on a Thin Line, 1984; Think Visual, 1987; How Are You, 1987; How Do I Get Close, 1989

Hard Rock—British

Kathy Kirby

Single: The Way of Love, 1965 **(88)**

Pop Vocal—British

The Knickerbockers

back row: **J. Charles, Randell;**
front row: **Walker, B. Charles**

Personnel: Buddy Randell (vocals, saxophones); Beau Charles (guitars); John Charles (bass); James Walker (drums)

Albums: Lloyd Thaxton Presents the Knickerbockers, 1965; Jerk & Twine, 1966; Lies, 1966; Stick with Us, 1967; Fabulous Knickerbockers, 1989

Singles: Lies, 1965 **(20)**; One Track Mind, 1966 **(46)**; High on Love, 1966 **(94)**; Chapel in the Fields, 1966 **(106)**; Love Is a Bird, 1966 **(133)**

Pop/Rock—New Jersey

Gladys Knight & The Pips

Personnel: Gladys Knight (vocals); Merald "Bubba" Knight (vocals); Brenda Knight (vocals) replaced (1959) by Edward Patten (vocals); William Guest (vocals); Eleanor Guest (vocals) replaced (1959) by Langston George (vocals) left group (1962)

Albums: Letter Full of Tears, 1961; Gladys Knight & the Pips, 1964; Everybody Needs Love, 1967; Feelin' Bluesy, 1968; Silk 'n' Soul, 1969; Nitty Gritty, 1969; Greatest Hits, 1970; All in a Knight's Work, 1970; If I Were Your Woman, 1971; Standing Ovation, 1972; Neither One of Us, 1973; All I Need Is Time, 1973; Imagination, 1973; Anthology, 1974; Knight Time, 1974; Claudine, 1974; I Feel a Song, 1974; A Little Knight Music, 1975; 2nd Anniversary, 1975; The Best of Gladys Knight & the Pips, 1976; Pipe Dreams, 1976; Still Together, 1977; The One and Only..., 1978; Bless This House, 1978; Miss Gladys Knight, 1979; About Love, 1980; Touch, 1981; Visions, 1983; Life, 1985

Singles: Every Beat of My Heart, 1961 **(6)**; Every Beat of My Heart, 1961 **(45)**; Letter Full of Tears, 1961 **(19)**; Operator, 1962 **(97)**; Giving Up, 1964 **(38)**; Lovers Always Forgive, 1964 **(89)**; Either Way I Lose, 1964 **(119)**; Stop and Get a Hold on Myself, 1965 **(123)**; Who Knows, 1965 **(129)**; Just Walk in My Shoes, 1966 **(129)**; Take Me in Your Arms and Love Me, 1967 **(98)**; Everybody Needs Love, 1967 **(39)**; I Heard It Through the Grapevine, 1967 **(2)**; The End of Our Road, 1968 **(15)**; It Should Have Been Me, 1968 **(40)**; I Wish It Would Rain, 1968 **(41)**; Didn't You Know (You'd Have to Cry Sometime), 1969 **(63)**; The Nitty Gritty, 1969 **(19)**; Friendship Train, 1969 **(17)**; You Need Love Like I Do (Don't You), 1970 **(25)**; If I Were Your Woman, 1970 **(9)**; I Don't Want to Do Wrong, 1971 **(17)**; Make Me the Woman That You Go Home To, 1971 **(27)**; Help Me Make It Through the Night, 1972 **(33)**; Neither One of Us (Wants to Be the First to Say Goodbye), 1973

(2); Daddy Could Swear, I Declare, 1973 **(19)**; Where Peaceful Waters Flow, 1973 **(28)**; All I Need Is Time, 1973 **(61)**; Midnight Train to Georgia, 1973 **(1)**; I've Got to Use My Imagination, 1973 **(4)**; Best Thing That Ever Happened to Me, 1974 **(3)**; On and On, 1974 **(5)**; Between Her Goodbye and My Hello, 1974 **(57)**; I Feel a Song (In My Heart)/Don't Burn Down the Bridge, 1974 **(21)**; Love Finds Its Own Way, 1975 **(47)**; The Way We Were/Try to Remember, 1975 **(11)**; Money, 1975 **(50)**; Part Time Love, 1975 **(22)**; So Sad the Song, 1976 **(47)**; Baby Don't Change Your Mind, 1977 **(52)**; Landlord, 1980 **(46)**; Save the Overtime (For Me), 1983 **(66)**; Love Overboard, 1988 **(13)**

Soul/Pop Vocal—Atlanta

Robert Knight

Album: Everlasting Love, 1967
Singles: Everlasting Love, 1967 **(13)**; Blessed Are the Lonely, 1968 **(97)**; Isn't It Lonely Together, 1968 **(97)**

Soul Vocal—Tennessee

Sonny Knight

Singles: Confidential, 1956 **(17)**; If You Want This Love, 1964 **(71)**; Love Me As Though There Were No Tomorrow, 1965 **(100)**

R & B Vocal—Illinois; real name is Joseph C. Smith

Terry Knight & The Pack

Personnel: Terry Knight (vocals, bass); Mark Farner (guitars, vocals); Don Brewer (drums, vocals)

Albums: Terry Knight & the Pack, 1966; Mark, Don & Terry, 1966–67, 1972
Singles: Better Man Than I, 1966 **(125)**; A Change on the Way, 1966 **(111)**; I (Who Have Nothing), 1966 **(46)**; This Precious Time, 1967 **(120)**; Love Love Love Love Love, 1967 **(117)**; St. Paul (The Legend Of), 1969 **(114)**

Hard Rock—Michigan

The Knockouts

Personnel: Bob D'Andrea (vocals)
Single: Darling Lorraine, 1959 **(46)**

Pop Vocal—New Jersey

Buddy Knox & The Rhythm Orchids

Personnel: Buddy Knox (guitars, vocals); Jimmy Bowen (bass); Don Lanier (guitars); Dave Alldred (drums)

Albums: Buddy Knox, 1957; Buddy Knox & Jimmy Bowen, 1958; Golden Hits, 1961; Buddy Knox, 1962; Buddy Knox in Nashville, 1963; Gypsy Man, 1970; Buddy Knox Rocks, 1973; Party Doll, 1978
Singles: Party Doll, 1957 **(1)**; Rock Your Little Baby to Sleep, 1957 **(17)**; Hula Love, 1957 **(9)**; Swingin' Daddy, 1958 **(80)**; Somebody Touched Me, 1958 **(22)**; That's Why I Cry, 1959 **(88)**; Teasable, Pleasable You, 1959 **(85)**; I Think I'm Gonna Kill Myself, 1959 **(55)**; Lovey Dovey, 1960 **(25)**; Ling-Ting-Tong, 1961 **(65)**; Hitchhike Back to Georgia, 1964 **(114)**

Rockabilly/Country—Texas

Kokomo

Personnel: Jimmy Wisner (piano)
Single: Asia Minor, 1961 **(8)**
Jazz/Pop — Philadelphia

The Koobas

Personnel: Stu Leatherwood (guitars); Keith Ellis (bass); Tony O'Riley (vocals); Roy Morris (drums)
Album: Koobas, 1969
Progressive Rock — British

Kool & the Gang

Personnel: Robert "Kool" Bell (bass, vocals); Ronald Bell (saxophones, keyboards); Dennis Thomas (saxophones, flutes); Robert Mickens (trumpet); Charles "Clay" Smith (guitars); Rick Westfield (keyboards) replaced (1977) by Kevin Lassiter (keyboards) replaced (1980) by Earl Toon (keyboards, vocals) replaced (1980) by Cutis Williams (keyboards); George Brown (drums); added (1978) James "JT" Taylor (vocals); added (1980) Cliff Adams (trombone); added (1980) Michael Ray (trumpet)
Albums: Kool & the Gang, 1969; Music Is the Message, 1970; Live at the Sex Machine, 1971; The Best of Kool & the Gang, 1971; Live at P.J.'s, 1972; Good Times, 1973; Wild and Peaceful, 1973; Kool Jazz, 1974; Light of Worlds, 1974; Kool & the Gang Greatest Hits, 1975; Spirit of the Boogie, 1975; Love & Understanding, 1976; Open Sesame, 1976; Behind the Eyes, 1977; Spin Their Top Hits, 1978; The Force, 1978; Ladies Night, 1979; Everybody's Dancin', 1979; Celebrate!, 1980; Something Special, 1981; Kool Kuts, 1982; As One, 1982; In the Heart, 1983; Twice As Kool, 1983; Emergency, 1984; Forever, 1986; Everything's Kool & the Gang, 1987; Sweat, 1989
Singles: Kool & the Gang, 1969 **(59)**; The Gang's Back Again, 1969 **(85)**; Let the Music Take Your Mind, 1970 **(78)**; Funky Man, 1970 **(87)**; Who's Gonna Take That Weight, 1971 **(113)**; I Want to Take You Higher, 1971 **(105)**; Love the Life You Live, 1972 **(107)**; Funky Stuff, 1973 **(29)**; Jungle Boogie, 1973 **(4)**; Hollywood Swinging, 1974 **(6)**; Higher Plane, 1974 **(37)**; Rhyme Tyme People, 1975 **(63)**; Spirit of the Boogie, 1975 **(35)**; Summer Madness, 1975 **(90)**; Caribbean Festival, 1975 **(55)**; Love and Understanding, 1976 **(77)**; Universal Sound, 1976 **(101)**; Open Sesame, 1976 **(55)**; Super Band, 1977 **(101)**; Slick Superchick, 1978 **(102)**; Ladies Night, 1979 **(8)**; Too Hot, 1980 **(5)**; Hangin' Out, 1980 **(103)**; Celebration, 1980 **(1)**; Take It to the Top, 1981; Jones vs. Jones, 1981 **(39)**; Take My Heart, 1981 **(17)**; Steppin' Out, 1982 **(89)**; Get Down On It, 1982 **(10)**; Big Fun, 1982 **(21)**; Let's Go Dancin' (Ooh La, La, La), 1982 **(30)**; Hi De Hi, Hi De Ho, 1982; Street Kids, 1983; Joanna, 1983 **(2)**; Straight Ahead, 1983; Tonight, 1984 **(13)**; Straight Ahead, 1984 **(104)**; Misled, 1984 **(10)**; Fresh, 1985 **(9)**; Cherish, 1985 **(2)**; Emergency, 1985 **(18)**; Victory, 1986 **(10)**; Stone Love, 1987 **(10)**; Holiday, 1987 **(66)**; Special Way, 1987 **(72)**
Dance/Pop — New Jersey

Al Kooper

Albums: Super Session, 1969 (with Stephen Stills and Michael Bloomfield); I Stand Alone, 1969;

Live Adventures, 1969 (with Michael Bloomfield); You Never Know Who Your Friends Are, 1970; Kooper Sessions, 1970; Easy Does It, 1970; Landlord, 1971; New York City, 1971; Possible Projection of the Future, 1972; Naked Songs, 1973; Al's Big Deal (Unclaimed Freight), 1975; Act Like Nothing's Wrong, 1976; Four on the Floor, 1979; Championship Wrestling, 1982

Blues/Rock—New York; Kooper discovered Lynyrd Skynyrd and the Tubes

Billy J. Kramer & The Dakotas

Personnel: Billy J. Kramer (vocals); Mike Maxfield (guitars); Robin McDonald (guitars); Ray Jones (bass); Tony Mansfield (drums)

Albums: Listen to Billy J. Kramer & the Dakotas, 1963; I'll Keep You Satisfied, 1964; Little Children, 1964; Trains, Boats & Planes, 1965; The Best of Billy J. Kramer & the Dakotas, 1977; Billy J. Kramer, 1983; Best of Billy J. Kramer, 1984; The EMI Years, 1991

Singles: Little Children, 1964 **(7)**; Bad to Me, 1964 **(9)**; I'll Keep You Satisfied, 1964 **(30)**; From a Window, 1964 **(23)**; It's Gotta Last Forever, 1965 **(67)**; Trains and Boats and Planes, 1965 **(47)**

Pop/Rock—British; Billy's real name is William Ashton

Bob Kuban & The In-Men

Personnel: Bob Kuban (guitars, vocals); Walter Scott (vocals; deceased 1983)

Album: Look Out for the Cheater, 1966

Singles: The Cheater, 1966 **(12)**; The Teaser, 1966 **(70)**; Drive My Car, 1966 **(93)**

Pop/Rock—St. Louis

Kuf-Linx

Personnel: John Jennings (vocals); George McFadden (vocals); Leo Manley (vocals); Gaines Steele (vocals); Zena Aya (vocals)

Single: So Tough, 1958 **(76)**

Pop Vocal—American

Jim Kweskin Jug Band

Personnel: Jim Kweskin (guitars, vocals); Bill Keith (pedal steel guitar); Mel Lyman (harmonica); Fritz Richmond (jug, washtub bass); Richard Greene (fiddle); Maria D'Amato Muldaur (vocals, kazoo, tambourine); Geoff Muldaur (guitars, vocals); Rex Rakish (drums, percussion, vocals)

Albums: Unblushing Brassiness, 1963; Jug Band Music, 1965; Relax Your Mind, 1966; See Reverse Side for Title, 1966; Jump for Joy, 1967; Garden of Joy, 1967; Best of the Jim Kweskin Jug Band, 1968; Whatever Happened to Those Days, 1968; American Aviator, 1969; Greatest Hits, 1970; Jim Kweskin's America, 1971; Jim Kweskin, 1978; Lives Again, 1978; Side by Side, 1980; Swing On a Star, 1980

Folk/Rock—American

Patti LaBelle & The Blue Belles

Personnel: Patti LaBelle (vocals); Nona Hendryx (vocals); Sarah Dash (vocals); Cindy Birdsong (vocals) left group (1967)

Albums: Over the Rainbow, 1963; Patti LaBelle & the Blue Belles, 1964

Singles: Sold My Heart to the Junkman, 1962 (**15**); I Found a New Love, 1962 (**122**); Cool Water, 1963 (**127**); Down the Aisle (Wedding Song), 1963 (**37**); You'll Never Walk Alone, 1964 (**34**); Danny Boy, 1964 (**76**); All or Nothing, 1965 (**68**); Take Me for a Little While, 1966 (**89**); Always Something There to Remind Me, 1967 (**125**)

Soul/Pop Vocal—Philadelphia

Frankie Laine

Albums: Rockin', 1957; Hell Bent for Leather!, 1961; I'll Take Care of Your Cares, 1967; I Wanted Someone to Love, 1967; To Each His Own, 1968; You Gave Me a Mountain, 1969

Singles: Humming Bird, 1955 (**17**); Hawk-Eye, 1955 (**45**); A Woman in Love, 1955 (**19**); Don't Cry, 1956 (**83**); Moonlight Gambler, 1956 (**3**); Love Is a Golden Ring, 1957 (**10**); Don't Make My Baby Blue, 1963 (**51**); I'll Take Care of Your Cares, 1967 (**39**); Making Memories, 1967 (**35**); You Wanted Someone to Play With (I Wanted Someone to Love), 1967 (**48**); Laura, What's He Got That I Ain't Got, 1967 (**66**); You, No One but You, 1967 (**83**); To Each His Own, 1968 (**82**); I Found You, 1968 (**118**); Take Me Back, 1968 (**115**); You Gave Me a Mountain, 1969 (**24**); Dammit Isn't God's Last Name, 1969 (**86**)

Pop Vocal—Chicago; real name is Frank LoVecchio

Herb Lance & The Classics

Single: Blue Moon, 1961 (**50**)

R & B Vocal—American

Major Lance

Albums: The Monkey Time, 1963; Um, Um, Um, Um, Um, Um/The Best of Major Lance, 1964; Major's Greatest Hits, 1965

Singles: The Monkey Time, 1963 (**8**); Hey Little Girl, 1963 (**13**); Um, Um, Um, Um, Um, Um, 1964 (**5**); The Matador, 1964 (**20**); It Ain't No Use, 1964 (**68**); Girls, 1964 (**68**); Rhythm, 1964 (**24**); Sometimes I Wonder, 1964 (**64**); Come See, 1965 (**40**); Ain't It a Shame, 1965 (**91**); Too Hot to Hold, 1965 (**93**); Everybody Loves a Good Time, 1965 (**109**); Investigate, 1966 (**132**); It's the Beat, 1966 (**128**); Follow the Leader, 1969 (**125**); Stay Away from Me (I Love You Too Much), 1970 (**67**); Must Be Love Coming Down, 1971 (**119**)

Soul Vocal—Chicago

Mickey Lee Lane

Single: Shaggy Dog, 1964 (**38**)

Pop Vocal—New York

The Larks

Personnel: Don Julian (vocals); Ted Walters (vocals); Chris Morrison (vocals)

Album: The Jerk, 1965

Singles: The Jerk, 1964 (**7**); Mickey's East Coast Jerk, 1965 (**132**)

R & B Vocal—Los Angeles

The Larks

Personnel: Eugene Mulford (vocals); Thermon Ruth (vocals); Alden

Bunn (vocals); Raymond Barnes (vocals); Hadie Rowe, Jr. (vocals); David McNeil (vocals)

Single: It's Unbelievable, 1961 **(69)**

R & B Vocal—North Carolina; original name was the Jubilators

Rod Lauren

Single: If I Had a Girl, 1959 **(31)**

Pop Vocal—American

Linda Laurie

Single: Ambrose (Part Five), 1959 **(52)**

Pop Vocal—New York

Steve Lawrence

Albums: Here's Steve Lawrence, 1958; Portrait of My Love, 1961; Winners!, 1963; Academy Award Losers, 1964; Everybody Knows, 1964; The Steve Lawrence Show, 1965; Together on Broadway, 1967 (with Eydie Gorme); What It Was, Was Love, 1969 (with Eydie Gorme); Real True Lovin', 1969 (with Eydie Gorme)

Singles: The Banana Boat Song, 1957 **(18)**; Party Doll, 1957 **(5)**; (The Bad Donkey) Pum-Pa-Lum, 1957 **(45)**; Can't Wait for Summer, 1957 **(42)**; Fabulous, 1957 **(71)**; Fraulein, 1957 **(54)**; Uh-Huh, Oh Yeah, 1958 **(73)**; Many a Time, 1958 **(97)**; (I Don't Care) Only Love Me, 1959 **(62)**; Pretty Blue Eyes, 1959 **(9)**; Footsteps, 1960 **(7)**; Portrait of My Love, 1961 **(9)**; My Claire de Lune, 1961 **(68)**; In Time, 1961 **(94)**; Somewhere Along the Way, 1961 **(67)**; Our Concerto, 1962 **(107)**; Go Away Little Girl, 1962 **(1)**; The Lady Wants to Twist, 1962 **(120)**; Don't Be Afraid, Little Darlin', 1963 **(26)**; Poor Little Rich Girl, 1963 **(27)**; More (Theme from *Mondo Cane*), 1963 **(117)**; I Want to Stay Here, 1963 **(28)** (with Eydie Gorme); Walking Proud, 1963 **(26)**; I Can't Stop Talking About You, 1963 **(35)** (with Eydie Gorme); My Home Town, 1964 **(106)**; A Room Without Windows, 1964 **(120)**; Everybody Knows, 1964 **(72)**; Yet . . . I Know, 1964 **(77)**; Bewitched, 1965 **(103)**; I Will Wait for You, 1965 **(113)**; Last Night I Made a Little Girl Cry, 1965 **(126)**; Millions of Roses, 1965 **(106)**; The Week-End, 1966 **(131)**; Real True Lovin', 1969 **(119)** (with Eydie Gorme); We Can Make It Together, 1972 **(68)** (with Eydie Gorme & the Osmonds)

Pop Vocal—New York; real name is Sidney Leibowitz

Leapy Lee

Album: Little Arrows, 1969

Single: Little Arrows, 1968 **(16)**

Pop Vocal—British; real name is Lee Graham

The Leaves

Personnel: Bill Rheinhart (vocals) replaced (1967) by Robert Arlin (vocals); John Beck (guitars, vocals); Robert Lee Reiner (guitars); James Pons (bass); Tom Ray (drums)

Albums: Hey Joe, 1966; All the Good That's Happening, 1967

Single: Hey Joe, 1966 **(31)**

Psychedelic Rock—Los Angeles

Led Zeppelin

Personnel: Robert Plant (vocals); Jimmy Page (guitars); John Paul Jones (bass, piano); John Bonham (drums; deceased 1980)

The Leaves: Beck, Pons, Ray, Reiner, Rheinhart

Led Zeppelin: Page, Bonham, Plant, Jones

Albums: Led Zeppelin, 1968; Led Zeppelin II, 1969; Led Zeppelin III, 1970; Led Zeppelin IV, 1971; Houses of the Holy, 1973; Physical Graffiti, 1975; Presence, 1976; The Song Remains the Same, 1976; In Through the Out Door, 1979; Coda, 1982; Led Zeppelin (Box), 1990

Singles: Good Times, Bad Times, 1969 **(80)**; Whole Lotta Love, 1969 **(4)**; Living Loving Mad, 1970 **(65)**; The Immigrant Song, 1970 **(16)**; Stairway to Heaven, 1971; Black Dog, 1971 **(15)**; Rock & Roll, 1972 **(47)**; Over the Hills and Far Away, 1973 **(51)**; D'Yer Mak'er, 1973 **(20)**; Trampled Underfoot, 1975 **(38)**; Kashmir, 1975; All My Love, 1979; Fool in the Rain, 1979 **(21)**

Hard/Blues Rock—British; Bonham's son Jason leads the hard rock band Bonham

Brenda Lee

Albums: Brenda Lee, 1960; Grandma, What Great Songs, 1960; This Is ... Brenda, 1960; Emotions

Brenda Lee

1961; All the Way, 1961; Sincerely,
1962; Brenda, That's All, 1962; All
Alone Am I, 1963; Let Me Sing,
1963; By Request, 1964; Merry
Christmas, 1964; Top Teen Hits,
1965; Versatile, 1965; Too Many
Rivers, 1965; Bye Bye Blues, 1966;
10 Golden Years, 1966; Coming On
Strong, 1966; Reflections in Blue,
1967; Let It Be Me, 1967; For the
First Time, 1968 (with Pete Foun-
tain); Johnny One Time, 1969;
Memphis Portrait, 1970; A Whole
Lotta Brenda Lee, 1972; Brenda,
1973; Brenda Lee Story, 1974; New
Sunrise, 1974; Now, 1975; L.A. Ses-
sion, 1977; 25th Anniversary, 1982;
The Early Years, 1984; Love Songs
Just for You, 1984; Christmas in a
New Old-Fashioned Way, 1991

Singles: One Step at a Time, 1957
(**43**); Dynamite, 1957 (**72**); Sweet
Nothin's, 1959 (**4**); I'm Sorry, 1960

(**1**); That's All You Gotta Do, 1960
(**6**); I Want to Be Wanted, 1960 (**1**);
Just a Little, 1960 (**40**); Rockin'
Around the Christmas Tree, 1960
(**14**); Emotions, 1961 (**7**); I'm Learn-
ing About Love, 1961 (**33**); It's
Never Too Late, 1961 (**101**); You
Can Depend on Me, 1961 (**6**); Dum
Dum, 1961 (**4**); Eventually, 1961
(**56**); Fool #1, 1961 (**3**); Anybody but
Me, 1961 (**31**); Rockin' Around the
Christmas Tree, 1961 (**50**); Break It
to Me Gently, 1962 (**4**); So Deep,
1962 (**52**); Everybody Loves Me but
You, 1962 (**6**); Here Comes That
Feelin', 1962 (**89**); Heart in Hand,
1962 (**15**); It Started All Over
Again, 1962 (**29**); All Alone Am I,
1962 (**3**); Save All Your Lovin' for
Me, 1962 (**53**); Rockin' Around the
Christmas Tree, 1962 (**59**); Your
Used to Be, 1963 (**32**); She'll Never
Know, 1963 (**47**); Losing You, 1963
(**6**); He's So Heavenly, 1963 (**73**);
My Whole World Is Falling Down,
1963 (**24**); I Wonder, 1963 (**25**); The
Grass Is Greener, 1963 (**17**); Sweet
Impossible You, 1963 (**70**); As
Usual, 1963 (**12**); Think, 1964 (**25**);
The Waiting Game, 1964 (**101**);
Alone with You, 1964 (**48**); My
Dreams, 1964 (**85**); When You Loved
Me, 1964 (**47**); He's Sure to Re-
member Me, 1964 (**135**); Is It True,
1964 (**17**); Thanks a Lot, 1965 (**45**);
The Crying Game, 1965 (**87**); Truly,
Truly, True, 1965 (**54**); Too Many
Rivers, 1965 (**13**); No One, 1965
(**98**); Rusty Bells, 1965 (**33**); Time
and Time Again, 1966 (**126**); Too
Little Time, 1966 (**123**); Ain't Gonna
Cry No More, 1966 (**77**); Coming
On Strong, 1966 (**11**); Ride, Ride,
Ride, 1967 (**37**); Take Me, 1967
(**126**); Where Is Love, 1967 (**134**);
Where's the Melody?, 1967 (**105**);
That's All Right, 1968 (**118**); Johnny

One Time, 1969 **(41)**; You Don't Need Me for Anything Anymore, 1969 **(84)**; I Think I Love You Again, 1970 **(97)**; Nobody Wins, 1973 **(70)**

Pop Vocal—Georgia; real name is Brenda Mae Tarpley

Curtis Lee

Album: Pretty Little Angel Eyes, 1961

Singles: Pledge of Love, 1961 **(110)**; Pretty Little Angel Eyes, 1961 **(7)**; Under the Moon of Love, 1961 **(46)**; Just Another Fool, 1962 **(110)**

Pop Vocal—Arizona

Dickey Lee

Album: The Tale of Patches, 1962
Singles: Patches, 1962 **(6)**; I Saw Linda Yesterday, 1962 **(14)**; Don't Wanna Think About Paula, 1963 **(68)**; The Day the Sawmill Closed Down, 1963 **(104)**; Big Brother, 1964 **(101)**; Laurie (Strange Things Happen), 1965 **(14)**; The Girl from Peyton Place, 1965 **(73)**; Red, Green, Yellow and Blue, 1968 **(107)**; 9,999,999 Tears, 1976 **(52)**

Rockabilly—Memphis; real name is Dick Lipscomb

Jackie Lee

Album: The Duck, 1966
Singles: The Duck, 1965 **(14)**; Your P-E-R-S-O-N-A-L-I-T-Y, 1966 **(111)**; Do the Temptation Walk, 1966 **(113)**; African Boo-Ga-Loo, 1968 **(121)**

R & B Vocal—Louisiana; real name is Earl Nelson

Laura Lee

Albums: Laura Lee, 1967; Women's Love Rights, 1971; The Rip Off, 1972
Singles: Dirty Man, 1967 **(68)**; Wanted: Lover, No Experience Necessary, 1967 **(84)**; Up Tight, Good Man, 1967 **(93)**; As Long As I Got You, 1968 **(123)**; Women's Love Rights, 1971 **(36)**; Love and Liberty, 1972 **(94)**; Since I Fell for You, 1972 **(76)**; Rip Off, 1972 **(68)**; If You Can Beat Me Rockin' (You Can Have My Chair), 1972 **(65)**; Crumbs Off the Table, 1972 **(107)**

Soul Vocal—Chicago; full name is Laura Lee Rundless

Left Banke

back row: **Finn, Cameron, Brand;** *front row:* **Martin, Brown**

Personnel: Steve Martin (vocals); Rick Brand (guitars); Michael Brown (keyboards) replaced (1969)

by Jeff Winfield (keyboards);
Thomas Finn (bass); George Came-
ron (drums)
   Albums: Walk Away Renee, 1967;
Too, 1969; And Suddenly It's Left
Banke, 1984
   Singles: Walk Away Renee, 1966
(5); Pretty Ballerina, 1967 **(15)**; Ivy,
Ivy, 1967 **(119)**; She May Call You
Up Tonight, 1967 **(120)**; Desiree,
1967 **(98)**; Queen of Paradise/And
One Day, 1980
   Pop/Rock — New York

The Lemon Pipers

Personnel: R. G. Nave (organ,
tambourine); Ivan Browne (guitars,
vocals); Bill Bartlett (guitars); Steve
Walmsley (bass); Bill Albaugh
(drums)
   Albums: Green Tambourine,
1968; Jungle Marmalade, 1968
   Singles: Turn Around and Take a
Look, 1967 **(132)**; Green Tambourine, 1967 **(1)**; Rice Is Nice, 1968
(46); Jelly Jungle (of Orange
Marmalade), 1968 **(51)**
   Bubblegum Pop — Ohio

John Lennon

Albums: Two Virgins, 1968; Life
with the Lions, 1969; Wedding
Album, 1969; Live Peace in Toronto, 1969; Plastic Ono Band, 1970;
Imagine, 1971; Sometime in New
York City, 1972; Mind Games,
1973; Walls & Bridges, 1974; Rock
'n' Roll, 1975; Shaved Fish, 1975;
Double Fantasy, 1980 (with Yoko
Ono); The John Lennon Collection, 1982; Milk & Honey, 1984;
Live in New York City, 1986; Lennon, 1990
   Singles: Give Peace a Chance,
1969 **(14)**; Cold Turkey, 1969 **(30)**;

John Lennon

Instant Karma (We All Shine On),
1970 **(3)**; Mother, 1971 **(43)**; Power
to the People, 1971 **(11)**; Imagine,
1971 **(3)**; Woman Is the Nigger of
the World, 1972 **(57)**; Mind Games,
1973 **(18)**; Whatever Gets You
Through the Night, 1974 **(1)**; #9
Dream, 1974 **(9)**; Stand by Me, 1975
(20); (Just Like) Starting Over, 1980
(1); Woman, 1980 **(2)**; Watching the
Wheels, 1980 **(10)**; Nobody Told
Me, 1984 **(5)**; I'm Steppin' Out,
1984 **(55)**; Borrowed Time, 1984;
Every Man Has a Woman Who
Loves Him, 1984; Jealous Guy, 1988
(80)
   Pop/Rock — British; John was shot
to death outside his New York
apartment on December 8, 1980

Ketty Lester

Album: Love Letters, 1962
   Singles: Love Letters, 1962 **(5)**;
But Not for Me, 1962 **(41)**; You
Can't Lie to a Liar, 1962 **(90)**; This
Land Is Your Land, 1962 **(97)**;
Some Things Are Better Left Un-
said, 1964 **(127)**

Pop Vocal—Arkansas; real name is Revoyda Frierson

The Lettermen

Personnel: Tony Butala (vocals); Jim Pike (vocals); Bob Engemann (vocals) replaced (1968) by Gary Pike (vocals)

Albums: A Song for Young Love, 1962; Once Upon a Time, 1962; Jim, Tony and Bob, 1962; College Standards, 1963; The Lettermen in Concert, 1963; A Lettermen Kind of Love, 1964; The Lettermen Look at Love, 1964; She Cried, 1964; Portrait of My Love, 1965; The Hit Sounds of the Lettermen, 1965; You'll Never Walk Alone, 1965; More Hit Sounds of the Lettermen, 1966; A New Song for Young Love, 1966; The Best of the Lettermen, 1966; Warm, 1967; Spring!, 1967; The Lettermen!!! . . . and "Live!," 1967; Goin' Out of My Head, 1968; Special Request, 1968; Put Your Head on My Shoulder, 1968; The Best of the Lettermen, Volume 2, 1969; I Have Dreamed, 1969; Close-Up, 1969; Hurt So Bad, 1969; Traces/Memories, 1970; Reflections, 1970; Everything's Good About You, 1971; Feelings, 1971; Love Book, 1971; Lettermen 1, 1972; "Alive" Again . . . Naturally, 1973; All-Time Greatest Hits, 1974

Singles: The Way You Look Tonight, 1961 **(13)**; When I Fall in Love, 1961 **(7)**; Come Back Silly Girl, 1962 **(17)**; How Is Julie?, 1962 **(42)**; Turn Around Look at Me, 1962 **(105)**; Silly Boy (She Doesn't Love You), 1962 **(81)**; Again, 1962 **(120)**; Heartache Oh Heartache, 1963 **(122)**; Allentown Jail, 1963 **(123)**; Where or When, 1963 **(98)**; Put Away Your Tear Drops, 1964 **(132)**; Girl with a Little Tin Heart, 1965 **(135)**; Theme from *A Summer Place,* 1965 **(16)**; Secretly, 1965 **(64)**; Sweet September, 1966 **(114)**; I Only Have Eyes for You, 1966 **(72)**; Chanson d'Amour, 1966 **(112)**; Our Winter Love, 1967 **(72)**; Goin' Out of My Head/Can't Take My Eyes Off You, 1967 **(7)**; Sherry Don't Go, 1968 **(52)**; All the Gray-Haired Men, 1968 **(109)**; Put Your Head on My Shoulder, 1968 **(44)**; I Have Dreamed, 1969 **(129)**; Hurt So Bad, 1969 **(12)**; Shangri-La, 1969 **(64)**; Traces/Memories Medley, 1969 **(47)**; Hang on Sloopy, 1970 **(93)**; She Cried, 1970 **(73)**; Hey Girl, 1970 **(104)**; Everything Is Good About You, 1971 **(74)**; Love, 1971 **(42)**

Pop Vocal—Los Angeles

Barbara Lewis

Albums: Baby I'm Yours, 1965; Don't Forget About Me, 1966

Singles: Hello Stranger, 1963 **(3)**; Straighten Up Your Heart, 1963 **(43)**; If You Love Her, 1963 **(131)**; Snap Your Fingers, 1963 **(71)**; Puppy Love, 1964 **(38)**; Someday We're Gonna Love Again, 1964 **(124)**; Spend a Little Time, 1964 **(119)**; Pushin' a Good Thing Too Far, 1964 **(113)**; Baby I'm Yours, 1965 **(11)**; Make Me Your Baby, 1965 **(11)**; Don't Forget About Me, 1966 **(91)**; Make Me Belong to You, 1966 **(28)**; Baby What Do You Want Me to Do, 1966 **(74)**; I'll Make Him Love Me, 1967 **(72)**

Pop Vocal—Detroit

Bobby Lewis

Albums: Tossin' and Turnin', 1961; Tossin' and Turnin' Again, 1962

Singles: Tossin' and Turnin', 1961 **(1)**; One Track Mind, 1961 **(9)**; What a Walk, 1961 **(77)**; Mamie in the Afternoon, 1962 **(110)**; I'm Tossin' and Turnin' Again, 1962 **(98)**

Blues/Boogie Rock—Detroit

Gary Lewis & The Playboys

Personnel: Gary Lewis (drums); Al Ramsey (guitars) replaced (1970) by Tom Tripplehorn (guitars); John R. West (guitars) replaced (1970) by James Karstein (guitars); David Walker (keyboards); David Costello (bass) replaced (1970) by Carl Radle (bass)

Albums: This Diamond Ring, 1965; A Session with Gary Lewis & the Playboys, 1965; Everybody Loves a Clown, 1965; She's Just My Style, 1966; Hits Again, 1966; Golden Greats, 1966; Paint Me a Picture, 1967; New Directions, 1967; Now, 1968; More Golden Greats, 1968; Rhythm of the Rain, 1969; I'm on the Right Road Now, 1969; Playboys, 1969; Rhythm, 1969; At Their Best, 1970; 20 Golden Greats, 1979

Singles: This Diamond Ring, 1964 **(1)**; Count Me In, 1965 **(2)**; Save Your Heart for Me, 1965 **(2)**; Everybody Loves a Clown, 1965 **(4)**; She's Just My Style, 1965 **(3)**; Sure Gonna Miss Her, 1966 **(9)**; Green Grass, 1966 **(8)**; My Heart's Symphony, 1966 **(13)**; (You Don't Have to) Paint Me a Picture, 1966 **(15)**; Where Will the Words Come From, 1966 **(21)**; Ice Melts in the Sun, 1967 **(121)**; The Loser (With a Broken Heart), 1967 **(43)**; Girls in Love, 1967 **(39)**; Jill, 1967 **(52)**; Sealed with a Kiss, 1968 **(19)**; Main Street, 1968 **(101)**; Rhythm of the Rain, 1969 **(63)**

Pop/Rock—California; Lewis is the son of comedian and film star Jerry Lewis; group appeared in *A*

The Playboys: *back row:* **Walker, Ramsey, West, Costello;** *front row:* **Lewis**

Swingin' Summer and *Out of Sight* films

Jerry Lee Lewis

Albums: Jerry Lee Lewis, 1957; Greatest, 1960; The Golden Hits of Jerry Lee Lewis, 1964; Live at the Star Club Hamburg, 1964; The Greatest Live Show on Earth, 1964; The Return of Rock, 1965; Country Songs for City Folk, 1964; Memphis Beat, 1966; By Request, 1967; Soul My Way, 1967; Another Place Another Time, 1968; She Still Comes Around (to What's Left of Me), 1969; I'm on Fire, 1969; Sings the Country Music Hall of Fame Hits, Vol. 1, 1969; Sings the Country Music Hall of Fame Hits, Vol. 2, 1969; Original Golden Hits— Volume 1, 1969; Original Golden Hits—Volume 2, 1969; Together, 1969 (with Linda Gail); She Even Woke Me Up to Say Goodbye, 1970; The Best of Jerry Lee Lewis, 1970; Live at the International, Las Vegas, 1970; There Must Be More to Love Than This, 1971; Touching Home, 1971; Original Golden Hits—Volume 3, 1971; Would You Take Another Chance On Me?, 1971; The "Killer" Rocks On, 1972; The Session, 1973; Fan Club Choices, 1974; Southern Roots, 1974; Boogie Woogie Country Man, 1975; I'm a Rocker, 1975; Odd Man In, 1976; Country Class, 1976; Country Memories, 1977; Best of Jerry Lee Lewis, Volume 2, 1978; Keeps on Rockin', 1978; Jerry Lee Lewis, 1979; When Two Worlds Collide, 1980; Killer Country, 1980; Best of Country Hall of Fame, 1981; I Am What I Am, 1984

Singles: Whole Lot of Shakin' Going On, 1957 (**3**); Great Balls of Fire, 1957 (**2**); You Win Again, 1958 (**95**); Breathless, 1958 (**7**); High School Confidential, 1958 (**21**); Break-Up, 1958 (**52**); I'll Make It Up to You, 1958 (**85**); I'll Sail My Ship Alone, 1959 (**93**); What'd I Say, 1961 (**30**); Sweet Little Sixteen, 1962 (**95**); How's My Ex Treating You, 1962 (**114**); Hit the Road Jack, 1963 (**103**); I'm on Fire, 1964 (**98**); High Heel Sneakers, 1964 (**91**); Baby, Hold Me Close, 1965 (**129**); Another Place, Another Time, 1968 (**97**); What's Made Milwaukee Famous (Has Made a Loser Out of Me), 1968 (**94**); Touching Home, 1971 (**110**); Me and Bobby McGee, 1971 (**40**); Chantilly Lace, 1972 (**43**); Turn on Your Love Light, 1972 (**95**); Drinking with Spo-Dee O'Dee, 1973 (**41**); No Headstone on My Grave, 1973 (**104**); Rockin' My Life Away, 1979 (**101**)

Rockabilly—Louisiana

Lewis & Clarke Expedition

Personnel: Travis "Michael Murphey" Lewis (guitars, vocals); Boomer "Owen Castleman" Clarke (vocals)

Album: Lewis & Clarke Expedition, 1967

Singles: I Feel Good (I Feel Bad), 1967 (**64**); Chain Around the Flowers, 1968 (**131**)

Pop/Rock—Northwest

Lifetime

Personnel: John McLaughlin (guitars) replaced (1971) by Tom Dunbar (guitars) replaced (1971) by Tequila (guitars, vocals) replaced (1975) by Allan Holdsworth (guitars); Jack Bruce (bass) replaced

(1970) by Ron Carter (bass) replaced (1971) by Juni Booth (bass) replaced (1971) by Herb Bushler (bass) replaced (1975) by Tony Newton (bass); Larry Young (organ) replaced (1971) by David Horowitz (keyboards) replaced (1975) by Alan Pasqua (keyboards); Tony Williams (drums); added (1971) Don Alias (percussion); added (1971) Warren Smith (percussion) replaced (1971) by Webster Lewis (organ); added (1971) Tillmon Williams (saxophones) left group (1973)

Albums: Lifetime, 1965; Spring, 1966; Emergency, 1969; Turn It Over, 1970; Ego, 1970; The Old Bum's Rush, 1972; Lifetime, 1975; Believe It, 1976; Million Dollar Legs, 1976; Lifetime, 1978; Joy of Flying, 1979

Jazz/Rock — British

Gordon Lightfoot

Albums: Lightfoot, 1966; Way I Feel, 1967; Lightfoot, 1968; Did She Mention My Name, 1968; Back Here On Earth, 1969; Early Lightfoot, 1969; Sunday Concert, 1969; Sit Down Young Stranger, 1970; The Summer Side of Life, 1971; Don Quixote, 1972; Old Dan's Records, 1972; Sundown, 1974; Cold on the Shoulder, 1975; Gord's Gold, 1975; Very Best of Gordon Lightfoot, 1975; Early Morning Rain, 1976; Summertime Dream, 1976; Classic Lightfoot, 1977; Endless Wire, 1978; Dream Street Rose, 1980; The Best of Gordon Lightfoot, 1981; Shadows, 1982; Salute, 1983; East of Midnight, 1986; Gord's Gold Volume 2, 1988

Singles: If You Could Read My Mind, 1970 **(5)**; If I Could, 1971; Talking in Your Sleep, 1971 **(64)**; The Summer Side of Life, 1971 **(98)**; Beautiful, 1972 **(58)**; The Same Old Obsession, 1972 **(102)**; You Are What I Am, 1973 **(101)**; Sundown, 1974 **(1)**; Carefree Highway, 1974 **(10)**; Rainy Day People, 1975 **(26)**; The Wreck of the Edmund Fitzgerald, 1976 **(2)**; Race Among the Ruins, 1977 **(65)**; The Circle Is Small (I Can See It in Your Eyes), 1978 **(33)**; Dream Street Rose, 1980; If You Need Me, 1980; Baby Step Back, 1982 **(50)**; Blackberry Wine, 1982; Shadows, 1982; Salute (A Lot More Livin' to Do), 1983; Without You, 1983

Folk Pop/Rock — Canadian

The Limeliters

Personnel: Glen Yarbrough (vocals); Lou Gottlieb (vocals); Alex Hassilev (vocals)

Albums: Tonight: In Person, 1961; The Limeliters, 1961; The Slightly Fabulous Limeliters, 1961; Sing Out!, 1962; Through Children's Eyes, 1962; Folk Matinee, 1962; Our Men in San Francisco, 1963; Makin' a Joyful Noise, 1963; Fourteen 14K

Folk Songs, 1963; More of Everything!, 1964
  Single: A Dollar Down, 1961 **(60)**
  Folk/Pop Vocal—California

Bob Lind

Albums: This Is Bob Lind, 1965; Don't Be Concerned, 1966; Photographs of Feelings, 1966; Since There Were Circles, 1967
  Singles: Elusive Butterfly, 1966 **(5)**; Remember the Rain, 1966 **(64)**; Truly Julie's Blues (I'll Be There), 1966 **(65)**; I Just Let It Take Me, 1966 **(123)**; San Francisco Woman, 1966 **(135)**
  Folk/Pop Vocal—Baltimore

Kathy Linden

Singles: Billy, 1958 **(7)**; You'd Be Surprised, 1958 **(50)**; Goodbye Jimmy, Goodbye, 1959 **(11)**; You Don't Know Girls, 1959 **(92)**
  Pop Vocal—New Jersey

Mark Lindsay

Albums: Arizona, 1969; Silverbird, 1970; You've Got a Friend, 1971
  Singles: First Hymn from Grand Terrace, 1969 **(81)**; Arizona, 1969 **(10)**; Miss America, 1970 **(44)**; Silver Bird, 1970 **(25)**; And the Grass Won't Pay No Mind, 1970 **(44)**; Problem Child, 1970 **(80)**; Been Too Long on the Road, 1971 **(98)**; Are You Old Enough, 1971 **(87)**
  Pop Vocal—Idaho; former lead vocalist with Paul Revere & the Raiders

Liquid Smoke

Personnel: Sandy Pantaleo (vocals); Vince Fersak (guitars); Mike Archeleta (bass); Benny Ninmann (keyboards); Chas Kimbrell (drums)
  Album: Liquid Smoke, 1969
  Single: I Who Have Nothing, 1970 **(82)**
  Psychedelic Pop—American

Litter

Personnel: Mark Gallagher (vocals); Dan Rinaldi (guitars, vocals); Tom Caplan (guitars) replaced (1969) by Ray Melina (guitars); Jim Kane (bass, keyboards); Tom Murray (drums); added (1968) Denny Waite (keyboards, vocals)
  Albums: Distortions, 1967; $100 Fine, 1968; Emerge, 1969
  Hard Rock—Detroit

Little Anthony & The Imperials

Personnel: Anthony Gourdine (vocals); Ernest Wright, Jr. (vocals) left group (1964); Clarence Collins (vocals); Tracy Lord (vocals) replaced (1964) by Sammy Strain (vocals) replaced (1964) by Kenny Seymour (vocals); Glouster Rogers (vocals) left group (1964)
  Albums: We Are the Imperials, 1958; Shades of the 40's, 1959; Forever Yours, 1960; Greatest Hits, 1961; I'm on the Outside (Looking In), 1964; Goin' Out of My Head, 1965; The Best of Little Anthony & the Imperials, 1966; Payin' Our Dues, 1967; Reflections, 1967; Movie Grabbers, 1967; The Best of Little Anthony & the Imperials, Volume 2, 1967; On the Outside, 1968; Out of Sight, Out of Mind, 1969; On a New Street, 1974; Daylight, 1980
  Singles: Tears on My Pillow, 1958 **(4)**; So Much, 1958 **(87)**;

Wishful Thinking, 1959 **(79)**; A Prayer and a Juke Box, 1959 **(81)**; Shimmy, Shimmy, Ko-Ko-Bop, 1959 **(24)**; My Empty Room, 1960 **(86)**; Please Say You Want Me, 1961 **(104)**; I'm on the Outside (Looking In), 1964 **(15)**; Goin' Out of My Head, 1964 **(6)**; Hurt So Bad, 1965 **(10)**; Take Me Back, 1965 **(16)**; I Miss You, 1965 **(34)**; Hurt, 1966 **(51)**; Better Use Your Head, 1966 **(54)**; You Better Take It Easy Baby, 1966 **(125)**; It's Not the Same, 1966 **(92)**; Don't Tie Me Down, 1967 **(123)**; I'm Hypnotized, 1968 **(98)**; Out of Sight, Out of Mind, 1969 **(52)**; The Ten Commandments of Love, 1969 **(82)**; Don't Get Close, 1970 **(116)**; World of Darkness, 1970 **(121)**; Help Me Find a Way (to Say I Love You), 1970 **(92)**; I'm Falling in Love with You, 1974 **(86)**; Hold On (Just a Little Bit Longer), 1975 **(105)**

Pop Vocal — New York

Little Caesar & The Consuls

Single: (My Girl) Sloopy, 1965 **(50)**

Bar Rock — Canadian

Little Caesar & The Romans

Personnel: David Johnson (vocals)
Singles: Those Oldies But Goodies (Remind Me of You), 1961 **(9)**; Hully Gully Again, 1961 **(54)**; Memories of Those Oldies But Goodies, 1961 **(101)**

R & B Vocal — Los Angeles

The Little Dippers

Personnel: Delores Dinning (vocals); Emily Gilmore (vocals); Darrell McCall (vocals); Hurshel Wigintin (vocals)
Single: Forever, 1960 **(9)**

Pop Vocal — American

Little Eva

Album: Llllloco-Motion, 1962
Singles: The Loco-Motion, 1962 **(1)**; Keep Your Hands Off My Baby, 1962 **(12)**; Let's Turkey Trot, 1963 **(20)**; Swingin' on a Star, 1963 **(38)** (with Big Dee Irwin); Old Smokey Locomotion, 1963 **(48)**; What I Gotta Do (to Make You Jealous), 1963 **(101)**; Let's Start the Party Again, 1963 **(123)**

Pop Vocal — North Carolina; real name is Eva Boyd

Little Joe & The Thrillers

Personnel: Joe Cook (vocals); Farris Hill (vocals); Richard Frazier (vocals); Donald Burnett (vocals); Harry Pascle (vocals)
Single: Peanuts, 1957 **(22)**

R & B Vocal — New York

Little Joey & The Flips

Personnel: Joey Hall (vocals)
Single: Bongo Stomp, 1962 **(33)**

R & B Vocal — Philadelphia

Little Milton

Albums: We're Gonna Make It, 1965; Sings Big Blues, 1968; Grits & Groceries, 1969; If Walls Could Talk, 1969; Friend of Mine, 1971;

Greatest Hits, 1973; Blues & Soul, 1974; Montreux Festival, 1974; Golden Decade, 1974; Blues Master, 1976; Chronicle, 1979; Age Ain't Nothin' But a Number, 1983; His Greatest Sides, Volume 1, 1984

Singles: Blind Man, 1965 **(86)**; We're Gonna Make It, 1965 **(25)**; Who's Cheating Who?, 1965 **(43)**; Your People, 1965 **(106)**; We Got the Winning Hand, 1966 **(100)**; Man Loves Two, 1966 **(127)**; Feel So Bad, 1967 **(91)**; Grits Ain't Groceries (All Around the World), 1969 **(73)**; Just a Little Bit, 1969 **(97)**; Poor Man, 1969 **(103)**; If Walls Could Talk, 1970 **(71)**; Baby I Love You, 1970 **(82)**; That's What Love Will Make You Do, 1972 **(59)**

Blues Vocal—Mississippi; real name is Milton Campbell

Little Richard

Albums: Here's Little Richard, 1957; Little Richard 2, 1958; The Fabulous Little Richard, 1959; Biggest Hits, 1959; Greatest Hits, 1959; Well Alright, 1959; Little Richard Is Back, 1962; Greatest Hits, 1964; Mr. Big, 1964; Rip It Up, 1964; Slippin' & Slidin', 1964; Coming Home, 1964; Little Richard Story, 1965; King of Gospel Songs, 1965; Wild & Frantic, 1965; The Explosive, 1967; Greatest Hits, 1967; Every Hour with Little Richard, 1970; The Rill Thing, 1971; King of Rock and Roll, 1971; Second Coming, 1971; Little Richard, 1973; The One and Only, 1974; The Very Best of Little Richard, 1975; Cast a Long Shadow, 1975; Little Richard, 1976; Greatest Hits, 1976; 20 Original Hits, 1976; His Biggest Hits, 1977; Greatest Hits Live, 1978; Grooviest 17 Original Hits, 1979; 18 Greatest Hits, 1986; Compact Command Performances, 1987

Singles: Tutti-Frutti, 1956 **(17)**; Long Tall Sally, 1956 **(6)**; Slippin' and Slidin' (Peepin' and Hidin'), 1956 **(33)**; Rip It Up, 1956 **(17)**; Ready Teddy, 1956 **(44)**; The Girl Can't Help It, 1957 **(49)**; Lucille, 1957 **(21)**; Send Me Some Lovin', 1957 **(54)**; Jenny, Jenny, 1957 **(10)**; Miss Ann, 1957 **(56)**; Keep a Knockin', 1957 **(8)**; Good Golly, Miss Molly, 1958 **(10)**; Ooh! My Soul, 1958 **(31)**; True, Fine Mama, 1958 **(68)**; Baby Face, 1958 **(41)**; Kansas City, 1959 **(95)**; He's Not Just a Soldier, 1961 **(113)**; Crying in the Chapel, 1963 **(119)**; Bama Lama Bama Loo, 1964 **(82)**; Whole Lotta Shakin' Goin' On, 1964 **(126)**; Goodnight Irene, 1964 **(128)**; I Don't Know What You've Got But It's Got Me—Part 1, 1965 **(92)**; Poor Dog (Who Can't Wag His Own Tail), 1966 **(121)**; Freedom Blues, 1970 **(47)**; Greenwood Mississippi, 1970 **(85)**; Call My Name, 1976 **(106)**; Great Gosh a'Mighty! (It's a Matter of Time), 1986 **(42)**

R & B/Rock—Georgia; real name is Richard Penniman

Liverpool Scene

Personnel: Adrian Henri (vocals); Andy Roberts (guitars, vocals); Roger McGough (guitars, vocals) replaced (1968) by Mike Evans (saxophones, vocals); Mike Hart (guitars, vocals); Percy Jones (bass) replaced (1972) by Dave Richards (bass); Brian Dodson (drums) replaced (1972) by Mike Kellie (drums)

Albums: Incredible New Liverpool Scene, 1967; Amazing Adventures of Liverpool Scene, 1968;

Bread of the Night, 1969; St. Adrian & Co., 1969; Heirloom, 1970; Recollections, 1972
   Pop Rock — British

Lollipop Shoppe

Personnel: Fred Cole (vocals); Ron Buzzel (guitars, vocals); Ed Bowen (guitars, vocals); Bob Atkins (bass); John the Greek (keyboards); Tim Rockson (drums)
   Album: Just Colour, 1967
   Single: You Must Be a Witch, 1967
   Psychedelic Pop — American

Jackie Lomax

Albums: Is This What You Want?, 1969; Home Is in My Head, 1971; Three, 1972; Livin' for Lovin', 1976; Did You Ever Have That Feeling?, 1977
   Singles: Sour Milk Sea, 1968 **(117)**; The Eagle Laughs at You, 1968 **(125)**
   Pop Vocal — British; became a member of Badger

Laurie London

Single: He's Got the Whole World (in His Hands), 1958 **(1)**
   Pop Vocal — British

Shorty Long

Singles: Devil with the Blue Dress, 1964 **(125)**; Function at the Junction, 1966 **(97)**; Night Fo' Last, 1968 **(75)**; Here Comes the Judge, 1968 **(8)**
   Soul Vocal — Alabama; Shorty drowned in June, 1969

Long Island Sound

Personnel: Tony Pragano (vocals); Angelo Frisketti (guitars); Tom Hanlon (guitars); Fred O'Brien (bass); Bob Pasternak (organ); Jack Russell (drums)
   Album: Long Island Sound, 1966
   Single: 1, 2, 3 and I Fell, 1966
   Folk/Rock — Connecticut

Trini Lopez

Albums: Trini Lopez at PJ's, 1963; More Trini Lopez at PJ's, 1963; On the Move, 1964; The Latin Album, 1964; Live at Basin St. East, 1964; The Folk Album, 1965; The Love Album, 1965; The Rhythm & Blues Album, 1965; The Sing-Along World of Trini Lopez, 1966; The Second Latin Album, 1966; Greatest Hits!, 1966; Trini Lopez in London, 1967; Trini Lopez — Now!, 1967
   Singles: If I Had a Hammer, 1963 **(3)**; Kansas City, 1963 **(23)**; Jailer, Bring Me Water, 1964 **(94)**; What

Have I Got of My Own, 1964 **(43)**;
Michael, 1964 **(42)**; Sinner Not a
Saint, 1964 **(103)**; Lemon Tree, 1965
(20); Sad Tomorrows, 1965 **(94)**;
Are You Sincere, 1965 **(85)**; Sinner
Man, 1965 **(54)**; Made in Paris,
1966 **(113)**; I'm Comin' Home,
Cindy, 1966 **(39)**; La Bamba—
Part 1, 1966 **(86)**; Gonna Get
Along Without Ya' Now, 1967 **(93)**;
Up to Now, 1967 **(123)**; Sally Was a
Good Old Girl, 1968 **(99)**; Come a
Little Bit Closer, 1969 **(121)**; Don't
Let the Sun Catch You Cryin', 1969
(133)

Pop/Folk Vocal—Dallas; full
name is Trinidad Lopez, III

Los Bravos

Personnel: Michael Kogel (gui-
tars, vocals); Antonio Martinez (gui-
tars); Miguel Vicens Danus (bass);
Manuel Fernandez (keyboards);
Pablo Sanllehi (drums)
Albums: Los Bravos, 1966; Bring
a Little Lovin', 1968; Black Is Black,
1974
Singles: Black Is Black, 1966 **(4)**;
Going Nowhere, 1966 **(91)**; Bring a
Little Lovin', 1968 **(51)**
Psychedelic Rock—Spain; Kogel
recorded under the name Mike
Kennedy in the 1970s

Los Pop Tops

Personnel: Phil Tris (vocals)
Singles: Oh Lord, Why Lord,
1968 **(78)**; Mammy Blue, 1971
(57)
Pop/Rock—Spain

Lothar & The Hand People

Personnel: John Emelin (vocals);
Kim King (guitars); Rusty Ford
(bass); Paul Conley (keyboards);
Tom Flye (drums)
Albums: Presenting Lothar & The
Hand People, 1968; Space Hymn,
1969
Psychedelic Rock—American

John D. Loudermilk

Albums: Language of Love, 1961;
12 Sides of J. D. Loudermilk, 1962;
Sings a Bizarre Collection of the
Most Unusual Songs, 1966; Subur-
ban Attitudes, 1967; Country Love
Songs, 1968; The Open Mind of
J. D. Loudermilk, 1969; Elloree
Volume 1, 1971; Best of J. D.
Loudermilk, 1973; Encores,
1975; Just Passing Through,
1978
Singles: Sittin' in the Balcony,
1957 **(38)**; Language of Love,
1961 **(32)**; Thou Shalt Not Steal,
1962 **(73)**; Callin' Doctor Casey,
1962 **(83)**; Road Hog, 1962 **(65)**;
Blue Train (of the Heartbreak
Line), 1964 **(132)**; Tobacco Road,
1965
Country/Pop—North Carolina;
recorded first hit under the name
Johnny Dee

Darlene Love

Singles: (Today I Met) The
Boy I'm Gonna Marry, 1963 **(39)**;
Wait Til' My Bobby Gets Home,
1963 **(26)**; A Fine Fine Boy, 1963
(53)
Pop Vocal—Philadelphia

Love

Maclean, Forssi, Lee, Echols, Pfisterer

Personnel: Arthur Lee (guitars, vocals); Bryan Maclean (guitars, vocals) replaced (1969) by Paul Martin (guitars); John Echols (guitars) replaced (1969) by Jay Donnellan (guitars) replaced (1969) by Gary Rowles (guitars); Ken Forssi (bass) replaced (1969) by Frank Fayad (bass); Don Conka (percussion) replaced (1966) by Michael Stuart (drums, percussion) replaced (1969) by Drachen Theaker (drums); Tjay Cantrelli (percussion) left group, 1967; Alban "Snoopy" Pfisterer (drums, keyboards) replaced (1969) by George Suranovich (drums)
Albums: Love, 1966; Da Capo, 1967; Forever Changes, 1967; Four Sail, 1969; Out Here, 1969; Love Revisited, 1970; False Start, 1970; Love Masters, 1972; Real to Real, 1974; Best of Love, 1980; Love Live, 1981
Singles: My Little Red Book, 1966 **(52)**; 7 and 7 Is, 1966 **(33)**; Alone Again Or, 1968 **(123)**; Alone Again Or, 1970 **(99)**
Psychedelic Rock—L.A.

Love Exchange

Album: Love Exchange, 1967
Single: Swallow the Sun, 1967
Folk/Rock—American

Love Sculpture

Personnel: Dave Edmunds (guitars, keyboards, vocals); John Williams (bass, vocals, keyboards); Bob Jones (drums, vocals)
Albums: Blues Helping, 1968; Forms and Feelings, 1969; Classic Tracks, 1974; Singles, 1980
Pub Rock—British

The Lovers

Personnel: Alden Bunn (vocals; deceased 1977); Anna Sandford (vocals)
Single: Darling It's Wonderful, 1957 **(48)**
R & B Vocal—North Carolina

The Lovin' Spoonful

Personnel: John Sebastian (guitars, vocals, harmonica); Zalman Yanovksy (guitars) replaced (1967) by Jerry Yester (guitars); John Boone (bass); Joe Butler (drums) replaced (1970) by Glen Cove (drums)
Albums: Do You Believe in Magic, 1965; Daydreams, 1966;

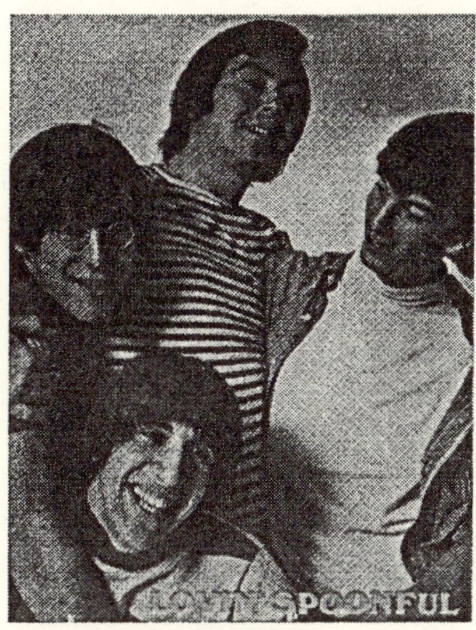

The Lovin' Spoonful: Sebastian, Yanovksy, Boone, Butler

What's Up Tiger Lilly, 1966; Hums, 1966; Best of Volume 1, 1967; You're a Big Boy Now, 1967; Everything Plaything, 1967; Best of Volume 2, 1968; Revelation Revolution, 1968; The Very Best of Lovin' Spoonful, 1969; Greatest Hits, 1970; More Golden Spoonful, 1974; Anthology, 1980

Singles: Do You Believe in Magic, 1965 **(9)**; You Didn't Have to Be So Nice, 1965 **(10)**; Daydream, 1966 **(2)**; Did You Ever Have to Make Up Your Mind, 1966 **(2)**; Summer in the City, 1966 **(1)**; Rain on the Roof, 1966 **(10)**; Nashville Cats, 1966 **(8)**; Full Measure, 1967 **(87)**; Darling Be Home Soon, 1967 **(15)**; Six o'Clock, 1967 **(18)**; She's Still a Mystery, 1967 **(27)**; Money, 1968 **(48)**; Never Going Back, 1968 **(73)**; (Till I) Run with You, 1968 **(128)**; Me About You, 1969 **(91)**

Pop/Rock—New York

Jim Lowe

Singles: Close the Door, 1955 **(42)**; The Green Door, 1956 **(1)**; By You, By You, By You, 1957 **(43)**; I Feel the Beat, 1957 **(84)**; Four Walls, 1957 **(15)**; Talkin' to the Blues, 1957 **(20)**; Hootenanny Granny, 1963 **(103)**

R & B Vocal—Missouri; former New York City D.J.

Trevor Lucas

Album: Overlander, 1966

Folk/Rock—British; member of Fairport Convention Eclection and Fotheringay

Robin Luke

Album: Susie Darlin', 1958
Single: Susie Darlin', 1958 **(5)**
Pop Vocal—Los Angeles

Lulu

Albums: Something to Shout About, 1965; Lulu, 1967; To Sir with Love, 1967; Love Loves to Love Lulu, 1967; Lulu's Album,

1969; World of Lulu, 1969; It's Lulu, 1970; New Routes, 1970; Melody Fair, 1970; Make Believe World, 1973; Don't Take Our Love for Granted, 1979; Boy, 1980; Lulu, 1981; Take Me to Your Heart Again, 1982; Shout, 1983

Singles: Shout, 1964 **(94)**; I'll Come Running, 1964 **(105)**; The Boat That I Row, 1967 **(115)**; To Sir with Love, 1967 **(1)**; Shout, 1967 **(96)**; Best of Both Worlds, 1967 **(32)**; Me, the Peaceful Heart, 1968 **(53)**; Boy, 1968 **(108)**; Morning Dew, 1968 **(52)**; Oh Me Oh My (I'm a Fool for You Baby), 1969 **(22)**; Hum a Song (from Your Heart), 1970 **(54)**; After the Feeling Is Gone, 1970 **(117)**; I Could Never Miss You (More Than I Do), 1981 **(18)**; If I Were You, 1981 **(44)**

Pop Vocal—Scotland; real name is Marie McDonald McLaughlin Lawrie; appeared in the film *To Sir with Love;* was formerly married to Bee Gee Maurice Gibb

Bob Luman

Albums: Let's Think About Living, 1960; Ain't Got Time, 1968; Come on Home, 1969; Getting Back to Nora, 1970; Is It Any Wonder That I Love You, 1971; A Chain Don't Take to Me, 1971; Livin' Lovin' Sounds, 1971; When You Say Love, 1972; Lonely Women Make Good Lovers, 1972; Bob Luman, 1973; Neither One of Us, 1973; Greatest Hits, 1974; Red Cadillac & Black Mustache, 1975; A Satisfied Mind, 1976; Alive and Well, 1977; The Pay Phone, 1978; The Rockers, 1979; More of the Rockers, 1979; Still Rockin', 1984

Singles: Let's Think About Living, 1960 **(7)**; Oh, Lonesome Me, 1960 **(105)**; Why, Why, Bye, Bye, 1960 **(106)**

Rockabilly—Texas; died in 1978

Arthur Lyman

Albums: Taboo, 1958; Yellow Bird, 1961; I Wish You Love, 1963

Singles: Taboo, 1959 **(55)**; Yellow Bird, 1961 **(4)**; Love for Sale, 1963 **(43)**; Cotton Fields, 1963 **(129)**

Instrumental Pop—Hawaii

Lyme & Cybelle

Personnel: Tule Livingston (vocals); Warren Zevon (guitars, vocals)

Album: Lyme & Cybelle, 1966

Singles: Follow Me, 1966 **(65)**; Like the Seasons, 1966

Pop Vocal—American

Frankie Lymon & The Teenagers

Personnel: Frankie Lymon (vocals; deceased 1968); Herman Santiago (vocals); Jimmy Merchant (vocals); Joe Negroni (vocals; deceased 1978); Sherman Garnes (vocals; deceased 1977)

Albums: Why Do Fools Fall in Love, 1956; Teenagers, 1957; Rock 'n' Roll Party, 1959; At the London Palladium, 1960; Greatest Hits, 1961

Singles: Why Do Fools Fall in Love, 1956 **(6)**; I Want You to Be My Girl, 1956 **(13)**; I Promise to Remember/Who Can Explain?, 1956 **(57)**; The ABC's of Love, 1956 **(77)**; Goody Goody, 1957 **(20)**; Little Bitty Pretty One, 1960 **(58)**

R & B Vocal—New York

Barbara Lynn

Albums: You'll Lose a Good Thing, 1962; Here Is Barbara Lynn, 1963

Singles: You'll Lose a Good Thing, 1962 **(8)**; Second Fiddle Girl, 1962 **(63)**; You're Gonna Need Me, 1962 **(65)**; Don't Be Cruel, 1963 **(93)**; To Love or Not to Love, 1963 **(135)**; (I Cried at) Laura's Wedding, 1963 **(68)**; Oh! Baby (We Got a Good Thing Goin'), 1964 **(69)**; Don't Spread It Around, 1964 **(93)**; It's Better to Have It, 1965 **(95)**; I'm a Good Woman, 1966 **(129)**; You Left the Water Running, 1966 **(110)**; This Is the Thanks I Get, 1968 **(65)**

R & B Vocal—Texas; full name is Barbara Lynn Ozen

MC5

Personnel: Rob Tyner (vocals, harmonica; deceased 1991); Wayne Kramer (guitars, vocals, keyboards); Fred "Sonic" Smith (guitars, vocals, keyboards); Mike Davis (bass, vocals); Dennis Thompson (drums, vocals)

Albums: Kick Out the Jams, 1969; Back in the USA, 1970; High Time, 1971; Babes in Arms, 1983

Single: Kick Out the Jams, 1969 **(82)**

Hard Rock—Detroit; MC5 is an abbreviation for Motor City 5

M.F.Q.

Personnel: Cyrus Farrar (guitars, vocals); Jerry Yester (guitars, vocals); Chip Douglas (bass, keyboards); Henry Diltz (banjo, guitars); Jim Copley (drums)

Album: M.F.Q., 1966

Singles: Nighttime Girl, 1966 **(122)**; This Could Be the Night, 1966

Folk/Rock—American

Modern Folk Quintet

Bobby McClure

Singles: Don't Mess Up a Good Thing, 1965 **(33)** (with Fontella Bass); You'll Miss Me (When I'm Gone), 1965 **(91)** (with Fontella Bass); Peak of Love, 1966 **(97)**

R & B Vocal—E. St. Louis

The McCoys

Personnel: Rick Zehringer (guitars, vocals); Bobby Peterson (keyboards) replaced (1967) by Ronnie Brandon (keyboards); Randy Jo Hobbs (bass); Randy Zehringer (drums)

Albums: Hang On Sloopy, 1965; You Make Me Feel So Good, 1966; Infinite McCoys, 1968; Human Ball, 1968

Singles: Hang On Sloopy, 1965 **(1)**; Fever, 1965 **(7)**; Up and Down, 1966 **(46)**; Come On Let's Go, 1966 **(22)**; You Make Me Feel So Good, 1966 **(53)**; Don't Worry Mother, Your Son's Heart Is Pure, 1966 **(67)**; I Got to Go Back (and Watch That Little Girl Dance), 1966 **(69)**;

Beat the Clock, 1967 **(92)**; Jesse Brady, 1968 **(98)**

Pop/Rock—Indiana; Rick Zehringer changed his last name to Derringer

Jimmy McCracklin

Albums: Jimmy McCracklin Sings, 1959; I Just Gotta Know, 1961; Twist with Jimmy McCracklin, 1962; Best of Jimmy McCracklin, 1963; Singer Man, 1964; Every Night, Every Day, 1965; Think, 1965; My Answer, 1966; New Soul of Jimmy McCracklin, 1967; Let's Get Together, 1968; Yesterday Is Gone, 1972

Singles: The Walk, 1958 **(7)**; Just Got to Know, 1961 **(64)**; Every Night, Every Day, 1965 **(91)**; Arkansas (Part 1), 1965 **(132)**; Think, 1965 **(95)**; My Answer, 1966 **(92)**; The Dog, 1966 **(112)**; Get Together, 1968 **(114)**

R & B Vocal—St. Louis

Gene McDaniels

Singles: A Hundred Pounds of Clay, 1961 **(3)**; A Tear, 1961 **(31)**; Tower of Strength, 1961 **(5)**; Chip Chip, 1962 **(10)**; Funny, 1962 **(99)**; Point of No Return, 1962 **(21)**; Spanish Lace, 1962 **(31)**; It's a Lonely Town (Lonely Without You), 1963 **(64)**

R & B Vocal—Kansas City

Chas. McDevitt

Single: Freight Train, 1957 **(40)** (with Nancy Wiskey)

Skiffle—British

McDonald & Giles

Personnel: Ian McDonald (keyboards, woodwinds, vocals); Peter Giles (bass, vocals); Michael Giles (drums, percussion)

Album: McDonald & Giles, 1969

Art Rock—British

Barry McGuire

Albums: Eve of Destruction, 1965; This Precious Time, 1966; World's Last Private Citizen, 1968; Barry McGuire & the Doctor, 1971; Seeds, 1974; Narnia, 1974; Lighten Up, 1975; To the Bride, 1976; C'mon Along, 1976; Have You Heard, 1976; Jubilation, 1977; Cosmic Cowboy, 1979; Inside Out, 1980; Finer Than Gold, 1981; Best of Barry, 1982

Singles: Eve of Destruction, 1965 **(1)**; Child of Our Times, 1965 **(72)**; Upon a Painted Ocean, 1965 **(117)**; Cloudy Summer Afternoon (Raindrops), 1966 **(62)**

Folk/Pop—Oklahoma

Lonnie Mack

Albums: The Wham of That Memphis Man, 1964; Glad I'm in the Band, 1969; Whatever's Right, 1969; The Hills of Indiana, 1972; Home at Last, 1977; Lonnie Mack with Pismo, 1978; Strike Like Lightning, 1985

Singles: Memphis, 1963 **(5)**; Wham!, 1963 **(24)**; Baby, What's Wrong, 1963 **(93)**; Where There's a Will, 1963 **(113)**; Lonnie on the Move, 1964 **(117)**; I've Had It, 1964 **(128)**; Honky Tonk '65, 1965 **(78)**

Instrumental Blues—Indiana

Scott McKenzie

Albums: The Voice of Scott Mc-
Kenzie, 1967; Stained Glass Morn-
ing, 1968
Singles: San Francisco (Be Sure to
Wear Flowers in Your Hair), 1967
(4); Look in Your Eyes, 1967 **(111)**;
Like an Old Time Movie, 1967
(24); Holy Man, 1968 **(126)**
　Folk/Rock — Florida; real name is
Philip Blondheim

Tommy McLain

Single: Sweet Dreams, 1966 **(15)**
Pop Vocal — Louisiana

Phil McLean

Single: Small Sad Sam, 1961 **(21)**
Novelty Pop — Detroit

Big Jay McNeely

Albums: Big Jay in 3D, 1961; Live
at Cisco's, 1963
Single: There Is Something on
Your Mind, 1959 **(44)** (with Little
Sonny Warner)
R & B — Los Angeles

Clyde McPhatter

Albums: Clyde McPhatter & the
Drifters, 1957; Love Ballads, 1958;
Clyde, 1959; Let's Start Over, 1960;
Ta Ta, 1960; Golden Blues Hits,
1960; Greatest Hits, 1961; Lover
Please, 1961; Rhythm and Soul,
1962; Best of Clyde McPhatter,
1963; Greatest Hits, 1963; Songs of
the Big City, 1964; Live at the
Apollo, 1964; May I Sing for You,
1966; 18 Original Hits, 1967; Wel-
come Home, 1971
Singles: Seven Days, 1956 **(44)**;
Treasure of Love, 1956 **(16)**; With-

out Love (There Is Nothing), 1957
(19); Just to Hold My Hand, 1957
(26); Long Lonely Nights, 1957
(49); Rock and Cry, 1957 **(93)**;
Come What May, 1958 **(43)**; A
Lover's Question, 1958 **(6)**; Lovey
Dovey, 1959 **(49)**; I Told Myself a
Lie, 1959 **(70)**; Since You've Been
Gone, 1959 **(38)**; Twice as Nice,
1959 **(91)**; You Went Back on Your
Word, 1959 **(72)**; Let's Try Again,
1959 **(48)**; Just Give Me a Ring,
1960 **(96)**; Think Me a Kiss, 1960
(66); Ta Ta, 1960 **(23)**; Tomorrow
Is a-Comin', 1961 **(103)**; I'll Love
You Till the Cows Come Home,
1961 **(110)**; I Never Knew, 1961 **(56)**;
Lover Please, 1962 **(7)**; Little Bitty
Pretty One, 1962 **(25)**; The Best
Man Cried, 1962 **(118)**; From One
to One, 1963 **(127)**; Deep in the
Heart of Harlem, 1964 **(90)**; Crying
Won't Help You Now, 1965 **(117)**
　R & B Vocal — North Carolina;
died from a heart attack in 1972

The Mad Lads

Personnel: John Gary Williams
(vocals) replaced (1966) by Sam Nelson (vocals); Robert Phillips (vocals); William Brown (vocals) replaced (1966) by Quincy Clifton
Billops, Jr. (vocals); Julius Green
(vocals)
Album: The Mad, Mad, Mad,
Mad, Mad Lads, 1969
Singles: Don't Have to Shop
Around, 1965 **(93)**; I Want Someone, 1966 **(74)**; By the Time I Get
to Phoenix, 1969 **(84)**
　R & B Vocal — American

Mad River

Personnel: Tom Manning (vocals); Rick Bochner (guitars); David

Robinson (guitars); Lawrence Hammond (bass, keyboards, vocals); Greg Dewey (drums, harmonica, vocals)

Albums: Mad River (EP), 1967; Mad River, 1968; Paradise Bar & Grill, 1969

Pop/Rock—American

Betty Madigan

Singles: There Should Be Rules (Protecting Fools Who Fall in Love), 1955 **(54)**; True Love Gone (Come on Home), 1957 **(78)**; Dance Everyone Dance, 1958 **(31)**

Pop Vocal—Washington, D.C.

Johnny Maestro

Singles: Model Girl, 1961 **(20)**; What a Surprise, 1961 **(33)**; Mr. Happiness, 1961 **(57)** (with the Coeds)

Pop Vocal—New York; real name is John Mastrangelo; lead singer of Brooklyn Bridge and the Crests

Magic Lanterns

Personnel: Bev Beverage (guitars, vocals); Peter Garner (guitars, vocals); Mike Osborne (bass, vocals); Jimmy Bilsbury (piano, vocals) replaced (1971) by Albert Hammond (keyboards, vocals); Harry Paul Ward (drums, vocals)

Albums: Shame, Shame, 1969; Magic Lanterns, 1971

Singles: Shame, Shame, 1968 **(29)**; One Night Stand, 1971 **(74)**; Let the Sunshine In, 1971 **(103)**; Country Woman, 1972 **(88)**

Pop/Rock—British

The Magic Mushrooms

Single: It's-a-Happening, 1966 **(93)**

Hard Rock—American

The Magicians

Personnel: Allan "Jake" Jacobs (guitars); Gary Bonner (guitars); Jerry Burnham (bass, vocals); Alan Gordon (drums)

Single: Invitation to Cry, 1966

Psychedelic Pop—American

Taj Mahal

Albums: Taj Mahal, 1967; The Natch'l Blues, 1969; Giant Step/De Ole Folks at Home, 1969; The Real Thing, 1971; Happy Just to Be Like I Am, 1972; Recyling the Blues & Other Related Stuff, 1972; Sounder (Soundtrack), 1972; Oooh So Good 'n' Blues, 1973; Mo Roots, 1974; Music Keeps Me Together, 1975; Satisfied 'n' Tickled Too, 1976; Anthology Volume 1 1966/76, 1976; Music fuh Ya' (Musica para Tu), 1977; Brothers, 1977; Evolution, 1978; Taj Mahal & the International Rhythm Band Live, 1979; Taj Mahal & the International Rhythm Band, 1980; Going Home, 1980; Live, 1981; Like Never Before, 1991

Single: Don't Call Us (We'll Call You), 1991

Blues/Rock—New York; real name is Henry St. Clair Fredericks

George Maharis

Albums: George Maharis Sings!, 1962; Portrait in Music, 1962; Just Turn Me Loose!, 1963; Where Can You Go for a Broken Heart?, 1963

Singles: Teach Me Tonight, 1962

(25); After the Lights Go Down Low, 1962 **(104)**; They Knew About You, 1962 **(111)**; Love Me As I Love You, 1962 **(54)**; Baby Has Gone Bye Bye, 1962 **(62)**; Don't Fence Me In, 1963 **(93)**; Where Can You Go (For a Broken Heart), 1963 **(102)**; That's How It Goes, 1963 **(88)**

Pop Vocal—New York; star of TV's "Route 66" and many film and TV projects

The Majors

Personnel: Ricky Cordo (vocals); Eugene Glass (vocals); Ronald Gathers (vocals); Frank Troutt (vocals); Idella Morris (vocals)

Albums: A Wonderful Dream, 1962; Anything You Can Do, 1963

Singles: A Wonderful Dream, 1962 **(22)**; A Little Bit Now (A Little Bit Later), 1962 **(63)**; She's a Troublemaker, 1962 **(83)**; Anything You Can Do, 1963 **(117)**; Your Life Begins (at Sweet 16), 1963 **(125)**; I'll Be There (to Bring You Love), 1964 **(113)**

R & B Vocal—Philadelphia

The Mamas & The Papas

Personnel: John Phillips (guitars, vocals); Denny Doherty (guitars, vocals); Michelle Phillips (vocals) replaced (1987) by Mackenzie Phillips (vocals); "Mama" Cass Elliott (vocals; deceased 1974) replaced

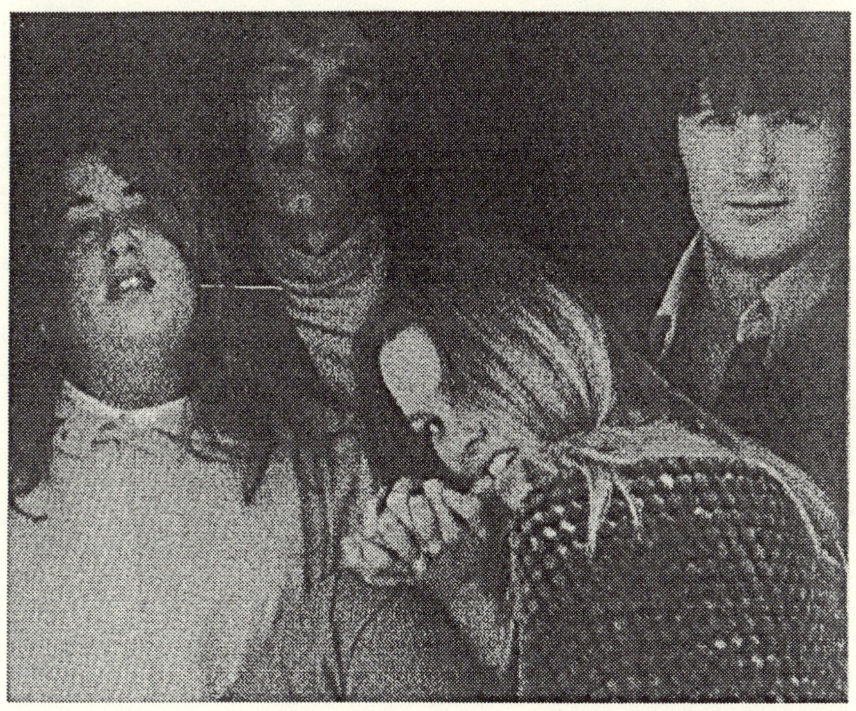

The Mamas & The Papas: Elliott, J. Phillips, M. Phillips, Doherty

(1987) by Elaine "Spanky" McFarlane (vocals)

Albums: If You Can Believe Your Eyes, 1966; Cass, John, Michelle & Denny, 1966; Deliver, 1967; Book of Songs, 1967; Farewell to the First Golden Era, 1968; Papas & Mamas, 1968; Golden Era Volume 2, 1968; Hits of Gold, 1969; 16 of the Greatest, 1969; A Gathering of Flowers, 1970; Monterrey Int'l Pop Festival, 1971; People Like Us, 1972; 20 Golden Hits, 1972; Best of the Mamas & the Papas, 1982

Singles: California Dreaming, 1966 **(4)**; Monday Monday, 1966 **(1)**; I Saw Her Again, 1966 **(5)**; Look Through My Window, 1966 **(24)**; Words of Love/Dancing in the Street, 1966 **(5)**; Dedicated to the One I Love, 1967 **(2)**; Creeque Alley, 1967 **(5)**; Twelve Thirty, 1967 **(20)**; Straight Shooter, 1967 **(130)**; Glad to Be Unhappy, 1967 **(26)**; Hey Girl, 1967 **(134)**; The Dancing Bear, 1967 **(51)**; Safe in My Garden, 1968 **(53)**; For the Love of Ivy, 1968 **(81)**; Do You Wanna Dance, 1968 **(76)**; Step Out, 1972 **(81)**

Folk/Pop—New York; Michelle Phillips has starred in TV's "Knots Landing"; daughter Chynna is part of Wilson Phillips

Mandala

Personnel: Roy Kenner (vocals); George Oliver (vocals); Domenic Troiano (guitars, vocals); Don Elliott (bass); Josef Chirowski (keyboards); Hugh Sullivan (keyboards); Pentti Whitey Glan (drums)

Album: Soul Crusade, 1968
Hard Rock—American

Harvey Mandel

Albums: Cristo Redentor, 1968; Righteous, 1969; Games Guitars Play, 1970; Baby Batter, 1971; Electronic Progress, 1971; Get Off in Chicago, 1972; The Snake, 1972; Shangrenade, 1973; Feel the Sound of Harvey Mandel, 1974; The Best of Harvey Mandel, 1975

Blues/Rock—American; former member of Canned Heat

Mandrake Memorial

Personnel: Craig Anderton (guitars); Randy Monaco (bass, vocals); Michael Kac (keyboards, vocals); Kevin Lally (drums)

Albums: Mandrake Memorial, 1968; Medium, 1969; Puzzle, 1970
Psychedelic Pop—American

The Manhattans

Personnel: Blue Lovett (vocals); Sonny Bivens (vocals); Kenny Kelly (vocals); Ricky Taylor (vocals); George Smith (vocals; deceased 1970) replaced (1970) by Gerry Alston (vocals)

Albums: Dedicated, 1965; For You and Yours, 1966; With These Hands, 1970; Million to One, 1972; There's No Me Without You, 1973; That's How Much I Love You, 1974; Manhattans, 1976; I Wanna Be Your Everything, 1976; It Feels So Good, 1978; There's No Good in Goodbye, 1978; Love Talk, 1979; After Midnight, 1980; Greatest Hits, 1980; Black Tie, 1981; Forever by Your Side, 1983

Singles: I Wanna Be Your Everything, 1964 **(68)**; Searchin' for My Baby, 1965 **(135)**; I'm the One Love Forgot, 1965 **(135)**; Follow Your Heart, 1966 **(92)**; Baby I Need You,

1966 **(96)**; I Bet'cha (Couldn't Love Me More), 1966 **(128)**; I Call It Love, 1967 **(96)**; If My Heart Could Speak, 1970 **(98)**; From Atlanta to Goodbye, 1970 **(113)**; A Million to One, 1972 **(114)**; One Life to Live, 1972 **(102)**; Back Up, 1973 **(107)**; There's No Me Without You, 1973 **(43)**; You'd Better Believe It, 1973 **(77)**; Don't Take Your Love, 1974 **(37)**; Hurt, 1975 **(97)**; Kiss and Say Goodbye, 1976 **(1)**; I Kinda Miss You, 1976 **(46)**; It Feels So Good to Be Loved So Bad, 1977 **(66)**; We Never Danced to a Love Song, 1977 **(93)**; Am I Losing You, 1978 **(101)**; Shining Star, 1980 **(5)**; Girl of My Dreams, 1980; I'll Never Find Another (Find Another Like You), 1980 **(109)**; Do You Really Mean Goodbye, 1981; Let Your Love Come Down, 1981; Honey Honey, 1982; Crazy, 1983 **(72)**; You Send Me, 1985 **(81)**

Soul/Pop Vocal—New Jersey; Smith died in 1970 from spinal meningitis

Carl Mann

Singles: Mona Lisa, 1959 **(25)**; Pretend, 1959 **(57)**

Rockabilly—Tennessee

Gloria Mann

Singles: Earth Angel (Will You Be Mine), 1955 **(18)**; Teen Age Prayer, 1955 **(19)**; Why Do Fools Fall in Love?, 1956 **(59)**

Pop Vocal—American; Gloria's son Bob Rosenberg leads the group Will to Power

Manfred Mann

Personnel: Manfred Mann (vocals, keyboards); Paul Jones (vocals) replaced (1968) by Mike D'Abo (vocals); Tom McGuinness (bass, guitars); Michael Vickers (guitars) replaced (1965) by Jack Bruce (bass, vocals) replaced (1967) by Klaus Voorman (bass) replaced (1968) by Dave Richmond (bass); Michael Hugg (drums)

Albums: Manfred Mann Album, 1964; Five Faces of Manfred Mann, 1964; Mann Made, 1964; My Little Red Book of Winners, 1965; Mann Made Hits, 1966; Pretty Flamingo, 1966; As Is, 1966; Greatest Hits, 1966; Soul of Mann, 1967; Up the Junction, 1968; Mighty Garvey, 1968; What a Man, 1968; Mighty Quinn, 1968; Manfred Mann Chapter Three, 1969; Chapter Three, Volume Two, 1970; This Is Manfred Mann, 1971

Singles: Do Wah Diddy Diddy, 1964 **(1)**; Sha La La, 1964 **(12)**; Come Tomorrow, 1965 **(50)**; My Little Red Book, 1965 **(124)**; Pretty Flamingo, 1966 **(29)**; Just Like a Woman, 1966 **(101)**; The Mighty Quinn, 1968 **(10)**; My Name Is Jack, 1968 **(104)**; Fox on the Run, 1969 **(97)**

Pop/Rock—British; Mann's real name is Michael Lubowitz; from South Africa; later formed Manfred Mann's Earth Band

The Marathons

Single: Peanut Butter, 1961 **(20)**

R & B Vocal—American

The Marcels

Personnel: Cornelius Harp (vocals); Fred Johnson (vocals); Ronald Mundy (vocals); Gene Bricker (vocals); Dick Knauss (vocals)

Album: Blue Moon, 1961
Singles: Blue Moon, 1961 **(1)**;
Summertime, 1961 **(78)**; Heartaches,
1961 **(7)**; My Melancholy Baby, 1962
(58); Twistin' Fever, 1962 **(103)**
R & B Vocal — Pittsburgh

Little Peggy March

Album: I Will Follow Him, 1963
Singles: I Will Follow Him, 1963
(1); I Wish I Were a Princess, 1963
(32); Hello Heartache, Goodbye
Love, 1963 **(26)**; The Impossible
Happened, 1963 **(57)**; (I'm Watching) Every Little Move You Make,
1964 **(84)**
Pop Vocal — Pennsylvania; real
name is Margaret Battavio; she was
only 15 when "I Will Follow Him"
hit #1; dropped "Little" when she
turned 16

Bobby Marchan

Singles: There's Something on
Your Mind, Part 2, 1960 **(31)**; I've
Got a Thing Going On, 1964 **(116)**
R & B Vocal — Ohio

Ernie Maresca

Single: Shout! Shout! Knock
Yourself Out, 1962 **(6)**
Pop Vocal — New York

The Mark IV

Singles: (Make With) The Shake,
1958 **(69)**; I Got a Wife, 1959 **(24)**
Pop/Rock — Chicago

The Marketts

Albums: Out of Limits, 1964; The
Batman Theme, 1966
Singles: Surfer's Stomp, 1962 **(31)**;
Balboa Blue, 1962 **(48)**; Out of
Limits, 1963 **(3)**; Vanishing Point,
1964 **(90)**; Batman Theme, 1966 **(17)**
Surf Rock — California

The Mar-Keys

Personnel: Steve Cropper (gui-
tars); Donald "Duck" Dunn (bass);
Jerry Lee "Smoochie" Smith (piano);
Charles "Pack" Axton (saxophones);
Don Nix (saxophones); Wayne Jack-
son (trumpet); Terry Johnson
(drums)
Albums: The Mar-Keys, 1961; Do
the People, 1962; Great Memphis
Sound, 1965; Back to Back, 1965;
Damnifiknew, 1969; Memphis
Horns, 1970; Memphis Experience,
1970; High on Music, 1976
Singles: Last Night, 1961 **(3)**;
Morning After, 1961 **(60)**; Pop-Eye
Stroll, 1962 **(94)**; Banana Juice, 1965
(121); Grab This Thing, Part 1, 1965
(111); Philly Dog, 1966 **(89)**
Soul/Rock — Memphis

Pigmeat Markham

Album: Here Comes the Judge,
1968
Singles: Here Comes the Judge,
1968 **(19)**; Sock It to 'em Judge, 1968
(103)
Novelty Pop — North Carolina;
real first name was Dewey; died in
1981

Martha & The Vandellas

Personnel: Martha Reeves (vocals); Annette Sterling (vocals) replaced (1963) by Betty Kelly (vocals)
replaced (1967) by Lois Reeves (vocals); Rosalind Ashford (vocals) replaced (1970) by Sandra Tilley (vocals)

Albums: Heat Wave, 1963; Dance Party, 1965; Greatest Hits, 1966; Watchout!, 1967; Martha & the Vandellas Live!, 1967; Ridin' High, 1968; Black Magic, 1972; Anthology, 1974

Singles: Come and Get These Memories, 1963 **(29)**; Heat Wave, 1963 **(4)**; Quicksand, 1963 **(8)**; Live Wire, 1964 **(42)**; In My Lonely Room, 1964 **(44)**; Dancing in the Street, 1964 **(2)**; Wild One, 1964 **(34)**; Nowhere to Run, 1965 **(8)**; You've Been in Love Too Long, 1965 **(36)**; Love (Makes Me Do Foolish Things), 1965 **(70)**; My Baby Loves Me, 1966 **(22)**; What Am I Going to Do Without Your Love, 1966 **(71)**; I'm Ready for Love, 1966 **(9)**; Jimmy Mack, 1967 **(10)**; Love Bug Leave My Heart Alone, 1967 **(25)**; Honey Chile, 1967 **(11)**; I Promise to Wait My Love, 1968 **(62)**; Forget Me Not, 1968 **(93)**; I Can't Dance to That Music You're Playin', 1968 **(42)**; Sweet Darlin', 1968 **(80)**; (We've Got) Honey Love, 1969 **(56)**; Taking My Love (and Leaving Me), 1969 **(102)**; I Gotta Let You Go, 1970 **(93)**; Bless You, 1971 **(53)**; In and Out of My Life, 1972 **(102)**; Tear It on Down, 1972 **(103)**

Pop/Soul Vocal — Detroit

Bobbi Martin

Albums: Don't Forget I Still Love You, 1965; For the Love of Him, 1970

Singles: Don't Forget I Still Love You, 1964 **(19)**; I Can't Stop Thinking of You, 1965 **(46)**; I Love You So, 1965 **(70)**; I Don't Want to Live (Without Your Love), 1965 **(115)**; Don't Take It Out on Me, 1966 **(119)**; Oh, Lonesome Me, 1966 **(134)**; Harper Valley P.T.A., 1968 **(114)**; For the Love of Him, 1970 **(13)**; Give a Woman Love, 1970 **(97)**; No Love at All, 1971 **(123)**

Pop Vocal — Baltimore; real first name is Barbara

Derek Martin

Single: You Better Go, 1965 **(78)**
Soul Vocal — American

Janis Martin

Single: Will You, Willyum, 1956 **(50)**
Rockabilly — Virginia

John Martyn

Albums: London Conversation, 1967; The Tumbler, 1968; Stormbringer, 1970; The Road to Ruin, 1970; Bless the Weather, 1971; Solid Air, 1973; Inside Out, 1973; Sunday's Child, 1975; Live at Leeds, 1975; So Far So Good, 1976; One World, 1977; Grace and Danger, 1980; Glorious Fool, 1982; The Electric, 1982; Philentropy, 1982; Well Kept Secret, 1983; Sapphire, 1985; Piece by Piece, 1986; Cooltide, 1991

Singles: I Couldn't Love You More, 1982; Piece by Piece, 1986

Folk/Jazz/Rock — Scotland

The Marvelettes

Personnel: Gladys Horton (vocals) replaced (1969) by Anne Bogan (vocals); Georgeanna Dobbins (vocals) left group (1961; deceased 1980); Juanita Cowart (vocals) left group (1961); Wanda Young (vocals) left group (1969); Katherine Anderson (vocals)

Albums: Please Mr. Postman,

1961; Marvelettes Sing, 1962; Playboy, 1963; Marvelous Marvelettes,
1963; Live on Stage, 1965; Greatest
Hits, 1966; The Marvelettes, 1967;
Sophisticated Soul, 1968; In Full
Bloom, 1970; Return of the Marvelettes, 1972; Best of the Marvelettes,
1975; Anthology, 1977

Singles: Please Mr. Postman, 1961
(1); Twistin' Postman, 1962 **(34)**;
Playboy, 1962 **(7)**; Beechwood
4-5789, 1962 **(17)**; Strange I Know,
1962 **(49)**; Locking Up My Heart,
1963 **(44)**; Forever, 1963 **(78)**; My
Daddy Knows Best, 1963 **(67)**; As
Long as I Know He's Mine, 1963
(47); He's a Good Guy (Yes He Is),
1964 **(55)**; You're My Remedy, 1964
(48); Too Many Fish in the Sea,
1964 **(25)**; I'll Keep Holding On,
1965 **(34)**; Danger Heartbreak Dead
Ahead, 1965 **(61)**; Don't Mess with
Bill, 1966 **(7)**; You're the One, 1966
(48); The Hunter Gets Captured by
the Game, 1967 **(13)**; When You're
Young and in Love, 1967 **(23)**; My
Baby Must Be a Magician, 1967
(17); Here I Am Baby, 1968 **(44)**;
What's Easy for Two Is Hard for
One, 1968 **(114)**; Destination: Any-
where, 1968 **(63)**; I'm Gonna Hold
on as Long as I Can, 1969 **(76)**;
That's How Heartaches Are Made,
1969 **(97)**

R & B Vocal—Detroit; Cowart
and Dobbins both left the group due
to illness

The Marvelows

Personnel: Melvin Mason
(vocals); Willie Stevenson (vocals);
Frank Paden (vocals); Johnny Paden
(vocals); added (1964) Jesse Smith
(vocals)

Single: I Do, 1965 **(37)**
R & B Vocal—Chicago

Barbara Mason

Albums: Yes, I'm Ready, 1965;
Give Me Your Love, 1973; Love's
the Thing, 1975

Singles: Yes, I'm Ready, 1965 **(5)**;
Sad, Sad Girl, 1965 **(27)**; If You
Don't (Love Me, Tell Me So), 1965
(85); Is It Me?, 1966 **(97)**; I Need
Love, 1966 **(98)**; Oh, How It Hurts,
1967 **(59)**; (I Can Feel Your Love)
Slipping Away, 1968 **(97)**; Rain-
drops Keep Fallin' on My Head/If
You Knew Him Like I Do, 1970
(112); Bed and Board, 1972 **(70)**;
Give Me Your Love, 1973 **(31)**; Yes,
I'm Ready, 1973 **(125)**; From His
Woman to You, 1974 **(28)**; Shackin'
Up, 1975 **(91)**

Pop Vocal—Philadelphia

The Masqueraders

Personnel: Lee Hatim (vocals);
Robert Wrightsill (vocals); Harold
Thomas (vocals); David Sanders
(vocals); Sammie Hutchins (vocals)

Albums: Everybody Wanna Live
On, 1976; Love Anonymous, 1977

Singles: I Ain't Got to Love Nobody Else, 1968 **(57)**; (Call Me) The
Travelling Man, 1976 **(101)**

Soul Vocal—Texas

Johnny Mathis

Albums: Wonderful Wonderful,
1957; Warm, 1957; Good Night,
Dear Lord, 1958; Johnny's Greatest
Hits, 1958; Swing Softly, 1958;
Merry Christmas, 1958; Open Fire,
Two Guitars, 1959; More Johnny's
Greatest Hits, 1959; Heavenly, 1959;
Faithfully, 1960; Johnny's Mood,
1960; The Rhythms and Ballads of
Broadway, 1960; I'll Buy You a
Star, 1961; Portrait of Johnny, 1961;
Live It Up!, 1962; Rapture, 1962;

Johnny's Newest Hits, 1963; Johnny, 1963; Romantically, 1963; Tender Is the Night, 1964; I'll Search My Heart and Other Great Hits, 1964; The Wonderful World of Make Believe, 1964; The Great Years, 1964; This Is Love, 1964; Love Is Everything, 1965; The Sweetheart Tree, 1965; The Shadow of Your Smile, 1966; So Nice, 1966; Johnny Mathis Sings, 1967; Up, Up and Away, 1967; Love Is Blue, 1968; Those Were the Days, 1968; The Impossible Dream, 1969; People, 1969; Love Theme from *Romeo and Juliet,* 1969; Raindrops Keep Fallin' on My Head, 1970; Close to You, 1970; Johnny Mathis Sings the Music of Bacharach & Kaempfert, 1971; Love Story, 1971; You've Got a Friend, 1971; Johnny Mathis in Person, 1972; The First Time Ever (I Saw Your Face), 1972; Johnny Mathis' All-Time Greatest Hits, 1972; Song Sung Blue, 1972; Me and Mrs. Jones, 1973; Killing Me Softly with Her Song, 1973; I'm Coming Home, 1973; The Heart of a Woman, 1974; When Will I See You Again, 1975; Feelings, 1975; I Only Have Eyes for You, 1976; Mathis Is..., 1977; You Light Up My Life, 1978; That's What Friends Are For, 1978 (with Deniece Williams); The Best Days of My Life, 1979; Different Kinda Different, 1980; The Best of Johnny Mathis 1975–1980, 1980; The First 25 Years—The Silver Anniversary Album, 1981; Friends in Love, 1982; Live, 1983; A Special Part of Me, 1984; Right from the Heart, 1985; Most Requested Songs, 1986; Once in a While, 1987; Love Songs, 1988; In the Still of the Night, 1989

Singles: Wonderful! Wonderful!, 1957 **(14)**; I'ts Not for Me to Say, 1957 **(5)**; Chances Are, 1957 **(1)**; The Twelfth of Never, 1957 **(9)**; No Love (But Your Love), 1957 **(21)**; Wild Is the Wind, 1957 **(22)**; Come to Me, 1958 **(22)**; All the Time, 1958 **(21)**; Teacher, Teacher, 1958 **(21)**; A Certain Smile, 1958 **(14)**; Call Me, 1958 **(21)**; Let's Love, 1959 **(44)**; You Are Beautiful, 1959 **(60)**; Someone, 1959 **(35)**; Small World, 1959 **(20)**; You Are Everything to Me, 1959 **(109)**; Misty, 1959 **(12)**; The Story of Our Love, 1959 **(93)**; The Best of Everything, 1959 **(62)**; Starbright, 1960 **(25)**; Maria, 1960 **(78)**; My Love for You, 1960 **(47)**; How to Handle a Woman, 1960 **(64)**; You Set My Heart to Music, 1961 **(107)**; Jenny, 1961 **(118)**; Wasn't the Summer Short?, 1961 **(89)**; Maria, 1961 **(88)**; Sweet Thursday, 1962 **(99)**; Marianna, 1962 **(86)**; Gina, 1962 **(6)**; What Will Mary Say, 1963 **(9)**; Every Step of the Way, 1963 **(30)**; Sooner or Later, 1963 **(84)**; Come Back, 1963 **(61)**; Your Teenage Dreams, 1963 **(68)**; I'll Search My Heart, 1963 **(90)**; Bye Bye Barbara, 1964 **(53)**; The Fall of Love, 1964 **(120)**; Taste of Tears, 1964 **(87)**; Listen Lonely Girl, 1964 **(62)**; Take the Time, 1965 **(104)**; Sweetheart Tree, 1965 **(108)**; On a Clear Day You Can See Forever, 1965 **(98)**; Venus, 1968 **(111)**; Love Theme from *Romeo and Juliet* (A Time for Us), 1969 **(96)**; Make It Easy on Yourself, 1972 **(103)**; I'm Coming Home, 1973 **(75)**; Life Is a Song Worth Singing, 1973 **(54)**; Too Much, Too Little, Too Late, 1978 **(1)** (with Deniece Williams); You're All I Need to Get By, 1978 **(47)** (with Deniece Williams); Friends in Love, 1982 **(38)** (with Dionne Warwick); Simple, 1984 **(81)**

Pop Vocal—San Francisco

John Mayall's Bluesbreakers

Personnel: John Mayall (guitars, vocals, keyboards); John McVie (bass) replaced (1965) by Jack Bruce (bass, vocals) replaced (1966) by John McVie (bass) replaced (1967) by Paul Williams (bass) replaced (1967) by Keith Tillman (bass) replaced (1968) by Andy Fraser (bass) replaced (1968) by Tony Reeves (bass) replaced (1968) by Steve Thompson (bass) replaced (1970) by Larry Taylor (bass) replaced (1972) by Victor Gaskin (bass) replaced (1977) by Edmond Lee (bass) replaced (1977) by Steve Thompson (bass) replaced (1979) by Bob Babitt (bass) replaced (1979) by Angus Thomas (bass) replaced (1981) by Kevin McCormick (bass) replaced (1982) by Tim Drummond (bass); Davy Graham (guitars) replaced (1963) by Sammie Prosser (guitars) replaced (1963) by Bernie Watson (guitars) replaced (1964) by John Gilbey (guitars) replaced (1964) by Roger Dean (guitars) replaced (1965) by Jeff Kribbit (guitars) replaced (1965) by Eric Clapton (guitars, vocals) replaced (1966) by Peter Green (guitars) replaced (1967) by Mick Taylor (guitars) replaced (1969) by Jon Mark (guitars) replaced (1970) by Harvey Mandel (guitars) replaced (1971) by Jimmy McCulloch (guitars; deceased 1979) replaced (1971) by Jerry McGee (guitars) replaced (1972) by Freddy Robinson (guitars) replaced (1975) by Hightide Harris (guitars) replaced (1975) by Rick Vito (guitars) replaced (1977) by James Smith (guitars) replaced (1979) by Cornell Dupree (guitars) replaced (1979) by Rick Vito (guitars) replaced (1984) by Mick Taylor (guitars); Peter Ward (drums) replaced (1963) by Hughie Flint (drums) replaced (1966) by Mickey Waller (drums) replaced (1966) by Aynsley Dunbar (drums) replaced (1967) by Mick Fleetwood (drums) replaced (1967) by Keef Hartley (drums) replaced (1968) by Jon Hiseman (drums) replaced (1968) by Colin Allen (drums) replaced (1969) by Hughie Flint (drums) replaced (1971) by Paul Lagos (drums) replaced (1972) by Keef Hartley (drums) replaced (1975) by Soho Richardson (drums) replaced (1977) by Frank Wilson (drums) replaced (1979) by Steve Jordan (drums) replaced (1979) by Rubin Alvarez (drums) replaced (1984) by Paul Gardiner (drums); Nigel Stanger (saxophones) replaced (1965) by Alan Skidmore (saxophones) replaced (1967) by Chris Mercer (saxophones) replaced (1967) by Dick Heckstall-Smith (saxophones) replaced (1969) by Johnny Almond (saxophones) replaced (1971) by Cliff Solomon (saxophones) replaced (1973) by Red Holloway (saxophones) replaced (1975) by Larry Blouin (saxophones) replaced (1976) by Jimmy Roberts (saxophones) replaced (1977) by Buddy McDaniels (saxophones) replaced (1979) by Jon Faddis (saxophones); Dennis Healey (trumpet) replaced (1967) by Rip Kant (trumpet) replaced (1968) by Henry Lowther (trumpet) replaced (1972) by Blue Mitchell (trumpet) replaced (1977) by Nolan Smith (trumpet) replaced (1979) by Lewis Soloff (trumpet) replaced (1979) by George Shaw (trumpet); added (1975) Dee McKinnie (vocals) replaced (1977) by Pepper Watkins (vocals) replaced (1978) by Beckie Burns (vocals) replaced (1981) by Maggie Parker (vocals); added (1975) Jay Spell (keyboards) replaced (1976) by Ronnie Barron (keyboards) replaced (1979) by Rob Mounsey (keyboards) replaced (1979) by Gordon Edwards (keyboards, bass) replaced (1980) by Ronnie Barron (keyboards)

Albums: John Mayall Plays John Mayall, 1964; Bluesbreakers, 1965; A Hard Road, 1967; Crusade, 1967; Blues Alone, 1967; Raw Blues, 1967; With Paul Butterfield (EP), 1967; Diary of a Band Volume 1, 1968; Diary of a Band Volume 2, 1968; Blues Giant, 1968; Bare Wires, 1968; Laurel Canyon, 1969; So Many Roads, 1969; Live, 1969; Best of John Mayall, 1969; Looking Back, 1970; Turning Point, 1970; Empty Rooms, 1970; U.S.A. Union, 1970; Live in Europe, 1970; World of John Mayall Volume 1, 1970; World of John Mayall Volume 2, 1971; Down the Line, 1971; Memories, 1971; Back to the Roots, 1971; Beyond the Turning Point, 1971; Jazz Blues Fusion, 1972; Through the Years, 1972; Moving On, 1973; Best of John Mayall Volume 2, 1973; Ten Years Gone, 1973; Latest Edition, 1975; New Year, New Band, New Company, 1975; Notice to Appear, 1975; John Mayall, 1976; Banquet in Blues, 1976; Lots of People, 1977; A Hard Core Package, 1977; Primal Solos, 1977; Blues Roots, 1978; Last of the British Blues, 1978; Bottom Line, 1979; No More Interviews, 1979; Roadshow Blues, 1981; Room to Move, 1984; Stormy Monday, 1984; Archives to Eighties, 1986; Chicago Line, 1988; A Sense of Place, 1990

Singles: Don't Waste My Time, 1969 **(81)**; Room to Move, 1970 **(102)**

Blues/Rock — British

Nathaniel Mayer & The Fabulous Twilights

Single: Village of Love, 1962 **(22)**

R & B Vocal — Detroit

Bill Medley

Albums: 100% Bill Medley, 1968; Soft and Soulful, 1969; Gone, 1970; Someone Is Standing Outside, 1970; Nobody Knows, 1970; A Song for You, 1972; Wings, 1973; Smile, 1973; Sweet Thunder, 1980; Right Here and Now, 1982; Best Of, 1988

Singles: I Can't Make It Alone, 1968 **(95)**; Brown Eyed Woman, 1968 **(43)**; Peace Brother Peace, 1968 **(48)**; This Is a Love Song, 1969 **(112)**; Don't Know Much, 1981 **(88)**; Right Here and Now, 1982 **(58)**; For You, 1983; Till Your Memory's Gone, 1983; I Still Do, 1984; I've Always Got the Heart to Sing the Blues, 1984; Is There Anything I Can Do, 1985; (I've Had) The Time of My Life, 1987 **(1)** (with Jennifer Warnes)

Pop/Country — California; one of the Righteous Brothers

Mel & Tim

Personnel: Mel Hardin (vocals); Tim McPherson (vocals)

Album: Starting All Over Again, 1973

Singles: Backfield in Motion, 1969 **(10)**; Good Guys Only Win in the Movies, 1970 **(45)**; Feelin' Bad, 1970 **(106)**; Starting All Over Again, 1972 **(19)**; I May Not Be What You Want, 1973 **(113)**

R & B Vocal — Mississippi

Melanie

Albums: Born to Be, 1969; Affectionately, 1969; Candles in the Rain, 1970; Leftover Wine, 1970; All the Right Noises, 1971; Garden in the City, 1971; Good Book, 1971; Gather Me, 1971; Stoneground Words, 1972; At Carnegie Hall, 1973; Four Sides of Melanie, 1974; The Very Best of Melanie, 1974; Please Love Me, 1974; Madrugada, 1974; As I See It Now, 1975; Sunset and Other Beginnings, 1975; From the Beginning, 1975; Best of Melanie, 1976; Phonogenic, 1978; Photograph, 1979; Ballroom Streets, 1979; Melanie, 1980; Favorite Songs, 1981; Arabesque, 1982; Seventh Wave, 1983; Am I Real or What, 1985

Singles: Beautiful People, 1967; Lay Down (Candles in the Rain), 1970 **(6)**; Peace Will Come, 1970 **(32)**; Stop! I Don't Want to Hear It Anymore, 1970 **(112)**; Ruby Tuesday, 1970 **(52)**; Look What They Did to My Song, 1971; Brand New Key, 1971 **(1)**; Nickel Song, 1972 **(35)**; Ring the Living Bell, 1972 **(31)**; Some Day I'll Be a Farmer, 1972 **(106)**; Together Alone, 1972 **(86)**; Do You Believe, 1973 **(115)**; Bitter Bad, 1973 **(36)**; Will You Love Me Tomorrow, 1973 **(82)**; Lover's Cross, 1974 **(109)**; Running After Love, 1978; One More Try, 1981 **(110)**; Detroit or Buffalo, 1981; Rag Doll, 1984; Who's Sleeping in My Bed?, 1985; Maybe I'm Lonely, 1985

Folk/Pop Vocal—New York; full name is Melanie Safka

Mello-Kings

Personnel: Robert Scholl (vocals; deceased 1975); Jerry Scholl (vocals); Eddie Quinn (vocals); Neil Arena (vocals); Larry Esposito (vocals)

Singles: Tonite, Tonite, 1957 **(77)**; Tonite, Tonite, 1961 **(95)**

Pop Vocal—New York; originally called Mello-Tones

The Mello-Tones

Single: Rosie Lee, 1957 **(24)**

Pop Vocal—American

Mercy

Personnel: Jack Sigler, Jr. (vocals)

Album: The Mercy & Love (Can Make You Happy), 1969

Singles: Love (Can Make You Happy), 1969 **(2)**; Forever, 1969 **(79)**

Pop/Rock—Florida

The Merry-Go-Round

Personnel: Michael Rice (guitars, vocals) replaced (1967) by Bill Rheinhart (guitars, vocals); Emitt

Merry-Go-Round: Rheinhart, Kato, Larson, Rhodes

Rhodes (guitars, keyboards, vocals); Gary Kato (bass, vocals); Joel Larson (drums, vocals)
Album: You're a Very Lovely Woman, 1967
Singles: Live, 1967 **(63)**; You're a Very Lovely Woman, 1967 **(94)**
Pop/Rock—California

Neil Merryweather

Albums: Neil Merryweather & the Boers, 1968; Word of Mouth, 1969; Ivar Avenue Reunion, 1970; Vacuum Cleaner, 1971; Space Rangers, 1974; Kryptonite, 1975
Pop/Rock—British

The Merseybeats

Personnel: Tony Crane (guitars, vocals); Aaron Williams (guitars, vocals) replaced (1966) by Joey Molland (guitars, vocals); Billy Kinsley (bass, vocals) replaced (1964) by John Gustafson (bass) replaced (1966) by Bob Gardner (bass); John Banks (drums) replaced (1966) by Peter Clarke (drums)
Albums: Merseybeats, 1964; Mersey Beats, 1965; England's Best Sellers, 1965; The Merseybeats Greatest Hits, 1977; Beat & Ballads, 1982
Singles: It's Love That Really Counts, 1963; Wishin' and Hopin', 1964; I Think of You, 1964; Don't Turn Around, 1964; Last Night, 1964; I Love You, Yes I Do, 1965; Sorrow, 1966; I Stand Accused, 1966
Pop/Rock—British

The Meters

Personnel: Arthur Neville (keyboards, vocals); Leo Nocentelli (guitars, vocals); George Porter (bass); Joseph Modeliste (drums); added (1975) Cyril Neville (percussion)
Albums: The Meters, 1971; Look Ka Py Py, 1972; Cabbage Alley, 1972; Rejuvenation, 1974; Cissy Strut, 1974; Fire on the Bayou, 1975; Best of the Meters, 1975; Trick Bag, 1976; New Direction,

1977; Good Old Funky Music,
1979

Singles: Sophisticated Cissy, 1969
(34); Cissy Strut, 1969 **(23)**; Ease
Back, 1969 **(61)**; Look Ka Py Py,
1969 **(56)**; Chicken Strut, 1970 **(50)**;
Hand Clapping Song, 1970 **(89)**; Be
My Lady, 1977 **(78)**

R & B/Soul — New Orleans

Lee Michaels

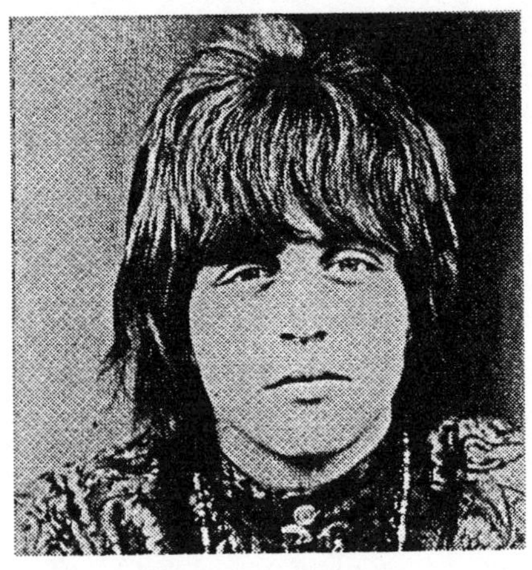

Albums: Carnival of Life, 1968;
Recital, 1969; Lee Michaels, 1969;
Barrel, 1970; 5th, 1971; Life, 1972;
Space and First Takes, 1972; Nice
Day for Something, 1973; Taliface,
1974; Saturn Rings, 1975

Singles: Hello, 1968; Heighty Hi,
1969 **(106)**; Stormy Monday, 1969;
Do You Know What I Mean, 1971
(6); Can I Get a Witness, 1971 **(39)**

Pop/Rock — Los Angeles

Michelle & Jeff

Album: Michelle & Jeff, 1968
Single: Baby Make It Soon, 1968
Pop Vocal — American

Mickey & Sylvia

Personnel: McHouston "Mickey"
Barker (vocals); Sylvia Vanderpool
(vocals)

Singles: Love Is Strange, 1957
(11); There Oughta Be a Law, 1957
(47); Dearest, 1957 **(85)**;
Bewildered, 1958 **(57)**; What Would
I Do, 1960 **(46)**; This Is My Story,
1960 **(100)**; Baby You're So Fine,
1961 **(52)**; Lovedrops, 1961 **(97)**

Pop Vocal — American

Mighty Baby

Personnel: Pete Watson (guitars)
replaced (1971) by Martin Stone
(guitars); Alan King (guitars, vocals); Reg King (vocals); Mike
Evans (bass); Roger Powell (drums);
added (1971) Ian Whiteman (vocals,
keyboards)

Albums: Mighty Baby, 1969; A
Jug of Love, 1971

Pub Rock — British

Buddy Miles

Albums: Expressway to Your
Skull, 1968; Electric Church, 1969;
Them Changes, 1970; We Got to
Live Together, 1970; Message to the
People, 1970; Live, 1971; Carlos
Santana & Buddy Miles Live, 1972;
Chapter VII, 1973; Booger Bear,
1973; All the Faces of Buddy Miles,
1974; More Miles Per Gallon, 1975;
Bicentennial Gathering, 1976; Sneak
Attack, 1981

Singles: Memphis Train, 1969
(100); Them Changes, 1970 **(81)**;
Down by the River, 1970 **(68)**;
Dreams, 1970 **(86)**; We Got to Live
Together, 1970 **(86)**; Wholesale
Love, 1971 **(71)**; Them Changes,
1971 **(62)**; We Got Love, 1974 **(108)**;

Rockin' and Rollin' on the Streets of Hollywood, 1975 **(91)**

Jazz/Rock—Nebraska; former member of Electric Flag and the Jimi Hendrix Experience

Garry Miles

Single: Look for a Star, 1960 **(16)**

Pop Vocal—Nashville; real name is James Cason

Lenny Miles

Singles: Don't Believe Him, Donna, 1960 **(41)**; In Between Tears, 1961 **(84)**

Pop Vocal—Texas

Chuck Miller

Singles: The House of Blue Lights, 1955 **(9)**; The Auctioneer, 1956 **(59)**

Boogie Woogie—California

Jody Miller

Albums: Queen of the House, 1965; He's So Fine, 1971

Singles: He Walks Like a Man, 1964 **(66)**; Queen of the House, 1965 **(12)**; Silver Threads and Golden Needles, 1965 **(54)**; Home of the Brave, 1965 **(25)**; Magic Town, 1965 **(125)**; He's So Fine, 1971 **(53)**; Baby, I'm Yours, 1971 **(91)**; There's a Party Goin' On, 1972 **(115)**

Pop Vocal—Phoenix

Ned Miller

Album: From a Jack to a King, 1963

Singles: From a Jack to a King, 1962 **(6)**; Invisible Tears, 1964 **(131)**; Do What You Do Well, 1964 **(52)**

Country Vocal—Utah; real first name is Henry

Roger Miller

Albums: Roger and Out, 1964; The Return of Roger Miller, 1965; The 3rd Time Around, 1965; Golden Hits, 1965; Words and Music, 1966; Walkin' in the Sunshine, 1967; A Tender Look at Love, 1968; Roger Miller, 1969; Roger Miller 1970, 1970

Singles: Dang Me, 1964 **(7)**; Chug-a-Lug, 1964 **(9)**; Do-Wacka-Do, 1964 **(31)**; King of the Road, 1965 **(4)**; Engine Engine #9, 1965 **(7)**; One Dyin' and a Buryin', 1965 **(34)**; It Happened Just That Way, 1965 **(105)**; Kansas City Star, 1965 **(31)**; England Swings, 1965 **(8)**; Husbands and Wives, 1966 **(26)**; I've Been a Long Time Leavin' (But I'll Be a Long Time Gone), 1966 **(103)**; You Can't Roller Skate in a Buffalo Herd, 1966 **(40)**; My Uncle Used to Love Me but She Died, 1966 **(58)**; Heartbreak Hotel, 1966 **(84)**; Walkin' in the Sunshine, 1967 **(37)**; The Ballad of Waterhole #3 (Code of the West), 1967 **(102)**; Little Green Apples, 1968 **(39)**; Vance, 1968 **(80)**; Me and Bobby McGee, 1969 **(122)**; Open Up Your Heart, 1973 **(105)**

Country/Pop—Texas

The Steve Miller Band

Personnel: Steve Miller (vocals, guitars, synthesizer); Lonnie Turner (bass) replaced (1969) by Bobby Winkelman (bass, vocals) replaced (1970) by Lonnie Turner (bass) replaced (1971) by Ross Valory (bass) replaced (1972) by Gerald Johnson

Steve Miller

(bass) replaced (1973) by Lonnie Turner (bass) replaced (1981) by Gerald Johnson (bass); James "Curly" Cooke (guitars, vocals) replaced (1968) by Boz Scaggs (guitars, vocals) replaced (1971) by Jesse Ed Davis (guitars) replaced (1976) by Curly Cooke (guitars) replaced (1977) by Greg Douglas (guitars) replaced (1982) by Kenny Lee Lewis (guitars); Jim Peterman (keyboards) replaced (1969) by Ben Sidran (keyboards, vocals) replaced (1972) by Dicky Thompson (keyboards) replaced (1977) by Byron Allred (keyboards); Tim Davis (drums) replaced (1971) by Jack King (drums) replaced (1972) by Gary Mallaber (drums, keyboards); added (1977) David Denny (guitars) replaced (1982) by John Massaro (guitars)

Albums: Children of the Future, 1968; Sailor, 1969; Brave New World, 1969; Your Saving Grace, 1970; Number Five, 1970; Rock Love, 1971; Recall the Beginning, 1972; Anthology, 1973; The Joker, 1973; The Legend, 1975; Fly Like an Eagle, 1976; Best of 1968–1973, 1977; Book of Dreams, 1977; Greatest Hits 1974–1978, 1978; Circle of Love, 1981; Abracadabra, 1982; Live, 1983; Italian X-Rays, 1984; Living in the 20th Century, 1987; Born 2B Blue, 1988

Singles: Living in the U.S.A., 1968 **(94)**; My Dark Hour, 1969 **(126)**; Going to the Country, 1970 **(69)**; Steve Miller's Midnight Tango, 1970 **(117)**; Space Cowboy, 1972; The Joker, 1973 **(1)**; Your Cash Ain't Nothin' but Trash, 1974 **(51)**; Living in the U.S.A., 1974 **(49)**; Take the Money and Run, 1976 **(11)**; Rock'n Me, 1976 **(1)**; Fly Like an Eagle, 1976 **(2)**; Jet Airliner, 1977 **(8)**; Jungle Love, 1977 **(23)**; Swingtown, 1977 **(17)**; Serenade, 1978; Heart Like a Wheel, 1981 **(24)**; Circle of Love, 1982 **(55)**; Abracadabra, 1982 **(1)**; Cool Magic, 1982 **(57)**; Give It Up, 1982 **(60)**; Living in the U.S.A., 1983; Shangri-La, 1984 **(57)**; Bongo Bongo, 1985 **(84)**; Italian X-Rays, 1985; I Want to Make the World Turn Around, 1986 **(97)**

Pop/Rock — Texas

Garry Mills

Single: Look for a Star — Part I, 1960 **(26)**

Pop Vocal — British

Hayley Mills

Album: The Parent Trap (Soundtrack), 1961

Singles: Let's Get Together, 1961

(8); Johnny Jingo, 1962 **(21)**; Ching-Ching and a Ding Ding Ding, 1962 **(118)**

Pop Vocal—British; Hayley starred in *The Parent Trap* along with other feature films

Garnet Mimms & The Enchanters

Personnel: Garnet Mimms (vocals); Sam Bell (vocals); Charles Boyer (vocals); Zola Pearnell (vocals)

Albums: Cry Baby and 11 Other Hits, 1963; As Long as I Have You, 1964; I'll Take Good Care of You, 1966; Remember (EP), 1973; Garnet Mimms Has It All, 1977

Singles: I Lied to My Heart, 1961 **(96)**; Cry Baby, 1963 **(4)**; For Your Precious Love, 1963 **(26)**; Baby Don't You Weep, 1963 **(30)**; Tell Me Baby, 1964 **(69)**; One Girl, 1964 **(67)**; I Wanna Thank You, 1964 **(91)**; A Quiet Place, 1964 **(78)**; Look Away, 1964 **(73)**; A Little Bit of Soap, 1965 **(95)**; It Was Easier to Hurt Her, 1965 **(124)**; That Goes to Show You, 1965 **(115)**; I'll Take Good Care of You, 1966 **(30)**; It's Been Such a Long Way Home, 1966 **(125)**; My Baby, 1966 **(132)**

Soul/Pop Vocal—Philadelphia

Sal Mineo

Singles: Start Movin' (in My Direction)/Love Affair, 1957 **(9)**; Lasting Love/You Shouldn't Do That, 1957 **(27)**; Party Time, 1957 **(45)**; Little Pigeon, 1958 **(45)**

Pop Vocal—Los Angeles; stabbed to death 2/12/76

The Miracles

Personnel: William "Smokey" Robinson (vocals) replaced (1972) by Billy Griffin (vocals); Ronnie White (vocals); Bobby Rogers (vocals); Pete Moore (vocals); Claudette Rogers Robinson (vocals) left group (1962)

Albums: Hi, We're the Miracles, 1961; Cookin' with the Miracles, 1962; Shop Around, 1962; I'll Try Something New, 1963; Christmas with the Miracles, 1963; The Fabulous Miracles, 1963; The Miracles on Stage, 1963; Doin' Mickey's Monkey, 1964; Greatest Hits from the Beginning, 1965; Going to a Go-Go, 1965; Away We Go-Go, 1966; Make It Happen, 1967; Greatest Hits, Volume 2, 1968; Special Occasion, 1968; Live!, 1969; Time Out for Smokey Robinson & the Miracles, 1969; Four in Blue, 1969; What Love Has . . . Joined Together, 1970; A Pocket Full of Miracles, 1970; The Tears of a Clown, 1970; One Dozen Roses, 1971; Flying High Together, 1972; 1957–1972, 1973; Renaissance, 1973; Smokey Robinson & the Miracles Anthology, 1974; Do It Baby, 1974; Don't Cha Love It, 1975; City of Angels, 1975; The Power of Music, 1976; Love Crazy, 1977; Miracles, 1977

Singles: Bad Girl, 1959 **(93)**; Shop Around, 1960 **(2)**; Ain't It, Baby, 1961 **(49)**; Mighty Good Lovin', 1961 **(51)**; Broken Hearted, 1961 **(97)**; Everybody's Gotta Pay Some Dues, 1961 **(52)**; What's So Good About Good-By, 1962 **(35)**; I've Been Good to You, 1962 **(103)**; I'll Try Something New, 1962 **(39)**; Way Over There, 1962 **(94)**; You've Really Got a Hold on Me, 1962 **(8)**; I Can Take a Hint, 1963 **(107)**; A Love She Can Count On, 1963 **(31)**; Mickey's Monkey, 1963 **(8)**; I Gotta

Dance to Keep from Crying, 1963 (35); (You Can't Let the Boy Over-power) The Man in You, 1964 (59); I Like It Like That, 1964 (27); That's What Love Is Made Of, 1964 (35); Come on Do the Jerk, 1964 (50); Ooh Baby Baby, 1965 (16); The Tracks of My Tears, 1965 (16); My Girl Has Gone, 1965 (14); Go-ing to a Go-Go, 1965 (11); Whole Lotta Shakin' in My Heart (Since I Met You), 1966 (46); (Come 'Round Here) I'm the One You Need, 1966 (17); The Love I Saw in You Was Just a Mirage, 1967 (20); More Love, 1967 (23); I Second That Emotion, 1967 (4); If You Can Want, 1968 (11); Yester Love, 1968 (31); Special Occasion, 1968 (26); Baby, Baby Don't Cry, 1969 (8); Doggone Right, 1969 (32); Here I Go Again, 1969 (37); Abraham, Martin and John, 1969 (33); Point It Out, 1969 (37); Darling Dear, 1970 (100); Who's Gonna Take the Blame, 1970 (46); The Tears of a Clown, 1970 (1); I Don't Blame You at All, 1971 (18); Crazy About the La La La, 1971 (56); Satisfaction, 1971 (49); We've Come Too Far to End It Now, 1972 (46); I Can't Stand to See You Cry, 1972 (45); Don't Let It End ('Til You Let It Begin), 1973 (56); Give Me Just Another Day, 1973 (111); Do It Baby, 1974 (13); Don't Cha Love It, 1974 (78); Gemini, 1975 (101); Love Machine (Part 1), 1975 (1); Spy for Brotherhood, 1977 (104)

Soul/Pop Vocal — Detroit

The Mirettes

Personnel: Vanetta Fields (vocals); Jessie Smith (vocals); Rob-bie Montgomery (vocals)

Single: In the Midnight Hour, 1968 (45)
Soul Vocal — American

Chad Mitchell Trio

Personnel: Chad Mitchell (vocals) replaced (1965) by John Denver (guitars, vocals); Mike Kobluk (vocals); Joe Frazier (vocals)

Albums: Mighty Day on Campus, 1962; The Chad Mitchell Trio at the Bitter End, 1962; Blowin' in the Wind, 1963; The Best of the Chad Mitchell Trio, 1963; Singin' Our Mind, 1963; Reflecting, 1964; The Slightly Irreverent Mitchell Trio, 1964; Typical American Boys, 1965

Singles: Lizzie Borden, 1962 (44); The John Birch Society, 1962 (99); The Marvelous Toy, 1963 (43)
Folk Vocal — Washington

Guy Mitchell

Singles: Ninety Nine Years (Dead or Alive), 1956 (23); Singing the Blues, 1956 (1); Crazy with Love, 1956 (53); Knee Deep in the Blues, 1957 (16); Take Me Back Baby, 1957 (47); Rock-a-Billy, 1957 (10); Sweet Stuff, 1957 (83); Heartaches by the Number, 1959 (1); The Same Old Me, 1960 (51); My Shoes Keep Walking Back to You, 1960 (45); Your Goodnight Kiss (Ain't What It Used to Be), 1961 (106); Charlie's Shoes, 1962 (110); Go Tiger, Go!, 1962 (101)
Pop Vocal — Detroit; real name is Al Cernik

Joni Mitchell

Albums: Joni Mitchell, 1968; Clouds, 1969; Ladies of the Canyon, 1970; Blue, 1971; For the Roses,

Joni Mitchell

1972; Court & Spark, 1974; Miles of
Aisles, 1974; Hissing of Summer
Lawns, 1975; Hejira, 1976; Don
Juan's Reckless Daughter, 1977;
Mingus, 1979; Shadows & Light,
1980; Wild Things Run Fast, 1982;
Dog Eat Dog, 1985; Chalkmarks in
a Rainstorm, 1986; Night Ride
Home, 1991

Singles: Big Yellow Taxi, 1970
(67); Carey, 1971 **(93)**; You Turn
Me On, I'm a Radio, 1972 **(25)**;
Raised on Robbery, 1973 **(65)**; Help
Me, 1974 **(7)**; Free Man in Paris,
1974 **(22)**; Big Yellow Taxi, 1974
(24); In France They Kiss on Main
Street, 1976 **(66)**; The Dry Cleaner
from Des Moines, 1979; Why Do
Fools Fall in Love, 1980 **(102)**;
(You're So Square) Baby I Don't
Care, 1982 **(47)**; Underneath the
Streetlight, 1983; Good Friends,
1985; Come in from the Cold, 1991

Folk/Rock—Canadian; real name
is Roberta Joan Anderson; has written songs for Judy Collins, Tom
Rush and Crosby, Stills & Nash

Moby Grape

Personnel: Jerry Miller (guitars,
vocals); Skip Spence (guitars, vocals) replaced (1969) by Gordon
Stevens (violin, mandolin, guitars)
replaced (1972) by Frank Reckard
(guitars, vocals) replaced (1973) by
Jeff Blackburn (guitars, vocals);
Peter Lewis (guitars, vocals); Bob
Mosley (bass, vocals) replaced (1970)
by Bob Moore (bass) replaced (1971)
by Bob Mosley (bass, vocals) replaced (1973) by Christian Powell
(bass); Don Stevenson (drums, vocals) replaced (1972) by Bob New-
kirk (drums) replaced (1973) by
John Craviotta (drums) replaced
(1973) by John Oxindine (drums);
added (1973) Cornelius Bumpus
(organ, saxophones)

Albums: Moby Grape, 1967;
Wow, 1968; Grape Jam, 1968;
Moby Grape '69, 1969; Truly Fine
Citizen, 1970; 20 Granite Creek,
1972; Great Grape, 1974; Best of
Moby Grape, 1976; Moby Grape
Live, 1979

Singles: Omaha, 1967 **(88)**; Hey
Grandma, 1967 **(127)**

Psychedelic Rock—San Francisco;
reformed in late 1974 under the
name Maby Grope

The Mojo Men

Personnel: Jim Alaimo (guitars,
vocals); Paul Curcio (guitars, vocals); Don Metchick (bass, vocals);
Dennis DeCarr (drums, vocals);
added (1967) Jan Ashton (drums,
vocals)

Albums: The Mojo Men, 1965;
Sit Down, I Think I Love You,
1967

Singles: Dance with Me, 1965
(61); She's My Baby, 1966; Sit
Down, I Think I Love You, 1967
(36); Me About You, 1967 **(83)**

Psychedelic Pop—California

The Moments

Personnel: Mark Greene (vocals) replaced (1970) by Johnny Morgan (vocals) replaced (1973) by Harry Ray (vocals); Billy Brown (vocals); Al Goodman (vocals)

Albums: The Moments Greatest Hits, 1971; The Moments Live at the New York State Woman's Prison, 1971; Look at Me, 1975

Singles: Not on the Outside, 1968 **(57)**; Sunday, 1969 **(90)**; I Do, 1969 **(62)**; Lovely Way She Looks, 1970 **(120)**; Love on a Two-Way Street, 1970 **(3)**; If I Didn't Care, 1970 **(44)**; All I Have, 1970 **(56)**; I Can't Help It, 1971 **(108)**; That's How It Feels, 1971 **(115)**; Lucky Me, 1971 **(98)**; To You with Love, 1971 **(107)**; Gotta Find a Way, 1973 **(68)**; Sexy Mama, 1974 **(17)**; Sho' Nuff Boogie (Part 1), 1974 **(80)** (with Sylvia); Look at Me (I'm in Love), 1975 **(39)**; Special Lady, 1980 **(5)**; Inside of You, 1980 **(76)**; My Prayer, 1980 **(47)**

Soul/Pop Vocal—New Jersey; began recording as Ray, Goodman and Brown in 1978

The Monarchs

Single: Look Homeward Angel, 1964 **(47)**

Pop/Rock—American

Zoot Money

Albums: It Should Have Been Me, 1965; Zoot, 1966; All Happening at the Klooks Kleek, 1967; Transition, 1968; Welcome to My Head, 1969; Zoot Money, 1970; Mr. Money, 1980; Big Roll Band, 1984

Jazz/Rock—British

The Monkees

Personnel: Davy Jones (vocals, percussion); Michael Nesmith (guitars, bass, vocals) left group (1970); Peter Tork (guitars); Mickey Dolenz (drums, vocals, guitars)

The Monkees: Nesmith, Dolenz, Jones, Tork

Albums: The Monkees, 1967; More of the Monkees, 1967; Headquarters, 1967; Pisces, Aquarius, Capricorn & Jones LTD, 1967; The Birds, the Bees & the Monkees, 1968; Head, 1968; Instant Replay, 1969; Greatest Hits, 1969; Changes, 1969; Golden Hits, 1970; Barrel Full of Monkees, 1970; Greatest Hits, 1976; Jones, Dolenz, Boyce & Hart, 1976; The Monkees, 1981; Monkee Business, 1982; Monkee Flips, 1984; More Greatest Hits, 1985; Live 1967, 1985; Missing Links, 1985; Missing Links Volume 2, 1986; Then & Now . . . Best of the Monkees, 1986; Pool It, 1987; Listen to the Band, 1991

Singles: Last Train to Clarksville, 1966 (**1**); I'm a Believer, 1966 (**1**); Stepping Stone, 1966 (**20**); A Little Bit Me, A Little Bit You, 1967 (**2**); The Girl I Knew Somewhere, 1967 (**39**); Pleasant Valley Sunday, 1967 (**3**); Words, 1967 (**11**); Daydream Believer, 1967 (**1**); Goin' Down, 1967 (**104**); Valleri, 1968 (**3**); Tapioca Tundra, 1968 (**34**); It's Nice to Be with You, 1968 (**51**); D. W. Washburn, 1968 (**19**); The Porpoise Song, 1968 (**62**); As We Go Along, 1968 (**106**); Teardrop City, 1969 (**56**); Someday Man, 1969 (**81**); Listen to the Band, 1969 (**63**); Good Clean Fun, 1969 (**82**); Mommy and Daddy, 1969 (**109**); Oh My My, 1970 (**98**); That Was Then, This Is Now, 1986 (**20**); Heart and Soul, 1987 (**87**); Daydream Believer, 1987 (**87**)

Pop/Rock—U.S./British

The Monotones

Personnel: Charles Patrick (vocals)
Single: Book of Love, 1958 (**5**)
Pop Vocal—New Jersey

Matt Monro

Albums: My Kind of Girl, 1961; Walk Away, 1965; Invitation to the Movies/Born Free, 1967
Singles: My Kind of Girl, 1961 (**18**); Why Not Now, 1961 (**92**); Softly as I Leave You, 1962 (**116**); Softly as I Leave You, 1964 (**121**); Walk Away, 1964 (**23**); For Mama, 1965 (**135**); Without You, 1965 (**101**); Born Free, 1966 (**126**)

Pop Vocal—British; died of liver cancer in 1985

Vaughn Monroe

Singles: Black Denim Trousers and Motorcyle Boots, 1955 (**38**); Don't Go to Strangers, 1956 (**38**); In the Middle of the House, 1956 (**11**); The Battle of New Orleans, 1959 (**87**); Queen of the Senior Prom, 1965 (**132**)

Pop Vocal—Ohio; died in 1973

Montage

Personnel: Bob Steurer (vocals); Mike Smyth (guitars, vocals); Lance Cornelius (bass, vocals); Michael Brown (keyboards); Vance Chapman (drums)
Albums: Montage, 1969; Hot Pants, 1970
Single: I Shall Call You Mary, 1969

Pop Rock—American

The Montanas

Singles: You've Got to Be Loved, 1968 (**58**); Run to Me, 1968 (**121**)
Pop/Rock—British

Chris Montez

Albums: Let's Dance, 1962; The

More I See You/Call Me, 1966; Time After Time, 1967; Foolin' Around, 1967; Watch What's Happened, 1968

Singles: All You Had to Do, 1962 **(108)**; Let's Dance, 1962 **(4)**; Some Kinda Fun, 1962 **(43)**; My Baby Loves to Dance, 1963 **(129)**; All You Had to Do (Is Tell Me), 1964 **(125)** (with Kathy Young); Call Me, 1966 **(22)**; The More I See You, 1966 **(16)**; There Will Never Be Another You, 1966 **(33)**; Time After Time, 1966 **(36)**; Because of You, 1967 **(71)**; Foolin' Around, 1967 **(135)**

Pop Vocal—Los Angeles; real last name is Montanez

The Moody Blues

back row: **Lodge, Hayward, Edge;** *front row:* **Thomas, Moraz**

Personnel: Denny Laine (guitars, vocals) replaced (1966) by Justin Hayward (guitars, vocals); Clint Warwick (bass, vocals) replaced (1966) by John Lodge (bass, vocals); Michael Pinder (keyboards, vocals) replaced (1980) by Patrick Moraz (keyboards) left group (1990); Ray Thomas (vocals, flute); Graeme Edge (drums, percussion)

Albums: The Moody Blues No. 1, 1965; Magnificent Moodies, 1966; Days of Future Passed, 1967; In Search of the Lost Chord, 1968; On the Threshold of a Dream, 1969; To Our Children's Children's Children, 1970; A Question of Balance, 1971; Every Good Boy Deserves Favour, 1972; Seventh Sojourn, 1973; This Is the Moody Blues, 1974; In the Beginning, 1975; Caught Live Plus Five, 1977; Octave, 1978; Out of This World, 1979; Long Distance Voyager, 1981; The Present, 1983; Early Blues, 1985; Voices in the Sky, 1985; The Other Side of Life, 1986; Sur la Mer, 1987; Greatest Hits, 1988; Legend of a Band, 1990; Keys of the Kingdom, 1991

Singles: Go Now, 1965 **(10)**; From the Bottom of My Heart, 1965 **(93)**; Stop, 1966 **(98)**; This Is My House (But Nobody Calls), 1966 **(119)**; Nights in White Satin, 1967 **(103)**; Legend of a Mind, 1968; Tuesday Afternoon, 1968 **(24)**; Ride My See-Saw, 1968 **(61)**; Simple Game, 1969; Never Comes the Day, 1969 **(91)**; Question, 1970 **(21)**; The Story in Your Eyes, 1971 **(23)**; Isn't Life Strange, 1972 **(29)**; Nights in White Satin, 1972 **(2)**; I'm Just a Singer (in a Rock and Roll Band), 1973 **(12)**; Steppin' in a Slide Zone, 1978 **(39)**; Driftwood, 1978 **(59)**; Gemini Dream, 1981 **(12)**; The Voice, 1981 **(15)**; Talking Out of Turn, 1981 **(65)**; Meanwhile, 1981; Sitting at the Wheel, 1983 **(27)**; Blue World, 1983 **(62)**; Running Water, 1984; Meet Me Halfway, 1984; Your Wildest

Dreams, 1986 **(9)**; The Other Side of Life, 1986 **(58)**; I Know You're Out There Somewhere, 1987 **(30)**; No More Lies, 1987; I Know, 1988; Say It with Love, 1991; Bless the Wings (That Bring You), 1991; Magic, 1991

Art Rock—British

The Moonglows

Personnel: Bobby Lester (vocals; deceased 1980); Harvey Fuqua (vocals); Alexander Graves (vocals); Prentiss Barnes (vocals); Billy Johnson (vocals)

Albums: Moonglows, 1955; The Return of the Moonglows, 1972

Singles: Sincerely, 1955 **(20)**; See Saw, 1956 **(25)**; Please Send Me Someone to Love, 1957 **(73)**; Ten Commandments of Love, 1958 **(22)**

R & B Vocal—Kentucky

Bob Moore

Album: Mexico and Other Great Hits!, 1961

Singles: Mexico, 1961 **(7)**; Kentucky, 1963 **(101)**

Instrumental—Nashville

Bobby Moore & The Rhythm Aces

Album: Searching for My Love, 1966

Singles: Searching for My Love, 1966 **(27)**; Try My Love Again, 1966 **(97)**

R & B Vocal—Alabama

Jaye P. Morgan

Singles: That's All I Want from You, 1954 **(3)**; Danger! Heartbreak Ahead/Softly, Softly, 1955 **(12)**; Chee Chee-Oo-Chee (Sang the Little Bird), 1955 **(12)** (with Perry Como); Two Lost Souls, 1955 **(18)** (with Perry Como); The Longest Walk/Swanee, 1955 **(6)**; Pepper-Hot Baby, 1955 **(12)**; If You Don't Want My Love, 1955 **(12)**; Not One Goodbye, 1955 **(48)**; Sweet Lips, 1956 **(85)**; Get Up! Get Up!, 1956 **(83)**; Lost in the Shuffle, 1956 **(69)**; Play for Keeps, 1956 **(79)**; Johnny Casanova, 1956 **(81)**; Just Love Me, 1956 **(97)**; Are You Lonesome Tonight, 1959 **(65)**; Miss You, 1959 **(78)**; I Walk the Line, 1960 **(66)**; A Heartache Named Johnny, 1962 **(119)**; Song for You, 1971 **(105)**

Pop Vocal—Colorado; Jaye P. is Mary Margaret Morgan

Van Morrison

Albums: Blowin' Your Mind, 1967; Astral Weeks, 1968; Best of Van Morrison, 1970; Moondance, 1970; His Band & Street Choir, 1970; Tupelo Honey, 1971; St. Dominic's Preview, 1972; Hard Nose the Highway, 1973; It's Too Late to Stop Now, 1974; TB Sheets, 1974; Veedon Fleece, 1974; This Is Where I Came In, 1976; Period of Transition, 1977; Wavelength, 1978; Into the Music, 1979; Charifellows, 1979;

Common One, 1980; Beautiful Visions, 1982; Inarticulate Speech of the Heart, 1983; Live at the Opera House Belfast, 1984; A Sense of Wonder, 1985; No Guru, No Method, No Teacher, 1986; Poetic Champions Compose, 1987; Irish Heartbeat, 1988 (with the Chieftains); Avalon Sunset, 1989; Best of Van Morrison, 1990; Bang Masters, 1991; Hymns to the Silence, 1991

Singles: Brown-Eyed Girl, 1967 **(10)**; Ro Ro Rosey, 1967 **(107)**; Come Running, 1970 **(39)**; Domino, 1970 **(9)**; Blue Money, 1971 **(23)**; Call Me Up in Dreamland, 1971 **(95)**; Wild Night, 1971 **(28)**; Tupelo Honey, 1972 **(47)**; (Straight to Your Heart) Like a Cannonball, 1972 **(119)**; Jackie Wilson Said (I'm in Heaven When You Smile), 1972 **(61)**; Redwood Tree, 1972 **(98)**; Gypsy, 1973 **(101)**; Moondance, 1977 **(92)**; Wavelength, 1978 **(42)**; Bright Side of the Road, 1979 **(110)**; Cleaning Windows, 1982; Tore Down a la Rimbaud, 1986; Everyday Is Like Sunday, 1988; Have I Told You Lately, 1989; Real Real Gone, 1990; Ordinary Love, 1991

Soul/Rock Vocal—Irish; former member of Them; real name is George Ivan

Mother Earth

Personnel: Tracy Nelson (keyboards, vocals); John Andrews (guitars); Bob Arthur (bass, vocals) replaced (1970) by Dave Zettner (bass) replaced (1971) by Tim Drummond (bass) replaced (1973) by Steve Mandell (bass); Martin Fierro (saxophones) replaced (1969) by Johnny Gimble (fiddle) replaced (1973) by Mac Gayden (guitars); R. P. St. John (vocals); replaced (1969)

by Scotty Moore (guitars) replaced (1970) by Bob Cardwell (guitars) replaced (1973) by Jack Lee (guitars); Mark Naftalin (keyboards) replaced (1969) by Shorty Lavender (fiddle) replaced (1970) by Andrew McMahon (keyboards); Lonnie Castille (drums) replaced (1968) by George Rains (drums) replaced (1969) by Clay Cotton (drums) replaced (1970) by Karl Himmel (drums) replaced (1973) by Jerry Carrigan (drums)

Albums: Revolution, 1968; Living with the Animals, 1968; Make a Joyful Noise, 1969; Tracy Nelson Country, 1969; Satisfied, 1970; Bring Me Home, 1971; Poor Man's Paradise, 1973

Blues/Rock—Nashville

Motherlode

Personnel: William "Smitty" Smith (vocals)
Albums: When I Die, 1969; Tuffed Out, 1973
Singles: When I Die, 1969 **(18)**; Memories of a Broken Promise/ What Does It Take (to Win Your Love), 1969 **(111)**

Pop Vocal—Canadian

Mouse & The Traps

Personnel: Ronnie Weiss (vocals)
Album: Mouse & the Traps, 1968
Singles: Public Execution, 1966 **(121)**; Sometimes You Just Can't Win, 1968 **(125)**; Maid of Sugar, Maid of Spice, 1968; Lie, Beg, Borrow and Steal, 1968

Psychedelic Rock—Texas

The Move

Personnel: Carl Wayne (vocals) replaced (1971) by Jeff Lynne

**Mouse & The Traps: Weiss,
*second from left***

(guitars, vocals, bass, keyboards);
Ace Kefford (bass, vocals) replaced
(1970) by Richard Tandy (keyboards, bass) left group (1972);
Trevor Burton (bass, guitars, vocals) replaced (1970) by Rick Price
(bass, vocals); Roy Wood (guitars,
vocals, woodwinds); Bev Bevan
(drums)
  Albums: The Move, 1967; Something Else (EP), 1968; Shazam!,
1969; Best of the Move, 1970; Looking On, 1970; Message from the
Country, 1971; Fire Brigade, 1971;
Split Ends, 1972; California Man,
1974; The Best of the Move, 1975;
Shines On, 1979; Best of the Move,
1991
  Singles: Blackberry Way, 1970;
California Man, 1972; Do Ya, 1972
(93)
  Art Rock—British; group evolved
into Electric Light Orchestra after
the completion of the Move's recording contract

Moving Fingers

Personnel: Ken Elliott (vocals,
keyboards); Bob Gibbons (guitars);
Nick South (bass); Kieran O'Connor
(drums)
  Album: Reality, 1969
  Hard Rock—British

The Mugwumps

Personnel: Cass Elliott (vocals;
deceased 1974); Denny Doherty
(vocals); Zal Yanovsky (guitars, vocals); James Hendricks (guitars,
vocals); John Sebastian (guitars, vocals)
  Album: Mugwumps, 1967
  Single: Jug Band Music, 1966
(127)
  Folk/Pop—American; group performed together before joining more
well known acts

The Murmaids

Personnel: Carol Fischer (vocals);
Terry Fischer (vocals); Sally Gordon
(vocals)
  Singles: Popsicles and Icicles, 1963
(3); Heartbreak Ahead, 1964 **(116)**
  Pop Vocal—Los Angeles

Mickey Murray

Single: Shout Bamalama, 1967
(54)
  Soul Vocal—American

Music Explosion

Personnel: James Lyons (vocals);
Rick Nesta (guitars); Don Atkins
(guitars); Butch Stahl (bass, organ);
Bob Avery (drums, harmonica)
  Album: Little Bit o' Soul, 1967
  Singles: Little Bit o' Soul, 1967
(2); Sunshine Games, 1967 **(63)**; We

Gotta Go Home, 1967 **(103)**; What You Want, 1968 **(119)**; Yes Sir, 1968 **(120)**

Pop/Rock—Ohio

The Music Machine

Personnel: Sean Bonniwell (guitars, vocals); Mark Landon (guitars, vocals); Keith Olsen (bass); Doug Rhodes (organ); Ron Edgar (drums)

Albums: Turn on the Music, 1966; Bonniwell Music Machine, 1968

Singles: Talk Talk, 1966 **(15)**; The People in Me, 1967 **(66)**; Double Yellow Line, 1967 **(111)**; The Eagle Never Hunts the Fly, 1967

Psychedelic Rock—Los Angeles

Billy Myles

Single: The Joker (That's What They Call Me), 1957 **(25)**

R & B Vocal—New York

The Mystics

Personnel: Phil Cracolici (vocals); Bob Ferrante (vocals); George Galfo (vocals); Albee Cracolici (vocals); Allie Contrera (vocals)

Singles: Hushabye, 1959 **(20)**; Don't Take the Stars, 1959 **(98)**; All Through the Night, 1960 **(107)**; Pain, 1969 **(116)**

Pop Vocal—New York

Napoleon XIV

Album: They're Coming to Take Me Away, 1966

Singles: They're Coming to Take Me Away, Ha-Haaa!, 1966 **(3)**; They're Coming to Take Me Away, Ha-Haaa!, 1973 **(87)**

Novelty Pop—New York; real name is Jerry Samuels

Johnny Nash

Albums: Johnny Nash, 1957; Quiet Hour, 1958; I Got Rhythm, 1959; Let's Get Lost, 1960; Starring Johnny Nash Studio Time, 1961; Soul Folk, 1965; Hold Me Tight, 1968; I Can See Clearly Now, 1972; My Merry-Go-Round, 1973; Celebrate Life, 1974; Greatest Hits, 1974; Tears on My Pillow, 1975; What a Wonderful World, 1977; The Johnny Nash Collection, 1977; Let's Go Dancing, 1979; The

The Music Machine: Bonniwell, Landon, unknown, Olsen, Edgar, **Rhodes**

Johnny Nash Album, 1980; Stir It Up, 1981

Singles: A Very Special Love, 1957 **(23)**; Almost in Your Arms, 1958 **(78)**; As Time Goes By, 1959 **(43)**; Some of Your Lovin', 1961 **(104)**; Ol' Man River, 1962 **(120)**; I'm Leaving, 1964 **(120)**; Let's Move & Groove (Together), 1965 **(88)**; Somewhere, 1966 **(120)**; Hold Me Tight, 1968 **(5)**; You Got Soul, 1968 **(58)**; Lovey Dovey, 1969 **(130)**; We Try Harder, 1969 **(135)** (with Kim Weston); Love and Peace, 1969 **(132)**; Cupid, 1969 **(39)**; (What a) Groovy Feeling, 1970 **(102)**; I Can See Clearly Now, 1972 **(1)**; Stir It Up, 1973 **(12)**; My Merry-Go-Round, 1973 **(77)**; Ooh What a Feeling, 1973 **(103)**; Loving You, 1974 **(91)**; You Can't Go Halfway, 1974 **(105)**; (What a) Wonderful World, 1974 **(103)**
Soul/Pop Vocal—Texas

The Nashville Teens

Personnel: John Allen (guitars); John Hawken (keyboards); Arthur Sharp (vocals); Peter Shannon (guitars); Ray Phillips (bass, harmonica); Barry Jenkins (drums)
Albums: Tobacco Road, 1963; Nashville Teens, 1964; Remembering, 1965; Live at the Red House, 1984
Singles: Tobacco Road, 1964 **(14)**; Google Eye, 1964 **(117)**; Find My Way Home, 1965 **(98)**; The Little Bird, 1965 **(123)**
Pop/Rock—British

The Nazz

Personnel: Todd Rundgren (vocals, guitars) replaced (1970) by Rick Nielsen (guitars, vocals); Car-son Von Osten (bass) replaced (1970) by Tom Petersson (bass); Robert Antoni (keyboards, vocals); Thomas Mooney (drums)
Albums: Nazz, 1968; Nazz Nazz, 1969; Nazz 3, 1969
Singles: Open My Eyes, 1968 **(112)**; Hello It's Me, 1969 **(66)**
Hard Rock—Philadelphia

Rick Nelson

Albums: Ricky, 1957; Ricky Nelson, 1958; Ricky Sings Again, 1959; Songs by Ricky, 1959; More Songs by Ricky, 1960; Rick Is 21, 1961; Album Seven by Rick, 1962; Best Sellers by Rick Nelson, 1963; It's Up to You, 1963; Million Sellers, 1963; For Your Sweet Love, 1963; A Long Vacation, 1963; Rick Nelson Sings "For You," 1964; The Very Thought of You, 1964; Spotlight on Rick, 1964; Best Always, 1965; Love & Kisses, 1965; Bright Lights & Country Fever, 1966; Country Fever, 1967; Another Side of Rick, 1968; Perspective, 1969; Rick Nelson in Concert, 1970; Rick Sings Nelson, 1970; The Very Best of Rick

Nelson, 1970; Legendary Masters, 1971; Rudy the Fifth, 1971; Garden Party, 1972; Rick Nelson Country, 1973; Windfall, 1974; Ricky Nelson Singles, 1977; Intakes, 1977; Ricky, 1980; Playing to Win, 1981; Live 1983–1985, 1989

Singles: I'm Walking, 1957 (**17**); A Teenager's Romance, 1957 (**2**); You're My One and Only Love, 1957 (**14**); Be-Bop Baby, 1957 (**3**); Have I Told You Lately That I Love You, 1957 (**29**); Stood Up, 1957 (**2**); Waitin' in School, 1957 (**18**); Believe What You Say, 1958 (**4**); My Bucket's Got a Hole in It, 1958 (**18**); Poor Little Fool, 1958 (**1**); Lonesome Town, 1958 (**7**); I Got a Feeling, 1958 (**10**); Never Be Anyone Else but You, 1959 (**6**); It's Late, 1959 (**9**); Just a Little Too Much, 1959 (**9**); Sweeter Than You, 1959 (**9**); I Wanna Be Loved, 1959 (**20**); Mighty Good, 1959 (**38**); Young Emotions, 1960 (**12**); Right by My Side, 1960 (**59**); I'm Not Afraid, 1960 (**27**); Yes Sir, That's My Baby, 1960 (**34**); You Are the Only One, 1960 (**25**); Milk Cow Blues, 1960 (**79**); Travelin' Man, 1961 (**1**); Hello Mary Lou, 1961 (**9**); A Wonder Like You, 1961 (**11**); Everlovin', 1961 (**16**); Young World, 1962 (**5**); Summertime, 1962 (**89**); Teen Age Idol, 1962 (**5**); I've Got My Eyes on You (and I Like What I See), 1962 (**105**); It's Up to You, 1962 (**6**); I Need You, 1962 (**83**); That's All, 1963 (**48**); I'm in Love Again, 1963 (**67**); You Don't Love Me Anymore (and I Can't Stand It), 1963 (**47**); I Got a Woman, 1963 (**49**); If You Can't Rock Me, 1963 (**100**); Old Enough to Love, 1963 (**94**); String Along, 1963 (**25**); Gypsy Woman, 1963 (**62**); A Long Vacation, 1963 (**120**); Fools Rush In, 1963 (**12**); There's Not a Minute, 1963 (**127**); Down Home, 1963 (**126**); Today's Teardrops, 1963 (**54**); For You, 1963 (**6**); Congratulations, 1964 (**63**); The Very Thought of You, 1964 (**26**); Lucky Star, 1964 (**127**); There's Nothing I Can Say, 1964 (**47**); Lonely Corner, 1964 (**113**); A Happy Guy, 1964 (**82**); Mean Old World, 1965 (**96**); Come Out Dancin', 1965 (**130**); You Just Can't Quit, 1966 (**108**); She Belongs to Me, 1969 (**33**); Easy to Be Free, 1970 (**48**); I Shall Be Released, 1970 (**102**); Life, 1971 (**109**); Garden Party, 1972 (**6**); Palace Guard, 1973 (**65**)

Pop Vocal — New Jersey; Rick was killed in a plane crash near Dallas on New Year's Eve, 1985 with his fiancée and band; real first name was Eric

Sandy Nelson

Albums: Teenbeat, 1960; He's a Drummer Boy, 1961; Let There Be Drums, 1961; Drums Are My Beat!, 1962; Drummin' Up a Storm, 1962; Compelling Percussion, 1962; Golden Hits, 1962; On the Wild Side, 1963; And Then There Were Drums, 1963; Teenage House Party, 1963; Best of the Beats, 1964; Beat That Drum, 1964; Sandy Nelson Plays, 1964; Be True to Your School, 1964; Live! In Las Vegas, 1964; Teen Beat '65, 1965; Drum Discotheque, 1965; Drums a Go-Go, 1965; Boss Beat, 1966; Superdrums, 1966; "In" Beat, 1966; Beat That *?!! Drum, 1967; Soul Drums, 1967; Boogaloo Beat, 1968; Rock 'n' Roll Revival, 1968; Manhattan Spiritual, 1969; Heavy Drums, 1969; Groovy, 1969; Golden Greats Volume 1,

1973; The Best of Sandy Nelson, 1974; Hocus Pocus, 1976

Singles: Teen Beat, 1959 **(4)**; Let There Be Drums, 1961 **(7)**; Drums Are My Beat, 1962 **(29)**; The Birth of the Beat, 1962 **(75)**; Drummin' Up a Storm, 1962 **(67)**; Drum Stomp, 1962 **(86)**; All Night Long, 1962 **(75)**; Live It Up, 1962 **(101)**; And Then There Were Drums, 1962 **(65)**; Let the Four Winds Blow, 1962 **(107)**; Teen Beat '65, 1964 **(44)**; Reach for a Star, 1965 **(133)**; Let There Be Drums '66, 1965 **(120)**; Drums a Go-Go, 1965 **(124)**; Manhattan Spiritual, 1969 **(119)**

Instrumental—California; super rock studio drummer

Nervous Norvus

Singles: Transfusion, 1956 **(8)**; Ape Call, 1956 **(24)**

Novelty Pop—California; real name is Jimmy Drake; died in 1968

Aaron Neville

Singles: Over You, 1960 **(111)**; Tell It Like It Is, 1966 **(2)**; She Took You for a Ride, 1967 **(92)**; Don't Know Much, 1989 **(2)** (with Linda Ronstadt); All My Life, 1990 **(11)** (with Linda Ronstadt); When Something Is Wrong with My Baby, 1990 **(78)** (with Linda Ronstadt)

R & B Vocal—New Orleans; former member of the Neville Brothers; father of Ivan Neville

The New Christy Minstrels

Personnel: Randy Sparks (vocals); Barry McGuire (vocals) replaced (1965) by Larry Ramos (vocals); Kenny Rogers (vocals) replaced

(1966) by John Denver (vocals); Gene Clark (vocals; deceased 1991) replaced (1964) by Terry Williams (vocals); Karen Black (vocals) replaced (1964) by Thelma Camacho (vocals) replaced (1966) by Kim Carnes (vocals)

Albums: The New Christy Minstrels, 1962; The New Christy Minstrels in Person, 1963; Tall Tales! Legends & Nonsense, 1963; Ramblin' Featuring Green, Green, 1963; Today, 1964; Land of the Giants, 1964; Cowboys and Indians, 1965; Chim Chim Cher-ee, 1965; The Wandering Minstrels, 1965; Greatest Hits, 1966; You Need Someone to Love, 1970

Singles: This Land Is Your Land, 1962 **(93)**; Denver, 1963 **(127)**; Green, Green, 1963 **(14)**; Saturday Night, 1963 **(29)**; Today, 1964 **(17)**; Silly Ol' Summertime, 1964 **(92)**; Gotta Get a Goin', 1965 **(111)**; Chim Chim Cher-ee, 1965 **(81)**; Chitty Chitty Bang Bang, 1969 **(114)**; You Angel You, 1969 **(58)**

Pop Vocal—American

New Colony Six

Personnel: Ray Graffia (vocals); Jerry Kollenberg (guitars, vocals); Pat McBride (vocals); Wally Kemp (bass) replaced (1968) by Chuck Lobes (keyboards); Craig Kemp (keyboards) replaced (1967) by Ronnie Rice (keyboards, bass, guitars, vocals); Chick James (drums) replaced (1970) by Billy Herman (drums, vocals)

Albums: Breakthrough, 1966; Colonization, 1967; Revelations, 1968; Attacking a Strawman, 1969; Roll On, 1971

Singles: I Confess, 1966 **(80)**; I Lie Awake, 1966 **(111)**; Love You So

Much, 1967 **(61)**; You're Gonna Be Mine, 1967 **(108)**; I'm Just Waitin' (Anticipatin' for Her to Show Up), 1967 **(128)**; I Will Always Think About You, 1968 **(22)**; Can't You See Me Cry, 1968 **(52)**; Things I'd Like to Say, 1968 **(16)**; I Could Never Lie to You, 1969 **(50)**; I Want You to Know, 1969 **(65)**; Barbara, I Love You, 1970 **(78)**; People and Me, 1970 **(116)**; Roll On, 1971 **(56)**; Long Time to Be Alone, 1971 **(93)**; Someone, Sometime, 1972 **(109)**

Pop/Rock — Chicago

New Vaudeville Band

Personnel: Geoff Stephens (vocals) replaced (1966) by Alan Klein (vocals); Mick Wilsher (guitars); Neil Korner (bass); Stan Heywood (keyboards); Hugh "Shuggy" Watts (trombone); Robert "Pops" Kerr (saxophones); Henry Harrison (drums)

Album: New Vaudeville Band, 1966

Singles: Winchester Cathedral, 1966 **(1)**; Peek-a-Boo, 1967 **(72)**; Finchley Central, 1967 **(102)**; Bonnie & Clyde, 1968 **(122)**

Pop — British; Stephens wrote "Tell Me When" for the Applejacks and "A Kind of Hush" for Herman's Hermits

The Newbeats

Personnel: Larry Henley (vocals); Dean Mathis (vocals); Marc Mathis (vocals)

Albums: Bread and Butter, 1964; Run, Baby, Run, 1966

Singles: Bread and Butter, 1964 **(2)**; Everything's Alright, 1964 **(16)**; Hey Daddy-O, 1965 **(118)**; Break

Away (from That Boy), 1965 **(40)**; (The Bees Are for the Birds) The Birds Are for the Bees, 1965 **(50)**; Run, Baby, Run (Back Into My Arms), 1965 **(12)**; Shake Hands (and Come Out Crying), 1966 **(92)**; Thou Shalt Not Steal, 1969 **(128)**; Groovin' (Out on Life), 1969 **(82)**; Laura (What's He Got That I Ain't Got), 1970 **(115)**

Pop Vocal — Texas/Georgia

The Nice

Personnel: Keith Emerson (keyboards); Lee Jackson (bass, vocals); David O'List (guitars, vocals) left group (1969); Brian Davison (drums)

Albums: The Thoughts of Emerlist Davyjack, 1967; Ars Longa Vita Brevis, 1968; Nice, 1969; Five Bridges Suite, 1970; Elegy, 1971; Autumn '67, Spring '68, 1972; The Immediate Story, 1975; Amoeni Redivivi, 1976; America, 1976; Greatest Hits, 1977

Progressive Rock — British

Nico

Albums: Chelsea Girl, 1968; Marble Index, 1968; Desert Shore, 1971; The End, 1974; June 1st, 1974, 1974; Drama of Exile, 1981; Do or Die, 1983

Avant Garde Rock — British; real name is Christa Paffga; former member of the Velvet Underground

The Nightcrawlers

Personnel: Chuck Conlon (guitars, vocals); Robbie Rouse (vocals); Sylvan Wells (guitars); Pete Thomason (bass); Tom Ruger (drums)

Album: The Nightcrawlers, 1967

The Nightcrawlers: Ruger, Rouse, Conlon, Wells, Thomason

Single: Little Black Egg, 1967 **(85)**
Psychedelic Rock—American

Harry Nilsson

Albums: Aerial Ballet, 1968;
Harry, 1969; Nilsson Sings Newman, 1969; The Point, 1970; Nilsson
Schmilsson, 1971; Son of Schmilsson, 1972; A Little Touch of Schmilsson in the Night, 1973; All-Time
Greatest Hits, 1974; Pussy Cats,
1975; That's the Way It Is, 1976;
Knillsson, 1977; The World's Greatest Lover, 1978

Singles: You Can't Do That, 1967
(122); Everybody's Talkin', 1968
(113); Everybody's Talkin', 1969 **(6)**;
I Guess the Lord Must Be in New
York City, 1969 **(34)**; Me & My Arrow, 1971 **(34)**; Without You, 1971
(1); Jump Into the Fire, 1972 **(27)**;
Coconut, 1972 **(8)**; Spaceman, 1972
(23); Remember, 1972 **(53)**; As
Time Goes By, 1973 **(86)**; Day-
break, 1974 **(39)**; Many Rivers to
Cross, 1974; Who Done It?, 1977;
Loneliness, 1984

Pop Vocal—New York; real name
is Harry Nelson III

1910 Fruitgum Company

Personnel: Joey Levine (vocals);
Bruce Shay (guitars, vocals); Frank
Jeckell (guitars, vocals); Pat Karwan
(guitars, vocals); Mark Gutkowski
(guitars); Chuck Travis (bass, gui-
tars, vocals); Larry Ripley (horns);
Rusty Oppenheimer (drums); Floyd
Marcus (drums, vocals)

Albums: Simon Says, 1968; A Red Light, 1968; Goody Goody Gumdrops, 1968; Indian Giver, 1969; Hard Rode, 1969; Juiciest Fruitgum, 1970

Singles: Simon Says, 1968 **(4)**; May I Take a Giant Step (Into Your Heart), 1968 **(63)**; 1-2-3 Red Light, 1968 **(5)**; Goody Goody Gumdrops, 1968 **(37)**; Indian Giver, 1969 **(5)**; Special Delivery, 1969 **(38)**; The Train, 1969 **(57)**; When We Get Married, 1969 **(118)**

Bubblegum Pop — New Jersey

Nino & The Ebb Tides

Personnel: Antonio "Nino" Aiello (vocals); Tony DiBari (vocals); Tony Imbimbo (vocals); Vinnie Drago (vocals)

Single: Juke Box Saturday Night, 1961 **(57)**

Pop Vocal — New York

The Nitty Gritty Dirt Band

Personnel: Jeff Hanna (vocals, guitars); Jimmie Fadden (vocals, harmonica, guitars); Ralph Barr (guitars, vocals) left group (1968) replaced (1976) by John Cable (guitars, vocals) replaced (1978) by Bob Carpenter (keyboards, vocals); Les Thompson (bass, guitars, banjo) left group (1974) replaced (1976) by Jackie Clark (bass, vocals) replaced (1978) by Richard Hathaway (bass,

Nitty Gritty Dirt Band: J. Hanna, Fadden, McEuen, Ibbotson

vocals) left group (1982); Jackson Browne (guitars, vocals) replaced (1966) by John McEuen (mandolin, guitars, fiddle, banjo) replaced (1987) by Bernie Leadon (guitars, vocals) left group (1988); Bruce Kunkel (guitars, banjo, fiddle) replaced (1968) by Chris Darrow (guitars, vocals, fiddle) left group (1968) replaced (1974) by Glen Grosclose (guitars) replaced (1976) by Geoffrey Morris (slide guitar) replaced (1978) by Al Garth (saxophones, fiddle) replaced (1981) by Bryan Savage (saxophones) left group (1982); David Hanna (drums, bass, percussion) replaced (1974) by Jimmy Ibbotson (drums, keyboards, guitars, vocals) replaced (1976) by Michael Buono (drums, percussion) replaced (1978) by Merle Bregante (drums, percussion) replaced (1980) by Rick Shlosser (drums, percussion) replaced (1981) by Vic Mastriani (drums, percussion) and Michael Gardner (drums, percussion) replaced (1983) by Jimmy Ibbotson (drums, percussion)

Albums: Nitty Gritty Dirt Band, 1967; Ricochet, 1967; Rare Junk, 1968; Pure Dirt, 1968; Alive, 1968; Uncle Charlie & His Dog Teddy, 1970; All the Good Times, 1971; Will the Circle Be Unbroken, 1972; Stars and Stripes Forever, 1974; Dream, 1975; Dirt, Silver and Gold, 1976; Wild Nights, 1978; An American Dream, 1979; Make a Little Magic, 1980; Jealousy, 1981; Let's Go, 1983; Plain Dirt Fashion, 1984; Partners, Brothers and Friends, 1985; Twenty Years of Dirt, 1986; Hold On, 1987; Workin' Band, 1988; More Great Dirt, 1989; Will the Circle Be Unbroken, Volume II, 1989; The Rest of the Dream, 1990; Live to Five, 1991

Singles: Buy for Me the Rain, 1967 **(45)**; Some of Shelly's Blues, 1969 **(106)**; Mr. Bojangles, 1970 **(9)**; The House at Pooh Corner, 1971 **(53)**; Some of Shelly's Blues, 1971 **(64)**; Jambalaya, 1972 **(84)**; Cosmic Cowboy, 1973 **(123)**; The Battle of New Orleans, 1974 **(72)**; (All I Have to Do Is) Dream, 1975 **(66)**; Hey Good Lookin', 1975; In for the Night, 1978 **(86)**; An American Dream, 1979 **(13)** (with Linda Ronstadt); Make a Little Magic, 1980 **(25)** (with Nicolette Larson); Badlands, 1980 **(107)**; High School Yearbook, 1980; Jealousy, 1981; Fire in the Sky, 1981 **(76)**; Jealousy, 1982; Shot Full of Love, 1983; Dance Little Jean, 1983; Colorado Christmas, 1983; Long Hard Road (The Sharecropper's Dream), 1984; I Love Only You, 1984; High Horse, 1985; Modern Day Romance, 1985; Black Days, Black Nights, 1985; Home Again in My Heart, 1985; Partners, Brothers and Friends, 1986; Baby's Got a Hold On Me, 1987; Fishin' in the Dark, 1987; Oh What a Love, 1987; Down That Road Tonight, 1988; When It's Gone, 1990; You Made Life Good Again, 1990; The Rest, 1990

Country/Rock—California; performed as the Dirt Band from 1978 through 1982; the "Circle" albums feature performances by many notable rock, country and bluegrass recording artists

Nick Noble

Singles: The Bible Tells Me So, 1955 **(22)**; To You, My Love, 1956 **(27)**; A Fallen Star, 1957 **(20)**; Moonlight Swim, 1957 **(37)**

Pop/Country Vocal—Chicago; real name is Nicholas Valkan

Cliff Nobles & Co.

Album: The Horse, 1968
Singles: The Horse, 1968 **(2)**;
Horse Fever, 1968 **(68)**; Switch It
On, 1969 **(93)**
Soul — Alabama

Jimmy Norman

Single: I Don't Love You No
More (I Don't Care About You),
1962 **(47)**
R & B Vocal — Nashville

NRBQ

Personnel: Steve Ferguson (guitars, vocals) replaced (1974) by
Donn Adams (trombone); Terry
Adams (keyboards, woodwinds,
vocals); Frank Gadler (vocals) left
group (1974); Joey Spampinato
(bass, vocals); G. T. Staley (drums,
percussion) replaced (1974) by Tom
Ardolino (drums); added (1971) Al
Anderson (guitars, vocals); added
(1974) Keith Spring (saxophones)
left group (1978); added (1974) Gary
Windo (saxophones) left group
(1978)
Albums: Stomp, 1968; NRBQ,
1969; Boppin' the Blues, 1970;
Scraps, 1972; Workshop, 1973;
NRBQ at Yankee Stadium, 1977;
All Hopped Up, 1978; Kick Me
Hard, 1979; Tiddlywinks, 1980;
Grooves in Orbit, 1983; Christmas
Wish, 1985; Uncommon Denomina-
tors, 1986; God Bless Us All, 1988;
Diggin' Uncle Q, 1989; Wild Week-
end, 1989; Peek-a-Boo/The Best of
NRBQ 1969–1989, 1990
Singles: Stomp, 1969 **(122)**; Get
That Gasoline Blues, 1974 **(70)**; I
Love Her, She Loves Me, 1978;
Rain at the Drive-In, 1983
Blues/Rock — New York

The Nu Tornados

Personnel: Eddie Dono (vocals);
Phil Dale (guitars); Tom Dell (gui-
tars); Mike Perna (bass); Louie
Mann (drums)
Single: Philadelphia U.S.A., 1958
(26)
Pop/Rock — Philadelphia

The Nutty Squirrels

Personnel: Don Elliot (vocals);
Sascha Burland (vocals)
Singles: Uh! Oh! Part 2, 1959
(14); Uh! Oh! Part 1, 1959 **(45)**
Novelty Pop — New York

Laura Nyro

Albums: More Than a Discovery,
1966; Eli and the Thirteenth Confession, 1968; New York Tendaberry,
1969; Christmas and the Beads of
Sweat, 1970; Gonna Take a Miracle,
1971; The First Songs, 1973; Smile,
1976; Season of Lights . . . Laura
Nyro in Concert, 1977; Nested, 1978;
Impressions, 1980; Mother's Spiritual, 1984; Live at the Bottom Line,
1988; Best of Laura Nyro, 1991
Singles: Wedding Bell Blues, 1966
(103); Up on the Roof, 1970 **(92)**;
It's Gonna Take a Miracle, 1972 **(103)**
Blue-Eyed Soul — New York; real
last name is Nigro

Phil Ochs

Albums: All the News That's Fit
to Sing, 1964; I Ain't Marchin' Anymore, 1965; In Concert, 1966; Pleasure of the Harbour, 1967; Tape
from California, 1968; Rehearsals
for Retirement, 1969; Greatest Hits,
1970; Gunfight at Carnegie Hall,
1971; Chords of Fame, 1974; Phil
Ochs Sings, 1976; Interviews, 1976;
Broadside Tapes, 1977; Then and
Now: Live in Vancouver 1968, 1991

Single: Outside a Small Circle of Friends, 1968 **(118)**

Folk/Rock—Texas; committed suicide in April, 1976; brother Michael is respected photographer/archivist of rock music and performers

October Country

Personnel: Michael Lloyd (guitars, keyboards, vocals)

Album: October Country, 1966

Single: October Country, 1966

Psychedelic Pop—California; Lloyd became a well known producer

Brooks O'Dell

Single: Watch Your Step, 1963 **(58)**

R & B Vocal—Philadelphia; vocalist with the Majestics

Kenny O'Dell

Singles: Beautiful People, 1967 **(38)**; Springfield Plane, 1968 **(94)**; Happy with You, 1968 **(118)**; My Honky Tonk Ways, 1975 **(105)**

Country/Pop—Oklahoma; real last name is Gist

Ohio Express

Personnel: Joey Levine (vocals); Dale Powers (guitars, vocals); Douglas Grassel (guitars); Dean Kastran (bass); James Pfayler (keyboards); Tim Corwin (drums)

Albums: Beg, Borrow & Steal, 1968; Ohio Express, 1968; Salt Water Taffy, 1968; Chewy Chewy, 1968; Mercy, 1969; The Very Best of the Ohio Express, 1969

Singles: Beg, Borrow & Steal, 1967 **(29)**; Try It, 1968 **(83)**; Yummy Yummy Yummy, 1968 **(4)**; Down at Lulu's, 1968 **(33)**; Chewy Chewy, 1968 **(15)**; Sweeter Than Sugar, 1969 **(96)**; Mercy, 1969 **(30)**; Pinch Me, 1969 **(99)**; Sausalito, 1969 **(86)**; Cowboy Convention, 1969 **(101)**

Bubblegum Pop—Ohio

The O'Jays

Personnel: Bobby Massey (vocals) left group (1972); Walter Williams (vocals); Eddie Levert (vocals); Bill Isles (vocals) left group (1965); William Powell (vocals; deceased 1977) replaced (1976) by Sam Strain

October Country

Ohio Express: Pfyaler, Kastran, Powers, Levine, Corwin

(vocals); replaced (1988) by Dwain Mitchell (vocals)

Albums: Comin' Through, 1965; Soul Sounds, 1967; Back on Top, 1968; Back Stabbers, 1972; The O'Jays in Philadelphia, 1973; Ship Ahoy, 1973; The O'Jays Live in London, 1974; Survival, 1975; Family Reunion, 1975; Message in the Music, 1976; Travelin' at the Speed of Thought, 1977; The O'Jays: Collectors' Items, 1978; So Full of Love, 1978; Identify Yourself, 1979; The Year 2000, 1980; Greatest Hits, 1981; My Favorite Person, 1982; When Will I See You Again, 1983; Let Me Touch You, 1988; Serious, 1989; Emotionally Yours, 1991; Home for Christmas, 1991

Singles: Lonely Drifter, 1963 (**93**); Stand Tall, 1964 (**131**); Lipstick Traces (on a Cigarette), 1965 (**48**); I've Cried My Last Tear, 1965 (**94**); Stand in for Love, 1965 (**95**); I'll Be Sweeter Tomorrow (Than I Was Today), 1967 (**66**); Look Over Your Shoulder, 1968 (**89**); The Choice, 1968 (**94**); One Night Affair, 1969 (**68**); Deeper (in Love with You), 1970 (**64**); Looky Looky (Look at Me Girl), 1970 (**98**); Back Stabbers, 1972 (**3**); 992 Arguments, 1972 (**57**); Love Train, 1973 (**1**); Time to Get Down, 1973 (**33**); Put Your Hands Together, 1973 (**10**); For the Love of Money, 1974 (**9**); Sunshine Part II, 1974 (**48**); Give the People What They Want, 1975 (**45**); Let Me Make Love to You, 1975 (**75**); I Love Music (Part 1), 1975 (**5**); Livin' for the Weekend, 1976 (**20**); Message in Our Music, 1976 (**49**); Darlin' Darlin' Baby (Sweet, Tender, Love), 1977 (**72**); Use Ta Be My Girl, 1978 (**4**); Brandy, 1978 (**79**); Sing a Happy Song, 1979 (**102**); Forever Mine, 1979 (**28**); Girl, Don't Let It Get You Down,

1980 (**55**); Emotionally Yours, 1991

Soul/Pop Vocal — Ohio

The O'Kaysions

Personnel: Donny Weaver (vocals); Ron Turner (vocals); Jim Spidel (vocals); Jimmy Hennant (vocals); Bruce Joyner (vocals); Wayne Pittman (vocals)

Album: Girl Watcher, 1968
Singles: Girl Watcher, 1968 (**5**); Love Machine, 1968 (**76**)

Blue-Eyed Soul — North Carolina

Oliver

Albums: Good Morning Starshine, 1969; Oliver Again, 1970; Prisms, 1971
Singles: Good Morning Starshine, 1969 (**3**); Jean, 1969 (**2**); Sunday Mornin', 1969 (**35**); Angelica, 1970 (**97**); Early Mornin' Rain, 1971 (**124**)

Pop Vocal — North Carolina; real name is William Oliver Swofford

Ollie & The Nightingales

Personnel: Ollie Hoskins (vocals); Quincy Clifton Billops, Jr. (vocals); Bill Davis (vocals); Nelson Lesure (vocals); Rochester Neal (vocals)
Singles: I Got a Sure Thing, 1968 (**73**); It's a Sad Thing, 1971 (**121**)

R & B Vocal — American

The Olympics

Personnel: Walter Ward (vocals); Charles Fizer (vocals) replaced (1958) by Melvin King (vocals) left group (1966) replaced (1970) by Kenny Sinclair (vocals); Eddie Lewis (vocals); Walter Hammond (vocals) replaced (1959) by Charles Fizer (vocals; deceased 1963) replaced (1963) by Julius McMichael (vocals)

Albums: Hully Gully, 1960; Dance by the Light of the Moon, 1961; Party Time, 1961; The Olympics, 1962; Do the Bounce, 1963; Something Old, Something New, 1965; The Olympics Sing, 1966
Singles: Western Movies, 1958 (**8**); (I Wanna) Dance with the Teacher, 1958 (**71**); Private Eye, 1959 (**95**); (Baby) Hully Gully, 1960 (**72**); Big Boy Pete, 1960 (**50**); Shimmy Like Kate, 1960 (**42**); Dance by the Light of the Moon, 1960 (**47**); Little Pedro, 1961 (**76**); Dooley, 1961 (**94**); The Bounce, 1963 (**40**); Dancin' Holiday, 1963 (**86**); Good Lovin', 1965 (**81**); Mine Exclusively, 1966 (**99**); Baby, Do the Philly Dog, 1966 (**63**)

R & B Vocal — California

Roy Orbison

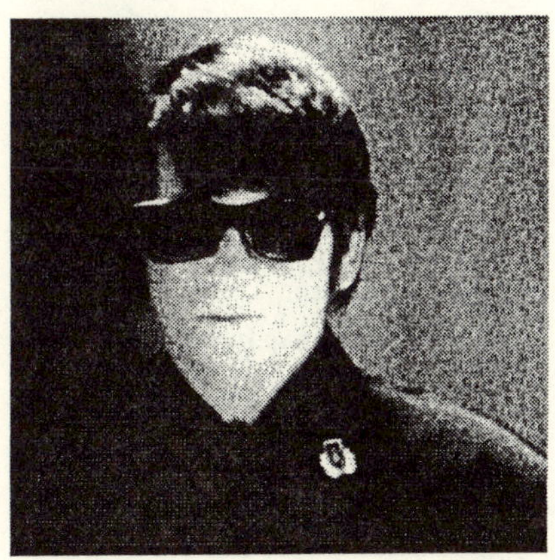

Albums: Lonely & Blue, 1961; Crying, 1962; Greatest Hits, 1962; In Dreams, 1963; Exciting Sounds, 1964; Oh Pretty Woman, 1964;

More of Roy Orbison's Greatest Hits, 1964; Early Orbison, 1964; There Is Only One, 1965; Orbisongs, 1965; The Very Best of Roy Orbison, 1966; The Orbison Way, 1966; The Classic, 1966; Sings Don Gibson, 1967; Greatest Hits, 1967; Cry Softly Lonely One, 1968; Fastest Guitar Alive, 1968; More Greatest Hits, 1969; Many Moods, 1969; Great Songs, 1969; Hank Williams' Songs, 1969; The Big O, 1970; Roy Orbison Sings, 1972; Memphis, 1973; All-Time Greatest Hits, 1973; Milestones, 1974; Monumental Hits, 1975; Monumental Hits Volume 2, 1975; I'm Still in Love with You, 1976; Regeneration, 1977; Laminar Flow, 1979; Golden Days, 1981; The Sun Years, 1984; Go Go Go, 1986; Mystery Girl, 1988; All Time Greatest Hits Volume 1, 1988; All Time Greatest Hits Volume 2, 1988; A Black and White Night, 1989; Singles Collection, 1989; Classic Roy Orbison, 1989; For the Lonely/18 Greatest Hits, 1989; In Dreams/Greatest Hits, 1989

Singles: Ooby Dooby, 1956 **(59)**; Up Town, 1960 **(72)**; Only the Lonely (Know How I Feel), 1960 **(2)**; Blue Angel, 1960 **(9)**; I'm Hurtin', 1960 **(27)**; Running Scared, 1961 **(1)**; Crying, 1961 **(2)**; Candy Man, 1961 **(25)**; Dream Baby (How Long Must I Dream), 1962 **(4)**; The Crowd, 1962 **(26)**; Leah, 1962 **(25)**; Workin' for the Man, 1962 **(33)**; In Dreams, 1963 **(7)**; Falling, 1963 **(22)**; Mean Woman Blues, 1963 **(5)**; Blue Bayou, 1963 **(29)**; Pretty Paper, 1963 **(15)**; It's Over, 1964 **(9)**; Oh, Pretty Woman, 1964 **(1)**; Goodnight, 1965 **(21)**; (Say) You're My Girl, 1965 **(39)**; Ride Away, 1965 **(25)**; Crawling Back, 1965 **(46)**; Let the Good Times Roll, 1965 **(81)**;

Breakin' Up Is Breakin' My Heart, 1966 **(31)**; Twinkle Toes, 1966 **(39)**; Too Soon to Know, 1966 **(68)**; Communication Breakdown, 1966 **(60)**; Cry Softly Lonely One, 1967 **(52)**; That Lovin' You Feelin' Again, 1980 **(55)** (with Emmylou Harris); In My Dreams, 1987; You Got It, 1989 **(9)**; She's a Mystery to Me, 1989; California Blue, 1989

Country/Rock — Texas; Roy died in 1988; was also a member of the Traveling Wilburys

The Original Caste

Personnel: Dixie Lee Innes (vocals)

Singles: One Tin Soldier, 1969 **(34)**; Mr. Monday, 1970 **(119)**; Nothing Can Touch Me, 1970 **(114)**; Ain't That Tellin' You People, 1970 **(117)**

Pop/Rock — American

The Original Casuals

Personnel: Gary Mears (vocals); Jay Joe Adams (vocals); Paul Kearney (vocals)

Single: So Tough, 1958 **(42)**

Pop Vocal — Dallas

The Originals

Personnel: Freddie Gorman (vocals); Crathman Spencer (vocals) replaced (1971) by Ty Hunter (vocals); Henry Dixon (vocals); Walter Gaines (vocals)

Albums: Green Grow the Lilacs, 1969; Baby, I'm for Real, 1970; Portrait, 1970; Naturally Together, 1971; Definitions, 1972; Game Called Love, 1974; California Sunset, 1975; Communique, 1976; Down to Love Town, 1977; Another Time Another

Place, 1978; Come Away with Me, 1978; Yesterday and Today, 1979

Singles: Baby, I'm for Real, 1969 **(14)**; The Bells, 1970 **(12)**; We Can Make It Baby, 1970 **(74)**; God Bless Whoever Sent You, 1970 **(53)**; I'm Someone Who Cares, 1972 **(113)**; Down to Love Town, 1976 **(47)**

Soul/R & B Vocal — Detroit

Tony Orlando

Singles: Halfway to Paradise, 1961 **(39)**; Bless You, 1961 **(15)**; Happy Times (Are Here to Stay), 1961 **(82)**; Chills, 1962 **(109)**; Shirley, 1963 **(133)**; I'll Be There, 1963 **(124)**; I Was a Boy (When You Needed a Man), 1969 **(109)**; Sweets for My Sweet, 1979 **(54)**

Pop Vocal — New York; real name is Michael Anthony Orlando Cassavitis

The Orlons

Personnel: Shirley Brickley (vocals; deceased 1977); Steve Caldwell (vocals) left group (1964); Rosetta Hightower (vocals); Marlena Davis (vocals) replaced (1964) by Audrey Brickley (vocals)

Albums: The Wah Watusi, 1962; All the Hits, 1962; South Street, 1963; Not Me, 1963; Biggest Hits, 1963; Golden Hits, 1964; Down Memory Lane, 1966; The Best of the Orlons, 1977

Singles: The Wah Watusi, 1962 **(2)**; Don't Hang Up, 1962 **(4)**; South Street, 1963 **(3)**; Not Me, 1963 **(12)**; Cross Fire!, 1963 **(19)**; Bon-Doo-Wah, 1963 **(55)**; Shimmy Shimmy, 1964 **(66)**; Rules of Love, 1964 **(66)**; Knock! Knock! (Who's

There?), 1964 **(64)**; I Ain't Comin' Back, 1965 **(129)**

Soul/Pop Vocal — Philadelphia

Orphan Egg

Personnel: Jim Bates (vocals); Pat Gallagher (guitars, vocals); Larry Smith (bass); Dave Monley (keyboards, guitars); George Lorix (drums)

Album: Orphan Egg, 1968

Hard Rock — American

Orpheus

Personnel: Jack McKenes (guitars, vocals) replaced (1969) by Elliott Sherman (keyboards); Bruce Arnold (guitars, vocals); Eric Gulliksen (bass, vocals) replaced (1969) by Howard Harsh (bass); Harry Sandler (drums, vocals) replaced (1969) by Bernard Purdie (drums)

Albums: Orpheus, 1967; Ascending, 1968; Joyful, 1968; Orpheus, 1969

Singles: Brown Arms in Houston, 1969 **(91)**; Can't Find the Time, 1969 **(80)**

Soft Pop/Rock — New York

Johnny Otis Show

Albums: The Johnny Otis Show, 1958; Cold Shot, 1969; Cuttin' Up, 1970; Live at Monterrey, 1971; Bulldog, 1975; Rock 'n' Roll History, 1979

Singles: Willie and the Hand Jive, 1958 **(9)**; Crazy Country Hop, 1958 **(87)**; Castin' My Spell, 1959 **(52)**; Mumblin' Mosie, 1960 **(80)**

R & B Vocal — California; Otis's real name is Veliotes

The Other Half

Personnel: Randy Holden (guitars, vocals); Mike Port (guitars, vocals)

Single: Mr. Pharmacist, 1967

Psychedelic Pop — American

The Outsiders

Geraci, King, Bruno, Baker, Masden

Personnel: Sonny Geraci (vocals); Tom King (guitars); Bill Bruno (guitars); Merdin Masden (bass, guitars); Ricky Baker (drums)

Albums: Time Won't Let Me In, 1965; Album 2, 1966; In, 1966; Happening Live, 1967

Singles: Time Won't Let Me, 1966 **(5)**; Girl in Love, 1966 **(21)**; Respectable, 1966 **(15)**; Help Me Girl, 1966 **(37)**; I'll Give You Time to Think It Over, 1967 **(118)**; Gotta Leave Us Alone, 1967 **(121)**; Little Bit of Lovin', 1967 **(117)**; Changes, 1970 **(107)**

Pop/Rock — Pennsylvania

The Ovations

Personnel: Louis Williams (vocals); Rochester Neal (vocals); Bill Davis (vocals); Quincy Clifton Billops, Jr. (vocals)

Singles: It's Wonderful to Be in Love, 1965 **(61)**; Touching Me, 1972 **(104)**; Having a Party, 1973 **(56)**

R & B Vocal — American

The Overlanders

Personnel: Paul Friswell (guitars, vocals)

Single: Yesterday's Gone, 1964 **(75)**

Pop/Rock — British

Donnie Owens

Single: Need You, 1958 **(25)**

Pop/Country — American

Pacific Gas & Electric

Personnel: Charlie Allen (vocals; deceased 1990); Glenn Schwartz (guitars) replaced (1971) by Ken Utterback (guitars) replaced (1973) by Robert Mann (guitars); Tom Marshall (guitars); Brent Black (bass) replaced (1971) by Frank Petricca (bass) replaced (1973) by Gordon Edwards (bass); Frank Cook (drums)

Albums: Pacific Gas & Electric, 1969; Get It On, 1969; Are You Ready, 1970; Pacific Gas & Electric Hard Burn, 1971; Pacific Gas & Electric with Charlie Allen, 1973; Best, 1973; Live and Kicking at Lexington, 1974

Singles: Are You Ready?, 1970 **(14)**; Father Come on Home, 1970 **(93)**; Thank God for You Baby, 1972 **(97)**

Hard/Blues Rock — California

The Packers

Personnel: Charles "Packy" Axton (vocals)

Single: Hole in the Wall, 1965
(43)
R & B Vocal—American

Patti Page

Albums: Manhattan Tower, 1956;
Golden Hits of the Boys, 1962; Say
Wonderful Things, 1963; Hush,
Hush, Sweet Charlotte, 1965; Gentle
on My Mind, 1968

Singles: Let Me Go, Lover!, 1954
(8); Piddily Patter Patter, 1955 **(47)**;
Croce di Oro (Cross of Gold), 1955
(16); Go on with the Wedding, 1956
(11); Too Young to Go Steady, 1956
(73); My First Formal Gown, 1956
(80); Allegheny Moon, 1956 **(2)**;
The Strangest Romance, 1956 **(93)**;
Mama from the Train, 1956 **(11)**;
Every Time (I Feel His Spirit), 1956
(87); Repeat After Me, 1957 **(53)**; A
Poor Man's Roses (or a Rich Man's
Gold), 1957 **(14)**; The Wall, 1957
(43); Old Cape Cod, 1957 **(3)**;
Wondering, 1957 **(12)**; I'll Remem-
ber Today, 1957 **(23)**; Belonging to
Someone, 1958 **(13)**; Another Time,
Another Place, 1958 **(20)**; Left Right
Out of Your Heart (Hi Lee Hi Lo
Hi Lup Up Up), 1958 **(9)**; Fibbin',
1958 **(39)**; Trust in Me, 1959 **(43)**;
The Walls Have Ears, 1959 **(77)**;
With My Eyes Wide Open I'm
Dreaming, 1959 **(59)**; Goodbye
Charlie, 1959 **(90)**; The Sound of
Music, 1959 **(90)**; Two Thousand,
Two Hundred, Twenty-Three
Miles, 1960 **(67)**; One of Us (Will
Weep Tonight), 1960 **(31)**; I Wish
I'd Never Been Born, 1960 **(52)**;
Don't Read the Letter, 1960 **(65)**; A
City Girl Stole My Country Boy,
1961 **(90)**; You'll Answer to Me, 1961
(46); Mom and Dad's Waltz, 1961
(58); Broken Heart and a Pillow
Filled with Tears, 1961 **(91)**; Go on

Home, 1961 **(42)**; Most People Get
Married, 1962 **(27)**; The Boys'
Night Out, 1962 **(49)**; Just a Simple
Melody, 1963 **(114)**; Pretty Boy
Lonely, 1963 **(98)**; Say Wonderful
Things, 1963 **(81)**; I'm Walkin', 1963
(127); I Adore You, 1964 **(131)**;
Hush, Hush, Sweet Charlotte, 1965
(8); You Can't Be True, Dear, 1965
(94); Custody, 1966 **(126)**; Till You
Come Back to Me, 1966 **(130)**; Gen-
tle on My Mind, 1968 **(66)**; Little
Green Apples, 1968 **(96)**; Stand by
Your Man, 1968 **(121)**; I Wish I
Had a Mommy Like You, 1970
(114)

Pop Vocal—Oklahoma; real name
is Clara Ann Fowler

The Palace Guard

Personnel: Emitt Rhodes (guitars,
vocals); Don Beaudine (guitars, vocals); Dave Beaudine (guitars, vocals); John Beaudine (bass, vocals);
Chuck McLing (keyboards, woodwinds); Rick Meser (keyboards,
vocals); Mike Conley (drums, percussion)

Album: The Palace Guard, 1966
Singles: Like Falling Sugar, 1966;
All Night Long, 1966
Pop/Rock—California

The Parade

Personnel: Jerry Riopelle (guitars, vocals); Smokey Roberts (bass); Murray MacLeod (drums)
Album: The Parade's Sunshine Girl, 1967
Singles: Sunshine Girl, 1967 **(20)**; The Radio Song, 1968 **(127)**
Pop/Rock—California

The Paradons

Personnel: West Tyler (vocals); Chuck Weldon (vocals); Billy Myers (vocals); William Powers (vocals)
Single: Diamonds and Pearls, 1960 **(18)**
R & B Vocal—California

The Paragons

Personnel: Julius McMichael (vocals)
Singles: Blue Velvet, 1960 **(103)**; If, 1961 **(82)**
R & B Vocal—New York

The Paris Sisters

Personnel: Albeth Paris (vocals); Priscilla Paris (vocals); Sherrell Paris (vocals)
Singles: Be My Boy, 1961 **(56)**; I Love How You Love Me, 1961 **(5)**; He Knows I Love Him Too Much, 1962 **(34)**; Let Me Be the One, 1962 **(87)**; Dream Lover, 1964 **(91)**
Pop Vocal—San Francisco

The Paramounts

Personnel: Robin Trower (guitars); Chris Copping (bass) replaced (1963) by Diz Derrick (bass); Gary Brooker (keyboards, vocals); B. J. Wilson (drums)
Album: The Paramounts (EP), 1963
Blues/Rock—British

Bobby Parker

Single: Watch Your Step, 1962 **(51)**
Pop Vocal—American

Fess Parker

Singles: Ballad of Davy Crockett, 1955 **(5)**; Wringle Wrangle, 1957 **(12)**
Pop Vocal—Texas; star of TV's "Daniel Boone"

Robert Parker

Album: Barefootin', 1966
Singles: All Nite Long (Part 1), 1959 **(113)**; Barefootin', 1966 **(7)**; The Scratch, 1966 **(128)**; Tip Toe, 1967 **(83)**
Soul—Louisiana

The Parliaments

Personnel: George Clinton (vocals); Clarence "Fuzzy" Haskins (vocals); Calvin Simon (vocals); Raymond Davis (vocals); Grady Thomas (vocals)
Singles: (I Wanna) Testify, 1967 **(20)**; All Your Goodies Are Gone (The Loser's Seat), 1967 **(80)**; Look at What I Almost Missed, 1968 **(104)**
Soul Vocal—American; evolved into Parliament

The Passions

Personnel: Jimmy Gallagher (vocals)
Singles: Just to Be with You, 1959 **(69)**; I Only Want You, 1960 **(113)**
R & B Vocal—New York

The Pastel Six

Single: The Cinnamon Cinder
(It's a Very Nice Dance), 1962 **(25)**
Folk/Pop—California

The Pastels

Personnel: Big Dee Irwin (vocals);
Richard Travis (vocals); Jimmy
Willingham (vocals); Tony Thomas
(vocals)
Single: Been So Long, 1958 **(24)**
R & B Vocal—American

Patience & Prudence

Personnel: Patience McIntyre
(vocals); Prudence McIntyre (vocals)
Singles: Tonight You Belong to
Me, 1956 **(4)**; Gonna Get Along
Without Ya Now, 1956 **(11)**; The
Money Tree, 1956 **(73)**
Pop Vocal—Los Angeles

Patty & The Emblems

Personnel: Patty Russell (vocals)
Single: Mixed-Up, Shook-Up,
Girl, 1964 **(37)**
Pop Vocal—New Jersey

Les Paul & Mary Ford

Albums: Hit Makers, 1954; Les
and Mary, 1955; Time to Dream,
1956; Lover, 1957; Hits of Les &
Mary, 1958; Les Paul and Mary
Ford, 1965; Les Paul Now, 1968;
Very Best of Les Paul, 1974; The
World Is Waiting for the Sunrise,
1974; Chester & Lester, 1977 (with
Chet Atkins); Guitar Monsters, 1978
(with Chet Atkins); Multi Trackin',
1979

Singles: Hummingbird, 1955 **(7)**;
Amukiriki (The Lord Willing), 1955
(38); Magic Melody, 1955 **(96)**;
Texas Lady, 1956 **(91)**; Moritat
(Theme from "Three Penny
Opera"), 1956 **(49)**; Nuevo Laredo,
1956 **(91)**; Cinco Robles, 1957 **(35)**;
Put a Ring on My Finger, 1958
(32); It's Been a Long, Long Time,
1961 **(105)**; Jura (I Swear I Love
You), 1961 **(37)**
Pop—American; divorced in 1963;
subsequent recordings were Les
solo; Mary's real name was Colleen
Summer; she died in 1977

Paul & Paula

Personnel: Ray "Paul" Hildebrand
(vocals); Jill "Paula" Jackson (vocals)
Albums: Paul & Paula Sing for
Young Lovers, 1963; We Got To-
gether, 1963
Singles: Hey Paula, 1962 **(1)**;
Young Lovers, 1963 **(6)**; First Quar-
rel, 1963 **(27)**; Something Old,
Something New, 1963 **(77)**; Flipped
Over You, 1963 **(108)**; A Perfect
Pair, 1963 **(105)**; First Day Back at
School, 1963 **(60)**; We'll Never
Break Up for Good, 1964 **(105)**
Pop Vocal—Texas; Hildebrand
retired in 1963 to raise a family in
Oregon

Pauper

Personnel: Adam Mitchell (gui-
tars, vocals, keyboards, drums);
Chuck Beal (guitars, mandolin);
Denny Gerrard (bass) replaced
(1968) by Brad Campbell (bass,
guitars, drums, vocals); Skip Prokop
(drums, vocals, guitars)
Albums: Magic People, 1967; Ellis
Island, 1968
Pop/Rock—Canadian

Rita Pavone

Album: Rita Pavone, 1964
Singles: Remember Me, 1964
(26); Just Once More, 1964 **(123)**;
Wait for Me, 1964 **(104)**
Pop Vocal—Italian

Tom Paxton

Albums: Ramblin' Boy, 1964;
Ain't That News, 1965; Outward
Bound, 1966; Morning Again, 1968;
Things I Notice Now, 1969;
Number 6, 1970; The Compleat
Tom Paxton, 1971; How Come the
Sun, 1971; Peace Will Come, 1972;
New Songs, Old Friends, 1973;
Children's Song Book, 1974;
Something in My Life, 1975; Satur-
day Night, 1976; New Songs from
the Briar Patch, 1977; Heroes, 1978;
Up & Up, 1980; Paxton Report,
1981; Even a Gray Day, 1983; The
Marvelous Toy and Other Galli-
maufry, 1984; One Million Lawyers,
1987; Politics, 1988
Folk/Rock—Oklahoma; Tom was
a popular Greenwich Village per-
former in the 1960s

Peaches & Herb

Personnel: Herb Fame (vocals);
Francine "Peaches" Barker (vocals)
replaced (1968) by Marlene
"Peaches" Mack (vocals) replaced
(1969) by Francine "Peaches" Barker
(vocals) retired (1971) replaced (1977)
by Linda "Peaches" Greene (vocals)
Albums: Let's Fall in Love, 1967;
For Your Love, 1967; Golden
Duets, 1968; Greatest Hits, 1968;
Peaches & Herb, 1977; 2 Hot, 1979;
Twice the Fire, 1979; Love Is
Strange, 1979; Worth the Wait,
1980; Sayin' Something, 1981
Singles: Let's Fall in Love, 1966

(21); Close Your Eyes, 1967 **(8)**; For
Your Love, 1967 **(20)**; Love Is
Strange, 1967 **(13)**; Two Little Kids,
1967 **(31)**; The Ten Commandments
of Love, 1968 **(55)**; United, 1968
(46); Let's Make a Promise, 1968
(75); So True, 1969 **(126)**; When
He Touches Me (Nothing Else Mat-
ters), 1969 **(49)**; Let Me Be the
One, 1969 **(74)**; It's Just a Game,
Love, 1970 **(110)**; The Sound of
Silence, 1971 **(100)**; We're Still Together, 1977 **(107)**; Shake Your
Groove Thing, 1978 **(5)**; Reunited,
1979 **(1)**; We've Got Love, 1979
(44); Roller Skatin' Mate, 1979
(66); I Pledge My Love, 1980 **(19)**;
One Child of Love, 1980; Surrender, 1981; Freeway, 1981
Soul—Washington, D.C.; Herb
was a policeman in Washington,
D.C.

Peanut Butter Conspiracy

Personnel: Sandi Robinson (vocals); Lance Fent (guitars); Bill Wolf
(guitars, harmonica); John Merrill
(guitars); Alan Brackett (bass); Jim
Voight (drums)
Albums: The Peanut Butter Conspiracy Is Spreading, 1967; Great

Conspiracy, 1968; For Children of All Ages, 1969

Singles: It's a Happening Thing, 1967 **(93)**; I'm a Fool, 1968 **(125)**

Psychedelic Pop—California

Pearls Before Swine

Personnel: Tom Rapp (guitars, vocals); Wayne Harley (banjo, vocals); Lane Lender (bass, guitars, vocals) replaced (1968) by William Salter (bass); Roger Krissinger (keyboards) replaced (1968) by Jim Bohanon (keyboards) replaced (1969) by Jim Fairs (guitars, keyboards, vocals); Warren Smith (drums) replaced (1968) by Grady Tate (drums)

Albums: One Nation Underground, 1967; Balaklava, 1968; These Things Too, 1969; The Use of Ashes, 1970; City of Gold, 1971; Beautiful Lies You Could Live, 1971

Country/Rock—American; Rapp replaced the group with studio musicians after 3rd album

Paul Peek

Singles: Brother-in-Law (He's a Moocher), 1961 **(84)**; Pin the Tail on the Donkey, 1966 **(91)**

Pop/Rock—American; former Blue Caps member

The Peels

Single: Juanita Banana, 1966 **(59)**

Pop/Rock—American

The Penguins

Personnel: Cleveland Duncan (vocals); Dexter Tisby (vocals); Bruce Tate (vocals); Curtis Williams (vocals)

Album: Cool Cool Penguins, 1955

Single: Earth Angel (Will You Be Mine), 1954 **(8)**

R & B Vocal—Los Angeles

The Pentagons

Personnel: Joe Jones (vocals)

Singles: To Be Loved (Forever), 1961 **(48)**; I Wonder (If Your Love Will Ever Belong to Me), 1961 **(84)**

R & B Vocal—California

The Pentangle

Personnel: Bert Jansch (vocals, guitars) replaced (1973) by Mike Pigott (guitars) replaced (1990) by Bert Jansch (guitars); John Renbourn (vocals, guitars) replaced (1990) by Peter Kirtley (guitars, vocals); Jacqui McShee (vocals); Danny Thompson (bass) replaced (1990) by Nigel Portman-Smith (bass, keyboards); Terry Cox (drums, percussion) replaced (1990) by Gerry Conway (drums)

Albums: The Pentangle, 1968; Sweet Child, 1968; Basket of Light, 1969; Cruel Sister, 1970; Reflections, 1971; Solomon's Seal, 1972; Pentangle History Book, 1972; Pentangling, 1973; Pentangle Collection, 1975; Anthology, 1978; At Their Best, 1983; Open the Door, 1985; Essential Volume 1, 1986; Essential Volume 2, 1987; Maid That's Deep in Love, 1987; In the Round, 1988; So Early in the Spring, 1989

Folk/Rock—British

People

Personnel: John Tristao (vocals); Gene Mason (vocals) left group (1969); Lawrence (vocals) left group (1969); Geoff Levin (guitars)

The Pentangle: Renbourn, Cox, McShee, Thompson, Jansch

People

replaced (1969) by Tom Tucker
(guitars); Robb Levin (bass); Albert
Ribisi (keyboards); Denny Fridkin
(drums)
Albums: I Love You, 1968; Both
Sides of People, 1968; There Are
People, 1969
Singles: I Love You, 1968 **(14)**;
Apple Cider, 1968 **(111)**
Psychedelic Pop—California

The Peppermint Rainbow

Album: Will You Be Staying
After Sunday?, 1969
Singles: Will You Be Staying
After Sunday?, 1968 **(32)**; Don't
Wake Me Up in the Morning,
Michael, 1968 **(54)**
Bubblegum Pop—American

The Peppermint Trolley Company

Album: Peppermint Trolley Company, 1968
Single: Baby You Come Rollin'
Across My Mind, 1968 **(59)**
Pop/Rock—American

Carl Perkins

Albums: Dance Album "Teenbeat," 1959; Whole Lotta Shakin',

1959; Country Boy Dreams, 1968; On Top, 1969; Blue Suede Shoes, 1969; Original Golden Hits, 1970; Boppin' the Blues, 1970 (with NRBQ); Carl Perkins, 1971; Brown-Eyed Handsome Man, 1972; Greatest Hits, 1973; My Kind of Country, 1974; Rockin' Guitar Man, 1975; Original Carl Perkins, 1976; From Jackson, Tennessee, 1977; Ol' Blue Suede's Back, 1978

Singles: Blue Suede Shoes, 1956 **(2)**; Boppin' the Blues, 1956 **(70)**; Your True Love, 1957 **(67)**; Pink Pedal Pushers, 1958 **(91)**; Pointed Toe Shoes, 1959 **(93)**

Rockabilly — Tennessee

Peter & Gordon

Peter Asher, Gordon Waller

Personnel: Peter Asher (vocals); Gordon Waller (vocals)

Albums: Peter & Gordon, 1964; A World Without Love, 1964; In Touch, 1964; I Don't Want to See You Again, 1965; I Go to Pieces, 1965; True Love Ways, 1965; Hurtin' 'n' Lovin', 1965; Woman, 1966; Peter & Gordon, 1966; Somewhere, 1966; Best of Peter & Gordon, 1966; Lady Godiva, 1966; Knights in Rusty Armour, 1967; In London for Tea, 1967; Hot, Cold & Custard, 1968; The Best of Peter & Gordon, 1977

Singles: A World Without Love, 1964 **(1)**; Nobody I Know, 1964 **(12)**; I Don't Want to See You Again, 1964 **(16)**; I Go to Pieces, 1965 **(9)**; True Love Ways, 1965 **(14)**; To Know You Is to Love You, 1965 **(24)**; Don't Pity Me, 1965 **(83)**; Woman, 1966 **(14)**; Stranger with a Black Dove, 1966 **(130)**; There's No Living Without Your Loving, 1966 **(50)**; To Show I Love You, 1966 **(98)**; Lady Godiva, 1966 **(6)**; Knight in Rusty Armour, 1966 **(15)**; Sunday for Tea, 1967 **(31)**; The Jokers, 1967 **(97)**; You've Had Better Times, 1968 **(118)**

Pop Vocal — British; Peter's sister was Paul McCartney's girlfriend; Paul wrote "A World Without Love"

Peter, Paul & Mary

Personnel: Peter Yarrow (guitars, vocals); Paul Stookey (guitars, vocals); Mary Travers (vocals)

Albums: Peter, Paul & Mary, 1962; (Moving), 1963; In the Wind, 1963; Peter, Paul & Mary in Concert, 1964; A Song Will Rise, 1965; See What Tomorrow Brings, 1965; Peter, Paul and Mary Album, 1966; Album 1700, 1967; Late Again, 1968; Peter, Paul and Mommy, 1969; 10 Years Together/The Best of Peter, Paul and Mary, 1970; Reunion, 1978; No Easy Walk to Freedom, 1989; Flowers and Stones, 1990

Singles: Lemon Tree, 1962 **(35)**; If I Had a Hammer, 1962 **(10)**; Big Boat, 1962 **(93)**; Settle Down (Goin'

Down That Highway), 1963 **(56)**; Puff the Magic Dragon, 1963 **(2)**; Blowin' in the Wind, 1963 **(2)**; Don't Think Twice, It's All Right, 1963 **(9)**; Stewball, 1963 **(35)**; Tell It on the Mountain, 1964 **(33)**; Oh, Rock My Soul, 1964 **(93)**; For Lovin' Me, 1965 **(30)**; When the Ship Comes In, 1965 **(91)**; Early Morning Rain, 1965 **(91)**; The Cruel War, 1966 **(52)**; The Other Side of This Life, 1966 **(100)**; Hurry Sundown, 1967 **(123)**; I Dig Rock and Roll Music, 1967 **(9)**; Too Much of Nothing, 1967 **(35)**; Love City (Postcard to Duluth), 1968 **(113)**; Day Is Done, 1969 **(21)**; Leaving on a Jet Plane, 1969 **(1)**

Folk/Pop — American

Paul Petersen

Album: Teen Age Triangle, 1963 (with James Darren and Shelley Fabares)

Singles: She Can't Find Her Keys, 1962 **(19)**; Keep Your Love Locked (Deep in Your Heart), 1962 **(58)**; Lollipops and Roses, 1962 **(54)**; My Dad, 1962 **(6)**; Amy, 1963 **(65)**; The Cheer Leader, 1963 **(78)**

Pop Vocal — California; played Jeff Stone on TV's "Donna Reed Show"

Ray Peterson

Albums: Ray Peterson, 1959; Tell Laura I Love Her, 1960; Missing You, 1961; Promises, 1964

Singles: The Wonder of You, 1959 **(25)**; Goodnight My Love (Pleasant Dreams), 1959 **(64)**; What Do You Want to Make Those Eyes at Me For, 1960 **(104)**; Tell Laura I Love Her, 1960 **(7)**; Corinna, Corinna, 1960 **(9)**; I'm Tired, 1961 **(104)**; Sweet Little Kathy, 1961 **(100)**;

Missing You, 1961 **(29)**; I Could Have Loved You So Well, 1961 **(57)**; Give Us Your Blessing, 1963 **(70)**; Promises, 1964 **(108)**; The Wonder of You, 1964 **(70)**; Oh No, 1964 **(128)**; Across the Street (Is a Million Miles Away), 1964 **(106)**

Pop Vocal — Texas

The Pets

Personnel: Richard Podolor (guitars)

Single: Cha-Hua-Hua, 1958 **(34)**

Instrumental Pop — American

James Phelps

Single: Love Is a 5-Letter Word, 1965 **(66)**

R & B Vocal — Louisiana; former Soul Stirrers vocalist

"Little Esther" Phillips

Albums: Release Me!, 1963; And I Love Him, 1965; Sings, 1966; Esther, 1967; Country Side, 1967; Burnin', 1971; From a Whisper to a Scream, 1972; Alone Again Naturally, 1972; Black-Eyed Blues, 1974; Performance, 1975; What a Difference a Day Makes, 1975 (with Joe Beck); Confessin' the Blues, 1976; For All We Know, 1976; Capricorn Princess, 1977; You've Come a Long Way Baby, 1977; Esther Phillips, 1978; Here's Esther, Are You Ready, 1979; Good Black Is Hard to Crack, 1981

Singles: Release Me, 1962 **(8)**; I Really Don't Want to Know, 1963 **(61)**; Am I That Easy to Forget, 1963 **(112)**; If You Want It (I've Got It), 1963 **(129)** (with Big Al Downing); You Never Miss Your Water

(Till the Well Runs Dry), 1963 **(73)** (with Big Al Downing); And I Love Him, 1965 **(54)**; Moonglow & Theme from Picnic, 1965 **(115)**; Let Me Know When It's Over, 1965 **(129)**; When a Woman Loves a Man, 1966 **(73)**; Release Me, 1967 **(93)**; Too Late to Worry, Too Blue to Cry, 1969 **(121)**; Set Me Free, 1970 **(118)**; Home Is Where the Hatred Is, 1972 **(122)**; I've Never Found a Man (to Love Me Like You Do), 1972 **(106)**; What a Diff'rence a Day Makes, 1975 **(20)**

R & B Vocal—Texas; died in 1984

Phil Phillips

Singles: Sea of Love, 1959 **(2)** (with the Twilights); What Will I Tell My Heart, 1960 **(108)**

R & B Vocal—Louisiana

Bobby "Boris" Pickett & The Crypt Kickers

Album: The Original Monster Mash, 1962

Singles: Monster Mash, 1962 **(1)**; Monsters' Holiday, 1962 **(30)**; Graduation Day, 1963 **(88)**; Monster Swim, 1964 **(135)**; Monster Mash, 1970 **(91)**; Monster Mash, 1973 **(10)**; King Kong (Your Song), 1976 **(107)** (with Pete Ferrara)

Novelty Pop—Massachusetts

Wilson Pickett

Albums: In the Midnight Hour, 1965; The Exciting Wilson Pickett, 1966; The Wicked Pickett, 1967; The Sound of Wilson Pickett, 1967; The Best of Wilson Pickett, 1967;

I'm in Love, 1968; The Midnight Mover, 1968; Hey Jude, 1969; Right On, 1970; Wilson Pickett in Philadelphia, 1970; The Best of Wilson Pickett, Volume II, 1971; Don't Knock My Love, 1971; Wilson Pickett's Greatest Hits, 1973; Mr. Magic Man, 1973; Tonight I'm My Biggest Audience, 1974; Miz Lena's Boy, 1974; Live in Japan, 1974; Join Me and Let's Be Free, 1975; Peace Breaker, 1975; Funky Situation, 1978; It's Too Late, 1979; I Want You, 1979; Right Track, 1981; Best of Wilson Pickett, 1981

Singles: If You Need Me, 1963 **(64)**; It's Too Late, 1963 **(49)**; I'm Down to My Last Heartbreak, 1963 **(95)**; I'm Gonna Cry, 1964 **(124)**; In the Midnight Hour, 1965 **(21)**; Don't Fight It, 1965 **(53)**; My Heart Belongs to You, 1965 **(109)**; 634-5789 (Soulville, U.S.A.), 1966 **(13)**; Ninety-Nine and a Half (Won't Do), 1966 **(53)**; Land of 1000 Dances, 1966 **(6)**; Mustang Sally, 1966 **(23)**; Everybody Needs Somebody to Love, 1967 **(29)**; I Found a Love—Part 1, 1967 **(32)**; Soul Dance Number Three, 1967 **(55)**; You Can't Stand Alone, 1967 **(70)**; Funky Broadway, 1967 **(8)**; Stag-O-Lee, 1967 **(22)**; I'm in Love, 1967 **(45)**; Jealous Love, 1968 **(50)**; I've Come a Long Way, 1968 **(101)**; She's Lookin' Good, 1968 **(15)**; I'm a Midnight Mover, 1968 **(24)**; I Found a True Love, 1968 **(42)**; A Man and a Half, 1968 **(42)**; Hey Jude, 1968 **(23)**; Mini-Skirt Minnie, 1969 **(50)**; Born to Be Wild, 1969 **(64)**; Hey Joe, 1969 **(59)**; You Keep Me Hanging On, 1969 **(92)**; Sugar Sugar/Cole, Cooke & Redding, 1970 **(25)**; She Said Yes, 1970 **(68)**; Engine Number 9, 1970 **(14)**; Don't Let the Green Grass Fool You, 1971

(17); Don't Knock My Love—Part 1, 1971 (13); Call My Name, I'll Be There, 1971 (52); Fire and Water, 1971 (24); Funk Factory, 1972 (58); Mama Told Me Not to Come, 1972 (99); Mr. Magic Man, 1973 (98); International Playboy, 1973 (104); Take a Closer Look at the Woman You're With, 1973 (90); Soft Soul Boogie Woogie, 1973 (103)

Soul Vocal—Alabama; former Falcons lead singer

Pieces of Eight

Single: Lonely Drifter, 1967 (59)
Pop/Rock—American

Pink Floyd

Personnel: Syd Barrett (guitars, vocals) replaced (1969) by David Gilmour (guitars, vocals); Roger Waters (bass, vocals) left group (1984); Richard Wright (keyboards, vocals); Nick Mason (drums, percussion)

Albums: The Piper at the Gates of Dawn, 1967; A Saucerful of Secrets, 1968; More, 1969; Ummagumma, 1969; Atom Heart Mother, 1970; Zabriskie Point (Soundtrack), 1970; Meddle, 1971; Relics, 1971; Obscured by the Clouds, 1972; Dark Side of the Moon, 1973; A Nice Pair (Piper & Saucerful), 1973; Wish You Were Here, 1975; Animals, 1977; The Best of Pink Floyd, 1978; The Wall, 1979; A Collection of Great Dance Songs, 1981; The Final Cut, 1983; Works, 1983; A Momentary Lapse of Reason, 1987; The Delicate Sound of Thunder, 1988

Singles: Arnold Layne, 1967; See Emily Play, 1969 (134); One of These Days, 1971; Money, 1973 (13); Time, 1973 (43); Us and Them, 1974 (101); Have a Cigar, 1975; Shine on You Crazy Diamond, 1975; Sheep, 1977; Another Brick in the Wall, 1980 (1); Run Like Hell, 1980 (53); Comfortably

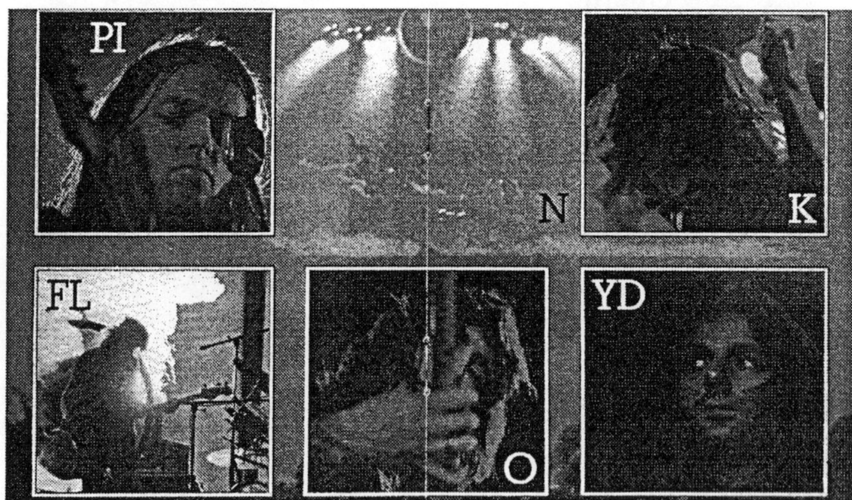

Pink Floyd; *counter-clockwise from top left:* **Gilmour, Gilmour, Waters, Wright, Mason**

Numb, 1980; When the Tigers Broke Free, 1982; Not Now John, 1983; Learning to Fly, 1987 **(70)**; On the Turning Away, 1987

Videos: The Wall, 1979; The Delicate Sound of Thunder, 1988

Progressive/Art Rock—British; the film *The Wall* was scored by Roger Waters and starred Boomtown Rats' Bob Geldof

Gene Pitney

Albums: Only Love Can Break a Heart, 1962; Gene Pitney Sings Just for You, 1963; World-Wide Winners, 1963; Blue Gene, 1963; Gene Pitney's Big Sixteen, 1964; It Hurts to Be in Love, 1964; George Jones & Gene Pitney, 1965; I Must Be Seeing Things, 1965; Big Sixteen, Volume 2, 1965; Looking Through the Eyes of Love, 1965; Big Sixteen, Volume 3, 1966; Greatest Hits of All Times, 1966; She's a Heartbreaker, 1968; The Best of Gene Pitney, 1968; Double Gold, 1968; Sings Bacharach, 1969; Anthology 1961–1968, 1978

Singles: (I Wanna) Love My Life Away, 1961 **(39)**; Every Breath I Take, 1961 **(42)**; Town Without Pity, 1961 **(13)**; (The Man Who Shot) Liberty Valance, 1962 **(4)**; Only Love Can Break a Heart, 1962 **(2)**; If I Didn't Have a Dime (to Play the Jukebox), 1962 **(58)**; Half Heaven—Half Heartache, 1962 **(12)**; Mecca, 1963 **(12)**; Teardrop by Teardrop, 1963 **(130)**; True Love Never Runs Smooth, 1963 **(21)**; Twenty Four Hours to Tulsa, 1963 **(17)**; That Girl Belongs to Yesterday, 1964 **(49)**; Who Needs It, 1964**(131)**; Yesterday's Hero, 1964 **(64)**; It Hurts to Be in Love, 1964 **(7)**; I'm Gonna Be Strong, 1964 **(9)**; I Must Be Seeing Things, 1965 **(31)**; I've Got Five Dollars and It's Saturday Night, 1965 **(99)** (with George Jones); Last Chance to Turn Around, 1965 **(13)**; I'm a Fool to Care, 1965 **(115)** (with George Jones); Looking Through the Eyes of Love, 1965 **(28)**; Princess in Rags, 1965 **(37)**; Nessuno Mi Puo' Giudcare, 1966 **(115)**; Backstage, 1966 **(25)**; (In the) Cold Light of Day, 1966 **(115)**; Just One Smile, 1966 **(64)**; Animal Crackers in My Soup, 1967 **(106)**; Something's Gotten Hold of My Heart, 1967 **(130)**; She's a Heartbreaker, 1968 **(16)**; Billy You're My Friend, 1968 **(92)**; She Lets Her Hair Down (Early in the Morning), 1969 **(89)**

Pop Vocal—Connecticut

The Pixies Three

Album: Birthday Party, 1963
Singles: Birthday Party, 1963 **(40)**; Cold Cold Winter, 1963 **(79)**; 442 Glenwood Avenue, 1964 **(56)**; Gee, 1964 **(87)**; It's Summer Time U.S.A., 1964 **(116)**

Pop Vocal—Pennsylvania

Plastic Penny

Personnel: Brian Keith (vocals); Mick Grabham (guitars); Tony Murray (bass); Paul Raymond (organ); Nigel Olsson (drums)
Albums: 2 Sides of Penny, 1968; Currency, 1969; Heads I Win, Tails You Lose, 1970

Hard Rock—British

The Platters

Personnel: Tony Williams (vocals) replaced (1961) by Sonny Turner (vocals); David Lynch (vocals; deceased 1981); Herbert Reed (vocals); Alex Hodge (vocals) replaced (1955) by Paul Robi (vocals; deceased 1989) replaced (1966) by Nate Nelson (vocals); added (1954) Zola Taylor (vocals) replaced (1966) by Sandra Dawn (vocals)

Albums: The Platters, 1956; The Platters, Volume Two, 1957; Remember When?, 1959; Encore of Golden Hits, 1960; More Encore of Golden Hits, 1960; The Flying Platters, 1960; The Flying Platters Around the World, 1961; Life Is Just a Bowl of Cherries, 1961; I Love You, 1000 Times, 1966; The Platters, 1966; Remember When, 1967; Going Back to Detroit, 1967; Songs for Only the Lonely, 1967; New Golden Hits of the Platters, 1967; Sweet Sweet Lovin', 1967; I Get the Sweetest Feeling, 1968; Only You, 1968; Moonlight Memories, 1968; The Platters Sing Latino, 1968; Reflections, 1968; Tenth Anniversary Album, 1968; New Soul of the Platter, 1969; Best of the Platters Volume 1, 1973; Best of the Platters Volume 2, 1973; Twenty Classic Hits, 1976

Singles: Only You (and You Alone), 1955 (5); The Great Pretender, 1955 (1); I'm Just a Dancing Partner, 1956 (87); (You've Got) The Magic Touch, 1956 (4); Winner Take All, 1956 (50); My Prayer, 1956 (1); Heaven on Earth, 1956 (39); You'll Never Never Know, 1956 (11); It Isn't Right, 1956 (13); On My Word of Honor, 1956 (20); One in a Million, 1956 (20); I'm Sorry, 1957 (11); He's Mine, 1957 (16); My Dream, 1957 (24); I Wanna, 1957 (24); Only Because, 1957 (65); Helpless, 1958 (56); Twilight Time, 1958 (1); You're Making a Mistake, 1958 (50); I Wish, 1958 (42); It's Raining Outside, 1958 (93); Smoke Gets in Your Eyes, 1958 (1); Enchanted, 1959 (12); Remember When, 1959 (41); Where, 1959 (44); Wish It Were Me, 1959 (61); Harbor Lights, 1960 (8); Sleepy Lagoon, 1960 (65); Ebb Tide, 1960 (56); I'll Be with You (In Apple Blossom Time), 1960 (102); Red Sails in the Sunset, 1960 (36); To Each His Own, 1960 (21); If I Didn't Care, 1961 (30); Trees, 1961 (62); I'll Never Smile Again, 1961 (25); Song for the Lonely, 1961 (115); You'll Never Know, 1961 (109); It's Magic, 1962 (91); I Love You 1000 Times, 1966 (31); Devri, 1966 (111); I'll Be Home, 1966 (97); With This Ring, 1967 (14); Washed Ashore (on a Lonely Island in the Sea), 1967 (56); Sweet, Sweet Lovin', 1967 (70); Hard to Get a Thing Called Love, 1968 (125)

Soul/Pop Vocal—Los Angeles

The Playboys

Personnel: Don Canton (vocals); Freddy James (vocals); Tony Starr (vocals); Gregory Carroll (vocals); Leonard Puzey (vocals)

Single: Over the Weekend, 1958 (62)

Pop Vocal—Philadelphia

The Playmates

Personnel: Donny Conn (vocals); Morey Carr (vocals); Chic Hetti (vocals)

Singles: Jo-Ann, 1958 (19); Let's Be Lovers, 1958 (87); Don't Go

Home, 1958 **(22)**; The Day I Died, 1958 **(81)**; Beep Beep, 1958 **(4)**; Star Love, 1959 **(75)**; What Is Love?, 1959 **(15)**; Wait for Me, 1960 **(37)**; Little Miss Stuck-Up, 1961 **(70)**; Keep Your Hands in Your Pockets, 1962 **(88)**

Pop Vocal—Connecticut

Poco

Personnel: Rusty Young (vocals, steel guitar, guitars); Jim Messina (guitars, vocals) replaced (1971) by Paul Cotton (vocals, guitars) re-placed (1989) by Jim Messina (gui-tars, vocals); Richie Furay (guitars, vocals) replaced (1975) by Al Garth (violin, saxophones) replaced (1978) by Kim Bullard (keyboards, vocals) replaced (1989) by Richie Furay (guitars, vocals); Randy Meisner (bass, vocals) replaced (1970) by Timothy B. Schmit (bass, vocals) replaced (1978) by Charlie Harrison (bass, vocals) replaced (1989) by Randy Meisner (bass, vocals); George Grantham (drums, vocals) replaced (1978) by Steve Chapman (drums, vocals) replaced (1989) by George Grantham (drums, vocals)

Albums: Picking Up the Pieces, 1969; Poco, 1970; Deliverin', 1971; From the Inside, 1971; A Good Feelin' to Know, 1973; Crazy Eyes, 1973; Seven, 1974; Cantamos, 1975; The Very Best of Poco, 1975; Head Over Heels, 1975; Live, 1975; Rose of Cimmaron, 1976; Indian Sum-mer, 1977; Legend, 1979; Under the Gun, 1980; Songs of Richie Furay, 1980; Songs of Paul Cotton, 1980; Blue and Gray, 1981; Cowboys and Englishmen, 1982; Backtracks, 1982; Ghost Town, 1982; Inamorata, 1984; Legacy, 1989; Crazy Loving/Best of

Poco: Grantham, Young, Messina, Furay, Meisner

Poco 1975–82, 1989; The Forgotten Trail 1969–1974, 1991

Singles: You'd Better Think Twice, 1970 **(72)**; C'mon, 1971 **(69)**; Just for Me & You, 1971 **(110)**; A Good Feelin' to Know, 1972; Crazy Eyes, 1973; Keep on Tryin', 1975 **(50)**; Rose of Cimmaron, 1976 **(94)**; Indian Summer, 1977 **(50)**; Crazy Love, 1979 **(17)**; Heart of the Night, 1979 **(20)**; Legend/Little Darlin', 1979 **(103)**; Under the Gun, 1980 **(48)**; Midnight Rain, 1980 **(74)**; The Everlasting Kind, 1980; Widowmaker, 1981; Sea of Heartbreak, 1982 **(109)**; Ghost Town, 1982 **(110)**; Shoot for the Moon, 1982 **(50)**; Break of Hearts, 1983; Days Gone By, 1984 **(80)**; This Old Flame, 1984; Save a Corner of Your Heart, 1984; Call It Love, 1989 **(18)**; Nothin' to Hide, 1989 **(39)**; When It All Began, 1990

Country/Rock — California

The Poets

Personnel: Ronnie Lewis (vocals); Melvin Bradford (vocals); Paul Fulton (vocals); Johnny James (vocals)

Single: She Blew a Good Thing, 1966 **(45)**

R & B Vocal — American

The Poni-Tails

Personnel: Toni Cistone (vocals); LaVerne Novak (vocals); Patti McCabe (vocals)

Singles: Born Too Late, 1958 **(7)**; Seven Minutes in Heaven, 1958 **(85)**; I'll Be Seeing You, 1959 **(87)**

Pop Vocal — Ohio

The Poppies

Personnel: Dorothy Moore (vocals); Petsye McCune (vocals); Rosemary Taylor (vocals)

Singles: Lullaby of Love, 1966 **(56)**; He's Ready, 1966 **(106)**

R & B Vocal — Mississippi

Sandy Posey

Albums: Born a Woman, 1966; I Take It Back, 1967

Singles: Born a Woman, 1966 **(12)**; Single Girl, 1966 **(12)**; What a Woman in Love Won't Do, 1967 **(31)**; I Take It Back, 1967 **(12)**; Are You Never Coming Home, 1967 **(59)**; Something I'll Remember, 1968 **(102)**

Pop Vocal — Memphis

Joey Powers

Single: Midnight Mary, 1963 **(10)**

Pop Vocal — Pennsylvania

Pozo Seco Singers

Personnel: Don Williams (vocals); Susan Taylor (vocals); Lofton Kline (vocals)

Albums: Time, 1966; I Can Make It with You, 1967

Singles: Time, 1966 **(47)**; I'll Be Gone, 1966 **(92)**; I Can Make It with You, 1966 **(32)**; Look What You've Done, 1966 **(32)**; Excuse Me Dear Martha, 1967 **(102)**; I Believed It All, 1967 **(96)**; Louisiana Man, 1967 **(97)**; Strawberry Fields/ Something (medley), 1970 **(115)**

Pop Vocal — Texas

The Precisions

Personnel: Bobby Brooks (vocals)

Single: If This Is Love (I'd Rather Be Lonely), 1967 **(60)**
Soul Vocal—American

The Premiers

Single: Farmer John, 1964 **(19)**
Latin Rock—California

Elvis Presley

Albums: Elvis Presley, 1956; Elvis, 1956; Elvis Rock 'n' Roll, 1956; Elvis Rock 'n' Roll 2, 1956; Peace in the Valley, 1957; Loving You, 1957; Loving You, Volume II, 1957; Love Me Tender, 1957; Just for You, 1957; Elvis' Christmas Album, 1957; Elvis' Golden Records, 1958; King Creole, 1958; For LP Fans Only, 1959; A Date with Elvis, 1959; 50,000,000 Elvis Fans Can't Be Wrong—Elvis' Gold Records, Volume 2, 1960; Elvis Is Back!, 1960; G.I. Blues, 1960; His Hand in Mine, 1961; Something for Everybody, 1961; Blue Hawaii, 1961;

Pot Luck, 1962; Girls! Girls! Girls!, 1962; It Happened at the World's Fair, 1963; Elvis' Golden Records, Volume 3, 1963; Fun in Acapulco, 1963; Kissin' Cousins, 1964; Roustabout, 1964; Girl Happy, 1964; Elvis for Everyone!, 1965; Harum Scarum, 1965; Frankie and Johnny, 1966; Paradise, Hawaiian Style, 1966; Californian Holiday, 1966; Spinout, 1966; How Great Thou Art, 1967; Double Trouble, 1967; Clambake, 1967; Elvis' Gold Records, Volume 4, 1968; Speedway, 1968; Elvis, 1968; Elvis Sings Flaming Star, 1969; From Elvis in Memphis, 1969; From Memphis to Vegas/From Vegas to Memphis, 1969; Let's Be Friends, 1970; On Stage—February 1970, 1970; Worldwide 50 Gold Award Hits, Volume 1, 1970; Almost in Love, 1970; Elvis Back in Memphis, 1970; Elvis—That's the Way It Is, 1970; Elvis Country ("I'm 10,000 Years Old"), 1971; You'll Never Walk Alone, 1971; Love Letters from Elvis, 1971; C'mon Everybody, 1971; The Other Sides—Worldwide Gold Award Hits, Volume 2, 1971; I Got Lucky, 1971; Wonderful World of Christmas, 1971; Elvis Now, 1972; He Touched Me, 1972; Elvis As Recorded at Madison Square Garden, 1972; Elvis Sings Hits from His Movies, Volume 1, 1972; Burning Love and Other Hits from His Movies, Volume 2, 1972; Separate Ways, 1973; Aloha from Hawaii Via Satellite, 1973; Elvis, 1973; Raised on Rock/For Ol' Times Sake, 1973; Elvis—A Legendary Performer, Volume 1, 1974; Good Times, 1974; Elvis Recorded Live on Stage in Memphis, 1974; Having Fun with Elvis on Stage, 1974; Promised Land, 1975; Today, 1975; Pictures of Elvis, 1975; Elvis—A Legendary Performer, Volume 2, 1976; The Sun Sessions, 1976; From Elvis Presley Boulevard, Memphis, Tennessee, 1976; Welcome to My World, 1977; Moody Blue, 1977; Elvis in Concert, 1977; He Walks Beside Me, 1978; Elvis Sings for Children and Grownups Too, 1978; Elvis—A Canadian Tribute, 1978; The '56 Sessions, 1978; The '56 Sessions, Volume 2, 1979; Elvis—A Legendary Performer, Volume 3, 1979; Our Memories of Elvis, 1979; Our Memories of Elvis, Volume 2, 1979; Elvis Aron Presley, 1980; Guitar Man, 1981; This Is Elvis, 1981; Elvis—Greatest Hits, Volume One, 1981; The Elvis Medley, 1982; I Was the One, 1983; Magic Moments, 1984; Elvis: The First Live Recordings, 1984; Elvis—A Golden Celebration, 1984; Rocker, 1984; A Valentine Gift for You, 1985; Return of the Rocker, 1985; Reconsider Baby, 1985; Number One Hits, 1986; Top Ten Hits, 1987; Elvis in Nashville, 1988; Alternate Aloha, 1988; Elvis Gospel 1957–71: Known Only to Him, 1989

Singles: Heartbreak Hotel, 1956 (**1**); I Was the One, 1956 (**19**); Blue Suede Shoes, 1956 (**20**); Money Honey, 1956 (**76**); I Want You, I Need You, I Love You, 1956 (**1**); My Baby Left Me, 1956 (**31**); Hound Dog, 1956 (**1**); Don't Be Cruel, 1956 (**1**); Blue Moon, 1956 (**55**); I Don't Care If the Sun Don't Shine, 1956 (**74**); Love Me Tender, 1956 (**1**); Anyway You Want Me (That's How I Will Be), 1956 (**20**); Love Me, 1956 (**2**); When My Blue Moon Turns to Gold Again, 1956 (**19**); Paralyzed, 1956 (**59**); Poor Boy, 1956 (**24**); Old Shep, 1956 (**47**); Too Much, 1957 (**1**); Playing

for Keeps, 1957 (**21**); All Shook Up, 1957 (**1**); That's When Your Heartaches Begin, 1957 (**58**); (There'll Be) Peace in the Valley (For Me), 1957 (**25**); Let Me Be Your Teddy Bear, 1957 (**1**); Loving You, 1957 (**20**); Jailhouse Rock, 1957 (**1**); Treat Me Nice, 1957 (**18**); Don't, 1958 (**1**); I Beg of You, 1958 (**8**); Wear My Ring Around Your Neck, 1958 (**2**); Doncha' Think It's Time, 1958 (**15**); Hard Headed Woman, 1958 (**1**); Don't Ask Me Why, 1958 (**25**); One Night, 1958 (**4**); I Got Stung, 1958 (**8**); (Now and Then There's) A Fool Such as I, 1959 (**2**); I Need Your Love Tonight, 1959 (**4**); A Big Hunk o' Love, 1959 (**1**); My Wish Came True, 1959 (**12**); Stuck On You, 1960 (**1**); Fame and Fortune, 1960 (**17**); It's Now or Never, 1960 (**1**); A Mess of Blues, 1960 (**32**); Are You Lonesome Tonight, 1960 (**1**); I Gotta Know, 1960 (**20**); Surrender, 1961 (**1**); Lonely Man, 1961 (**32**); Flaming Star, 1961 (**14**); I Feel So Bad, 1961 (**5**); Wild in the Country, 1961 (**26**); Little Sister, 1961 (**5**); (Marie's the Name) His Latest Flame, 1961 (**4**); Can't Help Falling in Love, 1962 (**2**); Rock-a-Hula Baby, 1962 (**23**); Good Luck Charm, 1962 (**1**); Anything That's Part of You, 1962 (**31**); Follow That Dream, 1962 (**15**); She's Not You, 1962 (**5**); Just Tell Her Jim Said Hello, 1962 (**55**); King of the Whole Wide World, 1962 (**30**); Return to Sender, 1962 (**2**); Where Do You Come From, 1962 (**99**); One Broken Heart for Sale, 1963 (**11**); They Remind Me Too Much of You, 1963 (**53**); (You're the) Devil in Disguise, 1963 (**3**); Bossa Nova Baby, 1963 (**8**); Witchcraft, 1963 (**32**); Kissin' Cousins, 1964 (**12**); It Hurts Me, 1964 (**29**); Kiss Me Quick, 1964

(**34**); What'd I Say, 1964 (**21**); Viva Las Vegas, 1964 (**92**); Suspicion, 1964 (**103**); Such a Night, 1964 (**16**); Never Ending, 1964 (**111**); Ask Me, 1964 (**12**); Ain't That Loving You Baby, 1964 (**16**); Wooden Heart, 1964 (**107**); Do the Clam, 1965 (**21**); You'll Be Gone, 1965 (**121**); Crying in the Chapel, 1965 (**3**); (Such an) Easy Question, 1965 (**11**); It Feels So Right, 1965 (**55**); Tickle Me, 1965 (**70**); I'm Yours, 1965 (**11**); (It's a) Long Lonely Highway, 1965 (**112**); Puppet on a String, 1965 (**14**); Wooden Heart, 1965 (**110**); Tell Me Why, 1966 (**33**); Blue River, 1966 (**95**); Frankie and Johnny, 1966 (**25**); Please Don't Stop Loving Me, 1966 (**45**); Love Letters, 1966 (**19**); Come What May, 1966 (**109**); Spinout, 1966 (**40**); All That I Am, 1966 (**41**); Indescribably Blue, 1967 (**33**); Fools Fall in Love, 1967 (**102**); Long Legged Girl (with the Short Dress On), 1967 (**63**); That's Someone You Never Forget, 1967 (**92**); There's Always Me, 1967 (**56**); Judy, 1967 (**78**); Big Boss Man, 1967 (**38**); You Don't Know Me, 1967 (**44**); Guitar Man, 1968 (**43**); U.S. Male, 1968 (**28**); Stay Away, 1968 (**67**); You'll Never Walk Alone, 1968 (**90**); We Call on Him, 1968 (**106**); Let Yourself Go, 1968 (**71**); Your Time Hasn't Come Yet, Baby, 1968 (**72**); Almost in Love, 1968 (**95**); A Little Less Conversation, 1968 (**69**); If I Can Dream, 1968 (**12**); Edge of Reality, 1968 (**112**); Memories, 1969 (**35**); How Great Thou Art, 1969 (**101**); In the Ghetto, 1969 (**3**); Clean Up Your Own Back Yard, 1969 (**35**); Suspicious Minds, 1969 (**1**); Don't Cry Daddy/Rubberneckin', 1970 (**6**); Kentucky Rain, 1970 (**16**); The Wonder of You/ Mama Liked the Roses, 1970 (**9**); I've Lost You/The Next Step Is Love, 1970 (**32**); You Don't Have to Say You Love Me/Patch It Up, 1970 (**11**); I Really Don't Want to Know/There Goes My Everything, 1971 (**21**); Where Did They Go, Lord/Rags to Riches, 1971 (**33**); Life/Only Believe, 1971 (**53**); I'm Leavin', 1971 (**36**); It's Only Love, 1971 (**51**); Until It's Time for You to Go, 1972 (**40**); An American Trilogy, 1972 (**66**); Burning Love, 1972 (**2**); Separate Ways, 1973 (**20**); Steamroller Blues/Fool, 1973 (**17**); Raised on Rock/For Ol' Times Sake, 1973 (**41**); I've Got a Thing About You Baby/Take Good Care of Her, 1974 (**39**); If You Talk in Your Sleep, 1974 (**17**); Promised Land, 1974 (**14**); My Boy, 1975 (**20**); T-R-O-U-B-L-E, 1975 (**35**); Bringing It Back, 1975 (**65**); Hurt, 1976 (**28**); For the Heart, 1976 (**95**); Moody Blue, 1977 (**31**); She Thinks I Still Care, 1977 (**95**); Way Down, 1977 (**18**); My Way, 1977 (**22**); Softly, As I Leave You, 1978 (**109**); (Let Me Be Your) Teddy Bear, 1978 (**105**); Guitar Man, 1981 (**28**); The Elvis Medley, 1982 (**71**)

Films: Love Me Tender, 1957; Loving You, 1957; King Creole, 1958; G.I. Blues, 1960; Blue Hawaii, 1961; Girls! Girls! Girls!, 1962; It Happened at the World's Fair, 1963; Fun in Acapulco, 1963; Kissin' Cousins, 1964; Roustabout, 1964; Girl Happy, 1965; Harum Scarum, 1965; Frankie and Johnny, 1966; Paradise, Hawaiian Style, 1966; Spinout, 1966; Double Trouble, 1967; Clambake, 1967; Speedway, 1968; Elvis—That's the Way It Is, 1970; This Is Elvis, 1981

Rockabilly—Memphis; Elvis was born in Tupelo, Mississippi on

01/08/35 and died in Memphis on 08/16/77; known as "The King of Rock & Roll"

Billy Preston

Albums: Most Exciting Organ Ever, 1965; Wildest Organ in Town, 1966; Gospel in My Soul, 1968; The Apple of Their Eye, 1969; That's the Way God Planned It, 1969; Encouraging Words, 1969; I Wrote a Simple Song, 1971; Music Is My Life, 1972; Everybody Likes Some Kind of Music, 1973; The Kids and Me, 1974; Live European Tour, 1974; It's My Pleasure, 1975; Billy Preston, 1976; Billy's Bag, 1976; Whole New Thing, 1977; Behold, 1979; Late at Night, 1979; Universal Love, 1980; Billy Preston & Syreeta, 1981; The Way I Am, 1981; Press'n On, 1982; Best of Billy Preston, 1985

Singles: That's the Way God Planned It, 1969 **(62)**; All That I've Got, 1970 **(108)**; My Sweet Lord, 1971 **(90)**; I Wrote a Simple Song, 1972 **(77)**; Outa-Space, 1972 **(2)**; That's the Way God Planned It, 1972 **(65)**; Slaughter, 1972 **(50)**; Will It Go Round in Circles, 1973 **(1)**; Space Race, 1973 **(4)**; You're So Unique, 1973 **(48)**; Nothing from Nothing, 1974 **(1)**; Struttin', 1974 **(22)**; Fancy Lady, 1975 **(71)**; Get Back, 1978 **(86)**; Go for It, 1979 **(108)** (with Syreeta); With You I'm Born Again, 1979 **(4)** (with Syreeta); Searchin', 1980 **(106)** (with Syreeta); One More Time for Love, 1980 **(52)** (with Syreeta); I'm Never Gonna Say Goodbye, 1982 **(88)**; And Dance, 1984; If You Let Me Love You, 1984

Soul/Boogie Rock—Texas; toured and recorded with the Beatles as their keyboardist in the late 1960s and shared label credit on "Get Back"

Johnny Preston

Albums: Running Bear, 1959; Free Me, 1961

Singles: Running Bear, 1959 **(1)**; Cradle of Love, 1960 **(7)**; Feel So Fine, 1960 **(14)**; Charming Billy, 1960 **(105)**; Leave My Kitten Alone, 1961 **(73)**; Free Me, 1961 **(97)**

Pop Vocal—Texas

The Pretty Things

Personnel: Dick Taylor (guitars, vocals) replaced (1970) by Victor Unitt (guitars, vocals) replaced (1971) by Peter Tolson (guitars, vocals) replaced (1980) by Dick Taylor (guitars, vocals); Phil May (vocals); John Stax (bass) replaced (1967) by Wally Allen Walter (bass, vocals) replaced (1972) by Stuart Brooks (bass, vocals) replaced (1973) by Jack Green (bass, vocals) replaced (1980) by Wally Allen Walter (bass, guitars, vocals); Brian Pendleton

(guitars) replaced (1967) by John
Povey (keyboards, vocals); Peter
Kirtley (drums) replaced (1964) by
Viv Andrews (drums) replaced
(1965) by Viv Prince (drums) replaced (1965) by Skip Allen (drums,
vocals) replaced (1968) by John
"Twink" Alder (drums) replaced
(1970) by Skip Allen (drums, vocals); added (1974) Gordon Edwards
(keyboards) left group (1976)

Albums: The Pretty Things, 1965;
Get the Picture, 1965; We Want
Your Love, 1966; Emotions, 1967;
S.F. Sorrow, 1968; Parachute, 1970;
Attention, 1971; Freeway Madness,
1973; Silk Torpedo, 1974; Savage
Eye, 1975; Greatest Hits, 1975; Vin-
tage Years, 1976; The Singles A's &
B's, 1977; Live, 1978; Real Pretty,
1979; Cross Talk, 1980; Best Of:
1967–1971, 1983; Get a Buss, 1984;
Live at Heartbreak Hotel, 1984

Hard Rock—British

Alan Price

Albums: The Price to Play, 1966;
The Price on His Head, 1967; Price
Is Right, 1968; The World of Alan
Price, 1970; Fame & Price, 1971; O
Lucky Man, 1973; Between Yester-
day & Today, 1974; Metropolitan
Man, 1975; Performing Price, 1975;
Shouts Across the Street, 1976;
Rainbow's End, 1977; England My
England, 1978; Alan Price, 1978;
Focus On, 1979; Lucky Day, 1979;
Rising Sun, 1980; In a Word, 1980;
Geordie Roots and Branches, 1983;
Best of Alan Price, 1984; Together,
1985

Singles: I Put a Spell on You,
1966 **(80)**; I Don't Feel Pain No
More (Time and Tide), 1984

Pop/Rock—British; former
member of the Animals

Lloyd Price

Albums: Exciting Lloyd Price,
1958; Mr. Personality, 1959; Mr.
Personality Sings the Blues, 1959;
Mr. Personality's Big 15, 1959; Fan-
tastic, 1960; Sings the Million Sel-
lers, 1960; Cookin', 1961; Lloyd
Price Orchestra, 1962; Misty, 1963;
This Is My Band, 1964; Lloyd
Price, 1965; Lloyd Price Swings for
Sammy, 1965; Sixteen Greatest
Hits, 1966; Now, 1968

Singles: Just Because, 1957 **(29)**;
Lonely Chair, 1957 **(88)**; Stagger
Lee, 1958 **(1)**; Where Were You (on
Our Wedding Day)?, 1959 **(23)**;
Personality, 1959 **(2)**; I'm Gonna
Get Married, 1959 **(3)**; Come into
My Heart, 1959 **(20)**; Wont'cha
Come Home, 1959 **(43)**; Lady Luck,
1960 **(14)**; Never Let Me Go, 1960
(82); No If's—No And's, 1960 **(40)**;
For Love, 1960 **(43)**; Question, 1960
(19); Who Coulda' Told You (They
Lied), 1960 **(103)**; Just Call Me (and
I'll Understand), 1960 **(79)**;
(You Better) Know What You're
Doin', 1960 **(90)**; Mary and Man-O,
1961 **(110)**; Under Your Spell Again,
1962 **(123)**; Misty, 1963 **(21)**; Billie
Baby, 1964 **(84)**; I Love You (I Just
Love You), 1964 **(123)**; Amen, 1964
(124); If I Had My Life to Live
Over, 1965 **(107)**; Love Music, 1973
(102)

R & B Soul/Louisiana

Primrose Circus

Album: Primrose Circus, 1967
Single: P.S. Call Me Lulu, 1967
Psychedelic Pop—American

P. J. Proby

Albums: I Am P. J. Proby, 1964;
P. J. Proby's in Town, 1965;

Somewhere, 1965; P. J. Proby, 1965; Enigma, 1967; Phenomenon, 1967; What's Wrong with My World, 1968; Believe It or Not, 1968; California License, 1969; Three Week Hero, 1969; I'm Yours, 1973; Let's Dance, 1975; Elvis, 1978; The Hero, 1979

Singles: Hold Me, 1964 **(70)**; Together, 1964 **(117)**; Somewhere, 1965 **(91)**; Niki Hoeky, 1966 **(23)**; I Can't Make It Alone, 1966 **(131)**; Work with Me Annie, 1967 **(119)**; Just Holding On, 1967 **(130)**; I Apologize Baby, 1968 **(135)**

Pop/Rock Vocal — Houston; real name is James Marcus Smith; former member of Focus

Procession

Personnel: Mick Rogers (guitars, vocals, bass); Brian Peacock (bass, guitars, keyboards); Trevor Griffin (keyboards, vocals); Craig Collinge (drums)

Album: Procession, 1968

Hard Rock — British

Procol Harum

Personnel: Ray Royer (guitars) replaced (1967) by Robin Trower (guitars) replaced (1972) by Dave Ball (guitars) replaced (1973) by Mick Grabham (guitars) replaced (1990) by Robin Trower (guitars); Gary Brooker (keyboards, vocals); Bobby Harrison (drums) replaced (1967) by Barry Wilson (drums; deceased 1990) replaced (1990) by Mark Brzezicki (drums); David Knights (bass) replaced (1969) by Chris Copping (bass, keyboards) replaced (1990) by Dave Bronze (bass); Matthew Fisher (keyboards) left group (1969) replaced (1972) by

Alan Cartwright (bass) left group (1976) replaced (1990) by Matthew Fisher (keyboards); Keith Reid (lyrics) left group (1973) rejoined (1990); added (1977) Pete Solley (organ) replaced (1990) by Jerry Stevenson (guitars, mandolin)

Albums: Procol Harum, 1967; Shine on Brightly, 1968; A Salty Dog, 1969; Home, 1970; Broken Barricades, 1971; The Best of Procol Harum, 1972; Live with the Edmonton Symphony Orchestra, 1972; Grand Hotel, 1973; Exotic Birds and Fruit, 1974; Procol's Ninth, 1975; Best of Procol Harum, 1975; Something Magic, 1976; Classics, 1986; Chrysalis Years 1973–1977, 1989; The Prodigal Stranger, 1991

Singles: A Whiter Shade of Pale, 1967 **(5)**; Homburg, 1967 **(34)**; Conquistador, 1972 **(16)**; Grand Hotel, 1973 **(117)**; Pandora's Box, 1976; All Our Dreams Are Sold, 1991

Blues/Progressive Rock — British

Professor Morrison's Lollipop

Single: You Got the Love, 1968 **(88)**

Bubblegum Pop/New Jersey

Arthur Prysock

Albums: Coast to Coast, 1963; A Portrait of Arthur Prysock, 1963; Everlasting Songs for Everlasting Lovers, 1964; A Double Header with Arthur Prysock, 1965; Arthur Prysock/Count Basie, 1966; Art & Soul, 1967; This Is My Beloved, 1968; Best of Arthur Prysock, 1969; Arthur Prysock '74, 1973; Love Makes It Right, 1974; All My Life, 1976; Silk & Satin, 1977; Does It Again, 1978; Unforgettable, 1978

Singles: Our Love Will Last, 1963 **(128)**; Close Your Eyes, 1964 **(124)**; Without the One You Love, 1964 **(126)**; It's Too Late, Baby Too Late, 1965 **(56)**; Only a Fool Breaks His Own Heart, 1965 **(125)**; Let It Be Me, 1966 **(124)**; You Don't Have to Say You Love Me, 1967 **(120)**; A Working Man's Prayer, 1968 **(74)**; Maman, 1968 **(134)**; In the Rain, 1973 **(110)**; When Love Is New, 1976 **(64)**

R & B Vocal—South Carolina

Gary Puckett & The Union Gap

Personnel: Gary Puckett (guitars, vocals); Kerry Chater (bass, vocals); Dwight Bement (saxophones); Gary Withem (keyboards); Paul Wheatbread (drums)

Albums: Woman, Woman, 1967; Young Girl, 1968; Incredible, 1969; New Album, 1970; Greatest Hits, 1970; The Gary Puckett Album, 1971; Lady Willpower, 1972

Singles: Woman, Woman, 1967 **(4)**; Young Girl, 1968 **(2)**; Lady Willpower, 1968 **(2)**; Over You, 1968 **(7)**; Don't Give in to Him, 1969 **(15)**; This Girl Is a Woman Now, 1969 **(9)**; Let's Give Adam and Eve Another Chance, 1970 **(41)**; I Just Don't Know What to Do with Myself, 1970 **(61)**; Keep the Customer Satisfied, 1971 **(71)**

Pop/Rock—San Diego

Bernard Purdie

Albums: Soul Finders, 1968; Soul Drums, 1968; Stand by Me, 1971; Purdie Good, 1974; Soul Is . . . Pretty Purdie, 1972; Shaft, 1974; Delights of the Garden, 1976

Single: Funky Donkey, 1968 **(87)**

Jazz/Rock—British; former drummer for the Jeff Beck Group and Hummingbird

James & Bobby Purify

Personnel: James Purify (vocals); Robert Lee Dickey (vocals) replaced (1974) by Ben Moore (vocals)

Albums: I'm Your Puppet, 1966; Pure Sound of James & Bobby Purify, 1967; James & Bobby Purify, 1977; You & Me Together Forever, 1978

Singles: I'm Your Puppet, 1966 **(6)**; Wish You Didn't Have to Go, 1967 **(38)**; Shake a Tail Feather, 1967 **(25)**; I Take What I Want, 1967 **(41)**; Let Love Come Between Us, 1967 **(23)**; Do Unto Me, 1968 **(73)**; I Can Remember, 1968 **(51)**; Help Yourself (to All of My Lovin'), 1968 **(94)**; Do Your Thing, 1975 **(101)**

R & B Vocal—Florida

The Purple Gang

Personnel: Pete Walker (vocals, kazoo); James Beard (guitars); Ank Langley (banjo); Del Robinson (mandolin, harmonica); Tony Moss (bass); Geoff Bourjer (keyboards); Keith Bailey (drums)

Album: The Purple Gang Strikes, 1968

Progressive Rock—British

The Pyramids

Personnel: Skip Mercer (guitars); Willie Glover (guitars); Steve Leonard (guitars); Ron McMullen (bass); Tom Pittman (drums)

Album: The Original Penetration! and Other Favorites, 1964

Single: Penetration, 1964 **(18)**
Surf Rock—California

Quaker City Boys

Personnel: Tommy Reilly (vocals)
Single: Teasin', 1958 **(39)**
Pop Vocal—Philadelphia

Quatrain

Personnel: Eric Pease (guitars,
vocals); Don Senneville (guitars,
vocals); Buff Lindsay (bass, vocals);
Jim Lekas (drums, vocals)
Album: Quatrain, 1968
Hard Rock—British

? & The Mysterians

Personnel: Rudy "?" Martinez
(vocals); Larry Borjas (guitars) re-
placed (1966) by Rob Balderamma
(guitars); Frank Lugo (bass); Frank
Rodriguez (keyboards); Robert
Martinez (drums) replaced (1966) by
Ed Serrato (drums)
Albums: 96 Tears, 1966; Action,
1966
Singles: 96 Tears, 1966 **(1)**; I
Need Somebody, 1966 **(22)**; Can't
Get Enough of You Baby, 1967
(56); Girl (You Captivate Me), 1967
(98); Do Something to Me, 1967
(110)
Hard Rock—Michigan

Quicksilver Messenger Service

Personnel: David Freiberg (vocals, bass) replaced (1972) by Mark
Ryan (bass) replaced (1974) by John
Nicholas (bass) replaced (1975) by
Skip Olsen (bass); John Cipollina
(guitars, vocals; deceased 1989)
replaced (1972) by Chuck Steaks

(keyboards) replaced (1974) by Bob
Hogan (keyboards) replaced (1975)
by Michael Lewis (keyboards); Gary
Duncan (guitars, vocals, bass); Jim
Murray (vocals, harmonica) left
group (1967); Casey Sonoban
(drums) replaced (1966) by Greg
Elmore (drums); Skip Spence (guitars, vocals) left group (1965) replaced (1970) by Dino Valenti (gui-
tars, vocals); added (1974) Harold
Aceves (drums) left group (1975);
added (1974) Bob Flurrie (guitars)
left group (1975); added (1969)
Nicky Hopkins (keyboards) left
group (1972)
Albums: Quicksilver Messenger
Service, 1968; Happy Trails, 1969;
Shady Grove, 1969; Just for Love,
1970; What About Me, 1971; Quick-
silver, 1972; Comin' Thru', 1972;
Anthology, 1973; Solid Silver, 1975;
Best of Quicksilver Messenger Ser-
vice, 1976; Maiden of the Cancer
Moon, 1983; Sons of Mercury, 1991
Singles: Stand by Me, 1968 **(110)**;
Who Do You Love, 1969 **(91)**; Fresh
Air, 1970 **(49)**; What About Me,
1971 **(100)**
Hard Rock—San Francisco

Quintessence

Personnel: Raja Ram (vocals,
flutes, piano); Dave Codling (guitars) left group (1972); Alan Mostert
(guitars); Sambhu Babaji (bass)
Shiva Shankar Jones (keyboards,
vocals) left group (1972); Jake
Milton (drums)
Albums: In Blissful Company,
1969; Quintessence, 1970; Dive
Deep, 1970; Self, 1971; Indweller,
1972
Progressive Rock—British

The Quin-Tones

Personnel: Roberta Haymon (vocals); Carolyn Holmes (vocals); Phyllis Carr (vocals); Jeannie Crist (vocals); Kenny Sexton (vocals); Ronnie Scott (piano)
Single: Down the Aisle of Love, 1958 **(18)**
Pop Vocal—Pennsylvania

The Radiants

Personnel: Maurice McAlister (vocals)
Singles: Father Knows Best, 1962 **(100)**; Shy Guy, 1963 **(104)**; Voice Your Choice, 1964 **(51)**; It Ain't No Big Thing, 1965 **(91)**; Whole Lot of Woman, 1965 **(116)**; Hold On, 1968 **(68)**
R & B Vocal—Chicago

The Rag Dolls

Singles: Society Girl, 1964 **(91)**; Dusty, 1965 **(55)**
Pop Vocal—American

Rainbow Press

Personnel: Marc Ellis (guitars, vocals); Larry Milton (guitars, keyboards); Dave Troup (bass); Charlie Osborne (keyboards); Joe Groff (percussion); Billy Yergin (drums)
Album: Sunday Funnies, 1969
Pop/Rock—British

The Raindrops

Personnel: Jeff Barry (vocals); Ellie Greenwich (vocals)
Album: The Raindrops, 1963
Singles: What a Guy, 1963 **(41)**; The Kind of Boy You Can't Forget, 1963 **(17)**; That Boy John, 1963 **(64)**; Book of Love, 1964 **(62)**; Let's

Go Together, 1964 **(109)**; One More Tear, 1964 **(97)**
Pop Vocal—American

Marvin Rainwater

Singles: Gonna Find Me a Bluebird, 1957 **(18)**; The Majesty of Love, 1957 **(93)** (with Connie Francis); Whole Lotta Woman, 1958 **(60)**; Half-Breed, 1959 **(66)**; I Can't Forget, 1961 **(119)**
Rockabilly—Kansas; real last name is Percy

The Rainy Daze

Personnel: Tim Gilbert (vocals, guitars); Mac Ferris (guitars); Sam Fuller (bass); Bob Heckendorf (keyboards); Kip Gilbert (drums)
Album: That Acapulco Gold, 1967
Single: That Acapulco Gold, 1967 **(70)**
Pop/Rock—Denver

Eddie Rambeau

Album: Concrete and Clay, 1965
Singles: Lover's Medley, 1963 **(132)** (with Marcy Joe); Concrete and Clay, 1965 **(35)**; My Name Is Mud, 1965 **(112)**; The Train, 1965 **(129)**; Clock, 1966 **(122)**
Pop Vocal—Pennsylvania; real last name is Flurie

The Ramrods

Personnel: Vincent Bell Lee (guitars); Eugene Morrow (bass); Claire Lane (keyboards); Richard Lane (drums)
Single: (Ghost) Riders in the Sky, 1961 **(30)**
Instrumental—Connecticut

Teddy Randazzo

Singles: Little Serenade, 1958 **(66)**; The Way of a Clown, 1960 **(44)**; Big Wide World, 1963 **(51)**; Lost Without You, 1964 **(130)**
   Pop Vocal — New York

The Ran-dells

Personnel: Steve Rappaport (vocals); Robert Rappaport (vocals); John Spirit (vocals)
   Single: Martian Hop, 1963 **(16)**
   Pop Vocal — New Jersey

Randy & The Rainbows

Personnel: Randy Safuto (vocals); Frank Safuto (vocals); Sal Zero (vocals); Mike Zero (vocals); Ken Arcipowski (vocals)
   Singles: Denise, 1963 **(10)**; Why Do Kids Grow Up, 1963 **(97)**; Little Star, 1964 **(133)**
   Pop Vocal — New York

Rare Breed

Personnel: Joey Levine (vocals)
   Single: Beg, Borrow & Steal, 1966
   Bubblegum Pop — American; changed name to Ohio Express and hit #29 with same record

Rare Earth

Personnel: Rob Richards (guitars, vocals) replaced (1971) by Ray Monette (guitars, vocals) replaced (1977) by Dan Ferguson (guitars); John Persh (bass, vocals) replaced (1973) by Mike Urso (bass) replaced (1975) by Reggie McBride (bass) replaced (1977) by Mike Urso (bass); Gil Bridges (saxophones, flutes, percussion); Ken James (keyboards) replaced (1971) by Mark Olson (keyboards) replaced (1975) by Gabriel Katona (keyboards, vocals) replaced (1976) by Frank Westbrook (keyboards) replaced (1977) by Ron Fransen (keyboards); Pete Rivera (drums) replaced (1975) by Barry Frost (percussion) left group (1975); added (1971) Edward Guzman (percussion); added (1973) Peter Hoorelbeke (drums, vocals)
   Albums: Dream Answers, 1968; Get Ready, 1970; Ecology, 1971; One World, 1971; In Concert, 1972; Willie Remembers, 1973; Ma, 1973; Back to Earth, 1975; Midnight Lady, 1976; Rare Earth, 1977; Band Together, 1978; Grand Slam, 1978
   Singles: Get Ready, 1970 **(4)**; I'm Losing You, 1970 **(7)**; Born to Wander, 1970 **(17)**; I Just Want to Celebrate, 1971 **(7)**; Hey, Big Brother, 1971 **(19)**; What'd I Say, 1972 **(61)**; Good Time Sally, 1972 **(67)**; We're Gonna Have a Good Time, 1973 **(93)**; Ma, 1973 **(108)**; Hum Along and Dance, 1973 **(110)**; It Makes You Happy (But It Ain't Gonna Last Too Long), 1975 **(106)**; Warm Ride, 1978 **(39)**; I Can Feel My Love Rising, 1978
   Soul/Rock — Michigan

The (Young) Rascals

Personnel: Gene Cornish (guitars, vocals) replaced (1971) by Buzz Feiten (guitars); Felix Cavalierre (keyboards, vocals); Eddie Brigati (bass, percussion, vocals) replaced (1969) by Chuck Rainey (bass) replaced (1971) by Robert Popwell (bass); Dino Danelli (drums)
   Albums: The Young Rascals, 1966; Collections, 1966; Groovin', 1967; Once Upon a Dream, 1968; Timepeace/Greatest Hits, 1968;

The Rascals: Danelli, Cavalierre, Cornish, Brigati

Freedom Suite, 1969; Search and Nearness, 1969; See, 1970; Peaceful World, 1971; Island of Real, 1972

Singles: I Ain't Gonna Eat Out My Heart Anymore, 1965 **(52)**; Good Loving, 1966 **(1)**; You Better Run, 1966 **(20)**; Come On Up, 1966 **(43)**; I've Been Lonely Too Long, 1967 **(16)**; Groovin', 1967 **(1)**; A Girl Like You, 1967 **(10)**; How Can I Be Sure, 1967 **(4)**; It's Wonderful, 1967 **(20)**; A Beautiful Morning, 1968 **(3)**; People Got to Be Free, 1968 **(1)**; A Ray of Hope, 1968 **(24)**; Heaven, 1969 **(39)**; See, 1969 **(27)**; Carry Me Back, 1969 **(26)**; Hold On, 1970 **(51)**; Glory, Glory, 1970 **(58)**; Right On, 1971 **(119)**; Love Me, 1971 **(95)**

Blue-Eyed Soul—New York; dropped "Young" from name, 1967

Lou Rawls

Albums: Black and Blue, 1963; Tobacco Road, 1964; Lou Rawls Live!, 1966; Lou Rawls Soulin', 1966; Lou Rawls Carryin' On, 1967; Too Much!, 1967; That's Lou, 1967; Feelin' Good, 1968; You're Good for Me, 1968; The Best of Lou Rawls, 1968; The Way It Was—The Way It Is, 1969; Close Up, 1969; Your Good Thing, 1969; You've Made Me So Very Happy, 1970; Natural Man, 1971; Silk & Soul, 1972; All Things in Time, 1976; Unmistak-ably Lou, 1977; When You Hear Lou, You've Heard It All, 1977; Lou Rawls Live, 1978; Let Me Be Good to You, 1979; Sit Down and Talk to Me, 1980; Shades of Blue, 1981; When the Night Comes, 1983

Singles: Three O'Clock in the Morning, 1965 **(83)**; Love Is a Hurtin' Thing, 1966 **(13)**; You Can Bring Me All Your Heartaches, 1966 **(55)**; Trouble Down Here Below, 1967 **(92)**; Dead End Street, 1967 **(29)**; Show Business, 1967 **(45)**; My Ancestors, 1968 **(113)**; You're Good for Me, 1968 **(103)**; Down Here on the Ground, 1968 **(69)**; The Split, 1968 **(123)**; Your Good Thing (Is About to End), 1969 **(18)**; I Can't Make It Alone, 1969 **(63)**; You've Made Me So Very Happy, 1970 **(95)**; Bring It on Home, 1970 **(96)**; A Natural Man, 1971 **(17)**; His Song Shall Be Sung, 1972 **(105)**; Walk On In, 1972 **(106)**; You'll Never Find Another Love Like Mine, 1976 **(2)**; Groovy People, 1976 **(64)**; See You When I Git There, 1977 **(66)**; Lady Love, 1978 **(24)**; You're My Blessing, 1980 **(77)**; Wind Beneath My Wings, 1983 **(65)**

Soul/Pop Vocal—Chicago

Diane Ray

Single: Please Don't Talk to the Lifeguard, 1963 **(31)**

Pop Vocal—North Carolina

Johnnie Ray

Albums: Johnnie Ray, 1952; The Big Beat, 1957

Singles: Whiskey and Gin, 1951; Cry, 1952 **(1)**; Please Mr. Sun, 1953; Such a Night, 1953; Johnnie's Comin' Home, 1955 **(100)**; Just Walking in the Rain, 1956 **(2)**; You Don't Owe Me a Thing, 1957 **(10)**; Look Homeward, Angel, 1957 **(36)**; Yes Tonight, Josephine, 1957 **(12)**; Build Your Love (On a Strong Foundation), 1957 **(58)**; Up Until Now, 1958 **(81)**; I'll Never Fall in Love Again, 1959 **(75)**

Pop Vocal—Oregon; died from liver failure in 1990

Margie Rayburn

Single: I'm Available, 1957 **(9)**

Pop Vocal—California; former Sunnysiders vocalist

The Rays

Personnel: Harold Miller (vocals); Walter Ford (vocals); David Jones (vocals); Harry James (vocals)

Singles: Silhouettes/Daddy Cool, 1957 **(3)**; Mediterranean Moon, 1960 **(95)**; Magic Moon (Clair de Lune), 1961 **(49)**

R & B Vocal—New York

Red Crayola

Personnel: Mayo Thompson (vocals, guitars); Rick Barthelme (guitars) replaced (1977) by Jesse Chamberlain (guitars, vocals); Steve Cunningham (bass) replaced (1977) by Tony Maimone (bass); Tommy Smith (drums) replaced (1977) by Scott Krauss (drums); added (1977) Alan Ravenstine (keyboards); added (1977) Tom Herman (guitars); added (1977) David Thomas (vocals)

Albums: Parable of Arable Land, 1967; God Bless the Red Crayola, 1968; Soldier Talk, 1979; Kangaroo, 1981; Black Snakes, 1983

Psychedelic Rock—American

Otis Redding

Albums: Pain in My Heart, 1964; The Great Otis Redding Sings Soul Ballads, 1965; Otis Blue/Otis Redding Sings Soul, 1965; The Soul Album, 1966; Complete & Unbelievable . . . The Otis Redding Dictionary of Soul, 1966; King & Queen, 1967 (with Carla Thomas); Otis Redding Live in Europe, 1967; History of Otis Redding, 1967; The Dock of the Bay, 1968; The Immortal Otis Redding, 1968; Otis Redding in Person at the Whiskey a-Go-Go, 1968; Love Man, 1969; Tell the Truth, 1970; Monterrey International Pop Festival, 1970 (with Jimi Hendrix Experience); The Best of Otis Redding, 1972; Otis Redding Volume 1, 1981; Recorded Live, 1982

Singles: These Arms of Mine, 1963 **(85)**; Pain in My Heart, 1963 **(61)**; Come to Me, 1964 **(69)**; Security, 1964 **(97)**; Chained and Bound, 1964 **(70)**; That's How Strong My Love Is, 1965 **(74)**; Mr. Pitiful, 1965 **(41)**; I've Been Loving You Too Long (to Stop Now), 1965 **(21)**; Respect, 1965 **(35)**; Just One More Day, 1965 **(85)**; Satisfaction, 1966 **(31)**; My Lover's Prayer, 1966 **(61)**; Fa-Fa-Fa-Fa-Fa (Sad Song), 1966 **(29)**; Try a Little Tenderness, 1966 **(25)**; I Love You More Than Words Can Say, 1967 **(78)**; Tramp, 1967 **(26)** (with Carla Thomas); Shake, 1967 **(47)**; Glory of Love, 1967 **(60)**; Knock on Wood, 1967

(**30**) (with Carla Thomas); (Sittin' on) The Dock of the Bay, 1968 (**1**); Lovey Dovey, 1968 (**60**) (with Carla Thomas); The Happy Song (Dum-Dum), 1968 (**25**); Amen, 1968 (**36**); Hard to Handle, 1968 (**51**); I've Got Dreams to Remember, 1968 (**41**); Papa's Got a Brand New Bag, 1968 (**21**); A Lover's Question, 1969 (**48**); When Something Is Wrong with My Baby, 1969 (**109**) (with Carla Thomas); Love Man, 1969 (**72**); Free Me, 1969 (**103**); (Your Love Has Lifted Me) Higher & Higher, 1969 (**110**); Demonstration, 1970 (**105**); I've Been Loving You Too Long, 1971 (**110**)

Soul/Pop Vocal — Georgia; Otis died in a plane crash 12/10/67

Jimmy Reed

Albums: I'm Jimmy Reed, 1957; Rockin' with Jimmy Reed, 1958; Found Love, 1959; Now Appearing, 1960; Jimmy Reed at Carnegie Hall, 1961; The Best of Jimmy Reed, 1962; Just Jimmy Reed, 1962; T'Ain't No Big Thing, 1963; Sings the Best of the Blues, 1963; Plays 12 String Guitar Blues, 1964; Boss Man of the Blues, 1964; At Soul City, 1965; The Legend, the Man, 1966; Soulin', 1968; Soul Greats, 1968; Jimmy Reed, 1969; Soulful Sound, 1969; The Best, 1970; New Jimmy Reed, 1971; Wailin' the Blues, 1972; Big Boss Man, 1973; Down in Virginia, 1973; I Ain't from Chicago, 1973; The Ultimate, 1974; Jimmy Reed Is Back, 1976; Cold Chills, 1976; Upside Your Head, 1980; Shame Shame Shame, 1980; Funky Funky Soul, 1981; High and Lonesome, 1981; Got Me Dizzy, 1982

Singles: The Sun Is Shining, 1957 (**65**); Honest I Do, 1957 (**32**); Down in Virginia, 1958 (**93**); Baby What You Want Me to Do, 1960 (**37**); Found Love, 1960 (**88**); Going by the River (Part II), 1960 (**104**); Hush-Hush, 1960 (**75**); Close Together, 1961 (**68**); Big Boss Man, 1961 (**78**); Bright Lights Big City, 1961 (**58**); Aw Shucks, Hush Your Mouth, 1962 (**93**); Good Lover, 1962 (**77**); Shame, Shame, Shame, 1963 (**52**); Mary-Mary, 1963 (**119**); Two Ways to Skin a Cat, 1967 (**125**)

R & B Vocal — Mississippi; died from epilepsy in 1976

Jim Reeves

Albums: He'll Have to Go, 1960; A Touch of Velvet, 1962; Moonlight and Roses, 1964; The Best of Jim Reeves, 1964; The Jim Reeves Way, 1965; The Best of Jim Reeves, Volume 2, 1966; Distant Drums, 1966; Blue Side of Lonesome, 1967

Singles: Four Walls, 1957 (**11**); Anna Marie, 1958 (**93**); Blue Boy, 1958 (**45**); Billy Bayou, 1958 (**95**); He'll Have to Go, 1959 (**2**); I'm Gettin' Better, 1960 (**37**); I Know One, 1960 (**82**); Am I Losing You, 1960 (**31**); I Missed Me, 1960 (**44**); The Blizzard, 1961 (**62**); What Would You Do?, 1961 (**73**); Losing Your Love, 1961 (**89**); (How Can I Write on Paper) What I Feel in My Heart, 1961 (**92**); Adios Amigo, 1962 (**90**); I'm Gonna Change Everything, 1962 (**95**); Is This Me?, 1963 (**103**); Guilty, 1963 (**91**); Welcome to My World, 1964 (**102**); Look Who's Talking, 1964 (**121**) (with Dottie West); Love Is No Excuse, 1964 (**115**); I Guess I Am Crazy, 1964 (**82**); I Won't Forget You, 1964 (**93**); This Is It, 1965 (**88**); Is It

Really Over?, 1965 **(79)**; Snow Flake, 1966 **(66)**; Distant Drums, 1966 **(45)**; Blue Side of Lonesome, 1966 **(59)**; I Won't Come in While He's There, 1967 **(112)**

Country/Pop Vocal — Texas; killed in a plane crash in 1964

The Reflections

Personnel: Tony Micale (vocals, guitars); Dan Bennie (guitars); Phil Castrodale (bass); John Dean (drums)

Album: The Reflections, 1964

Singles: (Just Like) Romeo and Juliet, 1964 **(6)**; Like Columbus Did, 1964 **(96)**; (I'm Just) A Henpecked Guy, 1964 **(124)**; Shabby Little Hut, 1965 **(121)**; Poor Man's Son, 1965 **(55)**

Pop/Rock — Detroit

The Regents

Personnel: Guy Villari (vocals); Sal Cuomo (vocals); Charles Fassert (vocals); Don Jacobucci (vocals); Tony Gravagna (vocals)

Singles: Barbara-Ann, 1961 **(13)**; Runaround, 1961 **(28)**

Pop Vocal — New York

Terry Reid

Albums: Bang Bang, You're Terry Reid, 1968; Move Over for Terry Reid, 1969; The Most of Terry Reid, 1971; River, 1973; Seeds of Memory, 1976; Rogue Waves, 1979

Hard Rock — British

The Remains

Personnel: Barry Tashian (guitars, vocals); Vern Miller (bass, gui-

The Remains: Miller, Briggs, Tashian, Damiani

tars); William Briggs (keyboards); Chip Damiani (drums)

Album: The Remains, 1967

Single: Don't Look Back, 1967

Psychedelic Rock — American

Diane Renay

Album: Navy Blue, 1964

Singles: Navy Blue, 1964 **(6)**; Kiss Me Sailor, 1964 **(29)**; Growin' Up Too Fast, 1964 **(124)**; It's in Your Tears, 1964 **(131)**; Watch Out, Sally, 1964 **(101)**

Pop Vocal — Philadelphia; real name is Renee Diane Kushner

John Renbourn

Albums: John Renbourn, 1965; Another Monday, 1967; Sir John —

Alot of Merrie Englandes, 1968; The Lady and the Unicorn, 1970; John Renbourn Sampler, 1971; Faro Annie, 1972; So Clear, 1973; Heads & Tails, 1974; The Hermit, 1976; Maid in Bedlam, 1977; John Renbourn & Stefan Grossman, 1978; Black Balloon, 1979; Enchanted Garden, 1980; Under the Volcano, 1980; Essential Collection, Volume 1, 1982; Essential Collection, Volume 2, 1983; Ship of Fools, 1987

Folk/Rock—British; former Pentangle guitarist

Rene & Ray

Personnel: Paul "Rene" Venezuela (vocals); Ray Quinones (vocals)
Single: Queen of My Heart, 1962 **(79)**

Pop Vocal—American; former Velveteens vocalists

Rene & Rene

Personnel: Rene Ornelas (vocals); Rene Herrera (vocals)
Album: Lo Mucho Que Te Quiero, 1968
Singles: Angelito, 1964 **(43)**; Lo Mucho Que Te Quiero (The More I Love You), 1968 **(14)**; Las Cosas, 1969 **(128)**

Pop Vocal—Texas

Reparata & The Delrons

Personnel: Mary "Reparata" Aiese (vocals); Sheila Reillie (vocals) replaced (1966) by Lorraine Mazzola (vocals); Carol Drobnicki (vocals)
Singles: Whenever a Teenager Cries, 1965 **(60)**; Tommy, 1965

(92); Captain of Your Ship, 1968 **(127)**

Pop Vocal—New York

The Revels

Personnel: John Kelly (vocals)
Single: Midnight Stroll, 1959 **(35)**

R & B Vocal—Philadelphia

Paul Revere & The Raiders

Personnel: Paul Revere (piano, vocals); Mark Lindsay (vocals, keyboards, saxophones); Drake Levin (guitars) replaced (1965) by Jim Valley (guitars) replaced (1969) by Freddy Weller (guitars, vocals); Phil Volk (bass) replaced (1969) by Keith Allison (bass) replaced (1970) by Charlie Coe (bass); Mike Smith (drums) replaced (1969) by Joe Correro, Jr. (drums, vocals)
Albums: Paul Revere & the Raiders, 1961; Here They Come!, 1965; Just Like Us!, 1966; Midnight Ride, 1966; The Spirit of '67, 1967; Greatest Hits, 1967; Revolution!, 1967; Goin' to Memphis, 1968; Something Happening, 1968; Christmas, Past and Present, 1968; Hard 'n' Heavy (with Marshmallow), 1969; The Spirit of '69, 1969; Alias Pink Puzz, 1969; Collage, 1970; Indian Reservation, 1971; Good Thing, 1971; All-Time Greatest Hits, 1972; Movin' On, 1972; Country Wine, 1972; Kicks, 1984
Singles: Like Longhair, 1961 **(38)**; Louie, Louie, 1963 **(103)**; Louie, Go Home, 1964 **(118)**; Over You, 1964 **(133)**; Sometimes, 1965 **(131)**; Steppin' Out, 1965 **(46)**; Just Like Me, 1965 **(11)**; Kicks, 1966 **(4)**; Hungry, 1966 **(6)**; The Great Airplane Strike, 1966 **(20)**; Good Thing, 1966 **(4)**;

The Raiders: Valley, Volk, Revere, Lindsay, Smith

Ups and Downs, 1967 **(22)**; Him or Me, What's It Gonna Be, 1967 **(5)**; I Had a Dream, 1967 **(17)**; Peace of Mind, 1967 **(42)**; Do Unto Others, 1967 **(102)**; Too Much Talk, 1968 **(19)**; Don't Take It So Hard, 1968 **(27)**; Cinderella Sunshine, 1968 **(58)**; Mr. Sun, Mr. Moon, 1968 **(18)**; Let Me, 1969 **(20)**; We Gotta All Get Together, 1969 **(50)**; Just Seventeen, 1970 **(82)**; Gone Movin' On, 1970 **(120)**; Indian Reservation, 1971 **(1)**; Birds of a Feather, 1971 **(23)**; Country Wine, 1972 **(51)**; Powder Blue Mercedes Queen, 1972 **(54)**; Song Seller, 1972 **(96)**; Love Music, 1973 **(97)**

Pop/Rock — Oregon

Debbie Reynolds

Albums: Tammy, 1957; The Singing Nun, 1966

Singles: Tammy, 1957 **(1)**; A Very Special Love, 1958 **(20)**; Am I That Easy to Forget, 1960 **(25)**; City Lights, 1960 **(55)**

Pop Vocal — Texas; film and TV star; mother of actress Carrie Fisher

Jody Reynolds

Singles: Endless Sleep, 1958 **(5)**;
Fire of Love, 1958 **(66)**
Rockabilly — Arizona

Lawrence Reynolds

Single: Jesus Is a Soul Man, 1969
(28)
Soul Vocal — Alabama

Rhinoceros

Personnel: John Finley (vocals);
Doug Hastings (guitars) replaced
(1970) by Larry Leishman (guitars);
Jerry Penrod (bass) replaced (1969)
by Steve Weis (bass) replaced (1969)
by Peter Hodgson (bass); Alan
Gerber (keyboards, vocals) left
group (1970); Danny Weis (keyboards, guitars); Michael Fonfara
(keyboards); Billy Mundi (drums)
replaced (1970) by Duke Edwards
(drums)
Albums: Rhinoceros, 1969; Satin
Chicken, 1969; Better Times Are
Coming, 1970
Jazz/Rock — California; group was
assembled by Elektra producer Paul
Rothchild in 1968

Cliff Richard

Albums: Cliff, 1959; Cliff Sings,
1959; Me & My Shadows, 1960;
Listen to Cliff, 1961; The Young
Ones, 1961; 21 Today, 1961; 32
Minutes 17 Seconds, 1962; When in
Spain, 1963; Summer Holiday,
1963; Wonderful Life, 1963; Hit
Album, 1963; It's All in the Game,
1964; Swinger's Paradise, 1964;
Aladdin & His Wonderful Lamp,
1965; Cliff Richard, 1965; When in
Rome, 1965; More Hits, 1965; Love
Is Forever, 1965; Kinda Latin, 1966;

Cliff Richard

Finders Keepers, 1966; Cinderella,
1967; Don't Stop Me Now, 1967;
Good News, 1967; Cliff in Japan,
1968; Two a Penny, 1968; Estab-
lished 1958, 1968; Best of Cliff
Richard, 1969; Sincerely, 1969;
About That Man, 1970; All My
Love, 1970; Tracks & Grooves,
1970; His Land, 1970; Best of Cliff
Richard Vol. 2, 1972; Take Me
High, 1973; Help It Along, 1974;
31st of February, 1974; Live, 1976;
I'm Nearly Famous, 1976; Every
Face Tells a Story, 1977; My Kind
of Life, 1977; 40 Golden Greats,
1977; Small Corners, 1978; Green
Light, 1978; Rock 'n' Roll Juvenile,
1979; Thank You Very Much, 1979;
We Don't Talk Anymore, 1979; I'm
No Hero, 1980; Love Songs, 1981;
Wired for Sound, 1981; Now You
See Me, Now You Don't, 1982;
Dressed for the Occasion, 1983;
Silver, 1983; Give a Little Bit More,

1983; Always Guaranteed, 1987; Private Collection, 1988; Stronger, 1989; From a Distance . . . The Event, 1990; Together, 1991

Singles: Living Doll, 1959 **(30)**; Lucky Lips, 1963 **(62)**; It's All in the Game, 1963 **(25)**; I'm the Lonely One, 1964 **(92)**; Bachelor Boy, 1964 **(99)**; I Only Have Eyes for You, 1964 **(109)**; Congratulations, 1968 **(99)**; Power to All Our Friends, 1973 **(109)**; Devil Woman, 1976 **(6)**; I Can't Ask for Anything More Than You Baby, 1976 **(80)**; My Kinda Life, 1977; Don't Turn the Light Out, 1977 **(57)**; Try a Smile, 1977; Hey Mr. Dreammaker, 1977; Miss You Nights, 1978; We Don't Talk Anymore, 1979 **(7)**; Carrie, 1980 **(34)**; Dreaming, 1980 **(10)**; Suddenly, 1980 **(20)** (with Olivia Newton-John); A Little in Love, 1980 **(17)**; Give a Little Bit More, 1981 **(41)**; Wired for Sound, 1981 **(71)**; Daddy's Home, 1981 **(23)**; The Only Way Out, 1982 **(64)**; Little Town, 1982; She Means Nothing to Me, 1983 (with Phil Everly); True Love Ways, 1983; Never Say Die (Give a Little Bit More), 1983 **(73)**; Please Don't Fall in Love, 1983; Donna, 1984; Baby You're Dynamite, 1984; She's So Beautiful, 1985; Living Doll, 1986; My Pretty One, 1987; Some People, 1987; Remember Me, 1987;Mistletoe and Wine, 1988; The Best of Me, 1989; Saviour's Day, 1990

Pop Vocal — British; real name is Harry Roger Webb

Frank Ricotti

Album: Our Point of View, 1969
Progressive Rock — British; also recorded with Mike D'Albuquerque of ELO

The Righteous Brothers

Bill Medley, Bobby Hatfield

Personnel: Bill Medley (vocals); Bobby Hatfield (vocals)

Albums: Right Now!, 1964; Some Blue Eyed Soul, 1965; You've Lost That Lovin' Feelin', 1965; Just Once in My Life, 1965; This Is New!, 1965; Back to Back, 1965; Soul & Inspiration, 1966; Best of the Righteous Brothers, 1966; Go Ahead and Cry, 1966; Sayin' Somethin', 1967; Greatest Hits, 1967; Souled Out, 1967; Standards, 1967; One for the Road, 1968; Greatest Hits Volume 2, 1969; Rebirth, 1970; Righteous Brothers, 1970; 2 x 2, 1973; Give It to the People, 1974; Sons of Mrs. Righteous, 1975; Portrait, 1975; Unchained Melody, 1975; History, 1977; Anthology, 1989; Best of the Righteous Brothers, 1990

Singles: Little Latin Lupe Lu, 1963 **(49)**; My Babe, 1963 **(75)**; Try to Find Another Man, 1964 **(119)**; This Little Girl of Mine, 1964 **(114)**; You've Lost That Lovin' Feeling, 1964 **(1)**; Bring Your Love to Me, 1965 **(83)**; My Babe, 1965 **(101)**; Fannie Mae, 1965 **(117)**; You Can Have Her, 1965 **(67)**; Just Once in My Life, 1965 **(9)**; Justine, 1965,

(85); Hung on You, 1965 (47); Unchained Melody, 1965 (4); For Your Love, 1965 (106); Ebb Tide, 1965 (5); Georgia on My Mind, 1966 (62); (You're My) Soul and Inspiration, 1966 (1); He Will Break Your Heart, 1966 (91); He, 1966 (18); Go Ahead and Cry, 1966 (30); On This Side of Goodbye, 1966 (47); White Cliffs of Dover, 1966 (118); Along Came Jones, 1967 (108); Melancholy Music Man, 1967 (43); Been So Nice, 1967 (128); Stranded in the Middle of Noplace, 1967 (72); Here I Am, 1968 (121); Rock and Roll Heaven, 1974 (3); Give It to the People, 1974 (20); Dream On, 1974 (32); Women in Love, 1985; Unchained Melody, 1990 (13); Unchained Melody (Different Version), 1990 (19)

Blue-Eyed Soul—American; Jimmy Walker replaced Medley from 1968 to 1974

Jeannie C. Riley

Albums: Harper Valley P.T.A., 1968; Yearbooks and Yesterdays, 1969; Things Go Better with Love, 1969

Singles: Harper Valley P.T.A., 1968 (1); The Girl Most Likely, 1968 (55); There Never Was a Time, 1969 (77); The Rib, 1969 (111); Things Go Better with Love, 1969 (111); Country Girl, 1970 (106); Oh, Singer, 1971 (74); Good Enough to Be Your Wife, 1971 (97)

Country/Pop Vocal—Texas; real name is Jeanne Stephenson

Terry Riley

Albums: Reed Streams, 1967; Keyboard Studies, 1969; In C', 1970; Church of Anthrax, 1971 (with

John Cale); Rainbow in Curved Air, 1971; Persian Surgery Dervishes, 1972; Happy Ending, 1975; Le Secret de la Vie, 1975; Shri Camel, 1980; Descending Moonshine Dervishes, 1982; Songs for the Ten Voices of the Two Prophets, 1984

Progressive Rock—American

The Rip-Chords

Personnel: Bruce Johnston (keyboards, guitars, vocals); Phil Stewart (guitars, vocals); Bernie Bringas (bass, vocals) replaced (1965) by Arnie Markus (bass); Terry Melcher (keyboards, vocals); Rich Rotkin (drums)

Albums: Hey Little Cobra and Other Hot Rod Hits, 1963; Three Window Coupe, 1964

Singles: Here I Stand, 1963 (51); Gone, 1963 (88); Hey Little Cobra, 1963 (4); Three Window Coupe, 1964 (28); One Piece Topless Bathing Suit, 1964 (96)

Surf Rock—California; Melcher is the son of Doris Day

Johnny Rivers

Albums: At the Whiskey a Go-Go, 1964; Here We Go-Go Again, 1964; In Action, 1965; Meanwhile Back at the Whiskey a Go-Go, 1965; Rocks the Folk, 1965; And I Know You Wanna Dance, 1966; Changes, 1966; Golden Hits, 1966; Rewind, 1967; Realization, 1968; Sensational, 1968; A Touch of Gold, 1969; John Lee Hooker, 1970; Slo Slim Slider, 1970; Home Grown, 1971; Johnny Rivers, 1972; Go Johnny Go, 1972; L.A. Reggae, 1973; History of Johnny Rivers, 1973; Super Pak, 1973; Blue Suede Shoes, 1973; Last

Boogie in Paris, 1974; Road, 1974; Very Best of Johnny Rivers, 1975; Help Me Rhonda, 1975; New Loves and Old Friends, 1975; Wild Night, 1976; Outside Help, 1978; Borrowed Time, 1980

Singles: Memphis, 1964 **(2)**; Oh What a Kiss, 1964 **(120)**; Maybelline, 1964 **(12)**; Mountain of Love, 1964 **(9)**; Midnight Special, 1965 **(20)**; Cupid, 1965 **(76)**; The Seventh Son, 1965 **(7)**; Where Have All the Flowers Gone, 1965 **(26)**; Under Your Spell Again, 1965 **(35)**; Secret Agent Man, 1966 **(3)**; Muddy Water, 1966 **(19)**; Poor Side of Town, 1966 **(1)**; Baby, I Need Your Loving, 1967 **(3)**; The Tracks of My Tears, 1967 **(10)**; Summer Rain, 1967 **(14)**; Look to Your Soul, 1968 **(49)**; Right Relations, 1968 **(61)**; These Are Not My People, 1969 **(55)**; Muddy River, 1969 **(41)**; One Woman, 1969 **(89)**; Into the Mystic, 1970 **(51)**; Fire & Rain, 1970 **(94)**; Sea Cruise, 1971 **(84)**; Think His Name, 1971 **(65)**; Rockin' Pneumonia & Boogie Woogie Flu, 1972 **(6)**; Blue Suede Shoes, 1973 **(38)**; Searchin'/So Fine, 1973 **(113)**; Six Days on the Road, 1974 **(106)**; Help Me Rhonda, 1975 **(22)**; Ashes and Sand, 1975 **(96)**; Swayin' to the Music (Slow Dancin'), 1977 **(10)**; Curious Mind (The Um Um Song), 1977 **(41)**; Romance (Give Me a Chance), 1980; China, 1980; Heartbreak Love, 1984

Pop Vocal — New York; real name is John Ramistella; discovered the Fifth Dimension

The Rivieras

Personnel: Homer Dunn (vocals); Charles Allen (vocals); Ronald Cook (vocals); Andrew Jones (vocals)

Singles: Count Every Star, 1958 **(73)**; Moonlight Serenade, 1959 **(47)**; Our Love, 1959 **(103)**; Since I Made You Cry, 1960 **(93)**; Moonlight Cocktails, 1960 **(103)**

R & B Vocal — New Jersey

The Rivieras

Personnel: Bill Dobslaw (vocals); Jim Boal (guitars); Willie Gaut (guitars); Doug Gean (bass); Otto Nuss (keyboards); Paul Dennert (drums)

Album: Let's Have a Party, 1964

Singles: California Sun, 1964 **(5)**; Little Donna, 1964 **(93)**; Let's Have a Party, 1964 **(99)**; Rockin' Robin, 1964 **(96)**

Pop/Rock — Indiana

The Rivingtons

Personnel: Carl White (vocals; deceased 1980); Sonny Harris (vocals); Al Frazier (vocals); Rocky Wilson (vocals)

Album: Papa-Oom-Mow-Mow, 1962

Singles: Papa-Oom-Mow-Mow, 1962 **(48)**; Mama-Oom-Mow-Mow, 1963 **(106)**; The Bird's the Word, 1963 **(52)**

Pop Vocal — California

Marty Robbins

Albums: Gunfighter Ballads and Trail Songs, 1959; More Gunfighter Ballads and Trail Songs, 1961; Devil Woman, 1962; Greatest Hits, 1963; Greatest Hits, Volume II, 1967; I Walk Alone, 1968; It's a Sin, 1969; My Woman, My Woman, My Wife, 1970; Greatest Hits, Volume III, 1971; Today, 1971; Biggest Hits, 1973; Lifetime of a Song, 1975; American Originals, 1977

Singles: Singing the Blues, 1956 **(17)**; A White Sport Coat (And a Pink Carnation), 1957 **(2)**; The Story of My Life, 1957 **(15)**; Just Married, 1958 **(26)**; Stairway of Love, 1958 **(68)**; She Was Only Seventeen (He Was One Year More), 1958 **(27)**; The Hanging Tree, 1959 **(38)**; Cap and Gown, 1959 **(45)**; El Paso, 1959 **(1)**; Big Iron, 1960 **(26)**; Is There Any Chance, 1960 **(31)**; Five Brothers, 1960 **(74)**; Ballad of the Alamo, 1960 **(34)**; Don't Worry, 1961 **(3)**; Jimmy Martinez, 1961 **(51)**; It's Your World, 1961 **(51)**; I Told the Brook, 1961 **(81)**; Sometimes I'm Tempted, 1962 **(109)**; Love Can't Wait, 1962 **(69)**; Devil Woman, 1962 **(16)**; Ruby Ann, 1962 **(18)**; Cigarettes and Coffee Blues, 1963 **(93)**; Not So Long Ago, 1963 **(115)**; Begging to You, 1963 **(74)**; Girl from Spanish Town, 1964 **(106)**; The Cowboy in the Continental Suit, 1964 **(103)**; One of These Days, 1964 **(105)**; Ribbon of Darkness, 1965 **(103)**; Tonight Carmen, 1967 **(114)**; I Walk Alone, 1968 **(65)**; My Woman, My Woman, My Wife, 1970 **(42)**; Jolie Girl, 1970 **(108)**; Padre, 1971 **(113)**; The Chair, 1971 **(121)**; I Don't Know Why (I Just Do), 1977 **(108)**

Country Vocal—Arizona; real last name was Robinson; died from a heart attack in 1982

The Robbs

Personnel: David "Dee Robb" Donaldson (vocals); Bruce Robb (guitars); Robert "Joe Robb" Donaldson (bass); Craig "Robb" Krampf (drums)

Albums: The Robbs, 1966; The Robbs, 1968

Singles: Race with the Wind, 1966 **(103)**; Rapid Transit, 1967 **(123)**; Movin', 1969 **(131)**; Last of the Wine, 1970 **(114)**; I'll Never Get Enough, 1970 **(106)**

Pop/Rock—Milwaukee

Robert & Johnny

Personnel: Robert Carr (vocals); Johnny Mitchell (vocals)

Singles: We Belong Together, 1958 **(32)**; I Believe in You, 1958 **(93)**; We Belong Together, 1961 **(104)**

R & B Vocal—New York

The Robins

Personnel: Ty Terrell (vocals); Billy Richards (vocals); Bobby Nunn (vocals); Roy Richards (vocals); added (1954) Carl Gardner (vocals); added (1954) Grady Chapman (vocals)

Singles: Smokey Joe's Cafe, 1955 **(79)**; White Cliffs of Dover, 1961 **(108)**

R & B Vocal—Los Angeles

Alvin Robinson

Singles: Something You Got, 1964 **(52)**; Fever, 1964 **(108)**

R & B Vocal—New Orleans; died in 1989

Floyd Robinson

Single: Makin' Love, 1959 **(20)**

Pop Vocal—Nashville

Rochell and The Candles

Personnel: Rochell Henderson (vocals); Melvin Sasso (vocals);

T. C. Henderson (vocals); Johnny Wyatt (vocals; deceased 1983)
Single: Once Upon a Time, 1961 **(26)**
R & B Vocal — Los Angeles

The Rock 'n' Roll Dubble Bubble Trading Card Co. of Philadelphia 1941

Single: Bubble Gum Music, 1969 **(74)**
Bubblegum Pop — American; another studio group produced by Kasenetz and Katz

Rock-a-Teens

Personnel: Vic Mizelle (guitars)
Single: Woo-Hoo, 1959 **(16)**
Instrumental Pop — Virginia

The Rockets

Personnel: Danny Whitten (guitars, vocals; deceased 1972); Leon Whitsell (guitars, vocals); George Whitsell (guitars, vocals); Billy Talbot (bass); Bobby Notkoff (violin); Ralph Molina (drums)
Album: Rockets, 1968
Country/Rock — American

Rockin' Rebels

Personnel: Bill Pennell (saxophones)
Album: Wild Weekend, 1963
Singles: Wild Weekend, 1962 **(8)**; Rockin' Crickets, 1963 **(87)**
Instrumental Rock — Canadian

The Rockin' R's

Personnel: Ron Valz (guitars); Ron Wernsman (bass); Ted Minar (drums)

Single: The Beat, 1959 **(57)**
Instrumental Pop — Illinois

The Rocky Fellers

Personnel: Eddie Feller (vocals); Albert Feller (vocals); Tony Feller (vocals); Junior Feller (vocals)
Singles: Killer Joe, 1963 **(16)**; Like the Big Guys Do, 1963 **(55)**
Pop Vocal — Phillipines

Jimmie Rodgers

Albums: Jimmie Rodgers, 1957; It's Over, 1966; Child of Clay, 1968; Windmills of Your Mind, 1969
Singles: Honeycomb, 1957 **(1)**; Kisses Sweeter Than Wine, 1957 **(3)**; Oh-Oh, I'm Falling in Love Again, 1958 **(7)**; The Long Hot Summer, 1958 **(77)**; Secretly, 1958 **(3)**; Make Me a Miracle, 1958 **(16)**; Are You Really Mine, 1958 **(10)**; The Wizard, 1958 **(45)**; Bimbombey, 1958 **(11)**; I'm Never Gonna Tell, 1959 **(36)**; Because You're Young, 1959 **(62)**; Ring-a-Ling-a-Lario, 1959 **(32)**; Wonderful You, 1959 **(40)**; Tucumcari, 1959 **(32)**; Wistful Willie, 1959 **(112)**; T.L.C. Tender Love and Care, 1960 **(24)**; Waltzing Matilda, 1960 **(41)**; Just a Closer Walk with Thee, 1960 **(44)**; The Wreck of the "John B," 1960 **(64)**; A Little Dog Cried, 1961 **(71)**; No One Will Ever Know, 1962 **(43)**; Rainbow at Midnight, 1962 **(62)**; Face in a Crowd, 1963 **(129)**; Two-Ten, Six-Eighteen (Doesn't Anybody Know My Name), 1963 **(78)**; Mama Was a Cotton Picker, 1963 **(131)**; The World I Used to Know, 1964 **(51)**; It's Over, 1966 **(37)**; Child of Clay, 1967 **(31)**; Today, 1968 **(104)**; The Windmills of Your Mind, 1969 **(123)**

Pop Vocal—Washington; had own TV series in 1959

Tommy Roe

Albums: Sheila, 1962; Something for Everybody, 1963; Sweet Pea, 1966; It's Now Winter's Day, 1967; Phantasy, 1967; Dizzy, 1969; 12 in a Roe/Greatest Hits, 1969; We Can Make Music, 1970; Beginnings, 1971; 16 Greatest Hits, 1971; Energy, 1976; Full Bloom, 1978

Singles: Sheila, 1962 **(1)**; Susie Darlin', 1962 **(35)**; Piddle De Pat, 1962 **(108)**; The Folk Singer, 1963 **(84)**; Everybody, 1963 **(3)**; Come On, 1964 **(36)**; Carol, 1964 **(61)**; Party Girl, 1964 **(85)**; Sweet Pea, 1966 **(8)**; Hooray for Hazel, 1966 **(6)**; It's Now Winters Day, 1966 **(23)**; Sing Along with Me, 1967 **(91)**; Little Miss Sunshine, 1967 **(99)**; Dottie I Like It, 1968 **(114)**; Dizzy, 1969 **(1)**; Heather Honey, 1969 **(29)**; Jack and Jill, 1969 **(53)**; Jam Up Jelly Tight, 1969 **(8)**; Stir It Up and Serve It, 1970 **(50)**; Pearl, 1970 **(50)**; We Can Make Music, 1970 **(49)**; Brush a Little Sunshine,

1970 **(117)**; Little Miss Goodie Two Shoes, 1971 **(104)**; Pistol Legged Woman, 1971 **(124)**; Stagger Lee, 1971 **(25)**; Mean Little Woman, Rosalie, 1972 **(92)**; Working Class Hero, 1973 **(97)**

Pop Vocal—Atlanta

Julie Rogers

Singles: The Wedding, 1964 **(10)**; Like a Child, 1965 **(67)**

Pop Vocal—British; real name is Julie Rolls

Kenny Rogers & The First Edition

back row: Settle, Williams; **front row:** Rogers, Camacho

Personnel: Kenny Rogers (vocals); Thelma Camacho (vocals) replaced (1968) by Mary Arnold (vocals); Mike Settle (guitars); Terry Williams (guitars); added (1967) Kin Vassey (guitars, bass, keyboards); added (1966) Mickey Jones (drums)

Albums: The First Edition, 1968; The First Edition '69, 1969; Ruby, Don't Take Your Love to Town, 1969; Something's Burning, 1970; Tell It All Brother, 1970; Greatest

Hits, 1971; Transition, 1971; The Ballad of Calico, 1972

Singles: Just Dropped In (to See What Condition My Condition Was In), 1968 **(5)**; Only Me, 1968 **(133)**; Are My Thoughts Still with You, 1968 **(119)**; But You Know I Love You, 1969 **(19)**; Once Again She's All Alone, 1969 **(126)**; Ruby, Don't Take Your Love to Town, 1969 **(6)**; Reuben James, 1969 **(26)**; Something's Burning, 1970 **(11)**; Tell It All Brother, 1970 **(17)**; Heed the Call, 1970 **(33)**; Someone Who Cares, 1971 **(51)**; Take My Hand, 1971 **(91)**; School Teacher, 1972 **(91)**; Lady, Play Your Symphony, 1972 **(105)**

Country/Rock—American; had TV show "Rollin'" in 1972

The Rollers

Personnel: Johnny Torrence (vocals); Al Wilson (vocals); Eddie Wilson (vocals); Don Sampson (vocals); Willie Willingham (vocals)

Single: The Continental Walk, 1961 **(80)**

R & B Vocal—California

The Rolling Stones

Personnel: Mick Jagger (vocals); Keith Richards (guitars, vocals); Brian Jones (guitars; deceased 1969); replaced (1969) by Mick Taylor (guitars) replaced (1975) by Ron Wood (guitars, vocals); Dick Taylor (guitars, bass, vocals) left group (1963); Bill Wyman (bass, vocals); Charlie Watts (drums); added (1970) Ian Stewart (piano; deceased 1991) left group (1977)

The Rolling Stones: Wyman, Watts, Jagger, Wood, Richards

Albums: The Rolling Stones, 1964; 5 × 5, 1964; The Rolling Stones 2, 1965; 12 × 5, 1965; The Rolling Stones Now!, 1965; Out of Our Heads, 1965; December's Children, 1965; Aftermath, 1966; Big Hits (High Tide and Green Grass), 1966; Got Live If You Want It, 1967; Between the Buttons, 1967; Flowers, 1967; Their Satanic Majesties Request, 1967; Beggar's Banquet, 1968; Let It Bleed, 1969; Get Your Ya-Ya's Out, 1970; Through the Past Darkly (Big Hits Vol. 2), 1970; Hot Rocks: 1964–1971, 1971; Stone Age, 1971; Gimme Shelter, 1971; Milestones, 1971; Sticky Fingers, 1971; More Hot Rocks (Big Hits and Fazed Cookies), 1972; Exile on Main Street, 1972; Goat's Head Soup, 1973; It's Only Rock 'n Roll, 1974; Rolled Gold, 1975; Metamorphosis, 1975; Made in the Shade, 1975; Black and Blue, 1976; Love You Live, 1977; Some Girls, 1978; Emotional Rescue, 1980; Sucking in the Seventies, 1981; Tattoo You, 1981; Still Life, 1982; Undercover, 1983; Rewind, 1984; Dirty Work, 1986; Steel Wheels, 1989; Flashpoint, 1991

Singles: Not Fade Away, 1964 **(48)**; Tell Me, 1964 **(24)**; It's All Over Now, 1964 **(26)**; Time Is on My Side, 1964 **(6)**; Heart of Stone, 1965 **(19)**; What a Shame, 1965 **(124)**; The Last Time, 1965 **(9)**; Play with Fire, 1965 **(96)**; Satisfaction, 1965 **(1)**; Get Off My Cloud, 1965 **(1)**; As Tears Go By, 1965 **(6)**; 19th Nervous Breakdown, 1966 **(2)**; Paint It Black, 1966 **(1)**; Mother's Little Helper, 1966 **(8)**; Lady Jane, 1966 **(24)**; Have You Seen Your Mother Baby/Standing in the Shadows, 1966 **(9)**; Ruby Tuesday, 1967 **(1)**; Let's Spend the Night Together, 1967 **(55)**; We Love You, 1967 **(50)**; Dandelion, 1967 **(14)**; She's a Rainbow, 1967 **(25)**; Jumpin' Jack Flash, 1968 **(3)**; Street Fighting Man, 1968 **(48)**; Honky Tonk Woman, 1969 **(1)**; Brown Sugar, 1971 **(1)**; Wild Horses, 1971 **(28)**; Tumbling Dice, 1972 **(7)**; Happy, 1972 **(22)**; You Can't Always Get What You Want, 1973 **(42)**; Angie, 1973 **(1)**; Doo Doo Doo Doo Doo (Heartbreaker), 1974 **(15)**; It's Only Rock 'n Roll, 1974 **(16)**; Ain't Too Proud to Beg, 1974 **(17)**; I Don't Know Why, 1975 **(42)**; Out of Time, 1975 **(81)**; Fool to Cry, 1976 **(10)**; Hot Stuff, 1976 **(49)**; Miss You, 1978 **(1)**; Beast of Burden, 1978 **(8)**; Shattered, 1979 **(31)**; Emotional Rescue, 1980 **(3)**; She's So Cold, 1980 **(26)**; Start Me Up, 1981 **(2)**; Waiting on a Friend, 1981 **(13)**; Hangfire, 1982 **(20)**; Going to a Go-Go, 1982 **(25)**; Time Is on My Side (Live), 1982; Undercover of the Night, 1983 **(9)**; She Was Hot, 1984 **(44)**; Miss You (Live), 1984; Too Much Blood, 1984; Harlem Shuffle, 1986 **(5)**; One Hit (to the Body), 1986 **(28)**; Mixed Emotions, 1989 **(5)**; Rock and a Hard Place, 1989 **(23)**; Almost Hear You Sigh, 1990 **(50)**; High Wire, 1991

Hard Rock—British; considered to be the greatest touring rock band

Ronald & Ruby

Personnel: Lee "Ronald" Morris (vocals); Beverly "Ruby" Ross (vocals)

Single: Lollipop, 1958 **(20)**

Pop Vocal—New Jersey

The Ron-Dels

Personnel: Delbert McClinton (vocals, guitars); Ronnie Kelly (vocals)

Single: If You Really Want Me To, I'll Go, 1965 **(97)**
Pop/Rock—Texas

Don Rondo

Singles: Two Different Worlds, 1956 **(11)**; White Silver Sands, 1957 **(7)**; There's Only You, 1957 **(77)**
Pop Vocal—New York

The Ronettes

Personnel: Veronica "Ronnie Spector" Bennett (vocals); Estelle Bennett (vocals); Nedra Talley (vocals)
Albums: Today's Hits, 1963; Christmas Gift, 1963; Presenting the Fabulous Ronettes Featuring Veronica, 1964; The Ronettes, 1965; Cha Cha Cha, 1967; The Ronettes Sing Their Greatest Hits, 1975
Singles: Be My Baby, 1963 **(2)**; Baby, I Love You, 1963 **(24)**; (The Best Part of) Breakin' Up, 1964 **(39)**; Do I Love You?, 1964 **(34)**; Walking in the Rain, 1964 **(23)**; Born to Be Together, 1965 **(52)**; Is This What I Get for Loving You?, 1965 **(75)**; I Can Hear Music, 1966 **(100)**; You Came, You Saw, You Conquered, 1969 **(108)**
Pop Vocal—Philadelphia

Ronnie & The Hi-Lites

Personnel: Ronnie Goodson (vocals; deceased 1980)
Singles: I Wish That We Were Married, 1962 **(16)**; Be Kind, 1962 **(120)**; A Slow Dance, 1963 **(116)**
R & B Vocal—New Jersey

Ronny & The Daytonas

Personnel: John "Bucky" Wilkin (vocals); Chips Moman (guitars, vocals); Bobby Russell (bass, vocals); Johnny MacRae (drums, vocals)
Albums: G.T.O., 1964; Sandy, 1965
Singles: G.T.O., 1964 **(4)**; California Bound, 1964 **(72)**; Bucket "T," 1964 **(54)**; Sandy, 1965 **(27)**; Somebody to Love Me, 1966 **(115)**; Dianne, Dianne, 1966 **(69)**; I'll Think of Summer, 1966 **(133)**
Pop/Rock—Nashville

Linda Ronstadt

Albums: Linda Ronstadt & the Stone Poneys, 1968; Hand Sown, Home Grown, 1969; Silk Purse, 1970; Linda Ronstadt, 1972; Don't Cry Now, 1974; Heart Like a

Wheel, 1974; Different Drum, 1975; Prisoner in Disguise, 1975; Hasten Down the Wind, 1976; Greatest Hits, 1976; A Retrospective, 1977; Simple Dreams, 1977; Living in the U.S.A., 1978; Mad Love, 1980; Greatest Hits Volume 2, 1980; Get Closer, 1982; What's New, 1983; Lush Life, 1984; For Sentimental Reasons, 1986; Round Midnight, 1986; Trio, 1987 (with Emmylou Harris & Dolly Parton); Canciones de Mi Padre, 1988; Cry Like a Rainstorm, Howl Like the Wind, 1989; Mas Canciones, 1991

Singles: Different Drum, 1967 **(13)**; Up to My Neck High in Muddy Water, 1968 **(93)**; Will You Love Me Tomorrow, 1970 **(111)**; Long Long Time, 1970 **(25)**; (She's a) Very Lovely Woman, 1971 **(70)**; The Long Way Around, 1971 **(74)**; Rock Me on the Water, 1972 **(85)**; Love Has No Pride, 1973 **(51)**; Silver Threads and Golden Needles, 1974 **(67)**; Colorado, 1974 **(108)**; You're No Good, 1974 **(1)**; When Will I Be Loved, 1975 **(2)**; It Doesn't Matter Anymore, 1975 **(47)**; Love Is a Rose, 1975 **(63)**; Heat Wave, 1975 **(5)**; Tracks of My Tears, 1975 **(25)**; That'll Be the Day, 1976 **(11)**; Someone to Lay Down Beside Me, 1976 **(42)**; Lose Again, 1977 **(76)**; Blue Bayou, 1977 **(3)**; It's So Easy, 1977 **(5)**; Poor Poor Pitiful Me, 1978 **(31)**; Tumbling Dice, 1978 **(32)**; Back in the U.S.A., 1978 **(16)**; Ooh Baby Baby, 1978 **(7)**; Just One Look, 1979 **(44)**; How Do I Make You, 1980 **(10)**; Hurt So Bad, 1980 **(8)**; I Can't Let Go, 1980 **(31)**; Get Closer, 1982 **(29)**; I Knew You When, 1982 **(37)**; Easy for You to Say, 1983 **(54)**; What's New, 1983 **(53)**; I've Got a Crush on You, 1984; Someone to Watch Over Me, 1984; Skylark, 1984 **(103)**; When I Fall in Love, 1985; Somewhere Out There, 1987 **(2)** (with James Ingram); Don't Know Much, 1990 **(2)** (with Aaron Neville); All My Life, 1990 **(11)**; When Something Is Wrong with My Baby, 1990 **(78)** (with Aaron Neville); Adios, 1990; Dreams to Dream, 1991

Pop Vocal—Arizona

The Rooftop Singers

Personnel: Erik Darling (vocals, guitars); Bill Svanhoe (vocals, guitars); Lynne Taylor (vocals; deceased 1982)

Album: Walk Right In!, 1963

Singles: Walk Right In, 1963 **(1)**; Tom Cat, 1963 **(20)**; Mama Don't Allow, 1963 **(55)**

Folk/Pop—American

The Roommates

Personnel: Steve Susskind (vocals); Jack Sailson (vocals); Felix Alvarez (vocals); Bob Minsky (vocals)

Single: Glory of Love, 1961 **(49)**

Pop Vocal—New York; Cathy Jean's backup group

The Rose Garden

Personnel: Diana Di Rose (guitars, vocals); James Groshong (guitars); John Norden (guitars); William Fleming (bass); Bruce Boudin (drums)

Album: The Rose Garden, 1968

Single: Next Plane to London, 1967 **(17)**

Pop/Rock—West Virginia

Rosie & The Originals

Personnel: Rosalie Hamlin (vocals)
Singles: Angel Baby, 1960 **(5)**; Lonely Blue Nights, 1961 **(66)**
Pop Vocal—San Diego

Jackie Ross

Singles: Selfish One, 1964 **(11)**; I've Got the Skill, 1964 **(89)**; Haste Makes Waste, 1964 **(126)**; Jerk and Twine, 1965 **(85)**
R & B Vocal—St. Louis

Rotary Connection

Personnel: Minnie Ripperton (vocals; deceased 1979); Judy Hauf (vocals); Sidney Barnes (vocals); Kenny Venegas (vocals); Mitch Aliotta (vocals); Bobby Sims (vocals)
Albums: Rotary Connection, 1968; Aladdin, 1968; Peace at Last, 1969; Songs, 1969; Dinner Music, 1970; Hey Love, 1971; Trip One, 1973
Singles: Paper Castle, 1968 **(132)**; Aladdin, 1968 **(113)**
Pop Vocal—Canadian

The Routers

Personnel: Joe Saraceno (guitars); Mike Gordon (guitars)
Album: Let's Go! With the Routers, 1963
Singles: Let's Go (Pony), 1962 **(19)**; Half Time, 1963 **(115)**; Sting Ray, 1963 **(50)**
Instrumental Rock—American

The Rover Boys

Personnel: Billy Albert (vocals)
Singles: Graduation, 1956 **(16)**;
From a School Ring to a Wedding Ring, 1956 **(79)**
Pop Vocal—Canadian

Billy Joe Royal

Albums: Down in the Boondocks, 1965; Hush, 1967; Cherry Hill Park, 1970
Singles: Down in the Boondocks, 1965 **(9)**; I Knew You When, 1965 **(14)**; I've Got to Be Somebody, 1965 **(38)**; It's a Good Time, 1966 **(104)**; Heart's Desire, 1966 **(88)**; Campfire Girls, 1966 **(91)**; Yo-Yo, 1966 **(117)**; These Are Not My People, 1967 **(113)**; The Greatest Love, 1967 **(117)**; Hush, 1967 **(52)**; Storybook Children, 1968 **(117)**; Cherry Hill Park, 1969 **(15)**; Every Night, 1970 **(113)**; Tulsa, 1971 **(86)**; Poor Little Pearl, 1971 **(111)**; Under the Boardwalk, 1978 **(82)**
Pop/Country Vocal—Georgia

The Royal Guardsmen

Personnel: Chris Nunley (vocals); Barry Winslow (guitars, vocals); Tom Richards (guitars); Bill Balogh (guitars, bass); Billy Taylor (organ); John Burdette (drums)

Albums: Snoopy vs. the Red Baron, 1967; Return of the Red Baron, 1967; Snoopy and His Friends, 1967; Snoopy for President, 1968

Singles: Snoopy vs. the Red Baron, 1966 **(2)**; The Return of the Red Baron, 1967 **(15)**; Airplane Song (My Airplane), 1967 **(46)**; Wednesday, 1967 **(97)**; I Say Love, 1968 **(72)**; Snoopy for President, 1968 **(85)**; Baby Let's Wait, 1968 **(35)**; Mother, Where's Your Daughter, 1969 **(112)**

Pop/Rock — Florida

Royal Teens

Personnel: Bob Gaudio (vocals) replaced (1959) by Al Kooper (vocals); Billy Dalton (vocals); Bill Crandall (vocals) replaced (1958) by Larry Qualiano (vocals); Tom Austin (vocals); added (1958) Joseph Francavilla (vocals)

Singles: Short Shorts, 1958 **(3)**; Harvey's Got a Girl Friend, 1958 **(78)**; Believe Me, 1959 **(26)**

Pop Vocal — New Jersey

The Royalettes

Personnel: Anita Ross (vocals); Sheila Ross (vocals); Terry Jones (vocals); Ronnie Brown (vocals)

Singles: Blue Summer, 1963 **(121)**; Poor Boy, 1965 **(113)**; It's Gonna Take a Miracle, 1965 **(41)**; I Want to Meet Him, 1965 **(72)**; You Bring Me Down, 1966 **(116)**

R & B Vocal — Baltimore

The Royaltones

Personnel: George Katsakis (saxophones)

Singles: Poor Boy, 1958 **(17)**;

Flamingo Express, 1961 **(82)**; Our Faded Love, 1964 **(103)**

Instrumental Pop — Michigan

The Rubber Band

Albums: Cream Songbook, 1969; Hendrix Songbook, 1969

Instrumental Pop — American

Ruby & The Romantics

Personnel: Ruby Nash (vocals); Ed Roberts (vocals); George Lee (vocals); Leroy Fann (vocals; deceased 1973); Ronald Moseley (vocals)

Albums: Our Day Will Come, 1963; Greatest Hits, 1968

Singles: Our Day Will Come, 1963 **(1)**; My Summer Love, 1963 **(16)**; Hey There Lonely Boy, 1963 **(27)**; Young Wings Can Fly (Higher Than You), 1963 **(47)**; Our Everlasting Love, 1964 **(64)**; Baby Come Home, 1964 **(75)**; When You're Young and in Love, 1964 **(48)**; Does He Really Care for Me, 1965 **(87)**; Your Baby Doesn't Love You Anymore, 1966 **(108)**; We Can Make It, 1966 **(120)**; Hurting Each Other, 1969 **(113)**

Pop/Soul Vocal — Ohio

David Ruffin

Albums: My Whole World Ended, 1969; Feelin' Good, 1969; Doin' His Thing, 1970; I Am My Brother's Keeper, 1970 (with Jimmy Ruffin); David Ruffin, 1973; Me and Rock 'n' Roll Is Here to Stay, 1974; Who I Am, 1975; Everything's Coming Up Love, 1976; In My Stride, 1977; At His Best, 1978; So Soon We Change, 1979; Gentleman

Ruffin, 1981; Ruffin & Kendrick, 1985

Singles: My Whole World Ended (The Moment You Left Me), 1969 **(9)**; I've Lost Everything I've Ever Loved, 1969 **(58)**; I'm So Glad I Fell for You, 1969 **(53)**; Stand by Me, 1970 **(61)** (with Jimmy Ruffin); Don't Stop Loving Me, 1971 **(112)**; Walk Away from Love, 1975 **(9)**; Heavy Love, 1976 **(47)**; Everything's Coming Up Love, 1976 **(49)**; Just Let Me Hold You for a Night, 1977 **(106)**

Soul Vocal—Mississippi; died in June, 1991; brother of Jimmy Ruffin; was a member of the Temptations

Jimmy Ruffin

Albums: Jimmy Ruffin, 1966; Top Ten, 1967; Jimmy Ruffin Way, 1967; Ruff'n Ready, 1969; Forever, 1970; Groove Governor, 1970; I Am My Brother's Keeper, 1970 (with David Ruffin); Greatest Hits, 1974; Love Is All We Need, 1975; 20 Golden Classics, 1980; Sunrise, 1980

Singles: As Long as There Is L-O-V-E Love, 1966 **(120)**; What Becomes of the Brokenhearted, 1966 **(7)**; I've Passed This Way Before, 1966 **(17)**; Gonna Give Her All the Love I've Got, 1967 **(29)**; Don't You Miss Me a Little Baby, 1967 **(68)**; I'll Say Forever My Love, 1968 **(77)**; Don't Let Him Take Your Love from Me, 1968 **(113)**; Farewell Is a Lonely Sound, 1969 **(104)**; Stand by Me, 1970 **(61)** (with David Ruffin); Maria (You Were the Only One), 1971 **(97)**; Hold on to My Love, 1980 **(10)**

Soul Vocal—Mississippi; brother of David Ruffin

The Rugbys

Personnel: Steve McNicol (guitars, vocals); Mike Mormer (bass, vocals); Ed Vernon (keyboards); Glenn Howerton (drums)

Album: Hot Cargo, 1969
Single: You, I, 1969 **(24)**
Pop/Rock—British

The Rumblers

Personnel: Johnny Kirkland (guitars); Mike Kelishes (guitars); Wayne Matteson (bass); Bob Jones (saxophones); Adrian Lloyd (drums)

Single: Boss, 1963 **(87)**
Instrumental Pop—California

The Rumor

Album: The Rumor, 1966
Singles: Without Her, 1966; Hold Me Now, 1966
Psychedelic Pop—American

Merrilee Rush & The Turnabouts

Albums: Angel of the Morning, 1968; Save Me, 1977

Singles: Angel of the Morning, 1968 **(7)**; That Kind of Woman, 1968 **(76)**; Reach Out, 1968 **(79)**; Everyday Livin' Days, 1969 **(130)**; Sign for the Goodtimes, 1969 **(125)**; Angel on My Shoulder, 1970 **(122)**; Save Me, 1977 **(54)**

Pop Vocal—Seattle

Tom Rush

Albums: Mind Ramblin', 1963; Blues Songs & Ballads, 1965; Blues & Folk, 1965; Tom Rush, 1965; Take a Little Walk with Me, 1966; I Got a Mind to Ramble, 1968; The Circle Game, 1968; Tom Rush,

1970; Wrong End of the Rainbow, 1970; Classic Rush, 1971; Merrimack County, 1972; Ladies Love Outlaws, 1974; The Best of Tom Rush, 1976

Singles: Who Do You Love, 1971 **(105)**; Mother Earth, 1972 **(111)**

Folk — New Hampshire

Bobby Russell

Album: Saturday Morning Confusion, 1971

Singles: 1432 Franklin Pike Circle Hero, 1968 **(36)**; Carlie, 1969 **(115)**; Saturday Morning Confusion, 1971 **(28)**

Pop Vocal — Nashville

Ray Russell

Albums: Turn Circle, 1968; Dragon Hill, 1969; Rites & Rituals, 1971; June 11th, 1971, 1971; Secret Asylum, 1973; Ready or Not, 1977

Pop/Rock — British

Rustix

Album: Bedlam, 1969

Hard Rock — British

Barry Ryan

Album: Two of a Kind, 1967 (with Paul Ryan)

Single: Eloise, 1968 **(86)** (with Paul Ryan)

Pop/Rock — British; real last name is Sapherson

Bobby Rydell

Albums: Bobby's Biggest Hits, 1961; Rydell at the Copa, 1961; Bobby Rydell/Chubby Checker, 1961; All the Hits, 1962; Bobby Rydell's Biggest Hits, Volume 2, 1962; The Top Hits of 1963, 1964; Forget Him, 1964

Singles: Kissin' Time, 1959 **(11)**; We Got Love, 1959 **(6)**; I Dig Girls, 1959 **(46)**; Wild One, 1960 **(2)**; Little Bitty Girl, 1960 **(19)**; Swingin' School, 1960 **(5)**; Ding-a-Ling, 1960 **(18)**; Volare, 1960 **(4)**; Sway, 1960 **(14)**; Groovy Tonight, 1960 **(70)**; Good Time Baby, 1961 **(11)**; Cherie, 1961 **(54)**; That Old Black Magic, 1961 **(21)**; The Fish, 1961 **(25)**; I Wanna Thank You, 1961 **(21)**; The Door to Paradise, 1961 **(85)**; Jingle Bell Rock, 1961 **(21)** (with Chubby Checker); I've Got Bonnie, 1962 **(18)**; Lose Her, 1962 **(69)**; Teach Me to Twist, 1962 **(109)** (with Chubby Checker); Gee, It's Wonderful, 1962 **(109)**; I'll Never Dance Again, 1962 **(14)**; The Cha-Cha-Cha, 1962 **(10)**; Jingle Bell Rock, 1962 **(92)** (with Chubby Checker); Butterfly Baby, 1963 **(23)**; Wildwood Days, 1963 **(17)**; Will You Be My Baby, 1963 **(114)**; Let's Make Love Tonight, 1963 **(98)**; Forget Him, 1963 **(4)**; Make Me Forget, 1964 **(43)**; A World Without Love, 1964 **(80)**; I Just Can't Say Goodbye, 1964 **(94)**; Diana, 1965 **(98)**

Pop Vocal — Philadelphia; real last name is Ridarelli

Mitch Ryder & The Detroit Wheels

Personnel: Mitch Ryder (vocals); Jim McCarty (guitars); Joe Kubert (guitars); Earl Elliott (bass) replaced (1967) by Jim McCallister (bass); John Badanjek (drums)

Albums: Take a Ride, 1966; Breakout, 1967; Sock It to Me, 1967; What Now My Love, 1967; All Mitch Ryder Hits!, 1967; Mitch

Ryder Sings the Hits, 1968; The Detroit Memphis Experiment, 1969; Detroit, 1971; Greatest Hits, 1972; Rev Up/Best of Mitch Ryder, 1989

Singles: Jenny Take a Ride, 1965 **(10)**; Little Latin Lupe Lu, 1966 **(17)**; Breakout, 1966 **(62)**; Taking All I Can Get, 1966 **(100)**; Devil with the Blue Dress On/Good Golly Miss Molly, 1966 **(4)**; Sock It to Me Baby, 1967 **(6)**; Too Many Fish in the Sea & Three Little Fishes (medley), 1967 **(24)**; Joy, 1967 **(41)**; What Now My Love, 1967 **(30)**; You Are My Sunshine, 1967 **(88)**; Come See About Me, 1967 **(113)**; Personality/Chantilly Lace, 1968 **(87)**; Ruby Baby, 1968 **(106)**; The Lights of Night, 1968 **(122)**; Ring Your Bell, 1969 **(125)**; Rock & Roll, 1971 **(107)**; When You Were Mine, 1983 **(87)**

Hard Rock — Detroit; Mitch's real name is William Levise, Jr.

Terje Rypdal

Albums: Bleak House, 1968; Dream, 1969; Terje Rypdal, 1971; Sart, 1972; Afric Popperbird, 1974; What Comes After, 1974; Whenever I Seem to Be Far Away, 1974; Odyssey, 1975; After the Rain, 1976; Waves, 1978; Rypdal, Vitous, DeJohnette, 1979 (with Miroslav Vitous and Jack DeJohnette); Descendra, 1980; To Be Continued, 1981; EOS, 1984 (with David Darling); Works, 1986; Singles Collection, 1988; Undisonus, 1989

Jazz/Rock — Scandinavian

Staff Sgt. Barry Sadler

Albums: Ballads of the Green Beret, 1966; The "A" Team, 1966

Singles: The Ballad of the Green Beret, 1966 **(1)**; The "A" Team, 1966 **(28)**

Pop Vocal — New Mexico; member of the U.S. Army Special Forces; died 11/5/89

The Safaris

Personnel: Jim Stephens (vocals); Richard Clasky (vocals); Marvin Rosenberg (vocals); Shelly Briar (vocals)

Singles: Image of a Girl, 1960 **(6)**; The Girl with the Story in Her Eyes, 1960 **(85)**; Kick Out, 1963 **(120)**

Pop Vocal — Los Angeles

Sagittarius

Personnel: Curt Boetcher (vocals); Michael Fennelly (guitars, vocals); Glen Campbell (guitars, vocals); Gary Usher (guitars); Terry Melcher (guitars, vocals); Keith Olsen (bass, vocals); Doug Rhodes (keyboards, vocals); Bruce Johnston (keyboards, vocals); Lee Mallory (keyboards, guitars); Ron Edgar (drums, guitars)

Albums: Begin, 1968 (as Millenium); Present Tense, 1968; The Blue Marble, 1969

Singles: My World Fell Down, 1967 **(70)**; In My Room, 1969 **(86)**; I Guess the Lord Must Be in New York City, 1969 **(135)**

Pop/Rock — California

Crispian St. Peters

Album: The Pied Piper, 1966

Singles: The Pied Piper, 1966 **(4)**; Changes, 1966 **(57)**; Your Ever Changin' Mind, 1966 **(106)**; You Were on My Mind, 1967 **(36)**;

Look Into My Teardrops, 1968
(133)
   Pop Vocal — British; real name is
Peter Smith

Kirby St. Romain

Single: Summer's Comin', 1963
(49)
   Pop Vocal — Dallas

Buffy Sainte-Marie

Albums: It's My Way, 1964;
Many a Mile, 1965; Little Wheel
Spin, 1966; Fire, Fleet and Candle-
light, 1967; I'm Gonna Be a Coun-
try Girl Again, 1968; Illuminations,
1970; She Used to Wanna Be a Bal-
lerina, 1971; Moon Shot, 1972;
Quiet Places, 1973; Best of Buffy
Sainte-Marie, 1973; Native North
American Child, 1974; Best of Buffy
Sainte-Marie, Volume 2, 1974;
Buffy, 1974; Changing Woman,
1975; Golden Hour, 1976; Sweet
America, 1976
   Singles: The Circle Game, 1970
(109); I'm Gonna Be a Country Girl
Again, 1971 **(98)**; Mister Can't You
See, 1972 **(38)**; He's an Indian
Cowboy in the Rodeo, 1972 **(98)**
   Folk/Country — Canadian; Buffy is
a Cree Indian

Kyu Sakamoto

Album: Sukiyaki and Other Japa-
nese Hits, 1963
   Singles: Sukiyaki, 1963 **(1)**; China
Nights (Shina No Yoru), 1963 **(58)**
   Pop Vocal — Japan

Sallyangie

Personnel: Sally Oldfield (vocals);
Mike Oldfield (guitars, vocals); Ray

Warleigh (flute, saxophones); Terry
Cox (drums)
   Album: Children of the Sun, 1968
Folk/Rock — British

Sammy Salvo

Single: Oh Julie, 1958 **(23)**
Pop Vocal — Alabama

Sam & Dave

Personnel: Samuel Moore (vo-
cals); Dave Prater (vocals; deceased
1988)
   Albums: Sam & Dave, 1966; Hold
On I'm Comin', 1966; Double Dyna-
mite, 1967; Soul Men, 1967; I
Thank You, 1968; Best of Sam &
Dave, 1969; Back Atcha, 1975
   Singles: You Don't Know Like I
Know, 1966 **(90)**; Hold On! I'm a
Comin', 1966 **(21)**; Said I Wasn't
Gonna Tell Nobody, 1966 **(64)**; You
Got Me Hummin', 1966 **(77)**; When
Something Is Wrong with My Baby,
1967 **(42)**; Soothe Me, 1967 **(56)**;
Soul Man, 1967 **(2)**; I Thank You,
1968 **(9)**; You Don't Know What
You Mean to Me, 1968 **(48)**; Can't
You Find Another Way (of Doing
It), 1968 **(54)**; Everybody Got to
Believe in Somebody, 1968 **(73)**;
Soul Sister, Brown Sugar, 1968 **(41)**;
Born Again, 1969 **(92)**; Baby-Baby
Don't Stop Now, 1970 **(117)**; One
Part Love-Two Parts Pain, 1970
(123); Don't Pull Your Love, 1971
(102)
   Soul/Pop Vocal — Southern

Sam the Sham &
The Pharoahs

Personnel: Domingo Samudio
(vocals, keyboards); Ray Stinnet
(guitars); Dave Martin (bass); Butch

Gibson (saxophones); Jerry Paterson (drums)

Albums: Wooly Bully, 1965; Their Second Album, 1965; On Tour, 1966; Lil' Red Riding Hood, 1966; Best of Sam the Sham & the Pharaohs, 1967; Nefertiti (Revue), 1967; Ten of Pentacles, 1968; Sam, Hard and Heavy, 1970

Singles: Wooly Bully, 1965 (**2**); Ju Ju Hand, 1965 (**26**); Ring Dang Doo, 1965 (**33**); Red Hot, 1966 (**82**); Lil' Red Riding Hood, 1966 (**2**); The Hair on My Chinny Chin Chin, 1966 (**22**); How Do You Catch a Girl, 1966 (**27**); Oh That's Good, No That's Bad, 1967 (**54**); Black Sheep, 1967 (**68**); Banned in Boston, 1967 (**117**); Yakety Yak, 1967 (**110**); I Couldn't Spell !!*@!, 1968 (**120**)

Boogie Rock — Dallas

The Sandals

Album: The Endless Summer, 1967

Surf Rock — California

The Sandpebbles

Personnel: Calvin White (vocals); Andrea Bolden (vocals); Lonzine Wright (vocals)

Album: Sandpebbles, 1967

Singles: Forget It, 1967 (**81**); Love Power, 1968 (**22**); If You Don't Hear Me the First Time (I'll Say It Again), 1968 (**122**); Never My Love, 1968 (**98**)

R & B Vocal — American

The Sandpipers

Personnel: Jim Brady (vocals); Michael Piano (vocals); Richard Shoff (vocals)

Albums: Guantanamera, 1966; The Sandpipers, 1967; Misty Roses, 1968; Softly, 1968; The Wonder of You, 1969; Greatest Hits, 1970; Come Saturday Morning, 1970

Singles: Guantanamera, 1966 (**9**); Louie, Louie, 1966 (**30**); Glass, 1967 (**112**); Quando M'Innamora, 1968 (**124**); Come Saturday Morning, 1969 (**17**); Free to Carry On, 1970 (**94**)

Pop Vocal — Los Angeles

Evie Sands

Singles: Take Me for a Little While, 1965 (**114**); Billy Sunshine, 1968 (**133**); Any Way That You Want Me, 1969 (**53**); Crazy Annie, 1970 (**116**); But You Know I Love You, 1970 (**110**); You Brought the Woman Out of Me, 1975 (**50**); I Love Makin' Love to You, 1975 (**50**)

Pop Vocal — New York

Jodie Sands

Singles: With All My Heart, 1957 (**15**); Someday (You'll Want Me to Want You), 1958 (**95**)

Pop Vocal — Philadelphia

Tommy Sands

Albums: Steady Date with Tommy Sands, 1957; Sing Boy Sing, 1958

Singles: Teen-Age Crush, 1957 (**2**); Ring-a-Ding-a-Ding, 1957 (**50**); My Love Song, 1957 (**62**); Goin' Steady/Ring My Phone, 1957 (**16**); Sing Boy Sing, 1958 (**24**); Teen-Age Doll, 1958 (**81**); Blue Ribbon Baby, 1958 (**50**); The Worryin' Kind, 1958 (**69**); I'll Be Seeing You, 1959 (**51**); The Old Oaken Bucket, 1960 (**73**)

Pop Vocal — Chicago; formerly married to Nancy Sinatra; was in several films

Mongo Santamaria

Albums: Watermelon Man!, 1963;
El Pussy Cat, 1965; La Bamba,
1965; Hey! Let's Party, 1966; Soul
Bag, 1968; Stone Soul, 1969;
Workin' on a Groovy Thing, 1969;
Feelin' Alright, 1970; Mongo '70,
1970

Singles: Watermelon Man, 1963
(10); Yeh-Yeh!, 1963 **(92)**; El Pussy
Cat, 1965 **(97)**; Cloud Nine, 1969
(32); We Got Latin Soul, 1969
(132); Feeling Alright, 1969 **(96)**

Jazz/Pop—Cuban; real first name
is Ramon

Santana

Carlos Santana

Personnel: Carlos Santana (guitars, vocals); David Brown (bass)
replaced (1971) by Tom Rutley
(bass) replaced (1972) by Douglas
Rauch (bass) replaced (1974) by
David Holland (bass) replaced
(1976) by Ivory Stone (bass) replaced (1976) by Pablo Tellez (bass)
replaced (1980) by Ron Carter (bass)
replaced (1980) by David Margen
(bass) replaced (1985) by Alphonso
Johnson (bass); Gregg Rolie (keyboards, vocals) replaced (1972) by
Tom Coster (keyboards, vocals) replaced (1974) by Wendy Haas (keyboards) replaced (1974) by Tom
Coster (keyboards, vocals) replaced
(1979) by Chris Solberg (keyboards,
vocals) replaced (1981) by Richard
Baker (keyboards) replaced (1985)
by Chester D. Thompson (keyboards); Mike Carabello (percussion) replaced (1971) by Rico Reyes
(percussion) and Pete "Coke" Esco-
vedo (percussion) replaced (1973) by
Phil Browne (percussion) replaced
(1974) by Leon Patillo (percussion)
replaced (1980) by Orestes Vilato
(percussion); Jose Areas (percussion)
replaced (1971) by Greg Errico (percussion) replaced (1976) by Francisco Aquabella (percussion) replaced (1977) by Paul Rekow
(percussion); Michael Shrieve
(drums) replaced (1974) by Ndugu
Leon Chancler (drums) replaced
(1976) by Graham Lear (drums)
replaced (1985) by Craig Krampf
(drums); added (1971) Neal Schon
(guitars, vocals) replaced (1972) by
Armando Peraza (guitars, vocals)
left group (1982); added (1974)
Greg Walker (vocals) replaced (1976)
by Tom Croucher (vocals) replaced
(1979) by Alexander Ligertwood
(vocals); added (1971) James
"Mingo" Lewis (piano) left group
(1973)

Albums: Santana, 1968; Abraxas,
1970; Santana III, 1972; Caravan-
serai, 1972; Welcome, 1974; Greatest
Hits, 1974; Borboletta, 1975; Lotus,
1975; Amigos, 1976; Festival, 1977;
Moonflower, 1977; Inner Secrets,

1979; Marathon, 1979; Zebop, 1981; Shango, 1982; Beyond Appearances, 1985; Freedom, 1986; Viva Santana!, 1988

Singles: Jingo, 1969 **(56)**; Evil Ways, 1970 **(9)**; Black Magic Woman, 1970 **(4)**; Oye Como Va, 1971 **(13)**; Everybody's Everything, 1971 **(12)**; No One to Depend On, 1972 **(36)**; When I Look in Your Eyes, 1974 **(102)**; Let It Shine, 1976 **(77)**; Dance Sister Dance, 1976; Europa, 1976; Let the Children Play, 1977 **(102)**; Give Me Love, 1977; She's Not There, 1977 **(27)**; Well Alright, 1978 **(69)**; Stormy, 1979 **(32)**; One Chain (Don't Make No Prison), 1979 **(59)**; Stay Beside Me, 1979; You Know That I Love You, 1979 **(35)**; All I Ever Wanted, 1980; Winning, 1981 **(17)**; The Sensitive Kind, 1981 **(56)**; Searchin', 1981 **(108)**; Hold On, 1982 **(15)**; Nowhere to Run, 1982 **(66)**; Say It Again, 1985 **(46)**; I'm the One Who Loves You, 1985 **(102)**

Latin/Jazz Rock — California

Santo & Johnny

Personnel: Santo Farina (steel guitars); Johnny Farina (guitars)

Albums: Santo & Johnny, 1960; Encore, 1960; Hawaii, 1961

Singles: Sleep Walk, 1959 **(1)**; Tear Drop, 1959 **(23)**; Caravan, 1960 **(48)**; The Breeze and I, 1960 **(109)**; Twistin' Bells, 1960 **(49)**; Hop Scotch, 1961 **(90)**; Spanish Harlem, 1962 **(101)**; I'll Remember (In the Still of the Night), 1964 **(58)**; A Thousand Miles Away, 1964 **(122)**

Instrumental Pop — New York

The Sapphires

Personnel: Carol Jackson (vocals); George Gainer (vocals); Joe Livingston (vocals)

Singles: Where Is Johnny Now, 1963 **(133)**; Who Do You Love, 1964 **(25)**; Thank You for Loving Me, 1964 **(106)**; Gotta Have Your Love, 1965 **(77)**

R & B Vocal — Philadelphia

Peter Sarstedt

Singles: Where Do You Go To (My Lovely), 1969 **(70)**; Frozen Orange Juice, 1969 **(116)**

Pop Vocal — British

Savage Resurrection

Personnel: Stevie Lange (vocals); Randy Hammon (guitars); Bill Harper (bass); John Palmer (keyboards); Jeff Myer (drums)

Album: Savage Resurrection, 1968

Pop/Rock — American

Savage Rose

Personnel: Annisette (vocals); Flemming Ostermann (guitars) replaced (1968) by Nils Tuxen (guitars) replaced (1972) by John Uribe (guitars) replaced (1973) by Peer Frost (guitars); Anders Koppel (keyboards); Thomas Koppel (keyboards, vocals); Ilse Maria Koppel (keyboards) left group (1972); Jens Rugsted (bass) replaced (1973) by Rudolf Hansen (bass); Alex Riel (drums) replaced (1973) by Ken Gudmand (drums)

Albums: Savage Rose, 1968; In the Plain, 1968; Travellin', 1969; Your Daily Gift, 1971; Refugee, 1972; Dodens Truimi, 1972; Babylon, 1973; Wild Child, 1973; I'm Satisfied, 1975; Sole Varogsa, 1980

Progressive Rock — Germany

Savoy Brown

Personnel: Kim Simmonds (guitars, vocals); Martin Stone (guitars) replaced (1968) by Dave Peverett (guitars, vocals) replaced (1974) by Stan Webb (guitars, vocals) replaced (1981) by Barry Paul (guitars, vocals); Ray Chappell (bass) replaced (1968) by Rivers Jobe (bass) replaced (1968) by Tony Stevens (bass) replaced (1971) by Andy Sylvester (bass) replaced (1973) by Andy Pyle (bass) replaced (1974) by James Leverton (bass) replaced (1975) by Andy Rae (bass) replaced (1976) by Ian Ellis (bass, vocals) replaced (1981) by John Humphrey (bass, vocals); Bob Hall (keyboards) replaced (1971) by Paul Raymond (keyboards, guitars) replaced (1974) by Miller Anderson (keyboards, guitars, vocals) replaced (1975) by Paul Raymond (keyboards, guitars) left group (1977) replaced (1981) by John Sinclair (keyboards); Bryce Portius (vocals) replaced (1968) by Chris Youlden (vocals) replaced (1971) by Dave Walker (vocals) left group (1973) replaced (1981) by Ralph Morman (vocals) replaced (1990) by Dave Walker (vocals); Bill Bruford (drums) replaced (1967) by Leo Manning (drums) replaced (1968) by Roger Earl (drums) replaced (1971) by Dave Bidwell (drums) replaced (1973) by Ron Berg (drums) replaced (1974) by Eric Dillon (drums) replaced (1975) by Tom Farnell (drums) replaced (1981) by Keith Boyce (drums)

Albums: Shake Down, 1967; Getting to the Point, 1968; Blue Matter, 1968; A Step Further, 1969; Raw Sienna, 1970; Looking In, 1970; Street Corner Talking, 1971; Hellbound Train, 1972; Lion's Share, 1973; Jack the Toad, 1973; Boogie Brothers, 1974; Wire Fire, 1975; Skin 'n' Bone, 1976; Best of Savoy Brown, 1977; Savage Return, 1978; Blues Roots, 1978; Rock 'n' Roll Warriors, 1981; Greatest Hits/Live, 1981; Best of Savoy Brown, 1982; Live in Central Park, 1985; Slow Train, 1986; Make Me Sweat, 1987; Kings of Boogie, 1988; Live & Kickin', 1990

Singles: I'm Tired, 1969 **(74)**; Tell Mama, 1971 **(83)**; Lay Back in the Arms of Someone, 1981 **(107)**; Run to Me, 1981 **(68)**

Blues/Rock—British

Sky Saxon

Albums: Full Spoon of Seedy Blues, 1967; Destiny's Children, 1986 (with Firewall)

Hard Rock—Los Angeles; former leader of the Seeds; real name is Richard Marsh

Scaffold

Personnel: Mike McGear (vocals); Roger McGough (vocals); added (1968) John Gorman (vocals)

Albums: McGough & McGear, 1967; Thank You Very Much/An Evening with Scaffold, 1968; Lily the Pink, 1969; Fresh Liver, 1973; Sold Out, 1975; Singles A's & B's, 1982

Single: Thank U Very Much, 1967 **(69)**

Folk/Pop—British; McGear is Paul McCartney's brother

Boz Scaggs

Albums: Boz, 1965; Boz Scaggs, 1969; Moments, 1971; Boz Scaggs & His Band, 1971; My Time, 1972;

Boz Scaggs

Slow Dancer, 1974; Silk Degrees, 1976; Down Two Then Left, 1977; Middle Man, 1980; Hits!, 1980; Other Roads, 1988

Singles: We Were Always Sweet-Hearts, 1971 **(61)**; Near You, 1971 **(96)**; Dinah Flo, 1972 **(86)**; You Make It Hard (to Say No), 1975 **(107)**; It's Over, 1976 **(38)**; Lowdown, 1976 **(3)**; What Can I Say, 1976 **(42)**; Lido Shuffle, 1977 **(11)**; Hard Times, 1977 **(58)**; Hollywood, 1978 **(49)**; Breakdown Dead Ahead, 1980 **(15)**; Jo Jo, 1980 **(17)**; Look What You've Done to Me, 1980 **(14)**; Miss Sun, 1980 **(14)**; You Can Have Me Anytime, 1981; Heart of Mine, 1988 **(35)**

Pop/Rock—Texas; real name is William Royce Scaggs; former member of the Steve Miller Band

Bobby Scott

Single: Chain Gang, 1956 **(13)**
Jazz/Pop—New York; died from lung cancer in 1990

Freddie Scott

Albums: Hey Girl, 1963; Are You Lonely, 1966

Singles: Hey, Girl, 1963 **(10)**; I Got a Woman, 1963 **(48)**; Where Does Love Go, 1964 **(82)**; Are You Lonely for Me, 1966 **(39)**; Cry to Me, 1967 **(70)**; Am I Grooving You, 1967 **(71)**; He Will Break Your Heart, 1967 **(120)**; He Ain't Give You None, 1967 **(100)**

Soul Vocal—Rhode Island

Jack Scott

Albums: Jack Scott, 1958; What Am I Living For, 1959; What in the World, 1960; I Remember Hank Williams, 1960; The Spirit Moves Me, 1961; Burning Bridges, 1961; Jack Scott Greatest Hits, 1962; The Legendary Jack Scott, 1982

Singles: Leroy, 1958 **(25)**; My True Love, 1958 **(3)**; With Your Love, 1958 **(28)**; Geraldine, 1958 **(96)**; Goodbye Baby, 1958 **(8)**; Save My Soul, 1958 **(73)**; I Never Felt Like This, 1959 **(78)**; The Way I Walk, 1959 **(35)**; There Comes a Time, 1959 **(71)**; What in the World's Come Over You, 1960 **(5)**; Burning Bridges, 1960 **(3)**; Oh, Little One, 1960 **(34)**; It Only Happened Yesterday, 1960 **(38)**; Cool Water, 1960 **(85)**; Patsy, 1960 **(65)**; Is There Something on Your Mind, 1961 **(89)**; A Little Feeling Called Love, 1961 **(91)**; My Dream Come True, 1961 **(83)**; Steps 1 and 2, 1961 **(86)**

Pop Vocal—Canadian; real name is Jack Scafone, Jr.

Linda Scott

Albums: I've Told Every Little Star, 1961; Yessiree, 1961; Count Every Star, 1962

Singles: I've Told Every Little Star, 1961 **(3)**; Don't Bet Money Honey, 1961 **(9)**; Starlight, Starbright, 1961 **(44)**; I Don't Know Why, 1961 **(12)**; It's All Because, 1961 **(50)**; Yessiree, 1962 **(60)**; Bermuda, 1962 **(70)**; Town Crier, 1962 **(116)**; Count Every Star, 1962 **(41)**; Never in a Million Years, 1962 **(56)**; I Left My Heart in the Balcony, 1962 **(74)**; Let's Fall in Love, 1963 **(108)**; Who's Been Sleepin' in My Bed?, 1964 **(100)**; Patch It Up, 1965 **(135)**

Pop Vocal—New Jersey; real last name is Sampson

Neil Scott

Single: Bobby, 1961 **(58)**
Pop Vocal—New York; real name was Neil Bogart; former president of Buddah, Casablanca and Boardwalk record labels; died in 1982

Peggy Scott & Jo Jo Benson

Albums: Lover's Holiday, 1968; Soul Shake, 1969
Singles: Lover's Holiday, 1968 **(31)**; Pickin' Wild Mountain Berries, 1968 **(27)**; Soul Shake, 1969 **(37)**; Every Little Bit Hurts, 1969 **(127)**; I Want to Love You Baby, 1969 **(81)**
Soul Vocal—American

Johnny Sea

Album: Day for Decision, 1966
Singles: My Baby Walks All Over Me, 1964 **(121)**; Day for Decision, 1966 **(35)**
Country Vocal—Mississippi

The Searchers

Personnel: John McNally (vocals, guitars); Mike Pender (vocals, guitars); Tony Jackson (bass, vocals) replaced (1964) by Frank Allen (bass); Chris Curtis (drums, vocals) replaced (1965) by John Blunt (drums) replaced (1969) by Bill Adamson (drums); added (1976) Bob Jackson (keyboards) replaced (1977) by Mick Weaver (keyboards)
Albums: Meet the Searchers, 1963; Sugar and Spice, 1963; This Is the Searchers, 1964; New Searchers LP, 1964; It's the Searchers, 1964; Sounds Like the Searchers, 1964; Searchers Number 4, 1965; Take Me for What I'm Worth, 1965; Smash Hits, 1967; Smash Hits Volume 2, 1967; Needles and Pins, 1971; Golden Hour, 1972; Second Take, 1972; Golden Hour Volume 2, 1973; Hear Hear, 1975; The Searchers File, 1977; The Searchers, 1980; Play for Today, 1981; Love's Melodies, 1981; Spotlight on the Searchers, 1981; 100 Minutes, 1982; Greatest Hits, 1985
Singles: Needles and Pins, 1964 **(13)**; Ain't That Just Like Me, 1964 **(61)**; Sugar and Spice, 1964 **(44)**; Don't Throw Your Love Away, 1964 **(16)**; Someday We're Gonna Love Again, 1964 **(34)**; When You Walk in the Room, 1965 **(35)**; Love Potion #9, 1964 **(3)**; What Have They Done to the Rain, 1965 **(29)**; Bumble Bee, 1965 **(21)**; Goodbye My Lover Goodbye, 1965 **(52)**; He's Got No Love, 1965 **(79)**; Take Me for What I'm Worth, 1966 **(76)**; Have You Ever Loved Somebody, 1966 **(94)**; Desdemona, 1971 **(94)**; It's Too Late, 1980; Heart in Her Eyes, 1980; Love's Melody, 1981
Pop/Rock—British

Seastones

Personnel: Grace Slick (vocals); David Crosby (vocals); David Freiberg (vocals); Jerry Garcia (guitars); Phil Lesh (bass); Ned Lagin (keyboards); Mickey Hart (percussion); Spencer Dryden (drums)
Album: Seastones, 1969
Folk/Rock—California

Seatrain

Personnel: Richard Greene (violin) replaced (1973) by Bonnie Douglas (violin); Jim Roberts (keyboards) replaced (1973) by Bill Elliott (keyboards); Andy Kulberg (bass, flutes); John Gregory (guitars, vocals) replaced (1971) by Peter Rowan (guitars, vocals) replaced (1973) by Peter Walsh (guitars, vocals); Don Kretmar (saxophones) replaced (1970) by Lloyd Baskin (keyboards, vocals); Roy Blumenfeld (drums) replaced (1970) by Larry Atamanuik (drums) replaced (1973) by Julio Coronado (drums)
Albums: Seatrain, 1969; Seatrain, 1971; Marblehead Messenger, 1972; Watch, 1973
Single: Marblehead Messenger, 1971 **(108)**
Blues/Rock—American

Second Hand

Personnel: Rob Elliott (guitars, vocals); Ken Elliott (keyboards, vocals); Kieran O'Connor (drums)
Albums: Reality, 1968; Death May Be Your Santa Claus, 1970
Hard Rock—British

The Secrets

Personnel: Kragen Gray (vocals); Josie Allen (vocals); Carole Raymont (vocals); Pat Miller (vocals)
Album: The Secrets, 1963
Single: The Boy Next Door, 1963 **(18)**
Pop/Rock—Cleveland

Neil Sedaka

Albums: Neil Sedaka, 1959; I Go Ape, 1960; Calendar Girl, 1960; Happy Birthday, Sweet Sixteen, 1961; Breaking Up Is Hard to Do, 1962; The Dreamer, 1963; Neil Sedaka Sings His Greatest Hits, 1963; Solitaire, 1973; The Tra La Days Are Over, 1974; Laughter in the Rain, 1974; Sedaka's Back, 1975; The Hungry Years, 1975; Steppin' Out, 1976; A Song, 1977; Greatest Hits, 1977; In the Pocket, 1980; Now, 1980; Come See About Me, 1984; My Friend, 1986
Singles: The Diary, 1958 **(14)**; I Go Ape, 1959 **(42)**; Oh! Carol, 1959 **(9)**; Crying My Heart Out for You, 1959 **(111)**; Stairway to Heaven, 1960 **(9)**; You Mean Everything to Me,

1960 **(17)**; Run Samson Run, 1960 **(28)**; Calendar Girl, 1960 **(4)**; Little Devil, 1961 **(11)**; Sweet Little You, 1961 **(59)**; Happy Birthday, Sweet Sixteen, 1961 **(6)**; King of Clowns, 1962 **(45)**; Breaking Up Is Hard to Do, 1962 **(1)**; Next Door to an Angel, 1962 **(5)**; Alice in Wonderland, 1963 **(17)**; Let's Go Steady Again, 1963 **(26)**; The Dreamer, 1963 **(47)**; Bad Girl, 1963 **(33)**; The Closest Thing to Heaven, 1964 **(107)**; Sunny, 1964 **(86)**; I Hope He Breaks Your Heart, 1964 **(104)**; The World Through a Tear, 1965 **(76)**; Let the People Talk, 1965 **(107)**; The Answer to My Prayer, 1966 **(89)**; We Can Make It If We Try, 1967 **(121)**; Laughter in the Rain, 1974 **(1)**; The Immigrant, 1975 **(22)**; That's When the Music Takes Me, 1975 **(27)**; The Hungry Years, 1975; Bad Blood, 1975 **(1)** (with Elton John); Breaking Up Is Hard to Do, 1975 **(8)**; Love in the Shadows, 1976 **(16)**; Steppin' Out, 1976 **(36)**; You Gotta Make Your Own Sunshine, 1976 **(53)**; Amarillo, 1977 **(44)**; Alone at Last, 1977 **(104)**; Should've Never Let You Go, 1980 **(19)** (with Dara Sedaka); Letting Go, 1980 **(107)**; My World Keeps Slipping Away, 1981; Your Precious Love, 1983; New Orleans, 1984

Pop Vocal—New York; wrote many pop hits with partner Howard Greenfield

The Seeds

Personnel: Richard "Sky Saxon" Marsh (vocals, keyboards, bass); Darryl Hooper (guitars, keyboards); Jan Savage (guitars, bass); Rick Aldridge (drums); added (1966) Harvey Sharpe (bass) left group (1967)

Saxon, Savage, Aldridge, Hooper

Albums: The Seeds, 1966; Web of Sound, 1966; Future, 1967; Merlin's Music Box (Raw & Alive), 1967; Fallin' Off the Edge, 1968

Singles: Pushin' Too Hard, 1966 **(36)**; Mr. Farmer, 1967 **(86)**; Can't Seem to Make You Mine, 1967 **(41)**; A Thousand Shadows, 1967 **(72)**

Hard Rock—Los Angeles

The Seekers

Personnel: Judith Durham (vocals); Keith Potger (guitars, vocals); Bruce Woodley (guitars); Athol Guy (bass)

Albums: The Seekers, 1965; The New Seekers, 1965; A World of Our Own, 1966; Georgy Girl, 1967; The Best of the Seekers, 1967

Singles: I'll Never Find Another You, 1965 **(4)**; Chilly Winds, 1965 **(122)**; A World of Our Own, 1965 **(19)**; The Carnival Is Over, 1965 **(105)**; Georgy Girl, 1966 **(2)**; Morningtown Ride, 1967 **(44)**; On the Other Side, 1967 **(115)**; Love Is Kind, Love Is Wine, 1968 **(135)**

Pop/Soft Rock—Australian

The Bob Seger System

Personnel: Bob Seger (guitars, vocals); Dan Honaker (guitars, bass, vocals); Bob Schultz (keyboards, vocals, saxophones); Pep Perrine (drums, vocals); added (1969) Tom Neme (guitars, keyboards, vocals) replaced (1970) by Dan Watson (keyboards, vocals)
Albums: Ramblin' Gamblin' Man, 1969; Noah, 1969; Mongrel, 1970; Brand New Morning, 1971; Smokin' OPs, 1972; Back in '72, 1973; Seven, 1974; Beautiful Loser, 1975
Singles: Heavy Music, 1967 (**103**); Ramblin' Gamblin' Man, 1968 (**17**); Ivory, 1969 (**97**); Noah, 1969 (**103**); Lucifer, 1970 (**84**); Looking Back, 1971 (**96**); If I Were a Carpenter, 1972 (**76**); Get Out of Denver, 1974 (**80**); Beautiful Loser, 1975 (**103**); Katmandu, 1975 (**43**)
Hard Rock—Michigan

Ronnie Self

Single: Bop-a-Lena, 1958 (**63**)
Rockabilly—Missouri; wrote hits for Brenda Lee; died in 1981

The Sensations

Personnel: Yvonne Baker (vocals); Sam Armstrong (vocals); Richard Curtain (vocals); Alphonso Howell (vocals)
Album: Let Me In, 1962
Singles: Music, Music, Music, 1961 (**54**); Let Me In, 1962 (**4**); That's My Desire, 1962 (**69**)
R & B Vocal—Philadelphia

The Serendipity Singers

Albums: The Serendipity Singers, 1964; The Many Sides of the Serendipity Singers, 1964; Take Your Shoes Off with the Serendipity Singers, 1965
Singles: Don't Let the Rain Come Down (Crooked Little Man), 1964 (**6**); Beans in My Ears, 1964 (**30**); Down Where the Wind Blows (Chilly Winds), 1964 (**112**); Little Brown Jug, 1965 (**124**); Plastic, 1965 (**118**)
Pop Vocal—Colorado; group formed at the University of Colorado

David Seville

Singles: Armen's Theme, 1956 (**42**); Gotta Get to Your House, 1957 (**77**); Witch Doctor, 1958 (**1**); The Bird on My Head, 1958 (**34**); Little Brass Band, 1958 (**78**); Judy, 1959 (**86**)
Novelty Pop—California; real name was Ross Bagdasarian; creator of the Chipmunks; died in 1972

Shades of Blue

Album: Shades of Blue, 1966
Singles: Oh How Happy, 1966 (**12**); Lonely Summer, 1966 (**72**); Happiness, 1966 (**78**)
R & B Vocal—Detroit

The Shadows

Personnel: Hank Marvin (guitars, vocals); Bruce Welch (guitars, vocals) replaced (1968) by Adam Hawkshaw (guitars, vocals) replaced (1972) by Bruce Welch (guitars, vocals); Ian Samwell (bass) replaced (1959) by Jet Harris (bass) replaced (1962) by Brian Locking (bass) replaced (1963) by John Rostill (bass; deceased 1973) replaced (1972) by John Farrar (bass, vocals) replaced (1977) by Alan Jones (bass); Ken Payne (guitars) left group (1960); Terry Smart (drums) replaced (1959) by Tony Meehan (drums) replaced (1961) by Brian Bennett (drums); added (1977) Francis Monkman (keyboards) replaced (1979) by Cliff Hall (keyboards)

Albums: The Shadows, 1962; Out of the Shadows, 1962; Greatest Hits, 1963; Dance with the Shadows, 1964; The Sound of the Shadows, 1965; More Hits, 1965; Shadow Music, 1966; Jigsaw, 1967; Hank, Bruce, Brian & John, 1967; Established 1958, 1968; It'll Be Me, 1969; Something Else, 1969; Shades of Rock, 1970; Mustang, 1972; Best of the Shadows, 1973; Rockin' with Curly Leads, 1973; Specs Appeal, 1975; Live at the Paris Olympia, 1975; Rarities, 1976; Tasty, 1977; 20 Golden Greats, 1977; Best of the Shadows Volume 2, 1978; At the Movies, 1978; String of Hits, 1979; Change of Address, 1980; Another String of Hits, 1980; Hits Right Up Your Street, 1981; Life in the Jungle/Live at Abbey Road, 1982; XXV, 1983; Guardian Angel, 1984; Shadows (The Vocal), 1984; Moonlight Shadows, 1985; Simply Shadows, 1987; Steppin' to the Shadows, 1989; Reflection, 1990

Singles: Feelin' Fine, 1959; Apache, 1960; F.B.I., 1961; Kon Tiki, 1961; Atlantis, 1961; Frightened City, 1961; Shindig, 1963; Don't Make My Baby Blue, 1965; Jigsaw, 1967; Mustang, 1972; Theme from the Deer Hunter, 1979

Pop/Rock—British; began as Cliff Richard's backing band in the 1950s

Shadows of Knight

Personnel: Jim Sohns (vocals); Warren Rogers (guitars); Jerry McGeorge (guitars); Joe Kelley (bass); Tom Schiffour (drums)

Albums: Gloria, 1966; Back Door Man, 1967; Shadows of Knight, 1968

Singles: Gloria, 1966 **(10)**; Oh Yeah, 1966 **(39)**; Bad Little Woman, 1966 **(91)**; I'm Gonna Make You Mine, 1966 **(90)**; Shake, 1968 **(46)**

Psychedelic Rock—Chicago

The Shaggs

Personnel: Betty Wiggin (guitars, vocals); Dorothy Wiggin (guitars); Helen Wiggin (drums)

Albums: The Philosophy of the World, 1969; The Shaggs' Own Thing, 1982

Pop/Rock—New Hampshire

Shango

Personnel: Tommy Reynolds (keyboards, vocals); Richie

Hernandez (guitars); Malcolm Evan (bass); Joe Barile (drums)
Albums: Shango, 1969; Trampin', 1970
Singles: Day After Day (It's Slippin' Away), 1969 **(57)**; Some Things a Man's Gotta Do, 1970 **(107)**
Pop/Rock—Texas

The Shangri-Las

Personnel: Mary Ann Ganser (vocals; deceased 1971); Marge Ganser (vocals; deceased 1973); Betty Weiss (vocals); Mary Weiss (vocals)
Albums: Leader of the Pack, 1964; Shangri-Las '65, 1965; I Can Never Go Home, 1966; Golden Hits, 1966
Singles: Remember (Walkin' in the Sand), 1964 **(5)**; Leader of the Pack, 1964 **(1)**; Give Him a Great Big Kiss, 1964 **(18)**; Maybe, 1964 **(91)**; Out in the Streets, 1965 **(53)**; Give Us Your Blessings, 1965 **(29)**; Right Now and Not Later, 1965 **(99)**; I Can Never Go Home Anymore, 1965 **(6)**; Long Live Our Love, 1966 **(33)**; He Cried, 1966 **(65)**; Past, Present and Future, 1966 **(59)**; The Sweet Sounds of Summer, 1967 **(123)**
Pop Vocal—New York

Shannon

Single: Abergavenny, 1969 **(47)**
Pop Vocal—British; Shannon is actually Marty Wilde; father of singer Kim Wilde

Del Shannon

Albums: Hats Off to Larry, 1961; Runaway, 1961; Little Town Flirt, 1963; Handy Man, 1965; Sings Hank Williams, 1965; 1661 Seconds of Del Shannon, 1965; This Is My

Del Shannon

Bag, 1966; Total Commitment, 1966; Further Adventures of Charles Westover, 1967; Best of Del Shannon, 1967; 10th Anniversary, 1971; Live in England, 1973; And the Music Plays On, 1978; Hit Parade, 1980; Drop Down and Get Me, 1981; Del Shannon, 1982; Runaway Hits, 1984; Rock On, 1991
Singles: Runaway, 1961 **(1)**; Hats Off to Larry, 1961 **(5)**; So Long Baby, 1961 **(28)**; Hey! Little Girl, 1961 **(38)**; I Won't Be There, 1962 **(113)**; Ginny in the Mirror, 1962 **(117)**; Cry Myself to Sleep, 1962 **(99)**; The Swiss Maid, 1962 **(64)**; Little Town Flirt, 1962 **(12)**; Two Kinds of Teardrops, 1963 **(50)**; From Me to You, 1963 **(77)**; Sue's Gotta Be Mine, 1963 **(71)**; That's the Way Love Is, 1964 **(133)**; Handy Man, 1964 **(22)**; Do You Want to Dance, 1964 **(43)**; Keep Searchin' (We'll Follow the Sun), 1964 **(9)**; Stranger in Town, 1965 **(30)**; Break Up, 1965 **(95)**; Move It Over, 1965 **(128)**; The Big Hurt, 1966 **(94)**; Under My Thumb, 1966 **(128)**; She, 1967 **(131)**; Runaway, 1967 **(112)**; Comin' Back to Me, 1969 **(127)**; Sea of Love, 1981 **(33)**; To Love Someone, 1982; In My Arms

Again, 1985; Stranger on the Run, 1985

Pop/Rock Vocal—Michigan; Del died in 1990; real name was Charles Westover

Dee Dee Sharp

Albums: It's Mashed Potato Time, 1962; Down to Earth, 1962 (with Chubby Checker); Songs of Faith, 1962; All the Hits, 1963; Do the Bird, 1963; Biggest Hits, 1964; Down Memory Lane, 1964; 18 Golden Hits, 1966; Happy 'Bout, 1976; What Colour Is Love, 1978; The Cameo Parkway Sessions, 1979; Dee Dee, 1980

Singles: Mashed Potato Time, 1962 **(2)**; Slow Twistin', 1963 **(3)** (with Chubby Checker); Gravy (for My Mashed Potatoes), 1962 **(9)**; Ride!, 1962 **(5)**; Do the Bird, 1963 **(10)**; Rock Me in the Cradle of Love, 1963 **(43)**; Wild!, 1963 **(33)**; Where Did I Go Wrong, 1964 **(82)**; Willyam, Willyam, 1964 **(97)**; Never Pick a Pretty Boy, 1964 **(131)**; I Really Love You, 1965 **(78)**; It's a Funny Situation, 1966 **(126)**; We Got a Thing Going On, 1968 **(127)** (with Ben E. King)

Pop/Soul Vocal—Philadelphia; real name is Dione LaRue

Ray Sharpe

Single: Linda Lu, 1959 **(46)** (with Duane Eddy & Al Casey)

Rockabilly—Texas

Sharpees

Personnel: Herbert Reeves (vocals); Benny Sharp (vocals); Horise O'Toole (vocals) replaced (1966) by

Stacey Johnson (vocals); Vernon Guy (vocals)

Singles: Do the "45," 1965 **(117)**; Tired of Being Lonely, 1966 **(79)**; I've Got a Secret, 1966 **(133)**

R & B Vocal—St. Louis

Marlena Shaw

Albums: Who Is This Bitch, Anyway?, 1975; Sweet Beginnings, 1977; Acting Up, 1978

Singles: Mercy, Mercy, Mercy, 1967 **(58)**; It's Better Than Walkin' Out, 1976 **(103)**

Soul Vocal—New York

Sandie Shaw

Album: Sandie Shaw, 1964

Singles: (There's) Always Something There to Remind Me, 1964 **(52)**; Girl Don't Come, 1965 **(42)**; Long Live Love, 1965 **(97)**; I'll Stop at Nothing, 1965 **(123)**; How Can You Tell, 1965 **(131)**

Pop Vocal—British; real last name is Goodrich

Timmy Shaw

Single: Gonna Send You Back to Georgia (a City Slick), 1964 **(41)**

Pop Vocal—American

Sheep

Album: Sheep, 1966

Singles: Hide & Seek, 1966 **(58)**; I Feel Good, 1966 **(130)**

Pop Rock—American

The Shells

Personnel: Nathaniel Booknight (vocals); Gus Geter (vocals); Randy Alston (vocals); Bobby Nurse (vocals); Danny Small (vocals)

Single: Baby Oh Baby, 1960 **(21)**
Pop Vocal — New York

Shep & The Limelites

Personnel: James "Shep" Sheppard (vocals; deceased 1970); Clarence Bassett (vocals); Charles Baskerville (vocals)
Albums: Daddy's Home, 1961; Shep & the Limelites, 1962
Singles: Daddy's Home, 1961 **(2)**; Ready for Your Love, 1961 **(42)**; Three Steps from the Altar, 1961 **(58)**; Our Anniversary, 1962 **(59)**; What Did Daddy Do, 1962 **(94)**; Remember Baby, 1963 **(91)**; Why, Why Won't You Believe Me, 1964 **(125)**
R & B Vocal — New York

The Shepherd Sisters

Personnel: Martha Shepherd (vocals); Gayle Shepherd (vocals); Judy Shepherd (vocals); Mary Lou Shepherd (vocals)
Singles: Alone (Why Must I Be Alone), 1957 **(18)**; Don't Mention My Name, 1963 **(94)**
Pop Vocal — Ohio

Allan Sherman

Albums: My Son, the Folk Singer, 1962; My Son, the Celebrity, 1963; My Son, the Nut, 1963; Allan in Wonderland, 1964; Peter and the Commissar, 1964; For Swingin' Livers Only, 1964; My Name Is Allan, 1965; Best of Allan Sherman, 1977
Singles: Hello Mudduh, Hello Fadduh! (A Letter from Camp), 1963 **(2)**; Hello Mudduh, Hello Fadduh! (A Letter from Camp) (version 2), 1964 **(59)**; The End of a Sym-

phony, 1964 **(113)**; Crazy Downtown, 1965 **(40)**; The Drinking Man's Diet, 1965 **(98)**
Novelty Pop — Chicago; Allan died in 1973; was a TV comedy writer; real last name was Copelon; created game show "I've Got a Secret"

Bobby Sherman

Albums: Bobby Sherman, 1969; Here Comes Bobby, 1970; With Love, Bobby, 1970; Portrait of Bobby, 1971; Getting Together, 1971; Bobby Sherman's Greatest Hits, 1972
Singles: It Hurts Me, 1965 **(118)**; Little Woman, 1969 **(3)**; La La La (If I Had You), 1969 **(9)**; Easy Come, Easy Go, 1970 **(9)**; Hey, Mister Sun, 1970 **(24)**; Julie, Do Ya Love Me, 1970 **(5)**; Cried Like a Baby, 1971 **(16)**; The Drum, 1971 **(29)**; Waiting at the Bus Stop, 1971 **(54)**; Jennifer, 1971 **(60)**; Together Again, 1972 **(91)**; Early in the Morning, 1973 **(113)**
Pop Vocal — California; starred on TV's "Here Come the Brides" and "Shindig"

The Sherrys

Personnel: Dinell Cook (vocals); Delphine Cook (vocals)
Singles: Pop Pop Pop-Pie, 1962 **(35)**; Slop Time, 1963 **(97)**
Pop Vocal — Philadelphia

The Shields

Personnel: Frankie Ervin (vocals); Jesse Belvin (vocals); Johnny "Guitar" Watson (vocals); Mel Williams (vocals); Buster Williams (vocals)
Single: You Cheated, 1958 **(12)**
R & B Vocal — Los Angeles

The Shindogs

Personnel: Delaney Bramlett (guitars, vocals); Joey Cooper (guitars, vocals); James Burton (bass); Chuck Blackwell (drums)

Single: Who Do You Think You Are, 1966 **(91)**

Pop/Rock—California; house band on TV's "Shindig"

The Shirelles

Personnel: Shirley Owens Alston (vocals); Micki Harris (vocals; deceased 1982); Doris Coley Kenner (vocals); Beverly Lee (vocals)

Albums: Tonight's the Night, 1961; The Shirelles Sing, 1961; Baby It's You, 1962; Greatest Hits, 1962; Foolish Little Girl, 1963; It's a Mad, Mad, Mad, Mad World, 1964; Sing the Golden Oldies, 1965; Greatest Hits Volume 2, 1965; Spontaneous Combustion, 1966; Remember When, 1967; Eternally Soul, 1970; Happy in Love, 1971; The Shirelles, 1972; Golden Hour, 1973; Let's Give Each Other, 1976

Singles: I Met Him on a Sunday, 1958 **(49)**; Dedicated to the One I Love, 1959 **(83)**; Tonight's the Night, 1960 **(39)**; Will You Love Me Tomorrow, 1960 **(1)**; Dedicated to the One I Love, 1961 **(3)**; Mama Said, 1961 **(4)**; A Thing of the Past, 1961 **(41)**; What a Sweet Thing That Was, 1961 **(54)**; Big John, 1961 **(21)**; The Things I Want to Hear (Pretty Words), 1961 **(107)**; Baby It's You, 1961 **(8)**; Soldier Boy, 1962 **(1)**; Love Is a Swingin' Thing, 1962 **(109)**; Welcome Home Baby, 1962 **(22)**; Mama, Here Comes the Bride, 1962 **(104)**; Stop the Music, 1962 **(36)**; It's Love That Really Counts, 1962 **(102)**; Everybody Loves a Lover, 1962 **(19)**; Foolish Little Girl, 1963 **(4)**; Not for All the Money in the World, 1963 **(100)**; Don't Say Goodnight and Mean Goodbye, 1963 **(26)**; What Does a Girl Do?, 1963 **(53)**; It's a Mad, Mad, Mad, Mad World, 1963 **(92)**; 31 Flavors, 1963 **(97)**; Tonight You're Gonna Fall in Love with Me, 1964 **(57)**; Sha-La-La, 1964 **(69)**; Thank You Baby, 1964 **(63)**; Lost Love, 1964 **(125)**; Maybe Tonight, 1964 **(88)**; Are You Still My Baby, 1964 **(91)**; March (You'll Be Sorry), 1965 **(108)**; My Heart Belongs to You, 1965 **(125)**; Shades of Blue, 1966 **(122)**; Don't Go Home (My Little Darlin'), 1967 **(110)**; Last Minute Miracle, 1967 **(99)**

Pop/Soul Vocal—New Jersey

Shirley & Lee

Personnel: Shirley Goodman (vocals); Leonard Lee (vocals; deceased 1976)

Singles: Let the Good Times Roll, 1956 **(20)**; I Feel Good, 1956 **(38)**; I've Been Loved Before, 1960 **(88)**; Let the Good Times Roll, 1960 **(48)**; Well-A, Well-A, 1961 **(77)**

R & B Vocal—New Orleans

Shocking Blue

Personnel: Mariska Veres (vocals); Robby van Leeuwen (guitars); Klaaseje van der Wal (bass); Cornelius van der Beek (drums)

Albums: Shocking Blue, 1969; Scorpio's Dance, 1969; Pop Power, 1970; Shocking Blue, 1972; Greatest Hits, 1973

Singles: Venus, 1969 **(1)**; Mighty Joe, 1970 **(43)**; Long and Lonesome Road, 1970 **(75)**; Never Marry a

Railroad Man, 1970 **(102)**; Serenade, 1971 **(110)**

Pop/Rock—Netherlands

Troy Shondell

Album: This Time, 1961

Singles: This Time, 1961 **(6)**; Tears from an Angel, 1961 **(77)**; Island in the Sky, 1962 **(92)**; Na-Ne-No, 1962 **(107)**; Let's Go All the Way, 1969 **(129)**

Country/Pop—Indiana

The Showmen

Personnel: General Norman Johnson (vocals)

Singles: It Will Stand, 1961 **(61)**; It Will Stand, 1964 **(80)**; 39-21-46, 1967 **(101)**

R & B Vocal—Virginia

The Show Stoppers

Personnel: Laddie Burke (vocals); Alec Burke (vocals); Earl Smith (vocals); Timmy Smith (vocals)

Single: Ain't Nothin' but a House Party, 1968 **(87)**

R & B Vocal—Philadelphia

The Sidekicks

Personnel: Zack Bocelle (vocals); Randy Bocelle (guitars); Jon Spirt (bass); Mike Burke (drums)

Singles: Suspicions, 1966 **(55)**; Fifi the Flea, 1966 **(115)**

Pop Vocal—American

Siegel Schwall Band

Personnel: Corky Siegel (keyboards, vocals, harmonica); Jim Schwall (guitars, vocals); Jos Davidson (bass); Russ Chadwick (drums) replaced (1970) by Shel Plotkin (drums); added (1967) Jack Dawson (vocals) replaced (1971) by Rollow Radford (guitars, bass)

Albums: Siegel Schwall Band, 1966; Say Siegel Schwall, 1967; Shake, 1968; Siegel Schwall '70, 1970; The Siegel Schwall Band, 1971; Sleepy Hollow, 1972; 953 West, 1973; Live Last Summer, 1974; R I P Siegel Schwall, 1974; The Best of Siegel Schwall Band, 1974; Three Pieces for Blues & Orchestra, 1975; Siegel Schwall & Symphony Orchestra, 1980

Single: Blues Band Opus 50, Part 1, 1973 **(105)**

Folk/Blues/Rock—American

Bunny Sigler

Albums: Let the Good Times Roll, 1967; That's How Long I'll Be Loving, 1974; Keep Smiling, 1974; Des Chansons Sentimentales, 1974; My Music, 1975; Let Me Party with You, 1978; I've Always Wanted to Sing . . . Not Just Write Songs, 1979; Let It Snow, 1980

Singles: Let the Good Times Roll & Feel So Good, 1967 **(22)**; Lovey Dovey/You're So Fine, 1967 **(86)**; Tossin' and Turnin', 1973 **(97)**; That's How Long I'll Be Loving You, 1975 **(102)**; Let Me Party with You (Party, Party, Party)—Part 1, 1978 **(43)**; Only You, 1978 **(87)** (with Loleatta Holloway)

R & B Vocal—Philadelphia; real first name is Walter; became successful R & B producer in the 1980s

The Silhouettes

Personnel: William Horton (vocals); Richard Lewis (vocals); Earl Beal (vocals); Raymond Edwards (vocals)

Single: Get a Job, 1958 **(1)**
R & B Vocal—Philadelphia; formerly called the Tornadoes

Silkie

Personnel: Silvie "Silkie" Tatler (vocals); Mike Silkie (guitars); Kev Silkie (bass); Ivor Silkie (drums)
Album: You've Got to Hide Your Love Away, 1965
Singles: You've Got to Hide Your Love Away, 1965 **(10)**; The Keys to My Soul, 1966 **(124)**; Born to Be with You, 1966 **(133)**
Pop/Rock—British; John Lennon, George Harrison and Paul McCartney played on their album

Silver Apples

Personnel: Danny Taylor (vocals, percussion); Simeon (vocals, banjo)
Albums: Silver Apples, 1968; Contracts, 1969
Psychedelic Pop—American

Gene Simmons

Album: Jumpin' Gene Simmons, 1964
Singles: Haunted House, 1964 **(11)**; The Dodo, 1964 **(83)**
Country/Pop—Mississippi; nickname was "Jumpin' Gene"

Joe Simon

Albums: Joe Simon, 1968; The Chokin' Kind, 1969; Joe Simon . . . Better Than Ever, 1969; The Sounds of Simon, 1971; Drowning in the Sea of Love, 1972; The Best of Joe Simon, 1972; The Power of Joe Simon, 1973; Mood, Heart & Soul, 1974; Get Down, 1975; Today, 1976; Easy to Love, 1977; Bad Case of Love, 1978; Love Vibrations, 1979
Singles: My Adorable One, 1964 **(102)**; Teenager's Prayer, 1966 **(66)**; My Special Prayer, 1967 **(87)**; Put Your Trust in Me (Depend on Me), 1967 **(129)**; Nine Pound Steel, 1967 **(70)**; No Sad Songs, 1968 **(49)**; (You Keep Me) Hangin' On, 1968 **(25)**; Message from Maria, 1968 **(75)**; I Worry About You, 1968 **(98)**; Looking Back, 1968 **(70)**; The Chokin' Kind, 1969 **(13)**; Baby, Don't Be Looking in My Mind, 1969 **(72)**; San Francisco Is a Lonely Town, 1969 **(79)**; It's Hard to Get Along, 1969 **(87)**; Moon Walk—Part 1, 1970 **(54)**; Farther on Down the Road, 1970 **(56)**; Yours Love, 1970 **(78)**; That's the Way I Want Our Love, 1970 **(93)**; Your Time to Cry, 1970 **(40)**; To Lay Down Beside You, 1971 **(117)**; Help Me Make It Through the Night, 1971 **(69)**; You're the One for Me, 1971 **(71)**; All My Hard Times, 1971 **(93)**; Drowning in the Sea of Love, 1971 **(11)**; Pool of Bad Luck, 1972 **(42)**; Power of Love, 1972 **(11)**; Misty Blue, 1972 **(91)**; Trouble in My Home/I Found My Dad, 1972 **(50)**; Step by Step, 1973 **(37)**; Theme from *Cleopatra Jones,* 1973 **(18)** (with the Mainstreamers); River, 1973 **(62)**; Get Down, Get Down (Get on the Floor), 1975 **(8)**; Music in My Bones, 1975 **(92)**; Come Get to This, 1976 **(102)**
Soul/Pop Vocal—Louisiana

Simon & Garfunkel

Personnel: Paul Simon (guitars, vocals); Art Garfunkel (vocals)
Albums: Wednesday Morning 3 A.M., 1966; The Sounds of Silence, 1966; Parsley, Sage, Rosemary &

Paul Simon, Art Garfunkel

Thyme, 1967; Bookends, 1968; The Graduate (Soundtrack), 1969; Bridge Over Troubled Water, 1970; Greatest Hits, 1972; The Concert in Central Park, 1982; Collected Works, 1990

Singles: Hey Schoolgirl, 1958 **(49)** (as Tom & Jerry); The Sounds of Silence, 1965 **(1)**; Homeward Bound, 1966 **(5)**; That's My Story, 1966 **(123)**; I Am a Rock, 1966 **(3)**; The Dangling Conversation, 1966 **(25)**; A Hazy Shade of Winter, 1966 **(13)**; At the Zoo, 1967 **(16)**; Fakin' It, 1967 **(23)**; Scarborough Fair/Canticle, 1968 **(11)**; Mrs. Robinson, 1968 **(1)**; Baby Driver, 1969 **(101)**; The Boxer, 1969 **(7)**; Bridge Over Troubled Water, 1970 **(1)**; Cecilia, 1970 **(4)**; El Condor Pasa (If I Could), 1970 **(18)**; For Emily, Wherever I May Find Her, 1972 **(53)**; America, 1972 **(97)**; My Little Town, 1975 **(9)**; Wake Up Little Susie, 1982 **(27)**

Pop/Soft Rock — New York

The Sims Twins

Personnel: Bobby Sims (vocals); Kenneth Sims (vocals)

Single: Soothe Me, 1961 **(42)**

R & B Vocal — Los Angeles

Nancy Sinatra

Albums: Boots, 1966; How Does That Grab You?, 1966; Nancy in London, 1966; Sugar, 1967; Country, My Way, 1967; Movin' with

Nancy, 1968; Nancy & Lee, 1968 (with Lee Hazlewood); Nancy, 1969; Nancy's Greatest Hits, 1970; Fairy Tales & Fantasies: The Best Of, 1989; Hit Years, 1989

Singles: So Long Babe, 1965 **(86)**; These Boots Are Made for Walkin', 1966 **(1)**; How Does That Grab You Darlin'?, 1966 **(7)**; Friday's Child, 1966 **(36)**; In Our Time, 1966 **(46)**; Sugar Town, 1966 **(5)**; Summer Wine, 1967 **(49)** (with Lee Hazlewood); Somethin' Stupid, 1967 **(1)** (with Frank Sinatra); Love Eyes, 1967 **(15)**; You Only Live Twice, 1967 **(44)**; Jackson, 1967 **(14)** (with Lee Hazlewood); Lightning's Girl, 1967 **(24)**; Sand, 1967 **(107)** (with Lee Hazlewood); Lady Bird, 1967 **(20)** (with Lee Hazlewood); Tony Rome, 1967 **(83)**; Some Velvet Morning, 1968 **(26)** (with Lee Hazlewood); 100 Years, 1968 **(69)**; Happy, 1968 **(74)**; Good Time Girl, 1968 **(65)**; God Knows I Love You, 1969 **(97)**; Here We Go Again, 1969 **(98)**; Drummer Man, 1969 **(98)**; Down from Dover, 1972 **(120)**

Pop Vocal—New Jersey; daughter of Frank Sinatra; was in films *The Oscar, Speedway, Get Yourself a College Girl* and *For Those Who Think Young*

The Sir Douglas Quintet

Personnel: Doug Sahm (guitars, vocals); Frank Moran (vocals, horns) replaced (1973) by Atwood Allen (guitars, vocals) replaced (1981) by Alvin Crow (guitars, vocals) replaced (1983) by Louis Ortega (guitars); Harvey "Speedy Sparks" Kagan (bass) replaced (1971) by Jack Barber (bass) replaced (1973) by Jim Stallings (bass) re-placed (1976) by Harvey Kagan (bass); Augie Meyer (keyboards); Johnny Perez (drums) replaced (1973) by George Rains (drums) re-placed (1980) by Johnny Perez (drums)

Albums: Best of the Sir Douglas Quintet, 1965; Honky Blues, 1968; Mendocino, 1969; 1 + 1 + 1 = 4, 1970; Together After Five, 1970; The Return of Doug Saldana, 1971; Doug Sahm & the Band, 1973; Groovers Paradise, 1974; Texas Rock for Country Rollers, 1976; Live Love, 1977; Doug Sahm, 1979; Hell of a Spell, 1980; Best of the Sir Douglas Quintet, 1980; Border Wave, 1981; Quintessence, 1983; Midnight Sun, 1983

Singles: She's About a Mover, 1965 **(13)**; The Tracker, 1965 **(105)**; The Rains Came, 1966 **(31)**; Quarter to Three, 1966 **(129)**; She Digs My Love, 1966 **(132)**; Mendo-cino, 1968 **(27)**; It Didn't Even Bring Me Down, 1969 **(108)**; Dyna-mite Woman, 1969 **(83)**; At the Crossroads, 1969 **(104)**; (Is Anybody Going to) San Antone, 1973 **(115)**

Tex/Mex Rock—Texas; Doug's real last name is Saldana

The Six Teens

Personnel: Trudy Williams (vo-cals); Ed Wells (vocals); Darryl Lewis (vocals); Richard Owens (vocals); Beverly Pecot (vocals); Louise Williams (vocals)

Singles: A Casual Look, 1956 **(25)**; Arrow of Love, 1957 **(80)**

R & B Vocal—Los Angeles

Skip & Flip

Personnel: Clyde "Skip" Battin (guitars, vocals); Garry "Flip" Pax-ton (guitars, vocals)

Album: Skip & Flip, 1960
Singles: It Was I, 1959 **(11)**; Fancy Nancy, 1959 **(71)**; Cherry Pie, 1960 **(11)**; Hully Gully Cha Cha, 1960 **(109)**
Pop/Rock—American

Skip Bifferty

Personnel: John Turnbull (guitars); Colin Gibson (bass); Mick Gallagher (keyboards); Tom Jackman (drums)
Album: Skip Bifferty, 1967
Pub Rock—British

The Skyliners

Personnel: Jimmy Beaumont (vocals); Janet Vogel (vocals; deceased 1980); Wally Lester (vocals); Joe VerScharen (vocals); Jackie Taylor (vocals, guitars)
Singles: Since I Don't Have You, 1959 **(12)**; This I Swear, 1959 **(26)**; It Happened Today, 1959 **(59)**; Pennies from Heaven, 1960 **(24)**; Close Your Eyes, 1961 **(105)**; Comes Love, 1963 **(128)**; The Loser, 1965 **(72)**; Where Have They Gone, 1975 **(100)**
R & B Vocal—Pittsburgh

Slade

Personnel: Noddy Holder (vocals, guitars); Dave Hill (guitars, vocals); Jimmy Lea (bass, vocals, keyboards, violin); Don Powell (drums)
Albums: Ambrose Slade, 1969; Balzy, 1969; Play It Loud, 1970; Slade Alive!, 1971; Slayed?, 1972; Sladest, 1973; Old, New, Borrowed and Blue, 1974; In Flame (Soundtrack), 1975; The Best of Slade, 1975; Nobody's Fools, 1976; Whatever Happened to Slade?, 1977; Alive Volume 2, 1978; Stomp Your Hands Clap Your Feet, 1978; Return to Base, 1979; Slade Smashes, 1980; We'll Bring the House Down, 1981; Till Deaf Do Us Part, 1981; On Stage, 1982; The Amazing Kamikaze Syndrome, 1983; Slade's Greatz, 1984; Keep Your Hands Off My Power Supply, 1984; Rogue's Gallery, 1985; Crackers—The Slade Christmas Album, 1985; You Boyz Make Big Noize, 1987; The Slade Collection '81–'87, 1991
Singles: Take Me Back 'Ome, 1972 **(97)**; Mama Weer All Crazee Now, 1972 **(76)**; Gudbuy T'Jane, 1973 **(68)**; Cum on Feel the Noize, 1973 **(98)**; Let the Good Times Roll/ Feel So Fine, 1973 **(114)**; In for a Penny, 1976; Let's Call It Quits, 1976; Lock Up Your Daughters, 1981; Merry Xmas Everybody, 1981; Merry Xmas Everybody, 1983; Run Runaway, 1984 **(20)**; My Oh My, 1984 **(37)**; All Join Hands, 1984; 7 Year Bitch, 1985; Little Sheila, 1985 **(86)**
Hard Rock—British

The Slades

Personnel: Don Burch (vocals)
Single: You Cheated, 1958 **(42)**
Pop Vocal—Texas

Percy Sledge

Albums: When a Man Loves a Woman, 1966; Warm and Tender Soul, 1966; The Percy Sledge Way, 1967; Take Time to Know Her, 1968; The Best of Percy Sledge, 1969; I'll Be Your Everything, 1974; Golden Voice of Soul, 1974
Singles: When a Man Loves a Woman, 1966 **(1)**; Warm and Tender Love, 1966 **(17)**; It Tears

Me Up, 1966 **(20)**; Baby, Help Me, 1967 **(87)**; Out of Left Field, 1967 **(59)**; Love Me Tender, 1967 **(40)**; What Am I Living For, 1967 **(91)**; Just Out of Reach (Of My Two Empty Arms), 1967 **(66)**; Cover Me, 1967 **(42)**; Take Time to Know Her, 1968 **(11)**; Sudden Stop, 1968 **(63)**; You're All Around Me, 1968 **(109)**; My Special Prayer, 1969 **(93)**; Any Day Now, 1969 **(86)**; The Angels Listened In, 1969 **(126)**; Kind Woman, 1969 **(116)**; Sunshine, 1973; I'll Be Your Everything, 1974 **(62)**

Soul/Pop Vocal—Alabama

P. F. Sloan

Albums: Songs of Our Times, 1965; 12 More Times, 1966; Measure of Pleasure, 1968; Raised on Records, 1972

Singles: The Sins of a Family, 1965 **(87)**; From a Distance, 1966 **(109)**

Folk/Pop—Los Angeles; songwriter of "Eve of Destruction" and hits for the Turtles, the Grass Roots, the Searchers and Herman's Hermits; first name is Phillip

Sly & The Family Stone

Personnel: Sylvester "Sly" Stone (guitars, vocals, keyboards); Freddie Stone (guitars); Larry Graham (bass, vocals) replaced (1973) by Rusty Allen (bass); Jerry Martini (guitars, vocals, saxophones); Rose Stone (percussion, vocals); Cynthia Robinson (trumpet, vocals); Greg Errico (drums) replaced (1973) by Andy Newmark (drums); added (1973) Pat Rizzo (guitars)

Albums: Dance to the Music, 1968; Life, 1968; M'Lady, 1968; Stand, 1969; Whole New Thing, 1970; There's a Riot Going On, 1971; Greatest Hits, 1971; Fresh, 1973; Small Talk, 1974; High Energy, 1975; High on You, 1975; Heard You Missed Me, 1976; 10 Years Too Soon, 1979; Back on the Right Track, 1979; Anthology, 1980; Ain't But the One Way, 1983

Singles: Dance to the Music, 1968 **(8)**; Life, 1968 **(93)**; M'Lady, 1968 **(93)**; Everyday People, 1968 **(1)**; Sing a Simple Song, 1969 **(89)**; Stand!, 1969 **(22)**; I Want to Take You Higher, 1969 **(60)**; Hot Fun in the Summertime, 1969 **(2)**; Thank You (Falettinme Be Mice Elf Agin), 1969 **(1)**; Everybody Is a Star, 1970 **(40)**; I Want to Take You Higher, 1970 **(38)**; Family Affair, 1971 **(1)**; Runnin' Away, 1972 **(23)**; Smilin', 1972 **(42)**; If You Want Me to Stay, 1973 **(12)**; Frisky, 1973 **(79)**; Time for Livin', 1974 **(32)**; Loose Booty, 1974 **(84)**; I Get High on You, 1975 **(52)**; Remember Who You Are, 1979 **(104)**; Ha Ha, Hee Hee, 1983

Psychedelic Soul—San Francisco

Millie Small

Album: My Boy Lollipop, 1964
Singles: My Boy Lollipop, 1964 **(2)**; Sweet William, 1964 **(40)**

Pop Vocal—Jamaica

The Small Faces

(see the Faces entry for complete details)

Carl Smith

Singles: Your Name Is Beautiful, 1958 **(80)**; Guess I've Been Around Too Long, 1958 **(93)**; Ten Thousand

Drums, 1959 **(43)**; If the World Don't End Tomorrow (I'm Comin' After You), 1960 **(107)**

Country Vocal—Tennessee; father of Carlene Carter and former husband of June Carter

Huey Smith & The Clowns

Personnel: Huey "Piano" Smith (piano); Bobby Marchan (vocals) replaced (1960) by Curly Smith (vocals)

Albums: Having Fun, 1957; Having a Good Time, 1957; For Dancing, 1958; Night Before Christmas, 1958; Rock 'n' Roll Revival, 1959; Rockin' Pneumonia, 1978

Singles: Rocking Pneumonia and the Boogie Woogie Flu, 1957 **(52)**; Don't You Just Know It, 1958 **(9)**; Don't You Know Yockomo, 1958 **(56)**; Pop-Eye, 1962 **(51)**

R & B/Soul—New Orleans

O. C. Smith

Albums: Hickory Holler Revisited, 1968; For Once in My Life, 1969; O. C. Smith at Home, 1969; O. C. Smith's Greatest Hits, 1970; Help Me Make It Through the Night, 1971

Singles: That's Life, 1967 **(127)**; The Son of Hickory Holler's Tramp, 1968 **(40)**; Main Street Mission, 1968 **(105)**; Little Green Apples, 1968 **(2)**; Isn't It Lonely Together, 1968 **(63)**; Honey (I Miss You), 1969 **(44)**; Friend, Lover, Woman, Wife, 1969 **(47)**; Daddy's Little Man, 1969 **(34)**; Me and You, 1969 **(103)**; Moody, 1970 **(114)**; Primrose Lane, 1970 **(86)**; Baby, I Need Your Loving, 1970 **(52)**; Help Me Make It Through the Night,

1971 **(91)**; Don't Misunderstand, 1972 **(102)**; La La Peace Song, 1974 **(62)**

Pop/Soul Vocal—American; was once lead singer in Count Basie's orchestra

Ray Smith

Singles: Rockin' Little Angel, 1960 **(22)**; Put Your Arms Around Me Honey, 1960 **(91)**; One Wonderful Love, 1960 **(103)**

Pop Vocal—Kentucky; Ray died in 1979 at the age of 41

Roger Smith

Single: Beach Time, 1959 **(64)**

Pop Vocal—California; star of TV's "77 Sunset Strip"; married to Ann-Margret

Somethin' Smith & The Redheads

Personnel: Somethin' Smith (vocals, guitars); Saul Striks (piano); Major Short (violin)

Singles: It's a Sin to Tell a Lie, 1955 **(7)**; When All the Streets Are Dark, 1955 **(90)**; In a Shanty in Old Shanty Town, 1956 **(27)**; Heartaches, 1956 **(71)**

Pop/R & B—California

Verdelle Smith

Singles: In My Room, 1966 **(62)**; Tar and Cement, 1966 **(38)**

Soul Vocal—Florida

Smith

Personnel: Gayle McCormick (vocals); Rick Cliburn (guitars) replaced (1970) by Jade Hass (guitars);

Jerry Carter (bass); Larry Moss
(keyboards); Robert Evans (drums)
   Albums: A Group Called Smith,
1969; Minus Plus, 1970
   Singles: Baby It's You, 1969 **(5)**;
Take a Look Around, 1970 **(43)**;
What Am I Gonna Do, 1970 **(73)**;
Comin' Back to Me, 1970 **(101)**
   Blues/Rock—Los Angeles

Smokestack Lightnin'

Personnel: Ronnie Darling (vo-
cals); Ric Eiserling (guitars); Mike
Deasy (guitars); Kelly Green (bass);
Sandy Zevon (keyboards, guitars);
Art Guy (drums)
   Album: Off the Wall, 1969
Blues/Rock—American

The Smothers Brothers

Personnel: Tom Smothers (guitars, vocals); Dick Smothers (bass,
vocals)
   Albums: The Songs and Comedy
of the Smothers Brothers, 1962; The
Two Sides of the Smothers Brothers,
1962; (Think Ethnic!), 1963; Curb
Your Tongue, Knave!, 1963; It
Must Have Been Something I Said!,
1964; Tour de Farce American History and Other Unrelated Subjects,
1964; Aesop's Fables the Smothers
Brothers Way, 1965; Mom Always
Liked You Best!, 1965; Golden Hits
of the Smothers Brothers Volume 2,
1966; Smothers Brothers Comedy
Hour, 1968
   Single: Jenny Brown, 1963 **(84)**
   Comedy/Folk—American; hosted
their own TV comedy and variety
show, 1967–1970

Soft Machine

Allen, Wyatt, Ratledge, Ayers

Personnel: Daevid Allen (guitars)
replaced (1967) by Andy Summers
(guitars) left group (1968) replaced
(1981) by Alan Parker (guitars);
Larry Nolan (guitars) left group
(1966); Robert Wyatt (vocals,
drums, percussion) replaced (1971)
by Phil Howard (drums) replaced
(1972) by John Marshall (drums);
Kevin Ayers (vocals, bass) replaced
(1969) by Hugh Hopper (bass) replaced (1973) by Roy Babbington
(bass) replaced (1976) by Percy
Jones (bass) replaced (1976) by Steve
Cooke (bass) replaced (1981) by Jack
Bruce (bass); Mike Ratledge (keyboards) replaced (1976) by Rick
Sanders (violin) replaced (1981) by
John Taylor (keyboards); added
(1973) Allan Holdsworth (guitars)
replaced (1975) by John Etheridge
(guitars) replaced (1981) by Allan
Holdsworth (guitars); added (1968)
Brian Hopper (saxophones) replaced
(1969) by Elton Dean (saxophones)
left group (1972); added (1969)
Marc Charig (cornet) left group
(1969); added (1969) Nick Evans
(trombone) left group (1969); added
(1969) Lyn Dobson (saxophones,
flutes) left group (1970); added
(1972) Karl Jenkins (piano,

saxophones); added (1976) Alan Wakeman (saxophones) replaced (1981) by Ray Warleigh (saxophones, flutes)

Albums: The Soft Machine, 1968; Volume Two, 1969; Third, 1970; Fourth, 1971; Fifth, 1972; Sixth, 1973; Seventh, 1974; Bundles, 1975; Softs, 1976; Rubber Riff, 1976; Triple Echo, 1977; At the Beginning, 1977; Alive & Well in Paris, 1978; Land of Cockayne, 1981; The Untouchable, 1991

Art/Progressive Rock—British; Wyatt was paralyzed in an accident; Alan Wakeman is a cousin of Yes's Rick Wakeman

Joanie Sommers

Album: Johnny Get Angry, 1962
Singles: One Boy, 1960 **(54)**; Johnny Get Angry, 1962 **(7)**; When the Boys Get Together, 1962 **(94)**; Little Girl Bad, 1963 **(132)**
Pop Vocal—California

The Sonics

Personnel: Rob Lind (vocals, saxophones) replaced (1980) by Les Kingbeard (saxophones); Larry Parypa (guitars, vocals) replaced (1980) by George Wallace (guitars); Andy Parypa (bass, vocals) replaced (1980) by George Crowe (bass);

Gerry Roslie (keyboards, vocals); Bob Bennett (drums) replaced (1980) by Bill Shaw (drums, vocals); added (1980) Michael Gone (guitars)

Albums: Introducing the Sonics, 1966; Here Are the Sonics, 1966; Sonics Boom, 1967; Explosives, 1968; Sonics, 1977; Original Northwest Punk, 1979; Unreleased, 1980; Sinderella, 1980

Singles: Boss Hoss, 1965; He's Waiting, 1966; Strychnine, 1966

Hard Rock—Washington; group reformed in 1980 with Roslie as the only original member

Sonny & Cher

Albums: Look at Us, 1965; Baby Don't Go, 1965 (with the Lettermen and Bill Medley); The Wondrous World of Sonny & Cher, 1966; In Case You're in Love, 1967; Good Times, 1967; Best of Sonny & Cher, 1967; Sonny & Cher Live, 1971; All I Ever Need Is You, 1972; Live in Las Vegas, 1972; Mama Was a Rock 'n' Roll Singer, Papa Used to Write Her Songs, 1973; Sonny & Cher, Live in Las Vegas, Volume 2, 1973; Greatest Hits, 1974; The Beat Goes On, 1975

Singles: I Got You Babe, 1965 **(1)**; Baby Don't Go, 1965 **(8)**; Laugh at Me, 1965 **(10)** (Sonny solo); Just You, 1965 **(20)**; But You're Mine, 1965 **(15)**; The Letter, 1965 **(75)**; The Revolution Kind, 1965 **(70)** (Sonny solo); Love Is Strange, 1965 **(131)** (as Caesar & Cleo); What Now My Love, 1966 **(14)**; Have I Stayed Too Long, 1966 **(49)**; Little Man, 1966 **(21)**; Living for You, 1966 **(87)**; The Beat Goes On, 1967 **(6)**; A Beautiful Story, 1967 **(53)**; Plastic Man, 1967 **(74)**; It's the Little Things, 1967 **(50)**; Good

Combination, 1967 **(56)**; All I Ever Need Is You, 1971 **(7)**; A Cowboy's Work Is Never Done, 1972 **(8)**; When You Say Love, 1972 **(32)**; Mama Was a Rock and Roll Singer, Papa Used to Write Her Songs, 1973 **(77)**

Pop Vocal—American; Sonny and Cher divorced in 1974; hosted TV variety show in 1970s

Sons of Champlin

Personnel: Bill Champlin (guitars, keyboards, vocals, saxophones); Terry Haggerty (guitars, vocals); Tim Caine (saxophones) left group (1971); Geoffrey Palmer (keyboards, bass, vocals, saxophones); Al Strong (bass) replaced (1973) by David Schallock (bass, vocals) replaced (1977) by Rob Moitoza (bass, vocals); Bill Bowen (drums) replaced (1973) by James Preston (drums)

Albums: Loosen Up Naturally, 1969; The Sons, 1969; Minus Seeds & Stems, 1970; Follow Your Heart, 1971; Welcome to the Dance, 1973; The Sons of Champlin, 1975; A Circle Filled with Love, 1976; Loving Is Why, 1977

Singles: Sing Me a Rainbow, 1967 **(124)**; Lookout, 1975 **(103)**; Hold On, 1976 **(47)**; Imagination's Sake, 1976 **(107)**; Here Is Where Your Love Belongs, 1977 **(80)**

Country/Rock—San Francisco

Sopwith Camel

Personnel: Terry Macneil (guitars, keyboards); Martin Beard (bass); Peter Kraemer (keyboards, vocals); William Sievers (guitars) left group (1968); Norman Mayell (drums, sitar)

Albums: Sopwith Camel (Hello, Hello), 1967; The Miraculous Hump Returns from the Moon, 1973

Singles: Hello, Hello, 1967 **(26)**; Postcard from Jamaica, 1967 **(88)**

Psychedelic Pop—San Francisco

The Sorrows

Personnel: Don Fardon (vocals); Wez Price (guitars); Philip Witcher (guitars); Philip Packham (bass); Bruce Finley (drums)

Album: Take a Heart, 1965

Single: Take a Heart, 1965 **(129)**

Pop/Rock—British

Jimmy Soul

Album: Jimmy Soul, 1962

Singles: Twistin' Matilda, 1962 **(22)**; If You Wanna Be Happy, 1963 **(1)**; Treat 'em Tough, 1963 **(108)**

Soul Vocal—New York; real name is James McCleese

Soul Brothers Six

Personnel: Charles Armstrong (vocals); Harry Armstrong (vocals); John Ellison (vocals); Lester Peleman (vocals); Von Elle Benjamin (vocals); Joe Johnson (vocals)

Singles: Some Kind of Wonderful, 1967 **(91)**; What Can You Do When You Ain't Got Nobody, 1968 **(107)**

R & B Vocal—New York

The Soul Sisters

Personnel: Thresia Cleveland (vocals); Ann Gissendanner (vocals)

Singles: I Can't Stand It, 1964 **(46)**; Good Time Tonight, 1964 **(98)**; Loop de Loop, 1964 **(107)**; Just a Moment Ago, 1964 **(100)**

Soul Vocal—American

Soul Survivors

Personnel: Kenneth Jeremiah (vocals); Richard Ingui (vocals); Charles Ingui (vocals); Edward Leonetti (guitars); Paul Venturini (organ, bass); Joey Forigone (drums)

Albums: When the Whistle Blows Anything Goes, 1967; Mission Impossible, 1968

Singles: Expressway to Your Heart, 1967 **(4)**; Explosion to My Soul, 1967 **(33)**; Impossible Mission (Mission Impossible), 1968 **(68)**; Mama Soul, 1969 **(115)**

Pop/Soul Vocal — Northeast

Sounds Incorporated

Personnel: John St. John Gillard (guitars); Wes Hunter (bass); Griff West (woodwinds); Barry Cameron (saxophones); Alan Holmes (saxophones); Terry Fogg (drums)

Albums: Sounds Like, 1963; Sounds Incorporated, 1964; Twist at the Star Club Hamburg, 1964; Sounds Incorporated, 1966; Rinky Dink, 1973

Instrumental Rock — British

Sounds Nice

Personnel: Chris Spedding (guitars); Brian Odgers (guitars); Herbie Flowers (bass); Tim Mycroft (keyboards); Clem Cattini (drums)

Album: Love at First Sight, 1969

Hard Rock — British

Joe South

Albums: You're the Reason, 1961; Introspect, 1969; Don't It Make You Want to Go Home?, 1970; Joe South's Greatest Hits, 1970; So the Seeds Are Growing, 1970; Joe South, 1971

Singles: The Purple People Eater Meets the Witch Doctor, 1958 **(47)**; You're the Reason, 1961 **(87)**; Birds of a Feather, 1968 **(106)**; Games People Play, 1969 **(12)**; Leanin' on You, 1969 **(104)**; Birds of a Feather, 1969 **(96)**; Don't It Make You Want to Go Home?, 1969 **(41)**; Walk a Mile in My Shoes, 1970 **(12)**; Children, 1970 **(51)**; Why Does a Man Do What He Has to Do?, 1970 **(118)**; Fool Me, 1971 **(78)**

Soul/Pop Vocal — Atlanta; real last name is Souter

Southwest F.O.B.

Personnel: Dan Seals (vocals, guitars); John Ford Coley (vocals, keyboards)

Album: Smell of Incense, 1968

Singles: Smell of Incense, 1968 **(56)**; Feelin' Groovy, 1970 **(115)**

Psychedelic Pop — Texas

The Spacemen

Single: The Clouds, 1959 **(41)**

Instrumental Pop — American

The Spaniels

Personnel: James "Pookie" Hudson (vocals)

Single: Everyone's Laughing, 1957 **(69)**

R & B Vocal — Indiana

Spanky & Our Gang

Personnel: Elaine "Spanky" McFarlane (vocals); Malcolm Hale (guitars, vocals; deceased 1968) replaced (1975) by Marc McClure (guitars); Kenny Hodges (guitars, vocals, bass) left group (1967); Lefty Baker (guitars, vocals, banjo) replaced (1975) by Bill Plummer (guitars); Nigel Pickering (bass, guitars); John George Seiter (drums) replaced (1975) by James Moon (drums)

Albums: Spanky & Our Gang, 1967; Like to Get to Know You, 1968; Without Rhyme or Reason, 1969; Greatest Hits, 1970; Live, 1970; Change, 1975

Singles: Sunday Will Never Be the Same, 1967 **(9)**; Making Every Minute Count, 1967 **(31)**; Lazy Day, 1967 **(14)**; Sunday Mornin', 1967 **(30)**; Like to Get to Know You, 1968 **(17)**; Give a Damn, 1968 **(43)**; Yesterday's Rain, 1968 **(94)**; Anything You Choose, 1969 **(86)**; And She's Mine, 1969 **(97)**; I Won't Brand You, 1975; L.A. Freeway, 1975

Pop/Rock — Chicago

The Spats

Personnel: Dick Johnson (vocals)
Singles: Gator Tails and Monkey Ribs, 1964 **(96)**; She Done Moved, 1965

Psychedelic Pop — California

The Spellbinders

Personnel: Bob Shivers (vocals); Ben Grant (vocals); Elouise Pennington (vocals); Jimmy Wright (vocals); McArthur Munford (vocals)
Singles: For You, 1965 **(93)**; Chain Reaction, 1966 **(118)**; We're Acting Like Lovers, 1966 **(130)**; Help Me (Get Myself Back Together Again), 1966 **(100)**

Soul Vocal — New Jersey

Skip Spence

Album: Oar, 1968

Hard Rock — California; former member of Moby Grape and Jefferson Airplane

The Spinners

Personnel: Bobby Smith (vocals); Pervis Jackson (vocals); Henry Fambrough (vocals); Billy Henderson (vocals); George W. Dixon (vocals) replaced (1962) by Edgar Edwards (vocals) replaced (1967) by G. C. Cameron (vocals) replaced (1972) by Phillipe Wynne (vocals; deceased 1984); replaced (1977) by John Edwards (vocals)

Albums: The Spinners, 1969; 2nd Time Around, 1970; Spinners, 1973; The Best of the Spinners, 1973; Mighty Love, 1974; New and Improved, 1974; Pick of the Litter, 1975; Spinners Live!, 1975; Happiness Is Being with the Detroit Spinners, 1976; Yesterday, Today & Tomorrow, 1977; Spinners/8, 1977; The Best of the Spinners, 1978; From Here to Eternity, 1979; Dancin' and Lovin', 1980; Love Trippin', 1980; Labor of Love, 1981; Can't Shake This Feelin', 1982; Grand Slam, 1983; Crossfire, 1984; Down to Business, 1989

Singles: That's What Little Girls Are Made For, 1961 **(27)**; Love (I'm Glad) I Found You, 1961 **(91)**; I'll Always Love You, 1965 **(35)**; Truly Yours, 1966 **(111)**; It's a Shame, 1970 **(14)**; We'll Have Made It, 1971 **(89)**; How Could I Let You Get Away, 1972 **(77)**; I'll Be Around, 1972 **(3)**; Could It Be I'm Falling in Love, 1972 **(4)**; One of a Kind (Love Affair), 1973 **(11)**; Together We Can Make Such Sweet Music, 1973 **(91)**; Ghetto Child, 1973 **(29)**; Mighty Love — Pt. 1, 1974 **(20)**; I'm Coming Home, 1974 **(18)**; Then Came You,

1974 **(1)** (with Dionne Warwick); Love Don't Love Nobody—Pt. 1, 1974 **(15)**; Living a Little, Laughing a Little, 1975 **(37)**; Sadie, 1975 **(54)**; They Just Can't Stop It (the Games People Play), 1975 **(5)**; Love or Leave, 1976 **(36)**; Wake Up Susan, 1976 **(56)**; The Rubberband Man, 1976 **(2)**; You're Throwing a Good Love Away, 1977 **(43)**; Heaven on Earth (So Fine), 1977 **(89)**; If You Wanna Do a Dance, 1978 **(49)**; Body Language, 1979 **(103)**; Working My Way Back to You/Forgive Me, Girl, 1979 **(2)**; Cupid/I've Loved You for a Long Time, 1980 **(4)**; Yesterday Once More/Nothing Remains the Same, 1981 **(52)**; You Go Your Way (I'll Go Mine), 1981 **(110)**; Never Thought I'd Fall in Love, 1982 **(95)**; Funny How Time Slips Away, 1982 **(67)**; Put Us Together Again, 1985; She Does, 1985; Spaceballs, 1987

R & B Vocal—Detroit

Spiral Starecase

Personnel: Vinny Parello (vocals, guitars); Pat Upton (guitars, vocals); Harvey Kaplan (bass); Dick Lopes (keyboards); Bobby Raymond (drums)

Album: More Today Than Yesterday, 1969

Singles: Baby What I Mean, 1968 **(111)**; More Today Than Yesterday, 1969 **(12)**; No One for Me to Turn To, 1970 **(52)**; She's Ready, 1970 **(72)**

Psychedelic Pop—California

Spirit

Personnel: Randy California (guitars); Jay Ferguson (vocals, keyboards) replaced (1971) by Al

Spirit: *back row:* **Ferguson, Cassidy, Locke;** *front row:* **California, Andes**

Staehely (guitars, vocals) left group (1973) replaced (1975) by Matt Andes (guitars, vocals) left group (1976) replaced (1984) by Jay Ferguson (keyboards, vocals); Mark Andes (bass, vocals) replaced (1971) by Chris Staehely (bass, vocals) replaced (1973) by Rob Arkin (bass) replaced (1974) by John Arliss (bass) replaced (1975) by Barry Keene (bass, vocals) replaced (1976) by Mark Andes (bass, vocals) replaced (1977) by John Terlep (bass, vocals) replaced (1977) by Larry Knight (bass) replaced (1981) by Steve Loria (bass) replaced (1984) by Mark Andes (bass, vocals) replaced (1990) by Mike Nile (bass, vocals); John Locke (keyboards) left group (1972) rejoined (1984); Ed Cassidy (drums)

Albums: Spirit, 1968; The Family That Plays Together, 1968; Clear Spirit, 1969; The Twelve Dreams of Dr. Sardonicus, 1970; Feedback, 1971; The Best of Spirit, 1973; Spirit of '76, 1975; Son of Spirit, 1975; Farther Along, 1976; Future Games, 1977; Live I & Live II, 1978; Potato-land, 1980; Spirit of '84, 1984; Rapture in the Chambers, 1989; Time Circle (1968–1972), 1990; The Collection, 1991

Singles: Mechanical World, 1968 **(123)**; I Got a Line on You, 1969 **(25)**; Dark Eyed Woman, 1969 **(118)**; 1984, 1970 **(69)**; Animal Zoo, 1970 **(97)**; Nature's Way, 1971 **(111)**; Mr. Skin, 1973 **(92)**; Nature's Way, 1976; I Got a Line on You, 1984; Black Satin Nights, 1984

Hard Rock — Los Angeles

The Spokesmen

Personnel: Johnny Madara (vocals); Dave White (vocals); Roy Gilmore (vocals)

Singles: The Dawn of Correction, 1965 **(36)**; Michelle, 1966 **(106)**

Pop Vocal — American

Spooky Tooth

Personnel: Gary Wright (keyboards, vocals) replaced (1970) by John Hawken (keyboards) replaced (1970) by Chris Stainton (keyboards) replaced (1973) by Gary Wright (keyboards, vocals); Mike Harrison (keyboards, vocals); Luther Grosvenor (guitars) replaced (1972) by Mick Jones (guitars, vocals); Greg Ridley (bass) replaced (1969) by Andy Leigh (bass) replaced (1969) by Alan Spenner (bass, vocals) replaced (1970) by Steve Thompson (bass) replaced (1971) by Ian Herbert (bass) replaced (1972) by Chris Stewart (bass) replaced (1973) by Keith Ellis (bass) replaced (1974) by Val Burke (bass); Mike Kellie (drums) replaced (1972) by Bryson Graham (drums) replaced (1974) by Mike Kellie (drums); added (1974) Mike Patto (vocals); added (1970) Henry McCullough (guitars) left group (1972)

Albums: It's All About Spooky Tooth, 1968; Spooky Two, 1969; Ceremony, 1969; The Last Puff, 1970; You Broke My Heart So I Busted Your Jaw, 1973; Witness, 1973; The Mirror, 1974; The Best of Spooky Tooth, 1976

Single: Feelin' Bad, 1969 **(132)**

Progressive Rock — British

Dusty Springfield

Albums: Silver Threads and Golden Needles, 1962 (with Tom Springfield); A Girl Called Dusty, 1964; Stay Awhile, 1964; Dusty, 1964; Everything Is Coming Up Dusty, 1965; Ooooooeeeeeiiii, 1965; You Don't Have to Say You Love Me, 1966; Dusty Springfield's Golden Hits, 1966; The Look of Love, 1967; The Peking Medallion (Soundtrack), 1967; Where Am I Going, 1967; Dusty Definitely, 1968; Dusty in Memphis, 1969; Best of Bacharach, 1970; From Dusty with

Love, 1970; A Brand New Me, 1970; This Is Dusty Springfield, 1971; See All Her Faces, 1972; Magic Garden, 1973; Cameo, 1973; Sings Bacharach & King, 1975; It Begins Again, 1978; Living Without Your Love, 1979; Dusty in Memphis Plus, 1981; Son of a Preacher Man, 1984; Reputation, 1990

Singles: Silver Threads and Golden Needles, 1962 **(20)** (The Springfields); Dear Hearts and Gentle People, 1962 **(95)** (The Springfields); Gotta Travel On, 1962 **(114)** (The Springfields); Island of Dreams, 1963 **(129)** (The Springfields); I Only Want to Be with You, 1964 **(12)**; Stay Awhile, 1964 **(38)**; Wishin' and Hopin', 1964 **(6)**; All Cried Out, 1964 **(41)**; Guess Who, 1964 **(109)**; Live It Up, 1965 **(128)**; Losing You, 1965 **(91)**; In the Middle of Nowhere, 1965 **(108)**; You Don't Have to Say You Love Me, 1966 **(4)**; All I See Is You, 1966 **(20)**; I'll Try Anything, 1967 **(40)**; The Look of Love, 1967 **(22)**; Give Me Time, 1967 **(76)**; What's It Gonna Be, 1967 **(49)**; I Close My Eyes and Count to Ten, 1968 **(122)**; Son of a Preacher Man, 1968 **(10)**; Don't Forget About Me, 1969 **(64)**; Breakfast in Bed, 1969 **(91)**; I Don't Want to Hear It Anymore, 1969 **(105)**; The Windmills of Your Mind, 1969 **(31)**; Willie & Laura Mae Jones, 1969 **(78)**; In the Land of Make Believe, 1969 **(113)**; A Brand New Me, 1969 **(24)**; Silly, Silly, Fool, 1970 **(76)**; I Wanna Be a Free Girl, 1970 **(105)**; Who Gets Your Love, 1973 **(121)**; Mama's Little Girl, 1973 **(118)**; Let Me Love You Once Before You Go, 1977 **(100)**; What Have I Done to Deserve This, 1987 **(2)** (with Pet Shop Boys)

Pop Vocal — British; real name is Mary O'Brien; recorded with brother Tom Springfield and Tim Feild as the Springfields

S R C

Personnel: Scott Richardson (vocals); Gary Quackenbush (guitars) replaced (1970) by Ray Goodman (guitars); Robin Dale (bass, vocals) replaced (1969) by Alan Wilmot (bass, vocals); Glenn Quackenbush (keyboards, vocals); E. G. Clawson (drums, vocals)

Albums: SRC, 1968; Milestones, 1969; Traveller's Tale, 1970

Hard Rock — American

Clyde Stacy

Singles: So Young, 1957 **(68)**; So Young, 1959 **(99)**

Rockabilly — Oklahoma

Terry Stafford

Album: Suspicion!, 1964

Singles: Suspicion!, 1964 **(3)**; I'll Touch a Star, 1964 **(25)**; Follow the Rainbow, 1964 **(101)**

Rockabilly — Texas

The Standells

Personnel: Tony Valentino (guitars); Larry Tamblyn (guitars, vocals); Gary Lane (bass, vocals) replaced (1967) by Dave Burke (bass, guitars); Dick Dodd (drums, vocals)

Albums: Dirty Water, 1966; Why Pick on Me, 1966; Hot Ones, 1967; Try It, 1967; Live & Out of Sight, 1968; In Person at P. J.'s, 1969

Singles: The Boy Next Door, 1965 **(102)**; Dirty Water, 1966 **(11)**; Sometimes Good Guys Don't Wear

White, 1966 (**43**); Why Pick on Me, 1966 (**54**); Can't Help But Love You, 1967 (**78**); Try It, 1967

Psychedelic Rock—Los Angeles

The Staple Singers

Personnel: Roebuck "Pop" Staples (vocals); Pervis Staples (vocals) left group (1971); Cleotha Staples (vocals); Yvonne Staples (vocals); Mavis Staples (vocals)

Albums: The Staple Swingers, 1971; Bealtitude: Respect Yourself, 1972; Be What You Are, 1973; City in the Sky, 1974; Let's Do It Again, 1975; Pass It On, 1976

Singles: Why? (Am I Treated So Bad), 1967 (**95**); For What It's Worth, 1967 (**66**); Heavy Makes You Happy (Sha-Na-Boom-Boom), 1971 (**27**); You've Got to Earn It, 1971 (**97**); Respect Yourself, 1971 (**12**); I'll Take You There, 1972 (**1**); This World, 1972 (**38**); Oh La De Da, 1973 (**33**); Be What You Are, 1973 (**66**); If You're Ready (Come Go with Me), 1973 (**9**); Touch a Hand, Make a Friend, 1974 (**23**); City in the Sky, 1974 (**79**); My Main Man, 1974 (**76**); Let's Do It Again, 1975 (**1**); New Orleans, 1976 (**70**)

Soul Vocal—Mississippi

The Starlets

Personnel: Dynetta Boone (vocals); Jane Hall (vocals); Maxine Edwards (vocals); Jeanette Miles (vocals); Mickey McKinney (vocals); Bernice Williams (vocals)

Singles: P.S. I Love You, 1960 (**106**); Better Tell Him No, 1961 (**38**); I Sold My Heart to the Junkman, 1962 (**15**)

R & B Vocal—Chicago

Edwin Starr

Albums: Soul Master, 1969; 25 Miles, 1969; Just We Two, 1970; War and Peace, 1970; Involved, 1971; Hits of Edwin Starr, 1974; Hell Up in Harlem, 1974; Afternoon Sunshine, 1977; Edwin Starr, 1977; Clean, 1979; Happy Radio, 1979; Stronger Than You Think I Am, 1980

Singles: Agent Double-O-Soul, 1965 (**21**); Back Street, 1965 (**95**); Stop Her on Sight (S.O.S.), 1966 (**48**); Headline News, 1966 (**84**); I Want My Baby Back, 1967 (**120**); I Am the Man for You Baby, 1968 (**112**); Way Over There, 1968 (**119**); Twenty-Five Miles, 1969 (**6**); I'm Still a Struggling Man, 1969 (**80**); Oh How Happy, 1969 (**92**) (with Blinky); Time, 1970 (**117**); War, 1970 (**1**); Stop the War Now, 1970 (**26**); Funky Music Sho Nuff Turns Me On, 1971 (**64**); There You Go, 1973 (**80**); Ain't It Hell Up in Harlem, 1974 (**110**); Abyssinia Jones, 1976 (**98**); Contact, 1979 (**65**); H.A.P.P.Y. Radio, 1979 (**79**)

Soul Vocal—Cleveland; real name is Charles Hatcher; Blinky is female vocalist Sandra Williams

Kay Starr

Singles: Good and Lonesome, 1955 (**17**); Rock and Roll Waltz, 1955 (**1**); I've Changed My Mind a Thousand Times, 1956 (**73**); Second Fiddle, 1956 (**40**); Love Ain't Right, 1956 (**89**); The Good Book, 1956 (**89**); The Things I Never Had, 1956 (**89**); Jamie Boy, 1957 (**54**); A Little Loneliness, 1957 (**73**); My Heart Reminds Me, 1957 (**9**); Foolin' Around, 1961 (**49**); I'll Never Be Free, 1961 (**94**); Four Walls, 1962 (**92**)

Pop Vocal—Oklahoma; real name
is Katherine Starks

Randy Starr

Single: After School, 1957 **(32)**
Pop Vocal—New York; real name
is Warren Nadel

The Statues

Personnel: James "Buzz" Cason
(vocals); Hugh Jarrett (vocals);
Richard Williams (vocals)
Single: Blue Velvet, 1960 **(84)**
Pop Vocal—Nashville

Status Quo

Personnel: Francis Rossi (guitars,
vocals); Rick Parfitt (guitars, vocals); Alan Lancaster (bass) replaced
(1986) by John Edwards (bass); John
Coughlan (drums) replaced (1986)
by Peter Kirchner (drums) replaced
(1988) by Jeff Rich (drums); added
(1972) Roy Lynes (keyboards) replaced (1977) by Andy Bown (keyboards, vocals)
Albums: Picturesque Matchstick-
able Messages, 1968; Spare Parts,
1968; Messages from the Status
Quo, 1968; Status Quotation, 1969;
Ma Kelly's Greasy Spoon, 1970;
Dog of Two Heads, 1971; Best of
Status Quo, 1972; Piledriver, 1973;
Golden Hour, 1973; Hello, 1974;
Quo, 1974; On the Level, 1975;
Status Quo, 1975; Golden Hour 2,
1975; The Rest of Status Quo, 1976;
Blue for You, 1976; Status Quo
Live, 1977; Down the Dustpipe,
1977; Rockin' All Over the World,
1977; If You Can't Stand the Heat,
1978; Whatever You Want, 1979; 12
Gold Bars, 1979; Just for the
Record, 1979; Now Hear This,
1980; Just Supposin', 1980; Never
Too Late, 1981; Fresh Quote, 1981;
1982, 1982; From the Makers Of...,
1982; Back to Back, 1983; Works,
1983; 12 Gold Bars 2, 1984; Live at
the N E C, 1984; In the Army Now,
1985; Status Quo, 1986; Burning
Bridges, 1988; Rocking All Over the
Years, 1990; Rock 'til You Drop,
1991
Singles: Pictures of Matchstick
Men, 1968 **(12)**; Ice in the Sun, 1968
(70); Paper Plane, 1973; Rain, 1973;
Down, Down, 1974; Caroline, 1974;
Break the Rules, 1974; Again &
Again, 1975; Roll Over, Lay Down,
1975; Getting Better, 1975; Mystery
Song, 1976; Wild Side of Life, 1976;
Rockin' All Over the World, 1977;
Accident Prone, 1978; Whatever
You Want, 1979; Living on an
Island, 1979; What You're

Status Quo: Rossi, Edwards, Parfitt

Proposing, 1980; Living on an Island, 1980; Lies, 1980; Something 'Bout You Baby, 1981; Rock 'n' Roll, 1981; Dear John, 1982; She Don't Fool Me, 1982; Caroline, 1982; Ol' Rag Blues, 1983; A Mess of Blues, 1983; Marguerita Time, 1983; Going Down Town Tonight, 1984; The Wanderer, 1984; In the Army Now, 1985; Rollin' Home, 1986; Red Sky, 1986; Burning Bridges (On & Off), 1988; The Anniversary Waltz Part One, 1990; The Anniversary Waltz Part Two, 1990

Hard Rock—British; major stars in England; they have failed to chart in U.S. since their 1968 debut

Steam

Album: Steam, 1970
Singles: Na Na Hey Hey Kiss Him Goodbye, 1969 **(1)**; I've Gotta Make You Love Me, 1970 **(46)**

Pop/Rock—New York; British studio group formed by songwriters Paul Leka, Dale Frashuer and Gary DeCarlo; touring group was different

Steamhammer

Personnel: Kieran White (guitars, vocals) replaced (1972) by Micky Waller (guitars); Martin Pugh (guitars, vocals); Steve Davy (bass, vocals) replaced (1972) by Louis Cennamo (bass); Mike Rushton (drums) replaced (1970) by Mick Bradley (drums)
Albums: Steamhammer, 1968; Steamhammer Mark 2, 1970; Mountains, 1971; Speech, 1972; This Is Steamhammer, 1972

Progressive Rock—British

The Steelers

Personnel: Leonard Truss (vocals); Wes Wells (vocals); Alonzo Wells (vocals); George Wells (vocals); Wales Wallace (vocals)
Single: Get It from the Bottom, 1969

R & B Vocal—Chicago

Steppenwolf

Personnel: John Kay (guitars, vocals, keyboards); Mike Monarch (guitars) replaced (1969) by Larry Byrom (guitars) replaced (1971) by Kent Henry (guitars) replaced (1974) by Bobby Cochran (guitars) replaced (1977) by Dennis Edmonton (guitars) replaced (1979) by Michael Palmer (guitars) replaced (1989) by Rocket Ritchotte (guitars); Rushton Moreve (bass; deceased 1981) replaced (1968) by John Morgan (bass) replaced (1969) by Nick St. Nicholas (bass) replaced (1970) by George Biondo (bass, vocals); Goldy McJohn (keyboards) replaced (1975) by Andy Chapin (keyboards) replaced (1975) by Wayne Cook (keyboards) replaced (1979) by Michael Wilk (keyboards); Jerry Edmonton (drums) replaced (1979) by Steven Palmer (drums) replaced (1989) by Ron Hurst (drums)
Albums: Steppenwolf, 1968; The Second, 1968; At Your Birthday Party, 1969; Early Steppenwolf, 1969; Monster, 1970; Steppenwolf Live, 1970; Steppenwolf 7, 1970; For Ladies Only, 1971; Steppenwolf Gold, 1971; Rest in Peace, 1972; 16 Greatest Hits, 1974; Slow Flux, 1974; Hour of the Wolf, 1975; Skullduggery, 1976; Reborn to Be Wild, 1977; The ABC Collection, 1977; Gold, 1980; Wolf Tracks, 1983; Rock 'n' Roll Rebels, 1987; Rise and Shine,

Steppenwolf: *l-r,* **Biondo, Henry, Edmonton, Kay, McJohn**

1990; Born to Be Wild—A Retrospective, 1991

Singles: Born to Be Wild, 1968 **(2)**; Magic Carpet Ride, 1968 **(3)**; Rock Me, 1969 **(10)**; It's Never Too Late, 1969 **(51)**; Move Over, 1969 **(31)**; Monster, 1969 **(39)**; Hey Lawdy Mama, 1970 **(35)**; Screaming Night Hog, 1970 **(62)**; Who Needs You, 1970 **(54)**; Snow Blind Friend, 1971 **(60)**; Ride with Me, 1971 **(52)**; For Ladies Only, 1971 **(64)**; Straight Shootin' Woman, 1974 **(29)**; Smokey Factory Blues, 1975 **(108)**; Hot Night in a Cold Town, 1983; Hold On, 1987

Hard Rock—International; Kay's real name is Joachim F. Krauledat

April Stevens

Singles: Teach Me Tiger, 1959 **(86)**; Wake Up and Love Me, 1974 **(93)**

Pop Vocal—New York

Cat Stevens

Albums: Matthew & Son, 1967; New Masters, 1968; Very Young & Early Songs, 1969; The World of Cat Stevens, 1970; Mona Bone Jakon, 1970; Tea for the Tillerman, 1971; Teaser and the Firecat, 1971; Catch Bull at Four, 1972; Foreigner,

1973; Buddah and the Chocolate Box, 1974; Numbers, 1975; Greatest Hits, 1975; Izitso, 1977; Back to Earth, 1978; Footsteps in the Dark/ Greatest Hits Volume II, 1984; Classics, 1986

Singles: I Love My Dog, 1966 **(118)**; Matthew & Son, 1967 **(115)**; Wild World, 1971 **(11)**; Moonshadow, 1971 **(30)**; Peace Train, 1971 **(7)**; Morning Has Broken, 1972 **(6)**; Sitting, 1972 **(16)**; The Hurt, 1973 **(31)**; Oh Very Young, 1974 **(10)**; Another Saturday Night, 1974 **(6)**; Ready, 1974 **(26)**; Two Fine People, 1975 **(33)**; Banapple Gas, 1976 **(41)**; (Remember the Days of the) Old Schoolyard, 1977 **(33)**; Sweet Jamaica, 1977; Was Dog a Doughnut, 1977 **(70)**; Bad Breaks, 1978 **(83)**; If You Want to Sing Out, Sing Out, 1984; Father and Son, 1985

Pop/Rock—British; real name is Steven Dimitri Georgiou; now goes by the name Yusaf Islam

Connie Stevens

Albums: Sixteen Reasons, 1960; Connie Stevens, 1962

Singles: Kookie, Kookie (Lend Me Your Comb), 1959 **(4)** (with Edd Byrnes); Sixteen Reasons, 1960 **(3)**; Too Young to Go Steady, 1960 **(71)**; Why'd You Wanna Make Me Cry, 1962 **(52)**; Mr. Songwriter, 1962 **(43)**; Hey Good Lookin', 1962 **(104)**; Now That You've Gone, 1965 **(53)**

Pop Vocal—New York; starred in TV's "Hawaiian Eye" and in movies; was once married to Eddie Fisher; daughter Tricia Lee Fisher is a recording artist; real name is Concetta Ingolia

Dodie Stevens

Singles: Pink Shoe Laces, 1959 **(3)**; Yes-Sir-Ee, 1959 **(79)**; The Five Pennies, 1959 **(89)**; Miss Lonely Hearts, 1959 **(111)**; No, 1960 **(73)**; Yes, I'm Lonesome Tonight, 1960 **(60)**

Pop Vocal—California; real name is Geraldine Pasquale

Ray Stevens

Albums: 1,837 Seconds of Humor, 1962; Gitarzan, 1969; Everything Is Beautiful, 1970; Ray Stevens . . . Unreal!, 1970; Ray Stevens' Greatest Hits, 1971; Turn Your Radio On, 1972; Boogity Boogity, 1974; Misty, 1975; The Very Best of Ray Stevens, 1975; Greatest Hits Volume 2, 1977; Shriner's Convention, 1980; He Thinks He's Ray Stevens, 1985; I Have Returned, 1986; Surely You Joust, 1986; Crackin' Up, 1987; I Never Made a Record I Didn't Like, 1988; Beside Myself, 1989

Singles: Sergeant Preston of the Yukon, 1960 **(108)**; Jeremiah Peabody's Poly Unsaturated Quick Dissolving Fast Acting Pleasant Tasting Green & Purple Pills, 1961 **(35)**; Ahab, the Arab, 1962 **(5)**; Further More, 1962 **(91)**; Santa Claus Is Watching You, 1962 **(45)**; Funny Man, 1963 **(81)**; Harry the Hairy Ape, 1963 **(17)**; Speed Ball, 1963 **(59)**; Party People, 1965 **(130)**; Freddie Feelgood (and His Funky Little Five Piece Band), 1966 **(91)**; Unwind, 1968 **(52)**; Funny Man, 1968 **(122)**; Mr. Businessman, 1968 **(28)**; The Great Escape, 1968 **(114)**; Gitarzan, 1969 **(8)**; Along Came Jones, 1969 **(27)**; Sunday Mornin' Comin' Down, 1969 **(81)**; Have a Little Talk with Myself, 1969 **(123)**; I'll Be Your Baby Tonight, 1970

(112); Everything Is Beautiful, 1970
(1); America, Communicate with
Me, 1970 (45); Sunset Strip, 1970
(81); Bridget the Midget (The
Queen of the Blues), 1970 (50); A
Mama and a Papa, 1971 (82); All
My Trials, 1971 (70); Turn Your
Radio On, 1971 (63); The Streak,
1974 (1); Moonlight Special, 1974
(73); Misty, 1975 (14); Indian Love
Call, 1975 (68); Young Love, 1976
(93); You Are So Beautiful, 1976
(101); Lady of Spain, 1976 (108); In
the Mood, 1977 (40); I Need Your
Help Barry Manilow, 1979 (49);
Shriner's Convention, 1980 (101)
  Novelty Pop—Georgia

Al Stewart

Albums: Bedsitter Images, 1967;
Love Chronicles, 1969; Zero She
Flies, 1970; Orange, 1972; Past,
Present and Future, 1974; Modern
Times, 1975; The Year of the Cat,
1976; The Early Years, 1977; Time
Passages, 1978; 24 Carrots, 1980; In-
dian Summer, 1981; Live Indian
Summer, 1981; Russians and Ameri-
cans, 1984; Best of Al Stewart, 1987;
Last Days of the Century, 1988;

Best of Al Stewart, Volume 2, 1990;
Chronicles, 1991
  Singles: The Years of the Cat,
1976 (8); On the Border, 1977 (42);
Time Passages, 1978 (7); Song on
the Radio, 1979 (29); Midnight
Rocks, 1980 (24); Paint by Num-
bers, 1980; Running Man, 1981; In-
dian Summer, 1981; Russians and
Americans, 1984
  Progressive Rock—British

Billy Stewart

Albums: I Do Love You, 1965;
Unbelievable, 1966; Cross My
Heart, 1967
  Singles: Reap What You Sow,
1962 (79); Strange Feeling, 1963
(70); I Do Love You, 1965 (26); Sit-
ting in the Park, 1965 (24); How
Nice It Is, 1965 (97); Because I
Love You, 1966 (96); Mountain of
Love, 1966 (100); Summertime,
1966 (10); Secret Love, 1966 (29);
Every Day I Have the Blues, 1967
(74); Cross My Heart, 1967 (86); I
Do Love You, 1969 (94)
  R & B—Washington, D.C.; Billy
was killed in an auto crash on 1/17/
70

John Stewart

Albums: Signals Through the
Glass, 1968; California Bloodlines,
1969; Willard, 1970; Lonesome
Picker Rides Again, 1971; Sunstorm,
1972; Cannons in the Rain, 1973;
The Phoenix Concerts Live, 1974;
Wingless Angels, 1975; Fire in the
Wind, 1977; Bombs Away Dream
Babies, 1979; Dream Babies Go
Hollywood, 1980; In Concert, 1980;
Forgotten Songs, 1980; Blondes,
1982; Revenge of the Budgie, 1983;
Trancas, 1984; The Last Campaign,

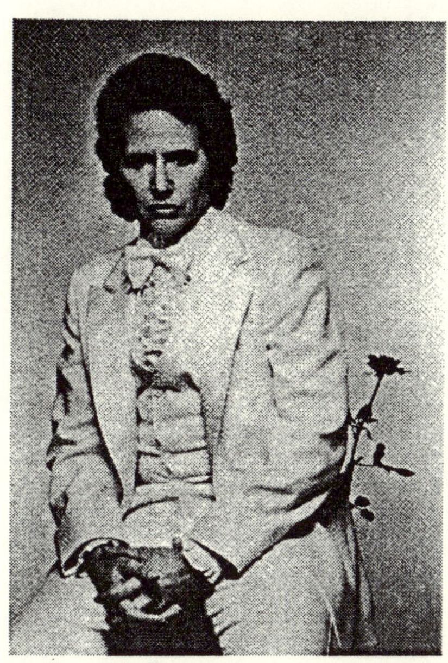

John Stewart

1984; Punch the Big Guy, 1987;
American Hero, 1989; Neon Beach/
Live 1990, 1991; Deep in the Neon/
Live at McCabe's, 1991
Singles: Armstrong, 1969 **(74)**;
Gold, 1979 **(5)**; Midnight Wind,
1979 **(28)**; Lost Her in the Sun,
1979 **(34)**; Odin (Spirit of the
Water), 1980; Wheels of Thunder,
1980; Hollywood Dreams, 1981; The
Queen of Hollywood High, 1983
   Folk/Rock—San Diego; former
member of the Kingston Trio

Sandy Stewart

   Album: My Coloring Book, 1963
   Single: My Coloring Book, 1962
(20)
   Pop Vocal—Philadelphia; real
name is Sandra Galitz

Gary Stites

Singles: Lonely for You, 1959
(24); A Girl Like You, 1959 **(80)**;
Starry Eyed, 1959 **(77)**; Lawdy Miss
Clawdy, 1960 **(47)**; Hurtin', 1966
(123)
   Pop/Rock—Denver

The Stompers

Personnel: Leonard Capizzi (vocals); Bill Capizzi (vocals); Ron
Deltorto (vocals); Lou Toscano (vocals); Bobby "Boris" Pickett (vocals)
replaced (1962) by Don Squire (vocals)
   Single: Quarter to Four Stomp,
1962 **(100)**
   Pop Vocal—American

The Stone Poneys

Personnel: Linda Ronstadt (vo-
cals); Bob Kimmell (guitars); Kenny
Edwards (guitars); James E. Bond,
Jr. (bass); Billy Mundi (drums)
   Albums: Stone Poneys, 1967;
Evergreen, Volume 2, 1967; Stone
Poneys & Friends, Volume 3, 1968
   Singles: Different Drum, 1967
(13); Up to My Neck in Muddy
Water, 1968 **(93)**
   Pop/Rock—American

The Storey Sisters

Personnel: Ann Storey (vocals);
Lillian Storey (vocals)
   Single: Bad Motorcycle, 1958 **(45)**
   Pop Vocal—Philadelphia

Billy Storm

Singles: I've Come of Age, 1959
(28); Love theme from *El Cid,* 1962
(105)
   Pop Vocal—Ohio

Gale Storm

Singles: I Hear You Knocking/ Never Leave Me, 1955 **(2)**; Memories Are Made of This, 1955 **(5)**; Teen Age Prayer, 1955 **(6)**; Why Do Fools Fall in Love, 1956 **(9)**; Ivory Tower, 1956 **(6)**; Tell Me Why, 1956 **(52)**; Now Is the Hour, 1956 **(59)**; A Heart Without a Sweetheart, 1956 **(79)**; On Treasure Island, 1957 **(74)**; Lucky Lips, 1957 **(77)**; Dark Moon, 1957 **(4)**

Pop Vocal—Texas; real name is Josephine Cottle; star of TV series "My Little Margie" and "Gale Storm Show"

The Strangeloves

Personnel: Richard Gottehrer (vocals); Robert Feldman (vocals); Jerry Goldstein (vocals)

Album: I Want Candy, 1965

Singles: Love, Love (That's All I Want from You), 1964 **(122)**; I Want Candy, 1965 **(11)**; Cara-Lin, 1965 **(39)**; Night Time, 1966 **(30)**; Hand Jive, 1966 **(100)**; Honey Do, 1968 **(120)**

Psychedelic Rock—New York; Gottehrer produced hit albums for Blondie and the Go-Gos; also recorded as the Sheep

The Strangers

Personnel: Joel Scott Hill (guitars)

Single: The Caterpillar Crawl, 1959 **(49)**

Pop/Rock—San Diego

Marcia Strassman

Single: The Flower Children, 1967 **(105)**

Folk/Pop Vocal—American; was a regular on the "M*A*S*H" and "Welcome Back Kotter" TV shows in the 1970s

Strawberry Alarm Clock

Personnel: Ed King (guitars, vocals) replaced (1982) by Leo

Strawberry Alarm Clock

Gaffney (guitars, vocals); Lee Freeman (guitars, bass, harmonica); Gary Lovetro (bass, vocals); George Bunnell (guitars, bass) replaced (1969) by Jimmy Pittman (guitars, vocals); Mark Weitz (keyboards); Randy Seol (drums) replaced (1969) by Gene Gunnels (drums)

Albums: Incense & Peppermints, 1968; Wake Up, It's Tomorrow, 1968; World in a Sea Shell, 1969; Good Morning Sunshine, 1969; Psych Out (Soundtrack), 1969; Best of Strawberry Alarm Clock, 1970; Changes, 1971

Singles: Incense & Peppermints, 1967 **(1)**; Tomorrow, 1967 **(23)**; Sit with the Guru, 1968 **(65)**; Barefoot in Baltimore, 1968 **(67)**; Good Morning Starshine, 1969 **(87)**

Psychedelic Rock—California; Freeman reformed the group in 1982; King rejoined Lynyrd Skynyrd in 1990

The Strawbs

Personnel: Dave Cousins (vocals, guitars) replaced (1979) by Roy Hill (guitars, vocals); Tony Hooper (guitars) replaced (1972) by Dave Lambert (vocals, guitars); Arthur Phillips (mandolin) replaced (1968) by Ron Chesterman (bass) replaced (1969) by John Ford (bass, vocals) replaced (1974) by Chas Cronk (bass); Sandy Denny (vocals) left group (1969) replaced (1970) by Claire Deniz (cello) left group (1971) replaced (1979) by John Knightsbridge (guitars); Ken Gudmand (drums) replaced (1969) by Richard Hudson (drums, vocals) replaced (1974) by Rod Coombes (drums) replaced (1978) by Tony Fernandez (drums); added (1969) Rick Wakeman (keyboards) replaced (1972) by

Blue Weaver (keyboards) replaced (1974) by John Hawken (keyboards) replaced (1976) by John Mealing (keyboards) replaced (1979) by Andy Richards (keyboards); added (1977) Robert Kirby (keyboards)

Albums: Sandy Denny & the Strawbs: All Our Own Work, 1968; Strawbs, 1969; Dragonfly, 1970; Just a Collection of Antiques and Curios, 1970; From the Witchwood, 1971; Grave New World, 1972; Bursting at the Seams, 1973; Hero and Heroine, 1974; Strawbs by Choice, 1974; Ghosts, 1975; Nomadness, 1976; Deep Cuts, 1976; Burning for You, 1977; Deadlines, 1978; Best of the Strawbs, 1978; Ringing Down the Years, 1990

Singles: Lemon Pie, 1971; Round and Round, 1972; Lay Down, 1972; Part of the Union, 1973 **(111)**; I Only Want My Love to Grow in You, 1976

Progressive/Folk Rock—British

The String-Alongs

Personnel: Keith McCormack (guitars); Aubrey Lee de Cordova (guitars); Richard Stephens (guitars); Jimmy Torres (bass); Don Allen (drums)

Album: Wheels, 1961

Singles: Wheels, 1961 **(3)**; Brass Buttons, 1961 **(35)**; Should I, 1961 **(42)**; Matilda, 1962 **(133)**

Instrumental Pop—American

Barrett Strong

Albums: Stronghold, 1975; Live & Love, 1976

Single: Money (That's What I Want), 1960 **(23)**

R & B Vocal—Mississippi; wrote hits for the Temptations

Chad & Jill Stuart

Single: The Cruel War, 1966 **(110)**
Pop Vocal—British; Chad, of
Chad & Jeremy, and his wife Jill

Sunny & The Sunglows

Personnel: Sunny Ozuna (vocals);
Tony Tostado (vocals); Jesse Villa-
nueva (vocals); Oscar Villanueva
(vocals); Ray Villanueva (vocals);
Alfred Luna (vocals); Gilbert Fer-
nandez (vocals)
Album: Talk to Me, 1963
Singles: Talk to Me, 1963 **(11)**;
Rags to Riches, 1963 **(45)**; Out of
Sight—Out of Mind, 1964 **(71)**;
Something's Got a Hold on Me,
1965 **(128)**
Pop Vocal—Texas

The Sunnysiders

Personnel: Freddy Morgan
(banjo; deceased 1970); Jad Paul
(guitars, vocals); Norman Milkin
(guitars, vocals); Margie Rayburn
(vocals)
Single: Hey, Mr. Banjo, 1955 **(12)**
Pop—American

The Sunrays

Personnel: Eddie Medora
(guitars, vocals); Byron Case
(guitars, vocals, drums); Vince
Hozier (bass, vocals); Marty Di
Giovanni (keyboards); Ricky Henn
(drums, vocals)
Albums: I Live for the Sun, 1965;
Andrea, 1966
Singles: I Live for the Sun, 1965
(51); Andrea, 1966 **(41)**; Still, 1966
(93)
Surf Rock—California

The Sunshine Company

Personnel: Maurice Manseau
(guitars, vocals, keyboards); Mary
Nance (vocals, percussion); Larry
Sims (guitars, vocals); Douglas
"Red" Mark (guitars, violin, vocals);
Merle Bregante (drums, vocals)
Albums: Happy Is the Sunshine
Company, 1967; Sunshine Com-
pany, 1968; Sunshine & Shadows,
1968
Singles: Happy, 1967 **(50)**; Back
on the Street Again, 1967 **(36)**;
Look, Here Comes the Sun, 1968
(56); Let's Get Together, 1968 **(112)**;
On a Beautiful Day, 1968 **(106)**;
Willie Jean, 1968 **(111)**
Bubblegum Pop—California

The Supremes

Personnel: Diana Ross (vocals)
replaced (1970) by Jean Terrell
(vocals) replaced (1973) by Sherri
Payne (vocals); Mary Wilson (vocals) replaced (1976) by Karen Jackson (vocals); Florence Ballard

The Supremes: Ballard, Ross, Wilson

(vocals; deceased 1976); replaced (1967) by Cindy Birdsong (vocals) replaced (1972) by Lynda Laurence (vocals) replaced (1975) by Susaye Green (vocals)

Albums: Meet the Supremes, 1964; Where Did Our Love Go, 1964; A Bit of Liverpool, 1964; The Supremes Sing, Country Western & Pop, 1965; We Remember Sam Cooke, 1965; More Hits by the Supremes, 1965; The Supremes at the Copa, 1965; I Hear a Symphony, 1966; The Supremes A'Go-Go, 1966; The Supremes Sing Holland-Dozier-Holland, 1967; The Supremes Sing Rodgers & Hart, 1967

(following recorded as Diana Ross & the Supremes)

Diana Ross & the Supremes Greatest Hits, 1967; Reflections, 1968; Live at London's Talk of the Town, 1968; Funny Girl, 1968; Diana Ross & the Supremes Join the Temptations, 1968 (with the Temptations); Love Child, 1968; TCB, 1968 (with the Temptations); Let the Sunshine In, 1969; Together, 1969 (with the Temptations); Cream of the Crop, 1969; On Broadway, 1969 (with the Temptations); Greatest Hits, Volume 2, 1970; Farewell, 1970

(following recorded as the Supremes)

Right On, 1970; The Magnificent 7, 1970 (with the Four Tops); New Ways but Love Stays, 1970; Touch, 1971; The Return of the Magnificent Seven, 1971 (with the Four Tops); Dynamite, 1972 (with the Four Tops); Floy Joy, 1972; The Supremes, 1972; Anthology (1962–1969), 1974; The Supremes, 1975; High Energy, 1976; Mary, Sherri & Susaye, 1976; The Supremes at Their Best, 1977; 20 Golden Greats, 1977

Singles: Your Heart Belongs to Me, 1962 **(95)**; Let Me Go the Right Way, 1962 **(90)**; My Heart Can't Take It No More, 1963 **(129)**

A Breath Taking Guy, 1963 **(75)**; When the Lovelight Starts Shining Through His Eyes, 1963 **(23)**; Run, Run, Run, 1964 **(93)**; Where Did Our Love Go, 1964 **(1)**; Baby Love, 1964 **(1)**; Come See About Me, 1964 **(1)**; Stop! In the Name of Love, 1965 **(1)**; Back in My Arms Again, 1965 **(1)**; Nothing but Heartaches, 1965 **(11)**; I Hear a Symphony, 1965 **(1)**; My World Is Empty Without You, 1966 **(5)**; Love Is Like an Itching in My Heart, 1966 **(9)**; You Can't Hurry Love, 1966 **(1)**; You Keep Me Hangin' On, 1966 **(1)**; Love Is Here and Now You're Gone, 1967 **(1)**; The Happening, 1967 **(1)**

(following recorded as Diana Ross & the Supremes)

Reflections, 1967 **(2)**; In and Out of Love, 1967 **(9)**; Forever Came Today, 1968 **(28)**; Some Things You Never Get Used To, 1968 **(30)**; Love Child, 1968 **(1)**; I'm Gonna Make You Love Me, 1968 **(2)** (with the Temptations); I'm Livin' in Shame, 1969 **(10)**; I'll Try Something New, 1969 **(25)** (with the Temptations); The Composer, 1969 **(27)**; No Matter What Sign You Are, 1969 **(31)**; The Young Folks, 1969 **(69)**; The Weight, 1969 **(46)** (with the Temptations); Someday We'll Be Together, 1969 **(1)**

(following recorded as the Supremes)

Up the Ladder to the Roof, 1970 **(10)**; Everybody's Got the Right to Love, 1970 **(21)**; Stoned Love, 1970 **(7)**; River Deep—Mountain High, 1970 **(14)** (with the Four Tops); Nathan Jones, 1971 **(16)**; You Gotta Have Love in Your Heart, 1971 **(55)** (with the Four Tops); Touch, 1971 **(71)**; Floy Joy, 1972 **(16)**;

Automatically Sunshine, 1972 **(37)**; Your Wonderful, Sweet Sweet Love, 1972 **(59)**; I Guess I'll Miss the Man, 1972 **(85)**; Bad Weather, 1973 **(87)**; I'm Gonna Let My Heart Do the Walking, 1976 **(40)**; You're My Driving Wheel, 1976 **(85)**

Pop/Soul Vocal—Detroit

The Surfaris

Personnel: Jim Fuller (guitars); Bob Berryhill (guitars); Jim Pash (guitars, woodwinds); Pat Connolly (bass, vocals); Ron Wilson (drums)

Albums: Wipe Out, 1963; Surfaris Play, 1963; Hit City '64, 1964; Fun City, 1964; Hit City '65, 1965; Wheels, 1966; Yesterday's Pop Scene, 1973; Surfers Rule, 1976; Gone with the Wave, 1977

Singles: Wipe Out, 1963 **(2)**; Surfer Joe, 1963 **(62)**; Point Panic, 1963 **(49)**; Wipe Out, 1966 **(16)**; Wipe Out, 1970 **(110)**

Surf Rock—California

The Surprise Package

Album: The Surprise Package, 1966

Single: Out of My Mind, 1966

Psychedelic Pop—Northwest

Bettye Swan

Albums: Make Me Yours, 1967; Don't Touch Me, 1969; Bettye Swan, 1972

Singles: Don't Wait Too Long, 1965 **(131)**; Make Me Yours, 1967 **(21)**; Fall in Love with Me, 1967 **(67)**; Don't Touch Me, 1969 **(38)**; Angel of the Morning, 1969 **(109)**; Don't You Ever Get Tired (Of Hurting Me), 1969 **(102)**; Little Things Mean a Lot, 1970 **(114)**;

Victim of a Foolish Heart, 1972
(63); Today I Started Loving You
Again, 1973 **(46)**

Pop/Soul Vocal—American; real
name is Betty Jean Champion

Sweeney's Men

Personnel: Johnny Moynihan
(woodwinds); Joe Dolan (guitars,
vocals) replaced (1967) by Terry
Woods (guitars, vocals, bass); Andy
Irvine (guitars) replaced (1969) by
Henry McCullough (guitars, vocals)
replaced (1970) by Al O'Donnell
(guitars)

Albums: Rattlin' & Roarin' Willy,
1968; Tracks of Sweeney, 1969;
Sweeney's Men, 1976

Pub Rock—Irish

Sweet Inspirations

Personnel: Cissy Houston
(vocals); Myrna Smith (vocals);
Estelle Brown (vocals); Sylvia
Shemwell (vocals)

Album: The Sweet Inspirations,
1968

Singles: Why (Am I Treated So
Bad), 1967 **(57)**; Let It Be Me, 1967
(94); That's How Strong My Love
Is, 1967 **(123)**; Sweet Inspiration,
1968 **(18)**; To Love Somebody, 1968
(74); Unchained Melody, 1968 **(73)**;
What the World Needs Now Is
Love, 1968 **(128)**; Crying in the
Rain, 1969 **(112)**; (Gotta Find) A
Brand New Lover—Part 1, 1969
(117); This World, 1970 **(123)**; Love
Is on the Way, 1979 **(104)**

R & B Vocal—American

Sweet Pain

Personnel: Annette Brox (vocals);
Alan Greed (vocals); Stuart Cowell

(guitars); Keith Tillman (bass); Sam
Crozier (keyboards, vocals); Junior
Dunn (drums)

Album: Sweet Pain, 1969

Blues/Rock—British

Sweet Thursday

Personnel: Alun Davies (guitars,
vocals); Jon Mark (guitars, vocals);
Brian Odgers (bass, woodwinds);
Nicky Hopkins (keyboards); Harvey
Burns (drums)

Album: Sweet Thursday, 1969

Hard Rock—British

Sweetwater

Personnel: Nansi Nevins (guitars,
vocals); Fred Herrera (bass, vocals);
Albert B. Moore (flutes, bass); Alex
Delzoppo (keyboards, vocals);
August Burns (cello); Elpidio Co-
bian (percussion); Alan Malarowitz
(drums)

Albums: Sweetwater, 1969; Just
for You, 1970; Melon, 1971

Folk/Rock—American

The Swinging
Blue Jeans

Personnel: Ray Ennis (guitars,
vocals); Ralph Ellis (guitars); Les
Braid (bass); Norman Kuhlke
(drums); added (1964) Terry Sylvester (guitars, vocals)

Albums: Tutti Frutti, 1964; Blue
Jeans a Swinging, 1964; Hippy
Hippy Shake, 1964; Shaking Time,
1964; Hey Hey Hey Hey (Live),
1965; The Swinging Blue Jeans,
1966; Brand New and Faded, 1974;
Swinging Blue Jeans, 1978

Singles: Hippy Hippy Shake, 1964
(24); Good Golly Miss Molly, 1964
(43); You're No Good, 1964 **(97)**;

Promise You'll Tell Her, 1964 **(130)**; Don't Make Me Over, 1966 **(116)**

Pop/Rock—British; band reformed in 1974 without Terry Sylvester

Swingin' Medallions

Personnel: Jimbo Doares (guitars); Jim Perkins (bass, saxophones); John McElrath (keyboards, vocals); Brent Fortson (keyboards, woodwinds); Steve Caldwell (saxophones, keyboards, drums); Carroll Bledsoe (trumpet); Charlie Webber (trumpet); Joe Morris (drums)

Album: Double Shot (of My Baby's Love), 1966

Singles: Double Shot (of My Baby's Love), 1966 **(17)**; She Drives Me Out of My Mind, 1966 **(71)**; I Found a Rainbow, 1967 **(107)**

Pop/Rock—North Carolina

The Syn

Personnel: Steve Nardella (vocals); Peter Banks (guitars) replaced (1967) by Peter Brockland (guitars); Chris Squire (bass); Andrew Jackman (keyboards); Chris Allen (drums) replaced (1967) by Gunnar Hakarnarson (drums)

Album: The Syn, 1967

Progressive Rock—British

Syndicate of Sound

Personnel: Jim Sawyer (guitars, vocals); Bob Gonzales (bass); Don Baskin (saxophones, vocals); John Sharkey (keyboards, guitars); John Duckworth (drums, vocals)

Album: Little Girl, 1966

Singles: Little Girl, 1966 **(8)**;

Syndicate of Sound

Rumors, 1966 **(55)**; Brown Paper Bag, 1970 **(73)**

Psychedelic Rock—California

The Tams

Personnel: Charles Pope (vocals); Joseph Pope (vocals); Robert Smith (vocals); Floyd Ashton (vocals); Horace Key (vocals)

Albums: The Tams, 1963; Hey Girl, 1964; Be Young, Be Foolish, Be Happy, 1968

Singles: Untie Me, 1962 **(60)**; What Kind of Fool (Do You Think I Am), 1963 **(9)**; You Lied to Your Daddy, 1964 **(70)**; It's All Right (You're Just in Love), 1964 **(79)**; Hey Girl Don't Bother Me, 1964 **(41)**; Find Another Love, 1964 **(129)**; Silly Little Girl, 1964 **(87)**; Be Young, Be Foolish, Be Happy, 1968 **(61)**; Trouble Maker, 1968 **(118)**

Soul/Pop Vocal—Atlanta

Norma Tanega

Albums: Walkin' My Cat Named Dog, 1966; I Don't Think It Will Hurt, 1977

Singles: Walkin' My Cat Named Dog, 1966 **(22)**; A Street That Rhymes at 6 A.M., 1966 **(129)**

Folk/Pop—California

The Tarriers

Personnel: Erik Darling (banjo, vocals); Bob Carey (guitars, bass); Alan Arkin (guitars, vocals)

Singles: Cindy, Oh Cindy, 1956 **(9)** (with Vince Martin); The Banana Boat Song, 1956 **(4)**

Pop/Folk—American; Arkin became an actor

The Tassels

Personnel: Rochelle Gaudet (vocals); John Gaudet (vocals); Leo Joyce (vocals); Joe Intelisano (vocals)

Single: To a Soldier Boy, 1959 **(55)**

Pop Vocal—New Jersey

Taste

Personnel: Rory Gallagher (guitars, vocals); Richard McCracken (bass); John Wilson (drums)

Albums: Taste, 1969; On the Boards, 1970; Live Taste, 1970; Taste at the Isle of Wight, 1972; In Concert at the Marquee '68, 1977

Hard/Blues Rock—Irish

Bobby Taylor & The Vancouvers

Personnel: Bobby Taylor (vocals); Tommy Chong (guitars); Eddie Patterson (guitars); Wes Henderson (bass); Robbie King (keyboards); Ted Lewis (drums)

Album: Does Your Mama Know About Us, 1968

Singles: Does Your Mama Know About Me, 1968 **(29)**; I Am Your Man, 1968 **(85)**; Malinda, 1968 **(48)**

Pop/Rock—Canadian; Chong formed comedy recording duo with Cheech Marin

Felice Taylor

Single: It May Be Winter Outside (But in My Heart It's Spring), 1967 **(42)**

Pop Vocal—California

Gloria Taylor

Single: You Got to Pay the Price, 1969 **(49)**

R & B Vocal—American

James Taylor

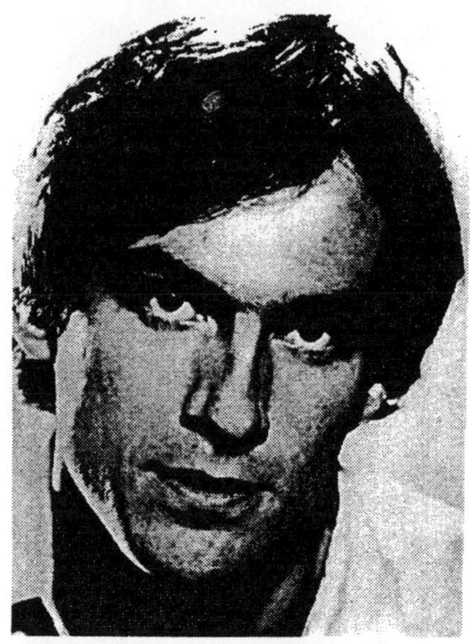

Albums: James Taylor, 1969; Sweet Baby James, 1970; Mud Slide Slim and the Blue Horizon, 1971;

One Man Dog, 1972; Walking Man, 1973; Gorilla, 1975; In the Pocket, 1976; Greatest Hits, 1976; JT, 1977; Flag, 1979; Dad Loves His Work, 1981; That's Why I'm Here, 1985; Never Die Young, 1988; New Moon Shine, 1991

Singles: Carolina in My Mind, 1969 (**118**); Sweet Baby James, 1970; Fire and Rain, 1970 (**3**); Carolina in My Mind, 1970 (**67**); Country Road, 1971 (**37**); You've Got a Friend, 1971 (**1**); Long Ago & Far Away, 1971 (**31**); Don't Let Me Be Lonely Tonight, 1972 (**14**); One Man Parade, 1973 (**67**); Mockingbird, 1975 (**5**) (with Carly Simon); How Sweet It Is (To Be Loved by You), 1975 (**5**); Mexico, 1975 (**49**); Shower the People, 1976 (**22**); Handy Man, 1977 (**4**); Your Smiling Face, 1977 (**20**); Honey Don't Leave L.A., 1978 (**61**); (What a) Wonderful World, 1978 (**17**) (with Paul Simon & Art Garfunkel); Woman's Gotta Have It, 1978; Devoted to You, 1978 (**36**) (with Carly Simon); Up on the Roof, 1979 (**28**); Her Town Too, 1981 (**11**) (with J. D. Souther); Hard Times, 1981 (**72**); Summer's Here, 1981; Everyday, 1985 (**61**); Only One, 1986; That's Why I'm Here, 1986; Baby Boom Baby, 1988; Never Die Young, 1988 (**80**); Copperline, 1991

Pop Vocal — Boston; formerly married to Carly Simon

Johnnie Taylor

Albums: Wanted One Soul Singer, 1968; Rare Stamps, 1968; Who's Making Love, 1969; Raw Blues, 1969; The Johnnie Taylor Philosophy Continues, 1969; Johnnie Taylor's Greatest Hits, 1970; One Step Beyond, 1971; Taylored in

Silk, 1973; Super Taylor, 1974; Eargasm, 1976; Rated Extraordinaire, 1977; Disco 9000, 1978; Ever Ready, 1978; The Johnnie Taylor Chronicle, Volume 1, 1978; The Johnnie Taylor Chronicle, Volume 2, 1978; Reflections, 1979; She's Killing Me, 1979; A New Day, 1980; Best of Johnnie Taylor, 1981

Singles: Rome (Wasn't Built in a Day), 1962 (**112**); Baby, We've Got Love, 1963 (**98**); Somebody's Been Sleeping in My Bed, 1967 (**95**); Who's Making Love, 1968 (**5**); Take Care of Your Homework, 1969 (**20**); Testify (I Wonna), 1969 (**36**); I Could Never Be President, 1969 (**48**); Just Keep on Loving Me, 1969 (**115**) (with Carla Thomas); Love Bones, 1969 (**43**); Steal Away, 1970 (**37**); I Am Somebody, Part II, 1970 (**39**); Jody's Got Your Girl and Gone, 1971 (**28**); I Don't Wanna Lose You, 1971 (**86**); Hijackin' Love, 1971 (**64**); Standing in for Jody, 1972 (**74**); Doin' My Own Thing, 1972 (**109**); Stop Doggin' Me, 1972 (**101**); I Believe in You (You Believe in Me), 1973 (**11**); Cheaper to Keep Her, 1973 (**15**); We're Getting Careless with Our Love, 1974 (**34**); I've Been Born Again, 1974 (**78**); Disco Lady, 1976 (**1**); Somebody's Gettin' It, 1976 (**33**); Love Is Better in the A.M. (Part 1), 1977 (**77**); Disco 9000, 1977 (**86**); Keep on Dancing, 1978 (**101**)

Soul Vocal — Arkansas; "Disco Lady" was banned on many radio stations due to the suggestive nature of the song

Little Johnny Taylor

Albums: Little Johnny Taylor, 1963; Everybody Knows About My Good Thing, 1971; Open House,

1973; Super Taylors, 1974; Little Johnny Taylor, 1979; As Long as I Don't See You, 1980; Part Time Love, 1980; I Shoulda Been a Preacher, 1981; Greatest Hits, 1982

Singles: You'll Need Another Favor, 1963 **(125)**; Part Time Love, 1963 **(19)**; Since I Found a New Love, 1964 **(78)**; If You Love Me (Like You Say), 1964 **(101)**; First Class Love, 1964 **(107)**; Nightingale Melody, 1964 **(109)**; Everybody Knows About My Good Thing, 1971 **(60)**

Soul/Blues Vocal—Memphis; real name is Johnny Young

Ted Taylor

Albums: Ted Taylor & Little Johnny, 1974; Shades of Blue, 1975; Ted Taylor, 1976; Keeping My Head Above Water, 1978; Keep on Walking, 1980

Single: Stay Away from My Baby, 1965 **(99)**

R & B Vocal—Oklahoma; former member of Mighty Clouds of Joy; died in 1987

The T-Bones

Personnel: Dan Hamilton (guitars); Joe Frank Carollo (bass); Tommy Reynolds (keyboards); Joe Correro, Jr. (drums)

Album: No Matter What Shape Your Stomach's In, 1966

Singles: No Matter What Shape (Your Stomach's In), 1965 **(3)**; Sippin' 'n' Chippin', 1966 **(62)**

Instrumental Pop—American; "No Matter What Shape" was from an Alka Seltzer TV commercial

Tea & Symphony

Personnel: Jeff Daw (guitars, flutes, vocals); James Langston (guitars, woodwinds, vocals); Dave "Clem" Clempson (guitars); Mick Hincks (bass, guitars); Ron Chesterman (bass); Nigel Phillips (keyboards, vocals); Bob Lamb (drums)

Albums: An Asylum for the Musically Insane, 1969; Jo Saga, 1970

Hard Rock—British

The Techniques

Single: Hey! Little Girl, 1957 **(29)**

Pop Vocal—American

Teddy & The Pandas

Album: Teddy & the Pandas, 1966

Singles: Once Upon a Time, 1966 **(134)**; We Can't Go on This Way, 1966 **(103)**; Searchin' for the Goodtimes, 1966

Pop/Rock—Massachusetts

The Teddy Bears

Personnel: Phil Spector (vocals); Annette "Carol Connors" Kleinbard (vocals); Marshall Leib (vocals)

Album: Teddy Bears Sing, 1958

Singles: To Know Him, Is to Love Him, 1958 **(1)**; I Don't Need You Anymore, 1959 **(98)**; Oh Why, 1959 **(91)**

Pop Vocal—Los Angeles

The Teen Queens

Personnel: Betty Collins (vocals); Rosie Collins (vocals)

Single: Eddie My Love, 1956 **(14)**

R & B Vocal—Los Angeles

Nino Tempo & April Stevens

Albums: Deep Purple, 1963; Stardust, 1964

Singles: Sweet and Lovely, 1962 **(77)**; Paradise, 1963 **(126)**; Deep Purple, 1963 **(1)**; Whispering, 1963 **(11)**; Stardust, 1964 **(32)**; Tea for Two, 1964 **(56)**; I'm Confessin' (That I Love You), 1964 **(99)**; Ooh La La, 1964 **(113)**; Swing Me, 1965 **(127)**; All Strung Out, 1966 **(26)**; You'll Be Needing Me Baby, 1967 **(133)**; My Old Flame, 1967 **(101)**; I Can't Go on Livin' Baby Without You, 1967 **(86)**; Let It Be Me, 1968 **(127)**; Love Story, 1972 **(113)**; Put It Where You Want It, 1973 **(122)**; Sister James, 1973 **(53)**

Pop Vocal—New York; real names are Antonio and Carol Lo Tiempo, brother and sister

The Tempos

Personnel: Mike Lazo (vocals); Jim Drake (vocals); Gene Schachter (vocals); Tom Minoto (vocals)

Single: See You in September, 1959 **(23)**

Pop Vocal—Pittsburgh

The Temptations

Personnel: Neil Stevens (vocals); Artie Martin (vocals); Larry Curtis (vocals); Artie Sands (vocals)

Single: Barbara, 1960 **(29)**

Pop Vocal—New York

The Temptations

Personnel: Otis "Miles" Williams (vocals); Eddie Kendricks (vocals) replaced (1970) by Ricky Owens (vocals) replaced (1971) by Damon Harris (vocals) replaced (1975) by Glenn Leonard (vocals) replaced (1988) by Ron Tyson (vocals); Paul Williams (vocals; deceased 1973) replaced (1971) by Richard Street (vocals); Melvin "David English" Franklin (vocals); Eldridge Bryant (vocals) replaced (1963) by David Ruffin (vocals; deceased 1991) replaced (1967) by Dennis Edwards (vocals) replaced (1977) by Louis Price (vocals) replaced (1979) by Dennis Edwards (vocals) replaced (1984) by Ali Ollie Woodson (vocals) replaced (1988) by Dennis Edwards (vocals)

Albums: Meet the Temptations, 1964; The Temptations Sing Smokey, 1965; Temptin' Temptations, 1965; Gettin' Ready, 1966; The Temptations Greatest Hits, 1966; Temptations Live!, 1967; With a Lot o' Soul, 1967; The Temptations in a Mellow Mood, 1967; Wish It Would Rain, 1968; Diana Ross & the Supremes Join the Temptations, 1968; TCB, 1968 (with Diana Ross & the Supremes); Live at the Copa, 1969; Cloud Nine, 1969; The Temptations Show, 1969; Puzzle People, 1969; Together, 1969 (with Diana Ross & the Supremes); On Broadway, 1969 (with Diana Ross & the Supremes); Psychedelic Shack, 1970; Live at London's Talk of the Town, 1970; Temptations Greatest Hits II, 1970; Sky's the Limit, 1971; Solid Rock, 1972; All Directions, 1972; Masterpiece, 1973; Anthology, 1973; 1990, 1973; A Song for You, 1975; House Party, 1975; Wings of Love, 1976; The Temptations Do the Temptations, 1976; Hear to Tempt You, 1977; Greatest Hits III, 1978; Bare Back, 1978; Power, 1980; 20 Golden Greats, 1980; The Temptations, 1981; Reunion, 1982; Surface Thrills, 1983; Back to Basics,

1984; Truly for You, 1984; To Be Continued, 1985; All the Million Sellers, 1986; 25th Anniversary, 1987; Milestone, 1991

Singles: Paradise, 1962 **(122)**; The Way You Do the Things You Do, 1964 **(11)**; The Girl's Alright with Me, 1964 **(102)**; I'll Be in Trouble, 1964 **(33)**; Girl (Why You Wanna Make Me Blue), 1964 **(26)**; My Girl, 1965 **(1)**; It's Growing, 1965 **(18)**; Since I Lost My Baby, 1965 **(17)**; You've Got to Earn It, 1965 **(123)**; My Baby, 1965 **(13)**; Don't Look Back, 1965 **(83)**; Get Ready, 1966 **(29)**; Ain't Too Proud to Beg, 1966 **(13)**; Beauty Is Only Skin Deep, 1966 **(3)**; (I Know) I'm Losing You, 1966 **(8)**; All I Need, 1967 **(8)**; You're My Everything, 1967 **(6)**; I've Been Good to You, 1967 **(124)**; (Loneliness Made Me Realize) It's You That I Need, 1967 **(14)**; I Wish It Would Rain, 1968 **(4)**; I Truly, Truly Believe, 1968 **(116)**; I Could Never Love Another (After Loving You), 1968 **(13)**; Please Return Your Love to Me, 1968 **(26)**; Cloud Nine, 1968 **(6)**; I'm Gonna Make You Love Me, 1968 **(2)**; Run Away Child, Running Wild, 1969 **(6)**; I'll Try Something New, 1969 **(25)**; Don't Let the Joneses Get You Down, 1969 **(20)**; I Can't Get Next to You, 1969 **(1)**; The Weight, 1969 **(46)** (with Diana Ross & the Supremes); Psychedelic Shack, 1970 **(7)**; Ball of Confusion (That's What the World Is Today), 1970 **(3)**; Ungena Za Ulimwnegu (Unite the World), 1970 **(33)**; Just My Imagination (Running Away with Me), 1971 **(1)**; It's Summer, 1971 **(51)**; Superstar (Remember How You Got Where You Are), 1971 **(18)**; Take a Look Around, 1972 **(30)**; Mother Nature, 1972 **(1)**;

Papa Was a Rollin' Stone, 1972 **(1)**; Masterpiece, 1973 **(7)**; The Plastic Man, 1973 **(40)**; Hey Girl (I Like Your Style), 1973 **(35)**; Let Your Hair Down, 1973 **(27)**; Heavenly, 1974 **(43)**; You've Got My Soul on Fire, 1974 **(74)**; Happy People, 1974 **(40)**; Shakey Ground, 1975 **(26)**; Glasshouse, 1975 **(37)**; Keep Holding On, 1976 **(54)**; Up the Creek (Without a Paddle), 1976 **(94)**; Power, 1980 **(43)**; Aiming at Your Heart, 1981 **(67)**; Oh What a Night, 1981 **(104)**; Standing on the Top — Part 1, 1982 **(66)** (with Rick James); Love on My Mind Tonight, 1983 **(88)**; Sail Away, 1984 **(54)**; Treat Her Like a Lady, 1984 **(48)**; Lady Soul, 1986 **(47)**

Soul/R & B Vocal — Detroit

Ten Wheel Drive

Personnel: Genya Ravan (vocals) replaced (1974) by Annie Sutton (vocals); Aram Schefrin (guitars, vocals); Bill Taxas (bass) replaced (1970) by Bob Piazza (bass) replaced (1971) by Blake Hines (bass); Michael Zager (keyboards); Dennis Parisi (trombone) replaced (1971) by Tom Malone (trombone) replaced (1974) by Gerry Chamberlain (trombone); Richard Meisterman (trumpet) replaced (1971) by Dean Pratt (trumpet); Louis Hoff (saxophones) replaced (1970) by David Liebman (saxophones) replaced (1971) by Alan Gauvin (saxophones) replaced (1974) by Ed Xiques (saxophones); Leon Rix (drums, cello) replaced (1970) by Allen Herman (drums) replaced (1971) by David Williams (drums) replaced (1974) by Barry Lararowitz (drums)

Albums: Construction #1, 1969; Brief Replies, 1970; Peculiar

Friends, 1971; Ten Wheel Drive, 1974

Single: Morning Much Better, 1970 **(74)**

Jazz/Blues Rock—New York; Ravan's real name is Goldie Zelkowitz

Ten Years After

Personnel: Alvin Lee (guitars, vocals); Leo Lyons (bass) replaced (1974) by Steve Thompson (bass) replaced (1975) by Andy Pyle (bass) replaced (1978) by Mick Hawksworth (bass) replaced (1980) by Mickey Feat (bass) replaced (1982) by Calvin "Fuzzy" Samuels (bass) replaced (1989) by Leo Lyons (bass); Chick Churchill (keyboards) replaced (1973) by Tim Hinkley (keyboards) replaced (1975) by Ronnie Leahy (keyboards) replaced (1980) by Steve Gould (guitars, vocals) replaced (1982) by Mick Taylor (guitars) replaced (1989) by Chick Churchill (keyboards); Ric Lee (drums) replaced (1973) by Ian Wallace (drums) replaced (1978) by Bryson Graham (drums) replaced (1978) by Tom Compton (drums) replaced (1989) by Ric Lee (drums)

Albums: Ten Years After, 1967; Undead, 1968; Stonehenge, 1969; Ssshh, 1969; Cricklewood Green, 1970; Watt, 1970; A Space in Time, 1972; Rock and Roll Music to the World, 1972; Recorded Live, 1973; Road to Freedom, 1973; Positive Vibrations, 1974; Alvin Lee & Company in Flight, 1974; Goin' Home, 1975; Pump Iron, 1975; Anthology, 1976; The Classic Performance, 1977; Saguitar, 1976; Rocket Fuel, 1978; Let It Rock, 1978; Ride On, 1979; Freefall, 1980; Hear Me Calling, 1981; RX5, 1981; About Time, 1989; The Essential Collection, 1991

Singles: Love Like a Man, 1970 **(98)**; I'd Love to Change the World, 1971 **(40)**; Baby, Won't You Let Me Rock 'n' Roll You, 1972 **(61)**; Choo Choo Man, 1972 **(89)**; Can't Stop, 1982

Hard Rock—British; original group reformed in 1989

Tammi Terrell

Albums: United, 1968; You're All I Need, 1968; Irresistible, 1969; Easy, 1969; Greatest Hits, 1970 (all above recorded with Marvin Gaye)

Singles: I Cried, 1963 **(99)**; I Can't Believe You Love Me, 1966 **(72)**; Come on and See Me, 1966 **(80)**; Ain't No Mountain High Enough, 1967 **(19)** (with Marvin Gaye); Your Precious Love, 1967 **(5)** (with Marvin Gaye); If I Could Build My Whole World Around You, 1967 **(10)** (with Marvin Gaye); If This World Were Mine, 1968 **(68)** (with Marvin Gaye); Ain't Nothing Like the Real Thing, 1968 **(8)** (with Marvin Gaye); You're All I Need to Get By, 1968 **(7)** (with Marvin Gaye); Keep on Lovin' Me Honey, 1968 **(24)** (with Marvin Gaye); This Old Heart of Mine (Is Weak for You), 1969 **(67)**; What You Gave Me, 1969 **(49)** (with Marvin Gaye); The Onion Song/ California Soul, 1970 **(50)** (with Marvin Gaye)

Soul/Pop Vocal—Philadelphia; Tammi died 3/16/70 from a brain tumor

Joe Tex

Albums: Hold What You've Got, 1965; The New Boss, 1965; The Love You Save, 1966; I've Got to Do a Little Bit Better, 1967; The Best of Joe Tex, 1967; Live and

Lively, 1968; Soul Country, 1968; Happy Soul, 1969; Buying a Book, 1969; Sings with Strings, 1970; From the Roots Came the Rapper, 1970; I Gotcha, 1972; Bumps & Bruises, 1977; Rub Down, 1978; Super Soul, 1979

Singles: All I Could Do Was Cry, 1960 **(102)**; Hold What You've Got, 1964 **(5)**; You Better Get It, 1965 **(46)**; You Got What It Takes, 1965 **(51)**; A Woman Can Change a Man, 1965 **(56)**; Don't Let Your Left Hand Know, 1965 **(95)**; One Monkey Don't Stop No Show, 1965 **(65)**; I Want To (Do Everything for You), 1965 **(23)**; A Sweet Woman Like You, 1965 **(29)**; The Love You Save (May Be Your Own), 1966 **(56)**; S.Y.S.L.J.F.M. (The Letter Song), 1966 **(39)**; I Believe I'm Gonna Make It, 1966 **(67)**; I've Got to Do a Little Bit Better, 1966 **(64)**; Papa Was Too, 1966 **(44)**; Show Me, 1967 **(35)**; Woman Like That, Yeah, 1967 **(54)**; A Woman's Hands, 1967 **(63)**; Skinny Legs and All, 1967 **(10)**; Men Are Gettin' Scarce, 1968 **(33)**; I'll Never Do You Wrong, 1968 **(59)**; Keep the One You Got, 1968 **(52)**; You Need Me, Baby, 1968 **(81)**; That's Your Baby, 1969 **(88)**; Buying a Book, 1969 **(47)**; That's the Way, 1969 **(94)**; It Ain't Sanitary, 1969 **(117)**; I Can't See You No More (When Johnny Comes Marching Home Again), 1969 **(105)**; Give the Baby Anything the Baby Wants, 1971 **(102)**; I Gotcha, 1972 **(2)**; You Said a Bad Word, 1972 **(41)**; Woman Stealer, 1973 **(103)**; Ain't Gonna Bump No More (with No Big Fat Woman), 1977 **(12)**

Soul/Funk Vocal—Texas; real name was Joseph Arrington, Jr.; died of heart attack 8/13/82

The Texans

Personnel: Johnny Burnette (vocals; deceased 1964); Dorsey Burnette (vocals; deceased 1979)
Single: Green Grass of Texas, 1961 **(100)**

Rockabilly—Memphis

Thee Prophets

Personnel: Brian Lake (vocals)
Album: Playgirl, 1969
Singles: Playgirl, 1969 **(49)**; Some Kind-a Wonderful, 1969 **(111)**

Pop/Rock—Milwaukee

Them

Personnel: Van Morrison (vocals, saxophones) replaced (1967) by Keith McDowell (vocals) replaced (1972) by Jerry Cole (vocals); William Harrison (guitars) replaced (1968) by Jim Armstrong (guitars) replaced (1973) by Jim Parker (guitars); Jackie McAuley (keyboards) replaced (1971) by Ray Elliot (keyboards) replaced (1972) by Peter Bardens (keyboards); Ronnie Millings (drums) replaced (1964) by Pat McAuley (drums) replaced (1968) by John Wilson (drums) replaced (1971) by David Harvey (drums) replaced (1973) by John Stark (drums); Alan Henderson (bass)
Albums: Angry Young Them, 1965; Them, 1965; Them Again, 1966; Now & Them, 1968; Time Out, Time in for Them, 1968; World of Them, 1970; Them, 1970; Them in Reality, 1971; The Beginning, 1972; Bad or Good, 1972; Them, 1973; Backtrackin', 1974; Rock Roots, 1976; Belfast Gypsies, 1977; Story of Them, 1977
Singles: Baby Please Don't Go, 1965 **(102)**; Here Comes the Night,

1965 **(24)**; Mystic Eyes, 1965 **(33)**;
Gloria, 1966 **(71)**
   Blues/Rock—Irish

Third Rail

Personnel: Joey Levine (vocals);
Kris Resnick (vocals); Artie Resnick
(keyboards, vocals)
   Album: In Music, 1967
   Singles: Run, Run, Run, 1967
(53); It's Time to Say Goodbye,
1968 **(113)**
   Bubblegum Pop—American

The 13th Floor Elevators

Personnel: Roky Erickson (vocals); Tommy Hall (jug); Stacy
Sutherland (guitars); Benny Thur-
man (bass, violin) replaced (1968) by
Don Galindo (bass); Ronnie
Leatherman (drums) replaced (1968)
by Danny Thomas (drums)
   Albums: The Psychedelic Sounds
of the Thirteenth Floor Elevators,
1966; Easter Everywhere, 1968; 13th
Floor Elevators Live, 1968; Bull of
the Woods, 1969; Avalon 66, 1977
   Single: You're Gonna Miss Me,
1966 **(55)**
   Pop/Rock—Texas

B. J. Thomas

Albums: I'm So Lonesome I
Could Cry, 1966; On My Way,
1969; Young and in Love, 1969;
Greatest Hits Volume 1, 1969; Raindrops Keep Fallin' on My Head,
1970; Everybody's Out of Town,
1970; Most of All, 1970; Greatest
Hits Volume 2, 1971; Billy Joe
Thomas, 1972; Rock 'n' Roll Lullaby, 1972; B. J. Thomas Country,
1972; Songs, 1973; Longhorn &

B. J. Thomas

London Bridges, 1974; Reunion,
1975; Help Me Make It, 1975; B. J.
Thomas, 1977; ABC Collection,
1977; Home Where I Belong, 1977;
Everybody Loves, 1978; Happy
Man, 1979; New Looks, 1983; Mid-
night Minute, 1989
   Singles: I'm So Lonesome I Could
Cry, 1966 **(8)**; Mama, 1966 **(22)**;
Billy and Sue, 1966 **(34)**; Bring
Back the Time, 1966 **(75)**; Tomor-
row Never Comes, 1966 **(80)**; Plain
Jane, 1966 **(129)**; I Can't Help It (If
I'm Still in Love with You), 1967
(94); The Eyes of a New York
Woman, 1968 **(28)**; Hooked on a
Feeling, 1968 **(5)**; It's Only Love,
1969 **(45)**; Pass the Apple Eve, 1969
(97); Raindrops Keep Fallin' on
My Head, 1969 **(1)**; Everybody's
Out of Town, 1970 **(26)**; I Just
Can't Help Believing, 1970 **(9)**;
Most of All, 1970 **(38)**; No Love at
All, 1971 **(16)**; Mighty Clouds of
Joy, 1971 **(34)**; Long Ago Tomor-
row, 1971 **(61)**; Rock and Roll Lul-
laby, 1972 **(15)**; That's What Friends
Are For, 1972 **(74)**; Happier Than
the Morning Sun, 1972 **(100)**;
Another Somebody Done Somebody
Wrong Song, 1975 **(1)**; Help Me
Make It (to My Rockin' Chair),

1975 **(64)**; Don't Worry Baby, 1977 **(17)**; Still the Lovin' Is Fun, 1977 **(77)**; Everybody Loves a Rain Song, 1978 **(43)**; Some Love Songs Never Die, 1981; I Recall a Gypsy Woman, 1981; The Unclouded Day, 1981; But Love Me, 1982; Whatever Happened to Old Fashioned Love, 1983 **(93)**; New Looks from an Old Lover, 1983; The Whole World's in Love When You're Lonely, 1984; The Girl Most Likely To, 1984; The Part of Me That Needs You Most, 1985; America Is, 1986

Pop/Soft Rock Vocal—Oklahoma; B. J. stands for Billy Joe

Carla Thomas

Albums: Gee Whiz, 1961; Comfort Me, 1966; Carla, 1966; King & Queen, 1967 (with Otis Redding); The Queen Alone, 1967; Memphis Queen, 1969; Best of Carla Thomas, 1969; Love Means, 1971; Chronicle, 1979

Singles: Gee Whiz (Look at His Eyes), 1961 **(10)**; A Love of My Own, 1961 **(56)**; I'll Bring It Home to You, 1962 **(41)**; What a Fool I've Been, 1963 **(93)**; That's Really Some Good, 1964 **(92)** (with Rufus Thomas); Night Time Is the Right Time, 1964 **(94)** (with Rufus Thomas); I've Got No Time to Lose, 1964 **(67)**; A Woman's Love, 1964 **(71)**; Stop! What You're Doing, 1965 **(92)**; Let Me Be Good to You, 1966 **(62)**; B-A-B-Y, 1966 **(14)**; Something Good (Is Going to Happen to You), 1967 **(74)**; Tramp, 1967 **(26)** (with Otis Redding); When Tomorrow Comes, 1967 **(99)**; I'll Always Have Faith in You, 1967 **(85)**; Knock on Wood, 1967 **(30)** (with Otis Redding); Pick Up the Pieces, 1967 **(68)**; Lovey Dovey,

1968 **(60)** (with Otis Redding); Dime a Dozen, 1968 **(114)**; Where Do I Go, 1968 **(86)**; I Like What You're Doing (To Me), 1969 **(49)**; When Something Is Wrong with My Baby, 1969 **(109)** (with Otis Redding); I Need You Woman, 1969 **(106)** (with William Bell); Just Keep on Loving Me, 1969 **(115)** (with Johnnie Taylor); I've Fallen in Love, 1969 **(117)**; Guide Me Well, 1970 **(107)**

Soul/Pop Vocal—Memphis; daughter of Rufus Thomas

Gene Thomas

Singles: Sometime, 1961 **(53)**; Baby's Gone, 1963 **(84)**

Pop Vocal—Texas

Irma Thomas

Albums: Wish Someone Would Care, 1964; Take a Look, 1965; Time Is on My Side, 1966; In Between Tears, 1973; Live, 1976; Soul Queen of New Orleans, 1977; Safe with Me, 1979; Irma Thomas Sings, 1979; Hip Shakin' Mama, 1980

Singles: Wish Someone Would Care, 1964 **(17)**; Anyone Who Knows What Love Is (Will Understand), 1964 **(52)**; Times Have Changed, 1964 **(98)**; He's My Guy, 1964 **(63)**; You Don't Miss a Good Thing, 1965 **(109)**; I'm Gonna Cry Till My Tears Run Dry, 1965 **(130)**; Take a Look, 1965 **(118)**; It's a Man's-Woman's World, 1966 **(119)**

Soul Vocal—Louisiana

Jon Thomas

Single: Heartbreak (It's Hurtin' Me), 1960 **(48)**

Blues/Soul—Cleveland

Rufus Thomas

Albums: Walking the Dog, 1963; May I Have Your Ticket Please, 1969; Funky Chicken, 1970; Rufus Thomas Live/Doing the Push & Pull at P. J.'s, 1971; Did You Hear Me, 1973; Clown Prince of Dance, 1974; I Ain't Gettin' Older, 1976; If There Were No Music, 1977; Chronicle, 1979 (with Carla Thomas)

Singles: The Dog, 1963 **(87)**; Walking the Dog, 1963 **(10)**; Can Your Monkey Do the Dog, 1964 **(48)**; Somebody Stole My Dog, 1964 **(86)**; That's Really Some Good, 1964 **(92)** (with Carla Thomas); Night Time Is the Right Time, 1964 **(94)** (with Carla Thomas); Jump Back, 1964 **(49)**; Do the Funky Chicken, 1970 **(28)**; (Do the) Push and Pull (Part 1) 1970 **(25)**; The Breakdown (Part 1), 1971 **(31)**; Do the Funky Penguin (Part 1), 1971 **(44)**

R & B Vocal—Memphis; father of Carla Thomas

Sue Thompson

Album: Paper Tiger, 1965

Singles: Sad Movies (Make Me Cry), 1961 **(5)**; Norman, 1961 **(3)**; Two of a Kind, 1962 **(42)**; If the Boy Only Knew, 1962 **(112)**; Have a Good Time, 1962 **(31)**; James (Hold the Ladder Steady), 1962 **(17)**; Willie Can, 1963 **(78)**; What's Wrong Bill, 1963 **(105)**; Big Daddy, 1964 **(132)**; Paper Tiger, 1965 **(23)**; Stop th' Music, 1965 **(115)**; Put It Back, 1966 **(131)**

Country/Pop Vocal—Missouri; real name Eva Sue McKee

The Three Chuckles

Personnel: Teddy Randazzo (accordion, vocals); Tom Romano (guitars, vocals); Russ Gilberto (bass, vocals)

Singles: Times Two, I Love You, 1955 **(67)**; And the Angels Sing, 1956 **(70)**

Pop—New York

Three Dog Night

Personnel: Chuck Negron (vocals); Danny Hutton (vocals); Cory Wells (vocals); Mike Allsup (guitars) replaced (1975) by James Smith (guitars); Joe Schermie (bass) replaced (1974) by Jack Ryland (bass) replaced (1975) by Dennis Belfield (bass); Jim Greenspoon (keyboards) replaced (1974) by Skip Konte (keyboards); Floyd Sneed (drums, percussion) replaced (1975) by Micky McMeel (drums)

Albums: Three Dog Night, 1969; Suitable for Framing, 1969; Live at the Forum, 1970; It Ain't Easy, 1970; Naturally, 1971; Golden Biscuits, 1971; Harmony, 1971; Seven Separate Fools, 1972; Around the World, 1973; Cyan, 1974; Hard Labor, 1974; Joy to the World/Greatest Hits, 1974; Dog Style, 1974; Coming Down Your Way, 1975; American Pastime, 1976; Golden Greats of 3 Dog Night, 1979; The Best of Three Dog Night, 1982; It's a Jungle, 1983

Singles: Nobody, 1969 **(116)**; Try a Little Tenderness, 1969 **(29)**; One, 1969 **(5)**; Easy to Be Hard, 1969 **(4)**; Eli's Coming, 1969 **(10)**; Celebrate, 1970 **(15)**; Mama Told Me Not to Come, 1970 **(1)**; Out in the Country, 1970 **(15)**; One Man Band, 1970 **(19)**; Joy to the World, 1971 **(1)**; It Ain't Easy, 1971; Liar, 1971 **(7)**; An Old Fashioned Love Song, 1971 **(4)**; Never Been to Spain, 1971 **(5)**; The Family of Man, 1972 **(12)**; I'd Be So

Three Dog Night: Hutton, Negron, Schermie, Allsup, Sneed, Wells, Greenspoon

Happy, 1972; Black and White, 1972 **(1)**; Pieces of April, 1972 **(19)**; Shambala, 1973 **(3)**; Let Me Serenade You, 1973 **(17)**; The Show Must Go On, 1974 **(4)**; Sure as I Am Sitting Here, 1974 **(16)**; Play Something Sweet, 1974 **(33)**; 'Til the World Ends, 1975 **(32)**; Everybody Is a Masterpiece, 1976; It's a Jungle Out There, 1983

Pop/Rock — Los Angeles

The Three G's

Personnel: Jerry Glasser (vocals); Robert Glasser (vocals); Ted Glasser (vocals)

Single: Let's Go Steady for the Summer, 1958 **(55)**

Pop Vocal — Los Angeles

Johnny Thunder

Album: Loop de Loop, 1962

Singles: Loop de Loop, 1962 **(4)**; The Rosy Dance, 1963 **(122)**; Hey Child, 1963 **(118)**; Send Her to Me, 1964 **(121)**; Everybody Do the Sloopy, 1965 **(67)**; My Prayer, 1966 **(106)**; Make Love to Me, 1967 **(96)** (with Ruby Winters); I'm Alive, 1969 **(122)**

R & B Vocal — Florida; real name is Gil Hamilton

Thunderclap Newman

Personnel: Andy Newman (keyboards); Jimmy McCulloch (guitars, vocals; deceased 1979); Jack McCulloch (drums); John "Speedy" Keen (vocals, drums); Jim Avery (bass)

Album: Hollywood Dream, 1969

Singles: Something in the Air, 1969 **(37)**; Something in the Air, 1970 **(120)**

Hard/Blues Rock — British

The Tikis

Personnel: Ted Templeman (guitars, vocals); Eddie James (guitars); Dick Scoppettone (guitars); Dick Yount (bass); John Peterson (drums)

Single: I Must Be Dreaming, 1966

Pop/Rock — California

Johnny Tillotson

Albums: Poetry in Motion, 1960; Without You, 1961; Johnny Tillotson's Best, 1962; It Keeps Right on a-Hurtin', 1962; Talk Back Trembling Lips, 1964; She Understands Me, 1965

Singles: Well I'm Your Man, 1958 **(87)**; Dreamy Eyes, 1958 **(63)**; True True Happiness, 1959 **(54)**; Why Do I Love You So, 1960 **(42)**; Earth Angel, 1960 **(57)**; Pledging My Love, 1960 **(63)**; Poetry in Motion, 1960 **(2)**; Jimmy's Girl, 1961 **(25)**; Without You, 1961 **(7)**; Dreamy Eyes, 1961 **(35)**; It Keep Right on a-Hurtin', 1962 **(3)**; Send Me the Pillow You Dream On, 1962 **(17)**; What'll I Do, 1962 **(106)**; I Can't Help It (If I'm Still in Love with You), 1962 **(24)**; I'm So Lonesome I Could Cry, 1962 **(89)**; Out of My Mind, 1963 **(24)**; You Can Never Stop Me from Loving You, 1963 **(18)**; Funny How Time Slips Away, 1963 **(50)**; Talk Back Trembling Lips, 1963 **(7)**; Please Don't Go Away, 1964 **(112)**; Worried Guy, 1964 **(37)**; I Rise, I Fall, 1964 **(36)**; Worry, 1964 **(45)**; She Understands Me, 1964 **(31)**; Angel, 1965 **(51)**; Then I'll Count Again, 1965 **(86)**; Heartaches by the Number, 1965 **(35)**; Our World, 1965 **(70)**; Hello Enemy, 1966 **(128)**; Tears on My Pillow, 1969 **(119)**; Apple Bend, 1971 **(127)**

Pop/Country Vocal — Florida; appeared in film *Just for Fun*

The Timetones

Personnel: Roger LaRue (vocals)
Single: In My Heart, 1961 **(51)**
Pop Vocal — New York

Tiny Tim

Album: God Bless Tiny Tim, 1968

Singles: Tip-Toe Thru' the Tulips with Me, 1968 **(17)**; Bring Back Those Rockabye Baby Days, 1968 **(95)**; Hello, Hello, 1968 **(122)**; Great Balls of Fire, 1969 **(85)**

Novelty Pop — New York; real name is Herbert Khaury

Nick Todd

Singles: Plaything, 1957 **(41)**; At the Hop, 1957 **(21)**

Pop Vocal — Florida; real name is Nick Boone; younger brother of Pat Boone

The Tokens

Personnel: Hank Medress (vocals) left group (1970); Neil Sedaka (vocals) replaced (1960) by Mitch Margo (vocals); Eddie Rabkin (vocals replaced (1956) by Jay Siegel (vocals); Cynthia Zolitin (vocals) replaced (1960) by Phil Margo (vocals)

Albums: The Lion Sleeps Tonight, 1962; I Hear Trumpets Blow, 1966; Back to Back, 1967 (with the Happenings)

Singles: Tonight I Fell in Love, 1961 **(15)**; The Taste of a Tear, 1961 **(112)**; Sincerely, 1961 **(120)**; The Lion Sleeps Tonight, 1961 **(1)**; B'wa Nina (Pretty Girl), 1962 **(55)**; La Bomba, 1962 **(85)**; Tonight I Met an Angel, 1963 **(126)**; Hear the Bells, 1963 **(94)**; Please Write, 1963 **(108)**; Swing, 1964 **(105)**; He's in Town, 1964 **(43)**; The Three Bells, 1965 **(120)**; I Hear Trumpets Blow, 1966 **(30)**; The Greatest Moments in a Girl's Life, 1966 **(102)**; Life Is Groovy, 1967 **(110)** (with the Kirby

Stone Four); Portrait of My Love, 1967 **(36)**; It's a Happening World, 1967 **(69)**; Go Away Little Girl/ Young Girl (medley), 1969 **(118)**; She Lets Her Hair Down (Early in the Morning), 1969 **(61)**; Don't Worry Baby, 1970 **(95)**
Pop Vocal — New York

Tom & Jerrio

Personnel: Robert "Tommy Dark" Tharp (vocals); Jerry "Jerrio" Murray (vocals)
Singles: Boo-Ga-Loo, 1965 **(47)**; Great Goo-Ga-Moo-Ga, 1965 **(123)**
R & B Vocal — American

Tomorrow

Personnel: Steve Howe (guitars); Keith West (vocals); John Wood (bass); Mark Wirtz (keyboards) replaced (1968) by John Burgess (keyboards, guitars); John "Twink" Alder (drums) replaced (1968) by Ken Lawrence (drums)
Album: Tomorrow, 1968
Progressive Rock — British

Oscar Toney, Jr.

Album: For Precious Love, 1967
Singles: For Your Precious Love, 1967 **(23)**; Turn on Your Love Light, 1967 **(65)**; You Can Lead Your Woman to the Altar, 1967 **(120)**; Without Love (There Is Nothing), 1968 **(90)**; Never Get Enough of Your Love, 1968 **(95)**
R & B Vocal — Alabama

Tony & Joe

Personnel: Tony Savonne (vocals); Joe Saraceno (vocals)
Single: The Freeze, 1958 **(33)**
Pop Vocal — New York

The Tornadoes

Personnel: George Bellamy (guitars); Heinz Burt (guitars, bass); Alan Caddy (guitars); Roger Laverne Jackson (keyboards); Clem Cattini (drums)
Albums: Sound of the Tornadoes, 1962; The Original Telstar, 1963; More Sounds from the Tornadoes, 1963; Tornado Rock, 1963; Away from It All, 1963
Singles: Telstar, 1962 **(1)**; Ridin' the Wind, 1963 **(63)**; Like Locomotion, 1963 **(119)**
Surf Rock — British

Mitchell Torok

Singles: Pledge of Love, 1957 **(25)**; Caribbean, 1959 **(27)**; Mexican Joe, 1959 **(102)**; Pink Chiffon, 1960 **(60)**
Country/Pop — Houston

Ed Townsend

Singles: For Your Love, 1958 **(13)**; When I Grow Too Old to Dream, 1958 **(59)**; Hold On, 1959 **(106)**; Stay with Me (A Little While

Longer), 1960 **(101)**; And Then
Came Love, 1961 **(114)**
　R & B Vocal—Tennessee

The Toy Dolls

Personnel: Susan Leslie (vocals);
Libby Redwine (vocals)
　Single: Little Tin Soldier, 1962
(84)
　Pop Vocal—Los Angeles

The Toys

Personnel: Barbara Harris (vocals); June Montiero (vocals); Barbara Parritt (vocals)
　Album: The Toys Sing "A
Lover's Concerto" and "Attack,"
1966
　Singles: A Lover's Concerto, 1965
(2); Attack, 1965 **(18)**; May My
Heart Be Cast Into Stone, 1966
(85); Silver Spoon, 1966 **(111)**; Baby
Toys, 1966 **(76)**; Sealed with a Kiss,
1968 **(112)**
　Pop/Soul Vocal—New York; appeared on "Shindig" TV show and
film *The Girl in Daddy's Bikini*

The Trade Winds

Personnel: Peter Anders (vocals);
Vinnie Poncia (vocals)
　Albums: The Tradewinds, 1965;
Mind Excursion, 1966
　Singles: New York's a Lonely
Town, 1965 **(32)**; The Girl from
Greenwich Village, 1965 **(129)**;
Mind Excursion, 1966 **(51)**; Catch
Me in the Meadow, 1966 **(132)**
　Pop Vocal—New York

The Tradewinds

Personnel: Ralph Rizzoli (vocals);
Angel Cifelli (vocals); Phil Mehill

(vocals); Sal Capriglione (vo-
cals)
　Single: Furry Murray, 1959 **(91)**
　Pop Vocal—New Jersey

Traffic

Personnel: Steve Winwood (keyboards, vocals, guitars); Dave
Mason (guitars, vocals) left group
(1968) rejoined (1971) left group
(1972); Chris Wood (saxophones,
flutes; deceased 1983); Jim Capaldi
(drums, vocals); added (1970) Ric
Grech (bass, vocals, violin) replaced
(1971) by David Hood (bass) replaced (1974) by Rosco Gee (bass);
added (1971) Reebop Kwaku Baah
(percussion) left group (1973); added
(1971) Jim Gordon (drums) replaced
(1971) by Roger Hawkins (drums)
left group (1974); added (1973) Barry
Beckett (keyboards) left group (1974)
　Albums: Mr. Fantasy, 1967;
Traffic, 1968; Last Exit, 1968; Best
of Traffic, 1969; John Barleycorn
Must Die, 1970; Live, 1970;
Welcome to the Canteen, 1971; The
Low Spark of High-Heeled Boys,
1972; Shootout at the Fantasy Factory, 1973; On the Road, 1974;
When the Eagle Flies, 1974; Heavy
Traffic, 1975; More Heavy Traffic,
1975; Hole in My Shoe, 1978
　Singles: Feelin' Alright, 1967;
Paper Sun, 1967 **(94)**; Feelin'
Alright, 1968 **(123)**; Empty Pages,
1970 **(74)**; Gimme Some Lovin',
1971 **(68)**; Rock & Roll Stew, 1972
(93); The Low Spark of High-
Heeled Boys, 1972
　Jazz/Blues Rock—British

Tramline

Personnel: John McCoy (vocals,
harmonica); Terry Sidgwick (bass,

vocals); Micky Moody (guitars); Terry Popple (drums)
Albums: Somewhere Down the Line, 1968; Moves of Vegetable Centuries, 1969
Hard Rock—British

The Trashmen

Personnel: Dal Winslow (guitars, vocals); Tony Andreason (guitars, vocals); Bob Reed (bass); Steve Wahrer (drums; deceased 1989)
Album: Surfin' Bird, 1964
Singles: Surfin' Bird, 1963 **(4)**; Bird Dance Beat, 1964 **(30)**; Bad News, 1964 **(124)**
Surf Rock—Minnesota

Travis & Bob

Personnel: Travis Pritchett (vocals); Bob Weaver (vocals)
Singles: Tell Him No, 1959 **(8)**; Little Bitty Johnny, 1959 **(114)**
Pop Vocal—Alabama

The Tree Swingers

Personnel: Art Polhemus (vocals); Terry Byrnes (vocals)
Single: Kookie Little Paradise, 1960 **(73)**
Novelty Pop—New Jersey

The Tremeloes

Personnel: Brian Poole (vocals) replaced (1966) by Aaron Woolley (vocals); Alan Blakely (guitars, vocals); Rick Westwood (guitars, vocals); Alan Howard (bass) replaced (1966) by Len Hawkes (bass, vocals); David Munden (drums); added (1970) Bob Benham (keyboards)
Albums: Big Hits of 1962, 1963; Twist and Shout, 1963; It's About Time, 1965; Here Come the Tremeloes, 1967; Here Comes My Baby, 1967; Even the Bad Times Are Good, 1967; Suddenly You Love Me, 1967; 58/68 World Explosion, 1968; Live in Cabaret, 1969; Master, 1970; Greatest Hits, 1970; Reach Out for the Tremeloes, 1973; Shiner, 1974; Don't Let the Music Die, 1976; Remembering, 1977
Singles: Someone, Someone, 1964 **(97)**; Here Comes My Baby, 1967 **(13)**; Silence Is Golden, 1967 **(11)**; Even the Bad Times Are Good, 1967 **(36)**; Suddenly You Love Me, 1968 **(44)**; Helule Helule, 1968 **(122)**; My Little Lady, 1968 **(127)**
Pop/Rock—British

The Troggs

Personnel: Reg Presley (vocals, bass); Tony Mansfield (guitars) replaced (1965) by Chris Britten (guitars); Dave Wright (guitars) replaced (1965) by Peter Staples (bass); Ronnie Bond (drums)
Albums: From Nowhere, 1966; Trogglodynamite, 1966; Wild Thing, 1966; Give It to Me, 1966; Cellophane, 1967; Best of the Troggs Volume 1, 1967; Best of the Troggs Volume 2, 1967; Love Is All Around, 1968; Mixed Bag, 1968; Trogglomania, 1969; Contrasts, 1970; The Troggs, 1975; A Girl Like You, 1975; The Trogg Tapes, 1976; The Original Trogg Tapes, 1976; Vintage Years, 1976; Live at Max's Kansas City, 1980; Black Bottom, 1981
Singles: Wild Thing, 1966 **(1)**; With a Girl Like You, 1966 **(29)**; I Can't Control Myself, 1966 **(43)**; Love Is All Around, 1968 **(7)**; You

The Troggs: Britten, Presley, Bond, Staples

Can Cry If You Want To, 1968 **(120)**; Good Vibrations, 1975 **(127)**
   Hard Rock—British

Doris Troy

Albums: Just One Look, 1963; Doris Troy, 1970; Stretching Out, 1974; Rainbow Testament, 1975
   Singles: Just One Look, 1963 **(10)**; Tomorrow Is Another Day, 1963 **(118)**; What'cha Gonna Do About It, 1963 **(102)**; Please Little Angel, 1964 **(128)**
   R & B Vocal—New York

Tommy Tucker

Singles: Hi-Heel Sneakers, 1964 **(11)**; Long Tall Shorty, 1964 **(96)**; Alimony, 1965 **(103)**
   R & B Vocal—Ohio; real name was Robert Higginbotham; died in 1982

The Tune Rockers

Single: The Green Mosquito, 1958 **(44)**
   Instrumental Pop—American

The Tune Weavers

Personnel: Margo Sylvia (vocals); Charlotte Davis (vocals); John Sylvia (vocals); Gilbert Lopez (vocals)
   Single: Happy, Happy Birthday Baby, 1957 **(5)**
   R & B Vocal—Boston

The Turbans

Personnel: Al Banks (vocals); Charles Williams (vocals); Matthew Platt (vocals); Andrew "Chet" Jones (vocals)
   Singles: When You Dance, 1955 **(33)**; When You Dance, 1961 **(114)**
   R & B Vocal—Philadelphia

Ike & Tina Turner

Albums: Soul of Ike & Tina Turner, 1960; Dance with Ike & Tina Turner, 1961; Dynamite, 1961; Don't Play Me Cheap, 1962; It's Gonna Work Out Fine, 1962; Greatest Hits, 1964; Live! The Ike & Tina Turner Show, 1965; River Deep—Mountain High, 1966; Fantastic, 1969; Outta Season, 1969; In Person, 1969; The Hunter, 1969; Come Together, 1970; Workin' Together, 1970; Live at Carnegie Hall/ What You Hear Is What You Get, 1971; 'Nuff Said, 1971; Feel Good, 1972; Nutbush City Limits, 1973; World of Ike & Tina Turner, 1973; Strange Fruit, 1974; Sixteen Great Performances, 1975; Delilah's Power, 1977; Airwaves, 1979

Singles: A Fool in Love, 1960 **(27)**; I Idolize You, 1960 **(82)**; I'm Jealous, 1961 **(117)**; It's Gonna Work Out Fine, 1961 **(14)**; Poor Fool, 1961 **(38)**; Tra La La La La, 1962 **(50)**; You Should'a Treated Me Right, 1962 **(89)**; You Can't Miss Nothing You Never Had, 1964 **(122)**; I Can't Believe What You Say (for Seeing What You Do), 1964 **(95)**; Tell Her, I'm Not Home, 1965 **(108)**; Goodbye, So Long, 1965 **(107)**; I Don't Need, 1965 **(134)**; River Deep-Mountain High, 1966 **(88)**; I'll Never Need More Than This, 1967 **(114)**; So Fine, 1968 **(117)**; I've Been Loving You Too Long, 1969 **(68)**; I'm Gonna Do All I Can (to Do Right by My Man), 1969 **(98)**; The Hunter, 1969 **(93)**; I Know, 1969 **(126)**; River Deep-Mountain High, 1969 **(112)**; Bold Soul Sister, 1969 **(59)**; Come Together, 1970 **(57)**; I Want to Take You Higher, 1970 **(34)**; Workin' Together, 1970 **(105)**; Proud Mary, 1971 **(4)**; Ooh Poo Pah Doo, 1971 **(60)**; I've Been Loving You Too Long, 1971 **(120)**; I'm Yours, 1971 **(104)**; Up in Heah, 1972 **(83)**; Nutbush City Limits, 1973 **(22)**; Sweet Rhode Island Red, 1974 **(106)**; Sexy Ida (Part 1), 1974 **(65)**; Baby-Get It On, 1975 **(88)**

Soul/R & B—American

Jesse Lee Turner

Single: The Little Space Girl, 1959 **(20)**

Rockabilly—Texas

Joe Turner

Singles: Corrine Corrina, 1956 **(41)**; Honey Hush, 1959 **(53)**; My Little Honey Dripper, 1960 **(102)**

R & B Vocal—Kansas City; died in 1985 from a heart attack

Sammy Turner

Singles: Sweet Annie Laurie, 1959 **(100)**; Lavender-Blue, 1959 **(3)**; Always, 1959 **(19)**; Symphony, 1959 **(82)**; Paradise, 1960 **(46)**

R & B Vocal—New Jersey; real last name is Black

Spyder Turner

Album: Stand by Me, 1967
Singles: Stand by Me, 1966 **(12)**; I Can't Make It Anymore, 1967 **(95)**

Soul Vocal—West Virginia; real first name is Dwight

The Turtles

Personnel: Mark Volman (vocals, guitars); Howard Kaylan (vocals, keyboards); Jim Tucker (guitars) left group (1967); G. Allan Nichol (guitars, keyboards, bass, vocals); Charlie Portz (bass) replaced (1966)

The Turtles: Barbata, Pons, Volman, Nichol, Kaylan

by Jim Pons (bass, guitars, vocals); Don Murray (drums) replaced (1966) by John Barbata (drums) replaced (1968) by John Seiter (drums, piano, vocals)

Albums: It Ain't Me Babe, 1965; You Baby, 1966; Happy Together, 1966; Golden Hits, 1967; Battle of the Bands, 1968; Turtle Soup, 1969; More Golden Hits, 1970; Wooden Head, 1970; Happy Together Again, 1975; 20 Greatest Hits, 1982; Turtle Wax/Best of Volume 2, 1987

Singles: It Ain't Me Babe, 1965 **(8)**; Let Me Be, 1965 **(29)**; You Baby, 1966 **(20)**; Grim Reaper of Love, 1966 **(81)**; Can I Get to Know You Better, 1966 **(89)**; Happy Together, 1967 **(1)**; She'd Rather Be with Me, 1967 **(3)**; You Know What I Mean, 1967 **(12)**; She's My Girl, 1967 **(14)**; Sound Asleep, 1968 **(57)**; The Story of Rock and Roll, 1968 **(48)**; Elenore, 1968 **(6)**; You Showed Me, 1968 **(6)**; You Don't

Have to Walk in the Rain, 1969 **(51)**; Love in the City, 1969 **(91)**; Lady-O, 1969 **(78)**; Eve of Destruction, 1970 **(100)**; Me About You, 1970 **(105)**

Pop/Rock—California

The Tymes

Personnel: George Williams (vocals); George Hilliard (vocals) replaced (1974) by Terri Gonzalez (vocals); Donald Banks (vocals); Albert Berry (vocals) replaced (1974) by Melanie Moore (vocals); Norman Burnett (vocals)

Albums: So Much in Love, 1963; The Sound of the Wonderful Tymes, 1963; Somewhere, 1964

Singles: So Much in Love, 1963 **(1)**; Wonderful! Wonderful!, 1963 **(7)**; Somewhere, 1963 **(19)**; To Each His Own, 1964 **(78)**; Wonderland of Love, 1964 **(124)**; The Magic of Our Summer Love, 1964 **(99)**; Here She Comes, 1964 **(92)**; People, 1968 **(39)**; Your Little Trustmaker, 1974 **(12)**; Ms. Grace, 1974 **(91)**; It's Cool, 1974 **(68)**

Pop/Soul Vocal—Philadelphia

T. Rex (Tyrannosaurus Rex)

Personnel: Marc Bolan (vocals, guitars; deceased 1977); Steve Took (guitars, vocals) replaced (1969) by Mickey Finn (guitars) replaced (1976) by Miller Anderson (guitars); added (1970) Steve Currie (bass) replaced (1973) by Jack Green (bass, guitars) replaced (1976) by Herbie Flowers (bass); added (1971) Bill Legend (drums) replaced (1974) by Dave Lutton (drums) replaced (1976) by Tony Newman (drums); added (1975) Dino Dines (keyboards); added (1975) Tyrone Scott (keyboards)

Albums: Beginning of Doves, 1966; My People Were Fair and Had Sky in Their Hair but Now They're Content to Wear Stars on Their Brows, 1968; Prophets Seers and Sages, the Angels of the Ages, 1969; Unicorn, 1969; Beard of Stars, 1970; T. Rex, 1970; Electric Warrior, 1971; The Best of T. Rex, 1971; Bolan Boogie, 1972; The Slider, 1972; Tanx, 1972; Great Hits, 1972; Zinc Alloy and the Hidden Riders of Tomorrow, 1974; Light of Love, 1974; Zip Gun Boogie, 1975; Futuristic Dragon, 1976; Dandy in the Underworld, 1977; Greatest Hits Volume 1, 1978; T. Rex Collection, 1978; Solid Gold, 1979; Solid Gold Easy Action, 1982; T. Rexstasy/The Best of T. Rex, 1985; The Ultimate Collection, 1991

Singles: Ride a White Swan, 1971 **(76)**; Hot Love, 1971 **(72)**; Bang a Gong, 1972 **(10)**; Telegram Sam, 1972 **(67)**; The Slider, 1972; Laser Love, 1974; I Love to Boogie, 1975; Dreamy Lady, 1976; Soul of My Suit, 1976; London Boys, 1976

Progressive/Hard Rock — British; Bolan's real name was Marc Feld

The Ultimate Spinach

Personnel: Geoffrey Winthrop (guitars, vocals, sitar) replaced (1969) by Jeff Baxter (guitars, vocals); Barbara Hudson (guitars, vocals); Ted Myers (guitars, vocals) left group (1968); Richard Nese (bass) replaced (1969) by Mike Levine (bass); Ian Bruce Douglas (keyboards, vocals, guitars) replaced (1969) by Tony Scheuren (key-

boards); Keith Lahteinen (drums, vocals) replaced (1969) by Russ Levine (drums)

Albums: Ultimate Spinach, 1968; Behold and See, 1968; Ultimate Spinach, 1969

Psychedelic Rock — Boston

The Underdogs

Single: Love's Gone Bad, 1967 **(122)**

Psychedelic Rock — American

Underground Sunshine

Personnel: Chris Connors (guitars, vocals); Jane Little (keyboards, vocals); Betty Kohl (bass, vocals); Frank Kohl (drums, vocals)

Album: Let There Be Light, 1969
Singles: Birthday, 1969 **(26)**; Don't Shut Me Out, 1969 **(102)**

Pop/Rock — International; Connors and Little are from Wisconsin, the Kohls from Germany

The Unifics

Personnel: Al Johnson (vocals); Hal Worthington (vocals; deceased 1990)

Album: The Unifics, 1968
Singles: Court of Love, 1968 **(25)**; The Beginning of My End, 1968 **(36)**; It's a Groovy World!, 1969 **(97)**

Soul — Washington, D.C.

The Uniques

Personnel: Joe Stampley (vocals)
Singles: Not Too Long Ago, 1965 **(66)**; All These Things, 1966 **(97)**; Run and Hide, 1966 **(126)**; How Lucky Can One Man Be, 1968

The Uniques

(115); Toys Are Made for Children, 1969 **(105)**; All These Things, 1970 **(112)**
Pop/Rock—Southern

Unit Four Plus Two

Personnel: Brian Parker (lyrics); Dave Meikle (guitars, vocals); Tommy Moeller (keyboards, vocals); Pete Moules (vocals); Howard Lubin (guitars, vocals) replaced (1968) by Russ Ballard (guitars, vocals); Bob Garwood (bass); Hugh Lem Halliday (drums) replaced (1968) by Robert Henrit (drums)
Albums: First Album, 1965; Unit Four Plus Two Featuring Concrete & Clay, 1965; Remembering, 1977
Singles: Concrete & Clay, 1965 **(28)**; You've Never Been in Love Like This Before, 1965 **(95)**; Hark, 1965 **(131)**
Pop/Rock—British

United States of America

Personnel: Dorothy Moskowitz (vocals); Gordon Marron (violin, vocals); Ed Bogas (keyboards); Joseph Byrd (keyboards); Rand Forbes (bass, vocals); Craig Woodson (drums, percussion)
Album: United States of America, 1968
Blues/Rock—American

The Unknowns

Personnel: Steve Alaimo (vocals); Mark Lindsay (vocals); Keith Allison (vocals)
Single: Melody for an Unknown Girl, 1966 **(74)**
Pop Vocal—American

The Unrelated Segments

Singles: The Story of My Life, 1966; Where You Gonna Go, 1966
Pop/Rock—Detroit

The Upbeats

Single: Just Like in the Movies, 1958 **(75)**
Pop Vocal—American

The Vacels

Single: You're My Baby (And Don't You Forget It), 1965 **(63)**
Pop/Rock—New York

The Vagrants

Personnel: Leslie "West" Weinstein (guitars, vocals); Gary Kato (bass); N. D. Smart (drums)
Single: Respect, 1966
Hard Rock—New York

Ritchie Valens

Albums: Ritchie Valens, 1959;
Ritchie, 1960; In Concert, 1960;
Greatest Hits, 1961
Singles: Come On, Let's Go, 1958
(42); Donna, 1958 **(2)**; La Bamba,
1958 **(22)**; That's My Little Suzie,
1959 **(55)**; Little Girl, 1959 **(92)**
Latin Rock—California; real
name was Richard Valenzuela; died
in the plane crash that also killed
Buddy Holly and the Big Bopper

Caterina Valente

Single: The Breeze and I, 1955
(8)
Pop Vocal—Italian

Mark Valentino

Single: The Push and Kick, 1962
(27)
Pop Vocal—Philadelphia

The Valentinos

Personnel: Bobby Womack (vo-
cals); Cecil Womack (vocals); Curtis
Womack (vocals); Harris Womack
(vocals); Friendly Womack, Jr. (vo-
cals)
Singles: Lookin' for a Love, 1962
(72); I'll Make It Alright, 1963 **(97)**;
It's All Over Now, 1964 **(94)**; I Can
Understand It, 1973 **(109)**
Soul Vocal—Cleveland

The Valiants

Personnel: Billy Storm (vocals)
Single: This Is the Nite, 1957 **(69)**
R & B Vocal—Los Angeles

Joe Valino

Single: Garden of Eden, 1956 **(12)**
Pop Vocal—American

Jim Valley

Single: Try, Try, Try, 1967 **(106)**
Pop/Rock—American; former
member of Paul Revere & the
Raiders

Frankie Valli

Albums: Frankie Valli—Solo,
1967; Timeless, 1968; Closeup, 1975;
Our Day Will Come, 1975; Gold,
1975; Fallen Angel, 1976; Frankie
Valli Is the Word, 1978
Singles: The Sun Ain't Gonna
Shine (Anymore), 1965 **(128)**;
(You're Gonna) Hurt Yourself, 1966
(39); You're Ready Now, 1966
(112); The Proud One, 1966 **(68)**;
Can't Take My Eyes Off You, 1967
(2); I Made a Fool of Myself, 1967
(18); To Give (the Reason I Live),
1968 **(29)**; The Girl I'll Never Know
(Angels Never Fly This Low), 1969
(52); My Eyes Adored You, 1974
(1); Swearin' to God, 1975 **(6)**; Our
Day Will Come, 1975 **(11)**; Fallen
Angel, 1976 **(36)**; We're All Alone,
1976 **(78)**; Boomerang, 1976; Easily,
1977 **(108)**; Second Thoughts, 1977;
Grease, 1978 **(1)**; Passion for Paris,
1978; Fancy Dancer, 1979 **(77)**;
Where Did We Go Wrong, 1980
(90)
Pop Vocal—New Jersey; member
of the Four Seasons; real name is
Francis Castellucio

June Valli

Singles: Unchained Melody, 1955
(29); The Wedding, 1958 **(43)**; The
Answer to a Maiden's Prayer, 1959

(71); Apple Green, 1960
(29)
Pop Vocal—New York

Van Der Graaf Generator

Personnel: Peter Hammill (vocals, guitars, piano); Keith Ellis (bass) replaced (1969) by Nic Potter (bass) left group (1972); Hugh Banton (piano, organ, bass) replaced (1977) by Graham Smith (violin); Guy Evans (drums); Chris J. Smith (saxophones) replaced (1969) by David Jackson (saxophones)

Albums: Aerosol Grey Machine, 1968; The Least We Can Do Is Wave to Each Other, 1969; H to He Who Am the Only One, 1970; Pawn Hearts, 1971; 1968/1971, 1973; Long Hello, 1973; Godbluff, 1975; Still Life, 1976; World Record, 1976; The Quiet Zone, 1977; Vital Live, 1978; Repeat Performance, 1980; The Long Hello Volume 1, 1980; The Long Hello Volume 2, 1981; The Long Hello Volume 3, 1982; Time Vaults, 1982
Progressive Rock—British

Leroy Van Dyke

Singles: Auctioneer, 1956 (19); Walk on By, 1961 (5); If a Woman Answers (Hang Up the Phone), 1962 (35)
Country Vocal—Missouri

The Van Dykes

Singles: Gift of Love, 1961 (91); The Bells Are Ringing, 1961 (99); No Man Is an Island, 1966 (94)
Pop Vocal—American

Vanilla Fudge

Appice, Stein, Martell, Bogert

Personnel: Tim Bogert (bass, vocals); Vince Martell (guitars, vocals); Mark Stein (keyboards, vocals); Carmine Appice (drums); added (1984) Paul Hanson (guitars)

Albums: Vanilla Fudge, 1967; The Beat Goes On, 1968; Renaissance, 1968; Near the Beginning, 1969; Rock 'n' Roll, 1970; While the World Was Eating (Pigeons), 1970; Best of Vanilla Fudge, 1982; Mystery, 1984

Singles: You Keep Me Hangin' On, 1967 (67); Where Is My Mind, 1968 (73); You Keep Me Hangin' On, 1968 (6); Take Me for a Little While, 1968 (38); Season of the Witch—Part 1, 1968 (65); Shotgun, 1969 (68); Some Velvet Morning, 1969 (103); Need Love, 1969 (111); Mystery, 1984
Blues/Soul Rock—New York

Vanity Fare

Personnel: Trevor Brice (vocals); Dick Allix (guitars); Tony Jarrett (guitars); Tony Goulden (bass); Barry Landeman (drums)

Album: Vanity Faire, 1969

Singles: Early in the Morning, 1969 **(12)**; Hitchin' a Ride, 1970 **(5)**; (I Remember) Summer Morning, 1970 **(98)**

Pop/Rock—British

Bobby Vee

Albums: Devil or Angel, 1960; With Strings and Things, 1960; Bobby Vee, 1961; Bobby Vee Sings Hits of the Rockin' '50s, 1961; Take Good Care of My Baby, 1962; Bobby Vee Meets the Crickets, 1962; A Bobby Vee Recording Session, 1962; Bobby Vee's Golden Greats, 1962; Merry Christmas from Bobby Vee, 1962; The Night Has a Thousand Eyes, 1963; Bobby Vee Meets the Ventures, 1963; I Remember Buddy Holly, 1963; Bobby Vee Sings the New Sound from England!, 1964; Hits of the '60s, 1964; Live on Tour, 1964; Golden Greats Volume 2, 1965; Look at Me Girl, 1966; Come Back When You Grow Up, 1967; Just Today, 1968; Do What You Gotta Do, 1968; Grits, Grills & Railings, 1969; Nothing Like a Sunny Day, 1970; Legendary Masters, 1974; The Very Best of Bobby Vee, 1975

Singles: Suzie Baby, 1959 **(77)**; What Do You Want?, 1960 **(93)**; One Last Kiss, 1960 **(112)**; Devil or Angel, 1960 **(6)**; Since I Met You Baby, 1960 **(81)**; Rubber Ball, 1960 **(6)**; Stayin' In, 1961 **(33)**; More Than I Can Say, 1961 **(61)**; Baby Face, 1961 **(119)**; How Many Tears, 1961 **(63)**; Take Good Care of My Baby, 1961 **(1)**; Run to Him, 1961 **(2)**; Walkin' with My Angel, 1961 **(53)**; Please Don't Ask About Barbara, 1962 **(15)**; I Can't Say Goodbye, 1962 **(92)**; Sharing You, 1962 **(15)**; Punish Her, 1962 **(20)**; Someday (When I'm Gone from You), 1962 **(99)** (with the Crickets); The Night Has a Thousand Eyes, 1962 **(3)**; Anonymous Phone Call, 1963 **(110)**; Charms, 1963 **(13)**; Be True to Yourself, 1963 **(34)**; A Letter from Betty, 1963 **(85)**; Yesterday and You (Armen's Theme), 1963 **(55)**; Never Love a Robin, 1963 **(99)**; Stranger in Your Arms, 1964 **(83)**; I'll Make You Mine, 1964 **(52)** (with the Eligibles); Hickory, Dick and Doc, 1964 **(63)**; Where Is She, 1964 **(120)**; (There'll Come a Day When) Ev'ry Little Bit Hurts, 1964 **(84)**; Pretend You Don't See Her, 1964 **(97)**; Cross My Heart, 1965 **(99)**; Keep on Trying, 1965 **(85)**; Run Like the Devil, 1965 **(124)**; A Girl I Used to Know, 1966 **(133)**; Look at Me Girl, 1966 **(52)**; Come Back When You Grow Up, 1967 **(3)**; Beautiful People, 1967 **(37)**; Maybe Just Today, 1968 **(6)** (with the Strangers); My Girl/Hey Girl, 1968 **(35)**; Do What You Gotta Do, 1968 **(83)**; I'm Lookin' for Someone to Love Me, 1968 **(98)**; Let's Call It a Day Girl, 1969 **(92)**; In and Out of Love, 1970 **(111)**; Sweet Sweetheart, 1970 **(88)**

Films: Swingin' Along, 1962; It's Trad, Dad, 1962; Play It Cool, 1963; C'mon Let's Live a Little, 1963; Just for Fun, 1964

Pop Vocal — North Dakota; real name is Robert Velline

The Vejtables

The Vejtables: *center,* Jan Ashton

Personnel: Jan Ashton (drums, vocals)

Album: The Vejtables, 1965

Singles: I Still Love You, 1965 **(84)**; The Last Thing on My Mind, 1965 **(117)**

Folk/Pop — San Francisco

The Velaires

Single: Roll Over Beethoven, 1961 **(51)**

R & B Vocal — American

The Velours

Personnel: Jerome Ramos (vocals)

Singles: Can I Come Over Tonight, 1957 **(83)**; Remember, 1958 **(83)**

R & B Vocal — New York

The Velvelettes

Personnel: Carol Gill (vocals); Bertha Barbee (vocals); Norma Barbee (vocals); Betty Kelly (vocals)

Singles: Needle in a Haystack, 1964 **(45)**; He Was Really Sayin' Somethin', 1965 **(64)**; These Things Will Keep Me Loving You, 1966 **(102)**

Soul/Pop Vocal — Michigan

Velvet Opera

Personnel: Jon Joyce (vocals); Colin Foster (guitars); John Ford (bass); Richard Hudson (drums)

Album: Ride a Hustler's Dream, 1969

Progressive Rock — British

The Velvet Underground

Personnel: Lou Reed (guitars, vocals) replaced (1970) by Walter Powers (vocals); Sterling Morrison (guitars, bass) replaced (1971) by Willie Alexander (guitars); Nico (Christa Paffga) (vocals) left group (1967); John Cale (bass, vocals, piano, viola) replaced (1968) by Doug Yule (bass, keyboards, vocals); Maureen Tucker (drums) replaced (1970) by Billy Yule (drums)

Albums: The Velvet Underground with Nico, 1967; White Light, White Heat, 1967; Velvet Underground, 1969; Loaded, 1970; Andy Warhol's Velvet Underground, 1971; Live at Max's Kansas City, 1972;

Squeeze, 1972; Velvet Underground, Lou Reed, 1973; Velvet Underground Live, 1974; Archetypes, 1974; Velvet Underground, 1976; VU, 1985; Live 1969 Volume 1, 1988; Live 1969 Volume 2, 1988
Psychedelic Rock — New York

The Velvets

Personnel: Virgil Johnson (vocals)
Singles: Tonight (Could Be the Night), 1961 **(26)**; Laugh, 1961 **(90)**; Let the Good Times Roll, 1962 **(102)**
R & B Vocal — Texas

The Ventures

Personnel: Bob Bogle (guitars, bass); Nokie Edwards (guitars, bass) replaced (1967) by Jerry McGee (bass, guitars) replaced (1970) by Nokie Edwards (guitars, bass) replaced (1985) by Jerry McGee (bass); Don Wilson (guitars); Howie Johnson (drums; deceased 1988) replaced (1963) by Mel Taylor (drums); added (1968) Johnny Durrill (keyboards) left group (1978)
Albums: Walk Don't Run, 1960; Another Smash, 1961; The Ventures, 1961; The Colorful Ventures, 1961; Twist Party, 1962; Twist with the Ventures, 1962; Twist Party Volume 2, 1962; Mashed Potatoes & Gravy, 1962; Dance Party, 1963; Play Telstar, 1963; Surfing, 1963; Country Classics, 1963; Let's Go, 1963; The Ventures in Space, 1963; The Fabulous Ventures, 1964; Walk Don't Run Volume 2, 1964; The Ventures Knock Me Out!, 1965; The Ventures on Stage, 1965; Play Guitar with the Ventures, 1965; The Ventures a Go-Go, 1965; Christmas Album, 1965; Where the Action Is, 1966; Batman Theme,

1966; Go with the Ventures, 1966; Wild Things!, 1966; Guitar Freakout!, 1967; Super Psychedelics, 1967; Best of the Ventures, 1967; Golden Greats, 1967; Million Dollar Weekend, 1967; Flights of Fantasy, 1968; I Like It Like That, 1968; The Horse, 1968; Underground Fire, 1969; More Golden Greats, 1969; Hawaii Five-O, 1969; Swamp Rock, 1969; 10th Anniversary Album, 1970; Ventures, 1971; Shaft, 1972; Joy/Ventures Play the Classics, 1972; Jim Croce Songbook, 1973; Legendary Masters, 1974; Best of the Pops, 1974; Very Best of the Ventures, 1975; Running Strong, 1976; Rocky Road, 1976; Rock 'n' Roll Forever, 1977; Greatest Hits, 1981; Stars on Guitars, 1983; NASA 25th Anniversary Commemorative Album, 1984; Best of the Ventures, 1986; Radical Guitars, 1987
Singles: Walk Don't Run, 1960 **(2)**; Perfidia, 1960 **(15)**; Ram-Bunk-Shush, 1961 **(29)**; Lullaby of the Leaves, 1961 **(69)**; (Theme from) Silver City, 1961 **(83)**; Blue Moon, 1961 **(54)**; Instant Mashed, 1962 **(104)**; Lolita Ya-Ya, 1962 **(61)**; The 2000 Pound Bee, 1963 **(91)**; Skip to M' Limbo, 1963 **(114)**; The Ninth Wave, 1963 **(122)**; Fugitive, 1964 **(126)**; Walk Don't Run '64, 1964 **(8)**; Slaughter on Tenth Avenue, 1964 **(35)**; Rap City, 1964 **(135)**; Diamond Head, 1965 **(70)**; Secret Agent Man, 1966 **(54)**; Blue Star, 1966 **(120)**; Green Hornet Theme, 1966 **(116)**; Wild Thing, 1966 **(116)**; Theme from the *Wild Angels,* 1966 **(110)**; Theme from *Endless Summer,* 1967 **(106)**; Hawaii Five-O, 1969 **(4)**; Theme from *A Summer Place,* 1969 **(83)**; Joy, 1971 **(109)**; Out of Limits, 1984
Instrumental Pop — Washington

Vik Venus

Single: Moonflight, 1969 **(38)**
Novelty Pop — American

Billy Vera

Singles: Storybook Children, 1967
(54) (with Judy Clay); Country
Girl, City Man, 1968 **(36)** (with
Judy Clay); With Pen in Hand,
1968 **(43)**; I've Been Loving You
Too Long, 1968 **(121)**; The Bible
Salesman, 1969 **(112)**
   Pop Vocal — California; real last
name is McCord

Larry Verne

Album: Mr. Custer, 1960
Singles: Mr. Custer, 1960 **(1)**;
Mister Livingston, 1960 **(75)**; Ab-
dul's Party, 1961 **(113)**
   Novelty Pop — Minnesota

The Vibrations

Personnel: James Johnson (vo-
cals); Carlton Fisher (vocals);
Richard Owens (vocals); Dave
Govan (vocals); Don Bradley (vo-
cals)
Albums: The Vibrations, 1961;
My Girl Sloopy, 1964; Misty, 1965
Singles: So Blue, 1960 **(110)**; The
Watusi, 1961 **(25)**; The Junkernoo,
1961 **(112)**; Stranded in the Jungle,
1961 **(117)**; My Girl Sloopy, 1964
(26); Sloop Dance, 1964 **(109)**; Keep
On Keeping On, 1965 **(118)**; End
Up Crying, 1965 **(130)**; Misty, 1965
(63); And I Love Her, 1966 **(118)**;
Love In Them There Hills, 1968
(93)
   R & B Vocal — Los Angeles

Michael Vickers

Albums: I Wish I Were a Group
Again, 1968; A Day at the Races,
1976
   Pop/Rock — British; former Manfred Mann member

The Videls

Personnel: Peter Anders (vocals);
Vinnie Poncia (vocals)
Single: Mister Lonely, 1960 **(73)**
Pop Vocal — Rhode Island

The Village Stompers

Album: Washington Square, 1963
Singles: Washington Square, 1963
(2); The La-Dee-Da Song, 1964
(104); From Russia with Love, 1964
(81); Oh! Marie, 1964 **(132)**; Fiddler
on the Roof, 1964 **(97)**; Those
Magnificent Men in Their Flying
Machines, 1965 **(130)**
   Dixieland Pop — New York

Gene Vincent & His Blue Caps

Albums: Bluejean Bop!, 1956;
Record Date, 1957; Sounds Like,
1958; Gene Vincent & the Blue
Caps, 1959; Vincent Rocks, Blue
Caps Roll, 1960; Crazy Times,
1960; Crazy Beat, 1961; Shakin' Up
a Storm, 1962; Gene Vincent, 1967;
Best of Gene Vincent, 1967; Best of
Gene Vincent, Volume 2, 1969; I'm
Back and I'm Proud, 1969; Gene
Vincent, 1970; The Day the World
Turned Blue, 1971; Bop That Won't
Stop, 1974; Greatest, 1977; Singles
Album, 1981; Bird Doggin', 1982
Singles: Be-Bop-a-Lula, 1956 **(7)**;
Race with the Devil, 1956 **(96)**;
Bluejean Bop, 1956 **(49)**; Lotta

Lovin'/Wear My Ring, 1957 **(13)**;
Dance to the Bop, 1957 **(23)**

Rock/Pop — Virginia; real name
was Vincent Eugene Craddock; died
in 1971

Bobby Vinton

Albums: Roses Are Red, 1962;
Bobby Vinton Sings the Big Ones,
1963; Blue Velvet, 1963; There! I've
Said It Again, 1964; Tell Me Why,
1964; Bobby Vinton's Greatest Hits,
1964; Mr. Lonely, 1965; Bobby Vin-
ton Sings for Lonely Nights, 1965;
Satin Pillows and Careless, 1966;
Please Love Me Forever, 1967; Take
Good Care of My Baby, 1968; I
Love How You Love Me, 1969;
Vinton, 1969; Bobby Vinton's
Greatest Hits of Love, 1970; My
Elusive Dreams, 1970; Ev'ry Day of
My Life, 1972; Sealed with a Kiss,
1972; Bobby Vinton's All-Time
Greatest Hits, 1972; Melodies of
Love, 1974; With Love, 1974; Bobby
Vinton Sings the Golden Decade of
Love, 1975; Heart of Hearts, 1975;

The Bobby Vinton Show, 1975; The
Name Is Love, 1977

Singles: Roses Are Red (My
Love), 1962 **(1)**; I Love You the
Way You Are, 1962 **(38)**; Rain
Rain Go Away, 1962 **(12)**; Trouble
Is My Middle Name, 1962 **(33)**;
Let's Kiss and Make Up, 1962 **(38)**;
Over the Mountain (Across the
Sea), 1963 **(21)**; Blue on Blue, 1963
(3); Blue Velvet, 1963 **(1)**; There!
I've Said It Again, 1963 **(1)**; My
Heart Belongs to You, 1964 **(9)**;
Tell Me Why, 1964 **(13)**; Clinging
Vine, 1964 **(17)**; Mr. Lonely, 1964
(1); Long Lonely Nights, 1965 **(17)**;
L-O-N-E-L-Y, 1965 **(22)**; Theme
from *Harlow* (Lonely Girl), 1965
(61); What Color (Is a Man), 1965
(38); Satin Pillows, 1965 **(23)**;
Careless, 1965 **(111)**; Tears, 1966
(59); Dum-De-Da, 1966 **(40)**; Pet-
ticoat White (Summer Sky Blue),
1966 **(81)**; Coming Home Soldier,
1966 **(11)**; For He's a Jolly Good
Fellow, 1967 **(66)**; Red Roses for
Mom, 1967 **(95)**; Please Love Me
Forever, 1967 **(6)**; Just as Much as
Ever, 1967 **(24)**; Take Good Care of
My Baby, 1968 **(33)**; Halfway to
Paradise, 1968 **(23)**; I Love How
You Love Me, 1968 **(9)**; To Know
You Is to Love You, 1969 **(34)**; The
Days of Sand and Shovels, 1969
(34); My Elusive Dreams, 1970
(46); No Arms Can Ever Hold You,
1970 **(93)**; Why Don't They Under-
stand, 1970 **(109)**; I'll Make You My
Baby, 1971 **(101)**; Every Day of My
Life, 1972 **(24)**; Sealed with a Kiss,
1972 **(19)**; But I Do, 1972 **(82)**;
Hurt, 1973 **(106)**; My Melody of
Love, 1974 **(3)**; Beer Barrel Polka/
Dick and Jane, 1975 **(33)**; Wooden
Heart, 1975 **(58)**; Moonlight Sere-
nade, 1976 **(97)**; Save Your Kisses
for Me, 1976 **(75)**; Only Love Can

Break a Heart, 1977 **(99)**; Make Believe It's Your First Time, 1980 **(78)**; Let Me Love You Goodbye, 1981 **(108)**

Pop Vocal—Pennsylvania; hosted TV variety show 1975–78

The Virtues

Personnel: Frank Virtuoso (guitars)

Album: Guitar Boogie Shuffle, 1959

Singles: Guitar Boogie Shuffle, 1959 **(5)**; Guitar Boogie Shuffle Twist, 1962 **(96)**

Instrumental Rock—Philadelphia

The Viscounts

Personnel: Harry Haller (saxophones); Bobby Spievak (guitars); Joe Spievak (bass); Larry Vecchio (organ); Clark Smith (drums)

Album: Harlem Nocturne, 1966

Singles: Harlem Nocturne, 1959 **(52)**; Night Train, 1960 **(82)**; Wabash Blues, 1960 **(77)**; Harlem Nocturne, 1965 **(39)**

Instrumental Pop—New Jersey

The Vogues

Personnel: William Burkette (vocals); Charles Blasko (vocals); Hugh Geyer (vocals); Dan Miller (vocals)

Albums: Five O'Clock World, 1966; Turn Around Look at Me, 1968; Till, 1969; Memories, 1969; Greatest Hits, 1970

Singles: You're the One, 1965 **(4)**; Five O'Clock World, 1965 **(4)**; Magic Town, 1966 **(21)**; The Land of Milk and Honey, 1966 **(29)**; Please Mr. Sun, 1966 **(48)**; That's the Tune, 1966 **(99)**; Turn Around,

Look at Me, 1968 **(7)**; My Special Angel, 1968 **(7)**; Till, 1968 **(27)**; Woman Helping Man, 1969 **(47)**; No, Not Much, 1969 **(34)**; Earth Angel (Will You Be Mine), 1969 **(42)**; Moments to Remember, 1969 **(47)**; Green Fields, 1969 **(92)**; God Only Knows, 1970 **(101)**; Hey, That's No Way to Say Goodbye, 1970 **(101)**; Love Song, 1971 **(118)**

Pop Vocal—Pennsylvania

The Volume's

Personnel: Ed Union (vocals)

Single: I Love You, 1962 **(22)**

R & B Vocal—Detroit

The Voxpoppers

Single: Wishing for Your Love, 1958 **(18)**

Pop Vocal—New York

Adam Wade

Albums: Adam Wade, 1960; Take Good Care of Her, 1961; As If I Didn't Know, 1961

Singles: Tell Her for Me, 1960 **(66)**; Ruby, 1960 **(58)**; I Can't Help It, 1960 **(64)**; Gloria's Theme, 1960 **(74)**; Take Good Care of Her, 1961 **(7)**; The Writing on the Wall, 1961 **(5)**; Point of No Return, 1961 **(85)**; As If I Didn't Know, 1961 **(10)**; Tonight I Won't Be There, 1961 **(61)**; Linda, 1961 **(94)**; Preview of Paradise, 1961 **(108)**; It's Good to Have You Back with Me, 1962 **(109)**; How Are Things in Lovers Lane, 1962 **(114)**; For the First Time in My Life, 1962 **(118)**; There'll Be No Teardrops Tonight, 1962 **(104)**; Don't Let Me Cross Over, 1963 **(117)**; Crying in the Chapel, 1965 **(88)**

Pop/Soul Vocal—Pittsburgh; hosted TV game show "Musical Chairs" in 1976

The Waikikis

Album: Hawaii Tattoo, 1965
Singles: Hawaii Tattoo, 1964 **(33)**; Hawaii Honeymoon, 1965 **(91)**
Instrumental—Belgian

The Wailers

Personnel: Rich Dangel (guitars); John Greek (guitars); Mark Marush (bass, saxophones); Kent Morrill (keyboards); Mike Burk (drums)
Albums: Fabulous Wailers at the Castle, 1959; Wailers Wailers Everywhere, 1960; Wailers & Company, 1961; Out of Our Tree, 1961; Outburst, 1962; Wailers, 1963; Tall Cool One, 1964; Walk Thru' the People, 1966
Singles: Tall Cool One, 1959 **(36)**; Mau-Mau, 1959 **(68)**; Hang Up, 1961; You Weren't Using Your Head, 1961; Tall Cool One, 1964 **(38)**; It's You Alone, 1966 **(118)**
Instrumental Rock—Tacoma

Gloria Walker

Singles: Talking About My Baby, 1968 **(60)**; Please Don't Desert Me Baby, 1969 **(98)**
R & B Vocal—American

Jr. Walker & The All Stars

Personnel: Jr. Walker (saxophones, vocals); Willie Woods (guitars); Vic Thomas (organ); James Graves (drums)
Albums: Shotgun, 1965; Soul Session, 1966; Road Runner, 1966; Live!, 1967; Home Cookin', 1969; Greatest Hits, 1969; What Does It Take to Win Your Love, 1970; A Gassss, 1971; Rainbow Funk, 1971; Moody Jr., 1972; Greatest Hits Volume 2, 1973; Peace & Understanding, 1973; Anthology, 1974; Jr. Walker & the All Stars, 1974; Hot Shot, 1976; Sax Appeal, 1976; Whopper Bopper Show Stopper, 1976; Smooth Soul, 1978; Back Street Boogie, 1979
Singles: Shotgun, 1965 **(4)**; Do the Boomerang, 1965 **(36)**; Shake and Fingerpop, 1965 **(29)**; Cleo's Back, 1965 **(43)**; Cleo's Mood, 1966 **(50)**; (I'm a) Road Runner, 1966 **(20)**; How Sweet It Is (to Be Loved by You), 1966 **(18)**; Money (That's What I Want)—Part 1, 1966 **(52)**; Pucker Up Buttercup, 1967 **(31)**; Shoot Your Shot, 1967 **(44)**; Come See About Me, 1967 **(24)**; Hip City—Part 2, 1968 **(31)**; Home Cookin', 1969 **(42)**; What Does It Take (to Win Your Love), 1969 **(4)**; These Eyes, 1969 **(16)**; Gotta Hold on to This Feeling, 1970 **(21)**; Do You See My Love (for You Growing), 1970 **(32)**; Holly Holy, 1970 **(75)**; Carry Your Own Load, 1971 **(117)**; Take Me Girl, I'm Ready, 1971 **(50)**; Way Back Home, 1971 **(52)**; Walk in the Night, 1972 **(46)**; Gimme That Beat, Part 1, 1973 **(101)**
R & B—Indiana; Walker's real name is Autry DeWalt II

The Walker Brothers

Personnel: Scott Engel (guitars, keyboards, vocals); Gary Leeds (drums, vocals); John Maus (guitars, vocals)
Albums: The Walker Brothers,

1965; Make It Easy on Yourself, 1965; The Sun Ain't Gonna Shine, 1966; Portrait, 1966; Images, 1967; The Walker Brothers Story, 1967; Immortal Walker Brothers, 1970; No Regrets, 1975; Greatest Hits, 1975; Lines, 1976; Nite Flights, 1978; Spotlight on the Walker Brothers, 1979

Singles: Make It Easy on Yourself, 1965 **(16)**; My Ship Is Comin' In, 1966 **(63)**; The Sun Ain't Gonna Shine (Anymore), 1966 **(13)**

Pop/Rock—Los Angeles

Jerry Wallace

Albums: In the Misty Moonlight, 1964; Do You Know What It's Like to Be Lonesome?, 1973

Singles: How the Time Flies, 1958 **(11)**; Diamond Ring, 1958 **(78)**; A Touch of Pink, 1959 **(92)**; Primrose Lane, 1959 **(8)**; Little Coco Palm, 1960 **(36)**; You're Singing Our Love Song to Somebody Else, 1960 **(115)**; Swingin' Down the Lane, 1960 **(79)**; There She Goes, 1960 **(26)**; Life's a Holiday, 1961 **(91)**; Lonesome, 1961 **(110)**; Shutters and Boards, 1962 **(24)**; In the Misty Moonlight, 1964 **(19)**; It's a Cotton Candy World, 1964 **(99)**; Spanish Guitars, 1964 **(132)**; Even the Bad Times Are Good, 1964 **(113)**; To Get to You, 1972 **(48)**; If You Leave Me Tonight I'll Cry, 1972 **(38)**

Country/Pop Vocal—Arizona

The Wanderers

Personnel: Ray Pollard (vocals)
Singles: For Your Love, 1961 **(93)**; I'll Never Smile Again, 1961 **(107)**; There Is No Greater Love, 1962 **(88)**

R & B Vocal—American

Billy Ward & His Dominoes

Personnel: Billy Ward (piano); Clyde McPhatter (vocals; deceased 1972) replaced (1953) by Jackie Wilson (vocals; deceased 1984) replaced (1957) by Gene Mumford (vocals); Charlie White (vocals); Joe Lamont (vocals); Bill Brown (vocals)
Singles: St. Therese of the Roses, 1956 **(13)**; Star Dust, 1957 **(12)**; Deep Purple, 1957 **(20)**; Jennie Lee, 1958 **(55)**

R & B/Soul—New York

Dale Ward

Single: Letter from Sherry, 1963 **(25)**

Country Vocal—American

Joe Ward

Single: Nuttin' for Xmas, 1955 **(20)**

Pop Vocal—Cincinnati

Robin Ward

Singles: Wonderful Summer, 1963 **(14)**; Winter's Here, 1964 **(123)**

Pop Vocal—Nebraska

Dee Dee Warwick

Albums: Dee Dee Warwick, 1965; I Want to Be with You, 1966; Foolish Fool, 1969; Suspicious Minds, 1971

Singles: You're No Good, 1963 **(117)**; Do It with All Your Heart, 1965 **(124)**; We're Doing Fine, 1965 **(96)**; I Want to Be with You, 1966 **(41)**; I'm Gonna Make You Love Me, 1966 **(88)**; When Love Slips Away, 1967 **(92)**; Foolish Fool, 1969 **(57)**; That's Not Love, 1969 **(106)**;

Ring of Bright Water, 1969 **(113)**; She Didn't Know (She Kept on Talking), 1970 **(70)**; Suspicious Minds, 1971 **(80)**

Soul/Pop Vocal—New Jersey; sister of Dionne Warwick

Dionne Warwick

Albums: Presenting Dionne Warwick, 1963; Anyone Who Had a Heart, 1964; Make Way for Dionne Warwick, 1964; The Sensitive Sound of Dionne Warwick, 1965; Here I Am, 1966; Dionne Warwick in Paris, 1966; Here Where There Is Love, 1967; On Stage and in the Movies, 1967; The Windows of the World, 1967; Magic of Believing, 1967; Dionne Warwick's Golden Hits, Part One, 1967; Valley of the Dolls, 1968; Promises, Promises, 1968; Soulful, 1969; Freewheelin', 1969; Dionne Warwick's Greatest Motion Picture Hits, 1969; Dionne Warwick's Golden Hits, Part Two, 1969; I'll Never Fall in Love Again, 1970; Very Dionne, 1970; The Dionne Warwick Story, 1971;

Dionne, 1972; From Within, 1972; Just Being Myself, 1973; Then Came You, 1975; Track of the Cat, 1975; A Man and a Woman, 1977 (with Isaac Hayes); Only Love Can Break a Heart, 1977; Love at First Sight, 1977; Dionne, 1979; No Night So Long, 1980; Hot! Live and Otherwise, 1981; Friends in Love, 1982; Heartbreaker, 1982; How Many Times Can We Say Goodbye, 1983; Finder of Lost Loves, 1985; Friends, 1985; Anthology, 1986; Reservations for Two, 1987; Collection—Her All Time Greatest Hits, 1989; Greatest Hits 1979–1990, 1990; Sings Cole Porter, 1990

Singles: Don't Make Me Over, 1962 **(21)**; This Empty Place, 1963 **(84)**; Make the Music Play, 1963 **(81)**; Anyone Who Had a Heart, 1963 **(8)**; Walk on By, 1964 **(6)**; A House Is Not a Home, 1964 **(71)**; You'll Never Get to Heaven (If You Break My Heart), 1964 **(34)**; Reach Out for Me, 1964 **(20)**; Who Can I Turn To, 1965 **(62)**; You Can Have Him, 1965 **(75)**; Here I Am, 1965 **(65)**; Looking with My Eyes, 1965 **(64)**; Are You There (With Another Girl), 1965 **(39)**; Message to Michael, 1966 **(8)**; Trains and Boats and Planes, 1966 **(22)**; I Just Don't Know What to Do with Myself, 1966 **(26)**; Another Night, 1966 **(49)**; Alfie, 1967 **(15)**; The Beginning of Loneliness, 1967 **(79)**; The Windows of the World, 1967 **(32)**; I Say a Little Prayer, 1967 **(4)**; (Theme from) Valley of the Dolls, 1968 **(2)**; Do You Know the Way to San Jose, 1968 **(10)**; Let Me Be Lonely, 1968 **(71)**; Who Is Gonna Love Me?, 1968 **(33)**; (There's) Always Something There to Remind Me, 1968 **(65)**; Promises, Promises, 1968 **(19)**; This Girl's in Love with

You, 1969 **(7)**; The April Fools, 1969 **(37)**; Odds and Ends, 1969 **(43)**; You've Lost That Lovin' Feeling, 1969 **(16)**; I'll Never Fall in Love Again, 1969 **(6)**; Let Me Go to Him, 1970 **(32)**; Paper Mache, 1970 **(43)**; Make It Easy on Yourself, 1970 **(37)**; The Green Grass Starts to Grow, 1970 **(43)**; Who Gets the Guy, 1971 **(57)**; Amanda, 1971 **(83)**; The Love of My Man, 1971 **(107)**; If We Only Have Love, 1972 **(84)**; I'm Your Puppet, 1972 **(113)**; Then Came You, 1974 **(1)** (with the Spinners); Once You Hit the Road, 1976 **(79)**; I Didn't Mean to Love You, 1976; Only Love Can Break Your Heart, 1977 **(109)**; I'll Never Love This Way Again, 1979 **(5)**; Deja Vu, 1979 **(15)**; After You, 1980 **(65)**; No Night So Long, 1980 **(23)**; Easy Love, 1980 **(62)**; Some Changes Are for Good, 1981 **(65)**; There's a Long Road Ahead of Us, 1981; Friends in Love, 1982 **(38)** (with Johnny Mathis); Heartbreaker, 1982 **(10)**; All the Love in the World, 1982; Take the Short Way Home, 1983 **(41)**; All the Love in the World, 1983 **(103)**; How Many Times Can We Say Goodbye, 1983 **(27)** (with Luther Vandross); Finder of Lost Loves, 1985; That's What Friends Are For, 1985 **(1)** (with Elton John, Gladys Knight and Stevie Wonder); Whisper in the Dark, 1986 **(72)**; Love Power, 1987 **(12)** (with Jeffrey Osborne); Reservations for Two, 1987 **(62)** (with Kashif)

Pop Vocal—New Jersey; co-hosted "Solid Gold" music TV show in the 1980s; most of her hits were written by Hal David and Burt Bacharach

Baby Washington

Albums: That's How Heartaches Are Made, 1963; Only Those in Love, 1965; The One and Only, 1966; Soul of Baby Washington, 1967; With You in Mind, 1968

Singles: Work Out, 1960 **(105)**; Nobody Cares (About Me), 1961 **(60)**; Handful of Memories, 1962 **(116)**; Hush Heart, 1962 **(102)**; That's How Heartaches Are Made, 1963 **(40)**; Leave Me Alone, 1963 **(62)**; Hey Lonely One, 1963 **(100)**; Who's Going to Take Care of Me, 1964 **(125)**; I Can't Wait Until I See My Baby, 1964 **(93)**; The Clock, 1964 **(100)**; It'll Never Be Over for Me, 1964 **(98)**; Run My Heart, 1965 **(121)**; Only Those in Love, 1965 **(73)**; No Time for Pity, 1965 **(125)**; Forever, 1973 **(119)**

R & B Vocal—South Carolina; recorded first hit as Jeanette "Baby" Washington, as Justine Washington from 1962–1964, then as Baby Washington

Johnny "Guitar" Watson

Albums: Johnny "Guitar" Watson, 1963; Blues Soul, 1965; Bad, 1966; Larry Williams Show with Johnny "Guitar" Watson, 1967; I Cried for You, 1967; In the Fats Bag, 1968; Listen, 1973; Gangster of Love, 1975; I Don't Want to Be a Lone Ranger, 1976; Captured Live, 1976; Ain't That a Bitch, 1976; A Real Mother for Ya, 1977; Funk Beyond the Call of Duty, 1977; Giant, 1978; What the Hell Is This, 1979; Love Jones, 1980; The Very Best of Johnny "Guitar" Watson, 1981; Johnny "Guitar" Watson and the

Family Clone, 1981; Hot Little Mama, 1982

Singles: Mercy, Mercy, Mercy, 1967 **(96)** (with Larry Williams); I Don't Want to Be a Lone Ranger, 1975 **(99)**; I Need It, 1976 **(101)**; Superman Lover, 1976 **(101)**; A Real Mother for Ya, 1977 **(41)**

R & B/Funk—Houston

Thomas Wayne with The DeLons

Singles: Tragedy, 1959 **(5)**; Eternally, 1959 **(92)**

Pop Vocal—Mississippi; last name was Perkins; died in 1971

We Five

Personnel: Beverly Bivens (vocals); Peter Fullerton (vocals); Jerry Burgan (vocals); Robert Jones (vocals); Michael Stewart (vocals)

Albums: You Were on My Mind, 1965; Make Someone Happy, 1968

Singles: You Were on My Mind, 1965 **(3)**; Let's Get Together, 1965 **(31)**; There Stands the Door, 1966 **(116)**

Pop Vocal—California; Michael Stewart is the brother of John Stewart

We the People

Album: We the People, 1966

Single: Mirror of Your Mind, 1966

Pop/Rock—Florida

The Weeds

Personnel: Fred Cole (guitars, vocals); Ed Bowen (guitars, bass, vocals); Tommy Wynne (drums, vocals)

Single: It's Your Time, 1967

Psychedelic Pop—Washington

Lenny Welch

Albums: Since I Fell for You, 1964; Two Different Worlds, 1965

Singles: You Don't Know Me, 1960 **(45)**; Since I Fell for You, 1963 **(4)**; Ebb Tide, 1964 **(25)**; If You See My Love, 1964 **(92)**; Darling Take Me Back, 1965 **(72)**; Two Different Worlds, 1965 **(61)**; Run to My Lovin' Arms, 1965 **(96)**; Rags to Riches, 1966 **(102)**; Since I Fell for You, 1967 **(134)**; The Right to Cry, 1967 **(128)**; Darling Stay with Me, 1968 **(112)**; Breaking Up Is Hard to Do, 1970 **(34)**; To Be Loved/Glory of Love (Medley), 1970 **(110)**; A Sunday Kind of Love, 1970 **(96)**

Pop/Soul Vocal—New Jersey

Freddy Weller

Album: Games People Play/These Are Not My People, 1969

Singles: These Are Not My People, 1969 **(113)**; The Promised Land, 1971 **(125)**; Indian Lake, 1971 **(108)**

Pop Vocal—American; former member of Paul Revere & the Raiders

Junior Wells

Albums: On Tap, 1966; It's My Life Baby, 1966; South Side Jam, 1967; Hoodoo Man Blues, 1967; Blue Hit Big Town, 1967; Coming at You, 1968; You're Tough Enough, 1968; Sings at the Golden Bear, 1968; In My Younger Days, 1971; Play the Blues, 1972

Blues Vocal—Chicago

Mary Wells

Albums: Bye Bye Baby, 1961; One Who Really Loves You, 1962; Two Lovers and Other Great Hits, 1962; On Stage, 1963; Together, 1964 (with Marvin Gaye); Greatest Hits, 1964; Mary Wells Sings My Guy, 1964; Mary Wells, 1965; My Baby Just Cares for Me, 1966; Love Songs of the Beatles, 1966; Ooh, 1966; Vintage Stock, 1967; Two Sides of Mary Wells, 1968; Servin' Up Some Soul, 1968

Singles: Bye Bye Baby, 1961 **(45)**; I Don't Want to Take a Chance, 1961 **(33)**; The One Who Really Loves You, 1962 **(8)**; You Beat Me to the Punch, 1962 **(9)**; Two Lovers, 1962 **(7)**; Laughing Boy, 1963 **(15)**; Two Wrongs Don't Make a Right, 1963 **(100)**; Your Old Stand By, 1963 **(40)**; You Lost the Sweetest Boy, 1963 **(22)**; What's Easy for Two Is So Hard for One, 1963 **(29)**; My Guy, 1964 **(1)**; Once Upon a Time, 1964 **(19)** (with Marvin Gaye); What's the Matter with You Baby, 1964 **(17)** (with Marvin Gaye); Ain't It the Truth, 1964 **(45)**; Stop Takin' Me for Granted, 1964 **(88)**; Use Your Head, 1965 **(34)**; Why Don't You Let Yourself Go, 1965 **(107)**; Never, Never Leave Me, 1965 **(54)**; He's a Lover, 1965 **(74)**; Me Without You, 1965 **(95)**; Dear Lover, 1966 **(51)**; Can't You See (You're Losing Me), 1966 **(94)**; Such a Sweet Thing, 1966 **(99)**; (Hey You) Set My Soul on Fire, 1967 **(122)**; The Doctor, 1968 **(65)**; Dig the Way I Feel, 1970 **(115)**

Soul/Pop Vocal — Detroit

West Coast Pop Art Experimental Band

Personnel: Michael Lloyd (keyboards, guitars, vocals); Dan Harris (guitars, vocals); Shaun Harris (bass, guitars, vocals); Bob Markley (drums)

Albums: Part One, 1967; Volume 2, 1967; A Child's Guide to Good and Evil, 1968; Where's My Daddy?, 1969; Legendary Unreleased Album, 1980

Singles: I Won't Hurt You, 1967; The Smell of Incense, 1967

Psychedelic Pop — California

Kim Weston

Singles: Love Me All the Way, 1963 **(88)**; What Good Am I Without You, 1964 **(61)** (with Marvin Gaye); Take Me in Your Arms (Rock Me a Little While), 1965 **(50)**; Helpless, 1966 **(56)**; It Takes Two, 1967 **(14)** (with Marvin Gaye); I Got What You Need, 1967 **(99)**; We Try Harder, 1969 **(135)** (with Johnny Nash); Lift Ev'ry Voice and Sing, 1970 **(120)**

Soul Vocal — Detroit; real name is Agatha Natalie Weston

Ian Whitcomb

Album: You Turn Me On!, 1965

Singles: This Sporting Life, 1964; This Sporting Life, 1965 **(100)**; You Turn Me On (Turn On Song), 1965 **(8)**; N-E-R-V-O-U-S!, 1965 **(59)**; Where Did Robinson Crusoe Go with Friday on Saturday Night?, 1966 **(101)**

Pop Vocal — British

Kitty White

Single: A Teen Age Prayer, 1955 **(68)**

Pop Vocal—American

Tony Joe White

Albums: Black and White, 1969; ...Continued, 1969; Tony Joe, 1970; Tony Joe White, 1971; The Train I'm On, 1972; Best of Tony Joe White, 1973; Home Made Ice Cream, 1973; Eyes, 1976; Tony Joe White, 1977; Real Thing, 1980

Singles: Polk Salad Annie, 1969 **(8)**; Roosevelt and Ira Lee (Night of the Mossacin), 1969 **(44)**; High Sheriff, 1970 **(112)**; Save Your Sugar for Me, 1970 **(94)**; Scratch My Back, 1970 **(117)**; It Must Be Love, 1976 **(108)**; I Get Off on It, 1980 **(79)**

Bayou Rock—Louisiana

Margaret Whiting

Album: The Wheel of Hurt, 1967

Singles: The Money Tree, 1956 **(20)**; I Can't Help It (If I'm Still in Love with You), 1958 **(74)**; The Wheel of Hurt, 1966 **(26)**; Just Like a Man, 1967 **(132)**; Only Love Can Break a Heart, 1967 **(96)**; I Almost Called Your Name, 1967 **(108)**; It Keeps Right on a-Hurtin', 1968 **(115)**; I Hate to See Me Go, 1968 **(127)**; Faithfully, 1968 **(117)**; Can't Get You Out of My Mind, 1968 **(124)**

Pop Vocal—Detroit

The Who

Personnel: Peter Townshend (guitars, keyboards, vocals); John Entwistle (bass, vocals); Roger Daltrey (vocals); Keith Moon (drums, percussion; deceased 1978) replaced (1978) by Kenney Jones (drums) left group (1983)

Albums: My Generation, 1965; A Quick One, 1966; Happy Jack, 1966; The Who Sell Out, 1967; Magic Bus, 1968; Direct Hits, 1969; Tommy, 1969; Live at Leeds, 1970; Who's Next, 1971; Quadrophenia, 1972; Meaty, Beaty, Big and Bouncy, 1972; Who Did It, 1973; Odds & Sods, 1974; Best of the Who 1964–1974, 1975; The Who by Numbers, 1975; The Story of the Who, 1976; Who Are You, 1978; The Kids Are Alright, 1979; Face Dances, 1981; Hooligans, 1981; It's Hard, 1982; Who's Greatest Hits, 1983; Who's Last, 1984; Who's Better, Who's Best, 1985; Who's Missing, 1985; Two's Missing, 1988; Join Together, 1989

Singles: I Can't Explain, 1965 **(93)**; My Generation, 1966 **(74)**; The Kids Are Alright, 1966 **(106)**; Happy Jack, 1967 **(24)**; Pictures of Lily, 1967 **(51)**; I Can See for Miles, 1967 **(9)**; Call Me Lightning, 1968 **(40)**; Magic Bus, 1968 **(25)**; Pinball Wizard, 1969 **(19)**; I'm Free, 1969 **(37)**; The Seeker, 1970 **(44)**; Summertime Blues, 1970 **(27)**; See Me, Feel Me, 1970 **(12)**; Baba O'Riley, 1971; Won't Get Fooled Again, 1971 **(15)**; Behind Blue Eyes, 1971 **(34)**; Join Together, 1972 **(17)**; The Relay, 1972 **(39)**; Love Reign Over Me, 1973 **(76)**; The Real Me, 1974 **(92)**; Squeeze Box, 1975 **(16)**; Slip Kid, 1976; Who Are You, 1978 **(14)**; Had Enough, 1978; Trick of the Light, 1979 **(107)**; Long Live Rock, 1979 **(54)**; 5:15, 1979 **(45)**; You Better You Bet, 1981 **(18)**; Don't Let Go the Coat, 1981 **(84)**; Athena, 1982 **(28)**; Eminence Front, 1982 **(68)**; It's Hard, 1983

The Who: *left to right,* Entwistle, Daltrey, Moon, Townshend

Hard Rock—British; "Quadrophenia" and "Tommy" became films

The Wild-Cats

Personnel: Dennis Gorgas (guitars); Frank Rainey (organ); Pat Piccininno (drums)
Single: Gazachstahagen, 1959 **(57)**
Instrumental Rock—New Jersey

Marty Wilde

Single: Bad Boy, 1960 **(45)**
Pop/Rock—British; real name is Reginald Smith; father of singer Kim Wilde

Wilde Flowers

Personnel: Richard Sinclair (guitars, vocals) replaced (1966) by Pye Hastings (guitars, vocals); Graham Flight (vocals) replaced (1965) by Kevin Ayers (vocals); Robert Wyatt (drums, vocals) replaced (1966) by Richard Coughlan (drums); Brian Hopper (guitars, saxophones); Hugh Hopper (bass) replaced (1966) by Dave Lawrence (bass); added (1965) Dave Sinclair (keyboards)
Album: The Wilde Flowers, 1967
Art Rock—British

The Wildweeds

Singles: No Good to Cry, 1967 **(88)**; And When She Smiles, 1971 **(113)**
Pop/Rock—American

Billy Williams

Singles: A Crazy Little Palace (That's My Home), 1956 **(49)**; The Pied Piper, 1957 **(50)**; I'm Gonna Sit Right Down and Write Myself a Letter/Date with the Blues, 1957 **(3)**; Got a Date with an Angel, 1957 **(78)**; Baby, Baby, 1958 **(78)**; I'll Get By (As Long as I Have You), 1958 **(87)**; Nola, 1959 **(39)**; Goodnight Irene, 1959 **(75)**

Pop Vocal — Texas; died in 1972

Danny Williams

Album: White on White, 1964
Singles: White on White, 1964 **(9)**; A Little Toy Balloon, 1964 **(84)**; More (Theme from *Mondo Cane*), 1964 **(110)**

Pop Vocal — South Africa

Larry Williams

Albums: Live, 1965; The Larry Williams Show, 1965; Here's Larry Williams, 1967; Two for the Price of One, 1967; Missing & Unissued Sides, 1968; Greatest Hits, 1969
Singles: Short Fat Fannie/High School Dance, 1957 **(5)**; Bony Moronie, 1957 **(14)**; You Bug Me, Baby, 1957 **(45)**; Dizzy, Miss Lizzy, 1958 **(69)**; Mercy, Mercy, Mercy, 1967 **(96)** (with Johnny "Guitar" Watson)

R & B/Rock — New Orleans; committed suicide in 1980

Mason Williams

Albums: Phonogram Record, 1969; Mason Williams' Ear Show, 1969; Music, 1969; Hand Made, 1970; Themes, Poems and Things, 1970; Sharepickers, 1971; Feudin' Banjos, 1971; Improved, 1971; Fresh Fish, 1972; Listening Matter, 1973
Singles: Classical Gas, 1968 **(2)**; Baroque Nova, 1968 **(96)**; Saturday Night at the World, 1969 **(99)**; Greensleeves, 1969 **(90)**; A Gift of Song, 1969 **(118)**

Folk/Pop — Texas; regular on "The Smothers Brothers Comedy Hour"; also a comedy writer

Maurice Williams & The Zodiacs

Personnel: Maurice Williams (vocals); Wiley Bennett (vocals); Henry Gaston (vocals); Charles Thomas (vocals); Albert Hill (vocals); Willie Morrow (vocals)
Albums: Stay, 1961; Best of Maurice Williams & the Zodiacs, 1979
Singles: Stay, 1960 **(1)**; I Remember, 1961 **(86)**; Come Along, 1961 **(83)**

Pop Vocal — South Carolina

Mike Williams

Single: Lonely Soldier, 1966 **(69)**
Pop Vocal — American

Chuck Willis

Album: Stoop Down Baby . . . Let Your Daddy See, 1972
Singles: C. C. Rider, 1957 **(12)**; Betty and Dupree, 1958 **(33)**; What Am I Living For, 1958 **(9)**; Hang Up My Rock and Roll Shoes, 1958 **(24)**; My Life, 1958 **(46)**

R & B Vocal — Atlanta; died from peritonitis in 1958

The Willows

Personnel: Tony Middleton (vocals)

Single: Church Bells May Ring, 1956 **(62)**
   R & B Vocal—New York

Al Wilson

Albums: Show and Tell, 1973; La La Peace Song, 1974; I've Got a Feeling, 1976

Singles: Do What You Gotta Do, 1968 **(102)**; The Snake, 1968 **(27)**; Poor Side of Town, 1969 **(75)**; I Stand Accused, 1969 **(106)**; Lodi, 1969 **(67)**; Show and Tell, 1973 **(1)**; Touch and Go, 1974 **(57)**; La La Peace Song, 1974 **(30)**; I Won't Last a Day Without You/Let Me Be the One, 1975 **(70)**; I've Got a Feeling (We'll Be Seeing Each Other Again), 1976 **(29)**
   Soul Vocal—Mississippi

J. Frank Wilson & The Cavaliers

Personnel: J. Frank Wilson (vocals); Phil Trunzo (vocals); Jerry Graham (vocals); Bobby Woods (vocals); George Croyle (vocals)

Album: Last Kiss, 1964

Singles: Last Kiss, 1964 **(2)**; Hey Little One, 1964 **(85)**; Six Boys, 1965 **(101)**; Last Kiss, 1973 **(92)**
   Pop Vocal—Texas

Jackie Wilson

Albums: He's So Fine, 1957; Lonely Teardrops, 1958; Dogging Around, 1959; Night, 1960; So Much, 1960; Jackie Wilson Sings the Blues, 1960; My Golden Favourites, 1960; A Woman, a Lover, a Friend, 1960; Try a Little Tenderness, 1961; You Ain't Heard Nothing Yet, 1961; By Special Request, 1961; Body & Soul, 1962; World's Greatest Melodies, 1962; Jackie Wilson at the Copa, 1962; Merry Christmas, 1962; Baby Workout, 1963; Shake a Hand, 1963; Something Else, 1964; Soul Time, 1964; Spotlight, 1965; Soul Galore, 1966; Whispers, 1966; Higher and Higher, 1967; Manufacturers of Soul, 1968 (with Count Basie); I Get the Sweetest Feeling, 1968; Greatest Hits, 1968; Do Your Thing, 1969; It's All Part of Love, 1971; You Got Me Walking, 1973; Greatest Hits, 1973; This Love Is Real, 1973; Beautiful Day, 1974; Very Best of Jackie Wilson, 1975; Nowstalgia, 1975; Nobody but You, 1977

Singles: Reet Petite (The Finest Girl You Ever Want to Meet), 1957 **(62)**; To Be Loved, 1958 **(22)**; We Have Love, 1958 **(93)**; Lonely Teardrops, 1958 **(7)**; That's Why (I Love You So), 1959 **(13)**; I'll Be Satisfied, 1959 **(20)**; You Better Know It, 1959 **(37)**; Talk That Talk, 1959 **(34)**; Night, 1960 **(4)**; Doggin' Around, 1960 **(15)**; (You Were Made for) All My Love, 1960 **(12)**; A Woman, a Lover, a Friend, 1960 **(15)**; Alone at Last, 1960 **(8)**; Am I the Man, 1960 **(32)**; My Empty Arms, 1961 **(9)**; The Tear of the Year, 1961 **(44)**; Please Tell Me Why, 1961 **(20)**; Your One and Only Love, 1961 **(40)**; I'm Comin' on Back to You, 1961 **(19)**; Lonely Life, 1961 **(80)**; Years from Now, 1961 **(37)**; You Don't Know What It Means, 1961 **(79)**; The Way I Am, 1961 **(58)**; My Heart Belongs to Only You, 1961 **(65)**; The Greatest Hurt, 1962 **(34)**; There'll Be No Next Time, 1962 **(75)**; I Found Love, 1962 **(93)** (with Linda Hopkins); Hearts, 1962 **(58)**; I Just Can't Help It, 1962 **(70)**; Forever and a Day, 1962 **(82)**;

Baby, That's All, 1962 **(119)**; What Good Am I Without You, 1963 **(121)**; Baby Workout, 1963 **(5)**; Shake a Hand, 1963 **(42)** (with Linda Hopkins); Shake! Shake! Shake!, 1963 **(33)**; Baby Get It (And Don't Quit It), 1963 **(61)**; I'm Travelin' On, 1964 **(123)**; Call Her Up, 1964 **(110)**; Big Boss Line, 1964 **(94)**; Squeeze Her—Tease Her (But Love Her), 1964 **(89)**; She's All Right, 1964 **(102)**; Danny Boy, 1964 **(94)**; No Pity (in the Naked City), 1965 **(59)**; I Believe I'll Love On, 1965 **(96)**; Think Twice, 1966 **(93)** (with Lavern Baker); Please Don't Hurt Me, 1966 **(128)** (with Lavern Baker); Whispers (Gettin' Louder), 1966 **(11)**; Just Be Sincere, 1967 **(91)**; I Don't Want to Lose You, 1967 **(84)**; I've Lost You, 1967 **(82)**; (Your Love Keeps Lifting Me) Higher and Higher, 1967 **(6)**; Since You Showed Me How to Be Happy, 1967 **(32)**; For Your Precious Love, 1968 **(49)** (with Count Basie); Chain Gang, 1968 **(84)** (with Count Basie); I Get the Sweetest Feeling, 1968 **(34)**; For Once in My Life, 1968 **(70)**; I Still Love You, 1969 **(105)**; Helpless, 1969 **(108)**; Let This Be a Letter (to My Baby), 1970 **(91)**; (I Can Feel Those Vibrations) This Love Is Real, 1970 **(56)**; Love Is Funny That Way, 1971 **(95)**; You Got Me Walking, 1972 **(93)**

Pop/Soul Vocal—Detroit; Jackie had a stroke in 1975 and spent the rest of his life in hospitals until he died on 1/21/84

Nancy Wilson

Albums: Nancy Wilson/Cannonball Adderley, 1962; Hello Young Lovers, 1962; Broadway—My Way, 1963; Hollywood—My Way, 1963; Yesterday's Love Songs/Today's Blues, 1964; Today, Tomorrow, Forever, 1964; How Glad I Am, 1964; The Nancy Wilson Show!, 1965; Today—My Way, 1965; Gentle Is My Love, 1965; From Broadway with Love, 1966; A Touch of Today, 1966; Tender Loving Care, 1966; Nancy—Naturally, 1967; Just for Now, 1967; Lush Life, 1967; Welcome to My Love, 1968; Easy, 1968; The Best of Nancy Wilson, 1968; The Sound of Nancy Wilson, 1968; Nancy, 1969; Son of a Preacher Man, 1969; Close-Up, 1969; Hurt So Bad, 1969; Can't Take My Eyes Off You, 1970; Now I'm a Woman, 1970; But Beautiful, 1971; Kaleidoscope, 1971; All in Love Is Fair, 1974; Come Get to This, 1975; This Mother's Daugther, 1976; I've Never Been to Me, 1977; The Two of Us, 1984 (with Ramsey Lewis)

Singles: Tell Me the Truth, 1963 **(73)**; (You Don't Know) How Glad I Am, 1964 **(11)**; I Wanna Be with You, 1964 **(57)**; And Satisfy, 1964 **(106)**; Don't Come Running Back to Me, 1965 **(58)**; Welcome, Welcome, 1965 **(125)**; Uptight (Everything's Alright), 1966 **(84)**; Face It Girl, It's Over, 1968 **(29)**; Peace of Mind, 1968 **(55)**; In a Long White Room, 1968 **(117)**; You'd Better Go, 1969 **(111)**; Got It Together, 1969 **(114)**; Can't Take My Eyes Off You, 1969 **(52)**; Now I'm a Woman, 1971 **(93)**

Jazz/Pop Vocal—Ohio

Wind

Personnel: Tony Orlando (vocals)
Single: Make Believe, 1969 **(28)**
Pop Vocal—New York

Wind in the Willows

Personnel: Deborah Harry (vocals); Paul Klein (guitars, vocals); Peter Brittain (guitars, vocals); Wayne Kirby (bass, keyboards, vocals); Steve DePhillips (bass, vocals); Harris Wiener (keyboards, vocals); Ida Andrews (woodwinds); Peter Leeds (percussion); Anton Carysforth (drums); Gil Fields (drums)

Album: Wind in the Willows, 1968

Progressive Rock—American

The Winstons

Personnel: Richard Spencer (vocals); Ray Maritano (vocals); Quincy Mattison (vocals); Phil Tolotta (vocals); Sonny Peckrol (vocals); G. C. Coleman (vocals)

Album: Color Him Father, 1969

Singles: Color Him Father, 1969 **(7)**; Love of the Common People, 1969 **(54)**; Say Goodbye to Daddy, 1970 **(107)**

Soul—Washington, D.C.

The Edgar Winter Group

Personnel: Edgar Winter (guitars, vocals); Randal Dolanon (guitars) replaced (1971) by Rick Derringer (guitars, vocals) replaced (1977) by Dan Minatre (guitars); Floyd Radford (guitars) replaced (1972) by Ronnie Montrose (guitars) left group (1974); Gene Kurtz (bass) replaced (1971) by George Sheck (bass) replaced (1972) by Randy Hobbs (bass) replaced (1973) by Dan Hartman (bass, vocals, guitars) replaced (1977) by Robert Arnold (bass); Jimmy Gillen (drums) re-

placed (1971) by Bobby Ramirez (drums) replaced (1973) by Chuck Ruff (drums, vocals) replaced (1977) by George Recile (drums)

Albums: Entrance, 1970; White Trash, 1971; Road Work, 1972; They Only Come Out at Night, 1973; Shock Treatment, 1974; Jasmine Nightdreams, 1975; Edgar Winter Group with Rick Derringer, 1975; Together . . . Live!, 1976 (with Johnny Winter); Recycled, 1977; Edgar Winter Album, 1979; Standing on Rock, 1981; Mission Earth, 1988; Edgar Winter Collection, 1989

Singles: Where Would I Be (Without You), 1971 **(128)**; Keep Playin' That Rock 'n' Roll, 1971 **(70)**; I Can't Turn You Loose, 1972 **(81)**; Frankenstein, 1973 **(1)**; Free Ride, 1973 **(14)**; Hangin' Around, 1973 **(65)**; River's Risin', 1974 **(33)**; Easy Street, 1974 **(83)**; Love Is Everywhere, 1981; Frankenstein '84, 1983; Cry Out, 1988

Hard Rock—Texas

Johnny Winter Band

Personnel: Johnny Winter (guitars, vocals, harmonica); Edgar Winter (keyboards, saxophones, vocals) left group (1969); Tommy Shannon (bass); John Turner (drums) replaced (1973) by Rich Hughes (drums)

Albums: The Progressive Blues Experiment, 1969; Johnny Winter, 1969; The Johnny Winter Story, 1969; First Winter, 1969; Second Winter, 1969; Johnny Winter and..., 1971 (with the McCoys); Live/Johnny Winter and..., 1971 (with the McCoys); About Blues, 1971; Early Times, 1971; Before the Storm, 1972; Still Alive and Well, 1973; Saints and Sinners, 1974; John

Dawson Winter III, 1974; Captured Live, 1976; Together . . . Live, 1976 (with Edgar Winter); Nothin' but the Blues, 1977; White Hot & Blue, 1978; Raising Cain, 1980; Guitar Slinger, 1984; Serious Business, 1986; Third Degree, 1987; Winter of '88, 1988; Birds Can't Row Boats, 1988; Let Me In, 1991

Singles: Rollin' Tumblin', 1969 **(129)**; Johnny B. Goode, 1970 **(92)**; Jumpin' Jack Flash, 1971 **(89)**; Raised on Rock, 1975 **(108)**

Blues/Rock—Texas; Johnny Winter recorded as a solo act after 1973

Ruby Winters

Singles: Make Love to Me, 1967 **(96)** (with Johnny Thunder); I Want Action, 1967 **(109)**; I Don't Want to Cry, 1969 **(97)**; Always David, 1969 **(121)**; Guess Who, 1969 **(99)**

Soul Vocal—Cincinnati

Bobby Womack

Albums: Live, 1971; Communication, 1972; Understanding, 1972; Facts of Life, 1973; Looking for Love Again, 1974; I Can Understand It, 1975; Greatest Hits, 1975; I Don't Know What the World Is Coming To, 1975; Safety Zone, 1976; B W Goes C W, 1976; Home Is Where the Heart Is, 1976; Pieces, 1978; Roads of Life, 1979; The Poet, 1982

Singles: Fly Me to the Moon, 1968 **(52)**; California Dreamin', 1968 **(43)**; I Left My Heart in San Francisco, 1969 **(119)**; How I Miss You Baby, 1969 **(93)**; More Than I Can Stand, 1970 **(90)**; The Preacher (Part 2), 1971 **(111)**; That's the Way I Feel About Cha, 1971 **(27)**; Woman's Gotta Have It, 1972 **(60)**; Sweet Caroline (Good Times Never Seemed So Good), 1972 **(51)**; Harry Hippie, 1972 **(31)**; Across 110th Street, 1973 **(56)**; Nobody Wants You When You're Down and Out, 1973 **(29)**; I'm Through Trying to Prove My Love to You, 1973 **(101)**; Lookin' for a Love, 1974 **(10)**; You're Welcome, Stop on By, 1974 **(59)**; Check It Out, 1975 **(91)**; Love Has Finally Come at Last, 1984 **(88)** (with Patti LaBelle)

Soul/R & B—Cleveland

The Womenfolk

Personnel: Elaine Gealer (vocals); Joyce James (vocals); Leni Ashmore (vocals); Barbara Cooper (vocals); Judy Fine (vocals)

Album: The Womenfolk, 1964

Singles: Little Boxes, 1964 **(83)**; Last Thing on My Mind, 1966 **(106)**

Folk/Pop—California

Stevie Wonder

Albums: Little Stevie Wonder/ The 12 Year Old Genius, 1963; Up-Tight Everything's Alright, 1966; Down to Earth, 1967; I Was Made to Love Her, 1967; Greatest Hits, 1968; For Once in My Life, 1969; My Cherie Amour, 1969; Stevie Wonder Live, 1970; Signed, Sealed and Delivered, 1970; Where I'm Coming From, 1971; Greatest Hits Volume 2, 1971; Music of My Mind, 1972; Talking Book, 1972; Innervisions, 1973; Fulfillingness' First Finale, 1974; Songs in the Key of Life, 1976; Looking Back, 1977; Journey Through the Secret Life of

Stevie Wonder

Plants, 1979; Hotter Than July, 1980; Stevie Wonder's Original Musiquarium 1, 1982; The Woman in Red, 1984; Love Songs/20 Classic Hits, 1985; In Square Circle, 1986; Characters, 1987; Music from Jungle Fever, 1991

Singles: Fingertips, 1963 (**1**); I Call It Pretty Music, 1963 (**101**); Workout Stevie, Workout, 1963 (**33**); Castles in the Sand, 1964 (**52**); Hey Harmonica Man, 1964 (**29**); High Heel Sneakers, 1965 (**59**); Uptight (Everything's Alright), 1965 (**3**); Nothing's Too Good for My Baby, 1966 (**20**); Blowin' in the Wind, 1966 (**9**); With a Child's Heart, 1966 (**131**); A Place in the Sun, 1966 (**9**); Travlin' Man, 1967 (**32**); Hey Love, 1967 (**90**); I Was Made to Love Her, 1967 (**2**); I'm Wondering, 1967 (**12**); Shoo-Be-Doo-Be-Doo-Da-Day, 1968 (**9**); You Met Your Match, 1968 (**35**); Alfie, 1968 (**66**); For Once in My Life, 1968 (**2**); I Don't Know Why, 1969 (**39**); My Cherie Amour, 1969 (**4**); Yester-Me, Yester-You, Yesterday, 1969 (**7**); Never Had a Dream Come True, 1970 (**26**); Signed, Sealed, Delivered (I'm Yours), 1970 (**3**); Heaven Help Us All, 1970 (**9**); We Can Work It Out, 1971 (**13**); Never Dreamed You'd Leave in Summer, 1971 (**78**); If You Really Love Me, 1971 (**8**); Superwoman, 1972 (**33**); Keep on Running, 1972 (**90**); Superstition, 1972 (**1**); You Are the Sunshine of My Life, 1972 (**1**); Higher Ground, 1973 (**4**); Living for the City, 1973 (**8**); Don't Worry 'Bout a Thing, 1974 (**16**); You Haven't Done Nothing, 1974 (**1**); Boogie on Reggae Woman, 1974 (**3**); I Wish, 1976 (**1**); Sir Duke, 1977 (**1**); Another Star, 1977 (**32**); As, 1977 (**36**); Pops, We Love You (A Tribute to Father), 1979 (**59**) (with Smokey Robinson, Marvin Gaye & Diana Ross); Send One Your Love, 1979 (**4**); Outside My Window, 1980 (**52**); Master Blaster, 1980 (**5**); I Ain't Gonna Stand for It, 1980 (**11**); Lately, 1981 (**64**); Did I Hear You Say You Love Me, 1981; That Girl, 1982 (**4**); Ebony and Ivory, 1982 (**1**) (with Paul McCartney); Do I Do, 1982 (**13**); Ribbon in the Sky, 1982 (**54**); Used to Be, 1982 (**46**) (with Charlene); Happy Birthday, 1983; I Just Called to Say I Love You, 1984 (**1**); Love Light in Flight, 1984 (**17**); Don't Drive Drunk, 1984; Part Time Lover, 1985 (**1**); Go Home, 1985 (**10**); Overjoyed, 1986 (**24**); Land of La La, 1986 (**86**); Skeletons, 1987 (**19**); You Will Know, 1988 (**77**); Get It, 1988 (**80**) (with Michael Jackson); My Love, 1988 (**80**) (with Julio Iglesias)

Soul/Pop/R & B—Michigan; real name is Steveland Morris

Wonder Who?

Singles: Don't Think Twice, 1965 **(12)**; On the Good Ship Lollipop, 1966 **(87)**; You're Nobody Till Somebody Loves You, 1966 **(96)**; Lonesome Road, 1967 **(89)**

Pop/Rock — New Jersey; group is the Four Seasons

Brenton Wood

Albums: Oogum Boogum, 1967; Baby You Got It, 1967

Singles: The Oogum Boogum Song, 1967 **(34)**; Gimme Little Sign, 1967 **(9)**; Baby You Got It, 1967 **(34)**; Lovey Dovey Kinda Lovin', 1968 **(99)**; Me and You, 1968 **(121)**; A Change Is Gonna Come, 1969 **(131)**

Soul/Pop Vocal — California; real name is Alfred Smith

Royston & Heather Wood

Albums: Galleries, 1968; Young Tradition Sampler, 1977; No Relation, 1977

Folk/Rock — British

Sheb Wooley

Singles: Are You Satisfied?, 1955 **(95)**; The Purple People Eater, 1958 **(1)**; Sweet Chile, 1959 **(70)**; That's My Pa, 1962 **(51)**; Don't Go Near the Eskimos, 1962 **(62)***; Hello Walls No. 2, 1963 **(131)***; Still No. 2, 1963 **(98)***; Detroit City No. 2, 1963 **(90)***; Almost Persuaded No. 2, 1966 **(58)***; Harper Valley P.T.A. (Later That Same Day), 1968 **(67)***

Novelty Pop — Oklahoma; real name is Shelby Wooley

**recorded as Ben Colder*

The Woolies

Personnel: Stormy Rice (vocals); Bee Metros (guitars); Ron English (guitars); Bob Baldori (bass); Jeff Baldori (drums)

Album: The Woolies, 1967

Singles: Who Do You Love, 1966; Who Do You Love, 1967 **(95)**

Pop/Rock — Michigan

Link Wray & His Ray Men

Albums: Link Wray & the Ray Men, 1960; Jack the Ripper, 1963; Link Wray, 1971; There's Good Rockin' Tonight, 1973; Be What You Want, 1973; Beans & Fatback, 1973; Rockin' & Handclappin', 1973; Rumble, 1974; Interstate 10, 1975; Stuck in Gear, 1976; Bullshot, 1979; Live at the Pasadiso, 1980

Singles: Rumble, 1958 **(16)**; Raw-Hide, 1959 **(23)**; Jack the Ripper, 1963 **(64)**

Rockabilly — North Carolina

Charles Wright & The Watts 103rd Street Rhythm

Albums: Together, 1969; In the Jungle Babe, 1969; Express Yourself, 1970; You're So Beautiful, 1971

Singles: Spreadin' Honey, 1967 **(73)**; Do Your Thing, 1969 **(11)**; Till You Get Enough, 1969 **(67)**; Comment, 1969 **(109)**; Must Be Your Thing, 1969 **(103)**; Love Land, 1970 **(16)**; Express Yourself, 1970 **(12)**; Solution for Pollution, 1971 **(96)**; Your Love (Means Everything to Me), 1971 **(73)**

Soul/Funk — Los Angeles

Dale Wright

Singles: She's Neat, 1958 **(38)**; Please Don't Do It, 1958 **(77)**

Rockabilly—Ohio; real name is Harlan Dale Riffe

O. V. Wright

Singles: That's How Strong My Love Is, 1964 **(109)**; You're Gonna Make Me Cry, 1965 **(86)**; Eight Men, Four Women, 1967 **(80)**; Ace of Spade, 1970 **(54)**; When You Took Your Love from Me, 1971 **(118)**; A Nickel and a Nail, 1971 **(103)**

Soul Vocal—Tennessee; O. V. stands for Overton Vertis; died in 1980

Bill Wyman

Albums: Monkey Grip, 1974; Stone Alone, 1976; Bill Wyman, 1981; Green Ice (Soundtrack), 1982

Single: In Another Land, 1967 **(87)**

Pop/Rock—British

Zal Yanovsky

Album: Alive & Well in Argentina, 1970

Single: As Long as You're Here, 1967 **(101)**

Pop/Rock—American; former member of the Lovin' Spoonful and the Mugwumps

Glenn Yarbrough

Albums: One More Round, 1964; Come Share My Life, 1965; Baby the Rain Must Fall, 1965; It's Gonna Be Fine, 1965; The Lonely Things, 1966; Live at the Hungry i, 1966; For Emily, Whenever I May Find Her, 1967; Honey & Wine, 1967; Each of Us Alone, 1968; Glenn Yarbrough Sings the Rod McKuen Songbook, 1969

Singles: Baby the Rain Must Fall, 1965 **(12)**; It's Gonna Be Fine, 1965 **(54)**

Pop/Folk Vocal—Wisconsin; former lead singer of the Limeliters

The Yardbirds

Personnel: Keith Relf (vocals, harmonica; deceased 1976); Tony 'Top' Topham (guitars) replaced (1963) by Eric Clapton (guitars, vocals) replaced (1965) by Jeff Beck (guitars) left group (1966); Chris Dreja (guitars, bass); Paul Samwell-Smith (bass) replaced (1966) by Jimmy Page (guitars, bass); Jim McCarty (drums)

Albums: Yardbirds with Sonny Boy Williamson, 1964; Five Live Yardbirds, 1965; For Your Love, 1965; Having a Rave Up with the Yardbirds, 1966; The Yardbirds, 1966; Over Under Sideways Down, 1966; Great Hits, 1967; Little Games, 1967; Live Yardbirds, 1971; The Yardbirds' Greatest Hits, 1973; Shapes of Things, 1977

Singles: For Your Love, 1965 **(6)**; Heart Full of Soul, 1965 **(9)**; I'm a Man, 1965 **(17)**; Shapes of Things, 1966; Over Under Sideways Down, 1966 **(13)**; Happenings Ten Years Time Ago, 1966 **(30)**; Little Games, 1967 **(51)**; Ha Ha Said the Clown, 1967 **(45)**; Ten Little Indians, 1967 **(96)**; Goodnight Sweet Josephine, 1968 **(127)**

Blues/Rock—British

The Yellow Balloon

Personnel: Alex Valdez (vocals); Don Grady (guitars, vocals)

The Yardbirds: Dreja, Clapton, Samwell-Smith, Relf, McCarty

Yellow Balloon: Don Grady on far left

Album: Yellow Balloon, 1967
Singles: Yellow Balloon, 1967
(25); Good Feelin' Time, 1967 **(101)**
   Psychedelic Pop—California;
Grady played Robbie Douglas on
TV's "My Three Sons"

Yes

Personnel: Jon Anderson (vocals)
replaced (1980) by Trevor Horn
(vocals, bass) replaced (1983) by Jon
Anderson (vocals); Chris Squire
(bass, vocals); Tony Kaye (keyboards) replaced (1971) by Rick
Wakeman (keyboards) replaced
(1974) by Vangelis Papathanasiou
(keyboards) replaced (1974) by
Patrick Moraz (keyboards) replaced
(1976) by Rick Wakeman (keyboards) replaced (1980) by Geoffrey
Downes (keyboards) replaced (1983)
by Tony Kaye (keyboards) replaced
(1983) by Eddie Jobson (keyboards)
replaced (1984) by Tony Kaye (keyboards); Peter Banks (guitars) replaced (1971) by Steve Howe
(guitars, vocals) replaced (1983) by
Trevor Rabin (guitars, vocals); Bill
Bruford (drums, percussion) replaced (1972) by Alan White
(drums, percussion); added (1990)
Rick Wakeman (keyboards); added

Yes: *back row:* **Squire, Wakeman, Anderson;** *front row:* **White, Howe**

(1990) Steve Howe (guitars, vocals); added (1990) Bill Bruford (drums percussion)

Albums: Yes, 1969; Time and a Word, 1970; The Yes Album, 1971; Fragile, 1972; Close to the Edge, 1972; Yessongs, 1973; Tales from Topographic Oceans, 1974; Relayer, 1974; Yesterdays, 1975; Going for the One, 1977; Tormato, 1978; Drama, 1980; Yesshows, 1980; Classic Yes, 1981; 90125, 1983; 90125 Live—The Solos, 1984; Big Generator, 1987; Union, 1991; Yes Years (box), 1991

Singles: Sweetness, 1970; Your Move, 1971 **(40)**; Roundabout/Long Distance Runaround, 1972 **(13)**; America, 1972 **(46)**; And You and I, 1972 **(42)**; Soon, 1975; Wond'rous Stories, 1977; Going for the One, 1977; Don't Kill the Whale, 1978; Into the Lens, 1980 **(104)**; Tempis Fugit, 1980; Owner of a Lonely Heart, 1983 **(1)**; Leave It, 1984 **(24)**; It Can Happen, 1984 **(51)**; Love Will Find a Way, 1987 **(30)**; Rhythm of Love, 1987 **(40)**; Lift Me Up, 1991; Saving My Heart, 1991

Progressive/Art Rock—British; Anderson, Bruford, Wakeman, Howe, Squire, Kaye, White and Rabin appear on the "Union" LP

"You Know Who" Group

Single: Roses Are Red My Love, 1964 **(43)**

Pop Vocal—American

Barry Young

Album: One Has My Name, 1966
Singles: One Has My Name (the Other Has My Heart), 1965 **(13)**;

Since You Have Gone from Me,
1966 **(130)**
Pop Vocal—American

Georgie Young &
The Rockin 'Bocs

Single: Nine More Miles (The
Faster-Faster Song), 1958 **(58)**
Pop/Rock—American

Jesse Colin Young

Albums: Youngblood, 1964; The
Soul of a City Boy, 1964; A Song
for Juli, 1973; Together, 1974; Light
Shine, 1974; Songbird, 1975; On the
Road, 1976; Love on a Wing, 1977;
American Dreams, 1978; The Per-
fect Stranger, 1982; The Highway Is
for Heroes, 1987
Singles: Higher and Higher, 1977
(109); Fight for It, 1982 (with Carly
Simon); Ophelia, 1982; Ophelia,
1983
Folk/Pop/Rock—California;
leader of the Youngbloods

Kathy Young &
The Innocents

Album: The Sound of Kathy
Young, 1961
Singles: A Thousand Stars, 1960
(3); Happy Birthday Blues, 1961
(30); Magic Is the Night, 1961 **(80)**
Pop Vocal—California

Neil Young &
Crazy Horse

Personnel: Neil Young (guitars,
vocals, keyboards, harmonica);
Danny Whitten (guitars, vocals; deceased 1972) replaced (1972) by Ben
Keith (guitars, vocals) replaced

Neil Young

(1974) by Frank Sampedro (guitars,
keyboards, vocals); Billy Talbot
(bass, vocals); Ralph Molina
(drums)
Albums: Neil Young, 1969;
Everybody Knows This Is Nowhere,
1969; After the Gold Rush, 1970;
Harvest, 1972; Journey Through the
Past, 1972; Time Fades Away, 1973;
On the Beach, 1974; Tonight's the
Night, 1975; Zuma, 1975; Long
May You Run, 1976 (The Stills-
Young Band); American Stars 'n'
Bars, 1976; Decade, 1977; Comes a
Time, 1978; Rust Never Sleeps,
1979; Live Rust, 1979; Hawks and
Doves, 1980; Re-Ac-Tor, 1981;
Trans, 1982; Everybody's Rockin',
1983; Greatest Hits, 1985; Old
Ways, 1985; Landing on Water,
1986; Life, 1987; This Note's for
You, 1988; Freedom, 1989; Ragged
Glory, 1990; Weld, 1991
Singles: Cinnamon Girl, 1970
(55); Only Love Can Break Your
Heart, 1970 **(33)**; When You Dance,
I Can Really Love, 1971 **(93)**; Heart
of Gold, 1972 **(1)**; Old Man, 1972

(31); War Song, 1972 **(61)** (with Graham Nash); Time Fades Away, 1973 **(108)**; Walk On, 1974 **(69)**; Lookin' for a Love, 1975; Hey Babe, 1976; Long May You Run, 1976 (The Stills-Young Band); Sugar Mountain, 1978; Four Strong Winds, 1978 **(61)**; Comes a Time, 1979; Hey, Hey, My My (Into the Black), 1979 **(79)**; Like a Hurricane, 1980; Hawks and Doves/Union Man, 1980; Stayin' Power, 1980; Southern Pacific, 1981 **(70)**; Opera Star, 1982; A Little Thing Called Love, 1982 **(71)**; Sample and Hold, 1983; Mr. Soul, 1983; Wonderin', 1983; Cry, Cry, Cry, 1983; Get Back to the Country, 1985; Old Ways, 1986; Long Walk Home, 1987; This Note's for You, 1988; Rockin' in the Free World, 1989; Mansion on the Hill, 1990; Over and Over, 1990

Country/Rock—Canadian; Neil hails from Toronto; performed at Live Aid

Young-Holt Unlimited

Personnel: Eldee Young (bass); Isaac "Red" Holt (drums); Don Walker (piano) left group (1968)

Albums: Wack Wack, 1967; Soulful Strut, 1969; Just a Melody, 1969

Singles: Wack Wack, 1966 **(40)**; Soulful Strut, 1968 **(3)**; Who's Making Love, 1969 **(57)**; Straight Ahead, 1969 **(110)**; Horoscope, 1969 **(115)**; Mellow Dreaming, 1970 **(106)**

R & B/Soul—Chicago; Young and Holt were ⅔ of the Ramsey Lewis Trio

The Youngbloods

Personnel: Jesse Colin Young (vocals, bass, guitars); Jerry Corbitt (guitars, bass) replaced (1971) by Michael Kane (bass); Lowell Levinger (guitars, keyboards); Joseph Bauer (drums)

Albums: Youngbloods, 1967; Earth Music, 1967; Elephant Mountain, 1969; Rock Festival, 1970; The Best of the Youngbloods, 1970; Two Trips, 1970; Crabtunes Noggins, 1971; Ride the Wind, 1971; Sunlight, 1971; Good and Dusty, 1972; High on a Ridgetop, 1972; This Is the Youngbloods, 1972

Singles: Grizzly Bear, 1967 **(52)**; Get Together, 1969 **(5)**; Darkness, Darkness, 1969 **(124)**; Sunlight, 1969 **(114)**; Darkness, Darkness, 1970 **(86)**; Sunlight, 1971 **(123)**

Pop/Folk Rock—California; Young's real name is Perry Miller

Timi Yuro

Albums: Timi Yuro, 1961; Hurt, 1961; Soul, 1962; What's a Matter Baby, 1962; Let Me Call You Sweetheart, 1963; Make the World Go Away, 1963; The Amazing Timi Yuro, 1964; Something's Bad in My Mind, 1968; In the Beginning, 1968; Best of Timi Yuro, 1968; The Timi Yuro Album, 1976

Singles: Hurt, 1961 **(4)**; I Apologize, 1961 **(72)**; Smile, 1961 **(42)**; She Really Loves You, 1961 **(93)**; Let Me Call You Sweetheart, 1962 **(66)**; What's a Matter Baby (Is It Hurting You), 1962 **(12)**; The Love of a Boy, 1962 **(44)**; Insult to Injury, 1963 **(81)**; Make the World Go Away, 1963 **(24)**; Gotta Travel On, 1963 **(64)**; Permanently Lonely, 1964 **(130)**; If, 1964 **(120)**; You Can Have Him, 1965 **(96)**; Once a Day, 1966

(118); Southern Lady, 1975
(108)

Pop Vocal—California; real name is Rosemarie Timothy Aurro Yuro

John Zacherle ("The Cool Ghoul")

Album: Monster Mash, 1962
Single: Dinner with Drac—Part 1, 1958 (6)

Novelty Pop—Philadelphia

Zager & Evans

Personnel: Denny Zager (vocals, guitars); Rick Evans (vocals, guitars)
Albums: In the Year 2525, 1969; Food for the Mind, 1970; The Early Writings of Zager & Evans, 1971
Singles: In the Year 2525, 1969 (1); Mr. Turnkey, 1969 (106)

Pop/Rock—Nebraska

Ricky Zahnd & The Blue Jeaners

Single: (I'm Getting') Nuttin' for Christmas, 1955 (21)

Pop Vocal—New York; was formerly a vice-president for the N.Y. Knicks and Rangers

Frank Zappa & The Mothers of Invention

Personnel: Frank Zappa (guitars, vocals); Ray Collins (vocals); Jim Sherwood (woodwinds); Buzz Gardner (woodwinds); Roy Estrada (bass, vocals); Don Preston (keyboards, bass); Jimmy Carl Black (drums); added (1967) Ian Underwood (guitars, keyboards, wood winds)

Albums: Freak Out, 1966; Absolutely Free, 1967; We're Only in It for the Money, 1967; Lumpy Gravy, 1967; Cruisin' with Ruben & the Jets, 1968; Mother Mania, 1969; Uncle Meat, 1969; Weasels Ripped My Flesh, 1970; Chunga's Revenge, 1970; Hot Rats, 1970; Burnt Weeny Sandwich, 1970; Live at Fillmore East, 1971; 200 Motels, 1971; Just Another Band from L.A., 1972; The Grand Wazoo, 1972; Waka Jawaka, 1972; Overnight Sensation, 1973; Apostrophe, 1974; Roxy & Elsewhere, 1974; One Size Fits All, 1974; Mother's Day, 1975; Zappa & the Mothers, 1975; Bongo Fury, 1975; Zoot Allures, 1976; In New York, 1978; Studio Tan, 1978; Sheik Yerbouti, 1979; Sleep Dirt, 1979; Orchestral Favourites, 1979; Joe's Garage Act I, 1980; Joe's Garage Acts II & III, 1980; Tinseltown Rebellion, 1981; You Are What You Is, 1981; Ship Arriving Too Late to Save a Drowning Witch, 1982; Man from Utopia, 1983; Rare Meat, 1983; The Perfect Stranger, 1984; Them or Us, 1984; Guitar, 1985; Meets the Mothers of Prevention, 1985; Jazz from Hell, 1986; Thing Fish, 1986; London Symphony Orchestra I, 1987; London Symphony Orchestra II, 1987; Broadway the Hard Way, 1988; You Can't Do That on Stage Anymore Volume 1, 1988; You Can't Do That on Stage Anymore Volume 2, 1988; You Can't Do That on Stage Anymore Volume 3, 1989; Make a Jazz Noise Hear, 1990; The Best Band You Never Heard in Your Life, 1991; Tis the Season to Be Jelly, 1991; The Ark, 1991; Freaks and Motherfu*$#%!, 1991; Piquantique, 1991;

Unmitigated Audacity, 1991; Saarbrucken 1978, 1991; Anyway the Wind Blows, 1991; As an Am, 1991; Beat the Boots (box), 1991

Singles: Don't Eat Yellow Snow, 1974 **(86)**; Disco Boy, 1977 **(105)**; Dancin' Fool, 1979 **(45)**; Joe's Garage, 1979; I Don't Wanna Get Drafted, 1980 **(103)**; Valley Girl, 1982 **(32)** (with Moon Zappa)

Psychedelic Rock—California; recorded as Frank Zappa after 1969; appeared in the films *Baby Snakes* and *200 Motels*

Danny Zella & His Zell Rocks

Single: Wicked Ruby, 1959 **(71)**
Pop/Rock—Detroit

Zephyr

Personnel: Tommy Bolin (guitars, vocals; deceased 1976) replaced (1972) by Jock Bartley (guitars, vocals); David Givens (bass, vocals); Candy Givens (keyboards, vocals); Robbie Chamberlain (drums) replaced (1970) by Bobby Berge (drums) replaced (1971) by P. M. Wooten (drums)

Albums: Zephyr, 1969; Going Back to Colorado, 1971; Sunset Ride, 1972

Hard Rock—American

The Zombies

Personnel: Rod Argent (keyboards, vocals) replaced (1990) by Sebastian Santa Maria (keyboards); Colin Blunstone (vocals); Paul Atkinson (guitars); Chris White (bass) replaced (1967) by Paul Arnold (bass) replaced (1990) by Chris White (bass); Hugh Grundy (drums)

Albums: Begins Here, 1965; Zombies, 1965; Earthdays, 1966; Odyssey and Oracle, 1968; World of the Zombies, 1970; Time of the Zombies, 1973; She's Not There, 1976;

The Zombies: Argent, Blunstone, Atkinson, White, Grundy

She's Not There (UK), 1981; The Zombies Greatest Hits, 1990; New World, 1991

Singles: She's Not There, 1964 **(2)**; Tell Her No, 1965 **(6)**; She's Coming Home, 1965 **(58)**; I Want You Back Again, 1965 **(95)**; Nothing's Changed, 1965; Whenever You're Ready, 1965 **(110)**; Just Out of Reach, 1965 **(113)**; Time of the Season, 1969 **(3)**; Imagine the Swan, 1969 **(109)**

Pop/Rock — British

The Birthday List

January

1 Country Joe McDonald
2 Chick Churchill
3 Stephen Stills
4 John McLaughlin
5 Thom Mooney
6 Syd Barrett, Sandy Denny
7 Kenny Loggins, Mike McCartney
8 David Bowie, Anthony Gourdine, Lee Jackson, Robbie
  Krieger, John Petersen, Elvis
  Presley, Terry Sylvester
9 Joan Baez, Bill Cowsill, Scott
  Engel, Kenneth Kelley,
  Jimmy Page, Dick Yount
10 Ronnie Hawkins, Bob Lang,
  Rod Stewart
11 none
12 Tom Ardolino, Long John
  Baldry, Cynthia Robinson
13 none
14 Tim Harris
15 Sonny Bivins, Captain Beefheart, Melvyn Gale
16 Donn Adams, Bob Bogle
17 Ted Dunbar, William Hart,
  Mick Taylor
18 Bobby Goldsboro, Dave Greenslade, David Ruffin, Larry
  Smith
19 Desi Arnaz, Jr., Joe Butler,
  Phil Everly, Janis Joplin

20 Eric Stewart, Ron Towson
21 Richie Havens, Jim Ibbotson
22 Sam Cooke, Micki Harris
23 Bill Cunningham
24 Neil Diamond, Warren Zevon
25 John Staehly
26 Derek Holt
27 Kim Gardner, Nick Mason,
  Nedra Talley
28 Rick Allen, Brian Keenan,
  Corky Laing
29 David Byron
30 Marty Balin, Sandy Deane,
  Steve Marriott, Joe Terranova
31 Phil Collins, Terry Kath, Curly
  Smith

February

1 Don Everly, Bob Shane
2 Skip Battin, Alan Caddy, Ronnie Goodson, Pete Lucia,
  Peter Macbeth, Graham Nash
3 Dave Davies, Angelo D'Aleo,
  Dennis Edwards, Melanie,
  Johnny Watson
4 Florence LaRue Gordon, Jerry
  Shirley, John Steel
5 J. R. Cobb, Al Kooper, Cory
  Wells, Chuck Winfield
6 none
7 Joe English, Jimmy Greenspoon, Alan Lancaster

8 Creed Bratton, Adolfo de la
   Parra, Tom Rush, Paul
   Wheatbread
9 Brian Bennett, Carole King
10 Ral Donner, Don Wilson
11 Tony Colton, Bobby "Boris"
   Pickett, Gene Vincent
12 Rick Frank, Steve Hackett,
   Ray Manzarek, Joe Schermie,
   John Ward
13 Roy Dyke, Peter Tork
14 Eric Andersen, Vic Briggs,
   Tim Buckley
15 Mick Avory
16 Sonny Bono
17 Bobby Lewis, Gene Pitney
18 none
19 Mark Andes, Lou Christie,
   William "Smokey" Robinson,
   Bobby Rogers
20 Randy California, Barbara
   Ellis, Buffy Sainte-Marie,
   Lewis Soloff
21 none
22 Oliver
23 Mike Maxfield, Johnny Winter,
   Rusty Young
24 Nicky Hopkins
25 George Harrison
26 Paul Cotton, Bob Hite
27 Eddie Gray
28 John Evan, Brian Jones, Ron
   Rosman, Marty Sanders, Joe
   South
29 Gretchen Christopher

March

1 Tony Ashton, Mike D'Abo,
   Roger Daltrey
2 John Cowsill, Tony Meehan,
   Lou Reed
3 Willie Chambers, Mike Pender
4 Eric Allan Dale, Chris Squire
5 none
6 Doug Dillard, David Gilmour,
   Hugh Grundy, Mary Wilson,

   Myron Yules
7 Matthew Fisher, Chris White
8 Mike Allsup, Micky Dolenz,
   Ralph Ellis, Randy Meisner
9 Trevor Burton, Jimmie Fadden, Mark Lindsay, Robin
   Trower
10 Dean Torrence
11 George Kooymans, Ric Rothwell
12 Jack Green, Paul Kantner,
   James Taylor
13 Neil Sedaka
14 James O'Rourke, Walter Parazaider
15 Ry Cooder, David Costell,
   Hughie Flint, Phil Lesh, Mike
   Love, Sly Stone
16 none
17 Clarence Collins, John Sebastian
18 Wilson Pickett, John Wilson
19 Paul Atkinson
20 Carl Palmer
21 Rose Stone, Viv Stanshall
22 George Benson, Jeremy Clyde,
   Howard Reitzes, Keith Relf,
   Harry Vanda
23 none
24 Mike Kellie
25 Johnny Burnette, Aretha
   Franklin, Elton John
26 Fred Parris, Diana Ross,
   Richard Tandy
27 Tony Banks
28 Chuck Portz, Richard Suss-
   man, Dean Webb
29 Gary Brooker
30 Dave Ball, Eric Clapton,
   Graeme Edge
31 Tony Brock, John D. Loudermilk, G. Allan Nichol, Mick
   Ralphs

April

1 Alan Blakely, Danny Brooks

Arthur Conley, Rudy Isley,
Ronnie Lane, Phil Margo
2 Marvin Gaye, Kurt Winter
3 Jeff Barry, Jan Berry, Richard
Manuel, Mel Schacher, Richard Thompson, Phillippe
Wynne
4 Peter Haycock, Dave Hill
5 David LaFlamme, Ronnie
White
6 Michelle Phillips
7 Mick Abrahams, Patricia Bennett, Spencer Dyrden, Bill
Kreutzmann
8 Roger Chapman, Steve Howe
9 none
10 Bobby Smith
11 none
12 David Cassidy, John Kay
13 Jack Casady, Lester Chambers
14 Ritchie Blackmore
15 Allan Clarke, Dave Edmunds,
Tony Williams
16 Dusty Springfield
17 Billy Fury
18 Harvey Kagan, Tony Reeves,
Skip Spence, Michael Vickers
19 Alan Price, Mark Volman
20 Craig Frost
21 Alan Warner, John Weider
22 Glen Campbell, Peter Frampton
23 Roy Orbison, Ray Peterson
24 Doug Clifford, Glenn Cornick
25 Michael Brown, Stu Cook,
Ronnie Gilbert, Michael
"Kennedy" Kogel
26 Duane Eddy, Bobby Rydell,
Maurice Williams, Gary
Wright
27 Peter Ham
28 Eddie Jobson
29 Lonnie Donnegan, Tommy
James, Francis Rossi, Klaus
Voorman
30 Johnny Horton, Wayne
Kramer, Bobby Vee

May

1 Judy Collins, Jerry Weiss
2 Randy Cain, Lesley Gore, Bob
Henrit, Goldy McJohn
3 Mary Hopkin, Peter Staples,
Frankie Valli
4 Ronnie Bond, Ed Cassidy,
Peggy McGannon
5 none
6 Dennis Cowan, Bob Seger
7 Janis Ian, Mitch Jayne, John
Mastrangelo, Rick Westwood
8 John Fred Gourrier, Rick Nelson, Paul Samwell-Smith
9 Pete Birrell, Don Danneman,
Richie Furay, Billy Joel,
Steven Katz, Dave Prater,
Tommy Roe
10 Fats Domino, Donovan, Henry
Fambrough, Jay Ferguson,
Graham Gouldman, Jackie
Lomax, Dave Mason, Danny
Rapp
11 Eric Burdon, John Chadwick,
Arnie Satin
12 Ian McLagan, James Purify,
David Walkes, Steve Win-
wood
13 Peter Gabriel, Danny Kirwan,
Mary Wells, Stevie Wonder
14 Jack Bruce, Al Ciner, Gene
Cornish, Bobby Darin, Derek
Leckenby, Warren Smith
15 Brian Eno, Mike Oldfield
16 Pervis Jackson, Barbara Lee
17 Bill Bruford, Malcolm Hale,
Taj Mahal
18 Rodney Dillard, Rick Wakeman, Bill Wallace
19 Jerry Hyman, Peter
Townshend
20 Cher, Joe Cocker, Sue Cowsill,
Jill Jackson
21 Ronald Isley, Hilton Valentine
22 none
23 none

24 Sarah Dash, Bob Dylan, Derek
    Quinn
25 Brian Davison, Mike Margo,
    John Palmer
26 Ray Ennis, Levon Helm, Stevie
    Nicks, Garry Peterson
27 Cilla Black
28 Papa John Creach, John Fog-
    erty, Tony Mansfield
29 Roy Crewsdon
30 Lenny Davidson
31 John Bonham, Augie Meyer,
    Peter Yarrow

June

1 Ron Wood
2 Charlie Watts
3 Michael Clarke, Ian Hunter,
   John Paul Jones, Curtis
   Mayfield
4 Roger Ball, Gordon Waller,
   Charlie Whitney
5 Floyd Butler, Freddie Stone
6 Pete Albin, Gary "U.S." Bonds,
   Howie Kane, Clarence White
7 Tom Jones
8 Mick Box, Chuck Negron, Boz
   Scaggs, Nancy Sinatra
9 Jon Lord, Jackie Wilson
10 Shirley Alston, Rick Price
11 Skip Allan, Joey Dee
12 Harold Cowart, Roy Harper,
    Norman Kuhlke, Reg Presley,
    John Wetton
13 Bobby Freeman
14 Rod Argent, Jim Lea, Alan
    White, Muff Winwood
15 Noddy Holder, Harry Nilsson,
    Nigel Pickering
16 Eddie Levert, John Rostill,
    Peppy "Castro" Thielheim
17 Chris Spedding
18 Don "Sugarcane" Harris, Paul
    McCartney
19 Tommy DeVito, Elaine
    "Spanky" McFarlane

20 Brian Wilson
21 Chris Britton, Miguel Vicens
    Danus, Ray Davies, Jon
    Hiseman, Joey Molland
22 Peter Asher, Howard Kaylan,
    Todd Rundgren, Steven
    Weber
23 none
24 Jeff Beck, Colin Blunstone, Ar-
    thur Brown, Mick Fleetwood,
    Bruce Johnston, Patrick
    Moraz, Chris Wood
25 Carly Simon, Clint Warwick
26 Billy Davis, Jr., Georgie Fame,
    Larry Taylor
27 none
28 Bobby Harrison
29 Billy Hinsche, Little Eva, Ian
    Paice, Roger Ruskin Spear
30 Florence Ballard, Dave Van
    Ronk

July

1 Delaney Bramlett, June
   Montiero
2 Paul Williams
3 Damon Harris
4 Jeremy Spencer, Alan Wilson
5 Michael Monarch, Robbie
   Robertson, Dick Scopettone
6 Byron Berline, Gene Chandler
7 Warren Entner, Larry Rhein-
   hardt, Jim Rodford, Ringo
   Starr, Rob Townsend
8 none
9 Joe Micelli, Ray Smith
10 Arlo Guthrie, Jerry Miller, Ian
    Whitcomb
11 Jeff Hanna
12 Phil Kramer, Christine McVie
13 Roger McGuinn
14 none
15 Peter Lewis, Linda Ronstadt
16 Tom Boggs, Tony Jackson
17 Stan Bronstein, Spencer Davis,
    Michael Vale

18 Brian Auger, Dion, Danny
    McCullough, Robin McDon-
    ald, Martha Reeves, Cesar
    Zuiderwijk
19 Alan Gorrie, Bernie Leadon
20 John Lodge, Carlos Santana
21 Cat Stevens, Barry Whitham
22 Estelle Bennett, Don Henley
23 Dino Danelli, Tony Joe White
24 Heinz Burt, Barbara Love
25 Mark Clarke, Mike Clarke,
    Tom Dawes, Jim McCarty
26 Al Anderson, Mick Jagger
27 Bobbie Gentry, Al Ramsey,
    Nick Reynolds
28 Michael Bloomfield, Simon
    Kirke, Richard Wright
29 none
30 Jeffrey Hammond-Hammond
31 Karl Greene, Gary Lewis,
    Hugh McDowell, Bob Welch,
    John R. West

August

1 Rick Coonce, Jerry Garcia
2 Garth Hudson, Doris Kenner
3 Beverly Lee
4 none
5 Rick Huxley, Greg Leskiw
6 Mike Elliot
7 Kerry Chater, Andy Fraser
8 Joe Tex
9 Marinus Gerritsen, Bill Hen-
    derson
10 Ian Anderson, Bobby Hatfield,
    Ronnie Spector
11 Erik Braunn, Mike Hugg, Jim
    Kale, Dennis Payton
12 none
13 Francisco Moran
14 Terry Adams, David Crosby,
    Larry Graham, George New-
    some
15 Billy Pinkney, Jimmy Webb,
    Peter York
16 Kevin Ayers, Gordon Fleet,

Barry Hay, Gary Lorzio, Joey
    Spampinato
17 John Seiter, Gary Talley
18 Barbara Harris, Nona Hen-
    dryx, Johnny Preston, Carl
    Wayne
19 Ginger Baker, Ian Gillan, Billy
    J. Kramer, Johnny Nash
20 John Lantree, James Pankow,
    Robert Plant, John Povey
21 Jackie DeShannon, Kenny
    Rogers
22 Fred Milano, Barry Withem
23 Keith Moon
24 Jim Capaldi, Joe Chambers,
    John Cipollina, Malcolm Dun-
    can, David Freiberg, Ken
    Hensley, Ernest Wright
25 Walter Williams
26 Bob Cowsill, Dick Cowsill,
    Chris Curtis
27 B. J. Thomas
28 Clem Cattini, Ann Lantree,
    Danny Seraphine
29 Richard Halligan
30 Charles Colbert
31 Van Morrison

September

1 Greg Errico, Barry Gibb
2 Rosalind Ashford, Bobby "Pur-
    ify" Dickey, Sam Gooden,
    Mik Kaminski
3 George Biondo, Don Brewer,
    Mike Harrison, Al Jardine,
    Gary Leeds
4 Gary Duncan, Greg Elmore
5 Chester Ayres, Dave Clemp-
    son, Buddy Miles, Al Stewart,
    John Stewart
6 James Litherland, Roger
    Waters
7 none
8 Dean Daughtry, Kelly Grou-
    cutt, Sal Valentino
9 Pete Gavin, Doug Ingle, Billy

Preston, Otis Redding, Freddy Weller
10　Barriemore Barlow, Danny Hutton, Don Powell, Pete Tolson
11　Bennie Dwyer, Leo Kottke
12　Maria Muldaur, Colin Young
13　Peter Cetera, David Clayton-Thomas
14　Barry Cowsill, Paul Kossoff
15　Les Braid
16　Bernie Calvert, Kenney Jones
17　Little Milton, LaMonte McLemore
18　none
19　Brook Benton, John Coghlan, Lee Dorman, Cass Elliott, Nick Massi, Bill Medley, Sylvia Tyson
20　none
21　Leonard Cohen, David Coverdale, Dickey Lee
22　none
23　Steve Boone, Ron Bushy
24　Barbara Allbut, Phyllis Allbut Meister, Jerry Donahue, Gerry Marsden, Linda McCartney, Carson Van Osten
25　John Locke, Onnie McIntyre, Ian Tyson
26　Joe Bauer, George Chambers, Dick Heckstall-Smith
27　Randy Bachman
28　Ben E. King, Nick St. Nicholas
29　Mark Farner, Manuel Fernandez, Mike Pinera
30　Marc Bolan, Dewey Martin, Johnny Mathis, Marilyn McCoo, Sylvia Peterson

October

1　Jerry Martini, Barbara Parritt
2　Ron Meagher, Michael Rutherford
3　Lindsey Buckingham, Chubby Checker, Antonio Martinez

4　Jim Fielder, Patti LaBelle
5　Carlo Mastrangelo, Steve Miller, Richard Street
6　none
7　Colin Cooper, Martin Murray
8　George Bellamy, Fred Cash, Ron McKernan, Ray Royer, Hamish Stuart
9　Jackson Browne, Pat Burke, John Entwistle, John Lennon, O. V. Wright
10　Alan Cartwright, Dennis Dalziel
11　none
12　Melvin Franklin, Sam Moore, Rick Parfitt
13　Chris Farlowe, Robert Lamm, Paul Simon
14　Justin Hayward, Cliff Richard
15　Barry McGuire, Don Stevenson
16　Bob Weir
17　Gary Puckett
18　Russ Giguere
19　Wilbert Hart, Jeannie C. Riley
20　Raymond Jones, Ric Lee, Jay Siegel
21　Elvin Bishop, Steve Cropper, Ron Elliott, Lee Loughnane, Manfred Mann
22　Eddie Brigatti, Bobby Fuller, Leslie West
23　Greg Ridley
24　Jerry Edmonton, Ted Templeman, Bill Wyman
25　Jon Anderson
26　Keith Hopwood
27　none
28　Wayne Fontana, Hank Marvin
29　Peter Green, Denny Laine, Peter Stampfel
30　Timothy B. Schmit, Grace Slick, Chris Williams
31　Russ Ballard, Tom Paxton

November

1　Keith Emerson, Ric Grech

2 Jay Black, Chip Hawkes, Dave Pegg, Bruce Welch

3 Tommy Dee, Bert Jansch, Lulu, Brian Poole

4 Harry Elston

5 Art Garfunkel, Rob Grill, Pete Hammill, Don McDougall, Peter Noone, Gram Parsons, Dennis Provisor, Pablo Sanllehi, Ike Turner

6 Glenn Frey, Bill Henderson, P. J. Proby, Doug Sahm, George Young

7 Joni Mitchell, Johnny Rivers, Mary Travers, Dino Valenti

8 Gerald Alston, Bonnie Bramlett, Don Murray, Johnny Perez, Minnie Ripperton, Rodney Desbrough Slater, Roy Wood

9 Tom Fogerty, Lee Graziano, Phil May

10 Greg Lake

11 Paul Cowsill, Chris Dreja, Chas Hodges, Roger Jackson, Vince Martell, Jesse Colin Young

12 Brian Hyland, John Maus, Neil Young

13 none

14 Freddy Garrity, Scherrie Payne

15 Petula Clark, Clyde McPhatter

16 Blue Lovett, Patti Santos

17 Robert Antoni, Martin Barre, Gene Clark, Bob Gaudio, Gordon Lightfoot, Dino Martin

18 none

19 Dave Guard, Fred Lipsius, Hank Medress, Pete Moore

20 George Grantham, Norman Greenbaum, Joe Walsh

21 none

22 Floyd Sneed

23 Freddie Marsden

24 Donald "Duck" Dunn, Lee Michaels, Robin Williamson

25 Bev Bevan, Val Fuentes

26 John McVie, Garnet Mimms, Tina Turner

27 Jimi Hendrix, Al Jackson

28 Clem Curtis, Gary Troxel

29 Felix Cavalierre, Denny Doherty, John Mayall

30 Roger Glover, Leo Lyons, Paul Stookey

December

1 John Densmore, Lou Rawls

2 Tom McGuinness, Dave Munden

3 John Cale, Ozzy Osbourne

4 Freddy Cannon, Chris Hillman, Bob Mosley, Dennis Wilson

5 Jim Messina

6 Len Barry, Mike Smith

7 none

8 Jerry Butler, Geoff Daking, Robert Elliott, Jim Morrison

9 Rick Danko, Dan Hicks, Neil Innes, Sam Strain, Kenny Vance

10 Jessica Cleaves, Ace Kefford, Chad Stuart

11 Booker T. Jones, Brenda Lee

12 Clive Bunker, Connie Francis, Mike Heron, Mike Pinder, Ralph Scala, Alan Ward, Dionne Warwick, Tony Williams

13 Tony Gomez, Ted Nugent

14 Frank Allen

15 Carmine Appice, Cindy Birdsong, Dave Clark

16 Tony Hicks

17 Paul Butterfield, Eddie Kendricks, Paul Rodgers

18 Sam Andrews, Chas Chandler, Keith Richard

19 Alvin Lee, John McEuen, Phil Ochs, Zal Yanovsky

20 Bobby Colomby, Stevie Wright

21 Ray Hildebrand, Albert Lee,
    Carl Wilson, Betty Wright,
    Frank Zappa
22 Maurice Gibb, Robin Gibb,
    Barry Jenkins
23 Luther Grosvenor, Tim Har-
    din, Jorma Kaukonen
24 Lee Dorsey, Henry Vestine
25 Alice Cooper, O'Kelly Isley,
    Chris Kenner, Trevor Lucas,
    Jacqui McShee, Phil Spector
26 Gordon Edwards
27 Larry Byrom, Les Maguire,
    Tracy Nelson, Peter Quaife,
    Dave Rowberry
28 Dorsey Burnette, Alex Chilton,
    Dick Diamonde, Keith
    Spring, Edgar Winter
29 Cozy Powell, Charlie Spinosa,
    Jerry Summers, Ray Thomas
30 Bo Diddley, John Hartford,
    Davy Jones, Jeff Lynne, Mike
    Nesmith, Del Shannon
31 Burton Cummings, John Den-
    ver, Andy Summers

The Deceased Performers List

1991

01/08	Steve Clark (Def Leppard)
02/00	Dave Guard (The Kingston Trio)
03/01	Frank Esler-Smith (Air Supply)
03/17	Scott McKay (The Blue Caps)
04/20	Steve Marriott (Humble Pie, The Small Faces)
04/23	Johnny Thunders
05/24	Gene Clark (The Byrds)
06/01	David Ruffin (The Temptations)
07/00	Ian Stewart (Rolling Stones)
09/17	Rob Tyner (MC5)
11/24	Freddie Mercury (Queen)
11/25	Eric Carr (Kiss)

1990

01/23	Allen Collins (Lynyrd Skynyrd)
02/08	Del Shannon
02/10	Hal Worthington (The Unifics)
02/25	Johnnie Ray
02/26	Cornelius Gunter
05/07	Charles Allen (Pacific Gas & Electric)
06/05	Jim Hodder (Steely Dan)
06/22	Corinthian Johnson (Dell-Vikings)
07/15	Bobby Day
07/23	Bert Sommer
07/26	Brent Mydland (The Grateful Dead)
08/15	Lew DeWitt (Statler Brothers)
08/27	Stevie Ray Vaughan
09/06	Tom Fogerty (Creedence Clearwater Revival)
11/05	Bobby Scott
11/10	Ronnie Dyson
12/07	Dee Clark

1989

01/21	Steve Wahrer (The Trashmen)
01/24	Alvin Robinson
01/26	Donnie Elbert
02/01	Paul Robi (The Platters)
03/16	John Simmons (The Reflections)
05/29	John Cipollina (Quicksilver Messenger Service)
07/00	Alan Murphy (Level 42)
11/05	SSgt. Barry Sadler
11/06	Dickie Goodman

1988

01/00	Howie Johnson (The Ventures)
03/10	Andy Gibb

04/09 Brook Benton
04/09 Dave Prater (Sam & Dave)
04/28 B. W. Stevenson
07/29 Pete Drake
10/22 Ted Taylor
10/25 Johnnie Louise Richardson (The Jaynetts)
11/00 Cathy Carr
11/22 Janet Ertel (The Chordettes)
12/06 Roy Orbison
12/10 Bill Harris (The Clovers)
12/16 Sylvester

1987

01/07 Bob McNelley (McGuffey Lane)
02/15 Jimmy Holiday
03/21 Dino Martin (Dino, Desi & Billy)
05/04 Paul Butterfield
07/01 Phil "Snakefinger" Lithman (The Residents)
09/11 Peter Tosh
09/21 Jaco Pastorius
12/07 Richard Taylor (The Manhattans)

1986

01/04 Phil Lynott (Thin Lizzy)
03/04 Richard Manuel (The Band)
03/22 Mark Dinning
03/31 O'Kelly Isley (The Isley Brothers)
09/27 Cliff Burton (Metallica)
11/05 Bobby Nunn (The Coasters)
12/01 Lee Dorsey

1985

01/31 Barbara Cowsill
02/07 Matt Monro
03/31 The Singing Nun
08/12 Kyu Sakamoto
10/12 Ricky Wilson (The B-52's)
11/24 Joe Turner
12/31 Rick Nelson

1984

00/00 Ron Tabak (Prism)
01/12 Stephen Douglas (McGuffey Lane)
01/21 Jackie Wilson
02/28 Joey Vann (The Duprees)
04/01 Marvin Gaye
04/06 Ral Donner
04/27 Z. Z. Hill
06/01 Nate Nelson (The Platters, Flamingos)
07/14 Phillippe Wynne (The Spinners)
08/07 "Little" Esther Phillips
08/15 Norman Petty
11/13 Don Addrisi (The Addrisi Brothers)

1983

00/00 Tom Evans (Badfinger)
01/00 Lamar Williams (The Allman Brothers Band)
01/28 Billy Fury
02/04 Karen Carpenter (The Carpenters)
04/08 Danny Rapp (Danny & the Juniors)
04/14 Peter Farndon (The Pretenders)
04/17 Felix Pappalardi (Mountain)
07/12 Chris Wood (Traffic)
12/27 Walter Scott (Bob Kuban & the In-Men)
12/28 Dennis Wilson (The Beach Boys)

1982

00/00 John Felten (Diamonds)
00/00 Lynne Taylor (The Rooftop Singers)
00/00 Abrim Tilmon (Detroit Emeralds)
01/22 Tommy Tucker
02/04 Alex Harvey (Sensational Alex Harvey Band)

03/17 Sam George
03/19 Randy Rhoads (Blizzard of Ozz)
05/10 Neil (Scott) Bogart
06/10 Micki Harris (The Shirelles)
06/16 James Honeyman-Scott (The Pretenders)
08/13 Joe Tex
08/17 George Barajas (Duke Jupiter)
12/02 David Blue (Country Joe & the Fish)
12/08 Marty Robbins

1981

01/02 David Lynch (The Platters)
02/09 Bill Haley
02/15 Michael Bloomfield (Electric Flag)
02/22 Kermit Chandler (The Sheppards)
02/24 Ty Hunter (The Glass House)
04/06 Bob Hite (Canned Heat)
05/11 Bob Marley
05/17 Alan Gowen (National Health, Gilgamesh)
07/01 Rushton Moreve (Steppenwolf)
07/11 Hubert Johnson (The Contours)
07/16 Harry Chapin
08/28 Ronnie Self
10/15 Jud Strunk
11/18 Doug Roberts (The Fireballs)

1980

00/00 Carl Radle (Derek & the Dominos)
01/06 Georgianna Dobbins (The Marvelettes)
01/07 Carl White (The Rivingtons)
01/07 Larry Williams

02/19 Bon Scott (AC/DC)
02/21 Janet Vogel (The Skyliners)
03/26 Jon Poulos (The Buckinghams)
04/22 Joe Crane (Hoodoo Rhythm Devils)
04/28 Tommy Caldwell (Marshall Tucker Band)
05/18 Ian Curtis (Joy Division)
06/09 Richard Perna (Lamont Cranston Band)
07/23 Keith Godchaux (The Grateful Dead)
09/25 John Bonham (Led Zeppelin)
10/15 Bobby Lester (The Moonglows)
11/04 Ronnie Goodson (Ronnie & the Hi-Lites)
11/16 O. V. Wright
12/08 John Lennon (The Beatles)
12/29 Tim Hardin

1979

00/00 Mike Patto (Spooky Tooth, Boxer)
01/13 Donny Hathaway
02/02 Sid Vicious (The Sex Pistols)
06/29 Lowell George (Little Feat)
07/06 Van McCoy
07/12 Minnie Ripperton (Rotary Connection)
08/19 Dorsey Burnette
09/27 Jimmy McCulloch (Wings, the Dukes, Stone the Crows, Thunderclap Newman)
11/17 John Glascock (Jethro Tull)
11/29 Ray Smith

1978

00/00 Greg Herbert (Blood, Sweat & Tears)
00/00 Larry Brownlee (C.O.D.s)
01/23 Terry Kath (Chicago)

04/21 Sandy Denny (Fairport Convention)
06/12 Johnny Bond
09/05 Joe Negroni (The Teenagers)
09/07 Keith Moon (The Who)
12/27 Bob Luman

1977

02/26 Sherman Garnes (The Teenagers)
05/26 William Powell (O'Jays)
08/16 Elvis Presley
08/21 Alden Bunn (The Lovers)
09/16 Marc Bolan (T. Rex)
09/30 Mary Ford
10/13 Shirley Brickley (The Orlons)
10/20 Ronnie Van Zant (Lynyrd Skynyrd)
10/20 Steve Gaines (Lynyrd Skynyrd)

1976

00/00 Johnny Will Hunter (The Hombres)
01/28 Chris Kenner
02/05 Rudy Pompili (The Comets)
02/12 Sal Mineo
02/22 Florence Ballard (The Supremes)
03/19 Paul Kossoff (Free, Crawler)
03/19 Garry Thain (Uriah Heep)
04/09 Phil Ochs
05/14 Keith Relf (The Yardbirds, Renaissance, Armageddon)
08/29 Jimmy Reed
10/23 Leonard Lee (Shirley & Lee)
12/04 Tommy Bolin (Deep Purple, Zephyr, the James Gang)
12/28 Freddie King

1975

04/23 Peter Ham (Badfinger)
06/29 Tim Buckley

08/02 Chan Daniels (The Highwaymen)
08/27 Robert Scholl (Mello-Kings)
10/01 Al Jackson (Booker T. & the MGs)

1974

02/28 Bobby Bloom
05/08 Graham Bond
07/29 Cass Elliott (The Mamas & the Papas, Mugwumps)
08/09 Bill Chase (Chase)
09/23 Robbie McIntosh (Average White Band)
11/08 Ivory Joe Hunter

1973

00/00 Roger Durham (Bloodstone)
00/00 Leroy Fann (Ruby & the Romantics)
00/00 Clarence White (The Byrds)
03/08 Rod McKernan (The Grateful Dead)
07/22 Larry Finnegan
08/17 Paul Williams (The Temptations)
09/19 Gram Parsons (Flying Burrito Brothers)
09/20 Jim Croce
11/21 Allan Sherman
11/26 John Rostill (The Shadows)
12/20 Bobby Darin

1972

00/00 Danny Whitten (Crazy Horse)
01/16 David Seville (The Chipmunks)
03/14 Linda Jones
06/13 Clyde McPhatter (The Drifters)
08/02 Brian Cole (The Association)
10/17 Billy Williams

11/11 Berry Oakley (The Allman Brothers Band)

1971

00/00 Arlester Christian (Dyke & the Blazers)
00/00 Mary Ann Ganser (The Shangri-Las)
07/03 Jim Morrison (The Doors)
07/04 Donald McPherson (Main Ingredient)
08/15 Thomas Wayne (The DeLons)
10/12 Gene Vincent
10/29 Duane Allman (The Allman Brothers Band)

1970

00/00 Tony Clarke
00/00 Freddy Morgan (Sunnysiders)
00/00 George Smith (The Manhattans)
02/00 Norman Johnson (Jive Five)
01/17 Billy Stewart
01/24 Jim Sheppard (Shep & the Limelites)
03/00 Darrell Banks
03/16 Tammi Terrell
06/10 Earl Grant
09/03 Alan Wilson (Canned Heat)
09/18 Jimi Hendrix
10/14 Janis Joplin

1969

00/00 Marge Ganser (The Shangri-Las)
00/00 Hank Majewski (The Four Seasons)
06/29 Shorty Long
07/03 Brian Jones (The Rolling Stones)
08/00 Martin Lamble (Fairport Convention)
10/23 Tommy Edwards

1968

00/00 Malcolm Hale (Spanky & Our Gang)
02/00 George "King" Scott
02/28 Frankie Lymon (The Teenagers)
08/13 Joe Hinton

1967

12/10 Otis Redding
12/10 Ronnie Caldwell (Bar-Kays)
12/10 Carl Cunningham (Bar-Kays)
12/10 Phalon Jones (Bar-Kays)
12/10 Jimmy King (Bar-Kays)

1966

00/00 Joe Henderson
07/18 Bobby Fuller (Bobby Fuller Four)

1965

02/15 Nat King Cole

1964

07/00 Rudy Lewis (The Drifters)
07/31 Jim Reeves
08/19 Johnny Burnette
12/11 Sam Cooke

1963

00/00 Charles Fizer (The Olympics)
12/14 Dinah Washington

1962

04/10 Stu Sutcliffe (The Beatles)

1961

none

1960

02/06   Jesse Belvin
04/17   Eddie Cochran
11/05   Johnny Horton

1959

02/03   Buddy Holly
02/03   J. P. Richardson (The Big Bopper)
02/03   Richie Valens

1958

04/10   Chuck Willis

1957

none

1956

none

1955

none

1954

12/24   Johnny Ace

References

Books:

The Rock Record (3rd Edition) by Terry Hounsome; 1987 Blandford Press Ltd., Oxford, England.

The Rolling Stone Encyclopedia of Rock & Roll; edited by Jon Pareles and Patricia Romanowski; 1983 Rolling Stone Press, Summit Books, New York, New York.

Periodicals

Billboard Magazine; BPI Communications, Inc., New York, New York.

CD Review; WGE Publishing, Inc., Hancock, New Hampshire.

Hit Parader; Charlton Publications, Inc., Derby, Connecticut.

Q; EMAP Metro; Frontline Ltd.; Peterborough, England.

Record Companies

Rhino Records of Santa Monica, California: The Nuggets series Volumes 1–12; Best of the Ohio Express and Other Bubblegum Smashes; Best of the 1910 Fruitgum Company and Other Bubblegum Smashes; The Box Tops Greatest Hits; Nancy Sinatra: The Hit Years; The Turtles 20 Greatest Hits; Best of the Beau Brummels; Best of the Chocolate Watchband; Best of Tim Buckley; Best of the Spencer Davis Group; Best of the Bobby Fuller Four; Best of Tommy James & the Shondells; Best of Love; Best of the Music Machine; Best of the Nazz; Best of the Olympics; Best of Allan Sherman; Best of the Standells; Best of the Troggs

GNP/Crescendo Records of Los Angeles, California; Greatest Hits of Petula Clark

Index

H

L

M

N